The Eurovision Song Contest

Lugano 1956 - Tel Aviv 2019

The Complete and Independent Guide

Silverthorn Publishing
12th Year of Publication

Simon Barclay
General Editor

2019 edition
© 2019 by Simon Barclay. All rights reserved

ISBN: 9780244790813

Contents		Page
Introduction to the 2019 Edition		5
Eurovision Winners		6
Section One: Qualifying for the 2019 Contest		9
Section Two: Contest Details & Votes		23
Contest performers and voting tables:	1950's	24
Contest performers and voting tables:	1960's	28
Contest performers and voting tables:	1970's	38
Contest performers and voting tables:	1980's	56
Contest performers and voting tables:	1990's	76
Contest performers and voting tables:	2000's	96
Contest performers and voting tables :	2010's	132
2019 First Semi-Final performers, jury voting, televoting and combined results		192
2019 Second Semi-Final performers, jury voting, televoting and combined results		196
2019 Final performers, jury voting, televoting and combined results		200
2019 Final: Voting Order & Spokespersons		204
Round by Round voting & changes to scoreboard: Jury Voting		205
Round by Round voting & changes to scoreboard: Public Televoting & combined results		211
Previous voting sytem: First Semi-Final results		215
Previous voting sytem: Second Semi-Final results		216
Previous voting sytem: Final results		217
Country-by-Country History		218
Section Three: Statistics & Analysis		251
Predicting the Winners, the history of votes for the best song		252
Predicting the Winners, who gives the most 12's and who gives nothing		254
Marcel Bezençon Awards		255
OGAE poll result		256
Internal selection or national competition		257
Winners' Ages & Genders since 1956		258
2019 Contestants profile - singers & backing performers		260
Language history by country		261
Most Successful Countries League Table		262
Least Successful Countries League Table		263
Most Finishes in Top 3		264
Most Finishes in Bottom 3		264
Best & worst at qualifying from the semi-finals		264
Best semi-final to compete in		265
Most consecutive semi-final failures		265
Unluckiest semi-finals for each country		266
Performance of the "Big 5"		268
Running Order analysis, where is best to perform? Previous voting system		269
Running Order analysis, where is best to perform? New voting System		270
Winners & losers position in the order of performance since 1975		272

[Continued..]

Contents (continued)

	Page
Double Douze!	273
Are You Sure? When Juries and the Public Disagree	274
Highest number of 12's received by one country	275
Lowest number of 12's received by a winning country	275
12 Points Go To... a 10 year history by country	276
History of 12 points from juries and public since 2016	278
Sharing The Love: the concentration of points awarded	279
The host country's performance since 1975	280
Nil Points!	281
Highest scores in finals	282
Largest and smallest winning margins	283
Performance of debutant countries since 1956	284
League Table of Appearances	284
Closest voting relationships	285
Each Country's Best Friends & their 10 year voting history	287
The most one-sided voting - who doesn't reciprocate?	288
And countries who have never voted for another	289
The least friendly pairs of countries: all results since 1975	290
The least friendly pairs of countries: the effect of the public vote from 2016 onwards	290
Jury/Public split of points in finals since 2016	291
Most Points Received since 1975	293
East v West - the impact of geographical voting	294
Bloc voting by juries and the public in the 2018 Final	296
Complete country-by-country voting analysis since 1975 - who votes for who?	297

Introduction to the 2019 Edition

The Eurovision Song Contest ventured outside Europe this year, with Israel hosting the contest following Netta's win in 2018 with "Toy". The organisers staged the 64th Contest in Tel Aviv's 9,000 capacity Expo Pavilion, which was watched by an estimated 182 million television viewers. Broadcaster IPBC chose two male and two female presenters to present the two semi-finals and final, Erez Tal, Bar Refaeli, Assi Azar and Lucy Ayoub. It was the first time Israel had hosted the contest since 1999 and the third time overall.

Forty-one countries participated, two fewer than last year, we lost Bulgaria to funding issues and Ukraine to a dispute over contract terms between the Ukrainian national broadcaster and the winner of their selection competition.

Congratulations to Duncan Laurence and to the Netherlands who won Eurovision for the first time since way back in 1975. This was Netherlands's fifth win overall. There were best-ever finishes by San Marino and the newly renamed North Macedonia who actually won the jury vote on the night.

There was controversy this year, when the Belarus jury was dismissed after they leaked details of their semi-final votes ahead of the Final. The EBU decided to use a representative calculated set of points in place of the Belarus jury but then managed to award them in reverse order by mistake. This led to Sweden being shown as the jury winners overall and not North Macedonia. The top four positions after both sets of points were fortunately not affected.

The "Big 5" continue to be mostly awful, with Germany receiving no points from the voting public and finishing second last, while the UK ended up rock bottom again. Italy proved it is possible to do well as an automatic qualifier though, finishing as runners-up. Hosts Israel received no points from the juries and finished a dismal 23rd.

Some interesting facts this year include Norway winning the public voting by some margin yet only finishing sixth. Netherlands' win was achieved with only two 12 points from public voting in the final, and six maximums in total, a record beaten only by Azerbaijan in 2011. There was massive bloc voting this year by the public, with the Balkan countries in particular benefitting – on average those countries received ten times more points from their neighbours than from the other countries.

The 2019 Edition of the Complete & Independent Guide is the 12th edition of the book and as usual it's packed with details of every Contest since 1956 along with plenty of analysis, in 348 pages. From next year we will start reducing the use of statistics based on scores recalculated under the pre-2016 system now that we have experienced the excitement of the new system for a few years.

As always, please get in touch if you have any comments or suggestions. The calculation of the statistics is a huge undertaking, as you can imagine, and we welcome feedback where corrections can be made for future editions.

Simon Barclay
Editor

@silverthornpub
silverthorn-publishing@outlook.com

Eurovision Winners

Year	Host City	Winner	Artist	Song
1956	Lugano, Switzerland	Switzerland	Lys Assia	Refrain
1957	Frankfurt, Germany	Netherlands	Corry Brokken	Net Als Toen
1958	Hilversum, Netherlands	France	André Claveau	Dors Mon Amour
1959	Cannes, France	Netherlands	Teddy Scholten	Een Beetje
1960	London, United Kingdom	France	Jacqueline Boyer	Tom Pillibi
1961	Cannes, France	Luxembourg	Jean-Claude Pascal	Nous Les Amoureux
1962	Luxembourg City, Luxembourg	France	Isabelle Aubret	Un Premier Amour
1963	London, United Kingdom	Denmark	Grethe & Jørgen Ingmann	Dansevise
1964	Copenhagen, Denmark	Italy	Gigliola Cinquetti	Non Ho L'étà
1965	Naples, Italy	Luxembourg	France Gall	Poupée De Cire, Poupée De Son
1966	Luxembourg City, Luxembourg	Austria	Udo Jürgens	Merci Chérie
1967	Vienna, Austria	United Kingdom	Sandie Shaw	Puppet On A String
1968	London, United Kingdom	Spain	Massiel	La, La, La
1969	Madrid, Spain	= France	Frida Boccara	Un Jour, Un Enfant
		= United Kingdom	Lulu	Boom Bang-a-bang
		= Netherlands	Lenny Kuhr	De Troubadour
		= Spain	Salomé	Vivo Cantando
1970	Amsterdam, Netherlands	Ireland	Dana	All Kinds Of Everything
1971	Dublin, Ireland	Monaco	Séverine	Un Banc, Un Arbre, Une Rue
1972	Edinburgh, United Kingdom	Luxembourg	Vicky Leandros	Après Toi
1973	Luxembourg City, Luxembourg	Luxembourg	Anne-Marie David	Tu Te Reconnaîtras
1974	Brighton, United Kingdom	Sweden	ABBA	Waterloo
1975	Stockholm, Sweden	Netherlands	Teach-In	Teach-In
1976	The Hague, Netherlands	United Kingdom	Brotherhood of Man	Save Your Kisses For Me
1977	London, United Kingdom	France	Marie Myriam	L'oiseau Et L'enfant
1978	Paris, France	Israel	Izhar Cohen & the Alphabeta	Abanibi
1979	Jerusalem, Israel	Israel	Milk and Honey	Hallelujah
1980	The Hague, Netherlands	Ireland	Johnny Logan	What's Another Year
1981	Dublin, Ireland	United Kingdom	Bucks Fizz	Making Your Mind Up
1982	Harrogate, United Kingdom	Germany	Nicole	Ein bißchen Frieden
1983	Munich, Germany	Luxembourg	Corinne Hermès	Si La Vie Est Cadeau
1984	Luxembourg City, Luxembourg	Sweden	Herrey's	Diggi-loo diggy-ley
1985	Gothenburg, Sweden	Norway	Bobbysocks	La Det Swinge
1986	Bergen, Norway	Belgium	Sandra Kim	J'aime La Vie
1987	Brussels, Belgium	Ireland	Johnny Logan	Hold Me Now
1988	Dublin, Ireland	Switzerland	Céline Dion	Ne Partez Pas Sans Moi
1989	Lausanne, Switzerland	Yugoslavia	Riva	Rock Me
1990	Zagreb, Yugoslavia	Italy	Toto Cutugno	Insieme: 1992
1991	Rome, Italy	Sweden	Carola	Fångad Av En Stormvind
1992	Malmö, Sweden	Ireland	Linda Martin	Why Me
1993	Millstreet, Ireland	Ireland	Niamh Kavanagh	In Your Eyes
1994	Dublin, Ireland	Ireland	P Harrington & C McGettigan	Rock 'n' Roll Kids
1995	Dublin, Ireland	Norway	Secret Garden	Nocturne
1996	Oslo, Norway	Ireland	Eimear Quinn	The Voice
1997	Dublin, Ireland	United Kingdom	Katrina and The Waves	Love shine a light
1998	Birmingham, United Kingdom	Israel	Dana International	Diva
1999	Jerusalem, Israel	Sweden	Charlotte Nilsson	Take me to your heaven
2000	Stockholm, Sweden	Denmark	Olsen Brothers	Fly on the wings of love
2001	Copenhagen, Denmark	Estonia	Tanel Padar, Dave Benton & 2XL	Everybody
2002	Tallinn, Estonia	Latvia	Marie N	I Wanna
2003	Riga, Latvia	Turkey	Sertab Erener	Everyway That I Can

Eurovision Winners

Year	Host City	Winner	Artist	Song
2004	Istanbul, Turkey	Ukraine	Ruslana	Wild Dances
2005	Kiev, Ukraine	Greece	Helena Paparizou	My Number One
2006	Athens, Greece	Finland	Lordi	Hard Rock Hallelujah
2007	Helsinki, Finland	Serbia	Marija Šerifovic	Molitva
2008	Belgrade, Serbia	Russia	Dima Bilan	Believe
2009	Moscow, Russia	Norway	Alexander Rybak	Fairytale
2010	Oslo, Norway	Germany	Lena Meyer-Landrut	Satellite
2011	Düsseldorf, Germany	Azerbaijan	Ell/Nikki	Running Scared
2012	Baku, Azerbaijan	Sweden	Loreen	Euphoria
2013	Malmö, Sweden	Denmark	Emmelie de Forest	Only Teardrops
2014	Copenhagen, Denmark	Austria	Conchita Wurst	Rise Like a Phoenix
2015	Vienna, Austria	Sweden	Måns Zelmerlöw	Heroes
2016	Stockholm, Sweden	Ukraine	Jamala	1944
2017	Kiev, Ukraine	Portugal	Salvador Sobral	Amar Pelos Dois
2018	Lisbon, Portugal	Israel	Netta	Toy
2019	Tel Aviv, Israel	Netherlands	Duncan Laurence	Arcade

SECTION 1

Qualification for the 2019 Contest

Notes on each country's national competitions

Eurovision 2019: Qualification

Albania

Representative:	Jonida Maliqi
Born:	26 March 1983 in Tirana, Albania (age 36 during ESC2019)
Previous appearances:	none

Selection Competition:	Festivali i Këngës 56	Broadcaster: RTSH
Selection Date:	Artist: 22 December 2018	Song: 22 December 2018
Format:	Semi-final with 22 artists, Final with 14 artists.	
Voting basis:	100% jury vote	

Top 3:

Artist	Song in Final	Points
Jonida Maliqi	Ktheju tokës	228
Lidia Lufi	Rrëfehem	219
Eranda Libohova	100 pyetje	181

Armenia

Representative:	Srbuhi Sargsyan
Born:	3 April 1994 in Yerevan, Armenia (age 25 during ESC2019)
Previous appearances:	none

Selection Competition:	Internal Selection	Broadcaster: AMPTV
Selection Date:	Artist: 30 November 2018	Song: 10 March 2019

Australia

Representative:	Kate Miller-Heidke
Born:	16 November 1981 in Brisbane, Australia (age 37 during ESC2019)
Previous appearances:	none

Selection Competition:	Eurovision - Australia Decides	Broadcaster: SBS
Selection Date:	Artist: 9 February 2019	Song: 9 February 2019
Format:	Final with 10 artists	
Voting basis:	50% jury/50% public vote.	

Top 3:

Artist	Song	Jury	Public	Total
Kate Miller-Heidke	Zero Gravity	48	87	135
Electric Fields	2000 And Whatever	44	70	114
Sheppard	On My Way	41	46	87

Austria

Representative:	Paenda (real name Gabriela Horn)
Born:	25 January 1988 in Deutschlandsberg, Austria (age 31 during ESC2019)
Previous appearances:	none

Selection Competition:	Internal Selection	Broadcaster: ORF
Selection Date:	Artist: 29 January 2019	Song: 29 January 2019

Eurovision 2019: Qualification

Azerbaijan

Representative:	Chingiz Mustafayev
Born:	11 March 1991 in Moscow, Russia (then USSR) (age 28 during ESC2019)
Previous appearances:	none

Selection Competition:	Internal Selection	Broadcaster:	İTV
Selection Date:	Artist: 8 March 2019	Song: 8 March 2019	

Belarus

Representative:	ZENA (real name Zinaida Kupriyanovich)
Born:	17 September 2002 in Minsk, Belarus (age 16 during ESC2019)
Previous appearances:	none

Selection Competition:	Nationalny Otbor	Broadcaster:	BTRC
Selection Date:	Artist: 7 March 2019	Song: 7 March 2019	
Format:	Final with 10 artists		
Voting basis:	100% jury voting		

Top 3:

Artist	Song	Points
ZENA	Like It	69
BLGN & Mirex	Champion	65
Sebastian Roos	Never Getting Close	62

Belgium

Representative:	Eliot Vassamillet
Born:	29 December 2000 in Mons, Belgium (age 18 during ESC2019)
Previous appearances:	none

Selection Competition:	Internal Selection	Broadcaster:	RTBF
Selection Date:	Artist: 14 January 2019	Song: 28 February 2019	

Croatia

Representative:	Roko Blažević
Born:	10 March 2000 in Split, Croatia (age 19 during ESC2019)
Previous appearances:	none

Selection Competition:	Dora 2019	Broadcaster:	HRT
Selection Date:	Artist: 16 February 2019	Song: 16 February 2019	
Format:	Final with 10 artists and two voting rounds		
Voting basis:	50% jury/50% public voting.		

Final: second round

Artist	Song	Jury	Public	Total
Roko Blažević	The Dream	12	12	24
Lorena Bućan	Tower of Babylon	10	8	18
Luka Nižetić	Brutalero	3	10	13

Eurovision 2019: Qualification

Cyprus

Representative:	Tamta Goduadze
Born:	10 January 1981 in Tbilisi, Georgia (then USSR) (age 38 during ESC2019)
Previous appearances:	none

Selection Competition:	Internal Selection	Broadcaster:	CyBC
Selection Date:	Artist: 21 December 2018	Song: 5 March 2019	

Czech Republic

Representative:	Lake Malawi
Group Members:	Albert Černý, Jeroným Šubrt, Antonín Hrabal
Previous appearances:	none

Selection Competition:	Eurovision Song CZ	Broadcaster:	ČT
Selection Date:	Artist: 28 January 2019	Song: 28 January 2019	
Format:	Final with 10 artists and two voting rounds		
Voting basis:	50% jury/50% public voting.		

Final: second round

Artist	Song	Jury	Public	Total
Lake Malawi	Friend of a Friend	12	10	22
Jakub Ondra	Space Sushi	6	12	18
Pam Rabbit	Easy to Believe	10	8	18

Denmark

Representative:	Leonora Jepsen
Born:	3 October 1998 in Hellerup, Denmark (age 20 during ESC2019)
Previous appearances:	none

Selection Competition:	Dansk Melodi Grand Prix 2019	Broadcaster:	DR
Selection Date:	Artist: 23 February 2019	Song: 23 February 2019	
Format:	Final with 10 artists and two voting rounds		
Voting basis:	50% jury/50% public voting.		

Final: second round

Artist	Song	Jury	Public	Total
Leonora	Love Is Forever	48%	36%	42%
Julie & Nina	League of Light	24%	46%	35%
Sigmund	Say My Name	28%	18%	23%

Eurovision 2019: Qualification

Estonia

Representative:	Victor Crone
Born:	31 January 1992 in Österåker, Sweden (age 27 during ESC2019)
Previous appearances:	none

Selection Competition:	Eesti Laul 2019	Broadcaster: ERR
Selection Date:	Artist: 16 February 2019	Song: 16 February 2019
Format:	2 Semi-Finals each with 12 artists, Final with 12 artists.	
Voting basis:	1st round: 50% jury/50% public voting. 2nd Round: 100% public voting	

Final: second round

Artist	Song	Public vote
Victor Crone	Storm	46%
Uku Suviste	Pretty Little Liar	30%
Stefan	Without You	24%

Finland

Representative:	Darude (real name Toni-Ville Henrik Virtanen) feat. Sebastian Rejman
Born:	Darude: 17 July 1975 in Eura, Finland (age 43 during ESC2019)
	Sebastian: 13 January 1978 in Helsinki, Finland (age 41 during ESC2019)
Previous appearances:	none

Selection Competition:	Uuden Musiikin Kilpailu 2019 (song only)	Broadcaster: YLE
Selection Date:	Artist: 29 January 2019 (internal selection)	Song: 2 March 2019
Format:	Final with chosen artist and 3 songs.	
Voting basis:	50% public vote/50% juries	

Top 3 Songs:

Artist	Song	Jury	Public	Total
Darude feat. Sebastian Rejman	Look Away	96	148	244
Darude feat. Sebastian Rejman	Superman	74	73	147
Darude feat. Sebastian Rejman	Release Me	70	19	89

France

Representative:	Bilal Hassani
Born:	9 September 1999 in Paris, France (age 19 during ESC2019)
Previous appearances:	none

Selection Competition:	Destination Eurovision 2019	Broadcaster: France Télévisions
Selection Date:	Artist: 26 January 2019	Song: 26 January 2019
Format:	Two semi-finals each with 9 artists, Final with 8 artists	
Voting basis:	50% public vote/50% jury	

Top 3 Songs:

Artist	Song	Jury	Public	Total
Bilal Hassani	Roi	50	100	200
Seemone	Tous les Deux	94	62	156
Chimène Badi	Là-haut	56	63	119

Eurovision 2019: Qualification

Georgia

Representative:	Oto Nemsadze
Born:	18 June 1989 in Gori, Georgia (then USSR) (age 29 during ESC2019)
Previous appearances:	none

Selection Competition:	Georgian Idol	Broadcaster:	GPB
Selection Date:	Artist: 3 March 2019	Song:	3 March 2019
Format:	5 elimination shows with 10 artists, leaving 4 artists in Final		
Voting basis:	100% public televote.		

Final Result:

Artist	Song	Public vote
Oto Nemsadze	Sul tsin iare	44.13%
Liza Kalandadze	Sevdisperi zgva	35.51%
Giorgi Nakashidze	Sul tsin iare	11.06%
Giogi Pruidze	Me mjera	9.30%

Germany

Representative:	S!sters
Group Members:	Laurita Spinelli, Carlotta Truman
Previous appearances:	none

Selection Competition:	Unser Lied für Israel	Broadcaster:	NDR
Selection Date:	Artist: 22 February 2019	Song:	22 February 2019
Format:	Final with 7 artists.		
Voting basis:	33% Jury/33% Public Televote/33% 100 member panel		

Top 3 Songs:

Artist	Song	Jury	Public	Panel	Total
S!sters	Sister	12	12	6	30
Makeda	The Day I Loved You Most	10	6	10	26
Lilly Among Clouds	Surprise	7	10	8	25

Greece

Representative:	Katerine Duska
Born:	6 November 1989 in Montreal, Canada (age 29 during ESC2019)
Previous appearances:	none

Selection Competition:	Internal selection	Broadcaster:	ERT
Selection Date:	Artist: 14 February 2019	Song:	6 March 2019

Eurovision 2019: Qualification

Hungary

Representative:	Joci Pápai
Born:	22 September 1981 in Tata, Hungary (age 37 during ESC2019)
Previous appearances:	Represented Hungary in ESC2017 in Kiev, finishing 8th in the Final.
Selection Competition:	A Dal 2019 Broadcaster: Duna TV
Selection Date:	Artist: 23 February 2019 Song: 23 February 2019
Format:	3 Heats, 2 Semi-finals & Final with 8 artists in 1st round, four in 2nd round.
Voting basis:	100% jury in first round of final, 100% public voting in second round

Top 4 in first round of final:

Artist	Song	Jury	Public vote
Joci Pápai	Az én apám	26	1st
Acoustic Planet	Nyári zápor	22	
Bence Vavra	Szótlanság	20	
Bogi Nagy	Holnap	16	

Iceland

Representative:	Hatari
Group members:	Klemens Nikulásson Hannigan, Matthías Tryggvi Haraldsson, Einar Hrafn Stefánsson
Previous appearances:	none
Selection Competition:	Söngvakeppnin 2019 Broadcaster: RÚV
Selection Date:	Artist: 2 March 2019 Song: 2 March 2019
Format:	2 Semi-finals, Final with 5 artists and two voting rounds.
Voting basis:	50% jury/50% public vote in 1st round of Final, 100% public vote in 2nd round.

Top 2:

Artist	Song	Public vote	Position
Hatari	Hatrið mun sigra	58%	1
Friðrik Ómar	Hvað ef ég get ekki elskað?	42%	2

Ireland

Representative:	Sarah McTernan
Born:	11 March 1994 in Scarriff, Ireland (age 25 during ESC2019)
Previous appearances:	none
Selection Competition:	Internal Selection Broadcaster: RTÉ
Selection Date:	Artist: 8 March 2019 Song: 8 March 2019

Eurovision 2019: Qualification

Israel

Representative:	Kobi Marimi
Born:	8 October 1991 in Ramat Gan, Israel (age 27 during ESC2019)
Previous appearances:	none
Selection Competition:	HaKokhav HaBa L'Eurovizion Broadcaster: IPBC/Keshet
Selection Date:	Artist: 12 February 2019 Song: 10 March 2019 (by internal selection)
Format:	Probably the most complicated of all selection competitions. 67 artists competed in 16 audition rounds, 4 shortlisting rounds, top 20 competed head to head in "duels". 12 then competed in themed duels in 4 heats. 4 semi-finals, then final with two rounds for 4 remaining artists.
Voting basis:	100% jury voting in first final, 50% jury/public voting in second final

Final: second round:

Artist	Song	Jury	Public	Total
Kobi Marimi	Let it be	102	113	215
Ketreyah	Impossible	78	87	165
Shefita	Broken	90	70	160

Italy

Representative:	Alessandro Mahmood
Born:	12 September 1992 in Milan, Italy (age 26 in ESC2019)
Previous appearances:	none
Selection Competition:	Sanremo 2019 Broadcaster: RAI
Selection Date:	Artist: 9 February 2019 Song: 9 February 2019
Format:	Final with 24 artists in first round, 3 in second round.
Voting basis:	50% juries/50% public voting

Top 3:

Artist	Song	Jury	Public	Average
Mahmood	Soldi	64%	21%	39%
Ultimo	I tuoi particolari	25%	49%	36%
Il Volo	Musica che resta	12%	30%	26%

Latvia

Representative:	Carousel
Group members:	Sabīne Žuga, Mārcis Vasiļevskis, Staņislavs Judins, Mareks Logins
Previous appearances:	none
Selection Competition:	Supernova 2019 Broadcaster: LTV
Selection Date:	Artist: 16 February 2019 Song: 16 February 2019
Format:	2 Semi-Finals with 16 artists, Final with 8 artists.
Voting basis:	50% jury/50% internet/televoting/streaming/in-person in a shopping centre!

Top 3:

Artist	Song	Jury	Public	Total
Carousel	That night	25%	2	3
Markus Riva	You Make Me So Crazy	24%	1	6
Laime Pilnīga	Awe	18%	5	7

Eurovision 2019: Qualification

Lithuania

Representative: Jurijus (real name Jurij Veklenko)
Born: 6 July 1990 in Klaipeda, Lithuania (age 28 during ESC2019)
Previous appearances: none

Selection Competition: "Eurovizijos" dainų konkurso nacionalinė atranka   Broadcaster: LRT
Selection Date: Artist: 23 February 2019   Song: 23 February 2019
Format: 4 Elimination Heats, 2 semi-finals & Final with 8 artists.
Voting basis: 50% jury/50% public vote

Top 3:

Artist	Song	Jury	Public	Total
Jurijus	Run With The Lions	12	12	24
Monika Marija	Light On	10	10	20
Antikvariniai Kašpirovskio Dantys	Mažulė	8	8	16

Malta

Representative: Michaela Pace
Born: 25 January 2001 in Gozo, Malta (age 18 during ESC2019)
Previous appearances: none

Selection Competition: X Factor Malta 2019   Broadcaster: PBS
Selection Date: Artist: 26 January 2019   Song: 26 January 2019
Format: 3 elimination semi-finals, with 12 artists, leaving 8 in the Final.
Voting basis: 100% public vote in the final, until two artists reamained, then jury decision which was tied, then decided by public votes.

Final two artists:

Artist	Final song (3 performed)	Result
Michela Pace	Shallow	1
Owen Leuellen	Believe	2

Moldova

Representative: Anna Odobescu
Born: 3 November 1991 in Dubăsari, Moldova (then USSR) (age 27 during ESC2019)
Previous appearances: none

Selection Competition: O Melodie Pentru Europa 2019   Broadcaster: TRM
Selection Date: Artist: 2 March 2019   Song: 2 March 2019
Format: Final with 10 artists.
Voting basis: 50% jury/50% public vote

Top 3:

Artist	Song	Jury	Public	Total
Anna Odobescu	Stay	12	10	22
Maxim Zavidia	I Will Not Surrender	5	12	17
Diana Brescan	Lies	10	5	15

Eurovision 2019: Qualification

Montenegro

Representative:	D mol
Group members:	Tamara Vujačić, Mirela Ljumić, Željko Vukčević, Ivana Obradović, Emel Franca, Rizo Feratović
Previous appearances:	none

Selection Competition: Montevizija 2019   Broadcaster: RTCG
Selection Date: Artist: 9 February 2019   Song: 9 February 2019
Format: Final with 5 artists in first round, 2 artists in Superfinal.
Voting basis: 100% jury in semi-final, 100% public voting in final

Superfinal:

Artist	Song	Public vote
D mol	Heaven	62%
Ivana Popović-Martinović	Nevinost	38%

Netherlands

Representative:	Duncan Laurence
Born:	11 April 1994 in Hellevoetsluis, Netherlands (age 25 during ESC2019)
Previous appearances:	None

Selection Competition: Internal Selection   Broadcaster: AVROTROS
Selection Date: Artist: 21 January 2019   Song: 7 March 2019

North Macedonia

Representative:	Tamara Todevska
Born:	1 June 1985 in Skopje, North Macedonia (then Yugoslavia) (age 33 during ESC2019)
Previous appearances:	Represented FYR Macedonia (now North Macedonia) in ESC 2008 in Belgrade, finishing 10th in the semi-final.

Selection Competition: Internal Selection   Broadcaster: MRT
Selection Date: Artist: 25 January 2019   Song: 8 March 2019

Norway

Representative:	KEiiNO
Group members:	Fred Buljo, Alexandra Rotan, Tom Hugo Hermansen
Previous appearances:	none

Selection Competition: Melodi Grand Prix 2019   Broadcaster: NRK
Selection Date: Artist: 2 March 2019   Song: 2 March 2019
Format: Final with 10 artists and three rounds of voting.
Voting basis: 100% public vote

Gold Duel'

Artist	Song	Public vote
KEiiNO	Spirit In The Sky	58.80%
Adrian Jørgensen	The Bubble	41.20%

Eurovision 2019: Qualification

Poland

Representative:	Tulia
Group members:	Joanna Sinkiewicz, Dominika Siepka, Patrycja Nowicka, Tulia Biczak
Previous appearances:	none
Selection Competition:	Internal Selection — Broadcaster: TVP
Selection Date:	Artist: 15 February 2019 — Song: 15 February 2019

Portugal

Representative:	Conan Osíris (real name Tiago Miranda)
Born:	5 January 1989 in Lisbon, Portugal (age 30 during ESC2019)
Previous appearances:	none
Selection Competition:	Festival da Canção 2019 — Broadcaster: RTP
Selection Date:	Artist: 2 March 2019 — Song: 2 March 2019
Format:	Two semi-finals each with 8 artists, Final with 8 artists.
Voting basis:	50% jury/50% public vote

Top 3:

Artist	Song	Jury	Public	Total
Conan Osíris	Telemóveis	12	12	24
NBC	Igual a ti	10	8	18
Matay	Perfeito	7	10	17

Romania

Representative:	Ester Peony
Born:	21 July 1993 in Câmpulung, Romania (age 25 during ESC2019)
Previous appearances:	none
Selection Competition:	Selecția Națională 2019 — Broadcaster: TVR
Selection Date:	Artist: 25 February 2018 — Song: 25 February 2018
Format:	2 semi-finals with 23 artists, Final with 12 artists.
Voting basis:	86% jury/14% public vote

Top 3:

Artist	Song	Jury	Public	Total
Ester Peony	On A Sunday	62	3	65
Laura Bretan	Dear Father	48	12	60
Bella Santiago	Army of Love	50	8	58

Russia

Representative:	Sergey Lazarev
Born:	1 April 1983 in Moscow, Russia (then Soviet Union) (age 36 during ESC2019)
Previous appearances:	3rd place in ESC2016 in Stockholm, representing Russia.
Selection Competition:	Internal Selection — Broadcaster: Channel One Russia
Selection Date:	Artist: 7 February 2019 — Song: 9 March 2019

Eurovision 2019: Qualification

San Marino

Representative:	Serhat (real name Ahmet Serhat Hacıpaşalıoğlu)
Born:	24 October 1964 in Instanbul, Turkey (age 54 during ESC2019)
Previous appearances:	12th place in semi-final in ESC2016 in Stockholm, representing San Marino.

Selection Competition:	Internal Selection	Broadcaster:	SMRTV
Selection Date:	Artist: 21 January 2019	Song: 7 March 2019	

Serbia

Representative:	Nevena Božović
Born:	15 June 1994 in Mitrovica, Kosovo (then Yugoslavia) (age 24 during ESC2019)
Previous appearances:	Represented Serbia as part of Moje 3, in ESC2013 in Malmö, finishing 11th in the semi-final.

Selection Competition:	Beovizija 2019	Broadcaster:	RTS
Selection Date:	Artist: 3 March 2019	Song: 3 March 2019	
Format:	Two semi-finals with 12 artists in each, final with 12 artists		
Voting basis:	50% jury/50% public vote		

Top 3:

Artist	Song	Jury	Public	Total
Nevena Božović	Kruna	12	8	20
Dženan Lončarević	Nema Suza	7	10	17
Sashka Janx	Da li čuješ moj glas	10	6	16

Slovenia

Representative:	Zala Kralj & Gašper Šantl
Born:	Unknown. Zala is age 19 during ESC2019 and Gasper is age 22.
Previous appearances:	none

Selection Competition:	EMA 2019	Broadcaster:	RTVSLO
Selection Date:	Artist: 24 February 2018	Song: 24 February 2018	
Format:	10 artists in Final, then two in Superfinal		
Voting basis:	100% public vote		

Superfinal:

Artist	Song	Public vote
Zala Kralj & Gašper Šantl	Sebi	72.89%
Raiven	Kaos	27.11%

Eurovision 2019: Qualification

Spain

Representative:	Miki (real name Miguel Núñez Pozo)
Born:	6 January 1996 in Barcelona, Spain (age 23 during ESC2019) ESC2019)
Previous appearances:	none

Selection Competition:	Operación Triunfo 2019	Broadcaster: TVE
Selection Date:	Artist: 20 January 2019	Song: 20 January 2019
Format:	Final with 10 artists.	
Voting basis:	100% public vote	

Second Round:

Artist	Song	Public vote
Miki	La Venda	34%
Maria	Muérdeme	22%
Miki & Natalia	Nadie Se Salva	14%

Sweden

Representative:	John Lundvik
Born:	27 January 1983 in London, United Kingdom (age 36 during ESC2019)
Previous appearances:	none

Selection Competition:	Melodifestivalen 2019	Broadcaster: SVT
Selection Date:	Artist: 9 March 2019	Song: 9 March 2019
Format:	4 Semi-Finals, 1 Second Chance Round, Final with 12 artists.	
Voting basis:	50% jury/50% public vote	

Top 3:

Artist	Song	Jury	Public	Total
John Lundvik	Too Late For Love	96	85	181
Bishara	On My Own	38	69	107
Hanna Ferm & LIAMOO	Hold You	48	59	107

Switzerland

Representative:	Luca Hänni
Born:	8 October 1994 in Bern, Switzerland (age 24 during ESC2019)
Previous appearances:	none

Selection Competition:	Internal Selection	Broadcaster: SRG SSR
Selection Date:	Artist: 7 March 2019	Song: 7 March 2019

Eurovision 2019: Qualification

United Kingdom

Representative: Michael Rice
Born: 25 October 1997 in Hartlepool, England (age 21 during ESC2019)
Previous appearances: none

Selection Competition: Eurovision: You Decide Broadcaster: BBC
Selection Date: Artist: 8 February 2019 Song: 8 February 2019
Format: Final with 6 artists, then 3 "duel" winners.
Voting basis: 100% public vote

Entries (only winner announced):

Artist	Song	Position
Michael Rice	Bigger Than Us	1
Kerri-Anne	Sweet Lies	
Jordan Clarke	Freaks	

SECTION 2

Contest Details and Voting Tables

Semi-Finals & Final results and votes awarded in each Contest

1956 Eurovision 1: Lugano, Switzerland   24 May 1956

Rank	Start	Country	Artist	Song	Writer	Composer
1	9	Switzerland	Lys Assia	Refrain	Emile Gardaz	Géo Voumard
2	10	Belgium	Mony Marc	Le Plus Beau Jour De Ma Vie	David Bée	Claude Alix
3	11	Germany	Freddy Quinn	So Geht Das Jede Nacht	Peter Mösser	Lothar Olias
4	12	France	Dany Dauberson	Il Est Là	Simone Vallauris	Simone Vallauris
5	14	Italy	Tonina Torielli	Amami Se Vuoi	Mario Panzeri	Vittorio Mascheroni
6	13	Luxembourg	Michèle Arnaud	Les Amants De Minuit	Pierre Lambry	Simone Laurencin
7	8	Netherlands	Corry Brokken	Voorgoed Voorbij	Jelle de Vries	Jelle de Vries
8	7	Italy	Franca Raimondi	Aprite Le Finestre	Pinchi	Virgilio Panzito
9	3	Belgium	Fud Leclerc	Messieurs Les Noyés De La Seine	Robert Montal	Jean Miret, Jacques Say
10	2	Switzerland	Lys Assia	Das Alte Karussell	Fernando Paggi	George Betz-Stahl
11	4	Germany	Walter Andreas Schwarz	Im Wartesaal Zum Großen Glück	Walter Andreas Schwarz	Walter Andreas Schwarz
12	5	France	Mathé Altéry	Le Temps Perdu	Rachèle Thoreau	André Lodge
13	6	Luxembourg	Michèle Arnaud	Ne Crois Pas	Jacques Lassry	Christian Guittreau
14	1	Netherlands	Jetty Paerl	De Vogels Van Holland	Annie Schmidt	Cor Lemaire

Note: Two songs were performed per country. Each country had 10 jurors who could award 1 point each to their favourite act, including those entries from their own country. The votes awarded have never been disclosed.

1957 Eurovision 2: Frankfurt, Germany   3 March 1957

Rank	Start	Country	Artist	Song	Writer	Composer	POINTS
1	6	Netherlands	Corry Brokken	Net Als Toen	Willy van Hemert	Guus Jansen	31
2	8	France	Paule Desjardins	La Belle Amour	Francis Carco	Guy Lefarge	17
3	9	Denmark	Birthe Wilke & Gustav Winckler	Skibet Skal Sejle I Nat	Paul Sörensen	Erik Fiehn	10
4	7	Germany	Margot Hielscher	Telefon, Telefon	Ralph Maria Siegel	Friedrich Meyer	8
5	2	Luxembourg	Danièle Dupré	Tant De Peine	Jacques Taber	Jean-Pierre Kemmer	8
6	4	Italy	Nunzio Gallo	Corde Della Mia Chitarra	Giuseppi Cavaliere	Mario Ruccione	7
7	3	United Kingdom	Patricia Bredin	All	Alan Stranks	Reynell Wreford	6
8	1	Belgium	Bobbejaan Schoepen	Straatdeuntje	Eric Franssen	Harry Frekin	5
9	10	Switzerland	Lys Assia	L'enfant Que J'étais	Emile Gardaz	Géo Voumard	5
10	5	Austria	Bob Martin	Wohin, Kleines Pony	Hans Werner, Kurt Svab	Kurt Svab	3

1957 Eurovision 2: Frankfurt, Germany

3 March 1957

	Austria	Belgium	Denmark	France	Germany	Italy	Monaco	Netherlands	Switzerland	United Kingdom	TOTAL
Belgium			2		2					1	5
Luxembourg	3	1				4					8
United Kingdom	1	1	1				1	1	1		6
Italy			1				2	1	2	2	7
Austria							1	1		2	3
Netherlands	6	5	3	4	1	1	3		7	1	31
Germany		1		6		1					8
France		2	2		6		1	4		2	17
Denmark						3	5			2	10
Switzerland			2		1	1		1			5

Note: each country had 10 jurors who could award 1 point each to their favourite act.

1958 Eurovision 3: Hilversum, Netherlands   12 March 1958

Rank	Start	Country	Artist	Song	Writer	Composer	POINTS
1	3	France	André Claveau	Dors Mon Amour	Hubert Giraud	Pierre Delanoë	27
2	10	Switzerland	Lys Assia	Giorgio	Fridolin Tschudi	Paul Burkhard	24
3	1	Italy	Domenico Modugno	Nel Blu Dipinto Di Blu	Franco Migliacci, Domenico Modugno	Domenico Modugno	13
4	5	Sweden	Alice Babs	Lilla Stjärna	Åke Gerhard	Åke Gerhard	10
5	9	Austria	Liane Augustin	Die Ganze Welt Braucht Liebe	Günther Léopold, Kurt Werner	Günther Léopold, Kurt Werner	8
6	7	Belgium	Fud Leclerc	Ma Petite Chatte	André Dohet	André Dohet	8
7	8	Germany	Margot Hielscher	Für Zwei Groschen Musik	Fred Rauch, Walter Brandin	Friedrich Meyer	5
8	6	Denmark	Raquel Rastenni	Jeg Rev Et Blad Ud Af Min Dagbog	Harry Jensen	Harry Jensen	3
9	2	Netherlands	Corry Brokken	Heel De Wereld	Benny Vreden	Benny Vreden	1
10	4	Luxembourg	Solange Berry	Un Grand Amour	Monique Laniece, Raymond Roche	Michel Eric	1

1959 Eurovision 4: Cannes, France   11 March 1959

Rank	Start	Country	Artist	Song	Writer	Composer	POINTS
1	5	Netherlands	Teddy Scholten	Een Beetje	Willy van Hemert	Dick Schallies	21
2	10	United Kingdom	Pearl Carr & Teddy Johnson	Sing Little Birdie	Syd Cordell	Stan Butcher	16
3	1	France	Jean Philippe	Oui, Oui, Oui, Oui	Pierre Cour	Hubert Giraud	15
4	8	Switzerland	Christa Williams	Irgendwoher	Lothar Löffler	Lothar Löffler	14
5	2	Denmark	Birthe Wilke	Uh-jeg Ville Ønske Jeg Var Dig	Carl Andersen	Otto Lington	12
6	11	Belgium	Bob Benny	Hou Toch Van Mij	Ke Riema	Hans Flower	9
7	3	Italy	Domenico Modugno	Piove	Dino Verde	Domenico Modugno	9
8	6	Germany	Alice & Ellen Kessler	Heut' Woll'n Wir Tanzen Geh'n	Astrid Voltmann	Helmut Zander	5
9	9	Austria	Ferry Graf	Der K Und K Kalypso Aus Wien	Günther Léopold	Norbert Pawlicki	4
10	7	Sweden	Brita Borg	Augustin	Åke Gerhard	Harry Sandin	4
11	4	Monaco	Jacques Pills	Mon Ami Pierrot	Raymond Bravard	Florence Veran	1

1958 Eurovision 3: Hilversum, Netherlands

12 March 1958

	Austria	Belgium	Denmark	France	Germany	Italy	Monaco	Netherlands	Sweden	Switzerland	TOTAL
Italy	1	4		1	4		1		1	1	13
Netherlands										1	1
France	7	1	9		1	6	1	1		1	27
Luxembourg										1	1
Sweden	1	1						3	2	3	10
Denmark				1			1		1		3
Belgium			1		5		1	1			8
Germany	1	1		2			1				5
Austria		1		3			1			3	8
Switzerland		2		3		4	4	5	6		24

1959 Eurovision 4: Cannes, France

11 March 1959

	Austria	Belgium	Denmark	France	Germany	Italy	Monaco	Netherlands	Sweden	Switzerland	United Kingdom	TOTAL
France	1	2			4	1		4		1	2	15
Denmark	2			4	1	1	1			1	2	12
Italy		1		3			1			3	1	9
Monaco	1											1
Netherlands	3	3	1	4	2	7	1				1	21
Germany		1		2		1	1					5
Sweden			1					3		1		4 or 5
Switzerland	1	1	2		1		1	3	2		5	14
Austria			1				1			1		4
United Kingdom	2	2	1	1	3		2	5		3		16
Belgium			2		3		1	1			2	9

Note: in both years each country had 10 jurors who could award 1 point each to their favourite act.

1960 Eurovision 5: London, United Kingdom

29 March 1960

Rank	Start	Country	Artist	Song	Writer	Composer	POINTS
1	13	France	Jacqueline Boyer	Tom Pillibi	Pierre Cour	André Popp	32
2	1	United Kingdom	Bryan Johnson	Looking High, High, High	John Watson	John Watson	25
3	8	Monaco	François Deguelt	Ce Soir-là	Pierre Dorsey	Hubert Giraud	15
4	6	Norway	Nora Brockstedt	Voi-voi	George Elgaaen	George Elgaaen	11
5	11	Germany	Wyn Hoop	Bonne Nuit, Ma Chérie!	Kurt Schwabach	Franz-Josef Breuer	11
6	5	Belgium	Fud Leclerc	Mon Amour Pour Toi	Robert Montal	Jack Say	9
7	7	Austria	Harry Winter	Du Hast Mich So Fasziniert	Robert Gilbert	Robert Stolz	6
8	12	Italy	Renato Rascel	Romantica	Dino Verde	Renato Rascel	5
9	9	Switzerland	Anita Traversi	Cielo E Terra	Mario Robbiani	Mario Robbiani	5
10	2	Sweden	Siw Malmkvist	Alla Andra Får Varann	Åke Gerhard	Ulf Kjellqvist	4
11	4	Denmark	Katy Bødtger	Det Var En Yndig Tid	Sven Buemann	Vilfred Kjær	4
12	10	Netherlands	Rudi Carrell	Wat Een Geluk	Willy van Hemert	Dick Schallies	2
13	3	Luxembourg	Camillo Felgen	So Laang We's Du Do Bast	Henri Mootz	Henri Mootz, Jean Roderes	1

1961 Eurovision 6: Cannes, France

18 March 1961

Rank	Start	Country	Artist	Song	Writer	Composer	POINTS
1	14	Luxembourg	Jean-Claude Pascal	Nous Les Amoureux	Maurice Vidalin	Jacques Datin	31
2	15	United Kingdom	The Allisons	Are You Sure?	John Alford, Bob Day	John Alford, Bob Day	24
3	10	Switzerland	Franca di Rienzo	Nous Aurons Demain	Emile Gardaz	Géo Voumard	16
4	9	France	Jean-Paul Mauric	Printemps (avril Carillonne)	Guy Favereau	Francis Baxter	13
5	16	Italy	Betty Curtis	Al Di Là	Giulio Rapetti	Carlo Donida	12
6	13	Denmark	Dario Campeotto	Angelique	Aksel Rasmussen	Aksel Rasmussen	12
7	12	Norway	Nora Brockstedt	Sommer I Palma	Egil Hagen	Jan Wølner	10
8	5	Yugoslavia	Ljiljana Petrovic	Neke Davne Zvezde	Miroslav Antic	Jože Privšek	9
9	1	Spain	Conchita Bautista	Estando Contigo	Antonio Guijarro	Augusto Algueró	8
10	6	Netherlands	Greetje Kauffeld	Wat Een Dag	Pieter Goemans	Dick Schallies	6
11	2	Monaco	Colette Deréal	Allons, Allons Les Enfants	Pierre Delanoë	Hubert Giraud	6
12	4	Finland	Laila Kinnunen	Valoa Ikkunassa	Sauvo Puhtila	Eino Hurme	6
13	8	Germany	Lale Andersen	Einmal Sehen Wir Uns Wieder	Ernst Bader	Rudolf Maluck	3
14	7	Sweden	Lill-Babs	April, April	Bo Eneby	Bobby Ericsson	2
15	3	Austria	Jimmy Makulis	Sehnsucht	Leopold Andrejewirsch	Leopold Andrejewirsch	1
16	11	Belgium	Bob Benny	September, Gouden Roos	Wim Brabants	Hans Flower	1

1960 Eurovision 5: London, United Kingdom — 29 March 1960

	Austria	Belgium	Denmark	France	Germany	Italy	Luxembourg	Monaco	Netherlands	Norway	Sweden	Switzerland	United Kingdom	TOTAL
United Kingdom	3	1			1	2	5	1	5	2	1	4		25
Sweden				2		1			1					4
Luxembourg						1								1
Denmark						1	1							4
Belgium	1				1	3					4		1	9
Norway	1	1	2	1						2			1	11
Austria		1	2				1						2	6
Monaco			2	3	7	1			1				1	15
Switzerland	2						1			1				5
Netherlands		1				1						1		2
Germany	2	2		4			1	2	1		1			11
Italy		3					1	2	2					5
France	1	3	4		1			5		5	4	1	5	32

1961 Eurovision 6: Cannes, France — 18 March 1961

	Austria	Belgium	Denmark	Finland	France	Germany	Italy	Luxembourg	Monaco	Netherlands	Norway	Spain	Sweden	Switzerland	United Kingdom	Yugoslavia	TOTAL
Spain					2				1	1	2		1	1	1		8
Monaco				3								1			1		6
Austria															1		1
Finland			1		1										2		6
Yugoslavia	3		1		2		2			1				1	1		9
Netherlands					2		2									2	6
Sweden													1				2
Germany	1		1										1				3
France						4	2		1	2		2	4		2		13
Switzerland	2							1	2			1			2	1	16
Belgium									1								1
Norway		5	2							1	8	1	2		1	1	10
Denmark		1	1			5				1			1				12
Luxembourg	4	1	1		3		3		4	3	1	2		1		5	31
United Kingdom		1					1	8					1	7			24
Italy		4	4		1	1			1	1		3			1	1	12

Note: in both years each country had 10 jurors who could award 1 point each to their favourite act.

1962 Eurovision 7: Luxembourg
18 March 1962

Rank	Start	Country	Artist	Song	Writer	Composer	POINTS
1	9	France	Isabelle Aubret	Un Premier Amour	Roland Valade	Claude Henri Vic	26
2	16	Monaco	François Deguelt	Dis Rien	René Rouzaud	Henri Salvador	13
3	14	Luxembourg	Camillo Felgen	Petit Bonhomme	Maurice Vidalin	Jacques Datin	11
4	13	United Kingdom	Ronnie Carroll	Ring-a-ding Girl	Stan Butcher	Syd Cordell	10
5	12	Yugoslavia	Lola Novakovic	Ne Pali Svetlo U Sumrak	Dragutin Britvic	Jozé Privšek	10
6	7	Germany	Conny Froboess	Zwei Kleine Italiener	Georg Buschor	Christian Bruhn	9
7	1	Finland	Marion Rung	Tipi-tii	Kari Tuomisaari	Kari Tuomisaari	4
8	6	Sweden	Inger Berggren	Sol Och Vår	Ulf Kjellqvist, Åke Gerhard	Ulf Kjellqvist, Åke Gerhard	4
9	15	Italy	Claudio Villa	Addio, Addio	Franco Migliacci	Domenico Modugno	3
10	11	Switzerland	Jean Philippe	Le Retour	Emile Gardaz	Géo Voumard	2
11	10	Norway	Inger Jacobsen	Kom Sol, Kom Regn	Ivar Andersen	Kjell Karlsen	2
12	5	Denmark	Ellen Winther	Vuggevise	Sejr Volmer-Sørensen	Kjeld Bonfils	2
13	8	Netherlands	De Spelbrekers	Katinka	Henry Hamhuis	Joop Stokkermans	0
14	2	Belgium	Fud Leclerc	Ton Nom	Tony Golan	Eric Channe	0
15	3	Spain	Victor Balaguer	Llámame	Miguel Portoles	Mario Selles	0
16	4	Austria	Eleonore Schwarz	Nur In Der Wiener Luft	Bruno Uher	Bruno Uher	0

1963 Eurovision 8: London, United Kingdom
23 March 1963

Rank	Start	Country	Artist	Song	Writer	Composer	POINTS
1	8	Denmark	Grethe & Jørgen Ingmann	Dansevise	Sejr Volmer-Sørensen	Otto Francker	42
2	10	Switzerland	Esther Ofarim	T'en Va Pas	Emile Gardaz	Géo Voumard	40
3	6	Italy	Emilio Pericoli	Uno Per Tutte	Alberto Testa, Giulio Rapetti	Tony Renis	37
4	1	United Kingdom	Ronnie Carroll	Say Wonderful Things	Norman Newell	Philip Green	28
5	11	France	Alain Barrière	Elle était Si Jolie	Alain Barrière	Alain Barrière	25
6	15	Monaco	Françoise Hardy	L'amour S'en Va	Françoise Hardy	Françoise Hardy	25
7	4	Austria	Carmela Corren	Vielleicht Geschieht Ein Wunder	Peter Wehle	Erwin Halletz	16
8	16	Luxembourg	Nana Mouskouri	A Force De Prier	Pierre Delanoë	Raymond Bernard	13
9	3	Germany	Heidi Brühl	Marcel	Charly Niessen	Charly Niessen	5
10	14	Belgium	Jacques Raymond	Waarom	Wim Brabants	Hans Flower	4
11	9	Yugoslavia	Vice Vukov	Brodovi	Mario Nardelli	Mario Nardelli	3
12	12	Spain	José Guardiola	Algo Prodigioso	Camillo Murillo Janero	Fernando Garcia Morcillo	2
13	5	Norway	Anita Thallaug	Solhverv	Dag Kristoffersen	Dag Kristoffersen	0
14	7	Finland	Laila Halme	Muistojeni Laulu	Börje Sundgren	Börje Sundgren	0
15	2	Netherlands	Annie Palmen	En Speeldoos	Pieter Goemans	Pieter Goemans	0
16	13	Sweden	Monica Zetterlund	En Gång i Stockholm	Beppe Wolgers	Bobbie Ericsson	0

1962 Eurovision 7: Luxembourg
18 March 1962

	Austria	Belgium	Denmark	Finland	France	Germany	Italy	Luxembourg	Monaco	Netherlands	Norway	Spain	Sweden	Switzerland	United Kingdom	Yugoslavia	TOTAL
Finland					2						1						4
Belgium	2																0
Spain																	0
Austria																	0
Denmark			3														2
Sweden			1												2		4
Germany				2					2								9
Netherlands													1				0
France	2	2				3	2	1	1	2	3	2	3	3	1	3	26
Norway					2	2											2
Switzerland		1		1													2
Yugoslavia			2	3	3		3					1	2				10
United Kingdom	1	3	2									3		2		2	10
Luxembourg									3					1		1	11
Italy								2		3							3
Monaco	3				1	1		3		3	2						13

Note: Each country awarded from 3 points to 1 point in descending order for their 3 favourite acts.

1963 Eurovision 8: London, United Kingdom
23 March 1963

	Austria	Belgium	Denmark	Finland	France	Germany	Italy	Luxembourg	Monaco	Netherlands	Norway	Spain	Sweden	Switzerland	United Kingdom	Yugoslavia	TOTAL
United Kingdom			3	3	3				1	3	5	5	2			3	28
Netherlands																	0
Germany									3		2		3	5			5
Austria	2		1	4	2				5	1		3		3	4		16
Norway																	0
Italy		3	5	2				4	5	5	3	3	5	4	2	4	37
Finland																	0
Denmark	3	5		5		2	2	5	4		4	2		3	3		42
Yugoslavia					1			3	2		1	4	1				3
Switzerland	5	4	4			4	5	3	4	5		1			5	5	40
France	2	1				1	4	1	2	4				4		2	25
Spain																	2
Sweden																	0
Belgium	4																4
Monaco	1		2	1		5	3	2		2			4	1	1	1	25
Luxembourg					4	3	1							2			13

Note: Each country awarded from 5 points to 1 point in descending order for their 5 favourite acts.

1964 Eurovision 9: Copenhagen, Denmark

21 March 1964

Rank	Start	Country	Artist	Song	Writer	Composer	POINTS
1	12	Italy	Gigliola Cinquetti	Non Ho L'étà	Mario Panzeri	Nicola Salerno	49
2	8	United Kingdom	Matt Monro	I Love The Little Things	Tony Hatch	Tony Hatch	17
3	10	Monaco	Romuald	Où Sont-elles Passées?	Pierre Barouh	Francis Lai	15
4	7	France	Rachel	Le Chant De Mallory	Pierre Cour	André Popp	14
5	1	Luxembourg	Hugues Aufray	Dès Que Le Printemps Revient	Jacques Plante	Hugues Aufray	14
6	6	Austria	Udo Jürgens	Warum Nur, Warum?	Udo Jürgen Bockelmann	Udo Jürgen Bockelmann	11
7	5	Finland	Lasse Mårtenson	Laiskotellen	Sauvo Puhtila	Lasse Mårtenson	9
8	3	Norway	Arne Bendiksen	Spiral	Egil Hagen	Sigurd Jansen	6
9	4	Denmark	Bjørn Tidmand	Sangen Om Dig	Morgens Dam	Aksel Rasmussen	4
10	15	Belgium	Robert Cogoi	Près De Ma Rivière	Robert Cogoi	Robert Cogoi	2
11	2	Netherlands	Anneke Grönloh	Jij Bent Mijn Leven	René de Vos	Ted Powder	2
12	16	Spain	Tim, Nelly & Tony	Caracola	Fina de Calderón	Fina de Calderón	1
13	14	Switzerland	Anita Traversi	I Miei Pensieri	Sanzio Chiesa	Giovanni Pelli	0
14	9	Germany	Nora Nova	Man Gewöhnt Sich So Schnell An Das Schöne	Niels Nobach	Rudi von der Dovenmühle	0
15	11	Portugal	António Calvário	Oração	Francisco Nicholson, Rogério Bracinha	João Nobre	0
16	13	Yugoslavia	Sabahudin Kurt	Zivot Je Sklopio Krug	Stevan Raickovic	Srcan Matijevic	0

1965 Eurovision 10: Naples, Italy

20 March 1965

Rank	Start	Country	Artist	Song	Writer	Composer	POINTS
1	15	Luxembourg	France Gall	Poupée De Cire, Poupée De Son	Serge Gainsbourg	Serge Gainsbourg	32
2	2	United Kingdom	Kathy Kirby	I Belong	Phil Peters	Peter Lee-Sterling	26
3	11	France	Guy Mardel	N'avoue Jamais	Françoise Dorin	Guy Mardel	22
4	6	Austria	Udo Jürgens	Sag Ihr, Ich Lass' Sie Grüßen	Frank Bohlen	Udo Jürgen Bockelmann	16
5	13	Italy	Bobby Solo	Se Piangi, Se Ridi	Giulio Rapetti	Roberto Satti, Gianni Marchetti	15
6	4	Ireland	Butch Moore	I'm Walking The Streets In The Rain	Teresa Conlon	Joe Harrigan, George Prendergast	11
7	14	Denmark	Birgit Brüel	For Din Skyld	Poul Henningsen	Jørgen Jersild	10
8	18	Switzerland	Yovanna	Non à Jamais Sans Toi	Jean Charles	Bob Calfati	8
9	9	Monaco	Marjorie Noël	Va Dire à L'amour	Jacques Mareuil	Raymond Bernard	7
10	10	Sweden	Ingvar Wixell	Absent Friend	Alf Henriksson	Dag Wiren	6
11	1	Netherlands	Conny Van den Bos	Het Is Genoeg	Karel Prior	Johnny Holshuyzen	5
12	17	Yugoslavia	Vice Vukov	Ceznja	Zarko Roje	Julijo Maric	2
13	7	Norway	Kirsti Sparboe	Karusell	Jolly Kramer-Johansen	Jolly Kramer-Johansen	1
14	12	Portugal	Simone de Oliveira	Sol De Inverno	Jeronimo Bragança	Carlos Nobrega e Sousa	1
15	3	Spain	Conchita Bautista	Qué Bueno, Qué Bueno	Antonio Figueroa Egea	Antonio Figueroa Egea	0
16	16	Finland	Viktor Klimenko	Aurinko Laskee Länteen	Reino Helismaa	Toivo Kärki	0
17	5	Germany	Ulla Wiesner	Paradies, Wo Bist Du?	Barbara Kist, Hans Blüm	Barbara Kist, Hans Blüm	0
18	8	Belgium	Lize Marke	Als Het Weer Lente Is	Jaak Dreesen	Jef van den Berg	0

1964 Eurovision 9: Copenhagen, Denmark — 21 March 1964

Receiving \ Voting	Austria	Belgium	Denmark	Finland	France	Germany	Italy	Luxembourg	Monaco	Netherlands	Norway	Portugal	Spain	Switzerland	United Kingdom	Yugoslavia	TOTAL
Luxembourg					3	5	3			3							14
Netherlands			1										1				2
Norway			5	1													6
Denmark				3	1												4
Finland											1	3		3		1	9
Austria		1				1	5	1	1	1		3					11
France	3			3					5		1		3			1	14
United Kingdom	1			3	1	1		3			5	3					17
Germany																	0
Monaco		3			5	3				5				1		3	15
Portugal																	0
Italy	5	5		5		3		5	3	5	5	5	5	3	5	5	49
Yugoslavia																	0
Switzerland																	0
Belgium																	2
Spain									1								1

1965 Eurovision 10: Naples, Italy — 20 March 1965

Receiving \ Voting	Austria	Belgium	Denmark	Finland	France	Germany	Ireland	Italy	Luxembourg	Monaco	Netherlands	Norway	Portugal	Spain	Sweden	Switzerland	United Kingdom	Yugoslavia	TOTAL
Netherlands												5							5
United Kingdom		6	5					1				1	3	5	3	5		3	26
Spain																			0
Ireland							5										3		11
Germany													3						0
Austria					5			5	3				5					3	16
Norway	1																		1
Belgium																			0
Monaco								1		5						1	5		7
Sweden			3	3						1								1	6
France						3	1		3		1			3	5			5	22
Portugal						1				3									1
Italy	3				3	5			1		3			1		3	1		15
Denmark				5				5											10
Luxembourg	5						3	3			5	5	5		5	3			32
Finland																			0
Yugoslavia				1	1														2
Switzerland	3				5														8

Note: In both years each country awarded their three favourite acts either 5 points, 3 points or 1 point, apart from Belgium in 1965 which chose only two favourites and awarded 6 and 3 points.

1966 Eurovision 11: Luxembourg City, Luxembourg 5 March 1966

Rank	Start	Country	Artist	Song	Writer	Composer	POINTS
1	9	Austria	Udo Jürgens	Merci Chérie	Udo Jürgen Bockelmann, Thomas	Udo Jürgen Bockelmann	31
2	10	Sweden	Lill Lindfors & Svante Thuresson	Nygammal Vals Eller Hip Man	Björn Lindroth	Bengt-Arne Wallin	16
3	6	Norway	Åse Kleveland	Intet Er Nytt Under Solen	Arne Bendiksen	Arne Bendiksen	15
4	17	Ireland	Dickie Rock	Come Back To Stay	Rowland Soper	Rowland Soper	14
5	3	Belgium	Tonia	Un Peu De Poivre, Un Peu De Sel	Phil van Cauwenbergh	Paul Quintens	14
6	12	Switzerland	Madeleine Pascal	Ne Vois-tu Pas?	Roland Schweizer	Pierre Brenner	12
7	5	Yugoslavia	Berta Ambroz	Brez Besed	Elza Budav	Mojmir Sepe	9
8	11	Spain	Raphael	Yo Soy Aquél	Manuel Alejandro	Manuel Alejandro	9
9	18	United Kingdom	Kenneth McKellar	A Man Without Love	Peter Callander	Cyril Ornadel	8
10	7	Finland	Ann-Christine Nyström	Play-boy		Ossi Runne	7
11	4	Luxembourg	Michèle Torr	Ce Soir Je T'attendais	Jacques Chaumelle	Bernard Kesslair	7
12	1	Germany	Margot Eskens	Die Zeiger Der Uhr	Hans Bradtke	Walter Dobschinski	7
13	8	Portugal	Madalena Iglesias	Ele E Ela	Carlos Canelhas	Carlos Canelhas	6
14	2	Denmark	Ulla Pia	Stop, Ja Stop - Ja Stop, Mens Legen Er	Erik Kåre	Erik Kåre	4
15	16	Netherlands	Milly Scott	Fernando En Philipo	Gerrit den Braber	Kees de Bruyn	2
16	15	France	Dominique Walter	Chez Nous	Jacques Plante	Claude Carrère	1
17	13	Monaco	Tereza	Bien Plus Fort	Jean-Max Rivière	Gérard Bourgeois	0
18	14	Italy	Domenico Modugno	Dio Come Ti Amo	Domenico Modugno	Domenico Modugno	0

1967 Eurovision 12: Vienna, Austria 8 April 1967

Rank	Start	Country	Artist	Song	Writer	Composer	POINTS
1	11	United Kingdom	Sandie Shaw	Puppet On A String	Bill Martin, Phil Coulter	Bill Martin, Phil Coulter	47
2	17	Ireland	Sean Dunphy	If I Could Choose	Wesley Burrows	Michael Coffey	22
3	4	France	Noëlle Cordier	Il Doit Faire Beau Là-bas	Pierre Delanoë	Hubert Giraud	20
4	2	Luxembourg	Vicky	L'amour Est Bleu	Pierre Cour	André Popp	17
5	14	Monaco	Minouche Barelli	Boum-badaboum	Serge Gainsbourg	Serge Gainsbourg, Michel Colombier	10
6	12	Spain	Raphael	Hablemos Del Amor	Manuel Alejandro	Manuel Alejandro	9
7	10	Belgium	Louis Neefs	Ik Heb Zorgen	Phil van Cauwenbergh	Paul Quintens	8
8	15	Yugoslavia	Lado Leskovar	Vse Roze Sveta	Milan Lindic	Urban Koder	7
9	9	Germany	Inge Brück	Anouschka	Hans Blüm	Hans Blüm	7
10	7	Sweden	Östen Warnebring	Som En Dröm	Curt Peterson, Marcus Österdahl, Patrice Hellberg	Curt Peterson, Marcus Österdahl, Patrice Hellberg	7
11	16	Italy	Claudio Villa	Non Andare Più Lontano	Vito Pallavicini	Gianni Mescoli	4
12	5	Portugal	Eduardo Nascimento	O Vento Mudou	João Magalhães Pereira	Nuño Nazareth Fernandes	3
13	8	Finland	Fredi	Varjoon-suojaan	Alvi Vuorinen	Lasse Mårtenson	3
14	3	Austria	Peter Horten	Warum Es Hunderttausend Sterne Gibt	Karin Bognar	Kurt Peche	2
15	13	Norway	Kirsti Sparboe	Dukkemann	Ola Johannessen	Tor Hultin	2
16	1	Netherlands	Thérèse Steinmetz	Ring-dinge	Gerrit den Braber	Johnny Holshuysen	2
17	6	Switzerland	Géraldine	Quel Coeur Vas-tu Briser?	Gérard Gray	Daniël Faure	0

1966 Eurovision 11: Luxembourg City, Luxembourg
5 March 1966

	Austria	Belgium	Denmark	Finland	France	Germany	Ireland	Italy	Luxembourg	Monaco	Netherlands	Norway	Portugal	Spain	Sweden	Switzerland	United Kingdom	Yugoslavia	TOTAL
Germany		1						1								5			7
Denmark				3									1						4
Belgium						5					5		3		1				14
Luxembourg	1				1	3									5				7
Yugoslavia	3			1		1		5			1								9
Norway										5			1	3				3	12
Finland			3						5			3							7
Portugal			1						1			5	5						6
Austria	5			5	3		3	3	5	3	1	5		5		3	3	5	31
Sweden			5											1		1		1	16
Spain																			9
Switzerland	5				5		3												12
Monaco																			0
Italy										1									0
France																			1
Netherlands											3								2
Ireland	3					1			3								1	3	14
United Kingdom																			8

1967 Eurovision 12: Vienna, Austria
8 April 1967

	Austria	Belgium	Finland	France	Germany	Ireland	Italy	Luxembourg	Monaco	Netherlands	Norway	Portugal	Spain	Sweden	Switzerland	United Kingdom	Yugoslavia	TOTAL
Netherlands		1				1	3		1							1	1	2
Luxembourg			2		2	2			2	4		1	1	4	1	2	1	17
Austria				1	1		1	2		1		1			1		4	2
France	1				2	1										2		20
Portugal			1	1									1		1			3
Switzerland						2					2	1		1			1	0
Sweden		1				1	1	5			7	1	1				1	7
Finland		3			1	1	1	1	3		1	1		1	1	1		3
Germany	3	2		3		1			2		1	1		1				7
Belgium	1		7			2	2	5	1	2	7	1		1			1	8
United Kingdom	1			1			1		1	1	2	2			7		1	47
Spain		1				1	1	1										9
Norway	2	3						1	1			1	5	1				2
Monaco			1			1	1					1	2	1			1	10
Yugoslavia		1	1				1	1		1	1		1		1	1		7
Italy	3				1							1		2	1	1	1	4
Ireland	3	3	2	4		1	1	1	2	1	1		1				1	22

Note: In 1966, each country awarded their three favourite acts either 5 points, 3 points or 1 point. In 1967, Ten jurors from each country each awarded 1 point to their favourite act

1968 Eurovision 13: London, United Kingdom
6 April 1968

Rank	Start	Country	Artist	Song	Writer	Composer	POINTS
1	15	Spain	Massiel	La, La, La	Ramón Arcusa, Manuel de la Calva	Ramón Arcusa, Manuel de la Calva	29
2	12	United Kingdom	Cliff Richard	Congratulations	Bill Martin, Phil Coulter	Bill Martin, Phil Coulter	28
3	10	France	Isabelle Aubret	La Source	Guy Bonnet, Henri Dijan	Daniël Faure	20
4	14	Ireland	Pat McGeegan	Chance Of A Lifetime	John Kennedy	John Kennedy	18
5	8	Sweden	Claes-Göran Hederström	Det Börjar Verka Kärlek, Banne Mej	Peter Himmelstrand	Peter Himmelstrand	15
6	16	Germany	Wencke Myhre	Ein Hoch Der Liebe	Carl Schäuble	Horst Jankowski	11
7	17	Yugoslavia	Luci Kapurso & Hamo Hajdarhodzic	Jedan Dan	Stijepo Strazicic	Djelo Jusic, Stipica Kalogjera	8
8	7	Monaco	Line & Willy	A Chacun Sa Chanson	Roland Valade	Jean-Claude Olivier	8
9	3	Belgium	Claude Lombard	Quand Tu Reviendras	Roland Dero	Jo van Wetter	8
10	11	Italy	Sergio Endrigo	Marianne	Sergio Endrigo	Sergio Endrigo	7
11	5	Luxembourg	Chris Baldo & Sophie Garel	Nous Vivrons D'amour	Jacques Demarny	Carlos Leresche	5
12	1	Portugal	Carlos Mendes	Verão	José Alberto Diogo	Pedro Osório	5
13	6	Switzerland	Gianni Mascolo	Guardando Il Sole	Sanzio Chiesa	Aldo d'Addario	2
14	13	Norway	Odd Børre	Stress	Ola Johannessen	Tor Hultin	2
15	4	Austria	Karel Gott	Tausend Fenster	Walter Brandin	Udo Jürgen Bockelmann	2
16	9	Finland	Kristina Hautala	Kun Kello Käy	Juha Vainio	Esko Linnavalli	1
17	2	Netherlands	Ronnie Tober	Morgen	Theo Strengers	Joop Stokkermans	1

1969 Eurovision 14: Madrid, Spain
29 March 1969

Rank	Start	Country	Artist	Song	Writer	Composer	POINTS
=1	14	France	Frida Boccara	Un Jour, Un Enfant	Eddy Marnay	Emile Stern	18
=1	7	United Kingdom	Lulu	Boom Bang-a-bang	Peter Warne	Alan Moorhouse	18
=1	8	Netherlands	Lenny Kuhr	De Troubadour	Lenny Kuhr	David Hartsema	18
=1	3	Spain	Salomé	Vivo Cantando	Aniano Alcalde	Maria José de Cerato	18
5	11	Switzerland	Paola del Medico	Bonjour, Bonjour	Jack Stark	Henry Mayer	13
6	4	Monaco	Jean-Jacques	Maman, Maman	Jo Perrier	Jo Perrier	11
7	10	Belgium	Louis Neefs	Jennifer Jennings	Phil van Cauwenbergh	Paul Quintens	10
8	5	Ireland	Muriel Day & the Lindsays	The Wages Of Love	Michael Reade	Michael Reade	10
9	13	Germany	Siw Malmkvist	Primaballerina	Hans Blüm	Hans Blüm	8
10	9	Sweden	Tommy Körberg	Judy, Min Vän	Britt Lindeborg	Roger Wallis	8
11	2	Luxembourg	Romuald	Cathérine	André Pascal	Paul Mauriat, André Borly	7
12	16	Finland	Jarkko & Laura	Kuin Silloin Ennen	Juha Vainio	Toivo Kärki	6
13	1	Yugoslavia	Ivan	Pozdrav Svijetu	Milan Lentic	Milan Lentic	5
14	6	Italy	Iva Zanicchi	Due Grosse Lacrime Bianche	Daiano	Piero Soffici	5
15	15	Portugal	Simone de Oliveira	Desfolhada Portuguesa	José Carlos Ary dos Santos	Nuño Nazareth Fernandes	4
16	12	Norway	Kirsti Sparboe	Oj, Oj, Oj, Så Glad, Jeg Skal Bli	Arne Bendiksen	Arne Bendiksen	1

Note: Four joint winners were declared. A tie-break system was introduced in 1970.

1968 Eurovision 13: London, United Kingdom — 6 April 1968

	Austria	Belgium	Finland	France	Germany	Ireland	Italy	Luxembourg	Monaco	Netherlands	Norway	Portugal	Spain	Sweden	Switzerland	United Kingdom	Yugoslavia	TOTAL
Portugal													3					5
Netherlands																1		1
Belgium		1					3											8
Austria	1																	2
Luxembourg	1			1					1							1		5
Switzerland																	2	2
Monaco			3			1				1					3			8
Sweden			1			4				2	1				2	2		15
Finland											1							1
France					2		2			3	6	1	1	1	3	1		20
Italy					2	1		1	5			1		3	2		2	7
United Kingdom	2	2	2	4	2	1	1	1	5	2		1	1	3	4		1	28
Norway	4				6			1		1		4	1	4			6	2
Ireland	2	1	3	4		1	3	1	4	1	1	4	2	4				18
Spain	2							1						2	1	5		29
Germany	1							1					1	1				11
Yugoslavia						3		1							1			8

1969 Eurovision 14: Madrid, Spain — 29 March 1969

	Belgium	Finland	France	Germany	Ireland	Italy	Luxembourg	Monaco	Netherlands	Norway	Portugal	Spain	Sweden	Switzerland	United Kingdom	Yugoslavia	TOTAL
Yugoslavia	1									1		1			1		5
Luxembourg	1			1				3	1	1						1	7
Spain	3	2		3			2	3	2	1	2		2			1	18
Monaco	1		1	1	1	4	2		2	2			2	1			11
Ireland		3					4	1	1				1				10
Italy		1			1		2			1							5
United Kingdom	1			1	1	3		1	1	1	1	2	5	3		1	18
Netherlands	1	6		1		3	2	1		3	1					2	18
Sweden	3									2		2		4			8
Belgium					3			1	1	2	1	2			3		10
Switzerland	2		2							1		2	2		2	2	13
Norway																	1
Germany	1	1			4		1	2		1	2	2	1	1		3	8
France	1								2	1	2		1	1	4		18
Portugal			1									2					4
Finland						1				1		1					6

Note: in both years, ten jurors from each country each awarded 1 point to their favourite act.

1970 Eurovision 15: Amsterdam, Netherlands

21 March 1970

Rank	Start	Country	Artist	Song	Writer	Composer	POINTS
1	12	Ireland	Dana	All Kinds Of Everything	Derry Lindsay, Jackie Smith	Derry Lindsay, Jackie Smith	32
2	7	United Kingdom	Mary Hopkin	Knock, Knock (who's there?)	John Carter, Geoff Stephens	John Carter, Geoff Stephens	26
3	11	Germany	Katja Ebstein	Wunder Gibt Es Immer Wieder	Günther Loose	Christian Bruhn	12
4	9	Spain	Julio Iglesias	Gwendolyne	Julio Iglesias	Julio Iglesias	8
5	6	France	Guy Bonnet	Marie Blanche	Pierre-André Dousset	Guy Bonnet	8
6	2	Switzerland	Henri Dès	Retour	Henri Dès	Henri Dès	8
7	1	Netherlands	Patricia & Hearts of Soul	Waterman	Pieter Goemans	Pieter Goemans	7
8	10	Monaco	Dominique Dussault	Marlène	Henri Dijan	Eddie Barclay, Jimmy Walter	5
9	3	Italy	Gianni Morandi	Occhi Di Ragazza	Gianfranco Baldazzi, Sergio Bardotti	Lucio Dalla	5
10	5	Belgium	Jean Vallée	Viens L'oublier	Jean Vallée	Jean Vallée	5
11	4	Yugoslavia	Eva Sršen	Pridi, Dala Ti Bom Cvet	Dušan Velkaverh	Mojmir Sepe	4
12	8	Luxembourg	David-Alexandre Winter	Je Suis Tombé Du Ciel	Eddy Marnay	Yves de Vriendt	0

Note: Only 12 countries participated due to a boycott over the voting system used in 1969.

1971 Eurovision 16: Dublin, Ireland

3 April 1971

Rank	Start	Country	Artist	Song	Writer	Composer	POINTS
1	3	Monaco	Séverine	Un Banc, Un Arbre, Une Rue	Yves Dessca	Jean-Pierre Bourtayre	128
2	6	Spain	Karina	En Un Mundo Nuevo	Tony Luz	Rafael Trabucchelli	115
3	5	Germany	Katja Ebstein	Diese Welt	Fred Jay	Dieter Zimmermann	100
4	9	United Kingdom	Clodagh Rodgers	Jack In The Box	David Myers	John Worsley	98
5	11	Italy	Massimo Ranieri	L'amore è Un Attimo	Gaetano Savio, Giancarlo Bigazzi	Federico Polito	91
6	12	Sweden	Family Four	Vita Vidder	Håkan Elmquist	Håkan Elmquist	85
7	14	Netherlands	Saskia & Serge	De Tijd	Gerrit den Braber	Joop Stokkermans	85
8	17	Finland	Markku Aro & the Koivisto Sisters	Tie Uuteen Päivään	Rauno Lehtinen	Rauno Lehtinen	84
9	15	Portugal	Tonicha	Menina Do Alto Da Serra	José Carlos Ary dos Santos	Nuño Nazareth Fernandes	83
10	7	France	Serge Lama	Un Jardin Sur La Terre	Henri Dijan, Jacques Demarny	Alice Dona	83
11	13	Ireland	Angela Farrell	One Day Love	Donald Martin, Ita Flynn	Donald Martin, Ita Flynn	79
12	4	Switzerland	Peter, Sue & Marc	Les Illusions De Nos Vingt Ans	Maurice Tézé	Peter Reber	78
13	8	Luxembourg	Monique Melsen	Pomme, Pomme, Pomme	Pierre Cour	Hubert Giraud	70
14	16	Yugoslavia	Krunoslav Slabinac	Tvoj Djecak Je Tuzan	Zvonimir Golob	Ivica Krajac	68
15	10	Belgium	Lily Castel & Jacques Raymond	Goeie Morgen, Morgen	Phil van Cauwenbergh	Paul Quintens	68
16	1	Austria	Marianne Mendt	Musik	Richard Schönherz, Manuel Rigoni	Richard Schönherz, Manuel Rigoni	66
17	18	Norway	Hanne Krogh	Lykken Er	Arne Bendiksen	Arne Bendiksen	65
18	2	Malta	Joe Grech	Marija L-maltija	Charles Misfud	Joe Grech	52

1970 Eurovision 15: Amsterdam, Netherlands — 21 March 1970

	Belgium	France	Germany	Ireland	Italy	Luxembourg	Netherlands	Spain	Sweden	Switzerland	United Kingdom	Yugoslavia	TOTAL
Netherlands		2	2		3								7
Switzerland			2				2				1		8
Italy						1		2				1	5
Yugoslavia											4		4
Belgium		3		1									5
France				3		2			2				8
United Kingdom		2	4	3	2	2	3		4	2		4	26
Luxembourg													0
Spain					3	2							8
Monaco	1	2						1	3	1			5
Germany		1		2	1	3		4	1	1			12
Ireland	9	1	2			2	5	3		6	4		32

Note: Ten jurors from each country each awarded 1 point to their favourite act.

1971 Eurovision 16: Dublin, Ireland — 3 April 1971

	Austria	Belgium	Finland	France	Germany	Ireland	Italy	Luxembourg	Malta	Monaco	Netherlands	Norway	Portugal	Spain	Sweden	Switzerland	United Kingdom	Yugoslavia	TOTAL
Austria		3	3	3	7	6	6	2	3	5	3	5	5	2	4	2	3	4	66
Malta	4	4	3	3	3	4	4	2	3	2	5	2		5	2	2	3	2	52
Monaco	4	10	7	8	10	9	4	4	5	4	9	10	8	2	10	10	8	10	128
Switzerland	5	3	4	6	6	5	7	2	5	4	5	4	6	2	4	6	6	4	78
Germany	6	7	5	8		5	6	2	8	10	6	4	7	8	6	6	6	7	100
Spain	4	4	9	10	7	9	4	4	2	8	9	8	7	5	6	5	7	7	115
France	3	3	3		5	6	5	2	7	8	3	5	5	5	4	8	5	5	83
Luxembourg	2	3	5	5	2	5	3	4	8	8	5	4	6	4	2	3	6	4	70
United Kingdom	4	8	6	8	5	7	3		2	8	6	6	7	2	5	6	8	6	98
Belgium	3		6	5	2	4		2	6	5	2	4	6	2	5	4	6	3	68
Italy	4	2	2	9	6	6	3	2	4	9	9	6	3		7	8	6	8	91
Sweden	7	6	4	5	4		6	2	6	4	5	4	4	6		9	5	6	85
Ireland	7	3	6	7	4	3		2	6		6	8	9	5	2	3	6	3	79
Netherlands	6	2	6	7	4	5	6	2	2	6		4	4	5	6	5	5	5	85
Portugal	4	4	5	8	5	3	4	5	3	6	5	8		10	2	2	6	5	83
Yugoslavia	6	4	2	7	7	7	5	2	2	4	4	5	4	6	2	4	3		68
Finland	4	10	3	4	4	6	4	2	4	4	3	6	8	3	4	4	10	6	84
Norway	3	6		5	2	7	2	2	3	6	2		5	2	2	4	7	4	65

Note: Two jurors from each country both awarded between 1 and 5 points per act.

39

1972 Eurovision 17: Edinburgh, United Kingdom   25 March 1972

Rank	Start	Country	Artist	Song	Writer	Composer	POINTS
1	17	Luxembourg	Vicky Leandros	Après Toi	Klaus Munro, Yves Dessca	Mario Panas, Klaus Munro	128
2	5	United Kingdom	The New Seekers	Beg, Steal Or Borrow	Tony Cole, Graeme Hall, Steve Wolfe	Tony Cole, Graeme Hall, Steve Wolfe	114
3	1	Germany	Mary Roos	Nur Die Liebe Läßt Uns Leben	Joachim Relin	Joachim Heider	107
4	18	Netherlands	Sandra & Andres	Als Het Om De Liefde Gaat	Hans van Hemert	Dries Holten	106
5	11	Austria	The Milestones	Falter Im Wind	Heinz Unger	Richard Schönherz, Manuel Rigoni	100
6	12	Italy	Nicola di Bari	I Giorni Dell' Arcobaleno	Dalmazio Masini	Piero Pintucci, Nicola di Bari	92
7	7	Portugal	Carlos Mendes	A Festa Da Vida	José Niza	José Calvário	90
8	8	Switzerland	Véronique Müller	C'est La Chanson De Mon Amour	Catherine Desage	Véronique Müller	88
9	13	Yugoslavia	Tereza	Muzika I Ti	Ivica Krajac	Nikica Kalogjera	87
10	4	Spain	Jaime Morey	Amanece	Ramón Arcusa	Augusto Algueró	83
11	2	France	Betty Mars	Comé-comédie	Frédéric Botton	Frédéric Botton	81
12	10	Finland	Päivi Paunu & Kim Floor	Muistathan	Juha Flinck	Juha Flinck, Nacke Johansson	78
13	14	Sweden	Family Four	Härliga Sommardag	Håkan Elmquist	Håkan Elmquist	75
14	6	Norway	Grethe Kausland & Benny Borg	Småting	Kåre Grøttum, Ivar Børsum	Kåre Grøttum, Ivar Børsum	73
15	3	Ireland	Sandie Jones	Ceol On Ghrá	Liam MacUistin	Joe Burkett	72
16	15	Monaco	Anne-Marie Godart & Peter MacLane	Comme On S'aime	Jean Drejac	Raymond Bernard	65
17	16	Belgium	Serge & Christine Ghisoland	À La Folie Ou Pas Du Tout	Daniël Nelis	Daniël Nelis, Bob Milan	55
18	9	Malta	Helen & Joseph	L-imħabba	Albert Cassola	Charles Camilleri	48

1972 Eurovision 17: Edinburgh, United Kingdom
25 March 1972

	Austria	Belgium	Finland	France	Germany	Ireland	Italy	Luxembourg	Malta	Monaco	Netherlands	Norway	Portugal	Spain	Sweden	Switzerland	United Kingdom	Yugoslavia	TOTAL
Germany	5	7	5	8		6	7	7	4	8	6	6	6	9	8	5	5	5	107
France	2	7	4		5	5	3	8	5	6	6	7	2	2	2	3	9	5	81
Ireland	4	4	3	3	4		3	6	6	5	5	6	4	4	5	3	4	3	72
Spain	5	3	4	5	7	5	3	5	4	8	5	8	6		7	3	3	2	83
United Kingdom	7	4	7	9	8	6	7	8	2	9	8	10	4	2	6	8		9	114
Norway	3	4	7	3	4	6	2	6	5	4	4		5	5	4	2	4	5	73
Portugal	4	7	2	4	3	7	9	10		4	5	2		7	7	6	4	4	90
Switzerland	8	4	7	5	4	6	5	7	5	6	5	7	2	5	4		4	5	88
Malta	2	2		2	3	4	2	2		3	4	2	2	2	3	2	6	2	48
Finland	3	8		3	4	3	3	6	3	5	8	6	4	6	4	3	5	4	78
Austria		4	4	6	6	6	6	5	5	6	9	5	5	6	10	7	3	8	100
Italy	6	6	6	5	4	3		6	6	6	5	6	7	2	8	9	3	4	92
Yugoslavia	3	8	3	4	7	5	2	8	4	9	6	4	5	8	4	2	5		87
Sweden	4	7	5	3	5	5	3	5	4		5	5	4	3		2	3	7	75
Monaco	3	4	5	3	4	4	3	4	5	3	5	6	2	3	3	2	5	4	65
Belgium	2		4	3	2	4	3		5	4	3	2	3	2	2	3	5	2	55
Luxembourg	8	8	6	8	9	9	9		4	7		8	7	2	8	6	10	10	128
Netherlands	6	2	9	6	6	8	3	7	3	5		8	5	8	6	6	9	9	106

Note: Two jurors from each country both awarded between 1 and 5 points per act.

1973 Eurovision 18: Luxembourg   7 April 1973

Rank	Start	Country	Artist	Song	Writer	Composer	POINTS
1	11	Luxembourg	Anne-Marie David	Tu Te Reconnaîtras	Vline Buggy	Claude Morgan	129
2	7	Spain	Mocedades	Eres Tú	Juan Carlos Calderón	Juan Carlos Calderón	125
3	15	United Kingdom	Cliff Richard	Power To All Our Friends	Guy Fletcher, Doug Flett	Guy Fletcher, Doug Flett	123
4	17	Israel	Ilanit	Ey-sham	Ehud Manor	Nurit Hirsh	97
5	12	Sweden	The Nova & The Dolls	You're Summer	Lars Forssell	Monica & Carl-Axel Dominique	94
6	1	Finland	Marion Rung	Tom Tom Tom	Rauno Lehtinen	Rauno Lehtinen	93
7	5	Norway	Bendik Singers	It's Just A Game	Arne Bendiksen	Arne Bendiksen	89
8	6	Monaco	Marie	Un Train Qui Part	Boris Bergman	Bernard Liamis	85
9	4	Germany	Gitte	Junger Tag	Stephan Lego	Günther-Eric Thöner	85
10	3	Portugal	Fernando Tordo	Tourada	José Carlos Ary dos Santos	Fernando Tordo	80
11	14	Ireland	Maxi	Do I Dream?	Jack Brierley, George Crosby	Jack Brierley, George Crosby	80
12	8	Switzerland	Patrick Juvet	Je Me Vais Marier, Marie	Pierre Delanoë	Patrick Juvet	79
13	10	Italy	Massimo Ranieri	Chi Sarà Con Te	Giancarlo Bigazzi	Federico Polito, Gaetano Savio	74
14	13	Netherlands	Ben Cramer	De Oude Muzikant	Pierre Kartner	Pierre Kartner	69
15	16	France	Martine Clémenceau	Sans Toi	Anne Gregory	Paul Koulak	65
16	9	Yugoslavia	Zdravko Colic	Gori Vatra	Kemal Monteno	Kemal Monteno	65
17	2	Belgium	Nicole & Hugo	Baby, Baby	Erik Marijsse	Ignace Baert	58

1973 Eurovision 18: Luxembourg

7 April 1973

	Belgium	Finland	France	Germany	Ireland	Israel	Italy	Luxembourg	Monaco	Netherlands	Norway	Portugal	Spain	Sweden	Switzerland	United Kingdom	Yugoslavia	TOTAL
Finland	9		4	6	5	5	2	6	5	5	6	5	6	7	6	9	7	**93**
Belgium		4	2	4	4	2	2	4	6	3	3	3	6	2	4	5	4	**58**
Portugal	6	4	6	5	4	5	3	4	4	5	5		8	2	8	5	6	**80**
Germany	5	2	7		6	4	3	7	5	5	4	6	9	6	7	5	4	**85**
Norway	5	8	6	6	3	9	5	7	7	3		5	6	3	7	3	6	**89**
Monaco	3	6	5	4	6	4	8	6		5	3	2	6	4	5	9	9	**85**
Spain	8	3	9	9	10	8	10	8	9	10	4	9		7	8	4	9	**125**
Switzerland	3	4	2	4	7	3	4	6	5	8	7	3	7	3		7	6	**79**
Yugoslavia	3	5	4	4	5	4	2	4	5	4	2	3	8	2	6	4		**65**
Italy	5	2	5	5	4	4		5	5	4	5	3	5	5	7	5	5	**74**
Luxembourg	6	6	10	7	8	8	9		7	9	8	8	6	8	10	10	9	**129**
Sweden	4	8	4	5	5	5	5	6	5	6	8	4	7		9	7	6	**94**
Netherlands	4	4	6	5	5	2	4	7	4		5	2	5	3	5	3	5	**69**
Ireland	7	3	4	4		4	5	6	6	6	6	6	7	5	5	5	1	**80**
United Kingdom	6	9	8	7	9	9	5	10	8	10	7	6	4	9	8		8	**123**
France	3	4		4	5	2	2	3	5	5	4	2	5	5	4	5	7	**65**
Israel	6	6	5	7	7		7	8	7	6	5	5	4	6	6	5	7	**97**

Note: Two jurors from each country both awarded between 1 and 5 points per act.

1974 Eurovision 19: Brighton, United Kingdom   6 April 1974

Rank	Start	Country	Artist	Song	Writer	Composer	POINTS
1	8	Sweden	ABBA	Waterloo	Stig Anderson	Benny Andersson, Björn Ulvæus	24
2	17	Italy	Gigliola Cinquetti	Sì	Mario Panzeri, Daniele Pace, Lorenzo Pilat, Corrado Conti	Mario Panzeri, Daniele Pace, Lorenzo Pilat, Corrado Conti	18
3	12	Netherlands	Mouth & MacNeal	I See A Star	Hans van Hemert	Hans van Hemert	15
4	10	Monaco	Romuald	Celui Qui Reste Et Celui Qui S'en Va	Michael Jourdan	Jean-Pierre Bourtayre	14
5	9	Luxembourg	Ireen Sheer	Bye, Bye, I Love You	Michael Kunze, Humbert Ibach	Ralph Siegel	14
6	2	United Kingdom	Olivia Newton-John	Long Live Love	Valerie Avon, Harold Spiro	Valerie Avon, Harold Spiro	14
7	6	Israel	Poogy	Natati La Khaiai	Dani Sanderson, Alon Oleartchick	Dani Sanderson	11
8	13	Ireland	Tina	Cross Your Heart	Paul Lyttle	Paul Lyttle	11
9	3	Spain	Peret	Canta Y Sé Feliz	Pedro Pubill Calaf	Pedro Pubill Calaf	10
10	11	Belgium	Jacques Hustin	Fleur De Liberté	Franck F Gérald	Jacques Hustin	10
11	5	Greece	Marinella	Krassi, Thalassa Ke T'agori Mou	Pythagoras	George Katsaros	7
12	7	Yugoslavia	Korni	Generacija 42	Kornelije Kovac	Kornelije Kovac	6
13	1	Finland	Carita	Äla Mene Pois (Keep Me Warm)	Hector	Eero Koivistoinen	4
14	16	Portugal	Paulo de Carvalho	E Depois Do Adeus	José Niza	José Calvário	3
15	14	Germany	Cindy & Bert	Die Sommermelodie	Kurt Feltz	Werner Scharfenberger	3
16	4	Norway	Anne-Karine Ström & the Bendik Singers	The First Day Of Love	Philip Kruse	Frode Thingnæs	3
17	15	Switzerland	Piera Martell	Mein Ruf Nach Dir	Pepe Ederer	Pepe Ederer	3

1974 Eurovision 19: Brighton, United Kingdom

6 April 1974

	Belgium	Finland	Germany	Greece	Ireland	Israel	Italy	Luxembourg	Monaco	Netherlands	Norway	Portugal	Spain	Sweden	Switzerland	United Kingdom	Yugoslavia	TOTAL
Finland					1	2										1		4
United Kingdom			2		1		3	1				2			1		4	14
Spain			1					1	3	1		2		1	1			10
Norway	1								1					1				3
Greece					1		3			4	2	1		2		2		11
Israel		1					2			2		1	1					6
Yugoslavia	1	5	2		1	2		1		3	2	1	1	1	5			24
Sweden	1		1	1	3	2	2		1		1	1	1				2	14
Luxembourg	2		2		1	1		2			1	1	2	1	1			14
Monaco				5				3			2							10
Belgium	1	1	1		1	1				3	1	1	2	3			3	15
Netherlands	1			2	1	1		2	1		2	1	2	2		1		11
Ireland	1			1											1			3
Germany	1				1								1		2	1		3
Switzerland												2						3
Portugal	1	2			1	1		1	4				2			5		18
Italy																		

Note: 10 jurors from each country awarded 1 point each to their favourite act

1975 Eurovision 20: Stockholm, Sweden
22 March 1975

Rank	Start	Country	Artist	Song	Writer	Composer	POINTS
1	1	Netherlands	Teach-In	Teach-In	Will Luikinga, Eddy Ouwens	Dick Bakker	152
2	9	United Kingdom	The Shadows	Let Me Be The One	Paul Curtis	Paul Curtis	138
3	19	Italy	Wess & Dori Ghezzi	Era	Andrea lo Vecchio	Shel Shapiro	115
4	3	France	Nicole Rieu	Et Bonjour à Toi L'artiste	Pierre Delanoë, Jeff Barnel	Pierre Delanoë, Jeff Barnel	91
5	5	Luxembourg	Géraldine	Toi	Pierre Cour, Bill Martin, Phil Coulter	Bill Martin, Phil Coulter	84
6	7	Switzerland	Simone Drexel	Mikado	Simone Drexel	Simone Drexel	77
7	15	Finland	Pihasoittajat	Old Man Fiddle	Hannu Karlsson	Kim Kuusi	74
8	18	Sweden	Lars Berghagen & the Dolls	Jennie, Jennie	Lars Berghagen	Lars Berghagen	72
9	2	Ireland	The Swarbriggs	That's What Friends Are For	Jimmy Swarbrigg, Tommy Swarbrigg	Jimmy Swarbrigg, Tommy Swarbrigg	68
10	17	Spain	Sergio y Estibaliz	Tú Volverás	Juan Carlos Calderón	Juan Carlos Calderón	53
11	12	Israel	Shlomo Artzi	At Ve'ani	Ehud Manor	Shlomo Artzi	40
12	10	Malta	Renato	Singing This Song	M Idris Misfud	Sammy Galea	32
13	8	Yugoslavia	Pepel In Kri	Dan Ljubezni	Dusan Velkaverh	Tadej Hrusovar	22
14	14	Monaco	Sophie	Une Chanson C'est Une Lettre	Boris Bergman	André Popp	22
15	11	Belgium	Ann Christy	Gelukkig Zijn	Mary Boduin	Mary Boduin	17
16	16	Portugal	Duarte Mendes	Madrugada	José Luis Tinoco	José Luis Tinoco	16
17	4	Germany	Joy Fleming	Ein Lied Kann Eine Brücke Sein	Michael Holm	Rainer Pietsch	15
18	6	Norway	Ellen Nikolaysen	You Touched My Life With Summer	Svein Hundnes	Svein Hundnes	11
19	13	Turkey	Semiha Yanki	Seninle Bir Dakika	Hikmet Munir Ebcioglu	Kemal Ebcioglu	3

Note: 1975 marked the introduction of the current 12, 10, 8, 7, 6, 5, 4, 3, 2 & 1 points system.

1975 Eurovision 20: Stockholm, Sweden   **22 March 1975**

	Belgium	Finland	France	Germany	Ireland	Israel	Italy	Luxembourg	Malta	Monaco	Netherlands	Norway	Portugal	Spain	Sweden	Switzerland	Turkey	United Kingdom	Yugoslavia	TOTAL
Netherlands	3	10	5	8	8	12	1	10	12	10		12	7	12	12	6	4	12	8	**152**
Ireland	12	1	6				4		4		6	4	7	3	10	7		6	1	**68**
France	2				12	7	8		7	7	8		4	8	8	3	1	8		**91**
Germany								8	3				12	4						**15**
Luxembourg		5	3		10	6	10		5		12		8	6	4		5	3	7	**84**
Norway							7			2	2									**11**
Switzerland	8	4	10	6	2		12	2	6	5	7	1	2		7		7			**77**
Yugoslavia	5			2	4						3		1					5		**22**
United Kingdom	10	7	12	10	3	10	3	12	8	12	4	7	5	10	5	8			12	**138**
Malta	7		8			1		5			1	2			2	4	2		2	**32**
Belgium				7							5								3	**17**
Israel	1	3	1	1	1		2	1			10	5			6	2	6	1		**40**
Turkey										3										**3**
Monaco	2	2		3		2	5	4	1				3	1	3	12		2		**22**
Finland				12	5	8		6		8		10		2		12	4	4	5	**74**
Portugal			2														12			**16**
Spain	4	8		5	7	4	6	7	2	4		3		5		5	3		4	**53**
Sweden		6	7			3			10	6	10	8	6	5		1	8	7	6	**72**
Italy	6	12	4	4	6	5		3		1		6	10	7	1	10	10	10	10	**115**

47

1976 Eurovision 21: The Hague, Netherlands
3 April 1976

Rank	Start	Country	Artist	Song	Writer	Composer	POINTS
1	1	United Kingdom	Brotherhood of Man	Save Your Kisses For Me	Tony Hiller, Lee Sheriden, Martin Lee	Tony Hiller, Lee Sheriden, Martin Lee	164
2	17	France	Catherine Ferry	Un, Deux, Trois	Jean Paul Cara	Tony Rallo	147
3	16	Monaco	Mary Christy	Toi, La Musique Et Moi	Gilbert Sinoué	Georges Costa, André Bars	93
4	2	Switzerland	Peter, Sue & Marc	Djambo, Djambo	Peter Reber	Peter Reber	91
5	14	Austria	Waterloo & Robinson	My Little World	Gerhard Heinz	Gerhard Heinz	80
6	4	Israel	Chocolate, Menta, Mastik	Emor Shalom	Ehud Manor	Matti Caspi	77
7	13	Italy	Romina & Al Bano	We'll Live It All Again	Al Bano, Romina Power	Detto Mariano	69
8	6	Belgium	Pierre Rapsat	Judy Et Cie	Eric van Hulse	Pierre Rapsat	68
9	8	Netherlands	Sandra Reemer	The Party's Over Now	Hans van Hemert	Hans van Hemert	56
10	7	Ireland	Red Hurley	When	Brendan J Graham	Brendan J Graham	54
11	11	Finland	Fredi & The Friends	Pump-pump	Matti Siitonen	Vexi Salmi	44
12	15	Portugal	Carlos do Carmo	Uma Flor De Verde Pinho	Manuel Alégre	José Niza	24
13	10	Greece	Mariza Koch	Panaghia Mou, Panaghia Mou	Michael Fotiades	Mariza Koch	20
14	5	Luxembourg	Jürgen Marcus	Chansons Pour Ceux Qui S'aiment	Vline Buggy, Fred Jay	Jack White	17
15	3	Germany	Les Humphries Singers	Sing, Sang, Song	Kurt Hertha	Ralph Siegel	12
16	12	Spain	Braulio	Sobran Las Palabras	Braulio	Braulio	11
17	9	Yugoslavia	Ambasadori	Ne Mogu Skriti Svoju Bol	Slobodan Djurasovic	Slobodan Vujovic	10
18	18	Norway	Anne-Karine Ström	Mata Hari	Philip Kruse	Frode Thingnaes	7

1976 Eurovision 21: The Hague, Netherlands

3 April 1976

	Austria	Belgium	Finland	France	Germany	Greece	Ireland	Israel	Italy	Luxembourg	Monaco	Netherlands	Norway	Portugal	Spain	Switzerland	United Kingdom	Yugoslavia	TOTAL
United Kingdom	10	12	10	7	8	12	3	12	4	8	10	10	12	12	12	12		10	164
Switzerland	8	7	7	6	5	2	1	4		1	4	6		7	4		12	7	91
Germany		1		2						2	1	2			2	2		3	12
Israel	6	5	8		3		4		10	7	1	5	7	2	1	7	6	8	77
Luxembourg		6					6					4		8					17
Belgium	3		12	5				1	8	3	8	4	6	6	5	6	7	1	68
Ireland	2	4		3	1	8		3	12	4	6		1	4	3	4	10	5	54
Netherlands	4				4	7	2	8	2		2			1					56
Norway												3							7
Greece		2	4	8	6		5	6	5		7	1	4		6		2		20
Finland	7					1	12	2			3		3	10		8	3	6	44
Spain				1			10	10	3	5	5	7	2			3	1	2	11
Italy	1	3	6	10	10	4				6					8		4		69
Austria		8	5		7		8	7	1	12	12	8	5	3	8	8	5		80
Portugal	5	8	2		12	5	7		7	10			5		7	5	6	4	24
Monaco	12	10	3	4	2	3		5	6			12	8	5	10	10	8	12	93
France																1			147
Yugoslavia																			10

49

1977 Eurovision 22: London, United Kingdom — 7 May 1977

Rank	Start	Country	Artist	Song	Writer	Composer	POINTS
1	18	France	Marie Myriam	L'oiseau Et L'enfant	Joe Garcy	Jean-Paul Cara	136
2	9	United Kingdom	Lynsey de Paul & Mike Moran	Rock Bottom	Lynsey de Paul, Mike Moran	Lynsey de Paul, Mike Moran	121
3	1	Ireland	The Swarbriggs Plus Two	It's Nice To Be In Love Again	Tommy Swarbrigg, Jimmy Swarbrigg	Tommy Swarbrigg, Jimmy Swarbrigg	119
4	2	Monaco	Michèle Torr	Une Petite Française	Jean Albertini	Paul de Senneville, Olivier Toussaint	96
5	10	Greece	Pascalis, Marianna, Robert & Bessy	Mathema Solfege	Sevy Tiliakou	Georges Hatzinassios	92
6	12	Switzerland	Pepe Lienhard Band	Swiss Lady	Peter Reber	Peter Reber	71
7	17	Belgium	Dream Express	A Million In One, Two, Three	Luc Smets	Luc Smets	69
8	6	Germany	Silver Convention	Telegram	Michael Kunze	Silvester Levay	55
9	14	Spain	Micky	Enseñame A Cantar	Fernando Arbex	Fernando Arbex	52
10	16	Finland	Monica Aspelund	Lapponia	Monica Aspelund	Aarno Raninen	50
11	11	Israel	Ilanit	Ah-haa-vah Hee Shir Lish-naa-yim	Edna Peleg	Eldad Shrim	49
12	3	Netherlands	Heddy Lester	De Mallemolen	Wim Hogenkamp	Frank Affolter	35
13	15	Italy	Mia Martini	Libera	Luigi Albertelli	Salvatore Fabrizio	33
14	8	Portugal	Os Amigos	Portugal No Coração	José Carlos Ary dos Santos	Fernando Tordo	18
15	5	Norway	Anita Skorgan	Casanova	Dag Nordtømme	Svein Strugstad	18
16	7	Luxembourg	Anne Marie B	Frère Jacques	Guy Béart, Pierre Cour	Guy Béart, Pierre Cour	17
17	4	Austria	Schmetterlinge	Boom Boom Boomerang	E. Lukas Resetarits	Schuri Herrnstadt, Willi Resetarits & Herbert Zöchling-Tampier	11
18	13	Sweden	Forbes	Beatles	Sven-Olof Bagge	Claes Bure	2

1977 Eurovision 22: London, United Kingdom — 7 May 1977

	Austria	Belgium	Finland	France	Germany	Greece	Ireland	Israel	Italy	Luxembourg	Monaco	Netherlands	Norway	Portugal	Spain	Sweden	Switzerland	United Kingdom	TOTAL
Ireland	5	3		10	5	10		12	8	8	8	1	12	1	4	12	8	12	**119**
Monaco	8	2	5	5	6	12	5	2	12	1			1	6	8	10	6	7	**96**
Netherlands		10		8		1	3	1			3				1		7	1	**35**
Austria			1			3					5		2						**11**
Norway	2	5		1					5					2		1		2	**18**
Germany			8	1		8	1	5	6	3	1	3		8	5	5		10	**55**
Luxembourg							2				2				7				**17**
Portugal				6					3	2	12	2	7			8	4		**18**
United Kingdom	12	12	4	12	10	6		8	2	12	10	7	4	12	3	7	1		**121**
Greece	4	6	6	3				3	1	6	7	10	5	10	12	3	10	5	**92**
Israel	3	1		2	4		7					5	10	4					**49**
Switzerland	10	8	10	2		4	6	4	4	5				3	6			4	**71**
Sweden					2					7	6	6							**2**
Spain	1	7	7		7	2	8		7								3	3	**52**
Italy	6		2	7	3		12	7				4	8	7	2	2	2		**33**
Finland				4		5	4	6			4	12	6	5		4	5		**50**
Belgium			3		8					4		8	3					10	**69**
France	7	4	12		12	7	10	10	10	10					10	6	12	6	**136**

1978 Eurovision 23: Paris, France

22 April 1978

Rank	Start	Country	Artist	Song	Writer	Composer	POINTS
1	18	Israel	Izhar Cohen & the Alphabeta	Abanibi	Ehud Manor	Nurit Hirsh	157
2	10	Belgium	Jean Vallée	L'amour ça Fait Chanter La Vie	Jean Vallée	Jean Vallée	125
3	6	France	Joël Prévost	Il Y Aura Toujours Des Violons	Didier Barbelivien	Gérard Stern	119
4	14	Monaco	Caline & Olivier Toussaint	Les Jardins De Monaco	Didier Barbelivien, Jean Albertini	Paul de Senneville, Olivier Toussaint	107
5	1	Ireland	Colm Wilkinson	Born To Sing	Colm Wilkinson	Colm Wilkinson	86
6	13	Germany	Ireen Sheer	Feuer	John Möring	Erich Leissman, Jean Frankfurter	84
7	17	Luxembourg	Baccara	Parlez-vous Français?	Frank Dostal, Peter Zenter	Rolf Soja	73
8	15	Greece	Tania Tsanaklidou	Charlie Chaplin	Yannis Xantoulis	Sakis Tsilikis	66
9	7	Spain	José Vélez	Bailemos Un Vals	Ramón Arcusa, Manuel de la Calva	Ramón Arcusa, Manuel de la Calva	65
10	9	Switzerland	Carole Vinci	Vivre	Pierre Alain	Alain Morisod	65
11	8	United Kingdom	Co-Co	The Bad Old Days	Stephanie de Sykes, Stuart Slater	Stephanie de Sykes, Stuart Slater	61
12	3	Italy	Ricchi e Poveri	Questo Amore	Sergio Bardotti	Dario Farina, Mario Luisini	53
13	11	Netherlands	Harmony	't Is Ok	Toon Gispen, Dick Bakker	Eddy Ouwens	37
14	20	Sweden	Björn Skifs	Det Blir Alltid Värre Framåt Natten	Peter Himmelstrand	Peter Himmelstrand	26
15	19	Austria	Springtime	Mrs Caroline Robinson	Walter Markel, Gerhard Markel, Norbert Niedermayer	Walter Markel, Gerhard Markel	14
16	16	Denmark	Mabel	Boom Boom	Mabel	Mabel	13
17	5	Portugal	Gemini	Dai-li-dou	Carlos Quintas	Victor Mamêde	5
18	4	Finland	Seija Simola	Anna Rakkaudelle Tilaisuus	Reijo Karvonen, Seija Simola	Reijo Karvonen	2
19	12	Turkey	Nazar	Sevince	Hulki Aktunç	Daghan Baydur, Onno Tunç	2
20	2	Norway	Jahn Teigen	Mil Etter Mil	Kai Eide	Kai Eide	0

1978 Eurovision 23: Paris, France
22 April 1978

	Austria	Belgium	Denmark	Finland	France	Germany	Greece	Ireland	Israel	Italy	Luxembourg	Monaco	Netherlands	Norway	Portugal	Spain	Sweden	Switzerland	Turkey	United Kingdom	TOTAL
Ireland	6	10		3	5	5	10				10			12			8	7	10		86
Norway																					0
Italy		1			4	2	2	10			3	8		6	1	8		1	1	6	53
Finland														2							2
Portugal										4						1					5
France	12	8	8	2		10	8	6	5	10	1	5	6	3	2	5	10	6	4	8	119
Spain	7	2		7		8	6	3	6		2	4	4				3	8	7		65
United Kingdom	5	4	3	1		6	3		2		5	7	2			3		2			61
Switzerland	10	7			2	3		12	1	1	8	2	8	5	6	4			6	2	65
Belgium	4			6	7		12			6	7	12	5	7		2	4	10		12	125
Netherlands			5						7	5	6	1			4		1			3	37
Turkey					12				12					1						1	2
Germany		5	1	12			7	1	3	3		10	7			10		3	8		84
Monaco	1	6	10	8	1	7	4	4	8	7	4		10	4	5	7	12	5	5	10	107
Greece	3		4	5	10	4		7	10	2					8		2	4			66
Denmark	2				6				4				1					6			13
Luxembourg			7	10	8		1	2		12		6	3	8	12	6	6		2	7	73
Israel	8	3	6			12	5	8		8	12	3	12		10			12	12	5	157
Austria		12	2	4	3	1									3				3		14
Sweden								5						10			5			4	26

1979 Eurovision 24: Jerusalem, Israel

31 March 1979

Rank	Start	Country	Artist	Song	Writer	Composer	POINTS
1	10	Israel	Milk and Honey	Hallelujah	Shimrit Orr	Kobi Oshrat	125
2	19	Spain	Betty Missiego	Su Canción	Fernando Moreno	Fernando Moreno	116
3	11	France	Anne-Marie David	Je Suis L'enfant-soleil	Eddy Marnay	Hubert Giraud	106
4	9	Germany	Dschinghis Khan	Dschinghis Khan	Bernd Meinunger	Ralph Siegel	86
5	4	Ireland	Cathal Dunne	Happy Man	Cathal Dunne	Cathal Dunne	80
6	3	Denmark	Tommy Seebach	Disco Tango	Keld Heick	Tommy Seebach	76
7	17	United Kingdom	Black Lace	Mary Ann	Peter Morris	Peter Morris	73
8	7	Greece	Elpida	Socrates	Sotia Tsotou	Doros Georghiades	69
9	1	Portugal	Manuela Bravo	Sobe, Sobe, Balão Sobe	Carlos Nobrega e Sousa	Carlos Nobrega e Sousa	64
10	8	Switzerland	Peter, Sue, Marc, Pfuri, Gorps & Kniri	Trödler Und Co	Peter Reber	Peter Reber	60
11	16	Norway	Anita Skorgan	Oliver	Philip Kruse	Anita Skorgan	57
12	14	Netherlands	Xandra	Colorado	Gerard Cox	Rob Bolland, Ferdi Bolland	51
13	13	Luxembourg	Jeane Manson	J'ai Déjà Vu ça Dans Tes Yeux	Jean Renard	Jean Renard	44
14	5	Finland	Katri-Helena	Katso Sineen Taivaan	Vexi Salmi	Matti Siitonen	38
15	2	Italy	Matia Bazar	Raggio Di Luna	Giancarlo Golzi, Salvatore Stellita	Carlo Marrale, Piero Cassano, Antoniella Ruggiero	27
16	6	Monaco	Laurent Vaguener	Notre Vie, C'est La Musique	Jean Albertini, Didier Barbelivien	P de Senneville, L Vaguener	12
17	15	Sweden	Ted Gärdestad	Satellit	Kenneth Gärdestad, Ted Gärdestad	Kenneth Gärdestad, Ted Gärdestad	8
18	12	Belgium	Micha Marah	Hey Nana	Guy Beyers	Charles Dumolin	5
19	18	Austria	Christina Simon	Heute In Jerusalem	André Heller	Peter Wolf	5

1979 Eurovision 24: Jerusalem, Israel — 31 March 1979

	Austria	Belgium	Denmark	Finland	France	Germany	Greece	Ireland	Israel	Italy	Luxembourg	Monaco	Netherlands	Norway	Portugal	Spain	Sweden	Switzerland	United Kingdom	TOTAL
Portugal	7	5		2	10	4				6	3	5	3	6		6	3	4		64
Italy	3			8											8	8				27
Denmark		7				10	12		12		4	3				4	1	1	3	76
Ireland		10	5	6	6	6	10		3	5	7			5			8	6	4	80
Finland					5	5	7			7	6							8		38
Monaco			4		3					2					1	2				12
Greece	2	1		10	4	2		4	10		5	7	7		10	7	2			69
Switzerland	12	4	7		7	7	2	1	4			2		8						60
Germany	8	2	12	3	12			5	6	1	1	12	2	12	2	12	6	5	8	86
Israel		6		12	1			12		10	8	8	1	7	12	10	12	10	12	125
France	5			1			8	12	5		12	10	12	7	6	3	5	6	6	106
Belgium						1													2	5
Luxembourg	4	3		4	2		5	3	7			4	4	2	7			3	10	44
Netherlands	3	8		5		3	3	10		3				4			4			51
Sweden							1	6	1											8
Norway	1		10					8	2	3	2	6	6		3	1	10		7	57
United Kingdom	6	8		7		8		7		8		1	5	10	4	5		2		73
Austria										4									1	5
Spain	10	12	3		8	12	6		8	12	10		10	1			7	12	5	116

55

1980 Eurovision 25: The Hague, Netherlands — 19 April 1980

Rank	Start	Country	Artist	Song	Writer	Composer	POINTS
1	17	Ireland	Johnny Logan	What's Another Year	Shay Healy	Shay Healy	143
2	12	Germany	Katja Ebstein	Theater	Bernd Meinunger	Ralph Siegel	128
3	13	United Kingdom	Prima Donna	Love Enough For Two	Stephanie de Sykes, Stuart Slater	Stephanie de Sykes, Stuart Slater	106
4	9	Switzerland	Paola	Cinéma	Peter Reber, Véronique Müller	Peter Reber	104
5	15	Netherlands	Maggie MacNeal	Amsterdam	Alex Alberts	Frans Smit, Sjoukje Smit, Robert Verwey	93
6	6	Italy	Alan Sorrenti	Non So Che Darei	Alan Sorrenti	Alan Sorrenti	87
7	14	Portugal	José Cid	Um Grande, Grande Amor	José Cid	José Cid	71
8	1	Austria	Blue Danube	Du Bist Musik	Klaus-Peter Sattler	Klaus-Peter Sattler	64
9	4	Luxembourg	Sophie & Magaly	Papa Pingouin	Pierre Delanoë, Jean-Paul Cara	Ralph Siegel, Bernd Meinunger	56
10	8	Sweden	Tomas Ledin	Just Nu!	Tomas Ledin	Tomas Ledin	47
11	16	France	Profil	Hé, Hé M'sieurs Dames	Richard de Bordeaux, Richard Joffo	Sylvano Santorio	45
12	18	Spain	Trigo Limpio	Qué Date Esta Noche	José Antonio Martin	José Antonio Martin	38
13	3	Greece	Anna Vishy & the Epikouri	Autostop	Rony Sofou	Jick Nakassian	30
14	7	Denmark	Bamses Venner	Tænker Altid På Dig	Flemming Jørgensen	Bjarne Gren-Jensen	25
15	2	Turkey	Ajda Pekkan	Petr'oil	Sanar Yurdatapan	Atilla Ozdemiroglu	23
16	11	Norway	Sverre Kjellsberg & Mattis Hætta	Sámiid Ædnan	Ragnar Olsen	Sverre Kjellsberg	15
17	19	Belgium	Telex	Euro-vision	Telex	Telex	14
18	5	Morocco	Samira Bensaïd	Bitakat Hob	Malou Rouanne	Abdel Ati Amenna	7
19	10	Finland	Vesa-Matti Loiri	Huilumies	Vexi Salmi	Aarno Raninen	6

1980 Eurovision 25: The Hague, Netherlands
19 April 1980

	Austria	Belgium	Denmark	Finland	France	Germany	Greece	Ireland	Italy	Luxembourg	Morocco	Netherlands	Norway	Portugal	Spain	Sweden	Switzerland	Turkey	United Kingdom	TOTAL
Austria		1	5	5	4	4	1	10	4		3	3	6	3	4	1	4		6	**64**
Turkey	3								8		12									**23**
Greece	5		2					4	2	1		8		1	3			1	3	**30**
Luxembourg	1	8	4	3	7			8				4	7			6			8	**56**
Morocco									7											**7**
Italy	2	10	3	6	2	7		2					1	12	10		8	6	4	**87**
Denmark				7		5	4									2	6		1	**25**
Sweden						2	10		5	5	6	10					5	2	2	**47**
Switzerland	6	2	8	12		10		12	3	5	7	10		6	2			2	7	**104**
Finland					1							2								**6**
Norway					3	6					4									**15**
Germany	8	7	7	2	10			5	12	3	10	12		8	12	5	7	10	10	**128**
United Kingdom	7	6	10	4	5	3		6		8	8	7	8	7	8	12	10	5		**106**
Portugal	4	4	6	1	6	1		7	10	4		5				8	2	4		**71**
Netherlands	12	3		10	12	8		1		12			5	4	5	3	3	12	2	**93**
France	5	5	1				7	3		2	1	4	3		6	4	1	3	5	**45**
Ireland	10	12	12	8	8	12	12		1	7		6	12	5	7	7	12		12	**143**
Spain	4								6	6	5			2				7		**38**
Belgium							3							10					1	**14**

1981 Eurovision 26: Dublin, Ireland

4 April 1981

Rank	Start	Country	Artist	Song	Writer	Composer	POINTS
1	14	United Kingdom	Bucks Fizz	Making Your Mind Up	Andy Hill	John Danter	136
2	3	Germany	Lena Valaitis	Johnny Blue	Bernd Meinunger	Ralph Siegel	132
3	9	France	Jean Gabilou	Humanahum	Joel Gracy	Jean-Paul Cara	125
4	19	Switzerland	Peter, Sue & Marc	Io Senza Tei	Peter Reber, Nella Martinetti	Peter Reber	121
5	12	Ireland	Sheeba	Horoscopes	Joe Burkett	Jim Kelly	105
6	18	Cyprus	Island	Monika	Stavros Sideras	Doros Georghiades	69
7	5	Israel	Habibi	Halaylah	Shlomit Aharon, Yuval Dor	Shuki Levi	56
8	17	Greece	Yiannis Dimitras	Feggari Kalokerino	Yiannis Dimitras	Giorgos Niachros	55
9	11	Netherlands	Linda Williams	Het Is Een Wonder	Bart van de Laar	Cees de Wit	51
10	20	Sweden	Björn Skifs	Fångad I En Dröm	Björn Skifs, Bengt Palmers	Björn Skifs, Bengt Palmers	50
11	4	Luxembourg	Jean-Claude Pascal	C'est Peut-être Pas L'amérique	Sophie Makhno, Jean-Claude Villemino	Sophie Makhno, Jean-Claude Villemino	41
12	6	Denmark	Debbie Cameron & Tommy Seebach	Krøller Eller Ej	Keld Heick	Tommy Seebach	41
13	16	Belgium	Emly Starr	Samson	Kick Dandy, Els van den Abeele	Kick Dandy, Giuseppe Marchese	40
14	10	Spain	Bacchelli	Y Solo Tú	Amado Jaén	Amado Jaén	38
15	7	Yugoslavia	Seid-Memic Vajta	Leila	Ranko Boban	Ranko Boban	35
16	8	Finland	Riki Sorsa	Reggae OK	Olli Ojala	Jim Pembroke	27
17	1	Austria	Marty Brem	Wenn Du Da Bist	Werner Böhmler	Werner Böhmler	20
18	15	Portugal	Carlos Paião	Play-back	Carlos Paião	Carlos Paião	9
19	2	Turkey	Modern Folk Trio & Ayseguil	Dönme Dolap	Ali Kocatepe	Ali Kocatepe	9
20	13	Norway	Finn Kalvik	Aldri I Livet	Finn Kalvik	Finn Kalvik	0

1981 Eurovision 26: Dublin, Ireland — 4 April 1981

	Austria	Belgium	Cyprus	Denmark	Finland	France	Germany	Greece	Ireland	Israel	Luxembourg	Netherlands	Norway	Portugal	Spain	Sweden	Switzerland	Turkey	United Kingdom	Yugoslavia	TOTAL
Austria				1		5									6	2		6			20
Turkey	5	10			5															3	9
Germany	10		8	8	7	8		5	6	8	3	3	4	12	12	12	6	12	7	2	132
Luxembourg	8	12			4	3	5		7	3		7	8	4	1	5	4		4		41
Israel					6		1				4	2		5	3	3	10	1	5		56
Denmark			3		8	4			2		7		1	2		4	5	4			41
Yugoslavia		5				1			5	2		5		1	2	6					35
Finland				2	10		12	8	4	7	12	6	5	10		10	12		1	4	27
France	12	3	7						3												125
Spain							3			6		4	10	3			2	10			38
Netherlands	3	2	2	7	2	2	3	3		4				7	7	7		5	6		51
Ireland	7	1	12	12		6	6	10		10	10	10			5		1	3		5	105
Norway																					0
United Kingdom	4	8	4	10	3	7	4	6	10	12	5	12	3	6	8	8	8	8		10	136
Portugal							8	1													9
Belgium	1		5	6	2			7		1	6						7	7	3	8	40
Greece	6	6	6	3		2	2		1	5		8	2		10		3		8	1	55
Cyprus		7				10		12	8				7						10	6	69
Switzerland	2		10	4	12	12	7	4	12		8	1	12	8	4	1		2	12	12	121
Sweden		4	1	5	1		10				2		6						2	7	50

59

1982 Eurovision 27: Harrogate, United Kingdom 24 April 1982

Rank	Start	Country	Artist	Song	Writer	Composer	POINTS
1	18	Germany	Nicole	Ein bißchen Frieden	Bernd Meinunger	Ralph Siegel	161
2	15	Israel	Avi Toledano	Hora	Yoram Tahar-Lev	Avi Toledano	100
3	7	Switzerland	Arlette Zola	Amour on t'aime	Pierre Alain	Alain Morisod	97
4	11	Belgium	Stella	Si tu aimes ma musique	Jo May	Fred Bekky, Rony Brack, Bobott	96
5	8	Cyprus	Anna Vishy	Mono i agapi	Anna Vishy	Anna Vishy	85
6	2	Luxembourg	Svetlana	Cours après le temps	Cyril Assous	Michel Jouveaux	78
7	4	United Kingdom	Bardo	One step further	Simon Jeffries	Simon Jeffries	76
8	9	Sweden	Chips	Dag efter dag	Monica Forsberg	Lasse Holm	67
9	10	Austria	Mess	Sonntag	Rudolph Leve	Michael Scheikl	57
10	12	Spain	Lucía	Él	Ignacio Román	Francisco Cepero	52
11	17	Ireland	The Duskeys	Here Today, Gone Tomorrow	Sally Keating	Sally Keating	49
12	3	Norway	Jahn Teigen & Anita Skorgan	Adieu	Herodes Falsk	Jahn Teigen	40
13	1	Portugal	Doce	Bem-bom	António Pinho, Tózé Brito, Pedro Brito	António Pinho, Tózé Brito, Pedro Brito	32
14	14	Yugoslavia	Aska	Halo Halo	Miro Zec	Aleksandar Sanja Ilic	21
15	5	Turkey	Neço	Hani	Olcayto Ahmet Tugsuz, Fait Tugsuz	Olcayto Ahmet Tugsuz	20
16	16	Netherlands	Bill van Dijk	Jij En Ik	Liselore Gerritsen	Dick Bakker	8
17	13	Denmark	Brixx	Video-video	Jens Brixtofte	Jens Brixtofte	5
18	6	Finland	Kojo	Nuku Pommiin	Juice Leskinen	Jim Pembroke, Otto Donner	0

1982 Eurovision 27: Harrogate, United Kingdom
24 April 1982

	Austria	Belgium	Cyprus	Denmark	Finland	Germany	Ireland	Israel	Luxembourg	Netherlands	Norway	Portugal	Spain	Sweden	Switzerland	Turkey	United Kingdom	Yugoslavia	TOTAL
Portugal	2	8			2		2	1	7	4				6	1	5	4		32
Luxembourg	6	2	4	4	7	8	10	5		7	7	6	5	4		3	6		78
Norway	12		3	2	4	10	6	2	6	1		4	2		5	10		6	40
United Kingdom	3				1	1	7		12	2	6		1		3				76
Turkey									8		3								20
Finland																			0
Switzerland	10	12	6	7		6	8	10	2	10	4	2		2		2	12	10	97
Cyprus	5	3			8	2	7	7	4	12	12	5	7		8		3	5	85
Sweden	8	5		8	3	2	5		3	5	8	7	4		4		5	2	67
Austria		6	7	6		4	4	4		3			8			7	10	4	57
Belgium	4		8	10	5	4	4	6	5		5	8	10	7	2	6	2	7	96
Spain		4	10		6	7		8	1						7	8		1	52
Denmark							1							1					5
Yugoslavia		1	1	3								3		12		4			21
Israel	7	7	2	1	12	12		3	10	8	1	10	6	10	10		1	3	100
Netherlands						5								3					8
Ireland			5	5		3		3		6	2	1	3	5	6	1	7	8	49
Germany	1	10	12	12	10		12	12			10	12	12	8	12	12	8	12	161

1983 Eurovision 28: Munich, Germany   23 April 1983

Rank	Start	Country	Artist	Song	Writer	Composer	POINTS
1	20	Luxembourg	Corinne Hermès	Si La Vie Est Cadeau	Alain Garcia	Jean-Pierre Millers	142
2	16	Israel	Ofra Haza	Hi	Ehud Manor	Avi Toledano	136
3	4	Sweden	Carola Häggkvist	Främling	Monica Forsberg	Lasse Holm	126
4	12	Yugoslavia	Danijel	Džuli	Mario Mihaljevic	Danijel Popovic	125
5	14	Germany	Hoffmann & Hoffmann	Rücksicht	Volker Lechtenbrink	Michael Reinecke	94
6	3	United Kingdom	Sweet Dreams	I'm Never Giving Up	Ron Roker, Jan Pulsford, Phil Wigger	Ron Roker, Jan Pulsford, Phil Wigger	79
7	11	Netherlands	Bernadette	Sing Me A Song	Martin Duiser	Piet Souer	66
8	1	France	Guy Bonnet	Vivre	Fulbert Cant	Guy Bonnet	56
9	18	Austria	Westend	Hurricane	Heli Deinboek, Heinz Nessizius	Peter Vieweger	53
10	2	Norway	Jahn Teigen	Do Re Mi	Herodes Falsk, Jahn Teigen	Anita Skorgan, Jahn Teigen	53
11	5	Italy	Riccardo Fogli	Per Lucia	Riccardo Fogli, Vincenzo Spampinato	Maurizio Fabrizio	41
12	9	Finland	Ami Aspelund	Fantasiaa	Kaisu Liuhala	Kari Kuusamo	41
13	17	Portugal	Armando Gama	Esta Balada Que Te Dou	Armando Gama	Armando Gama	33
14	10	Greece	Christie	Mou Les	Sophia Fildissi	Antonis Plessas, Mimis Plessas	32
15	8	Switzerland	Mariella Farré	Io Cosi Non Ci Sto	Nella Martinetti	Thomas Gonzenbach, Remo Kessler	28
16	13	Cyprus	Stavros & Constantina	I Agapi Akoma Zi	Stavros Sideras	Stavros Sideras	26
17	15	Denmark	Gry Johansen	Kloden Drejer	Flemming Gernyx, Christian Jacobsen	Flemming Gernyx, Christian Jacobsen, Lars Christensen	16
18	19	Belgium	Pas de Deux	Rendez-vous	Paul Peyskens	Walter Verdin	13
=19	6	Turkey	Çetin Alp and the Short Wave	Opera	Aysel Gürel	Bugra Ugur	0
=19	7	Spain	Remedios Amaya	¿quién Maneja Mi Barca?	Isidro Muñoz	José Miguel Evóras	0

1983 Eurovision 28: Munich, Germany
23 April 1983

	Austria	Belgium	Cyprus	Denmark	Finland	France	Germany	Greece	Israel	Italy	Luxembourg	Netherlands	Norway	Portugal	Spain	Sweden	Switzerland	Turkey	United Kingdom	Yugoslavia	TOTAL
France	3	7	4		6		4	7	1	10	3	2	3	3			10			3	56
Norway		7		8			1		4			8		6		3		6	5		53
United Kingdom	10	5	6	5	10	5	3	5		2	6	5	5	2		12	8	7		1	79
Sweden	8		7	10	1	6	12	10	8	8		3	12	4	2	2	5	4	8		126
Italy			1		1	7		2	6					7	3					8	41
Turkey																					0
Spain																					0
Switzerland	6	1					7		3	7	5		1		1				6	7	28
Finland	2		12		5	1	7	8	7		1		2				4	3	1		41
Greece						3									12						32
Netherlands	4	2	5	4	3	2	2	4	3	4	4		7			6	12	2		5	66
Yugoslavia	1	12	8	12	12		6	6	10	1	8	7	8		10		1	12	12		125
Cyprus		4		1			5		5				4							6	26
Germany	7	6	2	3	4	10		1		6	12	10	10	8		8	2		7		94
Denmark																7			2		16
Israel	12	10		7	7	8	10	3		3	10	12	6	10	6	5	7	1	10	10	136
Portugal					2	4					7	6			5	1	6		2	2	33
Austria		3	3	6			3	4	2	5		4		5		4		10	3	4	53
Belgium														1	8				4		13
Luxembourg	5	8	10	2	8	12	8	12	12	12		1	10	12	7	10	3	8		12	142

1984 Eurovision 29: Luxembourg City, Luxembourg   5 May 1984

Rank	Start	Country	Artist	Song	Writer	Composer	POINTS
1	1	Sweden	Herrey's	Diggi-loo diggy-ley	Britt Lindeborg	Torgny Söderberg	145
2	9	Ireland	Linda Martin	Terminal 3	Sean Sherrard	Sean Sherrard	137
3	4	Spain	Bravo	Lady, lady	Amaya Saizar	Miguel Blasco Larami	106
4	10	Denmark	Hot Eyes	Det' lige det	Keld Heick	Søren Bundgård	101
5	8	Belgium	Jacques Zegers	Avanti la vie	Jacques Zegers	Henri Seroka	70
6	18	Italy	Alice & Battiato	I treni di Tozeur	Rosario Cosentino	Franco Battiato	70
7	6	United Kingdom	Belle & the Devotions	Love games	Paul Curtis, Graham Sacher	Paul Curtis, Graham Sacher	63
8	3	France	Annick Thoumazeau	Autant d'amoureux que d'étoiles	Charel Level	Vladimir Cosma	61
9	16	Finland	Kirka	Hengaillaan	Jussi Tuominen	Jukka Siikavire	46
10	2	Luxembourg	Sophie Carle	100% d'amour	Jean-Michel Bériat, Patrick Jaymes	Jean-Pierre Goussaud	39
11	19	Portugal	Maria Guinot	Silêncio e tanta gente	Maria Guinot	Maria Guinot	38
12	15	Turkey	Bes Yil Önce, On Yil Sonra	Halay	Ulku Aker	Selcuk Basar	37
13	14	Germany	Mary Roos	Aufrecht geh'n	Michael Kunze	Michael Reinecke	34
14	11	Netherlands	Maribelle	Ik hou van jou	Peter van Asten, Richard De Bois	Peter van Asten, Richard De Bois	34
15	7	Cyprus	Andy Paul	Anna Mari-Elena	Andy Paul	Andy Paul	31
16	17	Switzerland	Rainy Day	Welche Farbe hat der Sonnenschein	Günther Loose	Günther Loose	30
17	5	Norway	Dollie de Luxe	Lenge leve livet	Ingrid Bjørnov, Benedicte Adrian	Ingrid Bjørnov, Benedicte Adrian	29
18	12	Yugoslavia	Vlado and Isolda	Ciao amore	Milan Peric	Slobodan Bucevac	26
19	13	Austria	Anita	Einfach weg	Walter Müller	Brigitte Seuberth, Ernst Seuberth	5

1984 Eurovision 29: Luxembourg
5 May 1984

	Austria	Belgium	Cyprus	Denmark	Finland	France	Germany	Ireland	Italy	Luxembourg	Netherlands	Norway	Portugal	Spain	Sweden	Switzerland	Turkey	United Kingdom	Yugoslavia	TOTAL
Sweden	12	7	12	12	8	6	12	12	6	6	10	10	4	4		10	3	7	4	145
Luxembourg		10	7	5				5	3					7			4		8	39
France	8	3	3	7		10	2	7	7	8	12	2	7		2	4	12	6		61
Spain	6		6	1	6		4	3	8	7	2	6	12		10	3	12	4	2	106
Norway		1	2	10	4	1	7	8	10	1	4		6		8	2	1		1	29
United Kingdom	2	2	2			12	10	4			8	3	10	3	3				12	63
Cyprus	2					1	5		1	12	7				4		5			31
Belgium	3		10	3	10	12	3		12	5	3	3	10	2		12	10	8		70
Ireland	10	12	5		7	3	10		5	3	7	4	2	10	12	1	2	12	6	137
Denmark	4	8		4	5	8	5	10		2	3	12	1	6	5	5		1	5	101
Netherlands						7		6						8			8	3		34
Yugoslavia			8		2		3													26
Austria				4				1												5
Germany	1	6		2		4			2		5	7	5		6	6		2		34
Turkey		4	10		3		1	2			1		3		7			5	10	37
Finland	5		1	6		5						5		1			6		3	46
Switzerland		5		8	1				4	10								10		30
Italy	7				12		6			4	6	1	8	12	1	7	7			70
Portugal							8							5		8			7	38

1985 Eurovision 30: Gothenburg, Sweden   3 May 1985

Rank	Start	Country	Artist	Song	Writer	Composer	POINTS
1	13	Norway	Bobbysocks	La Det Swinge	Rolf Løvland	Rolf Løvland	123
2	10	Germany	Wind	Für Alle	Hanne Haller	Hanne Haller	105
3	16	Sweden	Kikki Danielsson	Bra Vibrationer	Ingela "Pling" Forsman	Lasse Holm	103
4	14	United Kingdom	Vikki	Love Is....	Vikki Watson, James Kaleth	Vikki Watson, James Kaleth	100
5	11	Israel	Izhar Cohen	Olé Olé	Hamutal Ben Ze'ev	Kobi Oshrat	93
6	1	Ireland	Maria Christian	Wait Until The Weekend Comes	Brendan J. Graham	Brendan J. Graham	91
7	12	Italy	Al Bano & Romina Power	Magic, Oh Magic	Christiano Minellono	Dario Farina, Michael Hoffmann	78
8	17	Austria	Gary Lux	Kinder Dieser Welt	Michael Kunze	Mick Jackson, Geoff Bastow	60
9	2	Finland	Sonja Lumme	Eläköön Elämä	Veli-Pekka Lehto	Petri Laaksonen	58
10	6	France	Roger Bens	Femme Dans Ses Rêves Aussi	Didier Pascalis	Didier Pascalis	56
11	4	Denmark	Hot Eyes	Sku' Du Spør Fra No'n	Keld Heick	Søren Bundgård	41
12	15	Switzerland	Mariella Farré & Pino Gasparini	Piano Piano	Trudi Müller-Bosshard	Anita Kerr	39
13	18	Luxembourg	Margo, Franck Olivier, Diane Solomon, Ireen Sheer, Malcolm Roberts & Chris Roberts	Children, Kinder, Enfants	Bernd Meinunger, Jean-Michel Bériat	Ralph Siegel	37
14	5	Spain	Paloma San Basilio	La Fiesta Terminó	Juan Carlos Calderón	Juan Carlos Calderón	36
15	7	Turkey	MFÖ	Di Dai Di Dai (a'sik Oldum)	Mazhar Alanson, Fuat Güner, Özkan Ugur	Mazhar Alanson, Fuat Güner, Özkan Ugur	36
16	19	Greece	Takis Biniaris	Miazoume	Maro Bizani	Takis Biniaris	15
17	3	Cyprus	Lia Vishy	To Katalava Arga	Lia Vishy-Piliouri	Lia Vishy-Piliouri	15
18	9	Portugal	Adelaide	Penso Em Ti, Eu Sei	Adelaide Ferreira, Luis Fernando	Tózé Brito	9
19	8	Belgium	Linda Lepomme	Laat Me Nu Gaan	Bert Vivier	Pieter Verlinden	7

1985 Eurovision 30: Gothenburg, Sweden

3 May 1985

	Austria	Belgium	Cyprus	Denmark	Finland	France	Germany	Greece	Ireland	Israel	Italy	Luxembourg	Norway	Portugal	Spain	Sweden	Switzerland	Turkey	United Kingdom	TOTAL
Ireland	10	8	7	3	1	3	4			8	12		3	8	4	7	5	5	3	91
Finland	5	3	6					10	6	1	7				6	10	2	3	7	58
Cyprus								8	1		3						3			15
Denmark			3		8	10	6		2		2		6	1		5			4	41
Spain	3		1		5			6		3		1		2				12	2	36
France		1	4		2		2	12	7		10	3		3	3	6	12	1	8	56
Turkey																		skip	10	36
Belgium					10			7												7
Portugal														skip				7		9
Germany	7	10	12	10	6	8		2	4	7	5	10	8	7	10	8		2	1	105
Israel	6	2	5	4	4	12	7		8			6	10	5	8	2	7		5	93
Italy	12	12	10	1	7	5		1		4	skip	12		12	12			8		78
Norway	2	6		12	3	2	12	4	12	12	6	7	skip	6	1	12	6		12	123
United Kingdom	1	5	2	5		6	5	3	5	2	8	8	7	4	5	4	10	10	skip	100
Switzerland	4	7		6		7	1			6	4		5			1	skip			39
Sweden		4		8	12	1	8	5	10	10	8	2	12		2	skip	8	6	6	103
Austria	skip			7			10		3	5		5				3	1	4		60
Luxembourg	8			2		4	3				1	skip	4	10					10	37
Greece			8					skip				4			7					15

1986 Eurovision 31: Bergen, Norway — 3 May 1986

Rank	Start	Country	Artist	Song	Writer	Composer	POINTS
1	13	Belgium	Sandra Kim	J'aime La Vie	Rosario Marino Atria	Jean-Pierre Furnémont, Angelo	176
2	10	Switzerland	Daniela Simons	Pas Pour Moi	Nella Martinetti	Atilla Sereftug	140
3	1	Luxembourg	Sherisse Laurence	L'amour De Ma Vie	Alain Garcia, Frank Dostal	Rolf Soja	117
4	12	Ireland	Luv Bug	You Can Count On Me	Kevin Sheerin	Kevin Sheerin	96
5	17	Sweden	Lasse Holm & Monica Törnell	E' De' Det Här Du Kallar Kärlek	Lasse Holm	Lasse Holm	78
6	18	Denmark	Lise Haavik & Trax	Du Er Fuld Af Løgn	John Hatting	John Hatting	77
7	5	United Kingdom	Ryder	Runner In The Night	Maureen Darbyshire	Brian Wade	72
8	14	Germany	Ingrid Peters	Über Die Brücke Geh'n	Hans Blüm	Hans Blüm	62
9	8	Turkey	Klips ve Onlar	Halley	Ilhan Irem	Melih Kibar	53
10	9	Spain	Cadillac	Valentino	José Maria Guzmán	José Maria Guzmán	51
11	2	Yugoslavia	Doris Dragovic	Zeljo Moja	Zrinko Tutic	Zrinko Tutic	49
12	4	Norway	Ketil Stokkan	Romeo	Ketil Stokkan	Ketil Stokkan	44
13	7	Netherlands	Frizzle Sizzle	Alles Heeft Ritme	Peter Schön	Peter Schön, Rob ten Bokum	40
14	20	Portugal	Dora	Não Sejas Mau Para Mim	Guilherme Inês, Zé da Ponte, Luis Oliveira	Guilherme Inês, Zé da Ponte, Luis Oliveira	28
15	19	Finland	Kari Kuivalainen	Päivä Kahden Ihmisen	Kari Kuivalainen	Kari Kuivalainen	22
16	6	Iceland	Icy	Gleðibankinn	Magnús Eiríksson	Magnús Eiríksson	19
17	3	France	Cocktail Chic	Européennes	Georges Costa, Michel Costa	Georges Costa, Michel Costa	13
18	16	Austria	Timna Brauer	Die Zeit Ist Einsam	Peter Cornelius	Peter Janda	12
19	11	Israel	Moti Galadi & Sarai Tzuriel	Yavoh Yom	Moti Galadi	Yoram Zadok	7
20	5	Cyprus	Elpida	Tora Zo	Phivos Gavris, Petros Yiannaki	Petros Yiannaki	4

1986 Eurovision 31: Bergen, Norway — 3 May 1986

Country	Austria	Belgium	Cyprus	Denmark	Finland	France	Germany	Iceland	Ireland	Israel	Luxembourg	Netherlands	Norway	Portugal	Spain	Sweden	Switzerland	Turkey	United Kingdom	Yugoslavia	TOTAL
Luxembourg	10	10	8	2	4	8	12	1	7	4		8	12	6		10	2		8	5	117
Yugoslavia	1	4	12					5	3	1	2	7			3	1	2	3	7		49
France													3		3	3	7				13
Norway		5	6	5		4	6	4	6			2					6				44
United Kingdom	3	2	2	8	10	10	5		6	2	4			2	2	8	4	6		10	72
Iceland			4									5			6			2			19
Netherlands			1		3		10			8	1			7	1			7		2	40
Turkey	2	6		3	1	6	8	2	5	3	6	6	5	3			8		2	12	53
Spain	7	3		4	7	7		3	10	12	7	12	1	10			1	8	1	4	51
Switzerland	4	12	5			1					12				4	12		10	5	6	140
Israel						3							1				5				7
Ireland	12	2		12	8	3		8		6	3	10	2	8	12	7		5		8	96
Belgium	6		10	10	12	12	1	10	12	5	10	10	8	12	10	6	10	12	10	10	176
Germany	8	7		7	2				8		8			4		5			12	1	62
Cyprus									1											3	4
Austria		1			6		2		2					1							12
Sweden	5			6	5	2	4	12			5	3	7		7		12		3	7	78
Denmark						5	7	7	4	10		4	10	5	5	4	3		6		77
Finland	8		7				3	6				1	4					1			22
Portugal			3	1						7					8			4	4		28

1987 Eurovision 32: Brussels, Belgium   9 May 1987

Rank	Start	Country	Artist	Song	Writer	Composer	POINTS
1	20	Ireland	Johnny Logan	Hold Me Now	Sean Sherrard	Sean Sherrard	172
2	16	Germany	Wind	Laß Die Sonne In Dein Herz	Bernd Meinunger	Ralph Siegel	141
3	7	Italy	Umberto Tozzi & Raf	Gente Di Mare	Giancarlo Bigazzi	Umberto Tozzi, Raffaele Riefoli	103
4	21	Yugoslavia	Novi Fosili	Ja Sam Za Ples	Stevo Cvikic	Rajko Dujmic	92
5	12	Netherlands	Marcha	Rechtop In De Wind	Peter Koelewijn	Peter Koelewijn	83
6	19	Denmark	Anne-Catherine Herdorf & Bandjo	En Lille Melodi	Jacob Jonia	Helga Engelbrecht	83
7	17	Cyprus	Alexia	Aspro Mavro	Maria Papapavlou	Andreas Papapavlou	80
8	2	Israel	Datner & Kushnir	Shir Habatlanim	Zohar Laskov	Zohar Laskov	73
9	1	Norway	Kate Gulbrandsen	Mitt Liv	Hanne Krogh, Rolf Løvland	Rolf Løvland	65
10	11	Greece	Bang	Stop!	Thanos Kalliris, Vassilis Dertilis	Thanos Kalliris, Vassilis Dertilis	64
11	5	Belgium	Liliane Saint-Pierre	Soldiers Of Love	Liliane Keuninckx, Gyuri Spies, Marc de Coen	Liliane Keuninckx, Gyuri Spies, Marc de Coen	56
12	6	Sweden	Lotta Engberg	Boogaloo	Christer Lundh	Mikael Wendt	50
13	14	United Kingdom	Rikki	Only The Light	Richard Peebles	Richard Peebles	47
14	15	France	Christine Minier	Les Mots D'amour N'ont Pas De Dimanche	Gérard Curci	Marc Minier	44
15	18	Finland	Vicky Rosti	Sata Salamaa	Veli-Pekka Lehto	Petri Laaksonen	32
16	4	Iceland	Halla Margarét	Hægt Og Hljótt	Valgeir Guðjónsson	Valgeir Guðjónsson	28
17	22	Switzerland	Carole Rich	Moitié Moitié	Jean-Jacques Egli	Jean-Jacques Egli	26
18	8	Portugal	Nevada	Neste Barco à Vela	Alfredo Azinheira	Alfredo Azinheira, Jorge Mendes	15
19	9	Spain	Patricia Kraus	No Estás Solo	Patricia Kraus	Rafael Martínez, Rafael Trabucchelli	10
20	3	Austria	Gary Lux	Nur Noch Gefühl	Stefanie Werger	Kenneth Westmore	8
21	13	Luxembourg	Plastic Bertrand	Amour Amour	Roger Jouret, Alec Mansion	Roger Jouret, Alec Mansion	4
22	10	Turkey	Seyyal Tanner & Lokomotif	Sarkim Sevgi üstüne	Olcayto Ahmet Tugsuz	Olcayto Ahmet Tugsuz	0

1987 Eurovision 32: Brussels, Belgium
9 May 1987

	Austria	Belgium	Cyprus	Denmark	Finland	France	Germany	Greece	Iceland	Ireland	Israel	Italy	Luxembourg	Netherlands	Norway	Portugal	Spain	Sweden	Switzerland	Turkey	United Kingdom	Yugoslavia	TOTAL
Norway	4	7	3	3	5	4	7			2		7		4			3	10	6				65
Israel	1	6			7	10	8		5	5				3	2	10		4	8		4		73
Austria								7				1											8
Iceland		4					10	6							4		4			4			28
Belgium	3		5		3		4		8		2	6	5		5		4				7	4	56
Sweden		1	7	7		3			3		12	3				7	7			2			50
Italy	6	5	1		4		12	5	8	12	3		4			12	8	1	7	8	1	12	103
Portugal							2																15
Spain								10															10
Turkey																							0
Greece	2		12	6		7			1	6	5	8	7	5			5	6			5	5	64
Netherlands				2	2	12		3				10	8						10	7	3	8	83
Luxembourg																2					2		4
United Kingdom	5	3	2	4	1		5	4	4	3	10		1	5	1	3		5	2	3		2	47
France									12	10	8	5	12	1		5	1	7	1	6	10	7	44
Germany	10	10	6	12	10	6		12	6	7	8	4	6	10	3	5		2	4		10		141
Cyprus				10	6	5	3			8			2	2	6	4	2	3	4		6	10	80
Finland							1	1	7		6	2		8	10	1		3		1		1	32
Denmark	7				8	8	6	8		4				6	7	8	2	8	3	1	7	6	83
Ireland	12	12	8	5	12	1		2	10		4	12	10	12	8	8	10	12	12	10	12		172
Yugoslavia	8	8	10	8		2	6		2	1	7			7	12	6	6			12		3	92
Switzerland			4	1				5			1		3							5			26

1988 Eurovision 33: Dublin, Ireland 30 April 1988

Rank	Start	Country	Artist	Song	Writer	Composer	POINTS
1	9	Switzerland	Céline Dion	Ne Partez Pas Sans Moi	Nella Martinetti	Atilla Şereftuğ	137
2	4	United Kingdom	Scott Fitzgerald	Go	Julie Forsyth	Julie Forsyth	136
3	13	Denmark	Hot Eyes	Ka' Du Se Hva' Jeg Sa'	Keld Heick	Søren Bundgård	92
4	17	Luxembourg	Lara Fabian	Croire	Alain Garcia	Jacques Cardona	90
5	15	Norway	Karoline Krüger	For Vår Jord	Erik Hillestad	Anita Skorgan	88
6	21	Yugoslavia	Srebrna Krila	Mangup	Stevo Cvikic, Rajko Dujmic	Rajko Dujmic	87
7	8	Israel	Yardena Arazi	Ben Adam	Ehud Manor	Boris Dimitshtein	85
8	10	Ireland	Jump the Gun	Take Him Home	Peter Eades	Peter Eades	79
9	7	Netherlands	Gerard Joling	Shangri-la	Peter de Wijn	Peter de Wijn	70
10	19	France	Gérard Lenorman	Chanteur De Charme	Gérard Lenorman, Claude Lemesle	Gérard Lenorman	64
11	6	Spain	La Década	La Chica Que Yo Quiero (made In Spain)	Francisco Dondiego	Enrique Piero	58
12	2	Sweden	Tommy Körberg	Stad I Ljus	Py Bäckman	Py Bäckman	52
13	18	Italy	Luca Barbarossa	Ti Scrivo	Luca Barbarossa	Luca Barbarossa	52
14	11	Germany	Maxi & Chris Garden	Lied Für Einen Freund	Bernd Meinunger	Ralph Siegel	48
15	5	Turkey	MFÖ	Sufi (hey Ya Hey)	Mazhar Alanson	Mazhar Alanson, Fuat Güner, Özkan Ugu	37
16	1	Iceland	Beathoven	Sókrates	Sverrir Stormsker	Sverrir Stormsker	20
17	14	Greece	Aphroditi Fryda	Kloun	Dimitris Sakislis	Dimitris Sakislis	10
18	20	Portugal	Dora	Voltarei	José Calvário, José Niza	José Calvário, José Niza	5
19	16	Belgium	Reynaert	Laissez Briller Le Soleil	Joseph Reynaerts, Philippe Anciaux	Joseph Reynaerts, Dany Willem	5
20	3	Finland	Boulevard	Nauravat Silmät Muistetaan	Kirsti Willberg	Pepe Willberg	3
21	12	Austria	Wilfried	Lisa Mona Lisa	Wilfried Scheutz, Klaus Kofler, Ronnie Herbholzheimer	Wilfried Scheutz, Klaus Kofler, Ronnie Herbholzheimer	0

1988 Eurovision 33: Dublin, Ireland — 30 April 1988

	Austria	Belgium	Denmark	Finland	France	Germany	Greece	Iceland	Ireland	Israel	Italy	Luxembourg	Netherlands	Norway	Portugal	Spain	Sweden	Switzerland	Turkey	United Kingdom	Yugoslavia	TOTAL
Iceland	10		4		2						1		4		8		1					20
Sweden		1	8						5		10	3	8	12						2	4	52
Finland										3												3
United Kingdom		12	10	10	6	10	6	3	7	10	12	8		5	3	10	5	5	12		1	136
Turkey	8	6				8		1		8		4	1			5	4	6		6		37
Spain			1				8	2	2	2	8	6		2				7	5	4	7	58
Netherlands	2	10		6		6	12	6		7	5	12	3		10	6		6	6		1	70
Israel	6			5	10	5	3	7	1		3	5	10	8	12	8	12		10	10	6	85
Switzerland		4	7	2	1	12	10		10	4	7	1	6	7	5	12	7	10	2	4	1	137
Ireland		5			4	7		6		5				4	2	3	3	4	2	3	6	79
Germany			6				8		6						6		8	1	1	5	8	48
Austria																						0
Denmark	12	7		4	12	4		10	4	6			12	10	6	1	3					92
Greece				7	7										7				3			10
Norway	3	3	5			1	7	5	8	1	4		7	4			8			12	10	88
Belgium					5																	5
Luxembourg	1	8	2	12		2	2	4	12	12	2		5	6	4		10	12		7	3	90
Italy	5		3	8	8	3						2	2	3	1	7	2	8	4		5	52
France	7	2	3	3			5	2	12	12		10		1		2	2	3	8	3	12	64
Portugal							1									4						5
Yugoslavia	4		12	1	3		4	12	3	12	6	7					6	2	7	8		87

1989 Eurovision 34: Lausanne, Switzerland 6 May 1989

Rank	Start	Country	Artist	Song	Writer	Composer	POINTS
1	22	Yugoslavia	Riva	Rock Me	Stevo Cvikic	Rajko Dujmic	137
2	7	United Kingdom	Live Report	Why Do I Always Get It Wrong	Brian Hodgson	John Beeby	130
3	12	Denmark	Birthe Kjær	Vi Maler Byen Rød	Keld Heick	Søren Bundgård	111
4	10	Sweden	Tommy Nilsson	En Dag	Tim Norell, Ola Håkansson	Tim Norell, Ola Håkansson, Alexander Bard	110
5	13	Austria	Thomas Forstner	Nur Ein Lied	Joachim Horn-Bernges	Dieter Bohlen	97
6	16	Spain	Nina	Nacida Para Amar	Juan Carlos Calderón	Juan Carlos Calderón	88
7	14	Finland	Anneli Saaristo	La Dolce Vita	Turkka Mali	Matti Puurtinen	76
8	15	France	Nathalie Pâque	J'ai Volé La Vie	Sylvain Lebel	Guy Matteoni, G G Candy	60
9	1	Italy	Anna Oxa & Fausto Leali	Avrei Voluto	Franco Ciani, Franco Berlincioni	Franco Fasano	56
10	19	Greece	Marianna	To Diko Sou Asteri	Villy Sanianou	Yiannis Kyris, Marianna Efstratiou	56
11	17	Cyprus	Fanny Polymeri & Yiannis Savvidakis	Apopse As Vrethoume	Efi Meletiou	Marios Meletiou	51
12	2	Israel	Gili ve Galit	Derech Ha'melech	Shaike Paikov	Shaike Paikov	50
13	18	Switzerland	Furbaz	Viver Senza Tei	Marie-Louise Werth	Marie-Louise Werth	47
14	21	Germany	Nino de Angelo	Flieger	Joachim Horn-Bernges	Dieter Bohlen	46
15	4	Netherlands	Justine Pelmelay	Blijf Zoals Je Bent	Cees Bergman, Geert-Jan Hessing, Aart Mol, E van Prehn, E Veerhoff	Jan Kisjes	45
16	9	Portugal	Da Vinci	Conquistador	Pedro Luis	Ricardo	39
17	8	Norway	Britt Synnøve Johansen	Venners Nærhet	Leiv N Grøtte	Inge Enoksen	30
18	3	Ireland	Kiev Connolly & the Missing Passengers	The Real Me	Kiev Connolly	Kiev Connolly	21
19	6	Belgium	Ingeborg	Door De Wind	Stef Bos	Stef Bos	13
20	11	Luxembourg	Park Café	Monsieur	Maggie Parke, Bernard Loncheval, Yves Lacomblez	Maggie Parke, Gast Waltzing	8
21	5	Turkey	Pan	Bana Bana	Timur Selçuk	Timur Selçuk	5
22	20	Iceland	Daniel August Haraldsson	Það Sem Enginn Sér	Valgeir Guðjónsson	Valgeir Guðjónsson	0

1989 Eurovision 34: Lausanne, Switzerland — 6 May 1989

	Austria	Belgium	Cyprus	Denmark	Finland	France	Germany	Greece	Iceland	Ireland	Israel	Italy	Luxembourg	Netherlands	Norway	Portugal	Spain	Sweden	Switzerland	Turkey	United Kingdom	Yugoslavia	TOTAL
Italy			6		10		7	4				—				7	12		2			8	56
Israel		3		5	5		3		5	7	—	1		3				5	7		2	7	50
Ireland						7	4			—										7		2	21
Netherlands	4				4		6	1		3		10	2	—							3	4	45
Turkey													1				1			—			5
Belgium		—							1														13
United Kingdom	8		2	6	6	12	12	2	1	5	7	6	12	5		12	10	10	1		—	6	130
Norway		8							2		2				—			2					30
Portugal	12	2					8	6					7			—		3					39
Sweden		6	8	12	2	2		8		4	6	5	6			8	5	—	3	4	4	12	110
Luxembourg	7					5							—				3						8
Denmark		4	10	—	12	6	5	12	10	10	1	12	3	12	10	2				6	10	1	111
Austria		12	3	4	1			5	8	8	8			6			2	7	8	3	10	5	97
Finland	3		7	3	—	10		10	12	6	10		4	4		1	7	4		10		10	76
France	5	7	4	7	3	—	2	7			5	8	8		4			1		2		3	60
Spain	2			10	8	8	10	3	7	1	3	2		10		8	—	5	10		7		88
Cyprus	1		—	8						2	4			1		3			4	2	6		51
Switzerland		1		2		1						7			5	10			—	8	8		47
Greece			12					—	4	12				10	6	5	4	6	12	8	5		56
Iceland									—														0
Germany		5	1			3	—	3	6		12	4		8	7	4		8	5	12	1		46
Yugoslavia	10	10	5	1	7		1		3												12	—	137

75

1990 Eurovision 35: Zagreb, Yugoslavia — 5 May 1990

Rank	Start	Country	Artist	Song	Writer	Composer	POINTS
1	19	Italy	Toto Cutugno	Insieme: 1992	Toto Cutugno	Toto Cutugno	149
2	14	France	Joelle Ursull	White And Black Blues	Serge Gainsbourg	Georges Ougier de Moussac	132
3	17	Ireland	Liam Reilly	Somewhere In Europe	Liam Reilly	Liam Reilly	132
4	8	Iceland	Stjórnin	Eitt Lag Enn	Aðalsteinn Ásberg Sigurðsson	Hörður G Ólafsson	124
5	1	Spain	Azúcar Moreno	Bandido	José-Luis Abel	Raúl Orellana, Jaime Stinus	96
6	7	United Kingdom	Emma	Give A Little Love Back To The World	Paul Curtis	Paul Curtis	87
7	15	Yugoslavia	Tajci	Hajde Da Ludujemo	Alka Vuica	Zrinko Tutic	81
8	11	Denmark	Lonnie Devantier	Hallo Hallo	Keld Heick	John Hatting, Torben Lendager	64
9	13	Germany	Chris Kempers & Daniel Kovac	Frei Zu Leben	Michael Kunze	Ralph Siegel	60
10	20	Austria	Simone	Keine Mauern Mehr	Mario Botazzi	Wolfgang Berry, Nana Berry	58
11	12	Switzerland	Egon Egemann	Musik Klingt In Die Welt Hinaus	Cornelia Lackner	Cornelia Lackner	51
12	3	Belgium	Philippe Lafontaine	Macédomienne	Philippe Lafontaine	Philippe Lafontaine	46
13	6	Luxembourg	Céline Carzo	Quand Je Te Rêve	Thierry Delianis	Jean-Charles France	38
14	21	Cyprus	Haris Anastasiou	Milas Poli	Haris Anastasiou	John Vickers	36
15	5	Netherlands	Maywood	Ik Wil Alles Met Je Delen	Alice May	Alice May	25
16	18	Sweden	Edin-Ådahl	Som En Vind	Mikael Wendt	Mikael Wendt	24
17	4	Turkey	Kayahan	Gözlerinin Hapsindeyim	Kayahan Acar	Kayahan Acar	21
18	10	Israel	Rita	Shara Barechovot	Tzruya Lahav	Rami Kleinstein	16
19	2	Greece	Christos Callow & Wave	Horis Skopo	Giorgos Papagiannakis	Giorgos Paleokastriris	11
20	16	Portugal	Nucha	Há Sempre Alguém	Fancisco Teotonio Pereira	Jan van Dijck, Luis Filipe	9
21	22	Finland	Beat	Fri?	Stina Engblom	Kim & Janne Engblom, Tina Krause	8
22	9	Norway	Ketil Stokkan	Brandenburger Tor	Ketil Stokkan	Ketil Stokkan	8

1990 Eurovision 35: Zagreb, Yugoslavia
5 May 1990

	Austria	Belgium	Cyprus	Denmark	Finland	France	Germany	Greece	Iceland	Ireland	Israel	Italy	Luxembourg	Netherlands	Norway	Portugal	Spain	Sweden	Switzerland	Turkey	United Kingdom	Yugoslavia	TOTAL
Spain	8	1	8		10	5	12	8	4			8		2	5	5			6	10	1	3	96
Greece			6											5									11
Belgium						8	5						4	7	1	2		7	4	3		7	46
Turkey	4								2	1	2	2	1	3	4	1							21
Netherlands	5		2			6	3	4								3		4	3	3	4	2	25
Luxembourg	1	12	5	3		12						1						5	10			10	38
United Kingdom	10	10	3	10	7	10	1	5		6	10	6	3		10	12	7	8	7	1		4	87
Iceland								3		7	8	3	8			4	4	8			12		124
Norway				1	5		4			3	4							3					8
Israel	6	3	4						7	4		7		4	7	7	6	3	2	2		1	16
Denmark			1	12	3	1		12					2			8	1	4	1	6		5	64
Switzerland	3	6	7	4	12		10		1	10	6	5	12	12	12	4	8	5		4	7	12	51
Germany	2	4		5	1	2			12	8	12	10		12	3		5	1		12	5		60
France			10	7					10	5			7				3				2		132
Yugoslavia	12	7		8	4	7	7	7	8	12	1		6	10	8	6	10	12	5	5	10		81
Portugal	7																						9
Ireland		8	12	6	8	4	6	10	3		5	12	10	8	6	10	12	10	8	8	8	6	132
Sweden		2	2	2	2	3	2	2	6	2		4	5	1		2	2			7		8	24
Italy		5	6		6			6	5		3				2			6					149
Austria																							58
Cyprus																							36
Finland																							8

1991 Eurovision 36: Rome, Italy — 4 May 1991

Rank	Start	Country	Artist	Song	Writer	Composer	POINTS
1	8	Sweden	Carola	Fångad Av En Stormvind	Stephan Berg	Stephan Berg	146
2	9	France	Amina	C'est Le Dernier Qui A Parlé Qui A Raison	Amina Annabi	Wasis Diop	146
3	15	Israel	Duo Datz	Kan	Uzi Chitman	Uzi Chitman	139
4	19	Spain	Sergio Dalma	Bailar Pegados	Luis Gomez Escolar	Julio Seijas	119
5	5	Switzerland	Sandra Simó	Canzone Per Te	Renato Mascetti	Renato Mascetti	118
6	3	Malta	Paul Giordimaina & Georgina	Could It Be	Raymond Mahoney	Paul Abela	106
7	22	Italy	Peppino di Capri	Comme E' Ddoce 'o Mare	Giampiero Artegiani	Marcello Marocchi	89
8	12	Portugal	Dulce	Lusitana Paixão	Fred Micael, Zé da Ponte, J Quintela	Fred Micael, Zé da Ponte, J Quintela	62
9	21	Cyprus	Elena Patroclou	SOS	Andreas Christou	Kypros Charalambous	60
10	20	United Kingdom	Samantha Janus	A Message To Your Heart	Paul Curtis	Paul Curtis	47
11	11	Ireland	Kim Jackson	Could It Be That I'm In Love	Liam Reilly	Liam Reilly	47
12	10	Turkey	Izel Çeliköz, Rayhan Soykarçi & Can Ugurluér	Iki Dakika	Aysel Gürel	Sevket Ugurluér	44
13	4	Greece	Sofia Vossou	I Anixi	Andreas Mikroutsikos	Andreas Mikroutsikos	36
14	7	Luxembourg	Sarah Bray	Un Baiser Volé	Linda Lecomte, Mick Wersant	Patrick Hippert	29
15	2	Iceland	Stefán & Eyfi	Nina	Eyjólfur Kristjánsson	Eyjólfur Kristjánsson	26
16	18	Belgium	Clouseau	Geef Het Op	Bob Savenberg, Koen Wauters, Kris Wauters, Jan Leyers	Bob Savenberg, Koen Wauters, Kris Wauters, Jan Leyers	23
17	14	Norway	Just 4 Fun	Mrs Thompson	P G Roness, Kaare Skevik	Dag Kolsrud	14
18	17	Germany	Atlantis 2000	Dieser Traum Darf Niemals Sterben	Helmut Frey	Alfons Weindorf	10
19	13	Denmark	Anders Frandsen	Lige Der Hvor Hjertet Slår	Michael Elo	Michael Elo	8
20	16	Finland	Kaija	Hullu Yö	Jukka Välimaa	Ile Kallio	6
21	1	Yugoslavia	Baby Doll	Brazil	Dragana Saric	Zoran Vracevic	1
22	6	Austria	Thomas Forstner	Venedig Im Regen	Robby Musenbichler, Hubert Moser, Wolfgang Eltner	Robby Musenbichler, Hubert Moser, Wolfgang Eltner	0

Note: Sweden win on the higher number of '10' votes, after finishing level on total points and number of '12' votes.

1991 Eurovision 36: Rome, Italy — 4 May 1991

	Austria	Belgium	Cyprus	Denmark	Finland	France	Germany	Greece	Iceland	Ireland	Israel	Italy	Luxembourg	Malta	Norway	Portugal	Spain	Sweden	Switzerland	Turkey	United Kingdom	Yugoslavia	TOTAL
Yugoslavia														1									1
Iceland	4	4				2	5			12		7	10			2	6	10	4			1	26
Malta	2	1	10		1		10	2	4	1	4	10			6	7	5	12	6	7	7		106
Greece	8		8	5	5	4	6		5	2	8	2		5	1			8				4	36
Switzerland		12										4	12		3	6		8		2	8	5	118
Austria																							0
Luxembourg	5	2	2	4			3		4	3								1			3		29
Sweden	10	10	6	12	8		12		12		10		7	3	8	10	4		10	6	12	6	146
France	12	7	7		10		8	8	7	7	12			7	12	5	8	5	7		6	10	146
Turkey				8	2	7	2				7	8		7			2				5	3	44
Ireland	1	5		7	7				8		1	3	8	4					3	4	4		47
Portugal			4	1		10		4				1	2		2		10	7	1	5		3	62
Denmark															5			3					8
Norway				2			4		6				1							1			14
Israel		8	5	10	6	3		5	10	8			5	8	7	4	12	6	8	12	10	12	139
Finland								1	1	4							1						6
Germany	3		3	6	3	5		10	2		2	5		6		8	3	2			2		10
Belgium	7	6	12		4	6	7	3		6	5	6	6	10	4	1		4	12	8	1	8	23
Spain		3	1			1	1	12	3	5	6		3	12		8			5				119
United Kingdom				3		12							4		10	1							47
Cyprus	6				12	8		6		10	3			2		3	7		2	10		7	60
Italy																12							89

1992 Eurovision 37: Malmö, Sweden 9 May 1992

Rank	Start	Country	Artist	Song	Writer	Composer	POINTS
1	17	Ireland	Linda Martin	Why Me	Johnny Logan	Johnny Logan	155
2	16	United Kingdom	Michael Ball	One Step Out Of Time	Tony Ryan, Paul Davies, Victor Stratton	Tony Ryan, Paul Davies, Victor Stratton	139
3	10	Malta	Mary Spiteri	Little Child	Raymond Mahoney	Georgina Abela	123
4	19	Italy	Mia Martini	Rapsodia	Giancarlo Bigazzi	Giuseppe Dati	111
5	5	Greece	Cleopatra	Olou Tou Kosmou I Elpida	Christos Lagos	Christos Lagos	94
6	3	Israel	Dafna	Ze Rak Sport	Ehud Manor	Kobi Oshrat	85
7	11	Iceland	Heart 2 Heart	Nei Eða Já	Stefán Hilmarsson	Friðrik Karlsson, Grétar Örvarsson	80
8	6	France	Kali	Monté La Riviè	Remy Bellenchombre	Kali	73
9	23	Netherlands	Humphrey Campbell	Wijs Me De Weg	Edwin Schimscheimer	Edwin Schimscheimer	67
10	15	Austria	Tony Wegas	Zusammen Geh'n	Joachim Horn-Bernges	Dieter Bohlen	63
11	9	Cyprus	Evridiki	Teriazoume	George Theophanous	George Theophanous	57
12	18	Denmark	Lotte Nilsson & Kenny Lübcke	Ålt Det Som Ingen Ser	Carsten Warming	Carsten Warming	47
13	20	Yugoslavia	Extra Nena	Ljubim Te Pesmama	Gale Jankovic	Radivoje Radivojevic	44
14	1	Spain	Serafin	Todo Esto Es La Música	Luis Miguelez	Luis Miguelez, Alfredo Albuena	37
15	13	Switzerland	Daisy Auvray	Mister Music Man	Gordon Dent	Gordon Dent	32
16	22	Germany	Wind	Träume Sind Für Alle Da	Bernd Meinunger	Ralph Siegel	27
17	8	Portugal	Diná	Amor D'água Fresca	Rosa Lobato de Faria	Nandina Veloso	26
18	21	Norway	Merethe Trøan	Visjoner	Eva Jansen	Robert Morley	23
19	4	Turkey	Aylin Vatankos	Yaz Bitti	Aylin Üçanlar	Aldogan Simsekyay	17
20	2	Belgium	Morgane	Nous On Veut Des Violons	Anne-Marie Gaspard	Claude Barzotti	11
21	14	Luxembourg	Marion Welter & Kontinent	Sou Fräi	Jang Linster, Ab van Goor	Jang Linster, Ab van Goor	10
22	7	Sweden	Christer Björkmann	I Morgon är En Annan Dag	Niklas Strömstedt	Niklas Strömstedt	9
23	12	Finland	Pave	Yamma Yamma	Hector	Pave Maijanen	4

1992 Eurovision 37: Malmö, Sweden — 9 May 1992

	Austria	Belgium	Cyprus	Denmark	Finland	France	Germany	Greece	Iceland	Ireland	Israel	Italy	Luxembourg	Malta	Netherlands	Norway	Portugal	Spain	Sweden	Switzerland	Turkey	United Kingdom	Yugoslavia	TOTAL
Spain	2			1	3	6		4				7	3	2	1	5					1	1		37
Belgium						3							1					3			4			11
Israel	1	4	4	2		8	4						8	7	3	2	7	10	4	4	2	7	12	85
Turkey										3				8									6	17
Greece	4		12		5	7	3		2	5	7	12	8		4	8	5	6	3	10	8		7	94
France			3	4	7						12	6			6	10				12	3			73
Sweden				4		1						1											4	9
Portugal					2			2			8												5	26
Cyprus					8	2	8	10		6	3	4	12		8	3	2			2			8	57
Malta	8	10	1	8				7	8	10		3	5		5	1	12	12	12	5			10	123
Iceland	7	4		5			6	6			4	5			2		6	8	6	3				80
Finland											1												3	4
Switzerland	5								12	1		10		10								4		32
Luxembourg																			1					10
Austria	8	8		7		10	12	8	4	12	2	8	7	4	7		3	2	1			10		63
United Kingdom	12	12	6	12	6		10	12	7	7		2	10	6	10	7	4	5	5	8	10		2	139
Ireland	10	7	5	10	10		5		6		6		6	12	12	6	1	1	10	6	12	8		155
Denmark	3								10					5		6		4	7		5	3		47
Italy	6		10		12	12		3	5	4	10		2	3	12	12	8		8	7	6			111
Yugoslavia			2	6	4	5		1	1				4						2					44
Norway	3			6	1		2			2												5	1	23
Germany	6			3			7									4	10					6		27
Netherlands	5	2	7			4		5	3	8	5						7			1	7	2		67

1993 Eurovision 38: Millstreet, Ireland

15 May 1993

Qualification: 7 new applicant countries took part in a preliminary heat, the top 3 qualified for the main contest.

Rank	Start	Country	Artist	Song	Writer	Composer	POINTS
1	14	Ireland	Niamh Kavanagh	In your eyes	Jimmy Walsh	Jimmy Walsh	187
2	19	United Kingdom	Sonia	Better the devil you know	Dean Collinson, Red	Dean Collinson, Red	164
3	4	Switzerland	Annie Cotton	Moi, tout simplement	Jean-Jacques Egli	Christophe Dúc	148
4	12	France	Patrick Fiori	Mama Corsica	François Valéry	François Valéry	121
5	25	Norway	Silje Vige	Alle mine tankar	Björn-Erik Vige	Björn-Erik Vige	120
6	20	Netherlands	Ruth Jacott	Vrede	Henk Westbroek	Eric van Tijn, Jochem Fluitsma	92
7	13	Sweden	Arvingarna	Eloïse	Gert Lengstrand	Lasse Holm	89
8	8	Malta	William Mangion	This time	William Mangion	William Mangion	69
9	6	Greece	Katerina Garbi	Ellada, hora tou fotos	Dimosthenis	Dimosthenis	64
10	11	Portugal	Anabela	A cidade até ser dia	Paulo Dacosta, Marco Quelhas, Pedro Abrantes	Paulo Dacosta, Marco Quelhas, Pedro Abrantes	60
11	22	Spain	Eva Santamaria	Hombres	Carlos Toro	Carlos Toro	58
12	1	Italy	Enrico Ruggeri	Sole d'Europa	Enrico Ruggeri	Enrico Ruggeri	45
13	9	Iceland	Inga	Þá veistu svarið	Friðrik Sturlúson	Jon-Kjell Seljeseth	42
14	10	Austria	Tony Wegas	Maria Magdalena	Thomas Spitzer	Christian Kolonovits, Johann Bertl	32
15	21	Croatia	Put	Don't ever cry	Dorde Novkovic	Andrej Basa	31
16	18	Bosnia & H	Fazla	Sva bol svijeta	Fahrudin Pecikoza	Dino Dervishalidovic	27
17	17	Finland	Katri-Helena	Tule luo	Jukka Saarinen	Matti Puurtinen	20
18	3	Germany	Münchener Freiheit	Viel zu weit	Stefan Zauner	Stefan Zauner	18
19	23	Cyprus	Kyriakos Zymboulakis & Demos Van	Mi stamatas	Rodoula Papalambrianou	Aristos Moschovakis	17
20	15	Luxembourg	Modern Times	Donne-moi une chance	Patrick Hippert, Jimmy Martin	Patrick Hippert, Jimmy Martin	11
21	2	Turkey	Burak Aydos, Öztürk Baybora & Serter	Esmer yarim	Burak Aydos	Burak Aydos	10
22	16	Slovenia	1X Band	Tih dezeven dan	Tomaz Kosec	Cole Moretti	9
23	5	Denmark	Tommy Seebach Band	Under stjernerne på himlen	Keld Heick	Tommy Seebach	9
24	24	Israel	Lakahat Shiru	Shiru	Yoram Tahar-Lev	Shaike Paikov	4
25	7	Belgium	Barbara	Iemand als jij	Tobana	Marc Vliegen	3

Eurosong Qualifier: Ljubliana, Slovenia

3 April 1993

Rank	Start	Country	Artist	Song	Writer	Composer	POINTS
1	6	Slovenia	1X Band	Tih dezeven dan	Tomaz Kosec	Cole Moretti	54
2	1	Bosnia & H	Fazla	Sva bol svijeta	Fahrudin Pecikoza	Dino Dervishalidovic	52
3	2	Croatia	Put	Don't ever cry	Dorde Novkovic	Andrej Basa	51
4	7	Slovakia	Elán	Amnestia na neveru	Jan Baláž	Jožef Ráž	50
5	3	Estonia	Jaanika Sillamaa	Muretut meelt ja südametuld	Leelo Tungal	Andres Valkoneni	47
6	4	Hungary	Andrea Szulák	Arva reggel	Petar Ugrin	György Jakob, Emesi Hatvani	44
7	5	Romania	Dida Dragan	Nu pleca	Adrian Ordean	Dida Dragan	38

1993 Eurovision 38: Millstreet, Ireland — 15 May 1993

	Austria	Belgium	Bosnia & H	Croatia	Cyprus	Denmark	Finland	France	Germany	Greece	Iceland	Ireland	Israel	Italy	Luxembourg	Malta	Netherlands	Norway	Portugal	Slovenia	Spain	Sweden	Switzerland	Turkey	United Kingdom	TOTAL
Italy	6	8			12		8	5			1	4			10	7	2		10		2		1			45
Turkey					6																					10
Germany				2		3																				18
Switzerland	6				6	10	4	12	12	7	4	7	4	8	12	5	1	3	1	8	3	6				148
Denmark		5												10	3			7				1	2			9
Greece					12		6	7	2		4		7	2		6	8		2		8	6		2		64
Belgium									3					7												3
Malta	4	4	4	4	1	5		2	4	5	4	2	3								4	4	7	5	6	69
Iceland	1		12	5	2	4						1	2									7			2	42
Austria		3						3	1	1		6					7							4	3	32
Portugal	5				3	1	2				2		8		4			5		6		2	4		1	60
France	7			8	10	12	1			3	8		10		6		12	6	12	4	12	8		7	4	121
Sweden	10	10		3		7	7	8	8		7	10			5	4	3		4	12			8	1	7	89
Ireland	8	2	8	6	7	6	3	10	5	6	3		5	12	7	12	10	12	6	1	10	12	12		12	187
Luxembourg													12	4		10										11
Slovenia		1									5			3		1						3				9
Finland							4		3		5					2										20
Bosnia & H											12					4								12		27
United Kingdom	12	12	3	10	4	8	5	6	6		12	8	12	1	8		4	8	7	10	5	10	5	8		164
Netherlands	3	7	10	3				7	7		6	12		6		3		10		7	7	5		6	8	92
Croatia		4			5								6					4	5		1		3			31
Spain	2	5	6	7		2	10				10		1	5		8		1		2			6			58
Cyprus								1		10									3						5	17
Israel																										4
Norway	6		7	12	8		12		10	12	10	5			1		6		8	3			10	10		120

83

1994 Eurovision 39: Dublin, Ireland

30 April 1994

Qualification: Bottom 6 countries from 1993 relegated, replaced with 7 new applicant countries.

Rank	Start	Country	Artist	Song	Writer	Composer	POINTS
1	3	Ireland	P Harrington & C McGettigan	Rock 'n' roll kids	Brendan J. Graham	Brendan J. Graham	226
2	24	Poland	Edyta Górniak	To nie ja!	Jacek Cygan	Stanislas Syrewicz	166
3	14	Germany	MeKaDo	Wir geben 'ne Party	Bernd Meinunger	Ralph Siegel	128
4	22	Hungary	Friderika Bayer	Kinek mondjam el vétkeimet	Szilveszter Jenei	Szilveszter Jenei	122
5	12	Malta	Moira Stafrace & Christopher Scicluna	More than love	Moira Stafrace	Christopher Scicluna	97
6	17	Norway	E Andreasson & J W Danielsen	Duett	Hans Olav Mørk	Rolf Løvland	76
7	25	France	Nina Morato	Je suis un vrai garçon	Nina Morato	Bruno Maman	74
8	8	Portugal	Sara Tavares	Chamar a música	Rosa Lobato Faria	João Carlos Mota Oliveira	73
9	23	Russia	Youddiph	Vechni stranik	Youddiph	Lev Zemlinski	70
10	6	United Kingdom	Frances Ruffelle	We will be free (Lonely symphony)	George de Angelis, Mark Dean	George de Angelis, Mark Dean	63
11	4	Cyprus	Evridiki	Ime anthropos ke ego	George Theophanous	George Theophanous	51
12	5	Iceland	Sigga	Nætur	Stefán Hilmarsson	Friðrik Karlsson	49
13	1	Sweden	Marie Bergman & Roger Pontare	Stjärnorna	Mikael Littwold	Peter Bertilsson	48
14	19	Greece	Costas Bigalis & the Sea Lovers	To trehantiri (diri diri)	Costas Bigalis	Costas Bigalis	44
15	18	Bosnia & H	Alma & Dejan	Ostani kraj mene	Edu Mulahalilovic	Adi Mulahalilovic	39
16	7	Croatia	Tony Cetinski	Nek'ti bude ljubav sva	Zeljko Krznaric	Zeljen Klasterka	27
17	20	Austria	Petra Frey	Für den Frieden der Welt	Karl Brunner, Johann Brunner	Alfons Weindorf	19
18	21	Spain	Alejandro Abad	Ella no es ella	Alejandro Abad	Alejandro Abad	17
19	15	Slovakia	Martin Durinda & Tublatanka	Nekovecná piesen	Martin Sarvas	Martin Durinda	15
20	9	Switzerland	Duilio	Sto pregando	Giuseppe Scaramella	Giuseppe Scaramella	15
21	11	Romania	Dan Bittman	Dincolo de nori	Antoniu Furtuna, Dan Bittman	Antoniu Furtuna, Dan Bittman	14
22	2	Finland	CatCat	Bye bye baby	Kari Salli, Markku 'Make' Lentonen	Kari Salli, Markku 'Make' Lentonen	11
23	13	Netherlands	Willeke Alberti	Waar is de zon	Cooth van Doesburgh	Edwin Schimscheimer	4
24	10	Estonia	Silvi Vrait	Nagu merelaine	Leelo Tungal	Ivar Must	2
25	16	Lithuania	Ovidijus Vyšniauskas	Lopšine mylimai	Gintaras Zdebskis	Ovidijus Vyšniauskas	0

1994 Eurovision 39: Dublin, Ireland
30 April 1994

	Austria	Bosnia & H	Croatia	Cyprus	Estonia	Finland	France	Germany	Greece	Hungary	Iceland	Ireland	Lithuania	Malta	Netherlands	Norway	Poland	Portugal	Romania	Russia	Slovakia	Spain	Sweden	Switzerland	United Kingdom	TOTAL
Sweden	5				2					2	2		5	3	6	10						1		7		48
Finland		1							10																	11
Ireland	10	10	12	8	10	7	8	12		10	12		10	5	12	12	8	12	8	12	6	10	10	12	10	226
Cyprus						10	3		12								5	5		2		4	4	2		51
Iceland	3					1	4	4				6	3			5		3		1	1		8	3	6	49
United Kingdom	1	4	6		5					3	8	1					4	8				6		8		63
Croatia		3							5					10						5	3					27
Portugal						5	6			7	8	8		1	3	2	3			4	12	3	5	5	8	73
Switzerland							5							8		2						12				15
Estonia									2				2				1					2				2
Romania									6					6												14
Malta	4	12	7	2	7	6		3	7			10	7		1			4	10		10		4	6	1	97
Netherlands																4										4
Germany	2	7		6	3	3				12		5	4				7	10	12	7	7	8	6		7	128
Slovakia									3					12												15
Lithuania																										0
Norway	6	6	3	10	8		10	2	1	5	7	3	1		7				4	8		5	7	1	4	76
Bosnia & H			4			2		1		1				7		1					8	7				39
Greece				12		4											2		6		5		2	6		44
Austria		5	2	7					8	4			6	4	7	4			1				1		3	19
Spain							2				10	12							5		2					17
Hungary	8	3	5		4	12	7	7			4	4			10	8	12	1	2	3			12	4	2	122
Russia	6		1	3	1		1	6		6	6	4		2	5	3	10	2	3						5	70
Poland	12	8	8	1	12	8	12	10		8		7	12		8	6		7	7	6	4			10	12	166
France	7	2		4	6			8			5	2	8			7	6	6		10			3			74

1995 Eurovision 40: Dublin, Ireland　　　　　　　　　　　　　　　　　　　　　　　　　　　　　　　　13 May 1995

Qualification: Bottom 6 countries from 1994 relegated, replaced with the countries relegated in 1993.

Rank	Start	Country	Artist	Song	Writer	Composer	POINTS
1	5	Norway	Secret Garden	Nocturne	Petter Skavlan	Rolf Løvland	148
2	9	Spain	Anabel Conde	Vuelve conmigo	José María Purón	José María Purón	119
3	18	Sweden	Jan Johansen	Se på mej	Ingela Pling Forsman	Håkan Almqvist, Bobby Ljunggren	100
4	12	France	Nathalie Santamaria	Il me donne rendez-vous	Didier Barbelivien	François Bernheim	94
5	19	Denmark	Aud Wilken	Fra Mols til Skagen	Lise Cabble	Mette Mathiesen, Lise Cabble	92
6	11	Croatia	Magazin & Lidija	Nostalgija	Vjekoslava Huljic	Tonci Huljic	91
7	20	Slovenia	Darja Svajger	Prisluhni mi	Primoz Peterca	Primoz Peterca, Saso Fajon	83
8	21	Israel	Liora	Amen	Hamutal Ben Ze'ev	Moshe Datz	81
9	17	Cyprus	Alexandros Panayi	Sti fotia	Alexandros Panayi	Alexandros Panayi	79
10	22	Malta	Mike Spiteri	Keep me in mind	Alfred Sant	Ray Agius	76
11	15	United Kingdom	Love City Groove	Love City Groove	Paul Hardy, Steven Rudden, Tatsiana Mais, Jay Williams	Paul Hardy, Steven Rudden, Tatsiana Mais, Jay Williams	76
12	23	Greece	Elina Constantopoulou	Pia prossefchi	Antonis Pappas	Nikos Terzis	68
13	8	Austria	Stella Jones	Die Welt dreht sich verkehrt	Mischa Krausz	Mischa Krausz	67
14	2	Ireland	Eddie Friel	Dreamin'	Richard Abbott, Barry Woods	Richard Abbott, Barry Woods	44
15	7	Iceland	Bó Halldórsson	Núna	Jón Örn Marinósson	Bó Halldórsson, Ed Welch	31
16	10	Turkey	Arzu Ece	Sevi	Zeynep Talu	Melih Kibar	21
17	6	Russia	Philipp Kirkorov	Kolybelnaya dlya vulkana	Ilya Bershadsky	Ilya Reznyk	18
18	1	Poland	Justyna	Sama	Wojciech Waglewski	Mateusz Pospieszalski, Wojciech Waglewski	15
19	4	Bosnia & H	Davor Popovic	Dvadeset i prvi vijek	Zlatan Fazlic	Zlatan Fazlic, Sinan Alimanovic	14
20	14	Belgium	Frédéric Etherlinck	La voix est libre	Pierre Theunis	Pierre Theunis	8
21	16	Portugal	Tó Cruz	Baunilha e chocolate	Rosa Lobato De Faria	António Vitorino de Almeida	5
22	13	Hungary	Czaba Szigeti	Új név egy régi ház falan	Attila Horváth	Ferenc Balázs	3
23	3	Germany	Stone & Stone	Verliebt in Dich	Cheyenne Stone	Cheyenne Stone	1

1995 Eurovision 40: Dublin, Ireland — 13 May 1995

	Austria	Belgium	Bosnia & H	Croatia	Cyprus	Denmark	France	Germany	Greece	Hungary	Iceland	Ireland	Israel	Malta	Norway	Poland	Portugal	Russia	Slovenia	Spain	Sweden	Turkey	United Kingdom	TOTAL
Poland									3	1	6						1			3				15
Ireland			5			1	1	1	4		3				4			5	5	3	10	5	5	44
Germany				8										1										1
Bosnia & H		5			7	3		4														3		14
Norway		1	10	6	1	2	10	4	12	6	12	10	10	6	10	12	12	12	7	4		12	4	148
Russia	4										1													18
Iceland				6		8	2					6			2		2	3			6			31
Austria		10				10	8		7	4			2		3	2	2		3	6	4	4	5	67
Spain		12	8		10		7	6	6	2	5	2	12	8		8	7		12			8	8	119
Turkey		1											1	7						2			2	21
Croatia	10		10		5		12	8	5	10	10	3	4	12	7	7	4		8	12	3	7	1	91
France		6		3	2	6			2	8	8	5	7		6			2				2		94
Hungary	1											1								1				3
Belgium							7	8												7				8
United Kingdom	12	7	4			7	12		7	7		1	5		1	5	10	1			5			76
Portugal							4		1															5
Cyprus		8	2	1		5	3	3	8	12	2	12	6	4	5	1	8	4	4	5	8	1	3	79
Sweden	7	3	3		4	12		12			4			3	8	10	6	6	1			6	6	100
Denmark	3		6	2	3			7		3	7	7	3		12	3	5	10	6		12		10	92
Slovenia	6	4	7	4		8	8	5	10	8	8	8	2	2		4		7			7		10	83
Israel	2		4	12	8	10		10		5				5				8	10	10	2	10	12	81
Malta	2		12	6	4	4	6	2			5	4	7	10		6	3		2	10	1	7	7	76
Greece	5	2	7	12			5						8					2		8				68

1996 Eurovision 41: Oslo, Norway **18 May 1996**

Qualification: 1995 Winner plus 22 from 29 entries based on judged preselection

Rank	Start	Country	Artist	Song	Writer	Composer	POINTS
1	17	Ireland	Eimear Quinn	The voice	Brendan Graham	Brendan Graham	162
2	12	Norway	Elisabeth Andreasson	I evighet	Torhild Nigar	Torhild Nigar	114
3	23	Sweden	One More Time	Den vilda	Nanne Grönvall	Peter Grönvall	100
4	7	Croatia	Maja Blagdan	Sveta ljubav	Zrinko Tutic	Zrinko Tutic	98
5	11	Estonia	Ivo Linna & Maarja-Liis Ilus	Kaelakee hääl	Kaari Sillamaa	Priit Pajusaar	94
6	4	Portugal	Lúcia Moniz	O meu coração não tem cor	José Fanha	Pedro Osório	92
7	15	Netherlands	Maxine & Franklin Brown	De eerste keer	Peter van Asten, Piet Souer	Peter van Asten	78
8	2	United Kingdom	Gina G	Just a little bit	Simon Tauber	Steve Rodway	77
9	5	Cyprus	Constantinos	Mono gia mas	Rodoula Papalambrianou	Andreas Giorgallis	72
10	8	Austria	George Nußbaumer	Weil's Dr Guat Got	Mischa Krausz, George Nußbaumer	Mischa Krausz, George Nußbaumer	68
11	6	Malta	Miriam Christine	In a woman's heart	Alfred Sant	Paul Abela	68
12	1	Turkey	Sebnem Paker	Beşinçi mevsim	Dr. Çuhaci	Levent Çoker	57
13	19	Iceland	Anna Mjöll	Sjúbídú	Anna Mjöll Ólafsdóttir, Ólafur Gaukur	Anna Mjöll Ólafsdóttir, Ólafur Gaukur	51
14	10	Greece	Marianna Efstratiou	Emis forame to himona anixiatika	Iro Trigoni	Costas Bigalis	36
15	20	Poland	Kasia Kowalska	Chce znac swój grzech	Kasia Kowalska	Robert Amirian	31
16	9	Switzerland	Cathy Leander	Mon coeur l'aime	Régis Mounir	Régis Mounir	22
17	16	Belgium	Lisa del Bo	Liefde is een kaartspel	Daniel Ditmar	John Terra, Sarah Brogden	22
18	22	Slovakia	Marcel Palonder	Kým nás máš	Jozef Urban	Juraj Burian	19
19	13	France	Dan Ar Braz et l'Héritage des Celtes	Diwanit bugale	Dan Ar Braz	Dan Ar Braz	18
20	3	Spain	Antonio Carbonell	¡Ay, qué deseo!	Ketama	Ketama	17
21	14	Slovenia	Regina	Dan najlepših sanj	Aleksander Kogoj	Aleksander Kogoj	16
22	21	Bosnia & H	Amila Glamocak	Za našu ljubav	Sinan Alimanovic, Aida Frijak, Adnan Bajramovic	Sinan Alimanovic, Aida Frijak, Adnan Bajramovic	13
23	18	Finland	Jasmine	Niin kaunis on taivas	Timo Niemi	Timo Niemi	9

1996 Eurovision 41: Oslo, Norway — 18 May 1996

	Austria	Belgium	Bosnia & H	Croatia	Cyprus	Estonia	Finland	France	Greece	Iceland	Ireland	Malta	Netherlands	Norway	Poland	Portugal	Slovakia	Slovenia	Spain	Sweden	Switzerland	Turkey	United Kingdom	TOTAL
Turkey	3	5	5	1	1	2	5	4		4	3	10	7								6		6	57
United Kingdom		12		7	2	6	3	8		10	1	6			6	12		6		6	4	3		77
Spain					1							5												17
Portugal	1	6	1	10	12		3	5		4		2	6	12			4	10	7	4	10	5	2	92
Cyprus	2			8			6	2	12	10						3		12	10	2	5		12	72
Malta				12					8		1		5	1	6	10	4	5	5	5	1	10		68
Croatia		4	10		8	6		12	1	5	6	7	5	7	2		3	3		1		8	4	98
Austria			6		7		4		2		8	12	4		8	5	1					4		68
Switzerland		2								3	4	1	1	3	1		2	8		3			3	22
Greece	5				10					12				8							2		7	36
Estonia	8	8	3	5	7		12	1		8	2		3	8	10		8		4	12			10	94
Norway	8			3	3	5	7	7	10	8	7		10		4	2	10			10	7	2	8	114
France	7					3	2							4		1							1	18
Slovenia			8	6						1									1					16
Netherlands	12	1	2		5	4		10		2	5				7	7	5		6	8	3	1		78
Belgium				2		1							2						12				5	22
Ireland	7	3	12		6	12	10	6	10			4	12	10	12	8	12	7		7	12	12		162
Finland										7			2	2										9
Iceland	6				8				3		10		5	5	3	6	6	1	3					51
Poland	4	7					1		7						2			2	2			7		31
Bosnia & H			3		4							3										6		13
Slovakia									4			8			5				2					19
Sweden	10	10	4			10	8	3		6	12		8	6		4	7	4			8			100

1997 Eurovision 42: Dublin, Ireland 3 May 1997

Qualification: The 25 countries with the best average scores in the last 5 years qualified.

Rank	Start	Country	Artist	Song	Writer	Composer	POINTS
1	24	United Kingdom	Katrina and The Waves	Love shine a light	Kimberley Rew	Kimberley Rew	227
2	5	Ireland	Marc Roberts	Mysterious woman	John Farry	John Farry	157
3	2	Turkey	Sebnem Paker & Group Etnic	Dinle	Mehtap Alnitemiz	Levent Çoker	121
4	9	Italy	Jalisse	Fiumi di parole	Carmen di Domenico, Alessandra Drusian	Fabio Ricci	114
5	1	Cyprus	Chara & Andreas Konstantinou	Mana mou	Constantina Konstantinou	Constantina Konstantinou	98
6	10	Spain	Marcos Llunas	Sin rencor	Marcos Llunas	Marcos Llunas	96
7	22	France	Fanny	Sentiments songes	Jean-Paul Dreau	Jean-Paul Dreau	95
8	13	Estonia	Maarja-Liis Ilus	Keelatud maa	Kaari Sillamaa	Harmo Kallaste	82
9	18	Malta	Debbie Scerri	Let me fly	Ray Agius	Ray Agius	66
10	6	Slovenia	Tanja Ribic	Zbudi se	Zoran Predin	Sašo Lošic	60
11	12	Poland	Anna Maria Jopek	Ale jestem	Magda Czapinska	Tomasz Lewandowski	54
12	19	Hungary	VIP	Miert kell, hogy elmenj?	Krisztina Bokor Fekete, Attila Kornyei	Viktor Rakonczai, Sandor Jozsa	39
13	17	Greece	Marianna Zorba	Horepse	Manolis Manouselis	Manolis Manouselis	39
14	16	Sweden	Blond	Bara hon älskar mig	Stephan Berg	Stephan Berg	36
15	20	Russia	Alla Pugachova	Primadonna	Alla Pugachova	Alla Pugachova	33
16	21	Denmark	Kølig Kaj	Stemmen i mit liv	Thomas Laegård	Lars Pedersen	25
17	23	Croatia	ENI	Probudi me	Alida Sarar	Davor Tolja	24
18	11	Germany	Bianca Shomburg	Zeit	Bernd Meinunger	Ralph Siegel	22
19	14	Bosnia & H	Alma Cardzic	Goodbye	Milic Vukasinovic	Sinan Alimanovic, Milic Vukasinovic	22
20	25	Iceland	Paul Oscar	Minn hinsti dans	Paul Oscar	Trausti Haraldsson, Paul Oscar	18
21	4	Austria	Bettina Soriat	One step	Ina Siber, Marc Berry	Marc Berry	12
22	7	Switzerland	Barbara Berta	Dentro di me	Barbara Berta	Barbara Berta	5
23	8	Netherlands	Mrs. Einstein	Niemand heeft nog tijd	Ed Hooijmans	Ed Hooijmans	5
24	15	Portugal	Célia Lawson	Antes do adeus	Rosa Lobato de Faria	Thilo Krassmann	0
25	3	Norway	Tor Endresen	San Francisco	Tor Endresen	Tor Endresen, Arne Myksvol	0

1997 Eurovision 42: Dublin, Ireland — 3 May 1997

	Austria	Bosnia & H	Croatia	Cyprus	Denmark	Estonia	France	Germany	Greece	Hungary	Iceland	Ireland	Italy	Malta	Netherlands	Norway	Poland	Portugal	Russia	Slovenia	Spain	Sweden	Switzerland	Turkey	United Kingdom	TOTAL
Cyprus	7		4		7	1	4	5	12		12	3	4	7	10	2		3	1	4	10		4		5	98
Turkey		12				6	6	12	7	6	7	2	7	10	2		1	5	4		12	6	6		4	121
Norway																										0
Austria	10	8	6	8	10	8	10	8		5	3		10		3	3		10	3	1	6	10	7		12	157
Ireland		7	3	2		4	7		3	8			2	5	4		1	4	5		3			10		60
Slovenia											3								10							5
Switzerland													2	4												5
Netherlands	1	6	10	6	4		4	4	5	3	1	1	3		7		8	12	7	10	8	3	10	1	3	114
Italy	3	4	5	10	2		2	2	6	10		6	5	12	6		4	8	8	5			8	5		96
Spain	8			5	5		3	6	1	1	5		1	3	1			2		7			5	4		22
Germany		1		1							2					4	6	1		3	2	1	2			54
Poland	6						8	7	8	7		8	12								4	4		8	10	82
Estonia	4		1		8		3	3		4					8											22
Bosnia & H																										0
Portugal					6						4	5		6		8				6	7				7	36
Sweden		5	7	12	3				8		5	7	6			5	5		2		1		5			39
Greece	5		8	5			1			10		4		6		10				12				12		66
Malta					3	5	5						1		2									3	8	39
Hungary		3			1	7			2		12	10		8		1	12									33
Russia		2							4	2					5	7	3			2		7	1		2	25
Denmark						12					6			8		12				6		7	1			95
France	12	10	12	4	12	10		1	10	12	10	12	8	1	12	6	10	7	12	8	5	12	12	7	1	227
Croatia				7		2																				24
United Kingdom	2										6											8				18
Iceland																										

Page 91

1998 Eurovision 43: Birmingham, United Kingdom

9 May 1998

Qualification: Four automatic qualifiers (UK, Germany, Spain, France), along with those countries who failed to qualify for 1997 plus FYR Macedonia, the remaining places being given to the countries with the best average scores over the last 5 years.

Rank	Start	Country	Artist	Song	Writer	Composer	POINTS
1	8	Israel	Dana International	Diva	Yoav Ginai	Tzvika Pik	176
2	16	United Kingdom	Imaani	Where are you?	Scott English, Simon Stirling, Phil Manikiza	Scott English, Simon Stirling, Phil Manikiza	166
3	10	Malta	Chiara	The one that I love	Sunny Aquilina	Jason Paul Cassar	165
4	18	Netherlands	Edsilia Rombley	Hemel en aarde	Eric van Tijn, Jochem Fluitsma	Eric van Tijn, Jochem Fluitsma	150
5	1	Croatia	Danijela	Neka mi ne svane	Petar Grašo, Remi Kasinoti	Petar Grašo, Remi Kasinoti	131
6	20	Belgium	Mélanie Cohl	Dis oui	Philippe Swan	Philippe Swan	122
7	9	Germany	Guildo Horn	Guildo hat euch lieb	Stefan Raab	Stefan Raab	86
8	22	Norway	Lars A. Fredriksen	Alltid sommer	Linda Andernach Johannesen	David Eriksen	79
9	13	Ireland	Dawn	Is always over now?	Gerry Morgan	Gerry Morgan	64
10	19	Sweden	Jill Johnson	Kärleken är	Ingela "Pling" Forsman	Bobby Ljunggren, Håkan Almqvist	53
11	17	Cyprus	Michael Hajiyanni	Genesis	Zenon Zindilis	Michael Hajiyanni	37
12	23	Estonia	Koit Toome	Mere lapsed	Peeter Pruuli	Maria and Tomi Rahula	36
13	14	Portugal	Alma Lusa	Se eu te pudesse abraçar	José Cid	José Cid	36
14	24	Turkey	Tüzmen	Unutamazsin	Canan Tunç	Erdinç Tunç	25
15	21	Finland	Edea	Aava	Tommy Mansikka-Aho	Alexi Ahoniemi	22
16	4	Spain	Mikel Herzog	¿Qué voy a hacer sin ti?	Mikel Herzog	Alberto Estébanez	21
17	7	Poland	Sixteen	To takie proste	Olga Pruszkowska	Jaroslaw Pruszkowski	19
18	12	Slovenia	Vili Resnik	Naj bogovi slišijo	Urša Vlašic	Matjaz Vlašic	17
19	25	FYR Macedonia	Vlado Janevski	Ne zori, zoro	Vlado Janevski	Grigor Koprov	16
20	2	Greece	Dionysia & Thalassa group	Mia krifi evaisthissia	Yiannis Malachias	Yiannis Valvis	12
21	6	Slovakia	Katarína Hasprová	Modlitba	Anna Wepperyová	Gabriel Dušík	8
22	15	Romania	Malina Olinescu	Eu cred	Liliana Stefan	Adrian Romcescu	6
23	11	Hungary	Charlie	A holnap már ném lesz szomorú	Attila Horváth	István Lehr	4
24	3	France	Marie-Line	Où aller	Marie-Line Marolany	Marie-Line Marolany, Jean-Philippe Dary, Micaël Sene, Moïse Crespy	3
25	5	Switzerland	Gunvor	Lass ihn	Gunvor Guggisberg	Gunvor Guggisberg, Egon Egemann	0

1998 Eurovision 43: Birmingham, United Kingdom — 9 May 1998

	Belgium	Croatia	Cyprus	Estonia	Finland	France	FYR Macedonia	Germany	Greece	Hungary	Ireland	Israel	Malta	Netherlands	Norway	Poland	Portugal	Romania	Slovakia	Slovenia	Spain	Sweden	Switzerland	Turkey	United Kingdom	TOTAL
Croatia	5		7	3	3	8	12	10	5		3	10	10	4	6	6	2		12	10	1	3	5	4	2	131
Greece			12																							12
France			1				2																			3
Spain	3	1	4			4						3											6			21
Switzerland																										0
Slovakia		8																								8
Poland										2		7						10								19
Israel	10		10	7	10			5	10	7	6		12	6	3	10	12	7	7	4	10	5	10	5	8	172
Germany	7			1	1	12	8		3	6	8			12	12	8	10	6	8	2	12	6		10	6	86
Malta	8	7	5	5	5	6		8	6	7	12	7		8	2	3	5	1	3	12	5	6	8	10	12	165
Hungary						1																		3		4
Slovenia	3	3		4					2													1	2			17
Ireland				2		2	7	2	1	6		2			4	2	1	5	1					8		64
Portugal	1	2				10	4													2	6			6		36
Romania												6														6
United Kingdom	6	12	8	8	8	3	10	1	7	10	5	12	8	7	5	7	6	12	5	1	3	7	3	12		166
Cyprus	2	4				5	3		12	1	10	1	1	5		5	4	4		5				7	3	37
Netherlands	12	10		12	7			6	8	12	2	8	7	10	8	3	7		6	6	4	8	7	7	10	150
Sweden					6	7	6	4	4	8	7	5	4	5	10	12			6	7	7	2	4	2	1	53
Belgium			6	12			1	3		3	4	4	3	3	7	4	8		6		8	10	1	1	7	122
Finland				10							1				1	1	3				2	12				22
Norway	4		3	4	2					5		4	5	2				2	10	8	8	4			4	79
Estonia					12					4				1					2	3	2					36
Turkey		5					5											2	4							25
FYR Macedonia		6						12										3								16

1999 Eurovision 44: Jerusalem, Israel

29 May 1999

Qualification: Four automatic qualifiers (UK, Germany, Spain, France), along with those countries who failed to qualify for 1998, the remaining places being given to the countries with the best average scores over the last 5 years.

Rank	Start	Country	Artist	Song	Writer	Composer	POINTS
1	15	Sweden	Charlotte Nilsson	Take me to your heaven	Gert Lengstrand	Lars Diedricson	163
2	13	Iceland	Selma Björnsdóttir	All out of luck	Thorvaldur B. Thorvaldsson	S Björnsdóttir, T B. Thorvaldsson, S I. Baldvinsson	146
3	21	Germany	Sürpriz	Reise nach Jerusalem - Kudüs'e seyahat	Bernd Meinunger	Ralph Siegel	140
4	4	Croatia	Doris Dragovic	Marija Magdalena	Vjekoslava Huljic	Tonci Huljic	118
5	19	Israel	Eden	Yom huledeth	Moshe Datz, Gabriel Batler, Yaacov Lymay, Jacky Oved	Moshe Datz, Gabriel Batler, Yaacov Lymay, Jacky Oved	93
6	23	Estonia	Evelin Samuel and Camille	Diamond of night	Marian-Anna Kärmas & Kaari Sillamaa	Priit Pajusaar and Glen Pilvr	90
7	22	Bosnia & H	Dino and Beatrice	Putnici	Dino Dervišhalidovic	Dino Dervišhalidovic	86
8	9	Denmark	Trine Jepsen & Michael Teschl	This time (I mean it)	Ebbe Ravn	Ebbe Ravn	71
9	11	Netherlands	Marlayne	One good reason	Tjeerd Van Zanen and Alan Michael	Tjeerd Van Zanen and Alan Michael	71
10	18	Austria	Bobbie Singer	Reflection	Dave Moskin	Dave Moskin	65
11	6	Slovenia	Darja Svajger	For a thousand years	Primoz Peterca	Primoz Peterca	50
12	2	Belgium	Venessa Chinitor	Like the wind	Wim Claes, Emma Phillipa, Ilia Beyers, John Terra	Wim Claes, Emma Phillipa, Ilia Beyers, John Terra	38
13	5	United Kingdom	Precious	Say it again	Paul Varney	Paul Varney	38
14	8	Norway	Stig André Van Eijk	Living my life without you	Sem & Stig Van Eijk & Peter Brandt	Sem & Stig Van Eijk & Peter Brandt	35
15	20	Malta	Times 3	Believe 'n peace	Moira Stafrace	Chris Scicluna	32
16	7	Turkey	Tuba Önal & Grup Mystik	Dön artik	Canan Tunç	Erdinç Tunç	21
17	17	Ireland	The Mullans	When you need me	Bronagh Mullan	Bronagh Mullan	18
18	12	Poland	Mietek (Mieczyslaw) Szczesniak	Przytul mnie mocno	Wojciech Ziembicki	Seweryn Krajewski	17
19	10	France	Nayah	Je veux donner ma voix	Gilles Arcens & Luigi Rutigliano	Pascal Graczyk & René Colombies	14
20	1	Lithuania	Aiste Smilgeviciute	Strazdas	Sigitas Geda	Linas Rimša	13
21	14	Portugal	Marlain Angelidou	Tha'nai erotas	Andreas Karanikolas	George Kallis	12
22	16	Cyprus	Rui Bandeira	Como tudo começou	Tó Andrade	Jorge do Carmo	2
23	3	Spain	Lydia	No quiero escuchar	F R Fernández, A P Ramírez, A C Zamarreno, C L González	Fernando Rodriguez Fernández & Alejandro Piqueras Ramírez	1

1999 Eurovision 44: Jerusalem, Israel
29 May 1999

	Austria	Belgium	Bosnia & H	Croatia	Cyprus	Denmark	Estonia	France	Germany	Iceland	Ireland	Israel	Lithuania	Malta	Netherlands	Norway	Poland	Portugal	Slovenia	Spain	Sweden	Turkey	United Kingdom	TOTAL
Lithuania				2	5		2					3		1										13
Belgium			8	4			5	2			10	5												38
Spain			1																					1
Croatia	8	5			2		3	7	10	4	6	7	6	5	1		7	6	12	12	1	8		118
United Kingdom			1	5	4	1						4	5	8					2	4		4		38
Slovenia	2	5	5	12				1	12		12		10		6					2				50
Turkey						6		5		7						4					5			21
Norway				7	7		6			12	3			4			1	3	5		5		5	35
Denmark	5				8						7					8				5	8	2		71
France											2	2	2	4				2	3	3	4			14
Netherlands	4	12	4			7			4	6	1	6	4	2		10	4	4		10	12	5	10	71
Poland			6						3				7										2	17
Iceland	2	8			12	12	10		2		4	10	8	10	7	10	6	10	7	6	12	10	10	146
Cyprus																						2	2	2
Sweden	6	7	12		6	10	12	3	2	10	5	8	3	12	8	12	6	10				6	12	163
Portugal								12					12											12
Ireland					1	3	8	10		1				6	2	1	3	5	4			1	4	18
Austria	6	3	2	8	10	2	4	8	5		6				4	6	10	8	1	8	7	3	7	65
Israel	1	3	7	6	3	1		6	7	5	12		1	3	12	2	12	12	6	7	3	12		93
Malta	7	1	7			5	7	8	1	3		12	1		3	7	5	1	10	1	2	7	6	32
Germany	10	10	10	3	10	8		6				1	1	7	5	5	8	12	8	1	6	12	1	140
Bosnia & H	12	1		6	3				8	2	8							7			10	7		86
Estonia	3	4	3			4		4	6							5							3	90

95

2000 Eurovision 45: Stockholm, Sweden

13 May 2000

Qualification: Four automatic qualifiers (UK, Germany, Spain, France), along with those countries who failed to qualify for 1999, the remaining places being given to the countries with the best average scores over the last 5 years.

Rank	Start	Country	Artist	Song	Writer	Composer	POINTS
1	14	Denmark	Olsen Brothers	Fly on the wings of love	Jørgen Olsen	Jørgen Olsen	195
2	9	Russia	Alsou	Solo	Andrew Lane, Brandon Barnes	Andrew Lane, Brandon Barnes	155
3	21	Latvia	BrainStorm	My star	Renars Kaupers	Renars Kaupers	136
4	4	Estonia	Ines	Once in a lifetime	Jana Hallas	Pearu Paulus, Ilmar Laisaar, Alar Kotkas	98
5	15	Germany	Stefan Raab	Wadde hadde dudde da	Stefan Raab	Stefan Raab	96
6	23	Ireland	Eamonn Toal	Millennium of love	Raymond J. Smyth, Gerry Simpson	Raymond J. Smyth, Gerry Simpson	92
7	18	Sweden	Roger Pontare	When spirits are calling my name	Thomas Holmstrand, Linda Jansson, Peter Dahl	Thomas Holmstrand, Linda Jansson, Peter Dahl	88
8	7	Malta	Claudette Pace	Desire	Gerard James Borg	Philip Vella	73
9	17	Croatia	Goran Karan	Kada zaspu andeli	Nenad Nincevic	Zdenko Runjic	70
10	22	Turkey	Pinar Ayhan & S.O.S. band	Yorgunum anla	Sühan Ayhan, Pinar Ayhan, Orkun Yazgan	Sühan Ayhan, Pinar Ayhan, Orkun Yazgan	59
11	8	Norway	Charmed	My heart goes boom	Tore Madsen	Morten Henriksen	57
12	12	Iceland	Einer Ágúst Víðisson & Telma Ágústdóttir	Tell me! (Hvert sem er)	Sigurður Örn Jónsson	Örlygur Smári	45
13	2	Netherlands	Linda Wagenmakers	No goodbyes	John O'Hare	Ellert Driessen	40
14	24	Austria	The rounder girls	All to you	Dave Moskin	Dave Moskin	34
15	19	FYC Macedonia	XXL	100% te ljubam	Orce Zafirofski, Dragan Karanfilovski	Dragan Karanfilovski	29
16	3	United Kingdom	Nicki French	Don't play that song again	John Springate, Gary Shephard	John Springate, Gary Shephard	28
17	6	Romania	Taxi	The moon	Dan Teodorescu	Dan Teodorescu	25
18	13	Spain	Serafín Zubiri	Colgado de un sueño	José Maria Purón	José Maria Purón	18
19	20	Finland	Nina Åström	A little bit	Gerrit aan 't Goor	Luca Genta	18
20	16	Switzerland	Jane Bogaert	La vita cos'è?	Thomas Marin	Bernie Staub	14
21	11	Cyprus	Voice	Nomiza	Alexandros Panayi	Alexandros Panayi	8
22	1	Israel	Ping Pong	Sa'me'akh	Roi Arad, Guy Asif, Ronen Ben Tal	Roi Arad, Guy Asif	7
23	5	France	Sofia Mestari	On aura le ciel	Pierre Legay	Benoît Heinrich	5
24	10	Belgium	Nathalie Sorce	Envie de vivre	Silvio Pezzuto	Silvio Pezzuto	2

2000 Eurovision 45: Stockholm, Sweden — 13 May 2000

Receiving ↓ / Voting →	Austria	Belgium	Croatia	Cyprus	Denmark	Estonia	Finland	France	FYR Macedonia	Germany	Iceland	Ireland	Israel	Latvia	Malta	Netherlands	Norway	Romania	Russia	Spain	Sweden	Switzerland	Turkey	United Kingdom	TOTAL
Israel								6	1																7
Netherlands	8	2		5				2		1										4	6		3	3	40
United Kingdom	2		4	3		2					1	1		3									6	4	28
Estonia	6		6	6	4		8			5	5	7	6	10	7	7	4	3					2	4	98
France																2			3						5
Romania			7						12		5								6						25
Malta	2	1	8	8	3	1			8	3	7	3	3	4		1	2	7	8	1	3		5	2	73
Norway					7	3		5		7		4	7	6	3					5	7	2	10	3	57
Russia	7	7	12	12	6	10	5	5	7	4	8	10	10		12		8	12		5	5	2		8	155
Belgium									2																2
Cyprus			3						4						1										8
Iceland				10	12	6							5	7			7		2		8	1			45
Spain	10	10		4		8	10	7		12	12	12	12	12	8		10	5	12		12	10	1	12	195
Denmark	12	6	1		2		2	10	5	10	6	5		8		8	3		4	12		12		5	96
Germany	1													2		6			5						14
Switzerland	6						6	8	10	6	4	6			4		5	8	10	2		6	8	6	70
Croatia		5			10	5	7	1	6	8	4		4					10	7	6		3	12		88
Sweden			10	2														4							29
FYR Macedonia						7					10						5		7		2			6	18
Finland	8	12		1	8	12		3	3	7	10	8	4	12		4	4		1	7	10	7		7	136
Latvia	5	3			1	4	4	12	5	10		5	2			12	12			1	1	5		5	59
Turkey	4	4	5	7	5	4	1	4			2		2	1	10	3	6	2		3	4	8	7	10	92
Ireland							3			2	3			5	2					8		4	4	1	34
Austria																									

2001 Eurovision 46: Copenhagen, Denmark   12 May 2001

Qualification: Four automatic qualifiers (UK, Germany, Spain, France), along with those countries who failed to qualify for 2000, the remaining places being given to the countries with the best average scores over the last 5 years.

Rank	Start	Country	Artist	Song	Writer	Composer	POINTS
1	20	Estonia	Tanel Padar, Dave Benton & 2XL	Everybody	Maian-Anna Kärmas	Ivar Must	198
2	23	Denmark	Rollo & King	Never ever let you go	Stefan Nielsen	Søren Poppe	177
3	22	Greece	Antique	Die for you	Antonis Papas	Antonis Papas	147
4	14	France	Natasha Saint-Pier	Je n'ai que mon âme	Jill Kapler	Jill Kapler	142
5	7	Sweden	Friends	Listen to your heartbeat	Thomas G:son, Henrik Sethsson	Thomas G:son, Henrik Sethsson	100
6	13	Spain	David Civera	Dile que la quiero	Alejandro Abad	Alejandro Abad	76
7	17	Slovenia	Nuša Derenda	Energy	Lucienne Lonchina	Matjaz Vlasic	70
8	19	Germany	Michelle	Wer Liebe lebt	Eva Richter	Gino Trovatello, Matthias Stingl	66
9	21	Malta	Fabrizio Faniello	Another summer night	Georgina Abela	Paul Abela	48
10	10	Croatia	Vanna	Strings of my heart	Vjekoslava Huljic	Tonci Huljic	42
11	15	Turkey	Sedat Yüce	Sevgiliye son	Nurdan Güneri	Semih Güneri	41
12	6	Russia	Mumiy troll	Lady alpine blue	Ilia Lagoutenko	Ilia Lagoutenko	37
13	8	Lithuania	Skamp	You got style	Erica Quinn Jennings, Vilius Alesius, Viktoras Diawara	Viktoras Diawara, Linas Rimša	35
14	3	Bosnia & H	Nino	Hano	Nino Pršeš	Nino Pršeš	29
15	16	United Kingdom	Lindsay D.	No dream impossible	Russ Ballard, Chris Winter	Russ Ballard, Chris Winter	28
16	5	Israel	Tal Sondak	Ein davar	Shimrit Orr	Yair Klinger	25
17	11	Portugal	MTM	Só sei ser feliz assim	Marco Quelhas	Marco Quelhas	18
18	9	Latvia	Arnis Mednis	Too much	Gustavs Terzens, Arnis Mednis	Arnis Mednis	16
19	1	Netherlands	Michelle	Out on my own	André Remkes, Dirk Jan Vermeij	André Remkes, Dirk Jan Vermeij	16
20	18	Poland	Piasek	2 long	Andrzej Piaseczny	Robert Chojnacki	11
21	12	Ireland	Gary O'Shaughnessy	Without your love	Pat Sheridan	Pat Sheridan	6
22	2	Iceland	TwoTricky	Angel (Birta)	Einar Bárðarson	Einar Bárðarson	3
						Magnus Thor Sigmundsson	
23	4	Norway	Haldor Lagreid	On my own	Ole Henrik Antonsen, Tom-Steinar Hanssen, Ole Jørgen Olsen	Ole Henrik Antonsen, Tom-Steinar Hanssen	3

2001 Eurovision 46: Copenhagen, Denmark
12 May 2001

	Bosnia & H	Croatia	Denmark	Estonia	France	Germany	Greece	Iceland	Ireland	Israel	Latvia	Lithuania	Malta	Netherlands	Norway	Poland	Portugal	Russia	Slovenia	Spain	Sweden	Turkey	United Kingdom	TOTAL
Netherlands								6											4				6	16
Iceland			2												1									3
Bosnia & H	10	7																	7		4		1	29
Norway																	3							3
Israel	6				10		2	5			8	10	2									7		25
Russia				4			5	7	8	3	6	2	8											37
Sweden	3	4	10	7	2			1	1	8	5			5	2	5	5	10	2	5		8	8	100
Lithuania	2								1	4									2		1		4	35
Latvia		8		8								8												16
Croatia	7						7						10						5			10		42
Portugal					12	3														6				18
Ireland																	1						5	6
Spain	5			3	5	6	8	2	3	12	4		5	7	4	1	7		1	3	5	6	3	76
France	12	6	6	10		7	4	4	7	2	7		12	8	7	10	12	12	6		6	1	6	142
Turkey		7	3		7	7	10					7	4	3			2	3						41
United Kingdom	3			5	1	2		6	4		3	3	3	2	2	2	2	4		1	2			28
Slovenia	10	8				4			2	1		4		4	6	6			3		7			70
Poland			1			5								1							2			11
Germany	1		4	1	6		1		6		1		5	1	3	4	10	8		10		3	2	66
Estonia	4	2	8		8	10	12	10	10	6	12	12	12	12	10	12		6	12	8	8	12	12	198
Malta	1		12	2		1	3	3				1			5	3		7		4	3	2	1	48
Greece	8	5	5	6	3	8		8	5	10	2	5	7	6	8	8	4	5	8	12	12	5	7	147
Denmark		12		12	4	12	6	12	12	7	10	6	6	10	12	7	8	4	10	7	10	4	10	177

2002 Eurovision 47: Tallinn, Estonia — 25 May 2002

Qualification: Four automatic qualifiers (UK, Germany, Spain, France), along with the top 15 from the other participants in 2001, plus those countries which failed to qualify for the 2001 contest and Israel and Latvia by invitation.

Rank	Start	Country	Artist	Song	Writer	Composer	POINTS
1	23	Latvia	Marie N	I wanna	Marija Naumova, Marats Samauskis	Marija Naumova	176
2	20	Malta	Ira Losco	7th wonder	Gerard James Borg	Philip Vella	164
3	2	United Kingdom	Jessica Garlick	Come back	Martyn Baylay	Martyn Baylay	111
4	8	Estonia	Sahléne	Runaway	Jana Hallas	Pearu Paulus, Ilmar Laisaar, Alar Kotkas	111
5	17	France	Sandrine François	Il faut du temps	Patrick Bruel, Marie-Florence Gros	Rick Allison	104
6	1	Cyprus	One	Gimme	George Theophanous	George Theophanous	85
7	5	Spain	Rosa	Europe's living a celebration	Xasqui Ten	Toni Ten	81
8	21	Romania	Monica Anghel & Marcel Pavel	Tell me why	Mirela Fugaru	Ionel Tudor	72
9	12	Sweden	Afro-dite	Never let it go	Marcos Ubeda	Marcos Ubeda	72
10	7	Russia	Prime minister	Northern girl	Karen Kavaleryan, Evgene Fridlyand, Irina Antonyan	Kim Breitburg	55
11	6	Croatia	Vesna Pisarovic	Everything I want	Milana Vlaovic	Milana Vlaovic	44
12	10	Israel	Sarit Hadad	Light a candle	Yoav Ginai	Tzvika Pik	37
13	15	Bosnia & H	Maja Tatic	Na jastuku za dvoje	Ružica Cavic, Stevo Cvikic	Dragan Mijatovic	33
14	16	Belgium	Sergio & the Ladies	Sister	Dirk Paelinck	Mark Paelinck	33
15	22	Slovenia	Sestre	Samo ljubezen	Barbara Pešut	Robert Pešut	32
16	19	Turkey	Buket Bengisu & Saphire	Leylaklar soldu kalbinde	Sami Hodara, Figen Cakmak	Fani Hodara	29
17	4	Greece	Michalis Rakintzis	S.A.G.A.P.O.	Michalis Rakintzis	Michalis Rakintzis	27
18	3	Austria	Manuel Ortega	Say a word	Robert Pflugler	Alexander Kahr	26
19	9	FYR Macedonia	Karolina	Od nas zavisi	Vladimir Krstevski	Nikola Perevski	25
20	13	Finland	Laura	Addicted to you	Janina Frostell, Tracy Lipp	Maki Kolehmainen	24
21	18	Germany	Corinna May	I can't live without music	Bernd Meinunger	Ralph Siegel	17
22	11	Switzerland	Francine Jordi	Dans le jardin de mon âme	Francine Lehmann	Francine Lehmann	15
23	24	Lithuania	Aivaras	Happy You	Aivaras Stepukonis	Aivaras Stepukonis	12
24	14	Denmark	Malene	Tell me who you are	Michael Ronson	Michael Ronson	7

2002 Eurovision 47: Tallinn, Estonia — 25 May 2002

	Austria	Belgium	Bosnia & H	Croatia	Cyprus	Denmark	Estonia	Finland	France	FYR Macedonia	Germany	Greece	Israel	Latvia	Lithuania	Malta	Romania	Russia	Slovenia	Spain	Sweden	Switzerland	Turkey	United Kingdom	TOTAL
Cyprus	12	3		10								12		8		12	8	6	4	6	1			3	85
United Kingdom		6	7		1	6	6	8	1	4	8	7	5	5	8	10		1	8	10	2	6	2		111
Austria		5		1	12																		8		26
Greece	6			6	7				12								6	8		3	7	12			27
Spain	6	12	2	6				3			7	4		10		8			12			5		2	81
Croatia							10			5	3	5	2	12	6										44
Russia		4	10	5		8		10		6	4	2	1			8			6					7	55
Estonia	3			4	3			1		12			2	12	7	2	10	3		1	12		8		111
FYR Macedonia						1					5					5	12								25
Israel	5	2												3			5		7			1		5	37
Switzerland									10			1		1	10	1									15
Sweden	4	1	12	7		10	8	5	3	1			3	4			3		7				4	1	72
Finland			3		2	3	5					1	4								10				24
Denmark	7									3						3									7
Bosnia & H				7		2		7	2				7		2		4	7	2	3	6				33
Belgium		10	8			4				3	6	3		2	5		1			1	3	10	10	4	33
France						5	3	12				3	7			4	4	2	3	8	8	3	3	10	104
Germany	1						1			8							1		4	2			3		17
Turkey				3					7	8							7			4					29
Malta	8	7	4	12	10	12	7	2	6	10	10	6	10	7	3			5	10	10	4	4	5	12	164
Romania					8				5	12	1	8	8			6		12		5			7		72
Slovenia	2		1	8				6	4	2										7		2		6	32
Latvia	10	8	5	2	4	7	12		8	7	12	10	12		12	7		10	5	12	5	8	6	8	176
Lithuania							2							6				4							12

2003 Eurovision 48: Riga, Latvia   **24 May 2003**

Qualification: Four automatic qualifiers (UK, Germany, Spain, France), along with the top 15 from the other participants in 2002, plus those countries which failed to qualify for the 2002 contest and new entrant Ukraine.

Rank	Start	Country	Artist	Song	Writer	Composer	POINTS
1	4	Turkey	Sertab Erener	Everyway that I can	Demir Demirkan	Sertab Erener, Demir Demirkan	167
2	22	Belgium	Urban Trad	Sanomi	Yves Barbieux	Yves Barbieux	165
3	11	Russia	t.A.T.u.	Ne ver', ne boisia	Valeriy Polienko	Mars Lasar, Ivan Pogomalov	164
4	18	Norway	Jostein Hasselgård	I'm not afraid to move on	Arve Furset	Arve Furset	123
5	25	Sweden	Fame	Give me your love	Calle Kindbom, Carl Lösnitz	Calle Kindbom, Carl Lösnitz	107
6	2	Austria	Alf Poier	Weil der Mensch zählt	Alf Poier	Alf Poier	101
7	20	Poland	Ich Troje	Keine Grenzen - Zadnych granic	André Franke, J Horn-Bernges, Michal Wisniewski, Jacek Lagwa	André Franke, J Horn-Bernges, Michal Wisniewski, Jacek Lagwa	90
8	1	Iceland	Birgitta	Open your heart (Segðu mér allt)	Sveinbjörn Baldvinsson, Birgitta Haukdal	Hallgrímur Óskarsson	81
9	12	Spain	Beth	Dime	Amaya Martínez	Jesús-María Pérez	81
10	24	Romania	Nicola	Don't break my heart	Nicola	Mihai Alexandru	73
11	10	Germany	Lou	Let's get happy	Bernd Meinunger	Ralph Siegel	53
12	3	Ireland	Mickey Harte	We've got the world	Keith Molloy, Martin Brannigan	Keith Molloy, Martin Brannigan	53
13	14	Netherlands	Esther Hart	One more night	Alan Michael, Tjeerd van Zanen	Alan Michael, Tjeerd van Zanen	45
14	16	Ukraine	Olexandr	Hasta la vista	Mirit Shem-Ur	Tzvika Pik	30
15	8	Croatia	Claudia Beni	Više nisam tvoja	Andrej Babich	Andrej Babich	29
16	6	Bosnia & H	Mija Martina	Ne brini	Arjana Kunštek	Ines Prajo	27
17	17	Greece	Mando	Never let you go	Terry Siganos	Mando	25
18	19	France	Louisa Baileche	Monts et merveilles	Hocine Hallaf	Hocine Hallaf	19
19	13	Israel	Lior Narkis	Words for love	Yossi Gispan	Yoni Ro`en	17
20	9	Cyprus	Stelios Constantas	Feeling alive	Stelios Constantas	Stelios Constantas	15
21	23	Estonia	Ruffus	Eighties coming back	Vaiko Eplik	Vaiko Eplik	14
22	7	Portugal	Rita Guerra	Deixa-me sonhar	Paulo Martins	Paulo Martins	13
23	26	Slovenia	Karmen	Nanana	Karmen Stavec	Martin Stibernik	7
24	21	Latvia	F.L.Y.	Hello from Mars	Martin Freiman, Lauris Raynix	Martin Freiman, Lauris Raynix	5
25	5	Malta	Lynn Chirchop	To dream again	Cynthia Sammut	Alfred Zammit	4
26	15	United Kingdom	Jemini	Cry baby	Martin Isherwood	Martin Isherwood	0

2003 Eurovision 48: Riga, Latvia — 24 May 2003

	Austria	Belgium	Bosnia & H	Croatia	Cyprus	Estonia	France	Germany	Greece	Iceland	Ireland	Israel	Latvia	Malta	Netherlands	Norway	Poland	Portugal	Romania	Russia	Slovenia	Spain	Sweden	Turkey	Ukraine	United Kingdom	TOTAL
Iceland	12	3		6	5	1	1	1			7		3	12	6	12	1				4		7	8	4		81
Austria		2	5	5	4	6		2	2	10			4		8	8		10			7	8	6	6		8	101
Ireland		1	12	4	7		10			2			1	5	8	6		7			2	3		5	1	12	53
Turkey	12	12		10	8		10	10	7	3		7		4	12	10	2	8	10		10	3	8		2	7	167
Malta		4									3							1						12			4
Bosnia & H	7		8				6		1		2										8	2			3		27
Portugal			6						12		6						1		1					3			13
Croatia	5		6							8									7					3			29
Cyprus	1					2	7		10	8	4	1	2	2	2		5	4	5	6	12	4	10				15
Germany	8	7	3	12	10	12	7		5	4	4	10	12	3	1		4	4	3	5		6	2	10	12	4	53
Russia		10		7	6				5	6		12		1	5	2		12			1	6	4	2			164
Spain					1				3				5						5			1					81
Israel		8					8				5			7						10			5			1	17
Netherlands	8		2			3		5			5	4	5				10	5		8							45
United Kingdom																											0
Ukraine						3		5			1	4					10	5	2	8			12	4			30
Greece	2	6			12		3	7			12	3	7	6			6	2	3	1	5		12	4	7	6	25
Norway		5	8			10	5						8		4		3		6	4		5	3		8	2	123
France	10					4		12	6	7	10	8	10	10		4	12		4		3	5			10	5	19
Poland						5				1	8								8	2		12				3	90
Latvia	4		10		3	8	12	6	8			6		8	3	3	12	6	8	3	3	12		7	10	5	5
Belgium	6	7		1			4	4	4				6			1	8			2	6	10	1	1	6		165
Estonia	3	4	1	2	1	7	2	3		5		5	5	8	7	7	7	3	12	12	6	7	1		5	10	14
Romania			4	3																							73
Sweden																											107
Slovenia																											7

2004 Eurovision 49: Istanbul, Turkey — Semi-final: 12 May 2004

Rank	Start	Country	Artist	Song	Writer	Composer	POINTS
1Q	20	Serbia & Mont	Željko Joksimović	Lane moje	Leontina Vukmanoviæ	Željko Joksimović	263
2Q	11	Ukraine	Ruslana	Wild dances	Alexander Ksenofontov	Ruslana Lyzchicko	256
3Q	10	Greece	Sakis Rouvas	Shake it	Nektarios Tirakis	Nikos Terzis	238
4Q	13	Albania	Anjeza Shahini	The image of you	Agim Doçit	Edmon Zhulali	167
5Q	14	Cyprus	Lisa Andreas	Stronger every minute	Mike Konnaris	Mike Konnaris	149
6Q	22	Netherlands	Re-union	Without you	Angeline van Otterdijk	Ed van Otterdijk	146
7Q	21	Bosnia & H	Deen	In the Disco	Vesna Pisarovic	Vesna Pisarovic	133
8Q	8	Malta	Julie & Ludwig	On again….off again	Gerard James Borg	Philip Vella	74
9Q	18	Croatia	Ivan Mikulic	You are the only one	Duško Gruborovic & Marina Madrinic	Ivan Mikulic	72
10Q	15	FYR Macedonia	Tose Proeski	Life	Tose Proeski	Tose Proeski	71
11	5	Israel	David D'or	Le'ha'amin	David D'or	David D'or	57
12	17	Estonia	Neiokõsõ	Tii	Aapo Ilves	Priit Pajusaar, Glen Pilvre	57
13	19	Denmark	Tomas Thordarson	Shame on you	Ivar Lind Greiner	Ivar Lind Greiner	56
14	1	Finland	Jari Sillanpää	Takes 2 to tango	Jari Sillanpää	Mika Toivanen	51
15	7	Portugal	Sofia	Foi Magia	Paulo Neves	Paulo Neves	38
16	12	Lithuania	Linas ir Simona	What's happened to your love	Camden MS	Michalis Antonio, Linas Adomaitis	26
17	4	Latvia	Fomins & Kleins	Dziesma par laimi	Tomass Kleins	Guntars Racs	23
18	6	Andorra	Marta Roure	Jugarem a estimar-nos	Jofre Bardagi	Jofre Bardagi	12
19	2	Belarus	Aleksandra & Konstantin	My Galileo	Aleksey Solomaha	Aleksandra & Konstantin	10
20	9	Monaco	Maryon	Notre planète	Philippe Bosco	Philippe Bosco	10
21	16	Slovenia	Platin	Stay forever	Diana Lecnik	Simon Gomilsek	5
22	3	Switzerland	Piero Esteriore & the Music Stars	Celebrate	Greg Manning	Greg Manning	0

2004 Eurovision 49: Istanbul, Turkey
Semi-final: 12 May 2004

	Albania	Andorra	Austria	Belarus	Belgium	Bosnia & H	Croatia	Cyprus	Denmark	Estonia	Finland	France	FYR Macedonia	Germany	Greece	Iceland	Ireland	Israel	Latvia	Lithuania	Malta	Monaco	Netherlands	Norway	Poland	Portugal	Romania	Russia	Serbia & Mont	Slovenia	Spain	Sweden	Switzerland	Turkey	Ukraine	United Kingdom	TOTAL
Finland	7	5			1			6		7			2		5	3						6		3							3	8					51
Belarus		3	7						2	2						1																			5		10
Switzerland																																					0
Latvia		1	12					4		5																											23
Israel	5	3	10		2			2	2		2			1	3		4	2			6	2	2			7	5		3		4			4		2	57
Andorra																															12						12
Portugal	12				4		1	4	4	10												1									6		7				38
Malta	6	5													1	2	1	6	7	7		1	3			4	8		1						2	5	74
Monaco	2	4						4																													10
Greece	12	8	5		10	5	6	12	3	4	5		7	10		6	2	12	6	8	12	4	6	5		8	12		10	4	7	4	3	12	10	12	238
Ukraine	3	10	4		8	7	8	8	6	12			8	6	7	10	10	10	10	12	10	5	7	7		12	7		8	8	10	6	2	8	7	7	256
Lithuania			2				7							2			3		8		3																26
Albania		6			5	6			7	1	6		12	8	8	4	3	4	5		8	3	5	8		2	6		6	5	2	7	10	6	1	6	167
Cyprus	2	7			6				5		7			4	12	8	5	3	3		5	12	10	4		3	1		2	3	1	3	1	5	7	10	149
FYR Macedonia	8	2					2		1					3	4						1		1				4		12	6		2	5	3	6		71
Slovenia						1	3						1																								5
Estonia	1		8								12					7		5	12	10				1		5			4	7		1			3	1	57
Croatia		8	7			10		3			1		6	5					1	3	2	10	4			1	2		5			5	6	1	3	8	72
Denmark						3		3		3	4				12									6		10	10					12	12	5	8		56
Serbia & Mont	4	1	12		7	12	12	10	10	3	10		10	12	10		6	8	4	1	4	7	12	10		10				12	8	12	12	7	12	8	263
Bosnia & H	10	10	3		3		10		12				5	7		5	7				1	8	8	12					7	10		10	8	10	12	4	133
Netherlands	7	3	5		12	2	4	5	8	8	3		3	2	6	5	12	7	2	5		8		2		6	3		1	2	5		4	2	4	3	146

Note: France, Poland & Russia chose not to vote in the semi-final

2004 Eurovision 49: Istanbul, Turkey

Final: 12 May 2004

Final qualification rules:
Top 10 countries from the 2003 Final
Top 10 countries from the 2004 Semi-Final

Automatic qualification:
United Kingdom, France, Germany, Spain

Rank	Start	Country	Artist	Song	Writer	Composer	POINTS
1	10	Ukraine	Ruslana	Wild dances	Alexander Ksenofontov	Ruslana Lyzchicko	280
2	5	Serbia & Mont	Željko Joksimović	Lane moje	Leontina Vukmanoviæ	Željko Joksimoviæ	263
3	16	Greece	Sakis Rouvas	Shake it	Nektarios Tirakis	Nikos Terzis	252
4	22	Turkey	Athena	For Real	Gökhan & Hakan Özoğuz	Gökhan & Hakan Özoğuz	195
5	21	Cyprus	Lisa Andreas	Stronger every minute	Mike Konnaris	Mike Konnaris	170
6	24	Sweden	Lena Philipsson	It Hurts	Thomas Orup Eriksson	Thomas Orup Eriksson	170
7	9	Albania	Anjeza Shahini	The image of you	Agim Doçit	Edmon Zhulali	106
8	8	Germany	Max (Maximilian Mutzke)	Can't Wait Until Tonight	Stefan Raab	Stefan Raab	93
9	12	Bosnia & H	Deen	In the Disco	Vesna Pisarovic	Vesna Pisarovic	91
10	1	Spain	Ramón	Para Llenarme De Ti	Kike Santander	Kike Santander	87
11	14	Russia	Julia Savicheva	Believe Me	Brenda Loring	Maxim Fadeev	67
12	6	Malta	Julie & Ludwig	On again...off again	Gerard James Borg	Philip Vella	50
13	11	Croatia	Ivan Mikulic	You are the only one	Duško Gruborovic & Marina Madrinic	Ivan Mikulic	50
14	15	FYR Macedonia	Tose Proeski	Life	Tose Proeski	Tose Proeski	47
15	4	France	Jonatan Cerrada	A Chaque Pas	Jonatan Cerrada, Benjamin Robbins, Steve Balsamo	Jonatan Cerrada, Benjamin Robbins, Steve Balsamo	40
16	20	United Kingdom	James Fox	Hold On To Our Love	Gary Miller and Tim Woodcock	Gary Miller and Tim Woodcock	29
17	19	Poland	Blue Cafe	Love Song	Tatiana Okupnik	Pawel Rurak-Sokal	27
18	23	Romania	Sanda Ladosi	I Admit	Irina Gligor	George Popa	18
19	17	Iceland	Jónsi	Heaven	Magnús Þór Sigmundsson	Sveinn Rúnar Sigurðsson	16
20	7	Netherlands	Re-union	Without you	Angeline van Otterdijk	Ed van Otterdijk	11
21	2	Austria	Tie Break	Du Bist	Peter Zimmermann	Peter Zimmermann	9
22	13	Belgium	Xandee	1 Life	Dirk Paelinck	Marc Paelinck	7
23	18	Ireland	Chris Doran	If My World Stopped Turning	Brian McFadden, Jonathan Shorten	Brian McFadden, Jonathan Shorten	7
24	3	Norway	Knut Anders Sørum	High	Dan Attlerud	Thomas Thörnholm, Lars Andersson	3

2004 Eurovision 49: Istanbul, Turkey — Final: 12 May 2004

Order votes announced	2	1	3	6	5	4	18	9	11	12	14	15	25	10	17	21	19	20	23	22	26	24	27	28	29	30	31	32	8	34	13	33	7	35	36	16	TOTAL
	Albania	Andorra	Austria	Belarus	Belgium	Bosnia & H	Croatia	Cyprus	Denmark	Estonia	Finland	France	FYR Macedonia	Germany	Greece	Iceland	Ireland	Israel	Latvia	Lithuania	Malta	Monaco	Netherlands	Norway	Poland	Portugal	Romania	Russia	Serbia & Mont	Slovenia	Spain	Sweden	Switzerland	Turkey	Ukraine	United Kingdom	
Spain		12						7																		12	5				—		6	2		16	87
Austria			—																			3															9
Norway																								—								3					3
France	1	7			10							—	4					8					4			2		4			4						40
Serbia & Mont	7	2	12	7	3	—	12	10	7	1	10	10	10	10	8	7	3	7	5	2	6	1	10	6	5	7	8	10	—	12	6	12	12	8	12	3	263
Malta	3	6				1	2		1	6			3		1		6	4	6	4	—			1	3	1									1	2	50
Netherlands				6						3										2	2		—														11
Germany	2	10				3	1	2	4	2	3	7		—	10		4	3		1		7	3	3	6	8	4		8	3	12	7	10	5		4	93
Albania		5			1	4	6		4		3	1	12	5	10	4	2		1		10	1	1	1			1		4	4		7	7	6		1	106
Ukraine	5	10	4	10	5	6	8	8	5	12	8	2	8	6	7	12	7	12	12	12	8	6	7	7	12	10	6	12	10	8	8	10	7	12	—	5	280
Croatia			3	5		10	—	8			1		5			4	2		2		8		2	7		10		5	5	5			3				50
Bosnia & H	10		7			—	10		8		1		4				5					4		10					6	10		8	5	7	7		91
Belgium		1			—			1																													7
Russia				12				6		8	4				2				6	10	1					6		—	1				1	4	10		67
FYR Macedonia	6				8	8	5			5		6	—	7					10	8				2				2	12	7				3	3		47
Greece	12	8	2	6	8	5	7	12	3		6	6	7	7	—	6	5	10	7	10	12	10	6	2	7	6	12	7	7	6	7	4	4	10	8	12	252
Iceland									2	2						—						5	5	5				2									16
Ireland																	—																			7	7
Poland								2		4				4	4	3	8		3	7	4	2	8	4	—		2	1			1	1					27
United Kingdom			1											8	12	2	10		4		7	8	12	8		4	2			2		2			5	—	29
Cyprus	4	6	8	4	4		4	—	6	7	7	5	2	5	12	10	10	3	5	4	7	2		4	4	3	3	6	3	1	3	6	2	1	4	10	170
Turkey	3	8	8	12	2	7	3	4	10		5	12	6	12	6	5	1	2	2	3	5	8	12	8	8		10	8	2			5	8	—	6	6	195
Romania								3										1								4	—	3	4		10				2		18
Sweden	4	5	1	4	2	2		5	12	10	12	3	2	3		8	12	5	8	6	5			12	10	5	7	3	4	2	5	—		3	2	8	170

107

2005 Eurovision 50: Kiev, Ukraine — Semi-final: 19 May 2005

Rank	Start	Country	Artist	Song	Writer	Composer	POINTS
1Q	14	Romania	Luminița Anghel & Sistem	Let me try	Cristian Faur	Cristian Faur	235
2Q	4	Moldova	Zdob și Zdub	Boonika bate toba	Zdob și Zdub	Zdob și Zdub	207
3Q	24	Denmark	Jakob Sveistrup	Talking to you	Jacob Launbjerg & Andreas Mørck	Jacob Launbjerg & Andreas Mørck	185
4Q	20	Croatia	Boris Novkovic & Lado members	Vukovi umiru sami	Boris Novkovic	Franjo Valentiæ	169
5Q	15	Hungary	NOX	Forogj világ	Attila Valla	Szabolcs Harmath	167
6Q	13	Norway	Wig Wam	In my dreams	Trond "Teeny" Holter	Trond "Teeny" Holter	164
7Q	7	Israel	Shiri Maymon	Hasheket shenish'ar	Eyal Shachar & Pini Aronbayev	Pini Aronbayev	158
8Q	19	Switzerland	Vanilla Ninja	Cool vibes	David Brandes	David Brandes	114
9Q	17	FYR Macedonia	Martin Vucic	Make my day	Ognen Nedelkovski	Dragan Vucić	97
10Q	5	Latvia	Walter & Kazha	The war is not over	Martins Freimanis	Martins Freimanis	85
11	25	Poland	Ivan & Delfin	Czarna dziewczyna	Ivan Komarenko & Pawel Radziszewski	Lukasz Lazer	81
12	23	Slovenia	Omar Naber	Stop	Ursa Vlašič	Omar Naber	69
13	8	Belarus	Angelica Agurbash	Love me tonight	Nektarios Tyrakis	Nikos Terzis	67
14	22	Ireland	Donna and Joseph McCaul	Love?	Karl Broderick	Karl Broderick	53
15	9	Netherlands	Glennis Grace	My impossible dream	Bruce Smith	Robert D. Fisher	53
16	10	Iceland	Selma	If I had your love	Linda Thompson	Thorvaldur Bjarni Thorvaldsson, Vignir Snær Vigfússon	52
17	3	Portugal	2B	Amar	Jose da Ponte, Alexandre Honrado, Ernesto Leite	Jose da Ponte, Alexandre Honrado, Ernesto Leite	51
18	16	Finland	Geir Rönning	Why	Steven Stewart	Mika Toivanen	50
19	21	Bulgaria	Kaffe	Lorraine	Vesselin Ivanov, Orlin Pavlov	Vesselin Ivanov	49
20	12	Estonia	Suntribe	Let's get loud	Sven Lõhmus	Sven Lõhmus	31
21	1	Austria	Global.Kryner	Y así	Christof Spörk	Christof Spörk, Edi Köhldorfer	30
22	11	Belgium	Nuno Resende	Le grand soir	Alec Mansion & Frédéric Zeitoun	Alec Mansion & Frédéric Zeitoun	29
23	18	Andorra	Marian van de Wal	La mirada interior	Rafah Tanit, Daniel Aragay & Rafa Fernández	Rafah Tanit	27
24	6	Monaco	Lise Darly	Tout de moi	Phil Bosco	Didier Fabre	22
25	2	Lithuania	Laura and the Lovers	Little by little	Billy Butt	Bobby Ljunggren	17

2005 Eurovision 50: Kiev, Ukraine — Semi-final: 19 May 2005

	Albania	Andorra	Austria	Belarus	Belgium	Bosnia & H	Bulgaria	Croatia	Cyprus	Denmark	Estonia	Finland	France	FYR Macedonia	Germany	Greece	Hungary	Iceland	Ireland	Israel	Latvia	Lithuania	Malta	Moldova	Monaco	Netherlands	Norway	Poland	Portugal	Romania	Russia	Serbia & Mont	Slovenia	Spain	Sweden	Switzerland	Turkey	Ukraine	United Kingdom	TOTAL
Austria	5	10														1																	10			6				30
Lithuania																1			5		8																		4	17
Portugal	3		8	10	10								12	10	12																		7	5						51
Moldova				7	4	6							5						3	10	10	10				1				12	12	6		1			12	12	5	207
Latvia	7											10								6				2					4	1		1	6					2		85
Monaco		10																					12	2																22
Israel	7	12			3				3	4	5		1	8		3	6	8	3		10	3	6	5	12	10	1	4	6	8	8	3	7	4		3	6	5	6	158
Belarus		5			12		12	7						6			5	2	6		6		8		1			1		1	10		6				3	4		67
Netherlands	5			12					6	6									4	5				10			8									2			2	53
Iceland	6		10							10		6	2								12	5	7	3	8	6			12			3			10				3	52
Belgium	1								3				7				1		1	4			8	1									2							29
Estonia	2		3								6								10		12	5		3					1			2			2					31
Norway	2				2	2	4	4	4	12	12	4		2	4	12	12	12	8	7	6	6	3	8	7	2			7	3		4	3	12	8	5	2	6	7	164
Romania	4		10	3	8	7	1	5	12	7	1	5	6	5	7	4	12	5	8	12	6	6	10	12	8	8	7	8	1		3	5	1	12	5	4	7	1	8	235
Hungary	1		7	4	6	3	2	7	8	1	4	4	4	4	10	5	5	7		8	4	8	2	7	7	8	6	12	10	10	7	8	8	3	3	1	8	10	1	167
Finland	3						8			8	8												5		6	1	10		7			10			10	8				50
FYR Macedonia	12	4		2		10	10	12							2				1			5		4	3	3				4		10	8	10	1		10			97
Andorra	6																								4		7					2		10						27
Switzerland		1	12			2	3	3	5	2	12			3	6	3	3	6	2	3	7			6	2		2	5	2	2	2	2	5		4		2			114
Croatia	10	12		1	1	12					3	2	6	12	10	8	8	4	10		4	6	5	7	5	4	4	3	6	6		12	12		6	10	5	7	8	169
Bulgaria	4								10					8		7							5					2		1		1		6		5				49
Ireland		2		7		1	1	5	1		2	7		7			10		12	1		1			4		2		5	5				2			4		12	53
Slovenia	8		3	2		4																				4					6	6						3		69
Denmark	8	6						6			7	8			5	2	7	10	12	2	2	7	4		10	12	12	10	5	3	4			8	12	7			10	185
Poland		5	5					2				3	3		8	10	4	3		1	1	1		8		5	5			5	5			7	2		1	8		75

2005 Eurovision 50: Kiev, Ukraine

Final: 21 May 2005

Final qualification rules:
Top 10 countries from the 2004 Final
Top 10 countries from the 2005 Semi-Final

Automatic qualification:
United Kingdom, France, Germany, Spain

Rank	Start	Country	Artist	Song	Writer	Composer	POINTS
1	19	Greece	Helena Paparizou	My number one	Christos Dantis & Natalia Germanou	Christos Dantis	230
2	3	Malta	Chiara	Angel	Chiara Siracusa	Chiara Siracusa	192
3	4	Romania	Luminita Anghel & Sistem	Let me try	Cristian Faur	Cristian Faur	158
4	11	Israel	Shiri Maymon	Hasheket shenish'ar	Eyal Shachar & Pini Aronbayev	Pini Aronbayev	154
5	23	Latvia	Walter & Kazha	The war is not over	Martins Freimanis	Martins Freimanis	153
6	7	Moldova	Zdob si Zdub	Boonika bate toba	Zdob si Zdub	Zdob si Zdub	148
7	12	Serbia & Mont	No Name	Zauvijek moja	Milan Peric	Slaven Knezovic	137
8	22	Switzerland	Vanilla Ninja	Cool vibes	David Brandes	David Brandes	128
9	5	Norway	Wig Wam	In my dreams	Trond "Teeny" Holter	Trond "Teeny" Holter	125
10	13	Denmark	Jakob Sveistrup	Talking to you	Jacob Launbjerg & Andreas Mørck	Jacob Launbjerg & Andreas Mørck	125
11	18	Croatia	Boris Novkovic & Lado members	Vukovi umiru sami	Boris Novkoviæ	Franjo Valentiæ	115
12	1	Hungary	NOX	Forogj világ	Attila Valla	Szabolcs Harmath	97
13	6	Turkey	Gülseren	Rimi rimi ley	Göksan Arman	Erdinç Tunç	92
14	21	Bosnia & H	Feminnem	Call me	Andrej Babic	Andrej Babic	79
15	20	Russia	Natalia Podolskaya	Nobody hurt no one	M.S. Applegate, J.P. Chase	Victor Drobysh	57
16	8	Albania	Ledina Celo	Tomorrow I go	Pandi Laço	Adi Hila	53
17	15	FYR Macedonia	Martin Vucic	Make my day	Ognen Nedelkovski	Dragan Vucić	52
18	9	Cyprus	Constantinos Christoforou	Ela ela	Constantinos Christoforou	Constantinos Christoforou	46
19	16	Ukraine	Greenjolly	Razom nas bahato	Greenjolly	Greenjolly	30
20	14	Sweden	Martin Stenmarck	Las Vegas	Niklas Edberger, Johan Fransson, Tim Larsson & Tobias Lundgren	Niklas Edberger, Johan Fransson, Tim Larsson & Tobias Lundgren	30
21	10	Spain	Son de sol	Brujería	Alfredo Panebianco	Alfredo Panebianco	28
22	2	United Kingdom	Javine	Touch my fire	Javine Hilton & John Themis	Javine Hilton & John Themis	18
23	24	France	Ortal	Chacun pense à soi	Saad Tabainet, Ortal	Saad Tabainet, Ortal	11
24	17	Germany	Gracia	Run & hide	John O'Flynn	David Brandes, Jane Tempest	4

2005 Eurovision 50: Kiev, Ukraine
Final: 21 May 2005

	Order votes announced	Albania	Andorra	Austria	Belarus	Belgium	Bosnia & H	Bulgaria	Croatia	Cyprus	Denmark	Estonia	Finland	France	FYR Macedonia	Germany	Greece	Hungary	Iceland	Ireland	Israel	Latvia	Lithuania	Malta	Moldova	Monaco	Netherlands	Norway	Poland	Portugal	Romania	Russia	Serbia & Mont	Slovenia	Spain	Sweden	Switzerland	Turkey	Ukraine	United Kingdom	TOTAL
Hungary	23	11	1																																					17	97
United Kingdom			6		2																												6		5			1			18
Malta	4		5	6													10								4					2	8	3	6	1			7	1	8	10	192
Romania	5	7	6	1	7	2	8						4	6	10	8	8					3	1					12			8	3	3		12	6	2	3	8	10	158
Norway		2		4	3	3	1						12	7	3	5	5					2	7	5	7	4	3		7				2		2	3	8		6	5	125
Turkey	8		7		10	8	3													12			5								8				4	3	8		7	1	92
Moldova		2	7	1	4	6	1	2			5	6		2	5	1	7					4	8	10	2		4		12		3	10	3	5	3	8		4	7	12	2	148
Albania			3			8	3									10																		5	3		10	2			53
Cyprus	7							10							12									12	5			8			1	1					4	1		3	46
Spain		12												4									8								8										28
Israel	3	8	1	8	6						5	1	5	10		5	8					2	3	8	6	12	7	5		5	7	8		6	6	1	1	3	7	7	154
Serbia & Mont	6		12	3		10	4	12	10				6		10	3	6	2				3	1		1	6	4				6	6	8	10			4	12	3		137
Denmark		3	4									5	2		6		6		10			4	4		3		10	8	12	5	1					10	12			8	125
Sweden													6		6				7		8		3		5	3	1		5							2					30
FYR Macedonia	10						7	7	8						3										8					12	7		7	5	1		2	5			52
Ukraine																	8									2	2			7	2				1						30
Germany							12						2	1								2								2		2									4
Croatia	2	8				12		2	5			2		8				7				2	1		6	7	2	2	2		5	1		10		6	8	8	8	7	115
Greece	12	4	4	12	6	12	5	12	2	10		3	8	7	12		12	2	2	7		1	6	4		10	4	1	3	10	4	12	12	8	12	7	12	3	12	230
Russia				12								7	7								10	7		10												4		4	57
Bosnia & H		10					10			4			3				1										6	7				4				7	5	10		4	79
Switzerland		1		10				3	4	1	12	8		4	3	3	7	3		1		2	12	8	1	8		3	6	4		7	6		4			5	6	4	128
Latvia	10		6	6	5				7	1	6		10	4	1	1		3	12	6	10	12	10	12				8	4		5	7			7	3	5	1		6	153
France	1	5															5																							11

2006 Eurovision 51: Athens, Greece Semi-final: 18 May 2006

Rank	Start	Country	Artist	Song	Writer	Composer	POINTS
1Q	16	Finland	Lordi	Hard rock hallelujah	Mr. Lordi	Mr. Lordi	292
2Q	22	Bosnia & H	Hari Mata Hari	Lejla	Fahrudin Pecikoza & Dejan Ivanović	Željko Joksimović	267
3Q	13	Russia	Dima Bilan	Never let you go	Karen Kavaleryan, Irina Antonyan	Alexandr Lunyov	217
4Q	20	Sweden	Carola	Invincible	Thomas G:son, Carola Häggkvist	Thomas G:son, Bobby Ljunggren, Henrik Wikström	214
5Q	18	Lithuania	LT United	We are the winners	Andrius Mamontovas, Viktoras Diawara	Andrius Mamontovas, Saulius Urbonavicius	163
6Q	1	Armenia	André	Without your love	Catherine Bekian	Armen Martirosyan	150
7Q	15	Ukraine	Tina Karol	Show me your love	Tina Karol	Tina Karol	146
8Q	14	Turkey	Sibel Tüzün	Superstar	Sibel Tüzün	Sibel Tüzün	91
9Q	8	Ireland	Brian Kennedy	Every song is a cry for love	Brian Kennedy	Brian Kennedy	79
10Q	11	FYR Macedonia	Elena Risteska	Ninanajna	Rade Vrcakovski	Darko Dimitrov	76
11	12	Poland	Ich Troje	Follow my heart	Michael Wisnieski, Real McCoy, William Lennox	André Franke	70
12	7	Belgium	Kate Ryan	Je t'adore	Kate Ryan, Niklas Bergwall, Niclas Kings, Lisa Greene	Kate Ryan, Niklas Bergwall, Niclas Kings, Lisa Greene	69
13	23	Iceland	Silvia Night	Congratulations	Ágústa Eva Erlendsdóttir & Gaukur Úlfarsson	Þorvaldur Bjarni Þorvaldsson	62
14	6	Albania	Luiz Ejlli	Zjarr e ftohtë	Floran Kondi	Klodian Qafoku	58
15	9	Cyprus	Annet Artani	Why angels cry	Peter Yiannakis	Peter Yiannakis	57
16	3	Slovenia	Anžej Dežan	Mr. Nobody	Ursa Vlašić	Matjaz Vlašić	49
17	2	Bulgaria	Mariana Popova	Let me cry	Elina Gavrilova	Dani Milev	36
18	21	Estonia	Sandra	Through my window	Jana Hallas	Pearu Paulus, Ilmar Laisaar, Alar Kotkas	28
19	19	Portugal	Nonstop	Coisas de nada	José Manuel Afonso, Elvis Veiguinha	José Manuel Afonso, Elvis Veiguinha	26
20	17	Netherlands	Treble	Amambanda	Treble	Treble	22
21	10	Monaco	Séverine Ferrer	La coco-dance	J. Woodfeel, Iren Bo	J. Woodfeel, Iren Bo	14
22	5	Belarus	Polina Smolova	Mum	Andrey Kostiugov	Sergey Sukhomlin	10
23	4	Andorra	Jennifer	Sense tu	Joan Antoni Rechi	Rafael Artesero Herrero	8

2006 Eurovision 51: Athens, Greece — Semi-final: 18 May 2006

Receiving \ Voting	Alb	And	Arm	Bel	Bel	B&H	Bul	Cro	Cyp	Den	Est	Fin	Fra	FYR	Ger	Gre	Ice	Ire	Isr	Lat	Lit	Mal	Mol	Mon	Net	Nor	Pol	Por	Rom	Rus	S&M	Slo	Spa	Swe	Swi	Tur	Ukr	UK	TOTAL
Armenia	3			7	12				12				12		7	10			10	10			2		12		3		2	12			12	3	3	10	7	3	150
Bulgaria	8								8				4	6		3								3				1				5	5						36
Slovenia	7		2	2		7		6						3								5									7						2		49
Andorra																																	8						8
Belarus			1									1																									1		10
Albania				10		5		7						12	3			5				7				3				6		1	2	2	10	3		2	58
Belgium		7		8							6	3		6			4			4		6		6	7	6	4			2		5	2	5					69
Ireland	1		7		3					5											4		1		3		2	2		1	1	3		1	2		3	8	79
Cyprus	4	12														12	2			4	4	4		10				4	4		1	3		1	1			7	57
Monaco	3						2				2		8																										14
FYR Macedonia	12		8			10		8																					1		10	8			6				76
Poland			3	4	1		5					3	2		6	2	3	7	2	3			4		2	2				5	6		4		6	8		1	70
Russia			4	12	2	4	12		10	1	10		6	10	5	5	6	4	12	12	8	1	12	2	1	4	8	7	7		6	4		7	4	4	12		217
Turkey	6			8		12	1			6	4	6	10	2	8	4			3	6	12	8			10	1			10						8				91
Ukraine	6	10	10	10	8	3	3	2	6		2		5	7	12	8	5	3	8	6	6	3	5	4	6	8	6	10	3		5	2	3	5	5	6		12	146
Finland	10			8	10	8	7	10	7	10	12			5	12		12	10	7	8	10	10	10			12	12	8	5	8	8	10	10	12	10	6	6		292
Netherlands	2	2	4		4			10	3		8						1				1																		22
Lithuania	5			6	7	2	6	5	4	4	4	8		4	1		8	8	6	5			6	4	5	5	10	5	3	4	3	6	7	4	5	2	5	10	163
Portugal		12							2				7					1		7			7	5											7				26
Sweden	5	8	6	5	5	6	4	4	2	12	7	10		1	4		10	8	6	5	5	12	7	8	4	10	7	12	6	3	4	7	7	4	4			6	214
Estonia										2		5					1			7		2		5										8					28
Bosnia & H	10		5	3	6		10	12	5	8	1	12	6	10	10	6	7	6		2	3	2	8	12	8	12	5	6	12	7	12	12	1	10	12	12	8	4	267
Iceland						1				7	5	7	1		10			2		1	7					7		3						6	6			5	62

2006 Eurovision 51: Athens, Greece

Final: 20 May 2006

Final qualification rules:
Top 10 countries from the 2005 Final
Top 10 countries from the 2006 Semi-Final

Automatic qualification:
United Kingdom, France, Germany, Spain

Rank	Start	Country	Artist	Song	Writer	Composer	POINTS
1	17	Finland	Lordi	Hard rock hallelujah	Mr. Lordi	Mr. Lordi	292
2	10	Russia	Dima Bilan	Never let you go	Karen Kavaleryan, Irina Antonyan	Alexandr Lunyov	248
3	13	Bosnia & H	Hari Mata Hari	Lejla	Fahrudin Pecikoza & Dejan Ivanović	Željko Joksimović	229
4	12	Romania	Mihai Traistariu	Tornero	Cristian Hriscu, Mihaela Deac	Eduard Circotă	172
5	22	Sweden	Carola	Invincible	Thomas G:son, Carola Häggkvist	Thomas G:son, Bobby Ljunggren, Henrik Wikström	170
6	14	Lithuania	LT United	We are the winners	Andrius Mamontovas, Viktoras Diawara	Andrius Mamontovas, Saulius Urbonavicius	162
7	18	Ukraine	Tina Karol	Show me your love	Tina Karol	Tina Karol	145
8	24	Armenia	André	Without your love	Catherine Bekian	Armen Martirosyan	129
9	16	Greece	Anna Vissi	Everything	Anna Vissi	Nikos Karvelas	128
10	21	Ireland	Brian Kennedy	Every song is a cry for love	Brian Kennedy	Brian Kennedy	93
11	23	Turkey	Sibel Tüzün	Superstar	Sibel Tüzün	Sibel Tüzün	91
12	20	Croatia	Severina	Moja štikla	Severina Vučković	Boris Novković, Franjo Valentić	56
13	11	FYR Macedonia	Elena Risteska	Ninanajna	Rade Vrcakovski	Darko Dimitrov	56
14	8	Germany	Texas Lightning	No, no, never	Jane Comerford	Jane Comerford	36
15	5	Norway	Christine Guldbrandsen	Alvedansen	Kjetil Fluge, Christine Guldbrandsen	Kjetil Fluge, Atle Halstensen, Christine Guldbrandsen	36
16	1	Switzerland	Six4One	If we all give a little	Bernd Meinunger	Ralph Siegel	30
17	4	Latvia	Cosmos	I hear your heart	Molly-Ann Leikin, Guntars Račs	Reinis Sējāns, Andris Sējāns	30
18	9	Denmark	Sidsel Ben Semmane	Twist of love	Niels Drevsholt	Niels Drevsholt	26
19	15	United Kingdom	Daz Sampson	Teenage life	Daz Sampson, John Matthews	Daz Sampson, John Matthews	25
20	2	Moldova	Arsenium & Natalia Gordienko	Loca	Arsenium	Arsenium	22
21	6	Spain	Las Ketchup	Bloody Mary	Manuel Ruiz Gómez (Queco)	Manuel Ruiz Gómez (Queco)	18
22	19	France	Virginie Pouchin	Il était temps	Corneille	Corneille	5
23	3	Israel	Eddie Butler	Ze hazman	Osnat Tsabag, Orly Burg	Eddie Butler	4
24	7	Malta	Fabrizio Faniello	I do	Aldo Spiteri, Fabrizio Faniello	Aldo Spiteri, Fabrizio Faniello	1

2006 Eurovision 51: Athens, Greece
Final: 20 May 2006

Order votes announced	Albania	Andorra	Armenia	Belarus	Belgium	Bosnia & H	Bulgaria	Croatia	Cyprus	Denmark	Estonia	Finland	France	FYR Macedonia	Germany	Greece	Iceland	Ireland	Israel	Latvia	Lithuania	Malta	Moldova	Monaco	Netherlands	Norway	Poland	Portugal	Romania	Russia	Serbia & Mont	Slovenia	Spain	Sweden	Switzerland	Turkey	Ukraine	United Kingdom	TOTAL
	37	26	24	34	28	13	38	20	31	9	30	17	19	11	8	16	35	21	3	4	14	7	2	36	32	5	33	27	12	10	29	25	6	22	1	23	18	15	
Switzerland						4			3													12		6				1		3						1			30
Moldova																1												3	12				2						22
Israel													4																										4
Latvia			1	1							3							4			8		3	8						1			2				4	2	30
Norway										1		5				2	4			6				1						7				2			3		36
Spain	6	12																																					18
Malta	1																																						1
Germany	5																	3		3					3						5		5		7			5	36
Denmark												3					8									1								8					26
Russia	4	6	12	12	3	6	10	7	8	2	10	12	2	8	6	8	5	5	12	12	12	5	10		2	3	10	7	8		5	4	7	7		5	12	1	248
FYR Macedonia	3					8	6	8																							8	6		8	4	6			56
Romania	2	3	4	3	2	2	2	5	10	6	4	6	7	2	5	7	2	6	10	2	1	10	12	12	8	4	3	10		4	4	5	12	6	1	3	1	6	172
Bosnia & H	12		5	4	6		7	12	2	8	7	10	6	12	7	6	3	2	2		4		5		8	8	4	2	7	6	12	12	1	10	12	12	10		229
Lithuania		7		6		10	1	6	4	7	8	8		3	1	1	10	3	3	10		1	4	7	6	5	8	4		5	3	3	4	3			5	10	162
United Kingdom		2							1	4	2					4		8		1	3	3			2	2	1												25
Greece	8	1	8	2	10	1	12		12			1	5	7	8		5				3	8	1		5			6	10	4	6		4	4	5	4	7	7	128
Finland		10	7	7	8	7	5	10	5	12	12		8	6	10	12	12	10	7	8	10	7	6	12	7	12	12	6	4	8	7	8	10	12	8	7	7	12	292
Ukraine		5	10	10	5	5	3	4	6	10	5	2		5		5	6	1	5	5	7	2	8	2	1		6	12	3	10	2	2	3	1		8			145
France			2																			3																	5
Croatia						12								10	2									4							10	10			6				56
Ireland		4	3					2		5	6	4	1		4		1		8	4	6	4		10	4	7	2	5	10			1		5	3		2	8	93
Sweden	10	8	6	5	5	3		3		10	7	7	3	1	12		7	7	5	7	5	6	2	5	10	10	7	8	5	2	1	7	6		2	2	6	4	170
Turkey	7				7	10	4						12	4	12	3			1						12		5		6					10	10			3	91
Armenia				8	12		8		7				10		3	10			8		2		7		10				1	12			8			10	8		129

Notes: Serbia-Montenegro withdrew due to a dispute over the representing act, Croatia were awarded an automatic place in the Final

2007 Eurovision 52: Helsinki, Finland — Semi-final: 10 May 2007

Rank	Start	Country	Artist	Song	Writer	Composer	POINTS
1Q	15	Serbia	Marija Šerifovic	Molitva	Saša Milošević Mare	Vladimir Graić	298
2Q	22	Hungary	Magdi Rúzsa	Unsubstantial Blues	Imre Mózsik	Magdi Rúzsa	224
3Q	26	Turkey	Kenan Dogulu	Shake it up shekerim	Kenan Dogulu	Kenan Dogulu	197
4Q	4	Belarus	Dmitry Koldun	Work your magic	Karen Kavaleryan	Philip Kirkorov	176
5Q	28	Latvia	Bonaparti.lv	Questa Notte	Kjell Jennstig, Torbjörn Wassenius, Francesca Russo	Kjell Jennstig	168
6Q	1	Bulgaria	Elitsa Todorova, Stoyan Yankulov	Water	Elitsa Todorova	Elitsa Todorova, Stoyan Yankoulov	146
7Q	25	Slovenia	Alenka Gotar	Cvet z juga	Andrej Babiæ	Andrej Babiæ	140
8Q	6	Georgia	Sopho	My Story	Bibi Kvachadze	Beqa Jafaridze	123
9Q	18	FYR Macedonia	Karolina	Mojot Svet	Grigor Koprov, O Nedelkovski, V Dojcinovski	Grigor Koprov, O Nedelkovski, V Dojcinovski	97
10Q	9	Moldova	Natalia Barbu	Fight	Buga	Brasoveanu	91
11	17	Portugal	Sabrina	Dança comigo (vem ser feliz)	Emanuel, Tó Maria Vinhas	Emanuel	88
12	21	Andorra	Anonymous	Salvem el món	Anonymous	Anonymous	80
13	5	Iceland	Eirikur Hauksson	Valentine lost	Peter Fenner	Sveinn Rúnar Sigurðsson	77
14	14	Poland	The Jet Set	Time to party	Kamil Varen, David Junior Serame	Mateusz Krezan	75
15	3	Cyprus	Evridiki	Comme ci, comme ça	Poseidonas Giannopoulos	Dimitris Korgialas	65
16	13	Croatia	Dragonfly feat. Dado Topic	Vjerujem u ljubav	Dado Topic	Dado Topic	54
17	11	Albania	Aida & Frederik Ndoci	Hear my plea	Pandi Laço	Adrian Hila	49
18	19	Norway	Guri Schanke	Ven a bailar conmigo	Thomas G:son	Thomas G:son	48
19	12	Denmark	DQ	Drama Queen	Peter Andersen, Claus Christensen	Peter Andersen, Simon Munk	45
20	8	Switzerland	DJ BoBo	Vampires are alive	DJ BoBo	DJ BoBo	40
21	10	Netherlands	Edsilia Rombley	On top of the world	Tjeerd Oosterhuis, Martin Gijzemijter	Tjeerd Oosterhuis	38
22	23	Estonia	Gerli Padar	Partners in crime	Hendrik Sal-Saller	Berit Vaher	33
23	7	Montenegro	Stevan Faddy	Ajde kroci	Milan Periæ	Slaven Knezoviæ	33
24	2	Israel	Teapacks	Push the button	Kobi Oz	Kobi Oz	17
25	20	Malta	Olivia Lewis	Vertigo	Gerald James Borg	Philip Vella	15
26	24	Belgium	The KMG's	Love power	Paul Curtiz, Sexyfire	Paul Curtiz	14
27	27	Austria	Eric Papilaya	Get a life - Get alive	Austin Howard	Gerg Usek	4
28	16	Czech Rep	Kabát	Malá dáma	Kabát	Kabát	1

2007 Eurovision 52: Helsinki, Finland — Semi-final: 10 May 2007

Receiving ↓ / Voting →	UK	Ukraine	Turkey	Switzerland	Sweden	Spain	Slovenia	Serbia	Russia	Romania	Portugal	Poland	Norway	Netherlands	Montenegro	Moldova	Malta	Lithuania	Latvia	Israel	Ireland	Iceland	Hungary	Greece	Germany	Georgia	FYR Macedonia	France	Finland	Estonia	Denmark	Czech Republic	Cyprus	Croatia	Bulgaria	Bosnia & H	Belgium	Belarus	Austria	Armenia	Andorra	Albania	TOTAL
Bulgaria	6	2	12				3	5		1	5				5	5	3			6			8	10	4	3	7	8	2			10		6		3	2		6	1		1	146
Israel																		4				1						6		3		2	12				5			4		8	17
Cyprus	10		5		3			4	12	7	1	4	3		4	12	7	10	10	12	6		2	12	3	4	4	5	7			5	10			2	5	3		12		4	65
Belarus		12			12					3		3	12	5		8		5		8				6		1	4		12	10	10	1		5	6				8	7		3	176
Iceland		10	10			3			10					5			10	8	4	8		8	10	6			3		4	10			7		3		1	8					77
Georgia								8																	8		3			2	3		2	5		5		8		8	6	5	123
Montenegro		6	8			6	2		6	12	12									3			5	3	8	7	3				3		6	1	1					7	6		33
Switzerland				1							3		1	1	6										1						4						10				5		40
Moldova			4	7	4		8	3	12				4		7		8	5	4	5			5	8		7					4				7	4		10					91
Netherlands				5											1	6	6	8			5	8				6									1								38
Albania				7				3				5	8	10	12		1	3	1		10		3	5	1	6			8					12		4					5		49
Denmark			4	5	4			6						4				1	2		5	2			2			7					3						7				45
Croatia		5				5		6					8	10		6	6			7	10	8	3		5	2	12		8							10							54
Poland		8		12	10	5	12	2	8	6	4		8	10	12	6	1	1	2		2	10	12		10	8	12	7	8	1	6	8	8	12		12	4	10	8				75
Serbia				8	5	8	1		4	2		10		4	8		2	12	3		4		3	1			1	10			7	3	1		5		3			10	10	2	298
Czech Republic				6	6		10					2	2			1	12	2	3				1			12				1		6				10		6					1
Portugal		8	6		5	4	1	10		6		6			8		12			2	6																			12			88
FYR Macedonia	2		7	6	2	12		12	4	10	10		2				12			8	4		7	4	12	2					8	8		2			12	12		8			97
Norway	4	4	1	4	8	1	6											6	12			12	6		6									7			12			4			48
Malta								7		4			2						5																								15
Andorra		7	3		7	7	7		5		7	7	5	6	8	3	5		5		1	5	7				5			12	5								7		7		80
Hungary			2		2	12				4		6	6											4				6				7		2		5		4		3			224
Estonia			1	4	8	1	6	12		10		8	10			4		7	12		7		3			2											4						33
Belgium		4												2				6							12																		14
Slovenia		7	3	10	7	7		7	5	4	7	7		6	3	3	5		5		1	5			7		5				5				10			6					140
Turkey	12	1		10	2	2			7	5		1	6	12		10		12		10	8							12	7		8	1						12					197
Austria				3																																				1			4
Latvia	8	3		2	1	7	7		2	5		12	7	7	2	2		12		10			4			5			3	12	5	3	5	4					8		1		168

2007 Eurovision 52: Helsinki, Finland

Final: 12 May 2007

Final qualification rules:
Top 10 countries from the 2006 Final
Top 10 countries from the 2007 Semi-Final

Automatic qualification:
United Kingdom, France, Germany, Spain, Finland

Rank	Start	Country	Artist	Song	Writer	Composer	POINTS
1	17	Serbia	Marija Šerifovic	Molitva	Saša Milošević Mare	Vladimir Graić	268
2	18	Ukraine	Verka Serduchka	Dancing Lasha Tumbai	Andrei Danilko	Andrei Danilko	235
3	15	Russia	Serebro	Song # 1	Daniil Babichev	Maxim Fadeev	207
4	22	Turkey	Kenan Dogulu	Shake it up shekerim	Kenan Dogulu	Kenan Dogulu	163
5	21	Bulgaria	Elitsa Todorova, Stoyan Yankulov	Water	Elitsa Todorova	Elitsa Todorova, Stoyan Yankoulov	157
6	3	Belarus	Dmitry Koldun	Work your magic	Karen Kavaleryan	Philip Kirkorov	145
7	10	Greece	Sarbel	Yassou Maria	Mack	Alex Papakonstantinou, Marcus Englöf	139
8	23	Armenia	Hayko	Anytime you need	Karen Kavaleryan	Hayko	138
9	8	Hungary	Magdi Rúzsa	Unsubstantial Blues	Imre Mózsik	Magdi Rúzsa	128
10	24	Moldova	Natalia Barbu	Fight	Buga	Brasoveanu	109
11	1	Bosnia & H	Marija Sestic	Rijeka bez imena	Aleksandra Milutinovic, Goran Kovacic	Aleksandra Milutinovic, Goran Kovacic	106
12	11	Georgia	Sopho	My Story	Bibi Kvachadze	Beqa Jafaridze	97
13	20	Romania	Todomondo	Liubi, liubi, I love you	Mister M, Vlad Crepu, Ghedi Kamara	Mister M	84
14	6	FYR Macedonia	Karolina	Mojot Svet	Grigor Koprov, O Nedelkovski, V Dojcinovski	Grigor Koprov, O Nedelkovski, V Dojcinovski	73
15	7	Slovenia	Alenka Gotar	Cvet z juga	Andrej Babiæ	Andrej Babiæ	66
16	14	Latvia	Bonaparti.lv	Questa Notte	Kjell Jennstig, Torbjörn Wassenius, Francesca Russo	Kjell Jennstig	54
17	5	Finland	Hanna Pakarinen	Leave me alone	Martti Vuorinen, Hanna Pakarinen	Martti Vuorinen, Miikka Huttunen	53
18	12	Sweden	The Ark	The worrying kind	The Ark	The Ark	51
19	16	Germany	Roger Cicero	Frauen regieren die Welt	Frank Ramond, Matthias Hass	Frank Ramond, Matthias Hass	49
20	2	Spain	NASH	I love you mi vida	Tony Sanchez-Ohlsson, Rebeca Pous del Toro	Thomas G:son, Andreas Rickstrand	43
21	9	Lithuania	4Fun	Love or leave	Julija Ritčik	Julija Ritčik	28
22	13	France	Les Fatals Picards	L'amour à la Française	I Callot, L Honel, P Léger, J-M Sauvagnargues, Y Giraud	I Callot, L Honel, P Léger, J-M Sauvagnargues, Y Giraud	19
23	19	United Kingdom	Scooch	Flying the flag (for you)	Andrew Hill, Morten Schjolin, Russ Spencer, Paul Tarry	Andrew Hill, Morten Schjolin, Russ Spencer, Paul Tarry	19
24	4	Ireland	Dervish	They can't stop the spring	John Waters, Tommy Moran	John Waters, Tommy Moran	5

2007 Eurovision 52: Helsinki, Finland
Final: 12 May 2007

Order votes announced	Albania	Andorra	Armenia	Austria	Belarus	Belgium	Bosnia & H	Bulgaria	Croatia	Cyprus	Czech Republic	Denmark	Estonia	Finland	France	FYR Macedonia	Georgia	Germany	Greece	Hungary	Iceland	Ireland	Israel	Latvia	Lithuania	Malta	Moldova	Montenegro	Netherlands	Norway	Poland	Portugal	Romania	Russia	Serbia	Slovenia	Spain	Sweden	Switzerland	Turkey	Ukraine	United Kingdom	TOTAL
	16	4	3	5	2	14	13	32	19	18	26	7	30	11	6	41	9	22	8	42	37	28	21	36	23	29	39	1	27	24	31	15	17	35	10	20	38	33	25	12	34	40	
Bosnia & H	8			8		3			10		4	7			1	4		3										7	7	6		8			8	8		6	8	8			106
Spain	12		10		3		4	1		6	2		7		6	7	8		1	4	4		2	8	7	2	10	4	7		7	1	1	12	2			6	5	10	12		43
Belarus	2																					12	12			10	10	3						12			3		5		12		145
Ireland	5																																										5
Finland		7			1							4	6					1			12				5					4						10		12	1				53
FYR Macedonia	3						8	10	8		5											5		4	1	5		10			4			3	10	10	3		6	1	4		73
Slovenia		6			4	2	7		7							6						12		5	4			8			2	3		3	5				3				66
Hungary		6	2		2	5			4			8	4	10		3	5	7	5		8	1		5	1	1		8	4	8	4	2		3	12	5	3	8	3		4	2	128
Lithuania	1			2						12	3	1				3	4				5			10					5		2											3	28
Greece	7		8	3	3	8	3	12		2	1		5		3	3	4	10		7		1	1	6	12		6		5				10		4	2	2		4	5		10	139
Georgia			5		6	6	1			1	1		7					5	3	2	5	6	6	6		3	4		2				7	7		2			3	5	8	7	97
Sweden	2											12		8							10					12				12	5												51
France	4	8	2						1				2												3																		19
Latvia																						10				4			3	3	1	4	2			6	4					4	54
Russia	3	12		7	12		2	5	3	7	6		12	3	2	5	7	6	8	6	1	6	8	7	6	6	8	6	3	5	3	4	2		7		4	5	7	8	10	6	207
Germany	6	5								7		5	3	1	6			8	4		2								6		1		3				5	1				1	49
Serbia	1		7	12	7	7	12	6	12	3	8	6	8	12	8	12	6	8		12	7	4	3	3	10	8	5	12	8	10	8	5	6	5		12	1	10	12	8	6		268
Ukraine	12	6	4	10	1		5	3	5	4	12	3	8	6	4	2	10	5	7	3	6	8	10	12	8	3	7	2	1	2	12	12	4	8	3		7	3	2	3		8	235
United Kingdom																					7					12																	19
Romania	10			3		4	6	2		5					7				2	8	3		7	1		7	12					7		1			12			2	2		84
Bulgaria			4	6		4	6		6	10	7			5	5	8	5	4	12	10		5	2	2			3	5	12	3	3	6	5	4	10	7	10		6	6	3	5	157
Turkey	10		10		12	12	10		7			10		4	12	10	2	12	6	1						7	1	1	12				7	2		7		7	10		1	12	163
Armenia						10	8	4		8	10				10		12	2		3		5	5				2		10		10			10			8			12	5		138
Moldova	4	3	8				4			2			2	2		1	3		10	5		2	4		2					1	6	10	12	6	1	1	6	2	7	7	7		109

2008 Eurovision 53: Belgrade, Serbia — Semi-final 1: 20 May 2008

Votes are cast by countries participating in each semi-final plus two of the four automatically qualifying countries decided by draw: Germany & Spain in semi-final 1, United Kingdom & France in semi-final 2. The hosts, Serbia, were drawn to vote in semi-final 2. The top 9 countries ranked by televoting in each semi-final qualify for the final. The back-up jury also chose an additional act that finished outside the top 9 in each semi-final.

Rank	Start	Country	Artist	Song	Writer	Composer	POINTS
1Q	19	Greece	Kalomira	Secret Combination	Poseidon Yannopoulos	Konstantinos Pantzis	156
2Q	14	Armenia	Sirusho	Qele, Qele	Sirusho	H A Der-Hovagimian	139
3Q	18	Russia	Dima Bilan	Believe	Dima Bilan & Jim Beanz	Dima Bilan & Jim Beanz	135
4Q	9	Norway	Maria	Hold On Be Strong	Mira Craig	Mira Craig	106
5Q	2	Israel	Boaz	The Fire In Your Eyes	Dana International & Shai Kerem	Dana International	104
6Q	7	Azerbaijan	Elnur & Samir	Day After Day	Zahra Badalbeyli	Govher Hasanzadeh	96
7Q	17	Romania	Nico & Vlad	Pe-o Margine De Lume	Andreea Andrei & Adina Şuteu	Andrei Tudor	94
8Q	16	Finland	Teräsbetoni	Missä Miehet Ratsastaa	J Ahola	J Ahola	79
9Q	13	Bosnia & H	Laka	Pokušaj	Elvir Lakovic Laka	Elvir Lakovic Laka	72
10J	10	Poland	Isis Gee	For Life	Isis Gee	Isis Gee	42
12	4	Moldova	Geta Burlacu	A Century Of Love	Viorica Demici	Oleg Baraliuc	36
11	8	Slovenia	Rebeka Dremelj	Vrag Naj Vzame	Amon	Josip Miani-Pipi	36
13	15	Netherlands	Hind	Your Heart Belongs To Me	Hind Laroussi Tahiri & Tjeerd van Zanen	Hind Laroussi Tahiri, Tjeerd van Zanen & Bas van den Heuvel	27
14	1	Montenegro	Stefan Filipović	Zauvijek Volim Te	Ognen Nedelkovski	Grigor Koprov	23
15	11	Ireland	Dustin the Turkey	Irelande Douze Pointe	Darren Smith, Simon Fine & Dustin The Turkey	Darren Smith, Simon Fine & Dustin The Turkey	22
16	12	Andorra	Gisela	Casanova	Jordi Cubino	Jordi Cubino	22
17	6	Belgium	Ishtar	O Julissi	Michel Vangheluwe	Michel Vangheluwe	16
18	3	Estonia	Kreisiraadio	Leto Svet	Priit Pajusaar, Glen Pilvre, Peeter Oja, Hannes Võrno & Tarmo Leinatamm	Priit Pajusaar, Glen Pilvre, Peeter Oja, Hannes Võrno & Tarmo Leinatamm	8
19	5	San Marino	Miodio	Complice	Nicola Della Valle	Francesco Sancisi	5

2008 Eurovision 53: Belgrade, Serbia
Semi-final 1: 20 May 2008

	Andorra	Armenia	Azerbaijan	Belgium	Bosnia & H	Estonia	Finland	Germany	Greece	Ireland	Israel	Moldova	Montenegro	Netherlands	Norway	Poland	Romania	Russia	San Marino	Slovenia	Spain	TOTAL
Montenegro					12														1	10		23
Israel	7	7	10	7	5			4	5				5	6	10	4	6	8	2	4	4	104
Estonia							7					1										8
Moldova	1	6	5				10		4								10	5	5			36
San Marino	2								3													5
Belgium						6								10								16
Azerbaijan	8	2		5	3	4	5	8	7	5	5	10	3	4		10	7	10			2	96
Slovenia	4	4			10			1	2		2	2	10			2	1	2				36
Norway	10	8	7	1	4		12			8	6	3	4	5		7	4	7	7	2	3	106
Poland		1	3				2	5	1	12					2		2	3	10			42
Ireland				4	2	7					3			1	1	1					1	22
Andorra						3				1	4		1								12	22
Bosnia & H			4			1	8	7	3	3		6	12	7	12				8	12		72
Armenia	3			12	6	2	4	10	12	2	10	5	6	12	3	12	5	12	8	5	10	139
Netherlands		3	2	8							1				7		3		3			27
Finland	12			2	1	12		2	6	6		8	2	3	6	5		4	4	3	6	79
Romania	6	5	6	6			1	3	8	7	8	12		2	5	3		1	6	6	8	94
Russia	4	12	8	3	7	10	6	6	10	4	12	7	8	8	8	8	8		12	7	5	135
Greece	5	10	12	10	8	5	3	12		10	7	4	7	8	4	6	12	6		8	7	156

2008 Eurovision 53: Belgrade, Serbia

Semi-final 2: 22 May 2008

Votes are cast by countries participating in each semi-final plus two of the four automatically qualifying countries decided by draw: Germany & Spain in semi-final 1, United Kingdom & France in semi-final 2. The hosts, Serbia, were drawn to vote in semi-final 2. The top 9 countries ranked by televoting in each semi-final qualify for the final. The back-up jury also chose an additional act that finished outside the top 9 in each semi-final.

Rank	Start	Country	Artist	Song	Writer	Composer	POINTS
1Q	4	Ukraine	Ani Lorak	Shady Lady	Karen Kavaleryan	Philip Kirkorov	152
2Q	19	Portugal	Vânia Fernandes	Senhora Do Mar (Negras Águas)	Carlos Coelho	Andrej Babić	120
3Q	13	Denmark	Simon Mathew	All Night Long	Jacob Launbjerg, Svend Gudiksen & Nis Bøgvad	Jacob Launbjerg, Svend Gudiksen & Nis Bøgvad	112
4Q	11	Croatia	Kraljevi Ulice & 75 Cents	Romanca	Miran Hadži Veljković	Miran Hadži Veljković	112
5Q	14	Georgia	Diana Gurtskaya	Peace Will Come	Karen Kavaleryan	Kim Breitburg	107
6Q	10	Latvia	Pirates Of The Sea	Wolves Of The Sea	Jonas Liberg, Johan Sahlen, Claes Andreasson, Torbjorn Wassenius	Jonas Liberg, Johan Sahlen, Claes Andreasson, Torbjorn Wassenius	86
7Q	3	Turkey	Mor ve Ötesi	Deli	Mor ve Ötesi	Mor ve Ötesi	85
8Q	1	Iceland	Euroband	This Is My Life	Paul Oscar & Peter Fenner	Örlygur Smári	68
9Q	6	Albania	Olta Boka	Zemrën E Lamë Peng	Pandi Laço	Adrian Hila	67
10	18	FYR Macedonia	Tamara, Vrčak & Adrijan	Let Me Love You	Rade Vrchakovski-Vrcak	Rade Vrchakovski-Vrcak	64
11	12	Bulgaria	Deep Zone & Balthazar	DJ, Take Me Away	Dian Savov	Dian Savov	56
12J	2	Sweden	Charlotte Perrelli	Hero	Fredrik Kempe	Fredrik Kempe & Bobby Ljunggren	54
13	7	Switzerland	Paolo Meneguzzi	Era Stupendo	Pablo Meneguzzo & Vincenzo Incenzo	Pablo Meneguzzo	47
14	16	Malta	Morena	Vodka	Gerard James Borg	Philip Vella	38
15	17	Cyprus	Evdokia Kadi	Femme Fatale	Vangelis Evangelou	Nicos Evagelou	36
16	5	Lithuania	Jeronimas Milius	Nomads In The Night	Jeronimas Milius	Vytautas Diškevičius	30
17	9	Belarus	Ruslan Alehno	Hasta La Vista	Eleonora Melnik	Taras Demchuk	27
18	8	Czech Republic	Tereza Kerndlová	Have Some Fun	Gordon Pogoda	Gordon Pogoda & Stano Simor	9
19	15	Hungary	Csézy	Candlelight	Imre Mózsik	Viktor Rakonczai	6

2008 Eurovision 53: Belgrade, Serbia

Semi-final 2: 22 May 2008

	Albania	Belarus	Bulgaria	Croatia	Cyprus	Czech Republic	Denmark	France	FYR Macedonia	Georgia	Hungary	Iceland	Latvia	Lithuania	Malta	Portugal	Serbia	Sweden	Switzerland	Turkey	Ukraine	United Kingdom	TOTAL
Iceland	5	1			1		10	8			7		2	2	5	5		10	4	3	1	4	68
Sweden	1				4		12	1			1	8		3	7	3	3		3	2		6	54
Turkey	12	3	7				8	10		5	4				8			6	7		5	10	85
Ukraine		12	12	7	10	12	7	3	6		8	6	12	7	8	12			1	12			152
Lithuania									12	10												8	30
Albania		5		10		1		5				1				2		7	10	8	3	3	67
Switzerland	10			2	7		5	7	5						12					1			47
Czech Republic					2					4			5										9
Belarus				6		5	6		4	6		7		6							10		27
Latvia		6	1		6	3	3	2	10	8	10	4		12	6	10	2	8	6	5	2	5	86
Croatia		7	6		8	2		6	7		3	5	7	5	2	1	10	4		6	7		112
Bulgaria		2		1	8								1	1							6		56
Denmark	4	4	2	3	5	10		4	3	3	12	12	8	8	4	8		12	5		4	1	112
Georgia	8	10	4		12	8			2		2	2	10	10	10	7	7	1	12	10	12		107
Hungary							1			1							4						6
Malta	8	3		4		6	4				5	3	4			4	1		2			2	38
Cyprus	2		8				2			2							12		8	4		12	36
FYR Macedonia	7	10		12	4					7			3		3		6	5		7	8		64
Portugal	6	8	5	8	7	7		12			6	10		4					12			7	120

2008 Eurovision 53: Belgrade, Serbia

Final: 24 May 2008

Final qualification rules:
Top 9 countries from each semi-final decided by televoting,
plus one from each semi-final decided by a back-up jury.

Automatic qualification:
United Kingdom, France, Germany, Spain, Serbia

Rank	Start	Country	Artist	Song	Writer	Composer	POINTS
1	24	Russia	Dima Bilan	Believe	Dima Bilan & Jim Beanz	Dima Bilan & Jim Beanz	272
2	18	Ukraine	Ani Lorak	Shady Lady	Karen Kavaleryan	Philip Kirkorov	230
3	21	Greece	Kalomira	Secret Combination	Poseidon Yannopoulos	Konstantinos Pantzis	218
4	5	Armenia	Sirusho	Qele, Qele	Sirusho	H A Der-Hovagimian	199
5	25	Norway	Maria	Hold On Be Strong	Mira Craig	Mira Craig	182
6	23	Serbia	Jelena Tomašević & Bora Dugić	Oro	Dejan Ivanović	Željko Joksimović	160
7	12	Turkey	Mor ve Ötesi	Deli	Mor ve Ötesi	Mor ve Ötesi	138
8	20	Azerbaijan	Elnur & Samir	Day After Day	Zahra Badalbeyli	Govher Hasanzadeh	132
9	7	Israel	Boaz	The Fire In Your Eyes	Dana International & Shai Kerem	Dana International	124
10	6	Bosnia & H	Laka	Pokušaj	Elvir Lakovic Laka	Elvir Lakovic Laka	110
11	17	Georgia	Diana Gurtskaya	Peace Will Come	Karen Kavaleryan	Kim Breitburg	83
12	14	Latvia	Pirates Of The Sea	Wolves Of The Sea	Jonas Liberg, Johan Sahlen, Claes Andreasson, Torbjorn Wassenius	Jonas Liberg, Johan Sahlen, Claes Andreasson, Torbjorn Wassenius	83
13	13	Portugal	Vânia Fernandes	Senhora Do Mar (Negras Águas)	Carlos Coelho	Andrej Babić	69
14	11	Iceland	Euroband	This Is My Life	Paul Oscar & Peter Fenner	Örlygur Smári	64
15	16	Denmark	Simon Mathew	All Night Long	Jacob Launbjerg, Svend Gudiksen & Nis Bøgvad	Jacob Launbjerg, Svend Gudiksen & Nis Bøgvad	60
16	22	Spain	Rodolfo Chikilicuatre	Baila El Chiki Chiki	Rodolfo Chikilicuatre	Rodolfo Chikilicuatre	55
17	3	Albania	Olta Boka	Zemrën E Lamë Peng	Pandi Laço	Adrian Hila	55
18	15	Sweden	Charlotte Perrelli	Hero	Fredrik Kempe	Fredrik Kempe & Bobby Ljunggren	47
19	19	France	Sébastien Tellier	Divine	Sebastien Tellier, Amandine de La Richardière	Sebastien Tellier	47
20	1	Romania	Nico & Vlad	Pe-o Margine De Lume	Andreea Andrei & Adina Şuteu	Andrei Tudor	45
21	9	Croatia	Kraljevi Ulice & 75 Cents	Romanca	Miran Hadži Veljković	Miran Hadži Veljković	44
22	8	Finland	Teräsbetoni	Missä Miehet Ratsastaa	J Ahola	J Ahola	35
23	4	Germany	No Angels	Disappear	Remee, Hanne Sorvaag & Thomas Troelsen	Remee, Hanne Sorvaag & Thomas Troelsen	14
24	10	Poland	Isis Gee	For Life	Isis Gee	Isis Gee	14
25	2	United Kingdom	Andy Abraham	Even If	Andy Abraham, Andy Watkins & Paul Wilson	Andy Abraham, Andy Watkins & Paul Wilson	14

2008 Eurovision 53: Belgrade, Serbia — Final: 24 May 2008

Country (receiving)	Order votes announced	TOTAL
Romania	22	45
United Kingdom	25	14
Albania	33	55
Germany	38	14
Armenia	8	199
Bosnia & H	6	110
Israel	11	124
Finland	36	35
Croatia	14	44
Poland	26	14
Iceland	43	64
Turkey	5	138
Portugal	35	69
Latvia	17	83
Sweden	2	47
Denmark	42	60
Georgia	4	83
Ukraine	34	230
France	21	47
Azerbaijan	16	132
Greece	31	218
Spain	13	55
Serbia	10	160
Russia	39	272
Norway	30	182

Voting countries (order announced): Albania 7, Andorra 22, Armenia 25, Azerbaijan 33, Belarus 38, Belgium 8, Bosnia & H 6, Bulgaria 11, Croatia 36, Cyprus 14, Czech Republic 26, Denmark 43, Estonia 5, Finland 35, France 17, FYR Macedonia 2, Georgia 42, Germany 4, Greece 34, Hungary 21, Iceland 16, Ireland 31, Israel 13, Latvia 10, Lithuania 39, Malta 30, Moldova 15, Montenegro 41, Netherlands 28, Norway 20, Poland 23, Portugal 19, Romania 18, Russia 40, San Marino 9, Serbia 12, Slovenia 24, Spain 27, Sweden 37, Switzerland 32, Turkey 29, Ukraine 3, United Kingdom 1.

2009 Eurovision 54: Moscow, Russia

Semi-final 1: 12 May 2009

Votes are cast by countries participating in each semi-final plus two of the four automatically qualifying countries decided by draw: Germany & United Kingdom in semi-final 1, Spain & France in semi-final 2. The hosts, Russia, were drawn to vote in semi-final 2. The top 9 countries ranked by televoting in each semi-final qualify for the final. The back-up jury also chose an additional act that finished outside the top 9 in each semi-final.

Rank	Start	Country	Artist	Song	Writer	Composer	POINTS
1Q	12	Iceland	Yohanna	Is It True?	Óskar Páll Sveinsson, Chris Neil, Tinatin Japaridze	Óskar Páll Sveinsson, Chris Neil, Tinatin Japaridze	174
2Q	9	Turkey	Hadise	Düm Tek Tek	Sinan Akçıl, Hadise Açıkgöz, Stefaan Fernande	Sinan Akçıl	172
3Q	18	Bosnia & H	Regina	Bistra Voda	Aleksandar Čović	Aleksandar Čović	125
4Q	5	Sweden	Malena Ernman	La Voix	Fredrik Kempe and Malena Ernman	Fredrik Kempe	105
5Q	6	Armenia	Inga & Anush	Jan Jan	Vardan Zadoyan & Avet Barseghyan	Mane Hakobyan	99
6Q	17	Malta	Chiara	What If We	Gregory Bilsen	Marc Paelinck	86
7Q	10	Israel	Noa & Mira Awad	There Must Be Another Way	Noa, Mira Awad, Gil Dor	Noa, Mira Awad, Gil Dor	75
8Q	16	Portugal	Flor-de-lis	Todas As Ruas Do Amor	Pedro Marques	Pedro Marques, Paulo Pereira	70
9Q	14	Romania	Elena	The Balkan Girls	Laurenţiu Duţă, Alexandru Pelin	Laurenţiu Duţă, Ovidiu Bistriceanu, Daris Mangal	67
10	13	FYR Macedonia	Next Time	Neshto Shto Ke Ostane	Elvir Mekic	Jovan Jovanov & Damjan Lazarov	45
11	1	Montenegro	Andrea Demirovic	Just Get Out of My Life	Bernd Meinunger & Jose Juan Santana Rodriguez	Ralph Siegel	44
12J	15	Finland	Waldo's People	Lose Control	Waldo, A. Lehtonen, Karima, A. Kratz Gută	A. Lehtonen, Karima	42
13	4	Belarus	Petr Elfimov	Eyes That Never Lie	Valery Prokhozhy	Petr Elfimov	25
14	8	Switzerland	Lovebugs	The Highest Heights	Adrian Sieber, Thomas Rechberger, Florian Senn, Lovebugs	Adrian Sieber, Thomas Rechberger, Florian Senn, Lovebugs	15
15	7	Andorra	Susanne Georgi	La Teva Decisió (Get A Life)	Rune Braager, Lene Dissing, Marcus Winther-John, Pernille Georgi, Susanne Georgi	Rune Braager, Lene Dissing, Marcus Winther-John, Pernille Georgi, Susanne Georgi	8
16	11	Bulgaria	Krassimir Avramov	Illusion	Krassimir Avramov, William Tabanau, Casie Tabanau	Krassimir Avramov, William Tabanau	7
17	3	Belgium	Copycat	Copycat	Jacques Duvall	Benjamin Schoos	1
18	2	Czech Republic	Gipsy.cz	Aven Romale	Radoslav Gipsy Bang	Radoslav Gipsy Bang	0

2009 Eurovision 54: Moscow, Russia

Semi-final 1: 12 May 2009

	Andorra	Armenia	Belarus	Belgium	Bosnia & H	Bulgaria	Czech Republic	Finland	FYR Macedonia	Germany	Iceland	Israel	Malta	Montenegro	Portugal	Romania	Sweden	Switzerland	Turkey	United Kingdom	TOTAL
Montenegro	1	5	3		10				8	2		1	6		1			2	5		44
Czech Republic																					0
Belgium		1																			1
Belarus		4				1	1	4	6		1	4	1			4	1	4			25
Sweden		7	4	10	4		6	10	3	4	10	7	8	2	8	4	1	4	4	7	105
Armenia			10		1	8	12	1	2	10	2	10	3	4	4	8	5	1	10	5	99
Andorra										1											8
Switzerland	2		2		2			5							2		2				15
Turkey	5	10	6	12	12	12	5	7	12	12	7	6	10	8	5	12	7	12		12	172
Israel	8	7	4	3	4	4	4	6	1	5	6		4	5		3	6	5	3	1	75
Bulgaria									5										2		7
Iceland	10	12	12	7	7	6	10	12	4	6		12	12	7	12	10	12	7	8	8	174
FYR Macedonia					8	10	3			1				10	2	2		6	6		45
Romania	4	2	1	2	6	5		2	7		4	8	2	6	10	1		6	7	2	67
Finland	3			1			2	2		1	12		5	3	3	1	10			4	42
Portugal	12		6	6	3	2	2	2	7	7	8	2		6		7	3	10		6	70
Malta	6	3	4	8	5	3	7	3	3	3	5	5	7	1	6	6	4	3		10	86
Bosnia & H		6	5	5		7	8	8	10	8	3	3		12	7	5	8	8	12	3	125

2009 Eurovision 54: Moscow, Russia — Semi-final 2: 14 May 2009

Votes are cast by countries participating in each semi-final plus two of the four automatically qualifying countries decided by draw: Germany & United Kingdom in semi-final 1, Spain & France in semi-final 2. The hosts, Russia, were drawn to vote in semi-final 2. The top 9 countries ranked by televoting in each semi-final qualify for the final. The back-up jury also chose an additional act that finished outside the top 9 in each semi-final.

Rank	Start	Country	Artist	Song	Writer	Composer	POINTS
1Q	6	Norway	Alexander Rybak	Fairytale	Alexander Rybak	Alexander Rybak	201
2Q	12	Azerbaijan	AySel & Arash	Always	Arash Labaf, Robert Uhlmann, Elin Wrethov, Anders Wrethov	A Labaf, R Uhlmann, J Bejerholm, M Englof, A Papaconstantinou	180
3Q	18	Estonia	Urban Symphony	Rändajad	Sven Lõhmus	Sven Lõhmus	115
4Q	13	Greece	Sakis Rouvas	This Is Our Night	Graig Porteils & Cameron Giles-Webb	Dimitris Kontopoulos	110
5Q	15	Moldova	Nelly Ciobanu	Hora Din Moldova	Nelly Ciobanu	Veaceslav Daniliuc	106
6Q	17	Ukraine	Svetlana Loboda	Be my Valentine! (Anti-crisis Girl)	Yevgeny Matyushenko	Svetlana Loboda	80
7Q	16	Albania	Kejsi Tola	Carry Me In Your Dreams	Agim Doçi	Edmond Zhulali	73
8Q	9	Denmark	Brinck	Believe Again	Lars Halvor Jensen, Martin Michael Larsson, Ronan Keating	Lars Halvor Jensen, Martin Michael Larsson, Ronan Keating	69
9Q	14	Lithuania	Sasha Son	Love	Dmitrij Šavrov (Sasha Son)	Dmitrij Šavrov (Sasha Son)	66
10	4	Serbia	Marko Kon & Milaan	Cipela	Marko Kon, Aleksandar Kobac	Marko Kon, Aleksandar Kobac, Milan Nikolic	60
11	2	Ireland	Sinéad Mulvey & Black Daisy	Et Cetera	Niall Mooney, Jonas Gladnikoff, Daniele Moretti & Christina Schilling	Niall Mooney, Jonas Gladnikoff, Daniele Moretti & Christina Schilling	52
12	5	Poland	Lidia Kopania	I Don't Wanna Leave	Alex Geringas, Bernd Klimpel, Rike Boomgaarden, Dee Adam	Alex Geringas, Bernd Klimpel, Rike Boomgaarden, Dee Adam	43
13J	1	Croatia	Igor Cukrov featuring Andrea	Lijepa Tena	Vjekoslava Huljić	Tonči Huljić	33
14	7	Cyprus	Christina Metaxa	Firefly	Nikolas Metaxas	Nikolas Metaxas	32
15	11	Hungary	Zoli Ádok	Dance With Me	Kasai	Szabó Zé	16
16	10	Slovenia	Quartissimo featuring Martina	Love Symphony	Andrej Babić	Andrej Babić	14
17	19	Netherlands	The Toppers	Shine	Gordon Heuckeroth	Gordon Heuckeroth	11
18	8	Slovakia	Kamil Mikulčík & Nela Pocisková	Leť Tmou	Anna Žigová, Petronela Kolevská	Rastislav Dubovský	8
19	3	Latvia	Intars Busulis	Probka	Janis Elsbergs, Sergej Timofejev	Karlis Lacis	7

2009 Eurovision 54: Moscow, Russia
Semi-final 2: 14 May 2009

	Albania	Azerbaijan	Croatia	Cyprus	Denmark	Estonia	France	Greece	Hungary	Ireland	Latvia	Lithuania	Moldova	Netherlands	Norway	Poland	Russia	Serbia	Slovakia	Slovenia	Spain	Ukraine	TOTAL
Croatia	1			2		4	1		1				3				3	12		10		1	33
Ireland	7		1		10	1						7	2	3	4	3		3		2			52
Latvia				4							5	6									5		7
Serbia			12				12	5											3	12			60
Poland	6	1			3		4	1	2			3	1	6	2						5	6	43
Norway	8	12	8	8	12	12	3	8		10	10	12	10	2	3	10	10	8	10	8	12	10	201
Cyprus					7	6		12	10	8	1	1		12				2	1				32
Slovakia	4																1					2	8
Denmark	5	2	2	3		8		2	3	2	3	5		7		1			2	5	4		69
Slovenia	2	7	7							1					12			5					14
Hungary	3	8								7											3		16
Azerbaijan			6	10	8	10	10	7	12	6	8	10	12	8	6	12	12	6	12	6	7	12	180
Greece	12	4	3	12	2	5	6		6	12	4	4	6	10	1	2	4	10	5	4	6	4	110
Lithuania		6	5	1	5	7	2	6	5	5	7		4		7	4	5	7	7	3	1	5	66
Moldova		7		7		2	7	10	4		2			4	10	5	8	1	4	7	8	8	106
Albania		5	10		6	3	5	3	8	3	6	2	5	1	5	6	2	4	6		3	3	73
Ukraine		10		6				10	7	4	12	8	8			7	7		8	7	10		80
Estonia		3	4	5	4		8				12		7	5	8	8	6	4		1	2	7	115
Netherlands	10				1																		11

2009 Eurovision 54: Moscow, Russia

Final: 16 May 2009

Final qualification rules: Top 9 countries from each semi-final decided by televoting, plus one from each semi-final decided by a back-up jury.
Automatic qualification: United Kingdom, France, Germany, Spain, Russia

Final points scoring system: televoting by all countries participating in semi-finals/final equals 50% of points awarded, 50% also determined by a jury from each country.

Rank	Start	Country	Artist	Song	Writer	Composer	POINTS
1	20	Norway	Alexander Rybak	Fairytale	Alexander Rybak	Alexander Rybak	387
2	7	Iceland	Yohanna	Is It True?	Óskar Páll Sveinsson, Chris Neil, Tinatin Japaridze	Óskar Páll Sveinsson, Chris Neil, Tinatin Japaridze	218
3	11	Azerbaijan	AySel & Arash	Always	Arash Labaf, Robert Uhlmann, Elin Wrethov, Anderz Wrethov	A Labaf, R Uhlmann, J Bejerholm, M Englof, A Papaconstantinou	207
4	18	Turkey	Hadise	Düm Tek Tek	Sinan Akçıl, Hadise Açıkgöz, Stefaan Fernande	Sinan Akçıl	177
5	23	United Kingdom	Jade Ewen	It's My Time	Andrew Lloyd Webber & Diane Warren	Andrew Lloyd Webber & Diane Warren	173
6	15	Estonia	Urban Symphony	Rändajad	Sven Lõhmus	Sven Lõhmus	129
7	8	Greece	Sakis Rouvas	This Is Our Night	Graig Porteils & Cameron Giles-Webb	Dimitris Kontopoulos	120
8	3	France	Patricia Kaas	Et S'il Fallait Le Faire	Anse Lazio	Fred Blondin	107
9	12	Bosnia & H	Regina	Bistra Voda	Aleksandar Čović	Aleksandar Čović	106
10	9	Armenia	Inga & Anush	Jan Jan	Vardan Zadoyan, Avet Barseghyan	Mane Hakobyan	92
11	10	Russia	Anastasia Prikhodko	Mamo	Konstantin Meladzé, Diana Golde	Konstantin Meladzé	91
12	21	Ukraine	Svetlana Loboda	Be my Valentine! (Anti-crisis Girl)	Yevgeny Matyushenko	Svetlana Loboda	76
13	16	Denmark	Brinck	Believe Again	Lars Halvor Jensen, Martin Michael Larsson, Ronan Keating	Lars Halvor Jensen, Martin Michael Larsson, Ronan Keating	74
14	13	Moldova	Nelly Ciobanu	Hora Din Moldova	Nelly Ciobanu	Veaceslav Daniliuc	69
15	6	Portugal	Flor-de-lis	Todas As Ruas Do Amor	Pedro Marques	Pedro Marques, Paulo Pereira	57
16	2	Israel	Noa & Mira Awad	There Must Be Another Way	Noa, Mira Awad, Gil Dor	Noa, Mira Awad, Gil Dor	53
17	19	Albania	Kejsi Tola	Carry Me In Your Dreams	Agim Doçi	Edmond Zhulali	48
18	5	Croatia	Igor Cukrov featuring Andrea	Lijepa Tena	Vjekoslava Huljić	Tonči Huljić	45
19	22	Romania	Elena	The Balkan Girls	Laurențiu Duță, Alexandru Pelin	Laurențiu Duță, Ovidiu Bistriceanu, Daris Mangal	40
20	17	Germany	Alex Swings Oscar Sings!	Miss Kiss Kiss Bang	Alex Christensen, Steffen Haefeliger	Alex Christensen, Steffen Haefeliger	35
21	4	Sweden	Malena Ernman	La Voix	Fredrik Kempe & Malena Ernman	Fredrik Kempe	33
22	14	Malta	Chiara	What If We	Gregory Bilsen	Marc Paelinck	31
23	1	Lithuania	Sasha Son	Love	Dmitrij Šavrov (Sasha Son)	Dmitrij Šavrov (Sasha Son)	23
24	25	Spain	Soraya	La Noche Es Para Mi (The Night Is For Me)	Felipe Pedroso	Jason Gill, Dimitri Stassos, Irini Michas	23
25	24	Finland	Waldo's People	Lose Control	Waldo, A. Lehtonen, Karima, A. Kratz Gutā A. Lehtonen, Karima		22

2009 Eurovision 54: Moscow, Russia
Final: 16 May 2009

Order votes announced	Albania	Andorra	Armenia	Azerbaijan	Belarus	Belgium	Bosnia & H	Bulgaria	Croatia	Cyprus	Czech Republic	Denmark	Estonia	Finland	France	FYR Macedonia	Germany	Greece	Hungary	Iceland	Ireland	Israel	Latvia	Lithuania	Malta	Moldova	Montenegro	Netherlands	Norway	Poland	Portugal	Romania	Russia	Serbia	Slovakia	Slovenia	Spain	Sweden	Switzerland	Turkey	Ukraine	United Kingdom	TOTAL
	26	14	39	41	3	2	23	17	32	28	6	36	31	15	9	20	5	22	40	8	35	10	12	18	4	37	13	30	42	29	33	34	11	27	21	38	1	7	16	25	24	19	
Lithuania				1				1					1										7																				23
Israel	7		6				8				4		2	4	10		3	6			7			6			4	1	1				10	3	5	7			1		1	4	53
France	2	3			7	8	6						5	7		4		2		6	3	5	5	6	4		1	6	4							3	3		7	4	3	1	107
Sweden	1	2		5	1	1							6	2						3						2			1										1	1	3		33
Croatia							12					4		4	2			2							4	8	8		4							7			7				45
Portugal	6					6	1				7		3		7					1																	8	8	10				57
Iceland	6	8	5		2			5	2	5	2	10	8	10		2		7	4		12	10	8	8	12	3	5	7	12	1	8	10	3		6	5	8	10	5	2	1	8	218
Greece	12		10		5	5	5	12	7	12							6					8			7		2	1			2	8	4	6		5	1	2	2	6		5	120
Armenia					1	7		6		4	12			1		1		4		5						6		5		2	4	7	5		4	4	4	3			2		92
Russia			12	6	8						8		10				5													3							4			4	8		91
Azerbaijan	4		1		10	3	3	8	10	8	10	8	7	2	1	3		8	10		4	6	4	7	5	10	6	10	10	6	4	4	7	4	4	1		8	5	12	10	3	207
Bosnia & H	5				6			4	12					6		10	2			2				5	1		12	4			12			12	8	10		5	4	8			106
Moldova			2	7	4	4			3																	2			3			12	1							7	7		69
Malta																	4				5		1	1								3					5						31
Estonia		1								2	7	5		3			1	1	6	10			10	10		10		6		8	12	1	8	7	12			7	12		4	6	129
Denmark		5								6				12	5		5	5	3	4	4		3	2	6	5		3	6	7		2				8					5		74
Germany	3					2	2					7			3						1				6			2	8		1			1								7	35
Turkey	10		4	12		12	7	10	1	10	1	6	1	5	12	12	10	10	12		8	12	12	12	5	8	3		5	12		6	12	10	10	12	2	6	12			12	177
Albania								5	5		5					7			8					4		4	7			10		5				2		1	6				48
Norway	7	10	8	8	12	10	10	2	8	10	3	12	12	8	8	8	12	10	12	12	8	12	12	12	8	8	10	12		12	5	5	12	10	10	12	12	12	8	3	12	10	387
Ukraine			3	10	6		10				5								8			2		4	2	4		3	5	10	6		2	2	1		6	1	6			2	76
Romania				3		4		3		2			4			5			1		2		2		10	12				4	2		6				7						40
United Kingdom	8	4	7		3		4		4	7	6	3			4		8	12	1	8	10	4	2	3	3	1		3	2	4	10		6	8	7	3	10		8	5	6		173
Finland																																						4					22
Spain																		1																		3			3				23

2010 Eurovision 55: Oslo, Norway

Semi-final 1: 25 May 2010

Votes are cast by countries participating in each semi-final plus the four automatically qualifying countries decided by draw: Germany, France & Spain in semi-final 1, United Kingdom in semi-final 2. The hosts, Norway, were drawn to vote in semi-final 2. Points awarded are the combined totals of the televoting and jury votes. The top 10 countries in each semi-final qualify for the final.

Rank	Start	Country	Artist	Song	Writer	Composer	POINTS
1Q	10	Belgium	Tom Dice	Me And My Guitar	Tom Dice, Jeroen Swinnen & Ashley Hicklin	Tom Dice, Jeroen Swinnen & Ashley Hicklin	167
2Q	13	Greece	Giorgos Alkaios & Friends	OPA	Giannis Antoniou & Friends	Giorgos Alkaios	133
3Q	17	Iceland	Hera Björk	Je Ne Sais Quoi	Örlygur Smári & Hera Björk	Örlygur Smári & Hera Björk	123
4Q	14	Portugal	Filipa Azevedo	Há Dias Assim	Augusto Madureira	Augusto Madureira	89
5Q	7	Serbia	Milan Stanković	Ovo Je Balkan	Goran Bregović, Marina Tucaković & Ljiljana Jorgovanović	Goran Bregović	79
6Q	12	Albania	Juliana Pasha	It's All About You	Pirro Çako	Ardit Gjebrea	76
7Q	2	Russia	Peter Nalitch & Friends	Lost And Forgotten	Peter Nalitch	Peter Nalitch	74
8Q	8	Bosnia & H	Vukašin Brajić	Thunder And Lightning	Dino Šaran	Dino Šaran	59
9Q	16	Belarus	3+2	Butterflies	Malka Chaplin	Maxim Fadeev	59
10Q	1	Moldova	Sunstroke Project & Olia Tira	Run Away	Alina Galetskaya	Anton Ragoza & Sergey Stepanov	52
11	5	Finland	Kuunkuiskaajat	Työlki Ellää	Timo Kiiskinen	Timo Kiiskinen	49
12	11	Malta	Thea Garrett	My Dream	Sunny Aquilina	Jason Cassar	45
13	9	Poland	Marcin Mroziński	Legenda	Marcin Mroziński	Marcin Nierubiec	44
14	3	Estonia	Malcolm Lincoln	Siren	Robin Juhkental	Robin Juhkental	39
15	15	FYR Macedonia	Gjoko Taneski	Jas Ja Imam Silata	Kristijan Gabroski	Kristijan Gabroski	37
16	4	Slovakia	Kristina Pelakova	Horehronie	Kamil Peteraj	Martin Kavulic	24
17	6	Latvia	Aisha	What For?	Guntars Racs	Janis Lusens	11

2010 Eurovision 55: Oslo, Norway

Semi-final 1: 25 May 2010

	Albania	Belarus	Belgium	Bosnia & H	Estonia	Finland	France	FYR Macedonia	Germany	Greece	Iceland	Latvia	Malta	Moldova	Poland	Portugal	Russia	Serbia	Slovakia	Spain	TOTAL
Moldova	3	10	2	2			3	7		4			7			8	5	1		5	52
Russia	7	12	5			3			1	3		10	1	12	8	1		4			74
Estonia	6	1		1	12	12				1	2	12			5	4					39
Slovakia	4		1	5	2	2					5										24
Finland	2	7	7		10				3		6	6	2		1	5	3		2	2	49
Latvia					6	5															11
Serbia	3	4	3	12	1		12	10	4	7	3	3	3	3		2	4			6	79
Bosnia & Herzegovina	7	3	6				6	8	7	5				1	6		2	12	6	5	59
Poland	6	8		4			7				4	4	3	2		6	6		3		44
Belgium	4	2		6	8	10	10	4	12	10	12	8	12	6	12	12	10	7	10	8	167
Malta	2	2	8	7	3	1			2	2	4	1				3		2	12	1	45
Albania								6			10		6		4					4	76
Greece	10	5	8	8	2	4	2	12	5	12	8		8	7	7	10	7	10	8	10	133
Portugal	5		10	3	5	8	4	3	8		7	7	4	5	2			5	4	12	89
FYR Macedonia	12		4	10		6	8	2			1			4			1	8	1		37
Belarus		6			4		1	5	6	6		5	5	8	3	7	12	3	3	3	59
Iceland	8		12		7	7	5	1		8	1	2	10	10	10	6	8	3	7	7	123

133

2010 Eurovision 55: Oslo, Norway — Semi-final 2: 27 May 2010

Votes are cast by countries participating in each semi-final plus the four automatically qualifying countries decided by draw: Germany, France & Spain in semi-final 1, United Kingdom in semi-final 2. The hosts, Norway, were drawn to vote in semi-final 2. Points awarded are the combined totals of the televoting and jury votes. The top 10 countries in each semi-final qualify for the final.

Rank	Start	Country	Artist	Song	Writer	Composer	POINTS
1Q	17	Turkey	maNga	We Could Be The Same	Evren Özdemir, maNga, Fiona Movery Akıncı	maNga	118
2Q	7	Azerbaijan	Safura	Drip Drop	Sandra Bjurman	Anders Bagge, Stefan Örn	113
3Q	16	Georgia	Sofia Nizharadze	Shine	Hanne Sorvaag, Harry Sommerdahl & Christian Leuzzi	Hanne Sorvaag, Harry Sommerdahl & Christian Leuzzi	106
4Q	10	Romania	Paula Seling & Ovi	Playing With Fire	Ovidiu Cernăuțeanu	Ovidiu Cernăuțeanu	104
5Q	4	Denmark	Chanée & N'evergreen	In A Moment Like This	Thomas G:son, Henrik Sethsson & Erik Bernholm	Thomas G:son, Henrik Sethsson & Erik Bernholm	101
6Q	2	Armenia	Eva Rivas	Apricot Stone	Karen Kavaleryan	Armen Martirosyan	83
7Q	8	Ukraine	Alyosha	Sweet People	Olena Kucher	Olena Kucher, Borys Kukoba & Vadim Lisitsa	77
8Q	3	Israel	Harel Skaat	Milim	Noam Horev	Tomer Adaddi	71
9Q	12	Ireland	Niamh Kavanagh	It's For You	Niall Mooney, Mårten Eriksson, Jonas Gladnikoff & Lina Eriksson	Niall Mooney, Mårten Eriksson, Jonas Gladnikoff & Lina Eriksson	67
10Q	14	Cyprus	Jon Lilygreen & The Islanders	Life Looks Better In Spring	Nasos Lambrianides	Nasos Lambrianides, Melis Konstantinou	67
11	6	Sweden	Anna Bergendahl	This Is My Life	Kristian Lagerström	Bobby Ljunggren	62
12	1	Lithuania	InCulto	East European Funk	InCulto	InCulto	44
13	15	Croatia	Feminnem	Lako Je Sve	Neda Parmać, Pamela Ramljak	Branimir Mihaljević	33
14	9	Netherlands	Sieneke	Ik Ben Verliefd (Sha-la-lie)	Pierre Kartner	Pierre Kartner	29
15	13	Bulgaria	Miro	Angel Si Ti	Miroslav Kostadinov	Miroslav Kostadinov	19
16	11	Slovenia	Ansambel Žlindra & Kalamari	Narodnozabavni Rock	Leon Oblak	Marino Legovič	6
17	5	Switzerland	Michael von der Heide	Il Pleut de L'Or	Michael von der Heide, Heike Kospach, André Grüter	Michael von der Heide, Pele Loriano	2

2010 Eurovision 55: Oslo, Norway

Semi-final 2: 27 May 2010

	Armenia	Azerbaijan	Bulgaria	Croatia	Cyprus	Denmark	Georgia	Greece	Iceland	Ireland	Lithuania	Netherlands	Romania	Slovenia	Sweden	Switzerland	Turkey	Ukraine	United Kingdom	TOTAL
Lithuania	2			1	2	1	8		5	12					4	3	2	2	7	44
Armenia		7	8		12		10	12			1	10	10		5	3	4	8		83
Israel	8		1		4		5	7	7	4	5	12	3	5	8	5	6	6	5	71
Denmark	5	6	2	4	3		3	7	8			4	12	10	12			5		101
Switzerland							2													2
Sweden	3	2		2	1	12		5	12	5	3	6	1			10	2		3	62
Azerbaijan			7	10	10	5	12		2	10	2	1	8	8	3	6	12	12		113
Ukraine	10	8	6	6	6	3	7	2	4	2	10	2	5	1			3		2	77
Netherlands						4	1	4	3	3				6		2	5			29
Romania	4	5	4		8	8	4	8	10	6	6	3		4	7	4	8	3	12	104
Slovenia				5				1												6
Ireland	1	4		3		6		3	6		7	8	4	2		12	1	1	10	67
Bulgaria					5												7		6	19
Cyprus	6	3	5	12		7		10		4	4		6		6			4	4	67
Croatia	7	1	3			2				1				12		7				33
Georgia	12	10	10	7	7		6	6		7	12	5	2	7	2	1	10	7	1	106
Turkey		12	12	8		10	6		1	8	8	7	7	3	10	8		10	8	118

2010 Eurovision 55: Oslo, Norway

Final: 29 May 2010

Final qualification rules: Top 10 placed countries from each semi-final. Automatic qualification: United Kingdom, France, Germany, Spain, Norway.
Points awarded are the combined totals of the televoting and jury votes from each of the 39 participating countries.

Rank	Start	Country	Artist	Song	Writer	Composer	POINTS
1	22	Germany	Lena Meyer-Landrut	Satellite	Julie Frost & John Gordon	Julie Frost & John Gordon	246
2	14	Turkey	maNga	We Could Be The Same	Evren Özdemir, maNga, Fiona Movery Akıncı	maNga	170
3	19	Romania	Paula Seling & Ovi	Playing With Fire	Ovidiu Cernăuțeanu	Ovidiu Cernăuțeanu	162
4	25	Denmark	Chanée & N'evergreen	In A Moment Like This	Thomas G:son, Henrik Sethsson & Erik Bernholm	Thomas G:son, Henrik Sethsson & Erik Bernholm	149
5	1	Azerbaijan	Safura	Drip Drop	Sandra Bjurman	Anders Bagge, Stefan Örn	145
6	7	Belgium	Tom Dice	Me And My Guitar	Tom Dice, Jeroen Swinnen & Ashley Hicklin	Tom Dice, Jeroen Swinnen & Ashley Hicklin	143
7	21	Armenia	Eva Rivas	Apricot Stone	Karen Kavaleryan	Armen Martirosyan	141
8	11	Greece	Giorgos Alkaios & Friends	OPA	Giannis Antoniou & Friends	Giorgos Alkaios	140
9	13	Georgia	Sofia Nizharadze	Shine	Hanne Sorvaag, Harry Sommerdahl & Christian Leuzzi	Hanne Sorvaag, Harry Sommerdahl & Christian Leuzzi	136
10	17	Ukraine	Alyosha	Sweet People	Olena Kucher	Olena Kucher, Borys Kukoba & Vadim Lisitsa	108
11	20	Russia	Peter Nalitch & Friends	Lost And Forgotten	Peter Nalitch	Peter Nalitch	90
12	18	France	Jessy Matador	Allez Olla Olé	H Ducamin & J Ballue	H Ducamin & J Ballue	82
13	8	Serbia	Milan Stanković	Ovo Je Balkan	Goran Bregović, Marina Tucaković & Ljiljana Jorgovanović	Goran Bregović	72
14	24	Israel	Harel Skaat	Milim	Noam Horev	Tomer Adaddi	71
15	2	Spain	Daniel Diges	Algo Pequeñito (Something Tiny)	Jesús Cañadilla, Luis Miguel de la Varga, Alberto Jodar, Daniel Diges	Jesús Cañadilla, Luis Miguel de la Varga, Alberto Jodar, Daniel Diges	68
16	15	Albania	Juliana Pasha	It's All About You	Pirro Çako	Ardit Gjebrea	62
17	6	Bosnia & H	Vukašin Brajić	Thunder And Lightning	Dino Šaran	Dino Šaran	51
18	23	Portugal	Filipa Azevedo	Há Dias Assim	Augusto Madureira	Augusto Madureira	43
19	16	Iceland	Hera Björk	Je Ne Sais Quoi	Örlygur Smári & Hera Björk	Örlygur Smári & Hera Björk	41
20	3	Norway	Didrik Solli-Tangen	My Heart Is Yours	Hanne Sørvaag & Fredrik Kempe	Hanne Sørvaag & Fredrik Kempe	35
21	5	Cyprus	Jon Lilygreen & The Islanders	Life Looks Better In Spring	Nasos Lambrianides	Nasos Lambrianides, Melis Konstantinou	27
22	4	Moldova	Sunstroke Project & Olia Tira	Run Away	Alina Galetskaya	Anton Ragoza & Sergey Stepanov	27
23	10	Ireland	Niamh Kavanagh	It's For You	Niall Mooney, Mårten Eriksson, Jonas Gladnikoff & Lina Eriksson	Niall Mooney, Mårten Eriksson, Jonas Gladnikoff & Lina Eriksson	25
24	9	Belarus	3+2	Butterflies	Malka Chaplin	Maxim Fadeev	18
25	12	United Kingdom	Josh Dubovie	That Sounds Good To Me	Pete Waterman, Mike Stock, Steve Crosby	Pete Waterman, Mike Stock, Steve Crosby	10

2010 Eurovision 55: Oslo, Norway — Final: 29 May 2010

Receiving ↓ / Voting →	Albania	Armenia	Azerbaijan	Belarus	Belgium	Bosnia & H	Bulgaria	Croatia	Cyprus	Denmark	Estonia	Finland	France	FYR Macedonia	Georgia	Germany	Greece	Iceland	Ireland	Israel	Latvia	Lithuania	Malta	Moldova	Netherlands	Norway	Poland	Portugal	Romania	Russia	Serbia	Slovakia	Slovenia	Spain	Sweden	Switzerland	Turkey	Ukraine	United Kingdom	TOTAL
Voting announcement order	5	39	15	29	31	9	22	7	27	18	12	10	19	35	37	3	16	17	2	34	24	28	25	36	33	26	8	14	1	13	4	21	11	20	38	30	6	23	32	
Azerbaijan		7		6	5	7	12		10	2		4		3	8		1	4	3	7	2	8	12	7		7	8	12	2	8				7		2	12	12		**145**
Spain	7	7			1		2						5		2					1	5			4				3	2	4		5						4		**68**
Norway	2		6	4						5	7			6									3					6	10		3				4					**35**
Moldova							4	4	10	1				1	1							1									2									**27**
Cyprus	6															12													10					3	3		8			**27**
Bosnia & Herzegovina	3						4	10	1	10	3	6	7	6				10	10			1		3			10		4	5	10	12	4			7		1		**51**
Belgium						12		8	1				10	7											1			5				5	8	5						**143**
Serbia	12				12	4	1	1	12		2	1		5	3	2				6						1			7	5	10			5		6	3		7	**72**
Belarus	1	2																						3				1		2								7	12	**18**
Ireland	8	12	8	7	4	4	6	7	5	6	8	3	12	10	5	10	5	2	5		12	4		5	8	1	4	8	7	3		3	2	1	6	1	5	8		**25**
Greece			12		3	3	10	12						12	10	1	10	7	1	10	4			12	1	4	2		1		3		2		5	8	5	7		**140**
United Kingdom		2						5		3	4	5	2		7	4		7					6			6														**10**
Georgia			10	2	8		7		6	7	12	8				3		6		2	7		2	8	7	4	3	10	5	7	7	4	3	1	6	1	1			**136**
Turkey	10	1	10		4	3	8	12		1		3	12	10	5	1	10	5	1	8	3	4	5	12		3	6		6	3		6	2	1	5	3		2	2	**170**
Albania					3	5		5						12				8			8				8		2	2			6				5	8	4			**62**
Iceland		2	8							3	4	5					3		4		10	10	6	6	6				1						8	7	4	10	1	**41**
Ukraine	8	10	10				7		6	3		2	2		7	3		6	5	2		6		8		4	3	7	5			7		1			1		5	**108**
France	6					3		3	3	7	6	3	4			8	8	6	5	3			2			4			6	12	4	4	3	2					2	**82**
Romania	5	1	7	1	2		8		8	8		1		8	4			5	7			4	5	12		10	6	10		3	1	6	7	10	10	4	2	2	8	**162**
Russia		10	3	12		5					10				10					10	8	5		10		2		2			6						4	10		**90**
Armenia		4	5	5				8		7			6		10					12			4				5	7	6	12	4	1	6	8	1		6	6	5	**141**
Germany	10				10	8	3	6	4	12	12	12	3	8			2	3	8		12	10	8	6	4	12	12	1	3	6	12	8	10	12	12	12	10	5	4	**246**
Portugal	4					1				4			8		6		1	1			6		1									2	6	6	5					**43**
Israel	4	5		8	2				2		10		1	2		6								1	10	5			12	1	8		6	4				3	3	**71**
Denmark	2	5	4				2	2			5	2		2				12	12	4			8		2	8	12	4	12		7		12	4	8			6	6	**149**

2011 Eurovision 56: Düsseldorf, Germany

Semi-final 1: 10 May 2011

Votes are cast by countries participating in each semi-final plus the five automatically qualifying countries decided by draw: United Kingdom and Spain in semi-final 1, France, Germany and Italy in semi-final 2. Points awarded are based on the combined votes of the viewers and jury from each country voting in this semi-final. The top 10 countries in each semi-final qualify for the final.

Rank	Start	Country	Artist	Song	Writer	Composer	POINTS
1Q	19	Greece	Loucas Yiorkas feat Stereo Mike	Watch My Dance	Eleana Vrachali	Giannis Christodoulopoulos	133
2Q	18	Azerbaijan	Ell/Nikki	Running Scared	Stefan Örn, Sandra Bjurman	Stefan Örn, Sandra Bjurman, Iain Farquharson	122
3Q	10	Finland	Paradise Oskar	Da Da Dam	Axel Ehnström	Axel Ehnström	103
4Q	14	Iceland	Sjonni's Friends	Coming Home	Thorunn Clausen & Sjonni Brink	Sjonni Brink	100
5Q	17	Lithuania	Evelina Sašenko	C'est Ma Vie	Andrius Kairys	Paulius Zdanavičius	81
6Q	9	Georgia	Eldrine	One More Day	DJ Rock, Mikheil Chelidze	Beso Tsikhelashvili	74
7Q	15	Hungary	Kati Wolf	What About My Dreams?	Péter Geszti, Johnny K Palmer	Viktor Rakonczai, Gergő Rácz	72
8Q	6	Serbia	Nina	Čaroban	Kristina Kovač	Kristina Kovač	67
9Q	7	Russia	Alexej Vorobjov	Get You	Alexej Vorobjov, Nadir Khayat, AJ Junior, Bilal Hajji, Eric Sanicola	Alexej Vorobjov, Nadir Khayat, AJ Junior, Bilal Hajji, Eric Sanicola	64
10Q	8	Switzerland	Anna Rossinelli	In Love For A While	David Klein	David Klein	55
11	11	Malta	Glen Vella	One Life	Fleur Balzan	Paul Giordimaina	54
12	4	Armenia	Emmy	Boom Boom	Sosi Khanikyan	Hayk Harutyunyan, Hayk Hovhannisyan	54
13	5	Turkey	Yüksek Sadakat	Live It Up	Ergün Arsal	Kutlu Özmakinaci	47
14	3	Albania	Aurela Gaçe	Feel The Passion	Sokol Marsi	Shpetim Saraci	47
15	13	Croatia	Daria	Celebrate	Boris Djurdjevic & Marina Mudrinić	Boris Djurdjevic	41
16	12	San Marino	Senit	Stand By	Radiosa Romani	Radiosa Romani	34
17	2	Norway	Stella Mwangi	Haba Haba	Stella Mwangi	Big City/Beyond51	30
18	16	Portugal	Homens Da Luta	Luta É Alegria	Nuno Duarte	Vasco Duarte	22
19	1	Poland	Magdalena Tul	Jestem	Magdalena Tul	Magdalena Tul	18

2011 Eurovision 56: Düsseldorf, Germany

Semi-final 1: 10 May 2011

	Albania	Armenia	Azerbaijan	Croatia	Finland	Georgia	Greece	Hungary	Iceland	Lithuania	Malta	Norway	Poland	Portugal	Russia	San Marino	Serbia	Spain	Switzerland	Turkey	United Kingdom	TOTAL
Poland	1	1	1			4		4		2		3		2					2		5	18
Norway		1	2		8				10		4		1	2					2			30
Albania				7			12									8			6	8		47
Armenia			12			8	8		4		7					7		3		7	1	54
Turkey	12		5	12	7	3					2	7	2			10			5			47
Serbia	2	12		5	3	5	3	3	5	3	3	4		1	4	3		2	12	3		67
Russia	3	3		2	6			8	3	5		6	6	3		1	6				2	64
Switzerland			3					1	6	6			3	5		2	2	6				55
Georgia		8	7	3	1		10	6		12	8	12	5	8	5	2	4		10	10	6	74
Finland		6	7			6		2	12	7		2	10		12		3	4		1		103
Malta	6	7	4	4				6		1				8		12	5			2		54
San Marino	8	5	7	1		1	2	2			6									5		34
Croatia	7		4		10			12	1	8	12	10	4	10	1	4	12	12	8		7	41
Iceland		2		6	12		6		7		1	5	12		3	8	8	10	8	6	10	100
Hungary							5						8	6	7		10	10	4		3	72
Portugal	4					2	1		2			8			10	5		8	3			22
Lithuania		4			2	10	4	5	8		10	1	12	7	6	6	1	5	3	12	12	81
Azerbaijan	5			10	5	12	7	7		10	5		8	12	10	5		1	1	12	4	122
Greece	10	10		8	4	7		10	4	4			7		6	6	7	7	7	4	8	133

139

2011 Eurovision 56: Düsseldorf, Germany — Semi-final 2: 12 May 2011

Votes are cast by countries participating in each semi-final plus the five automatically qualifying countries decided by draw: United Kingdom and Spain in semi-final 1, France, Germany and Italy in semi-final 2. Points awarded are based on the combined votes of the viewers and jury from each country voting in this semi-final. The top 10 countries in each semi-final qualify for the final.

Rank	Start	Country	Artist	Song	Writer	Composer	POINTS
1Q	8	Sweden	Eric Saade	Popular	Fredrik Kempe	Fredrik Kempe	155
2Q	18	Denmark	A Friend in London	New Tomorrow	Lise Cabble, Jakob Schack Glæsner	Lise Cabble, Jakob Schack Glæsner	135
3Q	13	Slovenia	Maja Keuc	No One	Urša Vlašič	Matjaž Vlašič	112
4Q	14	Romania	Hotel FM	Change	Alexandra Ivan, Gabriel Băruța	Gabriel Băruța	111
5Q	1	Bosnia & H	Dino Merlin	Love in Rewind	Dino Merlin	Dino Merlin	109
6Q	6	Ukraine	Mika Newton	Angel	Maryna Skomorohova	Ruslan Kvinta	81
7Q	2	Austria	Nadine Beiler	The Secret is Love	Nadine Beiler	Thomas Rabitsch	69
8Q	19	Ireland	Jedward	Lipstick	Daniel Priddy, Lars Halvor Jensen, Martin Michael Larsson	Daniel Priddy, Lars Halvor Jensen, Martin Michael Larsson	68
9Q	15	Estonia	Getter Jaani	Rockefeller Street	Sven Lõhmus	Sven Lõhmus	60
10Q	7	Moldova	Zdob și Zdub	So Lucky	Andy Schuman, Marc Elsner	Mihai Gincu, Marc Elsner	54
11	4	Belgium	Witloof Bay	With Love Baby	Benoît Giaux, RoxorLoops	Benoît Giaux, RoxorLoops	53
12	10	Bulgaria	Poli Genova	Na Inat	Sebastian Arman, David Bronner, Borislav Milanov, Poli Genova	Sebastian Arman, David Bronner, Borislav Milanov, Poli Genova	48
13	5	Slovakia	TWiiNS	I'm Still Alive	Bryan Todd, Sandra Nordstrom, Branislav Jancich	Bryan Todd, Sandra Nordstrom, Branislav Jancich	48
14	16	Belarus	Anastasiya Vinnikova	I Love Belarus	Eugene Oleinik, Svetlana Geraskova	Eugene Oleinik	45
15	12	Israel	Dana International	Ding Dong	Dana International	Dana International	38
16	11	FYR Macedonia	Vlatko Ilievski	Rusinka	Marko Marinkovikj-Slatkaristika, Jovan Jovanov	Grigor Koprov, Vladimir Dojchinovski	36
17	17	Latvia	Musiqq	Angel in Disguise	Marats Ogleznevs	Marats Ogleznevs	25
18	9	Cyprus	Christos Mylordos	San Aggelos S'Agapisa	Mihalis Antoniou	Andreas Anastasiou	16
19	3	The Netherlands	3JS	Never Alone	Jaap Kwakman, Jan Dulles, Jaap de Witte	Jaap Kwakman, Jan Dulles, Jaap de Witte	13

2011 Eurovision 56: Düsseldorf, Germany — Semi-final 2: 12 May 2011

	Austria	Belarus	Belgium	Bosnia & H	Bulgaria	Cyprus	Denmark	Estonia	France	FYR Macedonia	Germany	Ireland	Israel	Italy	Latvia	Moldova	Netherlands	Romania	Slovakia	Slovenia	Sweden	Ukraine	TOTAL
Bosnia & Herzegovina	12		4			4	7		10	12	7	2	1	4	2		10		12	12	8	4	109
Austria		5		7	10		5	2	1		12	2	1	5			3		5	7	4	1	69
Netherlands			8		5																		13
Belgium	1			8	6	2		1	6			5	2	2	3	6	6	8		2			53
Slovakia	3	3	3	6	3	5	1	7		3				6		7			10	3		12	48
Ukraine	3	12		4						6	5	4	8	7	1	8		2	4	6	3		81
Moldova		10			2								4	3	7		12	12					54
Sweden	10	8	12	5		12	12	12	12	5	1	8	12			3	12	7	7	5		5	155
Cyprus											2			8								6	16
Bulgaria	2		1			10	4		3	1	4	1	3	10		5	2			4	1		48
FYR Macedonia		7		10						7				1		1				8		7	36
Israel		6	2			1	8	5	7	10	3	6			4	4	5	4			5		38
Slovenia	8			12	8	7	6	6	5	4	6	3	6	12	5	12	8	10	8		7		112
Romania	6		10		1	8	3		8			10	7		8		4		6		6	8	111
Estonia	5	1	6		4				4	8	8		5			12			1				60
Belarus	4			2		3	2	4				7			6	10		1			6	10	45
Latvia		2						8								2					2		25
Denmark	7	4	7	1	12	6		10	2		10	12	10		12	2	7	5	3	10	12	3	135
Ireland			5	3	7		10	3			8				10		1	6	2	1	10	2	68

141

2011 Eurovision 56: Düsseldorf, Germany

Final: 14 May 2011

Final qualification rules: Top 10 placed countries from each semi-final. Automatic qualification: United Kingdom, France, Germany, Spain, Italy.
Points awarded are based on the combined votes of the viewers and jury from each of the 43 participating countries.

Rank	Start	Country	Artist	Song	Writer	Composer	POINTS
1	19	Azerbaijan	Ell/Nikki	Running Scared	Stefan Örn, Sandra Bjurman	Stefan Örn, Sandra Bjurman, Iain Farquharson	221
2	12	Italy	Raphael Gualazzi	Madness of Love	Raphael Gualazzi	Raphael Gualazzi	189
3	7	Sweden	Eric Saade	Popular	Fredrik Kempe	Fredrik Kempe	185
4	23	Ukraine	Mika Newton	Angel	Maryna Skomorohova	Ruslan Kvinta	159
5	3	Denmark	A Friend in London	New Tomorrow	Lise Cabble, Jakob Schack Glæsner	Lise Cabble, Jakob Schack Glæsner	134
6	2	Bosnia & H	Dino Merlin	Love in Rewind	Dino Merlin	Dino Merlin	125
7	9	Greece	Loucas Yiorkas feat Stereo Mike	Watch My Dance	Eleana Vrachali	Giannis Christodoulopoulos	120
8	6	Ireland	Jedward	Lipstick	Daniel Priddy, Lars Halvor Jensen, Martin Michael Larsson	Daniel Priddy, Lars Halvor Jensen, Martin Michael Larsson	119
9	25	Georgia	Eldrine	One More Day	DJ Rock, Mikheil Chelidze	Beso Tsikhelashvili	110
10	16	Germany	Lena Meyer-Landrut	Taken by a Stranger	Gus Seyffert, Nicole Morier, Monica Birkenes	Gus Seyffert, Nicole Morier, Monica Birkenes	107
11	14	United Kingdom	Blue	I Can	Ciaron Bell, Ben Collier, Ian Hope, Duncan James, Liam Keenan, Lee Ryan, StarSign	Ciaron Bell, Ben Collier, Ian Hope, Duncan James, Liam Keenan, Lee Ryan, StarSign	100
12	15	Moldova	Zdob și Zdub	So Lucky	Andy Schuman, Marc Elsner	Mihai Gincu, Marc Elsner	97
13	20	Slovenia	Maja Keuc	No One	Urša Vlašič	Matjaž Vlašič	96
14	24	Serbia	Nina	Čaroban	Kristina Kovač	Kristina Kovač	85
15	11	France	Amaury Vassili	Sognu	Jean-Pierre Marcellesi, Julie Miller	Daniel Moyne, Quentin Bachelet	82
16	10	Russia	Alexej Vorobjov	Get You	Alexej Vorobjov, Nadir Khayat, AJ Junior, Bilal Hajji, Eric Sanicola	Alexej Vorobjov, Nadir Khayat, AJ Junior, Bilal Hajji, Eric Sanicola	77
17	17	Romania	Hotel FM	Change	Alexandra Ivan, Gabriel Băruţa	Gabriel Băruţa	77
18	18	Austria	Nadine Beiler	The Secret is Love	Nadine Beiler	Thomas Rabitsch	64
19	4	Lithuania	Evelina Sašenko	C'est Ma Vie	Andrius Kairys	Paulius Zdanavičius	63
20	21	Iceland	Sjonni's Friends	Coming Home	Thorunn Clausen & Sjonni Brink	Sjonni Brink	61
21	1	Finland	Paradise Oskar	Da Da Dam	Axel Ehnström	Axel Ehnström	57
22	5	Hungary	Kati Wolf	What About My Dreams?	Péter Geszti, Johnny K Palmer	Viktor Rakonczai, Gergő Rácz	53
23	22	Spain	Lucía Pérez	Que Me Quiten Lo Bailao	Rafael Artesero	Rafael Artesero	50
24	8	Estonia	Getter Jaani	Rockefeller Street	Sven Lõhmus	Sven Lõhmus	44
25	13	Switzerland	Anna Rossinelli	In Love For A While	David Klein	David Klein	19

142

2011 Eurovision 56: Düsseldorf, Germany — Final: 14 May 2011

Order votes announced	Albania	Armenia	Austria	Azerbaijan	Belarus	Belgium	Bosnia & H	Bulgaria	Croatia	Cyprus	Denmark	Estonia	Finland	France	FYR Macedonia	Georgia	Germany	Greece	Hungary	Iceland	Ireland	Israel	Italy	Latvia	Lithuania	Malta	Moldova	Netherlands	Norway	Poland	Portugal	Romania	Russia	San Marino	Serbia	Slovakia	Slovenia	Spain	Sweden	Switzerland	Turkey	Ukraine	United Kingdom	TOTAL
	31	9	15	20	29	42	36	2	28	5	14	40	7	26	10	25	19	24	34	11	37	39	4	43	35	32	41	3	8	16	33	30	1	18	27	12	21	38	17	23	22	6	13	
Finland											5	7					2		10		3				1				12	5									7					57
Bosnia & Herzegovina	7		12		1								12		12		7	7		10			4					8	4					4	12		12		8	5	10		5	125
Denmark						5		7	7	3		10	10	5				3		12	12	12		6	5			12	7	3		1	2	4		6	8		10	12	10		6	134
Lithuania									2							12						10		7				12	3	12			1		7	6	8	1						63
Hungary			2	2								12	12	2						5										1	6				8			6	5					53
Ireland			4			7		3			12	10					8			4				10		8		5	10	1	6	7	3	1				7	12			4	12	119
Sweden	4		3	4	4	4	5		4	10	10	12	6	10	6	1		6	10	7	4	12		4	6	6	3	10	10			3	1	6	1	10	4	5		1	4	1	3	185
Estonia					2	2					2		7				8				7	5		10	4	8	6															2		44
Greece	10	7		8		8		10		12					3	6			8			8	2		6		1					8	8	8	3					2		6		120
Russia	4	8		4	5			4		2		5			4	4	5	1	3	1				4	7		5		2				8	4		10			12			8		77
France	2	5		12		12	4		6	7		4			1	2		12					1	1	1	1	2						3	12								5		82
Italy	12	6	6	1	3	6	6			1		6	4	8		7		10	4	3				12	10	10				10	2		3	12	2		3	10		4			7	189
Switzerland																																			5	4							10	19
United Kingdom	6	2		5	2			12		4	3	1	1		1	5		2		2	2	6	10	5	3	7	4	7	5		3		4	2			1				6	3	8	100
Moldova		5	10	7	7	1								4							8		8	8	4							12	7			5		7	6		7	7		97
Germany			10		8	5	3		1	8	8	8		3		5	4	4		6		1	6	8	2	2		7									7	3	6	8	3	7	8	107
Romania			1	6		10		6			4	1	1	3					1		1		12	8	8	12	12	4										8	4		5			77
Austria		3					7	5	3		1		1		2		12		2		16		5		2		4	1		4						3	5		4	7	1	2		64
Azerbaijan	8		8		6	3	8		10	8	8	8	5	6		8		5	7	8		4		2	8	12	10	6		8	8	10	12	10		7			3	1	12	10	2	221
Slovenia			3				12		12	6	7	2			10		1		6		2	3		3	3	3	2				1	4	5	1	10	1		5			2			96
Iceland							1				6		8						12				5						8		4							2	1	10		4	4	61
Spain	5													12	4																12									3			1	50
Ukraine	3	12		12	10			8	5	5		7			7	10		7					7	5	12		8		6	2	7	2	10	6	6	12	6	2	2		7			159
Serbia	1	1	7		12		10		8				2	8				3										6	6	6				5		10	10			6				85
Georgia		10		10	12			1			3							8	5			2			12		7			7			6	7			4				8	12		110

2012 Eurovision 57: Baku, Azerbaijan

Semi-final 1: 22 May 2012

Votes are cast by countries participating in each semi-final plus the five automatically qualifying countries decided by draw: Italy and Spain in semi-final 1, France, Germany and the United Kingdom in semi-final 2. Hosts Azerbaijan voted in semi-final 1. Points awarded are based on the combined votes of the viewers and jury from each of the countries voting in this semi-final. The top 10 countries in each semi-final qualify for the final.

Rank	Start	Country	Artist	Song	Writer	Composer	POINTS
1Q	14	Russia	Buranovskiye Babushki	Party for Everybody	Olga Tuktareva, Mary S Applegate	Viktor Drobysh, Timofei Leontiev	152
2Q	5	Albania	Rona Nishliu	Suus	Rona Nishliu	Florent Boshnjaku	146
3Q	6	Romania	Mandinga	Zaleilah	Elena Ionescu, Dihigo Omar Secada, Costi Ionita	Costi Ionita	120
4Q	3	Greece	Eleftheria Eleftheriou	Aphrodisiac	Dimitri Stassos, Mikaela Stenström, Dajana Lööf	Dimitri Stassos, Mikaela Stenström, Dajana Lööf	116
5Q	17	Moldova	Pasha Parfeny	Lăutar	Pasha Parfeny	Pasha Parfeny, Alex Brashovean	100
6Q	18	Ireland	Jedward	Waterline	Nick Jarl & Sharon Vaughn	Nick Jarl & Sharon Vaughn	92
7Q	12	Cyprus	Ivi Adamou	La La Love	Alexandra Zakka, Björn Djupström, Alexandra Zakka & Viktor Svensson	Alex Papaconstantinou, Björn Djupström, Alexandra Zakka & Viktor Svensson	91
8Q	2	Iceland	Greta Salóme & Jónsi	Never Forget	Gréta Salóme	Gréta Salóme	75
9Q	13	Denmark	Soluna Samay	Should've Known Better	Chief 1, Remee & Isam B	Chief 1 & Remee	63
10Q	15	Hungary	Compact Disco	Sound of Our Hearts	Behnam Lotfi, Gábor Pál, Attila Sándor, Csaba Walkó	Behnam Lotfi, Gábor Pál, Attila Sándor, Csaba Walkó	52
11	7	Switzerland	Sinplus	Unbreakable	Gabriel Broggini, Ivan Broggini	Gabriel Broggini, Ivan Broggini	45
12	9	Finland	Pernilla	När Jag Blundar	Jonas Karlsson	Jonas Karlsson	41
13	10	Israel	Izabo	Time	Ran Shem-Tov & Shiri Hadar	Ran Shem-Tov & Shiri Hadar	33
14	11	San Marino	Valentina Monetta	The Social Network Song (Oh Oh - Uh - Oh Oh)	Timothy Touchton & José Santana Rodriguez	Ralph Siegel	31
15	1	Montenegro	Rambo Amadeus	Euro Neuro	Rambo Amadeus	Rambo Amadeus	20
16	4	Latvia	Anmary	Beautiful Song	Rolands Ūdris	Ivars Makstnieks	17
17	8	Belgium	Iris	Would You?	Nina Sampermans, Jean Bosco Safari, Walter Mannaerts	Nina Sampermans, Jean Bosco Safari, Walter Mannaerts	16
18	16	Austria	Trackshittaz	Woki Mit Deim Popo	Lukas Plöchl, Manuel Hoffelner	Lukas Plöchl	8

2012 Eurovision 57: Baku, Azerbaijan

Semi-final 1: 22 May 2012

	Albania	Austria	Azerbaijan	Belgium	Cyprus	Denmark	Finland	Greece	Hungary	Iceland	Ireland	Israel	Italy	Latvia	Moldova	Montenegro	Romania	Russia	San Marino	Spain	Switzerland	TOTAL
Montenegro	12																		8			20
Iceland		2		5	8	10	10	5	4			4	1	5	2	5		1	3	6	4	75
Greece	8	1	10	8	12	4				5	10	3	5		10	10	12	5	7	3	3	116
Latvia			3								4				4	2		4				17
Albania		12	12	10	10	7	5	10	10	3	1	5	12	4	1	12	4	2	10	4	12	146
Romania	5	5	7	4	6	1		8	3	4	12	8	10	7	12	7		8	6	12	2	120
Switzerland	3	3			2				8	2		1	8		8		2		1			45
Belgium						8	2				6											16
Finland	1			1	1	3			12		3	2		1								41
Israel		7						3		7						4	5	6		2	1	33
San Marino	10		5	3			3	2	5	12	5	10	3	3		6	7	7				31
Cyprus	6		1				1	12	7	8	7	12	7	8	6	8	3	3	4	8	10	91
Denmark		10		4	4		8	1		6	8		6	12	5		6			7		63
Russia	7	4	8	12	7	12	12	7				6	2				8		2			152
Hungary			2	6		5	4			1												52
Austria				2																		8
Moldova	4	6	6		5	6	6	6	2		2	6	4	2		3	10	12	5	10	6	100
Ireland		8	4	7	3	2	7	3	6	10		7		10		1		10	12	5	7	92

2012 Eurovision 57: Baku, Azerbaijan
Semi-final 2: 24 May 2012

Votes are cast by countries participating in each semi-final plus the five automatically qualifying countries decided by draw: Italy and Spain in semi-final 1, France, Germany and the United Kingdom in semi-final 2. Hosts Azerbaijan voted in semi-final 1. Points awarded are based on the combined votes of the viewers and jury from each of the countries voting in this semi-final. The top 10 countries in each semi-final qualify for the final.

Rank	Start	Country	Artist	Song	Writer	Composer	POINTS
1Q	11	Sweden	Loreen	Euphoria	Thomas G:son & Peter Boström	Thomas G:son & Peter Boström	181
2Q	1	Serbia	Željko Joksimović	Nije Ljubav Stvar	Marina Tucaković & Miloš Roganović	Željko Joksimović	159
3Q	18	Lithuania	Donny Montell	Love is Blind	Brandon Stone & Jodie Rose	Brandon Stone	107
4Q	14	Estonia	Ott Lepland	Kuula	Aapo Ilves	Ott Lepland	100
5Q	13	Turkey	Can Bonomo	Love Me Back	Can Bonomo	Can Bonomo	80
6Q	17	Bosnia & H	MayaSar	Korake Ti Znam	Maja Sarihodžić	Maja Sarihodžić	77
7Q	4	Malta	Kurt Calleja	This Is The Night	Johan Jämtberg, Mikael Gunnerås & Kurt Calleja	Johan Jämtberg, Mikael Gunnerås & Kurt Calleja	70
8Q	7	Ukraine	Gaitana	Be My Guest	Gaitana	Gaitana and KIWI Project	64
9Q	2	FYR Macedonia	Kaliopi	Crno I Belo	Kaliopi	Romeo Grill	53
10Q	16	Norway	Tooji	Stay	Tooji, Figge Boström & Peter Boström	Tooji, Figge Boström & Peter Boström	45
11	8	Bulgaria	Sofi Marinova	Love Unlimited	Donka Vasileva	Krum Geopriev & Iasen Kozev	45
12	10	Croatia	Nina Badrić	Nebo	Nina Badrić	Nina Badrić	42
13	6	Portugal	Filipa Sousa	Vida Minha	Carlos Coelho	Andrej Babic	39
14	12	Georgia	Anri Jokhadze	I'm A Joker	Bibi Kvachadze	Rusudan Chkhaidze	36
15	3	Netherlands	Joan Franka	You And Me	Joan Franka	Joan Franka, Jessica Hoogenboom	35
16	5	Belarus	Litesound	We Are The Heroes	Dmitry Kariakin, Vladimir Kariakin	Dmitry Kariakin, Vladimir Kariakin	35
17	9	Slovenia	Eva Boto	Verjamem	Igor Pirkovič	Vladimir Graić, Hari Mata Hari	31
18	15	Slovakia	Max Jason Mai	Don't Close Your Eyes	Max Jason Mai	Max Jason Mai	22

2012 Eurovision 57: Baku, Azerbaijan — Semi-Final 2: 26 May 2012

	Belarus	Bosnia & H	Bulgaria	Croatia	Estonia	France	FYR Macedonia	Georgia	Germany	Lithuania	Malta	Netherlands	Norway	Portugal	Serbia	Slovakia	Slovenia	Sweden	Turkey	Ukraine	United Kingdom	TOTAL
Serbia	8	10	12	10	1	12	12	10	10	2	5	10	10	8		8	12	8		8	3	159
FYR Macedonia	2	8	7	7				1			1				8		6		8	5		53
Netherlands					7				8	3			3			2	2	1	7		4	35
Malta	5		6	5	3		2	4		6		2			3	2	4	4	6	6	12	70
Belarus				2			1	8		7	4	1				5				12		35
Portugal	4	4		3		8			3	1	6	6	5			5	3	6	1			39
Ukraine	12	2	5	1	5	2	3	6		5	6		2	2	4	1		6			2	64
Bulgaria	3	3				3	6		2		2		6	6	2				10		5	45
Slovenia	5			8			4		4						10							31
Croatia	1	12					7		1						12	12	8			1		42
Sweden	7	7	10	6	12	6	8	12	12	10	8	12	12	10	7		10		5	7	8	181
Georgia	6				4		10			12			1	1		3			3	10		36
Turkey		6	8		2	7		3	6		12	7	8			10	1	7		2	6	80
Estonia	4	3				10		7	7	8		8	8	12				12		3	7	100
Slovakia				6	6	1					7	3		4	1			3				22
Norway	3	1	2		8		5	2	5	4	3	5	4	3	5	4	5	10	4			45
Bosnia & Herzegovina			1	12		4	5					4	7	5	6	6	7	5	12		1	77
Lithuania	10		4	4	10	5		5			10			7		7		2	2	4	10	104

2012 Eurovision 57: Baku, Azerbaijan

Final: 26 May 2012

Final qualification rules: Top 10 placed countries from each semi-final. Automatic qualification: United Kingdom, France, Germany, Spain, Italy & hosts Azerbaijan. Points awarded are based on the combined votes of the viewers and jury from each of the 42 participating countries.

Rank	Start	Country	Artist	Song	Writer	Composer	POINTS
1	17	Sweden	Loreen	Euphoria	Thomas G:son & Peter Boström	Thomas G:son & Peter Boström	372
2	6	Russia	Buranovskiye Babushki	Party For Everybody	Olga Tuktareva, Mary S Applegate	Viktor Drobysh, Timofei Leontiev	259
3	24	Serbia	Željko Joksimović	Nije Ljubav Stvar	Marina Tucaković & Miloš Roganović	Željko Joksimović	214
4	13	Azerbaijan	Sabina Babayeva	When The Music Dies	Anders Bagge, Sandra Bjurman, Stefan Örn, Johan Kronlund	Anders Bagge, Johan Kronlund, Sandra Bjurman, Stefan Örn	150
5	3	Albania	Rona Nishliu	Suus	Rona Nishliu	Florent Boshnjaku	146
6	11	Estonia	Ott Lepland	Kuula	Aapo Ilves	Ott Lepland	120
7	18	Turkey	Can Bonomo	Love Me Back	Can Bonomo	Can Bonomo	112
8	20	Germany	Roman Lob	Standing Still	Wayne Hector, Jamie Cullum, Steve Robson	Wayne Hector, Jamie Cullum, Steve Robson	110
9	10	Italy	Nina Zilli	L'Amore È Femmina (Out Of Love)	Nina Zilli, Christian Rabb, Kristoffer Sjökvist, Frida Molander & Charlie Mason	Christian Rabb, Kristoffer Sjökvist, Frida Molander & Charlie Mason	101
10	19	Spain	Pastora Soler	Quédate Conmigo (Stay With Me)	Antonio Sánchez	Antonio Sánchez, Thomas G:son & Erik Bernholm	97
11	26	Moldova	Pasha Parfeny	Lăutar	Pasha Parfeny	Pasha Parfeny, Alex Brashovean	81
12	14	Romania	Mandinga	Zaleilah	Elena Ionescu, Dihigo Omar Secada, Costi Ionita	Costi Ionita	71
13	22	FYR Macedonia	Kaliopi	Crno I Belo	Kaliopi	Romeo Grill	71
14	4	Lithuania	Donny Martell	Love Is Blind	Brandon Stone & Jodie Rose	Brandon Stone	70
15	25	Ukraine	Gaitana	Be My Guest	Gaitana	Gaitana and KIWI Project	65
16	8	Cyprus	Ivi Adamou	La La Love	A Papaconstantinou, B Djupström, A Zakka & V Svensson	A Papaconstantinou, B Djupström, A Zakka & V Svensson	65
17	16	Greece	Eleftheria Eleftheriou	Aphrodisiac	Dimitri Stassos, Mikaela Stenström, Dajana Lööf	Dimitri Stassos, Mikaela Stenström, Dajana Lööf	64
18	5	Bosnia & H	MayaSar	Korake Ti Znam	Maja Sarihodžić	Maja Sarihodžić	55
19	23	Ireland	Jedward	Waterline	Nick Jarl & Sharon Vaughn	Nick Jarl & Sharon Vaughn	46
20	7	Iceland	Greta Salóme & Jónsi	Never Forget	Gréta Salóme	Gréta Salóme	46
21	21	Malta	Kurt Calleja	This Is The Night	Johan Jämtberg, Mikael Gunnerås & Kurt Calleja	Johan Jämtberg, Mikael Gunnerås & Kurt Calleja	41
22	9	France	Anggun	Echo (You And I)	William Rousseau & Anggun	Jean Pierre Pilot & William Rousseau	21
23	15	Denmark	Soluna Samay	Should've Known Better	Chief 1, Remee & Isam B	Chief 1 & Remee	21
24	2	Hungary	Compact Disco	Sound Of Our Hearts	Behnam Lotfi, Gábor Pál,	Behnam Lotfi, Gábor Pál,	19
25	1	United Kingdom	Engelbert Humperdinck	Love Will Set You Free	Attila Sándor, Csaba Walkó	Attila Sándor, Csaba Walkó	12
26	12	Norway	Tooji	Stay	Martin Terefe & Sacha Skarbek	Martin Terefe & Sacha Skarbek	7

Last row writer/composer: Tooji, Figge Boström & Peter Boström

2012 Eurovision 57: Baku, Azerbaijan
Final: 26 May 2012

Order votes announced	Albania	Austria	Azerbaijan	Belarus	Belgium	Bosnia & H	Bulgaria	Croatia	Cyprus	Denmark	Estonia	Finland	France	FYR Macedonia	Georgia	Germany	Greece	Hungary	Iceland	Ireland	Israel	Italy	Latvia	Lithuania	Malta	Moldova	Montenegro	Netherlands	Norway	Portugal	Romania	Russia	San Marino	Serbia	Slovakia	Slovenia	Spain	Sweden	Switzerland	Turkey	Ukraine	United Kingdom	TOTAL
	1	4	8	6	7	15	17	21	20	31	30	34	11	23	35	38	14	40	26	42	41	36	32	29	9	16	2	24	28	25	3	39	10	37	22	19	33	27	18	13	5	12	
United Kingdom					1																																					12	12
Hungary																										1														1	5	7	19
Albania		8			10	6	4	5	4	5	3	6	3	12	3	6	10	8		4		12	1		1		10	1			7		12	2	8	3		1	1				146
Lithuania			4	8	8		5						3		12				7			4	4		4		1	1	6		1	5	12	1					12				70
Bosnia & Herzegovina		7						10				6		7		7		6				10			3		6						10	5	2	7			1	10			55
Russia	3	5	10	12	8	3	6	6	5	8	8	8	4	4	5	7	4	7	7	6	8	10	10	6	3	6	4	4	8	8	4		10	7	3	8	8		1	10	7	3	259
Iceland			12						1	6	6	7			5	3		6			3	5					6	4	5						4	4	4		12				46
Cyprus	6	2				2											12	5	8							5					2	2	7			5	5						65
France	7																		6	2						2											1	2					21
Italy				4				2	2	3	7		1		4	2	3	5		4	8		3	4	10	5	5	7	4	4	2	6	7	3		5	1	2	5		4	4	101
Estonia												10	10		5	4			10	8		8	8	8		2		7	7	2		6		10			6	8			1		120
Norway																			1									3										3					7
Azerbaijan	4			7		7	10		8				1	2			5			1	1			4	10	5	5			4	8	10	4	3	6					12	12	2	150
Romania		6	3						3	1			2		10	10	7			8	6			8	12	2					3	1							4				71
Denmark									12		2	5			1	5			5	5								2	2														21
Greece	12	5	2	1	1											1					2	7			6	4					8	3		4						3			64
Sweden	5	12	7	6	12	8	8	7	10	12	12	12	12	2	8	12	6	12	12	12	12	8	12	12	6	7		12	12	3	10	12	3	10	12	10	12		7	6	6	12	372
Turkey	10	3	12		7	4	7			2		3	5	5	7		7	3	1					10	1	12		8		12	3		5	3				6	3			1	112
Spain		6				5	3		6		4	6		8			12		2	5				1	8		8	6	3	12	6		1		4			4	8			8	97
Germany	2	4						4			10		7		2			10		10	10		7	3	2	3		2	3	10		4				2	3		4			6	110
Malta												4		1								1		7									2			1						5	41
FYR Macedonia	8		8	3		12	2	8		4							8			3			5		5		8	5					6		1	6							71
Ireland			1	1										1			1						6	2	7			10	1					12								4	46
Serbia	1	10		4	5	10	12	12	7		1		2	10		10	8	4	4						5	3	12	10	10	5	5	4	6		7	12		5	10			10	214
Ukraine		3	10			6	5			7		6		3	6		1	2	4	3	5		6	2	7	8		1	1	1		8		6	1	1	2		10				65
Moldova	1		5				1			7						2	2	2	3			4					3			6	12	7	8				7		2	8	2		81

2013 Eurovision 58: Malmö, Sweden

Semi-final 1: 14 May 2013

Votes are cast by countries participating in each semi-final plus the five automatically qualifying countries decided by draw: Italy and United Kingdom in semi-final 1, France, Germany and Spain in semi-final 2. Hosts Sweden voted in semi-final 1. Points awarded are based on the combined votes of the viewers and jury from each of the countries voting in this semi-final. The top 10 countries in each semi-final qualify for the

Rank	Start	Country	Artist	Song	Writer	Composer	POINTS
1Q	5	Denmark	Emmelie de Forest	Only Teardrops	Lise Cabble, Julia Fabrin Jakobsen, Thomas Stengaard	Lise Cabble, Julia Fabrin Jakobsen, Thomas Stengaard	167
2Q	6	Russia	Dina Garipova	What If	Gabriel Alares, Joakim Björnberg, Leonid Gutkin	Gabriel Alares, Joakim Björnberg, Leonid Gutkin	156
3Q	7	Ukraine	Zlata Ognevich	Gravity	Karen Kavaleryan	Mikhail Nekrasov	140
4Q	12	Moldova	Aliona Moon	O Mie	Yuliana Scutaru	Pasha Parfeny	95
5Q	15	Belgium	Roberto Bellarosa	Love Kills	Iain James, Jukka Immonen	Iain James, Jukka Immonen	75
6Q	8	Netherlands	Anouk	Birds	Anouk Teeuwe	Tore Johansson, Martin Gjerstad	75
7Q	11	Belarus	Alyona Lanskaya	Solayoh	Martin King	Marc Paelinck	64
8Q	13	Ireland	Ryan Dolan	Only Love Survives	Wez Devine, Ryan Dolan	Wez Devine, Ryan Dolan	54
9Q	10	Lithuania	Andrius Pojavis	Something	Andrius Pojavis	Andrius Pojavis	53
10Q	2	Estonia	Birgit Õigemeel	Et Uus Saaks Alguse	Mihkel Mattisen & Silvia Soro	Mihkel Mattisen	52
11	16	Serbia	Moje 3	Ljubav Je Svuda	Marina Tucaković	Saša Milošević Mare	46
12	9	Montenegro	Who See	Igranka	Dejan Dedovic, Mario Djordjevic, Djordje Miljenovic	Djordje Miljenovic	41
13	4	Croatia	Klapa s mora	Mižerja	Goran Topolovac	Goran Topolovac	38
14	1	Austria	Natália Kelly	Shine	Andreas Grass, Nikola Paryla, Alexander Kahr	Andreas Grass, Nikola Paryla, Alexander Kahr	27
15	14	Cyprus	Despina Olympiou	An Me Thimasai	Zenon Zintillis	Andreas Giorgallis	11
16	3	Slovenia	Hannah	Straight Into Love	Hannah Mancini, Marko Primuzak	Hannah Mancini, Gregor Zemljic, Erik Margan, Matija Rodic	8

2013 Eurovision 58: Malmö, Sweden

Semi-final 1: 14 May 2013

	Austria	Belarus	Belgium	Croatia	Cyprus	Denmark	Estonia	Ireland	Italy	Lithuania	Moldova	Montenegro	Netherlands	Russia	Serbia	Slovenia	Sweden	Ukraine	United Kingdom	TOTAL
Austria			3	4	2	4	1	4	2		3		4		2	1			1	27
Estonia		5	1			1		8	5	4	5			5			6	1	4	52
Slovenia				5	1							3								8
Croatia								1		1		5	3	4	10	2		6		38
Denmark	12	8	10	12	8		12	12	6	6	7	8	12	10	8	8	12	4	12	167
Russia	10	10	7	8	10		10	10	4	10	8	7	7		6	10	10	7	10	156
Ukraine	2	12	8	7	12		6	2	12	12	12	12	8	7	5	12	1		2	140
Netherlands	8		12			10	7	5	1	7		2		3	1	3	8		8	75
Montenegro		2		6		5			10		6				12		2	8		41
Lithuania		7	6		3	2	4	6	7		2	6	2	1	4	4		5	7	53
Belarus			5	1	6	6	3	3	8	8	10	4	6	2	7	7		12		64
Moldova	7	6		2	5	3	5			3	1		5	12			5	10	6	95
Ireland		4	4		7		2			5		4		6			3	3	3	54
Cyprus	1		2			7						1	10		3					11
Belgium	4	3		3		7	8	7	3	2	4	10	1	8		6	7	2	5	75
Serbia	6	1	12	10	4											5	4			46

151

2013 Eurovision 58: Malmö, Sweden
Semi-final 2: 16 May 2013

Votes are cast by countries participating in each semi-final plus the five automatically qualifying countries decided by draw: Italy and United Kingdom in semi-final 1, France, Germany and Spain in semi-final 2. Hosts Sweden voted in semi-final 1. Points awarded are based on the combined votes of the viewers and jury from each of the countries voting in this semi-final. The top 10 countries in each semi-final qualify for the

Rank	Start	Country	Artist	Song	Writer	Composer	POINTS
1Q	4	Azerbaijan	Farid Mammadov	Hold Me	John Ballard & Ralph Charlie Al Fahel	Dimitrios Kontopoulos	139
2Q	9	Greece	Koza Mostra feat. Agathon Iakovidis	Alcohol is Free	Stathis Pachidis, Ilias Kozas	Ilias Kozas	121
3Q	13	Norway	Margaret Berger	I Feed You My Love	Karin Park, Robin Lynch, Niklas Olovson	Karin Park, Robin Lynch, Niklas Olovson	120
4Q	6	Malta	Gianluca	Tomorrow	Boris Cezek & Dean Muscat	Boris Cezek & Dean Muscat	118
5Q	17	Romania	Cezar	It's My Life	Cristian Faur	Cristian Faur	83
6Q	8	Iceland	Eythor Ingi	Ég Á Líf	Örlygur Smári & Pétur Örn Gudmundsson	Örlygur Smári & Pétur Örn Gudmundsson	72
7Q	11	Armenia	Dorians	Lonely Planet	Vardan Zadoyan	Tony Iommi	69
8Q	12	Hungary	ByeAlex	Kedvesem (Zoohacker Remix)	Alex Márta	Alex Márta, Zoltán Palásti Kovács	66
9Q	5	Finland	Krista Siegfrids	Marry Me	Krista Siegfrids, Erik Nyholm, Kristoffer Karlsson, Jessica Lundström	Krista Siegfrids, Erik Nyholm, Kristoffer Karlsson, Jessica Lundström	64
10Q	15	Georgia	Nodi Tatishvili & Sophie Gelovani	Waterfall	Thomas G:son	Thomas G:son & Erik Bernholm	63
11	2	San Marino	Valentina Monetta	Crisalide (Vola)	Mauro Balestri	Ralph Siegel	47
12	7	Bulgaria	Elitsa Todorova feat. Stoyan Yankulov	Samo Shampioni (Only Champions)	Elitsa Todorova, Christian Talev	Elitsa Todorova, Christian Talev	45
13	16	Switzerland	Takasa	You And Me	Georg Schlunegger, Roman Camenzind, Fred Herrmann	Georg Schlunegger, Roman Camenzind, Fred Herrmann	41
14	10	Israel	Moran Mazor	Rak Bishvilo	Gal Sarig	Han Harari	40
15	14	Albania	Adrian Lulgjuraj & Bledar Sejko	Identitet	Eda Sejko	Bledar Sejko	31
16	3	FYR Macedonia	Esma & Lozano	Pred Da Se Razdeni	Magdalena Cvetkovska	Darko Dimitrov, Lazar Cvetkovski, Simeon Atanasov	28
17	1	Latvia	PeR	Here We Go	Ralfs Eilands	Ralfs Eilands, Arturas Burke	13

2013 Eurovision 58: Malmö, Sweden
Semi-final 2: 16 May 2013

	Albania	Armenia	Azerbaijan	Bulgaria	Finland	France	FYR Macedonia	Georgia	Germany	Greece	Hungary	Iceland	Israel	Latvia	Malta	Norway	Romania	San Marino	Spain	Switzerland	TOTAL
Latvia							2	7				3								1	13
San Marino		4	1		1	5	5	1		1	2		4	3	6	5	4		10		47
FYR Macedonia	12			5											5			2			28
Azerbaijan	8			12	3	8	8	12		12	12		12	7	12	8	12	3	2	3	139
Finland	1		3			7			3		5	8	1	8	1	12	3	7	8	2	64
Malta	6	7	12		5	2	12	6	5	5	8	7	2	6		12	7	10		7	118
Bulgaria	4	10	4			1	3	4		2		6				1	1	8	6		45
Iceland	10	1		10	12				12				6	10		10	10		7	10	72
Greece	3	8	7	4	7	4	6	2	8		10	2		5	8	7		12	5	6	121
Israel	3	6	6		2			5	4	7	3	1					2		3		40
Armenia				8		12		10	6				8	1	3	4	5	4			69
Hungary	7		5	6	8	3		3	10	4			3	2	8	2	6	2	3		66
Norway		5		7	10		7	8	2			12	5	12	4		8	5	12	12	120
Albania			2				10			8	7	4						6		8	31
Georgia	2	12	10	3						6	4	5	7	4				1	4	5	63
Switzerland	2	2		1	6	10	4		1	3	6				2	3					41
Romania	5	3	8	2	4	6	1		7	10		10	10		10	6		1	1		83

153

2013 Eurovision 58: Malmö, Sweden

Final: 18 May 2013

Final qualification rules: Top 10 placed countries from each semi-final. Automatic qualification: United Kingdom, France, Germany, Spain, Italy & hosts Sweden. Points awarded are based on the combined votes of the viewers and jury from each of the 39 participating countries.

Rank	Start	Country	Artist	Song	Writer	Composer	POINTS
1	18	Denmark	Emmelie de Forest	Only Teardrops	Lise Cabble, Julia Fabrin Jakobsen, Thomas Stengaard	Lise Cabble, Julia Fabrin Jakobsen, Thomas Stengaard	281
2	20	Azerbaijan	Farid Mammadov	Hold Me	John Ballard & Ralph Charlie Al Fahel	Dimitrios Kontopoulos	234
3	22	Ukraine	Zlata Ognevich	Gravity	Karen Kavaleryan	Mikhail Nekrasov	214
4	24	Norway	Margaret Berger	I Feed You My Love	Karin Park, Robin Lynch, Niklas Olovson	Karin Park, Robin Lynch, Niklas Olovson	191
5	10	Russia	Dina Garipova	What If	Gabriel Alares, Joakim Björnberg, Leonid Gutkin	Gabriel Alares, Joakim Björnberg, Leonid Gutkin	174
6	21	Greece	Koza Mostra feat. Agathon Iakovidis	Alcohol is Free	Stathis Pachidis, Ilias Kozas	Ilias Kozas	152
7	23	Italy	Marco Mengoni	L'Essenziale	Roberto Casalino	Francesco De Benedittis, Roberto Casalino, Marco Mengoni	126
8	9	Malta	Gianluca	Tomorrow	Boris Cezek & Dean Muscat	Boris Cezek & Dean Muscat	120
9	13	Netherlands	Anouk	Birds	Anouk Teeuwe	Tore Johansson, Martin Gjerstad	114
10	17	Hungary	ByeAlex	Kedvesem (Zoohacker Remix)	Alex Márta	Alex Márta, Zoltán Palásti Kovács	84
11	3	Moldova	Aliona Moon	O Mie	Yuliana Scutaru	Pasha Parfeny	71
12	6	Belgium	Roberto Bellarosa	Love Kills	Iain James, Jukka Immonen	Iain James, Jukka Immonen	71
13	14	Romania	Cezar	It's My Life	Cristian Faur	Cristian Faur	65
14	16	Sweden	Robin Stjernberg	You	Robin Stjernberg, Joy Deb, Linnea Deb, Joakim Harestad Haukaas	Robin Stjernberg, Joy Deb, Linnea Deb, Joakim Harestad Haukaas	62
15	25	Georgia	Nodi Tatishvili & Sophie Gelovani	Waterfall	Thomas G:son	Thomas G:son & Erik Bernholm	50
16	8	Belarus	Alyona Lanskaya	Solayoh	Martin King	Marc Paelinck	48
17	19	Iceland	Eythor Ingi	Ég Á Líf	Örlygur Smári & Pétur Örn Gudmundsson	Örlygur Smári & Pétur Örn Gudmundsson	47
18	12	Armenia	Dorians	Lonely Planet	Vardan Zadoyan	Tony Iommi	41
19	15	United Kingdom	Bonnie Tyler	Believe in Me	Desmond Child, Lauren Christy, Christopher Braide	Desmond Child, Lauren Christy, Christopher Braide	23
20	7	Estonia	Birgit Õigemeel	Et Uus Saaks Alguse	Mihkel Mattisen & Silvia Soro	Mihkel Mattisen	19
21	11	Germany	Cascada	Glorious	Yann Peifer, Manuel Reuter, Andres Ballinas, Tony Cornelissen	Yann Peifer, Manuel Reuter, Andres Ballinas, Tony Cornelissen	18
22	2	Lithuania	Andrius Pojavis	Something	Andrius Pojavis	Andrius Pojavis	17
23	1	France	Amandine Bourgeois	L'enfer Et Moi	Boris Bergman	David Salkin	14
24	4	Finland	Krista Siegfrids	Marry Me	Krista Siegfrids, Erik Nyholm, Kristoffer Karlsson, Jessica Lundström	Krista Siegfrids, Erik Nyholm, Kristoffer Karlsson, Jessica Lundström	13
25	5	Spain	ESDM	Contigo Hasta El Final (With You Until The End)	Raquel del Rosario, David Feito, Juan Suárez	Raquel del Rosario, David Feito, Juan Suárez	8
26	26	Ireland	Ryan Dolan	Only Love Survives	Wez Devine, Ryan Dolan	Wez Devine, Ryan Dolan	5

2013 Eurovision 58: Malmö, Sweden — Final: 18 May 2013

Receiver	Order	Albania	Armenia	Austria	Azerbaijan	Belarus	Belgium	Bulgaria	Croatia	Cyprus	Denmark	Estonia	Finland	France	FYR Macedonia	Georgia	Germany	Greece	Hungary	Iceland	Ireland	Israel	Italy	Latvia	Lithuania	Malta	Moldova	Montenegro	Netherlands	Norway	Romania	Russia	San Marino	Serbia	Slovenia	Spain	Sweden	Switzerland	Ukraine	United Kingdom	TOTAL
Order votes announced		3	15	5	13	19	22	21	37	36	31	25	17	28	35	34	26	29	10	27	30	7	16	20	39	24	12	32	4	14	11	23	1	8	33	18	2	38	9	6	
France	28	2																																							14
Lithuania	39				3	5																																	1		17
Moldova	12		2	1		4	3							4	7	1					1										12	6				2			8		71
Finland	17													3			1																3								13
Spain	18	6									2												2																		8
Belgium	22		3									5	2	3					4		4			2					12			8	5			1	7			3	71
Estonia	25												6											10	3										2						19
Belarus	19		5	7											5	5						3			1			3					10	5					12		48
Malta	24		6	8					3	3	3				5	3	5	3	8	5	1		10	5					8	10	5			8	10	6	5	3	2	7	120
Russia	23		7			8			5	5	4	5	7		6	6	2			1	10		1	12	7			7	4	6				8		3			4	10	174
Germany	26	3	6			2	8												3																1	3		1	6		18
Armenia	15													7		10								4		1	1					2	1					4	6		41
Netherlands	4	4	8	4	6		12	2				10	8		2			5	5	8	6	3		6	4	1	10	7		8	6	3			7		8	4		4	114
Romania	11	5	4	6							1	7		1		6		10		6	7	5	1		4	7	10	7										2			65
United Kingdom	6																			7	5			4	5	5		1	3	4	3				1		1				23
Sweden	2			5		10	5		1	1		8	4		5	5	3			4		5	3	4	5		5		3	12		3	6	1	6			3			62
Hungary	10	8		7			2	6	4		8	1	10	7			12			5	12		3	6	2				7	2			6	2			3	10			84
Denmark	31	1	4	5	5	1	10	2	10	7		8	7	12	12	7	10	7	10	12	12	8	12	6	2	6	6	10	10	7	6	4		12	12	8		3	5	12	281
Iceland	27							12					5				8		6											4				4	4		6	5		2	47
Azerbaijan	13	7	12			10			7	8	6			8		12	4	12	12	7	2	12		3	12	12	8	12	2	5	10	12	2	5	3	8	8	6	10	6	234
Greece	29	10	8	7	4	6	2	7	5	12		4			4		6		1	3	8	2	7	1	10	4		8	1	5	7	10	12	3	7			8		8	152
Ukraine	9		12		12	12	8	10	12	10	3		1	10	10	8		8	7	3	8	10	5	7	10	10	12	6	5	1	4	1	12	10	8	10		8		5	214
Italy	16	12	1		1	12	8		8	6		8				2	7	6	1		4			8	6	10	2	4	5	5	1	4	4	4	8	12	12		3	8	126
Norway	14	2	3			2	3	7			12	7	5		8	4		4	2	10	7	6	8	8	8	3	3	2	6		8	7	7	7	5	5	12	7	3	10	191
Georgia	34		10		10					2																					5	5					2	12	7		50
Ireland	30																				2																		1	1	5

2014 Eurovision 59: Copenhagen, Denmark

Semi-final 1: 6 May 2014

Votes are cast by countries participating in each semi-final plus the five automatically qualifying countries decided by draw: Spain and France in semi-final 1, Italy, Germany and the UK in semi-final 2. Hosts Denmark voted in semi-final 1. Points awarded are based on the combined votes of the viewers and jury from each of the countries voting in this semi-final. The top 10 countries in each semi-final qualify for the final.

Rank	Start	Country	Artist	Song	Writer	Composer	POINTS
1Q	14	Netherlands	The Common Linnets	Calm After the Storm	Ilse DeLange, JB Meijers, Rob Crosby, Matthew Crosby, Jake Etheridge	Ilse DeLange, JB Meijers, Rob Crosby, Matthew Crosby, Jake Etheridge	150
2Q	4	Sweden	Sanna Nielsen	Undo	Fredrik Kempe, David Kreuger, Hamed "K-One" Pirouzpanah	Fredrik Kempe, David Kreuger, Hamed "K-One" Pirouzpanah	131
3Q	16	Hungary	András Kállay-Saunders	Running	András Kállay-Saunders	András Kállay-Saunders & Krisztián Szakos	127
4Q	1	Armenia	Aram MP3	Not Alone	Garik Papoyan	Aram MP3	121
5Q	9	Ukraine	Mariya Yaremchuk	Tick-Tock	Mariya Yaremchuk & Sandra Bjurman	Mariya Yaremchuk	118
6Q	7	Russia	Tolmachevy Sisters	Shine	John Ballard, Ralph Charlie, Gerard James Borg	Philipp Kirkorov & Dimitris Kontopoulos	63
7Q	15	Montenegro	Sergej Ćetković	Moj Svijet	Sergej Ćetković & Emina Sandal	Sergej Ćetković	63
8Q	5	Iceland	Pollapönk	No Prejudice	Heidar Orn Kristjansson, Haraldur Freyr Gislason, John Grant	Heidar Orn Kristjansson	61
9Q	8	Azerbaijan	Dilara Kazimova	Start a Fire	Stefan Örn, Johan Kronlund, Alessandra Günthardt	Stefan Örn, Johan Kronlund, Alessandra Günthardt	57
10Q	12	San Marino	Valentina Monetta	Maybe (Forse)	Mauro Balestri	Ralph Siegel	40
11	13	Portugal	Suzy	Quero Ser Tua	Emanuel	Emanuel	39
12	3	Estonia	Tanja	Amazing	Tanja	Timo Vendt, Tanja	36
13	2	Latvia	Aarzemnieki	Cake to Bake	Guntis Veilands	Guntis Veilands	33
14	10	Belgium	Axel Hirsoux	Mother	Rafael Artesero & Ashley Hicklin	Rafael Artesero & Ashley Hicklin	28
15	6	Albania	Hersi	One Night's Anger	Jorgo Papingji	Gentian Lako	22
16	11	Moldova	Cristina Scarlat	Wild Soul	Lidia Scarlat	Ivan Akulov	13

2014 Eurovision 59: Copenhagen, Denmark

Semi-final 1: 10 May 2014

	Albania	Armenia	Azerbaijan	Belgium	Denmark	Estonia	France	Hungary	Iceland	Latvia	Moldova	Montenegro	Netherlands	Portugal	Russia	San Marino	Spain	Sweden	Ukraine	TOTAL
Armenia	5			3	5	5	12	8	3	6		10	12	4	12	10	6	8	12	121
Latvia		5	7		1	6		2	6					3		2		1		33
Estonia		4	5		10		4		5							3	2	5		36
Sweden	6			8	8	7	6	10	10	8	10	5	8	8	6	3	12		10	131
Iceland				4	2	2	8	6		5		12	7	1		7	3	7	3	61
Albania				2		1							1			5				22
Russia		7	10	1	4	4	2	5	2	4	12	4	4	5		6		2	6	63
Azerbaijan	7	12		7	7	10	2	1	1	2	6	7	5	2	10	4			5	57
Ukraine	3	6	12				1	3	7	7	8	8	3	7	7	1		6		118
Belgium	4		4						4	1	7	2			4					28
Moldova			6	6								6			1				2	13
San Marino	8	2	1		3	3	5	7			1	3	2		3		1			40
Portugal	1	3	3		3		10		12		3	1				12	8	4	4	39
Netherlands	2	10		10	12	12	7	12	12	12	2			12	2	12	7	12	7	150
Montenegro	12	8	2		6		7	4			5		6	6	5		4	3	1	63
Hungary	10	1	8	12		8	3		8	3	4	10	10	10	8	8	10	10	8	127

157

2014 Eurovision 59: Copenhagen, Denmark

Semi-final 2: 8 May 2014

Votes are cast by countries participating in each semi-final plus the five automatically qualifying countries decided by draw: Spain and France in semi-final 1, Italy, Germany and the UK in semi-final 2. Hosts Denmark voted in semi-final 1. Points awarded are based on the combined votes of the viewers and jury from each of the countries voting in this semi-final. The top 10 countries in each semi-final qualify for the final.

Rank	Start	Country	Artist	Song	Writer	Composer	POINTS
1Q	6	Austria	Conchita Wurst	Rise Like a Phoenix	Charly Mason, Joey Patulka, Ali Zuckowski, Julian Maas	Charly Mason, Joey Patulka, Ali Zuckowski, Julian Maas	169
2Q	15	Romania	Paul Seling & Ovi	Miracle	Ovi, Philip Halloun, Frida Amundsen, Beyond51	Ovi, Philip Halloun, Frida Amundsen, Beyond51	125
3Q	8	Finland	Softengine	Something Better	Henri Oskár, Topi Latukka	Topi Latukka	97
4Q	12	Switzerland	Sebalter	Hunter of Stars	Sebastiano Paù-Lessi	Sebastiano Paù-Lessi	92
5Q	10	Belarus	Teo	Cheesecake	Dmitry Novik	Yury Vashchuk (Teo)	87
6Q	3	Norway	Carl Espen	Silent Storm	Josefin Winther	Josefin Winther	77
7Q	13	Greece	Freaky Fortune feat. RiskyKidd	Rise Up	Freaky Fortune & RiskyKidd	Freaky Fortune	74
8Q	5	Poland	Donatan & Cleo	My Słowianie - We Are Slavic	Cleo	Donatan	70
9Q	1	Malta	Firelight	Coming Home	Richard Edwards Micallef	Richard Edwards Micallef	63
10Q	14	Slovenia	Tinkara Kovač	Round and Round	Tinkara Kovač, Hannah Mancini, Tina Piš	Raay	52
11	7	Lithuania	Vilija Matačiūnaitė	Attention	Vilija Matačiūnaitė	Vilija Matačiūnaitė & Viktoras Vaupšas	36
12	9	Ireland	Can-Linn (feat. Kasey Smith)	Heartbeat	Jonas Gladnikoff, Rasmus Palmgren, Patrizia Helander	Hazel Kaneswaran, Jonas Gladnikoff, Rasmus Palmgren, Patrizia Helander	35
13	11	FYR Macedonia	Tijana	To The Sky	Elena Risteska Ivanovska, Darko Dimitrov	Darko Dimitrov, Lazar Cvetkoski	33
14	2	Israel	Mei Finegold	Same Heart	Rami Talmid	Rami Talmid	19
15	4	Georgia	The Shin and Mariko	Three Minutes to Earth	Eugen Eliu	Zaza Miminoshvili	15

2014 Eurovision 59: Copenhagen, Denmark

Semi-final 2: 10 May 2014

	Austria	Belarus	Finland	FYR Macedonia	Georgia	Germany	Greece	Ireland	Israel	Italy	Lithuania	Malta	Norway	Poland	Romania	Slovenia	Switzerland	United Kingdom	TOTAL
Austria		7	12	6	10	4	12	12	10	12	10	10	8	10	12	10	12	12	169
Belarus	10		7	2	12		8	1	7		12	6	1	7	8	6			87
F.Y.R. Macedonia		1	1		2				2	2		3				12	10		33
Finland	8			10	1	5	4	10	3	8	5		12	8	5	2	8	8	97
Georgia		5				1	1				6	2							15
Greece	3	12	4		3	6		4	6	6		8	6	1	10	3	4	1	74
Ireland	4	1	3	7			2		1		5	4	3	5	7	1	1	5	35
Israel		2		5		2								2	2				19
Lithuania		6			7			5		1			5	4	1	3		10	36
Malta	1	4	5	12	8	3	7	3		5	1		2	6		4	5	7	63
Norway	5	10	10	4	5	7	6	8	4		8	7			3	5	2		77
Poland	2	8	6	3		12	1	2	12	10	4	1			4		3	4	70
Romania	12		2	8	6	8	10	7	8	4	2	12	7	3		7	7	6	125
Slovenia	7				4			6		7	3		10		6		6	2	52
Switzerland	6	3	8	1		10	5		5	3	7	5	4	12	10	8		3	92

159

2014 Eurovision 59: Copenhagen, Denmark

Final: 10 May 2014

Final qualification rules: Top 10 placed countries from each semi-final. Automatic qualification: United Kingdom, France, Germany, Spain, Italy & hosts Denmark. Points awarded are based on the combined votes of the viewers and jury from each of the 37 participating countries.

Rank	Start	Country	Artist	Song	Writer	Composer	POINTS
1	11	Austria	Conchita Wurst	Rise Like a Phoenix	Charly Mason, Joey Patulka, Ali Zuckowski, Julian Maas	Charly Mason, Joey Patulka, Ali Zuckowski, Julian Maas	290
2	24	The Netherlands	The Common Linnets	Calm After the Storm	Ilse DeLange, JB Meijers, Rob Crosby, Matthew Crosby, Jake Etheridge	Ilse DeLange, JB Meijers, Rob Crosby, Matthew Crosby, Jake Etheridge	238
3	13	Sweden	Sanna Nielsen	Undo	Fredrik Kempe, David Kreuger, Hamed "K-One" Pirouzpanah	Fredrik Kempe, David Kreuger, Hamed "K-One" Pirouzpanah	218
4	7	Armenia	Aram MP3	Not Alone	Garik Papoyan	Aram MP3	174
5	21	Hungary	András Kállay-Saunders	Running	András Kállay-Saunders	András Kállay-Saunders, Krisztián Szakos	143
6	1	Ukraine	Mariya Yaremchuk	Tick-Tock	Mariya Yaremchuk & Sandra Bjurman	Mariya Yaremchuk	113
7	15	Russia	Tolmachevy Sisters	Shine	John Ballard, Ralph Charlie, Gerard James Borg	Philipp Kirkorov & Dimitris Kontopoulos	89
8	5	Norway	Carl Espen	Silent Storm	Josefin Winther	Josefin Winther	88
9	23	Denmark	Basim	Cliché Love Song	Lasse Lindorff, Daniel Fält, Basim Moujahid, Kim Novak-Zorde	Lasse Lindorff, Daniel Fält, Basim Moujahid, Kim Novak-Zorde	74
10	19	Spain	Ruth Lorenzo	Dancing in the Rain	Ruth Lorenzo, Julian Emery, James Lawrence Irvin	Ruth Lorenzo, Julian Emery, James Lawrence Irvin	74
11	18	Finland	Softengine	Something Better	Henri Oskár, Topi Latukka	Topi Latukka	72
12	6	Romania	Paul Seling & Ovi	Miracle	Ovi, Philip Halloun, Frida Amundsen, Beyond51	Ovi, Philip Halloun, Frida Amundsen, Beyond51	72
13	20	Switzerland	Sebalter	Hunter of Stars	Sebastiano Paù-Lessi	Sebastiano Paù-Lessi	64
14	9	Poland	Donatan & Cleo	My Słowianie - We Are Slavic	Cleo	Donatan	62
15	4	Iceland	Pollapönk	No Prejudice	Heidar Orn Kristjansson, Haraldur Freyr Gislason, John Grant	Heidar Orn Kristjansson	58
16	2	Belarus	Teo	Cheesecake	Dmitry Novik	Yury Vashchuk (Teo)	43
17	26	United Kingdom	Molly	Children of the Universe	Molly Smitten-Downes, Anders Hansson	Molly Smitten-Downes, Anders Hansson	40
18	12	Germany	Elaiza	Is it Right?	Elzbieta Steinmetz, Adam Kesselhaut	Elzbieta Steinmetz, Frank Kretschmer	39
19	8	Montenegro	Sergej Ćetković	Moj Svijet	Sergej Ćetković & Emina Sandal	Sergej Ćetković	37
20	10	Greece	Freaky Fortune feat. RiskyKidd	Rise Up	Freaky Fortune & RiskyKidd	Freaky Fortune	35
21	16	Italy	Emma	La Mia Città	Emma Marrone	Emma Marrone	33
22	3	Azerbaijan	Dilara Kazimova	Start a Fire	Stefan Örn, Johan Kronlund, Alessandra Günthardt	Stefan Örn, Johan Kronlund, Alessandra Günthardt	33
23	22	Malta	Firelight	Coming Home	Richard Edwards Micallef	Richard Edwards Micallef	32
24	25	San Marino	Valentina Monetta	Maybe (Forse)	Mauro Balestri	Ralph Siegel	14
25	17	Slovenia	Tinkara Kovač	Round and Round	Tinkara Kovač, Hannah Mancini, Tina Piš	Raay	9
26	14	France	Twin Twin	Moustache	Lorent Ardouvin, François Ardouvin	Pierre Beyres, Kim N'Guyen	2

2014 Eurovision 59: Copenhagen, Denmark

Final: 10 May 2014

Order votes announced	Albania 4	Armenia 15	Austria 30	Azerbaijan 1	Belarus 19	Belgium 32	Denmark 6	Estonia 24	FYR Macedonia 17	France 12	Finland 28	Georgia 36	Germany 20	Greece 2	Hungary 25	Iceland 16	Ireland 27	Israel 21	Italy 33	Latvia 14	Lithuania 29	Malta 11	Moldova 26	Montenegro 7	Netherlands 10	Norway 23	Poland 3	Portugal 22	Romania 8	Russia 9	San Marino 5	Slovenia 37	Spain 31	Sweden 18	Switzerland 35	Ukraine 34	United Kingdom 13	TOTAL
Ukraine			5	10	8		6	8		2		6		5	2		5	5		7	5		10	7						7			6				13	113
Belarus	8			7			1					7						1			3		5	1		6			12		12		6			6		43
Azerbaijan					3														7				10						10						1			33
Iceland			2			5		6		7			2		5					5	8	8			6		7		1	1	8		1		5	1	4	58
Norway			1	4				3		2			5	3		1			7			2			10	6		3	1					3				88
Romania			8	6		5		5	4	7							2	8		5	8					4		1		4			8					72
Armenia			12	10			2					12			7	2		6		10		6	3	10			1	4	7	8	6		4			10		174
Montenegro		12							12																7													37
Poland	6		2		7	3		1	5		5		10	1		3		2	8		1		2	4							1				2			62
Greece	2	7	4							1		4						3	3				4			2											2	35
Austria	5		1	12	6	12		4	3	12	10	10	7	12	10	10	12	12	12	6	10	10	7	2	12	8		12	8	5	2		12	12	12	8	12	290
Germany	4	6		1								5													8				2	2				7	7	5		39
Sweden	7		6		10	10		10		10	4	2		2		7		10		8	7	7		3	8	8	8	4	8	12	2	10	8		6	5		218
France											1																					1						2
Russia												8		10				3	3	2	6	5	8		8			2			3				4	4		89
Italy	10		4							1												12		6								2						33
Slovenia									1															8														9
Finland		4				3	4	6		6			4	6	6	5	6	4	6	4	4	3		5	2	7	3		5		3		6	6	4		6	72
Spain	12	2				2		2					1				5	7		2	2				3	5	2		6		3		12	8	8	2	5	74
Switzerland		5	3				5		10		6		3				1		6								10	7	6	6			10				1	64
Hungary	8	7		8	5	7	3				3	1		4		6		7		1	2			12	4			6	10				2	7	1	3		143
Malta	1			5													3								5						4						10	32
Denmark		1				6										8					1				1	1	6	5	4		1		3	8	3		3	74
Netherlands																																						
San Marino	4	10		2		8	10	12	7	8	8			8	12	12	10		4	12	12				4	12	12	10	3	3		2		10	10		8	238
United Kingdom	3	3		3	1	1	7					3										4	1			3					5		5					40

2015 Eurovision 60: Vienna, Austria

Semi-final 1: 19 May 2015

Votes are cast by countries participating in each semi-final plus the five automatically qualifying countries decided by draw: France and Spain in semi-final 1, Italy, Germany and the UK in semi-final 2. Hosts Austria voted in semi-final 1. Special guests Australia voted in both semi-finals. Points awarded are based on the combined votes of the viewers and jury from each of the countries voting in this semi-final. The top 10 countries in each semi-final qualify for the final.

Rank	Start	Country	Artist	Song	Writer	Composer	POINTS
1Q	12	Russia	Polina Gagarina	A Million Voices	Gabriel Alares, Joakim Björnberg, Katrina Noorbergen, Leonid Gutkin, Vladimir Matetsky	Gabriel Alares, Joakim Björnberg, Katrina Noorbergen, Leonid Gutkin, Vladimir Matetsky	182
2Q	3	Belgium	Loïc Nottet	Rhythm Inside	Beverly Jo Scott	Loïc Nottet	149
3Q	7	Estonia	Elina Born & Stig Rästa	Goodbye to Yesterday	Stig Rästa	Stig Rästa	105
4Q	16	Georgia	Nina Sublatti	Warrior	Nina Sublatti	Nina Sublatti, Thomas G:son	98
5Q	15	Romania	Voltaj	De la capăt (All over Again)	Calin Gavril Goia, Gabriel Constantin, Adrian Cristescu, Paduraru Silviu-Marian, Alstani Victor-Razvan, Monica-Ana Stevens, Andrei-Madalin Leonte	Calin Gavril Goia, Gabriel Constantin, Adrian Cristescu, Paduraru Silviu-Marian, Alstani Victor-Razvan	89
6Q	6	Greece	Maria Elena Kyriakou	One Last Breath	Vangelis Konstantinidis, Evelina Tziora	Efthivoulos Theocharous, Maria-Elena Kyriakou	81
7Q	2	Armenia	Genealogy	Face the Shadow	Inna Mkrtchyan	Armen Martirosyan	77
8Q	10	Hungary	Boggie	Wars for Nothing	Sára Hélène Bori	Áron Sebestyén / Boglárka Csemer	67
9Q	9	Serbia	Bojana Stamenov	Beauty Never Lies	Charlie Mason	Vladimir Graić	63
10Q	14	Albania	Elhaida Dani	I'm Alive	Sokol Marsi	Arber Elshani, Kristijan Lekaj	62
11	1	Moldova	Eduard Romanyuta	I Want Your Love	Erik Lewander, Hayley Aitken, Tom Andrews	Erik Lewander, Hayley Aitken, Tom Andrews	41
12	11	Belarus	Uzari & Maimuna	Time	Gerylana/Maimuna	Uzari	39
13	13	Denmark	Anti Social Media	The Way You Are	Remee, Chief 1	Remee, Chief 1	33
14	4	Netherlands	Trijntje Oosterhuis	Walk Along	Anouk Teeuwe	Tobias Karlsson	33
15	8	FYR Macedonia	Daniel Kajmakoski	Autumn Leaves	Joacim Persson	Joacim Persson	28
16	5	Finland	Pertti Kurikan Nimipäivät	Aina mun pitää	Pertti Kurikan Nimipäivät	Pertti Kurikan Nimipäivät	13

2015 Eurovision 60: Vienna, Austria

Semi-final 1: 19 May 2015

	Albania	Armenia	Australia	Austria	Belarus	Belgium	Denmark	Estonia	Finland	France	FYR Macedonia	Georgia	Greece	Hungary	Moldova	Netherlands	Romania	Russia	Serbia	Spain	TOTAL
Moldova	2	6			5						5	10					8		5		41
Armenia	5				7	12				5	7	8	7		4	5	1	12		4	77
Belgium	6	1	8	6	6		12	10	12	12	6	5	6	10	5	12	7	8	7	10	149
Netherlands	1						7	5	3	2	1	2					4	5		3	33
Finland					1	6	2	4						2							13
Greece	12	8	6	4	3	3		1	2	3	4	4		3	3	6	6	5	6	2	81
Estonia		4	5	10	8	5	8		8	4	2	3	4	8	2	8	2	10	2	12	105
FYR Macedonia	10		3					2							1				12		28
Serbia		5	12	7	4	4	1	12	4	1	12		2	4		7		4			63
Hungary	3		2	5			4		7	6		8	3			4	10	2	8		67
Belarus		7					3								8			6			39
Russia	7	10	10	12	12	8	10	8	10	10	8	12	12	12	7	10	12		10	7	182
Denmark		2	4	1		1		7	1	7		7	1	7		3	5			1	33
Albania		3	1	3	10	10	6					6	10		6			3		6	62
Romania	8			8	2	7	5	3	6	8		1	5	5	12	2		1	3	8	89
Georgia	4	12	7	2	10	2		6	5		3		8	6	10	1	4	7	1	5	98

2015 Eurovision 60: Vienna, Austria

Semi-final 2: 21 May 2015

Votes are cast by countries participating in each semi-final plus the five automatically qualifying countries decided by draw: France and Spain in semi-final 1, Italy, Germany and the UK in semi-final 2. Hosts Austria voted in semi-final 1. Special guests Australia voted in both semi-finals. Points awarded are based on the combined votes of the viewers and jury from each of the countries voting in this semi-final. The top 10 countries in each semi-final qualify for the final.

Rank	Start	Country	Artist	Song	Writer	Composer	POINTS
1Q	13	Sweden	Måns Zelmerlöw	Heroes	Linnea Deb, Joy Deb, Anton Hård af Segerstad	Linnea Deb, Joy Deb, Anton Hård af Segerstad	217
2Q	10	Latvia	Aminata	Love Injected	Aminata Savadogo	Aminata Savadogo	155
3Q	9	Israel	Nadav Guedj	Golden Boy	Doron Medalie	Doron Medalie	151
4Q	6	Norway	Mørland & Debrah Scarlett	A Monster Like Me	Kjetil Mørland	Kjetil Mørland	123
5Q	16	Slovenia	Maraaya	Here for You	Charlie Mason, Raay	Raay, Marjetka Vovk	92
6Q	15	Cyprus	John Karayiannis	One Thing I Should Have Done	Mike Connaris	Mike Connaris	87
7Q	1	Lithuania	Monika Linkyte & Vaidas Baumila	This Time	Monika Liubinaitė	Vytautas Bikus	67
8Q	17	Poland	Monika Kuszyńska	In the Name of Love	Monika Kuszyńska	Kuba Raczyński	57
9Q	4	Montenegro	Knez	Adio	Marina Tucaković & Dejan Ivanović	Željko Joksimović	57
10Q	11	Azerbaijan	Elnur Hüseynov	Hour of the Wolf	Sandra Bjurman, Nicolas Rebscher, Nicklas Lif, Lina Hansson	Nicolas Rebscher, Nicklas Lif, Lina Hansson	53
11	5	Malta	Amber	Warrior	Matt Muxu Mercieca	Elton Zarb	43
12	2	Ireland	Molly Sterling	Playing with Numbers	Greg French & Molly Sterling	Greg French & Molly Sterling	35
13	8	Czech Republic	Marta Jandová & Václav Noid Bárta	Hope Never Dies	Tereza Šoralová	Václav Noid Bárta	33
14	7	Portugal	Leonor Andrade	Há um mar que nos separa	Miguel Gameiro	Miguel Gameiro	19
15	12	Iceland	María Ólafs	Unbroken	Ásgeir Orri Ásgeirsson, Sæþór Kristjánsson, María Ólafsdóttir, Pálmi Ragnar Ásgeirsson	Ásgeir Orri Ásgeirsson, Sæþór Kristjánsson, Pálmi Ragnar Ásgeirsson	14
16	3	San Marino	Michele Perniola & Anita Simoncini	Chain of Lights	John O'Flynn	Ralph Siegel	11
17	14	Switzerland	Mélanie René	Time to Shine	Mélanie René	Mélanie René	4

2015 Eurovision 60: Vienna, Austria

Semi-final 2: 21 May 2015

	Australia	Azerbaijan	Cyprus	Czech Republic	Germany	Iceland	Ireland	Israel	Italy	Latvia	Lithuania	Malta	Montenegro	Norway	Poland	Portugal	San Marino	Slovenia	Sweden	Switzerland	United Kingdom	TOTAL
Lithuania	4	7	7	1		4	7	4		10		4		10			3			3	3	67
Ireland		2	1	5	2					4	2		2				5	1	3		8	35
San Marino																				1		11
Montenegro		10														5						57
Malta	3		2	4				10		2			10				7		5	1		43
Norway	8		6	7	7	10	3	7		7	8	5	6		6	8	8	6	12	10	2	123
Portugal		3			1		4	1	1			1	4									19
Czech Republic					4	8		8		3			1		8	1	4					33
Israel	7	8	10	2	8				12		4	10	3	8	10	10	6	5			12	151
Latvia	10	6	8	8	10	7	12	2	8		12	7	7	7	10	7	10	8		8	10	155
Azerbaijan	2		5	10		2		3	8		6	8	7	2	3	3			4			53
Iceland		5					2				1			2	2				2			14
Sweden	12	4	12	12	12	12	10	12	10	12	10	12	8	12	12	12	12	12		12	7	217
Switzerland		1												1	1							4
Cyprus	6				5	5	6	5	7	6	3	2		6	4	6	2	7	6	5	6	87
Slovenia	5	12	3	3	6	6		6	3	8	7	3		4	5	4	1		5	4	4	92
Poland	1		4		3	3	5		5	5	5	6		5	4	2		2	5	2		57

165

2015 Eurovision 60: Vienna, Austria

Final: 23 May 2015

Final qualification rules: Top 10 placed countries from each semi-final. Automatic qualification: United Kingdom, France, Germany, Spain, Italy, hosts Austria and special guests Australia.
Points awarded are based on the combined votes of the viewers and jury from each of the 40 participating countries.

Rank	Start	Country	Artist	Song	Writer	Composer	POINTS
1	10	Sweden	Måns Zelmerlöw	Heroes	Linnea Deb, Joy Deb, Anton Hård af Segerstad	Linnea Deb, Joy Deb, Anton Hård af Segerstad	365
2	25	Russia	Polina Gagarina	A Million Voices	Gabriel Alares, Joakim Björnberg, Katrina Noorbergen, Leonid Gutkin, Vladimir Matetsky	Gabriel Alares, Joakim Björnberg, Katrina Noorbergen, Leonid Gutkin, Vladimir Matetsky	303
3	27	Italy	Il Volo	Grande amore	Ciro Esposito / Francesco Boccia	Ciro Esposito / Francesco Boccia	292
4	13	Belgium	Loïc Nottet	Rhythm Inside	Beverly Jo Scott	Loïc Nottet	217
5	12	Australia	Guy Sebastian	Tonight Again	Guy Sebastian, David Ryan Harris, Louis Schoorl	Guy Sebastian, David Ryan Harris, Louis Schoorl	196
6	19	Latvia	Aminata	Love Injected	Aminata Savadogo	Aminata Savadogo	186
7	4	Estonia	Elina Born & Stig Rästa	Goodbye to Yesterday	Stig Rästa	Stig Rästa	106
8	9	Norway	Mørland & Debrah Scarlett	A Monster Like Me	Kjetil Mørland	Kjetil Mørland	102
9	3	Israel	Nadav Guedj	Golden Boy	Doron Medalie	Doron Medalie	97
10	8	Serbia	Bojana Stamenov	Beauty Never Lies	Charlie Mason	Vladimir Graić	53
11	23	Georgia	Nina Sublatti	Warrior	Nina Sublatti	Nina Sublatti, Thomas G:son	51
12	24	Azerbaijan	Elnur Hüseynov	Hour of the Wolf	Sandra Bjurman, Nicolas Rebscher, Nicklas Lif, Lina Hansson	Nicolas Rebscher, Nicklas Lif, Lina Hansson	49
13	16	Montenegro	Knez	Adio	Marina Tucaković & Dejan Ivanović	Željko Joksimović	44
14	1	Slovenia	Maraaya	Here for You	Charlie Mason, Raay	Raay, Marjetka Vovk	39
15	20	Romania	Voltaj	De la capăt (All over Again)	C G Goia, G Constantin, A Cristescu, P Silviu-Marian, A Victor-Razvan, M-A Stevens, A-M Leonte	Calin Gavril Goia, Gabriel Constantin, Adrian Cristescu, Padururu Silviu-Marian, Alstani Victor-Razvan	35
16	6	Armenia	Genealogy	Face the Shadow	Inna Mkrtchyan	Armen Martirosyan	34
17	26	Albania	Elhaida Dani	I'm Alive	Sokol Marsi	Arber Elshani, Kristijan Lekaj (Zzap'n'Chriss)	34
18	7	Lithuania	Monika Linkyte & Vaidas Baumila	This Time	Monika Liubinaitė	Vytautas Bikus	30
19	15	Greece	Maria Elena Kyriakou	One Last Breath	Vangelis Konstantinidis, Evelina Tziora	Efthivoulos Theocharous, Maria-Elena Kyriakou	23
20	22	Hungary	Boggie	Wars for Nothing	Sára Hélène Bori	Áron Sebestyén / Boglárka Csemer	19
21	21	Spain	Edurne	Amanecer	Tony Sánchez-Ohlsson, Peter Boström & Thomas G:son	Tony Sánchez-Ohlsson, Peter Boström & Thomas G:son	15
22	11	Cyprus	John Karayiannis	One Thing I Should Have Done	Mike Connaris	Mike Connaris	11
23	18	Poland	Monika Kuszyńska	In the Name of Love	Monika Kuszyńska	Kuba Raczyński	10
24	5	United Kingdom	Electro Velvet	Still in Love with You	David Mindel & Adrian Bax White	David Mindel & Adrian Bax White	5
25	2	France	Lisa Angell	N'oubliez pas	Laure Izon / M. Albert	Michel Illouz / M. Albert	4
26	14	Austria	The Makemakes	I Am Yours	Jimmy Harry and The Makemakes	Jimmy Harry and The Makemakes	0
27	17	Germany	Ann Sophie	Black Smoke	Michael Harwood, Ella McMahon, Tonino Speciale	Michael Harwood, Ella McMahon, Tonino Speciale	0

2015 Eurovision 60: Vienna, Austria — Final: 23 May 2015

	Albania	Armenia	Australia	Austria	Azerbaijan	Belarus	Belgium	Cyprus	Czech Republic	Denmark	Estonia	Finland	France	FYR Macedonia	Georgia	Germany	Greece	Hungary	Iceland	Ireland	Israel	Italy	Latvia	Lithuania	Malta	Moldova	Montenegro	Netherlands	Norway	Poland	Portugal	Romania	Russia	San Marino	Serbia	Slovenia	Spain	Sweden	Switzerland	United Kingdom	TOTAL
Order votes announced	7	16	20	23	9	6	14	36	21	12	39	3	15	24	40	19	4	26	35	17	31	34	10	28	2	8	1	29	37	30	38	5	32	33	11	25	22	18	13	27	
Slovenia		3			3			6	2	6		1	3	8	1	5		7	2	1		8	3	4	5	3	4	5	1	1	7	1		1	5		1	1	3		39
France																																									4
Israel	5		2	2	7	2		6			3	3		2	1	5		7	5			8	1		5		3	5	4	4	7	1		2		6	1	4	3	5	97
Estonia	4	3	3	6	4	7	2	2		6		10		3	2	2			1		3	2	6	8	3		1	4	3	2	1		7		2	4	3	3		5	106
United Kingdom																																									5
Armenia						4	3		2				3	3	12		1			1													6							4	34
Lithuania			5	3				3	3	1	2				3				7	7	2	3	7		1		12	1												1	30
Serbia	2		4	4						3				10																									5		53
Norway		4	4			10		4		3	4	4	4	5	7	4		4	10	4	2	5	2	5	2	8	5	3		3	6	6	8	6	8	4			5		102
Sweden	7	7	12	7	6	10	12	10	10	12	10	12	8	5	7	10	10	10	12	10	10	12	12	10	10	8	5	10	12	12	8	8	8	7	8	12	8		12	12	365
Cyprus																	10																								11
Australia	3	1		12	5	6	4	4	5	8	5	5	2	2		7	5	8	8	5	7	6	2	5	6	4		8	10	8	2	2	4	8	3	2	2	7	4	2	196
Belgium	1	4	6	5		8		7	6	7	7	7	12	1		8	7	7	4	2	4	7	12	3	10	6	5	12	7	5	5	7	10	5	4	3	6	10	2	3	217
Austria																																									0
Greece	10	5						8						4					3	12																					23
Montenegro	6	8		2									4																					12	12	10		2			44
Germany																																									0
Poland																																								2	10
Latvia	2	7		1	5	5	7	3	5	4	4	6	7			4	6	5	7	3		4		12		2		2	8	10	2	5	2	12	1	7	4	5	4	7	186
Romania							5	1		2							1				5					12			4		4										35
Spain				1									5																	3	3		1					5	1		15
Hungary									1		8		1			1				3		1					2					4		4							19
Georgia	10	1		12	10				4		1			5			2	3	5	8	5			6		5		6	5				5						1		51
Azerbaijan				8		3	1			4					10				3					2	8	3	8	3				3	3								49
Russia	8	12	10	8	12	12	10	5	8	10	12	8	10	6	5	12	8	6	6	8	6	6	10	7	7	10	7	6	2	6	10	12		10	10	5	10	6	7	6	303
Albania							6							12			6										10														34
Italy	12	6	8	10	8	1	8	12	7	5	3	2	6	7	8	3	12	2	6	6	12		8	1	12	7	6	7	7	7	12	12	12	10	7	8	12	8	6	8	292

167

2016 Eurovision 61: Stockholm, Sweden

Semi-final 1: 10 May 2016

Votes are cast by countries participating in each semi-final plus the five automatically qualifying countries decided by draw: France and Spain in semi-final 1, Italy, Germany and the UK in semi-final 2. Hosts Sweden voted in semi-final 1. This semi-final marked the first time the new voting system was used, with each voting country now awarding two sets of points, one from their professional jury and one from their public vote. The top 10 countries in each semi-final qualify for the final.

Rank	Start	Country	Artist	Song	Writer	Composer	POINTS
1Q	9	Russia	Sergey Lazarev	You Are The Only One	John Ballard, Ralph Charlie	Dimitris Kontopoulos, Philip Kirkorov	342
2Q	7	Armenia	Iveta Mukuchyan	LoveWave	Iveta Mukuchyan, Stephanie Crutchfield	Lilith Navasardyan, Levon Navasardyan	243
3Q	18	Malta	Ira Losco	Walk On Water	Lisa Desmond, Tim Larsson, Tobias Lundgren, Molly Pettersson-Hammar & Ira Losco	Lisa Desmond, Tim Larsson, Tobias Lundgren, Molly Pettersson-Hammar & Ira Losco	209
4Q	4	Hungary	Freddie	Pioneer	Borbála Csarnai	Szabó Zé	197
5Q	6	Netherlands	Douwe Bob	Slow Down	Douwe Bob Posthuma, Jeroen Overman, Jan-Peter Hoekstra	Douwe Bob Posthuma, Jeroen Overman, Jan-Peter Hoekstra, Matthijs van Duijvenbode	197
6Q	14	Azerbaijan	Samra	Miracle	Amir Aly, Jakke Erixson, Henrik Wikström	Amir Aly, Jakke Erixson, Henrik Wikström	185
7Q	12	Austria	ZOË	Loin d'ici	Christof Straub & Zoe Straub	Christof Straub & Zoe Straub	170
8Q	11	Cyprus	Minus One	Alter Ego	Thomas G:son, Minus One	Thomas G:son, Minus One	164
9Q	10	Czech Republic	Gabriela Gunčíková	I Stand	Aidan O'Connor, Sara Biglert	Christian Schneider, Sara Biglert	161
10Q	5	Croatia	Nina Kraljić	Lighthouse	Andreas Grass & Nikola Paryla	Andreas Grass & Nikola Paryla	133
11	17	Bosnia & H	Dalal & Deen feat. Ana Rucner and Jala	Ljubav Je	Almir Ajanović, Jasmin Fazlić	Almir Ajanović	104
12	8	San Marino	Serhat	I Didn't Know	Nektarios Tyrakis	Olcayto Ahmet Tuğsuz	68
13	15	Montenegro	Highway	The Real Thing	Srdjan Sekulovic Skansi	Skansi, Luka Vojvodić, Maro Market	60
14	16	Iceland	Greta Salóme	Hear Them Calling	Greta Salóme Stefánsdóttir	Greta Salóme Stefánsdóttir	51
15	1	Finland	Sandhja	Sing It Away	Sandhja Kuivalainen, Petri Matara, Milos Rosas, Markus Savijoki	Heikki Korhonen, Markus Savijoki, Milos Rosas, Petri Matara, Sandhja Kuivalainen	51
16	2	Greece	Argo	Utopian Land	Vladimiros Sofianides	Vladimiros Sofianides	44
17	3	Moldova	Lidia Isac	Falling Stars	Gabriel Alares, Sebastian Lestapier, Ellen Berg, Leonid Gutkin	Gabriel Alares, Sebastian Lestapier, Ellen Berg, Leonid Gutkin	33
18	13	Estonia	Jüri Pootsmann	Play	Stig Rästa, Vallo Kikas, Fred Krieger	Stig Rästa, Vallo Kikas, Fred Krieger	24

2016 Eurovision 61: Stockholm, Sweden — **Combined Jury & Public Votes** — **Semi-final 1: 10 May 2016**

	Armenia	Austria	Azerbaijan	Bosnia & H	Croatia	Cyprus	Czech Republic	Estonia	Finland	France	Greece	Hungary	Iceland	Malta	Moldova	Montenegro	Netherlands	Russia	San Marino	Spain	Sweden	TOTAL
Finland	8	2					7	7				5	2	5			2			3	10	51
Greece	10		6			15										3		10				44
Moldova	6		5			2								4				11				33
Hungary	6	8	15	5	16	12	18	10	4	2	3		8	8	9	7	9	10	7	15	4	197
Croatia	5	13		17		8	8	3	7	12	14		7		7	15	17	5	1	2	4	133
Netherlands	8	16	4	1	7	4	13	20	18	7	4	3	22	7	4	2			18	10	16	197
Armenia		9		10	8	17	12	3	8	12	3	12	8	16	18	15	17	24	8	22	8	243
San Marino		5	13	10				4	3	15	18	7	1	11	4	2	4					68
Russia	19	15	24	15	16	22	8	13	14	10	22	20	22	22	22	18	9		15	16	20	342
Czech Republic	7	11	5	16	16	5		6	10	4	3	11	8	5	11	5	6	6	6	13	7	161
Cyprus	8	2	1	2	12		5	16	7	9	20	9	6	14	7	5	13	8	13	4	3	164
Austria	5		6	6	7		10	10	13	22	7	8	12	2	7		16	10	3	12	9	170
Estonia		1	3				13		13					2	3			2				24
Azerbaijan		4		16	3	12	13	7	2	7	5	19	10	10	12	12	7	17	16	5	8	185
Montenegro	10		7	11	6	1		7			6			7				3	10			60
Iceland		6			1		4	7	9	6		1		3			7		8	6	5	51
Bosnia & H	2	12	15		16		9				5	16			1	18		10	6	8	12	104
Malta	22	12	12	7	8	13	9	10	8	10	5		10		11	14	9	10	5	8	10	209

2016 Eurovision 61: Stockholm, Sweden

Semi-final 2: 12 May 2016

Votes are cast by countries participating in each semi-final plus the five automatically qualifying countries decided by draw: France and Spain in semi-final 1, Italy, Germany and the UK in semi-final 2. Hosts Sweden voted in semi-final 1. Each voting country now awards two sets of points, one from their professional jury and one from their public vote. The top 10 countries in each semi-final qualify for the final.

Rank	Start	Country	Artist	Song	Writer	Composer	POINTS
1Q	10	Australia	Dami Im	Sound of Silence	DNA (David Musumeci & Anthony Egizii)	DNA (David Musumeci & Anthony Egizii)	330
2Q	14	Ukraine	Jamala	1944	Jamala	Jamala	287
3Q	18	Belgium	Laura Tesoro	What's The Pressure?	Sanne Putseys, Birsen Uçar	Sanne Putseys, Louis Favre, Yannick Werther	274
4Q	9	Lithuania	Donny Montell	I've Been Waiting For This Night	Jonas Thander, Beatrice Robertsson	Jonas Thander, Beatrice Robertsson	222
5Q	12	Bulgaria	Poli Genova	If Love Was A Crime	Borislav Milanov, Sebastian Arman, Joacim Bo Persson	Borislav Milanov, Sebastian Arman, Joacim Bo Persson	220
6Q	2	Poland	Michał Szpak	Color Of Your Life	Kamil Varen	Andy Palmer	151
7Q	4	Israel	Hovi Star	Made of Stars	Doron Medalie	Doron Medalie	147
8Q	1	Latvia	Justs	Heartbeat	Aminata Savadogo	Aminata Savadogo	132
9Q	16	Georgia	Nika Kocharov & Young Georgian Lolitaz	Midnight Gold	Kote Kalandadze	Kote Kalandadze, Thomas G:Son	123
10Q	6	Serbia	Sanja Vučić ZAA	Goodbye (Shelter)	Ivana Peters	Ivana Peters	105
11	8	FYR Macedonia	Kaliopi	Dona	Kaliopi	Romeo Grill	88
12	5	Belarus	IVAN	Help You Fly	Alexander Ivanov, Timofei Leontiev, Mary Susane Applegate	Victor Drobysh	84
13	15	Norway	Agnete	Icebreaker	Agnete Johnsen, Gabriel Alares, Ian Curnow	Agnete Johnsen, Gabriel Alares, Ian Curnow	63
14	11	Slovenia	ManuElla	Blue And Red	Leon Oblak	Manuella Brechko, Marjan Hvala	57
15	7	Ireland	Nicky Byrne	Sunlight	Nicky Byrne, Wayne Hector, Ronan Hardiman	Nicky Byrne, Wayne Hector, Ronan Hardiman	46
16	17	Albania	Eneda Tarifa	Fairytale	Olsa Toqi	Olsa Toqi	45
17	13	Denmark	Lighthouse X	Soldiers Of Love	Søren Bregendal, Johannes Nymark, Martin Skriver, Sebastian Owens, Daniel Durn, Katrine Klith Andersen	Søren Bregendal, Johannes Nymark, Martin Skriver, Sebastian Owens, Daniel Durn, Katrine Klith Andersen	34
18	3	Switzerland	Rykka	The Last Of Our Kind	Christina Rieder, Mike James, Jeff Dawson, Warne Livesey	Christina Rieder, Mike James, Jeff Dawson, Warne Livesey	28

2016 Eurovision 61: Stockholm, Sweden

Combined Jury & Public Votes

Semi-final 2: 12 May 2016

	Albania	Australia	Belarus	Belgium	Bulgaria	Denmark	FYR Macedonia	Georgia	Germany	Ireland	Israel	Italy	Latvia	Lithuania	Norway	Poland	Serbia	Slovenia	Switzerland	Ukraine	United Kingdom	TOTAL
Latvia	1	5	5	3		5	9	13	8	11	7			19	5	11		10	6	9	5	132
Poland	2		6	12	6	6	1	10	12	10	6	13	4	10	14		2	7	7	13	10	151
Switzerland	3	1		1	7	2	6	7	1													28
Israel	4	16	2	11	7	5	6	7	14	9		8	2	6	6	8	7	4	10	9	6	147
Belarus	6	6			10	1		6		3			8	6		12	5	2	1	15	3	84
Serbia	8	5	5	2	13		22	2			3		5	1	5	1		12	15	3	3	105
Ireland	7		4			8					3	2	1			2				2	9	46
FYR Macedonia	24	6			8						10	2					24	10	4	2		88
Lithuania	4	15	20	11	6	17	5	12	7	15	9	5	22		20	6	5	1	8	14	20	222
Australia	16		15	22	19	20	8	12	17	14	24	15	16	17	20	20	11	11	18	19	16	330
Slovenia	7	4		7	1		10			8		6	3	1			10					57
Bulgaria	14	18	12	13		10	16	5	11	15	13	7	10	5	16	9	10	11	7	5	13	220
Denmark	5	1	3	5				4	3		4		2		5	1			1			34
Ukraine	10	3	19	11	16	6	16	24	14	4	17	22	22	18	10	24	16	16	10		9	287
Norway	10	5	9	4	1	16	2	1						6			3	2	2	1	1	63
Georgia	10	5	4	8	7		1		15	1	5	7		18	1	14	5	1	2	12	13	123
Albania											8							3	10	14	10	45
Belgium	8	24	16		20	20	8	13	14	18	14	9	10	9	14	8	10	19	15	14	11	274

171

2016 Eurovision 61: Stockholm, Sweden

FINAL: 14 May 2016

Final qualification rules: Top 10 placed countries from each semi-final. Automatic qualification: United Kingdom, France, Germany, Spain, Italy and hosts Sweden. Each of the 42 participating countries now awards two sets of points, one from their professional jury and one from their public vote.

Rank	Start	Country	Artist	Song	Writer	Composer	POINTS
1	21	Ukraine	Jamala	1944	Jamala	Jamala	534
2	13	Australia	Dami Im	Sound of Silence	DNA (David Musumeci & Anthony Egizii)	DNA (David Musumeci & Anthony Egizii)	511
3	18	Russia	Sergey Lazarev	You Are The Only One	John Ballard, Ralph Charlie	Dimitris Kontopoulos, Philip Kirkorov	491
4	8	Bulgaria	Poli Genova	If Love Was A Crime	Borislav Milanov, Sebastian Arman, Joacim Bo Persson	Borislav Milanov, Sebastian Arman, Joacim Bo Persson	307
5	9	Sweden	Frans	If I Were Sorry	Frans Jeppsson Wall, Fredrik Andersson, Michael Saxell, Oscar Fogelström	Frans Jeppsson Wall, Fredrik Andersson, Michael Saxell, Oscar Fogelström	261
6	11	France	Amir	J'ai cherché	Nazim Khaled, Amir Haddad	Nazim Khaled, Amir Haddad, Johan Errami	257
7	26	Armenia	Iveta Mukuchyan	LoveWave	Iveta Mukuchyan, Stephanie Crutchfield	Lilith Navasardyan, Levon Navasardyan	249
8	12	Poland	Michał Szpak	Color Of Your Life	Kamil Varen	Andy Palmer	229
9	16	Lithuania	Donny Montell	I've Been Waiting For This Night	Jonas Thander, Beatrice Robertsson	Jonas Thander, Beatrice Robertsson	200
10	1	Belgium	Laura Tesoro	What's The Pressure?	Sanne Putseys, Birsen Uçar	Sanne Putseys, Louis Favre, Yannick Werther	181
11	3	Netherlands	Douwe Bob	Slow Down	Douwe Bob Posthuma, Jeroen Overman, Jan-Peter Hoekstra	Douwe Bob Posthuma, Jeroen Overman, Jan-Peter Hoekstra, Matthijs van Duijvenbode	153
12	22	Malta	Ira Losco	Walk On Water	Lisa Desmond, Tim Larsson, Tobias Lundgren, Molly Pettersson-Hammar & Ira Losco	Lisa Desmond, Tim Larsson, Tobias Lundgren, Molly Pettersson-Hammar & Ira Losco	153
13	24	Austria	ZOË	Loin d'ici	Christof Straub & Zoë Straub	Christof Straub & Zoë Straub	151
14	7	Israel	Hovi Star	Made of Stars	Doron Medalie	Doron Medalie	135
15	20	Latvia	Justs	Heartbeat	Aminata Savadogo	Aminata Savadogo	132
16	6	Italy	Francesca Michielin	No Degree Of Separation	Francesca Michielin, Federica Abbate, Norma Jean Martine	Fabio Gargiulo, Federica Abbate, Cheope	124
17	4	Azerbaijan	Samra	Miracle	Amir Aly, Jakke Erixson, Henrik Wikström	Amir Aly, Jakke Erixson, Henrik Wikström	117
18	15	Serbia	Sanja Vučić ZAA	Goodbye (Shelter)	Ivana Peters	Ivana Peters	115
19	5	Hungary	Freddie	Pioneer	Borbála Csarnai	Szabó Zé	108
20	23	Georgia	Nika Kocharov & Young Georgian Lolitaz	Midnight Gold	Kote Kalandadze	Kote Kalandadze, Thomas G:Son	104
21	14	Cyprus	Minus One	Alter Ego	Thomas G:son, Minus One	Thomas G:son, Minus One	96
22	19	Spain	Barei	Say Yay!	Barei, Ruben Villanueva & Victor Pua	Barei, Ruben Villanueva & Victor Pua	77
23	17	Croatia	Nina Kraljić	Lighthouse	Andreas Grass & Nikola Paryla	Andreas Grass & Nikola Paryla	73
24	25	United Kingdom	Joe And Jake	You're Not Alone	Matt Schwartz, Justin Benson, Siva Kaneswaran	Matt Schwartz, Justin Benson, Siva Kaneswaran	62
25	2	Czech Republic	Gabriela Gunčíková	I Stand	Aidan O'Connor, Sara Biglert	Christian Schneider, Sara Biglert	41
26	10	Germany	Jamie-Lee	Ghost	Anna Leyne	Anna Leyne, Thomas Burchia, Conrad Hensel	11

2016 Eurovision 61: Stockholm, Sweden — Combined Jury & Public Votes

FINAL: 14 May 2016

Recipient	Albania	Armenia	Australia	Austria	Azerbaijan	Belarus	Belgium	Bosnia & H	Bulgaria	Croatia	Cyprus	Czech Republic	Denmark	Estonia	Finland	France	FYR Macedonia	Georgia	Germany	Greece	Hungary	Iceland	Ireland	Israel	Italy	Latvia	Lithuania	Malta	Moldova	Montenegro	Netherlands	Norway	Poland	Russia	San Marino	Serbia	Slovenia	Spain	Sweden	Switzerland	Ukraine	United Kingdom	TOTAL
Belgium		4	24	5		4						2	16			4	8	10	5			6	12	7			5			3	16	7	4			5	8		3	10	10		181
Czech Republic		1		4											3	1					2	5	2												4		1		3		10	5	41
Netherlands			3	6				6					7	14	10	7	2	7	7		8	18	8			3		3	8	7	1	6			4		1	3	7	5		3	153
Azerbaijan						10		9		10			14	6			1	1				1				3	2	6		1				16				2	10	5	17	13	117
Hungary	2	3			11	3		1			2			10		12				1	7			2	4			5		10	1	12	6	1	3	10	3			9		1	108
Italy	18						10			8	8	13		6	2		1	7	4	5		6				2	6	15		4	7			1	10		1	10		8	2		8	124
Israel	3	10			9					3	3				7	3	5	2			8		4		8	2	6	1		6	1	3			3	7	2	8	7	9	6		135
Bulgaria	12	7	18	5	16	5		11		7	5		2		4	15	20	3	12	7		15		14	7	2	2	18	2	7	7	13		10		12	12	1		8		6	3	307
Sweden	3	2	15	10	11	10	1	5			1		14	22	22	7		6	18	1	7		7	15	2	15	7	1	6		12	7	10	2	4	1	5	1			5	1	261
Germany			2														1																										11
France	10	19	13	8	4		16	11		10	13	5	2	3	4			4		10	1	7	3	20	12		4	8	6	6	9	1	1	10	8		4	17	11	3		6	6	257
Poland	5	1		12	5	6	12		6	4	2	7	5	1	5	7	11	4	4	3	8	10	10	4	10	5	9		1	1	10	11		5		4	9	5	10	5	8	10	229
Australia	24	5		15	9	7	16	13	13	17	15	1	20	14	15	6	8	9	11	12	15	6	6	15	6	11	17	15	19	18	17	18	17	6	5	13	10	12	24	13	9	14	511
Cyprus	12				1			7	1					7	1					20	5				7			5	2	1			1	11	5								96
Serbia			4			5		20	5	14							19								4	18				18		14	2		8			17		12		2	115
Lithuania	4		8	1	5	10		1	1		3	3	11	10	6			10	1		3	4	12	1	2	19			7	2			2	5	8	8			8	7	15	16	200
Croatia		1	6				14	8	12		1	8			5		11	2			8	7		3			1		1	6					4	4	8					1	73
Russia	14	14	5	11	24	6	16	11	18	14	22	10	4	12	8	7	8	8	12	22	10	15	8	10	8	19	17	14	19	18	3	6	8		17	13	10	12	14	6	12	7	491
Spain	6	3	7		1		6		7		7			7	1	4		3		22	5		8	4	12		8	2	8	7	7		5		6		10		2	2	2	4	77
Latvia					5			4					1	15	15			13	2		8			5	5		19	2	1			3	11		5		7		5	3	13	3	132
Ukraine	6	10	10	10	20	17	5	19	10	10	22	1	15	15	12	15	18	22	13	8	12	18	15	20	22	22	18	4	22	10	10	8	24		17	19	19	7	7	10		15	534
Malta	2	13	6	10	11	5			7		6	6	2	2	5		3		2	4	10				5	4			3	12		7		8	3	10	5	6	7		3	1	153
Georgia	18			5			7										3		8	5	6	3	1	3	6	6					14	3	8	5	6						9		104
Austria	4	3		11			8	5	4	6		4	3						7	1	6					2	4	4	4		14		4	8	1		6	2	5	14		12	151
United Kingdom	5	8																10										13						6	8	2							62
Armenia	2		2	2	10	7		2	20	4	16	8		4	3	14	7	12	2	18	1		10	8	1	6	4	7	12	10	10		2	24	2	5	4	18	4		7		249

173

2017 Eurovision 62: Kiev, Ukraine
Semi-final 1: 9 May 2017

Votes are cast by countries participating in each semi-final plus the five automatically qualifying countries decided by draw: Italy, Spain and United Kingdom in semi-final 1, France and Germany in semi-final 2. Hosts Ukraine also voted in semi-final 2. Each voting country awards two sets of points, one from their professional jury and one from their public vote. The top 10 countries in each semi-final qualify for the final.

Rank	Start	Country	Artist	Song	Writer	Composer	POINTS
1Q	9	Portugal	Salvador Sobral	Amar Pelos Dois	Luísa Sobral	Luísa Sobral	370
2Q	12	Moldova	Sunstroke Project	Hey Mamma	Alina Galetcaia	Anton Ragoza, Serghei Ialovitki, Seghei Stepanov, Mihail Cebotarenco	291
3Q	1	Sweden	Robin Bengtsson	I Can't Go On	David Kreuger, Hamed "K-One" Pirouzpanah, Robin Stjernberg	David Kreuger, Hamed "K-One" Pirouzpanah, Robin Stjernberg	227
4Q	5	Belgium	Blanche	City Lights	Pierre Dumoulin, Ellie DelVaux	Pierre Dumoulin, Emmanuel Delcourt	165
5Q	15	Cyprus	Hovig	Gravity	Thomas G:son	Thomas G:son	164
6Q	3	Australia	Isaiah	Don't Come Easy	DNA (David Musumeci & Anthony Egizii), Michael Angelo	DNA (David Musumeci & Anthony Egizii), Michael Angelo	160
7Q	16	Armenia	Artsvik	Fly With Me	Avet Barseghyan, David Tserunyan	Lilith Navasaryan, Levon Navasardyan	152
8Q	8	Azerbaijan	Dihaj	Skeletons	Sandra Bjurman	Isa Melikov	150
9Q	11	Poland	Kasia Moś	Flashlight	Kasia Moś, Rickard Bonde Truumeel, Pete Barringer	Kasia Moś, Rickard Bonde Truumeel, Pete Barringer	119
10Q	10	Greece	Demy	This Is Love	Romy Papadea, John Ballard	Dimitris Kontopoulos	115
11	2	Georgia	Tamara Gachechiladze	Keep The Faith	Tamara Gachechiladze	Anri Jokhadze	99
12	7	Finland	Norma John	Blackbird	Lasse Piirainen, Leena Tirronen	Lasse Piirainen, Leena Tirronen	92
13	14	Czech Republic	Martina Bárta	My Turn	DWB, Kyler Niko	DWB, Kyler Niko	83
14	4	Albania	Lindita	World	Lindita, Big Basta	Klodian Qafoku	76
15	13	Iceland	Svala	Paper	Svala Bjorgvinsdottir, Lily Elise	Svala Bjorgvinsdottir, Einar Egilsson, Lester Mendez, Lily Elise	60
16	6	Montenegro	Slavko Kalezić	Space	Adis Eminić, Iva Boršić, Momcilo Zekovic Zeko	Momčilo Zeković Zeko	56
17	17	Slovenia	Omar Naber	On My Way	Omar Naber	Omar Naber	36
18	18	Latvia	Triana Park	Line	Agnese Rakovska	Agnese Rakovska, Kristaps Ērglis, Kristians Rakovskis	21

2017 Eurovision 62: Kiev, Ukraine — Semi-final 1: 9 May 2017
Combined Jury & Public Votes

Contestant \ Voter	Albania	Armenia	Australia	Azerbaijan	Belgium	Cyprus	Czech Republic	Finland	Georgia	Greece	Iceland	Italy	Latvia	Moldova	Montenegro	Poland	Portugal	Slovenia	Spain	Sweden	United Kingdom	TOTAL
Sweden	14	9	16	6	17	13	12	19	12	5	18	11	9	9	9	9	15	12	9		3	227
Georgia	1	14		18	3	1		3		10	7	4		7		10	9	5		6	1	99
Australia	6	4		9	11	9	12	8	6		16	1	10	6	4	8	6	15	8	14	7	160
Albania				13						15		15	1	10	22			1				76
Belgium	11	6	4	7		7	9	10	5	5	9	11	15	6	2	15	8	10	10	13	8	165
Montenegro	5	1	7			6		3	7	7	2	5	5	8		5	14	6	1	1		56
Finland	7		9	13	3					1	6	12	3	3	13		9	8	5	15	3	92
Azerbaijan			4		5	14	16	22	22	8	6	14	24	16	11	24		10	5		20	150
Portugal	18	14	16	20	19	16	14	22	20	15	24	4	6	18	16	4	7	20	24	17		370
Greece	14	15	4		6	24			2	2	1	8		7			1	4	6	6	5	115
Poland	4	4	12	4	12	5	16	2	3		5	19	6	4	15			10	3	15	18	119
Moldova	19	18	22	15	11	7	16	14	9	10	8		14		15	10	22		17		20	291
Iceland	4	3	2	2	2	1		10	3				12	2		1		10	8	9	2	60
Czech Republic		4	4	4	6		9		1	18	5	6	7		2	3	14	4	10	4	8	83
Cyprus	3	24	6		12	1	5	13	12	20	8	6	6	7	5	7	3			12	9	164
Armenia			10		7	13	1	8	17				5	14	8	12	4	1	4	3	5	152
Slovenia	10				2			3	4		1				9	8	4		4	1		36
Latvia				5				1						5					2		7	21

175

2017 Eurovision 62: Kiev, Ukraine — Semi-final 2: 11 May 2017

Votes are cast by countries participating in each semi-final plus the five automatically qualifying countries decided by draw: Italy, Spain and United Kingdom in semi-final 1, France and Germany in semi-final 2. Hosts Ukraine also voted in semi-final 2. Each voting country awards two sets of points, one from their professional jury and one from their public vote. The top 10 countries in each semi-final qualify for the final.

Rank	Start	Country	Artist	Song	Writer	Composer	POINTS
1Q	15	Bulgaria	Kristian Kostov	Beautiful Mess	Borislav Milanov, Sebastian Arman, Joacim Persson, Alexander Blay, Alex	Borislav Milanov, Sebastian Arman, Joacim Persson, Alexander Blay, Alex	403
2Q	7	Hungary	Joci Pápai	Origo	József Pápai	József Pápai	231
3Q	18	Israel	IMRI	I Feel Alive	Dolev Ram, Penn Hazut	Dolev Ram, Penn Hazut	207
4Q	6	Netherlands	OG3NE	Lights And Shadows	Rick Vol	Rick Vol, Rory de Kievit	200
5Q	12	Norway	JOWST	Grab The Moment	Jonas McDonnell	Joakim With Steen	189
6Q	5	Romania	Ilinca ft. Alex Florea	Yodel It!	Alexa Niculae	Mihai Alexandru	174
7Q	2	Austria	Nathan Trent	Running On Air	Nathan Trent, Bernhard Penzias	Nathan Trent, Bernhard Penzias	147
8Q	11	Croatia	Jacques Houdek	My Friend	Jacques Houdek, Ines Prajo, Arjana Kunštek, Fabrizio Laucella	Jacques Houdek, Siniša Reljić,	141
9Q	14	Belarus	Naviband	Story Of My Life	Artem Lukyanenka	Artem Lukyanenka	110
10Q	8	Denmark	Anja	Where I Am	Anja Nissen, Michael D'Arcy, Angel Tupai	Anja Nissen, Michael D'Arcy, Angel Tupai	101
11	1	Serbia	Tijana Bogićević	In Too Deep	Borislav Milanov, Joacim Persson, Lisa Desmond, Johan Alkenae	Borislav Milanov, Joacim Persson, Lisa Desmond, Johan Alkenae	98
12	13	Switzerland	Timebelle	Apollo	Elias Näslin, Alessandra Günthardt, Nicolas Günthardt	Elias Näslin, Alessandra Günthardt, Nicolas Günthardt	97
13	9	Ireland	Brendan Murray	Dying To Try	Jörgen Elofsson, James Newman	Jörgen Elofsson, James Newman	86
14	17	Estonia	Koit Toome & Laura	Verona	Sven Lõhmus	Sven Lõhmus	85
15	3	FYR Macedonia	Jana Burčeska	Dance Alone	Joacim Persson, Alex Omar, Bobi-Leon Milanov, Florence A.	Joacim Persson, Alex Omar, Bobi-Leon Milanov, Florence A.	69
16	4	Malta	Claudia Faniello	Breathlessly	Gerard James Borg	Philip Vella, Sean Vella	55
17	16	Lithuania	Fusedmarc	Rain Of Revolution	Denis Zujev, Michail Levin	Denis Zujev, Viktoria Ivanovskaja, Michail Levin	42
18	10	San Marino	Valentina Monetta & Jimmie Wilson	Spirit Of The Night	Jutta Staudenmayer, Steven Barnacle	Ralph Siegel	1

176

2017 Eurovision 62: Kiev, Ukraine

Combined Jury & Public Votes

Semi-final 2: 11 May 2017

	Austria	Belarus	Bulgaria	Croatia	Denmark	Estonia	France	FYR Macedonia	Germany	Hungary	Ireland	Israel	Lithuania	Malta	Netherlands	Norway	Romania	San Marino	Serbia	Switzerland	Ukraine	TOTAL
Serbia	6	4	2	12	8	1	6	12	7	4	2			2	6	6		2		18		98
Austria		6	12	9	10	5	4	3	10	11	10	11	4	1	14	4	9	8	7	9		147
FYR Macedonia			12	6			8			2		5	1	8	3	3	1	4	15	3	3	69
Malta	6	5	7	1		4	6	8	3		5	2	6		9	8		1	2	7		55
Romania	7	5	7	7	8	12	12	13	7	7	12	13		11	9	8		8	6	7	9	174
Netherlands	12	8	9	14	17	8	5	8	13	16	8	4	5	9		11	12	15	8	12	6	200
Hungary	15	10	8	22	7	10	7	11	10		6	19	7	6	10	8	12	13	24	13	13	231
Denmark		2	4	8		8	2	7	1	6		4	6	5	11	14	10	5	4	3	2	101
Ireland	13	3	1		7	14	1	1	4	5		1	12	5	2	2	9	2		2	2	86
San Marino									1													1
Croatia	11	7	12			5	2	8	11	10	7		2	8	6	2	12	10	10	10	8	141
Norway	5	16	8	4	22	13	3		14	12	9	10	19		12		4	10	4	10	14	189
Switzerland	6	2	7	1	5	3	4	6	2	1	8	3	8	5	4	5	16	5	4		2	97
Belarus	8		5	10		6	13	22		5	1	13	11	7	3		1		2	1	24	110
Bulgaria	20	24		14	18	22	15	22	22	24	22	18	20	24	24	24	16	20	18	18	18	403
Lithuania		8				1		4			12					10		6		1	1	42
Estonia	2	9	2		3		6	6	3	4	3	13	12	5		5	3			1	8	85
Israel	5	7	20	8	11	4	22	7	8	9	10		3	20	12	14	11	7	12	9	8	207

2017 Eurovision 62: Kiev, Ukraine

FINAL: 13 May 2017

Final qualification rules: Top 10 placed countries from each semi-final. Automatic qualification: United Kingdom, France, Germany, Spain, Italy and hosts Ukraine. Each of the 42 participating countries awards two sets of points, one from their professional jury and one from their public vote.

Rank	Start	Country	Artist	Song	Writer	Composer	POINTS
1	11	Portugal	Salvador Sobral	Amar Pelos Dois	Luisa Sobral	Luisa Sobral	758
2	25	Bulgaria	Kristian Kostov	Beautiful Mess	Borislav Milanov, Sebastian Arman, Joacim Persson, Alexander Blay, Alex	Borislav Milanov, Sebastian Arman, Joacim Persson, Alexander Blay, Alex	615
3	7	Moldova	Sunstroke Project	Hey, Mamma!	Alina Galetcaia	Anton Ragoza, Serghei Ialovitki, Seghei Stepanov, Mihail Cebotarenco	374
4	23	Belgium	Blanche	City Lights	Pierre Dumoulin, Ellie Delvaux	Pierre Dumoulin, Emmanuel Delcourt	363
5	24	Sweden	Robin Bengtsson	I Can't Go On	David Kreuger, Hamed "K-One" Pirouzpanah, Robin Stjernberg	David Kreuger, Hamed "K-One" Pirouzpanah, Robin Stjernberg	344
6	9	Italy	Francesco Gabbani	Occidentali's Karma	Francesco Gabbani, Fabio Ilacqua, Luca Chiaravalli	Francesco Gabbani, Filippo Gabbani, Luca Chiaravalli	334
7	20	Romania	Ilinca ft. Alex Florea	Yodel It!	Alexa Niculae	Mihai Alexandru	282
8	8	Hungary	Joci Pápai	Origo	József Pápai	József Pápai	200
9	14	Australia	Isaiah	Don't Come Easy	DNA (David Musumeci & Anthony Egizii), Michael Angelo	DNA (David Musumeci & Anthony Egizii), Michael Angelo	173
10	17	Norway	JOWST	Grab The Moment	Jonas McDonnell	Joakim With Steen	158
11	6	Netherlands	OG3NE	Lights And Shadows	Rick Vol	Rick Vol, Rory de Kievit	150
12	26	France	Alma	Requiem	Nazim Khaled, Alexandra Maquet	Nazim Khaled	135
13	13	Croatia	Jacques Houdek	My Friend	Jacques Houdek, Ines Prajo, Arjana Kunštek, Fabrizio Laucella	Jacques Houdek, Siniša Reljić, Tony Malm	128
14	12	Azerbaijan	Dihaj	Skeletons	Sandra Bjurman	Isa Melikov	120
15	18	United Kingdom	Lucie Jones	Never Give Up On You	Emmelie de Forest, Daniel Salcedo, Lawrie Martin	Emmelie de Forest, Daniel Salcedo, Lawrie Martin	111
16	4	Austria	Nathan Trent	Running On Air	Nathan Trent, Bernhard Penzias	Nathan Trent, Bernhard Penzias	93
17	3	Belarus	Naviband	Story Of My Life	Artem Lukyanenka	Artem Lukyanenka	83
18	5	Armenia	Artsvik	Fly With Me	Avet Barseghyan, David Tserunyan	Lilith Navasaryan, Levon Navasardyan	79
19	15	Greece	Demy	This Is Love	Romy Papadea, John Ballard	Dimitris Kontopoulos	77
20	10	Denmark	Anja	Where I Am	Anja Nissen, Michael D'Arcy, Angel Tupai	Anja Nissen, Michael D'Arcy, Angel Tupai	77
21	19	Cyprus	Hovig	Gravity	Thomas G:son	Thomas G:son	68
22	2	Poland	Kasia Moś	Flashlight	Kasia Moś, Rickard Bonde Truumeel, Pete Barringer	Kasia Moś, Rickard Bonde Truumeel, Pete Barringer	64
23	1	Israel	IMRI	I Feel Alive	Dolev Ram, Penn Hazut	Dolev Ram, Penn Hazut	39
24	22	Ukraine	O Torvald	Time	Kamenchuk Yevhen	Zhenia Galych, Denys Miziuk	36
25	21	Germany	Levina	Perfect Life	Lindy Robbins, Dave Bassett, Lindsey Ray	Lindy Robbins, Dave Bassett, Lindsey Ray	6
26	16	Spain	Manel Navarro	Do It For Your Lover	Manel Navarro, Antonio Rayo	Manel Navarro, Antonio Rayo	5

2017 Eurovision 62: Kiev, Ukraine
FINAL: 13 May 2017
Combined Jury & Public Votes

Country	TOTAL
Israel	39
Poland	64
Belarus	83
Austria	93
Armenia	79
Netherlands	150
Moldova	374
Hungary	200
Italy	334
Denmark	77
Portugal	758
Azerbaijan	120
Croatia	128
Australia	173
Greece	77
Spain	5
Norway	158
United Kingdom	111
Cyprus	68
Romania	282
Germany	6
Ukraine	36
Belgium	363
Sweden	344
Bulgaria	615
France	135

Voting countries (columns, left to right as shown on page): United Kingdom, Ukraine, Switzerland, Sweden, Spain, Slovenia, Serbia, San Marino, Romania, Portugal, Poland, Norway, Netherlands, Montenegro, Moldova, Malta, Lithuania, Latvia, Italy, Israel, Ireland, Iceland, Hungary, Greece, Germany, Georgia, FYR Macedonia, France, Finland, Estonia, Denmark, Czech Republic, Cyprus, Croatia, Bulgaria, Belgium, Belarus, Azerbaijan, Austria, Australia, Armenia, Albania.

2018 Eurovision 63: Lisbon, Portugal

Semi-final 1: 8 May 2018

Votes are cast by countries participating in each semi-final plus the five automatically qualifying countries decided by draw: Spain and United Kingdom in semi-final 1, France, Italy and Germany in semi-final 2. Hosts Portugal voted in semi-final 1. Each voting country awards two sets of points, one from their professional jury and one from their public vote. The top 10 countries in each semi-final qualify for the final.

Rank	Start	Country	Artist	Song	Writer	Composer	POINTS
1Q	7	Israel	Netta	Toy	Doron Medalie & Stav Beger	Doron Medalie & Stav Beger	283
2Q	19	Cyprus	Eleni Foureira	Fuego	Alex Papaconstantinou, Geraldo Sandell, Anderz Wrethov, Didrick, Viktor Svensson	Alex Papaconstantinou, Geraldo Sandell, Anderz Wrethov, Didrick, Viktor Svensson	262
3Q	5	Czech Republic	Mikolas Josef	Lie To Me	Mikolas Josef	Mikolas Josef	232
4Q	13	Austria	Cesár Sampson	Nobody But You	Sebastian Arman, Cesár Sampson, Joacim Persson, Johan Alkenäs, Borislav Milanov	Sebastian Arman, Cesár Sampson, Joacim Persson, Johan Alkenäs, Borislav Milanov	231
5Q	9	Estonia	Elina Nechayeva	La Forza	Elina Nechayeva, Ksenia Kuchukova	Mihkel Mattisen, Timo Vendt	201
6Q	18	Ireland	Ryan O'Shaughnessy	Together	Ryan O'Shaughnessy, Mark Caplice, Laura Elizabeth Hughes	Ryan O'Shaughnessy, Mark Caplice, Laura Elizabeth Hughes	179
7Q	10	Bulgaria	Equinox	Bones	Borislav Milanov, Joacim Persson, Brandon Treyshun Campbell, Dag Lundberg	Borislav Milanov, Joacim Persson, Brandon Treyshun Campbell, Dag Lundberg	177
8Q	3	Albania	Eugent Bushpepa	Mall	Eugent Bushpepa	Eugent Bushpepa	162
9Q	6	Lithuania	Ieva Zasimauskaitė	When We're Old	Vytautas Bikus	Vytautas Bikus	119
10Q	15	Finland	Saara Aalto	Monsters	Saara Aalto, Joy Deb, Linnea Deb, Ki Fitzgerald	Saara Aalto, Joy Deb, Linnea Deb, Ki Fitzgerald	108
11	1	Azerbaijan	Aisel	X My Heart	Sandra Bjurman	Dimitris Kontopoulos	94
12	4	Belgium	Sennek	A Matter Of Time	Laura Groeseneken, Alex Callier, Maxime Tribeche	Laura Groeseneken, Alex Callier, Maxime Tribeche	91
13	17	Switzerland	ZiBBZ	Stones	Laurell Barker, Corinne Gfeller	Laurell Barker, Corinne Gfeller, Stefan Gfeller	86
14	14	Greece	Yianna Terzi	Oniro Mou	Yianna Terzi, Aris Kalimeris, Michalis Papathanasiou, Dimitris Stamatiou	Yianna Terzi, Aris Kalimeris, Michalis Papathanasiou, Dimitris Stamatiou	81
15	16	Armenia	Sevak Khanagyan	Qami	Anna Danielyan, Victoria Maloyan	Sevak Khanagyan	79
16	8	Belarus	Alekseev	Forever	Yevgeny Matyushenko	Kirill Pavlov	65
17	12	Croatia	Franka	Crazy	Franka Batelic	Branimir Mihaljevic	63
18	11	FYR Macedonia	Eye Cue	Lost And Found	Bojan Trajkovski	Bojan Trajkovski, Darko Dimitrov	24
19	2	Iceland	Ari Ólafsson	Our Choice	Thorunn Clausen	Thorunn Clausen	15

2018 Eurovision 63: Lisbon, Portugal — Semi-final 1: 8 May 2018

Jury Votes

Recipient	Albania	Armenia	Austria	Azerbaijan	Belarus	Belgium	Bulgaria	Croatia	Cyprus	Czech Republic	Estonia	Finland	FYR Macedonia	Greece	Iceland	Ireland	Israel	Lithuania	Portugal	Spain	Switzerland	United Kingdom	TOTAL
Azerbaijan	5								10		3		7	12			10						47
Iceland					7	1				4			2								1		15
Albania		5	6	7	12	4			7	5	1	6	10	8	12		4	1	5	4		7	114
Belgium	4	6	7				12	1		10	4	5			2	2		8	10				71
Czech Republic		7	8		10	10	7	10	1				8	2	5	4	3	5	3	7	8	10	98
Lithuania	1	2						8			10	2				2	2		12		7		57
Israel	10	12	12	4	6	7	5	12	12	3		12	5	4	10	10		7	2	12	5	8	167
Belarus	7	1		12																			20
Estonia		8	3	1	5			6	5				4	10	6	8		4	8	6	12	6	81
Bulgaria	6		4	2		2			6	7	7	10	12	6	2	6	6	3	7	3	3	12	107
FYR Macedonia	8			6										3			1						18
Croatia		4			8		4		4		2		6	5			6		1			5	46
Austria		4		5	1	12	8		3	1	12	8			7	7	12	10	6	8	6	10	115
Greece	3	2	10					3	8						1	1							28
Finland					3		1		2		5				4	5	7	2		1	2	3	35
Armenia			10		4	6	2			2		3					5		4			2	38
Switzerland	2	3	1	3		8		5		6	6	1	1		3	3	8	6		5	4	59
Ireland			5		2	5		7		8	4	4	3		8			12		2	10	1	71
Cyprus	12	10		8		3	3	2			8	7		7		12				10	4		89

181

2018 Eurovision 63: Lisbon, Portugal

Semi-final 1: 8 May 2018

Public Votes

	Albania	Armenia	Austria	Azerbaijan	Belarus	Belgium	Bulgaria	Croatia	Cyprus	Czech Republic	Estonia	Finland	FYR Macedonia	Greece	Iceland	Ireland	Israel	Lithuania	Portugal	Spain	Switzerland	United Kingdom	TOTAL
Azerbaijan	7		4					5		10			5	3	1	1	5		7			1	47
Iceland																							0
Albania			1					4		3	3	1	12	10		1	2	8		5	10	1	48
Belgium		3		2	2						3						2	8					20
Czech Republic	2	7	10	8	8	8	3	10	7		7	7	6	6	12	4	2	7	1	4	3	2	134
Lithuania				1	6	4	10		3		10	2			3	12	12		6	3		12	62
Israel	4	4	6	10	10	3	7	6	8	12	1	10	3	2	8	5		1	2	7	8	5	116
Belarus		10		12			2		5		6	3		1				6					45
Estonia	6	5	3	3	3	5	4	6	6	5		12	3	8	6	10	7	12	12	2	1	4	120
Bulgaria	5	2	5	4	5				10	2			8	7		3	3	2		8		6	70
FYR Macedonia							5	1															6
Croatia	3	1	2										10								4		17
Austria	3	6		5	4	10	8	7	1	6	8	8			7	8	8	10	5	4	12	2	116
Greece	10	8				1	10	3	12	4			4							2	2	3	53
Finland	8					2	1		4	1	12		2		10	6	6	3	4	6	5	7	73
Armenia					12	6	6			8				5									41
Switzerland	1		8					2	2		2	4	1		2	2	1		3	1			27
Ireland		5	12	6	1	12		8	2	4	5	6		4	4	4	4	4	8	12	6	10	108
Cyprus	12	12	7	7	7	7	12	12		7	4	5	7	12	5	7	10	5	10	10	7	8	173

2018 Eurovision 63: Lisbon, Portugal — Combined Jury & Public Votes — Semi-final 1: 8 May 2018

	Albania	Armenia	Austria	Azerbaijan	Belarus	Belgium	Bulgaria	Croatia	Cyprus	Czech Republic	Estonia	Finland	FYR Macedonia	Greece	Iceland	Ireland	Israel	Lithuania	Portugal	Spain	Switzerland	United Kingdom	TOTAL
Azerbaijan	12								10	10	3		12	15	1		15		7				94
Iceland					7	1				4			2								1		15
Albania		5	7	7	12	4	6	8	7	8	1	7	22	18	12	1	4	1	5	9	10	8	162
Belgium	4	9	7	2	2		12	1		10	7	5			2	2	2	16	10				91
Czech Republic	2	14	18	8	18	18	10	20	8		7	7	14	8	17	8	15	12	4	11	11	2	232
Lithuania	1	2	2	1	6	4	10	8	3	3	20	4			3	12	2		18	3	7	12	119
Israel	14	16	18	14	16	10	12	12	20	24	1	22	8	6	18	15		8	4	19	13	13	283
Belarus	7	11		24			2		5		6	3		1				6					65
Estonia	6	13	6	4	3	5	4	6	11	5		12	4	18	12	18	7	16	20	8	13	10	201
Bulgaria	11	2	9	6	10	2		6	16	9	7	10	20	13		9	3	5	7	11	3	18	177
FYR Macedonia	8			6			5	1						3			1						24
Croatia		1	2	5	8	4	4		4		2		16	5	6		6		1		4	5	63
Austria	3	10		5	5	22	16	7	4	7	20	16			14	15	20	20	11	8	18	10	231
Greece	13	10		10		1	10	6	20				4		1	1					2	3	81
Finland	8				3	2	2		2	1	17		2		14	11	13	5	4	7	7	10	108
Armenia			10		16	12	8		4	10		3		5			5		4			2	79
Switzerland	3	3	9	3		8		7		6	2	5	1	1	5	5	9	6	3	6		4	86
Ireland		17	17	6	3	17		15	2	12	11	10	1	4	12		4	16	8	14	16	11	179
Cyprus	24	22	7	15	7	10	15	14		7	12	12	10	19	5	19	10	5	10	20	11	8	262

2018 Eurovision 63: Lisbon, Portugal — Semi-final 2: 10 May 2018

Votes are cast by countries participating in each semi-final plus the five automatically qualifying countries decided by draw: Spain and United Kingdom in semi-final 1, France, Italy and Germany in semi-final 2. Hosts Portugal voted in semi-final 1. Each voting country awards two sets of points, one from their professional jury and one from their public vote. The top 10 countries in each semi-final qualify for the final.

Rank	Start	Country	Artist	Song	Writer	Composer	POINTS
1Q	1	Norway	Alexander Rybak	That's How You Write A Song	Alexander Rybak	Alexander Rybak	266
2Q	15	Sweden	Benjamin Ingrosso	Dance You Off	MAG, Louis Schoorl, K Nita, Benjamin Ingrosso	MAG, Louis Schoorl, K Nita, Benjamin Ingrosso	254
3Q	7	Moldova	DoReDos	My Lucky Day	John Ballard	Philipp Kirkorov	235
4Q	9	Australia	Jessica Mauboy	We Got Love	Anthony Egizii, David Musumeci, Jessica Mauboy	Anthony Egizii, David Musumeci	212
5Q	5	Denmark	Rasmussen	Higher Ground	Niclas Arn, Karl Eurén	Niclas Arn, Karl Eurén	204
6Q	18	Ukraine	Melovin	Under The Ladder	Mike Ryals	Melovin	179
7Q	8	Netherlands	Waylon	Outlaw In 'Em	Waylon, Ilya Toshinskiy, Jim Beaver	Waylon, Ilya Toshinskiy, Jim Beaver	174
8Q	17	Slovenia	Lea Sirk	Hvala, ne!	Lea Sirk	Lea Sirk, Tomy DeClerque	132
9Q	3	Serbia	Sanja Ilić & Balkanika	Nova Deca	Danica Krstajić	Aleksandar Sanja Ilić, Tatjana Karajanov Ilić	117
10Q	13	Hungary	AWS	Viszlát Nyár	Örs Siklósi	Bence Brucker, Dániel Kökényes, Áron Veress, Soma Schiszler	111
11	2	Romania	The Humans	Goodbye	Cristina Caramarcu	Alexandru Matei, Alin Neagoe	107
12	14	Latvia	Laura Rizzotto	Funny Girl	Laura Rizzotto	Laura Rizzotto	106
13	12	Malta	Christabelle	Taboo	Muxu, Christabelle	Thomas G:son, Johnny Sanchez	101
14	11	Poland	Gromee feat. Lukas Meijer	Light Me Up	Andrzej Gromala, Lukas Meijer, Mahan Moin, Christian Rabb	Andrzej Gromala, Lukas Meijer, Mahan Moin, Christian Rabb	81
15	6	Russia	Julia Samoylova	I Won't Break	Netta Nimrodi, Leonid Gutkin, Arie Burshtein	Netta Nimrodi, Leonid Gutkin, Arie Burshtein	65
16	16	Montenegro	Vanja Radovanović	Inje	Vladimir Radovanovic	Vladimir Radovanovic	40
17	4	San Marino	Jessika feat. Jenifer Brening	Who We Are	Mathias Strasser, Christof Straub, Zoe Straub, Jenifer Brening, Stefan Moessle	Mathias Strasser, Christof Straub, Zoe Straub, Jenifer Brening, Stefan Moessle	28
18	10	Georgia	Ethno-Jazz Band Iriao	For You	Irina Sanikidze	David Malazonia; Mikheil Mdinaradze	24

2018 Eurovision 63: Lisbon, Portugal — Jury Votes — Semi-final 2: 10 May 2018

	Australia	Denmark	France	Georgia	Germany	Hungary	Italy	Latvia	Malta	Moldova	Montenegro	Netherlands	Norway	Poland	Romania	Russia	San Marino	Serbia	Slovenia	Sweden	Ukraine	TOTAL
Norway	8		2	5	5	7	12	5	12	4	6	10		4	2	10	7	8	7	12	1	133
Romania	6		1	6		12		3	2	12	8	2	2	3		4		1	6	3	2	67
Serbia		1			1	6	1		1		12				6	7	6		4			45
San Marino							5		3						5	1						14
Denmark	6					5	10		8	1	1						10	5			4	40
Russia			3							7			4									14
Moldova	10	2		3	4	8	4	6	4	5	5	3			12	12	10		5	2		82
Netherlands	1	5	8	10	7		3	8			4		8	10	8		4	10	10	6	12	127
Australia		12	12		8	10	7	12	7	10	3	4	10	8		3		6	2	10	6	130
Georgia						1		2													8	11
Poland			4		2	4				2	7	5	1			2	2			1		21
Malta	3	8	6	4	6		8	7				1	6	1	10	8	8	4	8	4		93
Hungary	4			2										6	3	5			3			23
Latvia	5	7	10	8	10	2				3		7	7	7	1		5	3		7	10	92
Sweden	12	10	7	12	12	3	6	10	10		2	12	12	12		8	12	12	12		7	171
Montenegro									5						7			7	1		3	23
Slovenia	2	4	5	1	3		2	4		6	10	8	5	5	4	6	3	2		8	5	67
Ukraine	7	3	7	7				1	6	8		6	3	2		6	1			5		65

2018 Eurovision 63: Lisbon, Portugal

Public Votes — Semi-final 2: 10 May 2018

	Australia	Denmark	France	Georgia	Germany	Hungary	Italy	Latvia	Malta	Moldova	Montenegro	Netherlands	Norway	Poland	Romania	Russia	San Marino	Serbia	Slovenia	Sweden	Ukraine	TOTAL
Norway	6	12	4	5	4	8	1	4	6	6	5	10		7	6	8	7	6	10	10	8	133
Romania			8	8			12			12												40
Serbia			10		6	2	4			10	12				4	6			12	4		72
San Marino	2								12													14
Denmark	12		5	3	10	12	7	7	8	4	3	12	12	8	8	7	12	4	8	12	10	164
Russia				6			2	12	3	8	8			1	1		1	7			3	51
Moldova	10	6	12	12	5	10	10	8	4		4	7	5	2	12	12	6	5	6	5	12	153
Netherlands	1	7			3	4		1	5	3	2		7	1	3		2		1	6		47
Australia		8	6		7	3	10	2	10	5	2	4	8	3	7	1	4	3	4	7		82
Georgia								5								3						13
Poland		4	7		12		3		1			5	6							8	7	60
Malta	7	1																				8
Hungary	3			4	8		6	3		1	1	8	2	10	10	4	8	12	5	1	2	88
Latvia		2		7										4						1		14
Sweden	8	10	1	2				6	7	2	6	6	10	5	2	5	5	1	2		4	83
Montenegro											10						3	10	7			17
Slovenia	4	3	2			5	5		2	3	7	3	3	6	5	2	3	8		3	6	65
Ukraine	5	5	3	10	1	6	8	10	2	7	7	2	4	12	5	10	10	2	3	2		114

2018 Eurovision 63: Lisbon, Portugal — Combined Jury & Public Votes — Semi-final 2: 10 May 2018

	Australia	Denmark	France	Georgia	Germany	Hungary	Italy	Latvia	Malta	Moldova	Montenegro	Netherlands	Norway	Poland	Romania	Russia	San Marino	Serbia	Slovenia	Sweden	Ukraine	TOTAL
Norway	14	18	6	10	9	15	13	9	18	10	11	20		11	8	18	14	14	17	22	9	266
Romania			9	14		12	12	3	2	24	8	2	2	3		4		1	6	3	2	107
Serbia		1	10		7	8	5		1	10	24	1	1		10	13	6		16	4		117
San Marino	2						5		15						5	1						28
Denmark	18		5	3	10	17	17	7	16	5	4	12	12	8	8	7	12	9	8	12	14	204
Russia			3	6			2	12	3	15	8		4		1		1	7			3	65
Moldova	20	8	12	15	9	10	14	14	8		9	10	5	2	24	24	16	5	11	7	12	235
Netherlands	2	12	8	11	10	12	3	9	5	8	6		15	11	11		6	10	11	12	12	174
Australia		20	18		15	13	7	14	17	15	3	8	18	11	7	4	4	9	6	17	6	212
Georgia						1		7								3					13	24
Poland		4	11		14	11	3		1	2	7	10	7		10	2	2			9	7	81
Malta	10	9	6	4	6		8	7			1	1	6	1			8	4	8	4		101
Hungary	7			6	8		6	3		1	1	8	2	16	13	9	8	12	8	1	2	111
Latvia	5	9	10	15	10	2				3		7	7	11	1		5	3		7	11	106
Sweden	20	20	8	14	12	4	6	16	17	2	8	18	22	17	2	13	17	13	14		11	254
Montenegro									5						7			17	8		3	40
Slovenia	6	7	7	1	5	5	7	4	8	6	10	11	8	11	4	2	6	10		11	11	132
Ukraine	12	8	3	17	1	6	8	11		15	17	8	7	14	5	16	11	2	3	7		179

2018 Eurovision 63: Lisbon, Portugal
FINAL: 12 May 2018

Final qualification rules: Top 10 placed countries from each semi-final. Automatic qualification: United Kingdom, France, Germany, Spain, Italy and hosts Portugal. Each of the 43 participating countries awards two sets of points, one from their professional jury and one from their public vote.

Rank	Start	Country	Artist	Song	Writer	Composer	POINTS
1	22	Israel	Netta	Toy	Doron Medalie & Stav Beger	Doron Medalie & Stav Beger	529
2	25	Cyprus	Eleni Foureira	Fuego	Alex Papaconstantinou, Geraldo Sandell, Anderz Wrethov, Didrick, Viktor Svensson	Alex Papaconstantinou, Geraldo Sandell, Anderz Wrethov, Didrick, Viktor Svensson	436
3	5	Austria	Cesár Sampson	Nobody But You	Sebastian Arman, Cesár Sampson, Joacim Persson, Johan Alkenäs, Borislav Milanov	Sebastian Arman, Cesár Sampson, Joacim Persson, Johan Alkenäs, Borislav Milanov	342
4	11	Germany	Michael Schulte	You Let Me Walk Alone	Michael Schulte, Thomas Stengaard, Katharina Müller, Nisse Ingwersen	Michael Schulte, Thomas Stengaard, Katharina Müller, Nisse Ingwersen	340
5	26	Italy	Ermal Meta e Fabrizio Moro	Non Mi Avete Fatto Niente	Ermal Meta, Fabrizio Moro, Andrea Febo	Ermal Meta, Fabrizio Moro, Andrea Febo	308
6	14	Czech Republic	Mikolas Josef	Lie To Me	Mikolas Josef	Mikolas Josef	281
7	20	Sweden	Benjamin Ingrosso	Dance You Off	MAG, Louis Schoorl, K Nita, Benjamin Ingrosso	MAG, Louis Schoorl, K Nita, Benjamin Ingrosso	274
8	6	Estonia	Elina Nechayeva	La Forza	Elina Nechayeva, Ksenia Kuchukova	Mihkel Mattisen, Timo Vendt	245
9	15	Denmark	Rasmussen	Higher Ground	Niclas Arn, Karl Eurén	Niclas Arn, Karl Eurén	226
10	19	Moldova	DoReDos	My Lucky Day	John Ballard	Philipp Kirkorov	209
11	12	Albania	Eugent Bushpepa	Mall	Eugent Bushpepa	Eugent Bushpepa	184
12	4	Lithuania	Ieva Zasimauskaitė	When We're Old	Vytautas Bikus	Vytautas Bikus	181
13	13	France	Madame Monsieur	Mercy	Emilie Satt, Jean-Karl Lucas	Emilie Satt, Jean-Karl Lucas	173
14	18	Bulgaria	Equinox	Bones	Borislav Milanov, Joacim Persson, Brandon Treyshun Campbell, Dag Lundberg	Borislav Milanov, Joacim Persson, Brandon Treyshun Campbell, Dag Lundberg	166
15	7	Norway	Alexander Rybak	That's How You Write A Song	Alexander Rybak	Alexander Rybak	144
16	24	Ireland	Ryan O'Shaughnessy	Together	Ryan O'Shaughnessy, Mark Caplice, Laura Elizabeth Hughes	Ryan O'Shaughnessy, Mark Caplice, Laura Elizabeth Hughes	136
17	1	Ukraine	Melovin	Under The Ladder	Mike Ryals	Melovin	130
18	23	Netherlands	Waylon	Outlaw In 'Em	Waylon, Ilya Toshinskiy, Jim Beaver	Waylon, Ilya Toshinskiy, Jim Beaver	121
19	10	Serbia	Sanja Ilić & Balkanika	Nova Deca	Danica Krstajić	Aleksandar S Ilić, Tatjana K Ilić	113
20	16	Australia	Jessica Mauboy	We Got Love	Anthony Egizii, David Musumeci, Jessica Mauboy	Anthony Egizii, David Musumeci	99
21	21	Hungary	AWS	Viszlát Nyár	Örs Siklósi	Bence Brucker, Dániel Kökényes, Áron Veress, Soma Schiszler	93
22	3	Slovenia	Lea Sirk	Hvala, ne!	Lea Sirk	Lea Sirk, Tomy DeClerque	64
23	2	Spain	Amaia y Alfred	Tu Canción	Raul Gomez Garcia, Sylvia Ruth Santoro	Raul Gomez Garcia, Sylvia Ruth Santoro	61
24	9	United Kingdom	SuRie	Storm	Nicole Blair, Gil Lewis, Sean Hargreaves	Nicole Blair, Gil Lewis, Sean Hargreaves	48
25	17	Finland	Saara Aalto	Monsters	Saara Aalto, Joy Deb, Linnea Deb, Ki Fitzgerald	Saara Aalto, Joy Deb, Linnea Deb, Ki Fitzgerald	46
26	8	Portugal	Cláudia Pascoal	O Jardim	Isaura	Isaura	39

2018 Eurovision 63: Lisbon, Portugal — FINAL: 12 May 2018 — Jury Votes

Receiving Country	Order votes announced	Albania	Armenia	Australia	Austria	Azerbaijan	Belarus	Belgium	Bulgaria	Croatia	Cyprus	Czech Republic	Denmark	Estonia	Finland	France	FYR Macedonia	Georgia	Germany	Greece	Hungary	Iceland	Ireland	Israel	Italy	Latvia	Lithuania	Malta	Moldova	Montenegro	Netherlands	Norway	Poland	Portugal	Romania	Russia	San Marino	Serbia	Slovenia	Spain	Sweden	Switzerland	Ukraine	United Kingdom	TOTAL
Ukraine	15																																										1		11
Spain	30		7			6		1			7		6						6				1			1						2		2	10		3							1	43
Slovenia	26				5		4					7				2	2									4					1			3	1		6								41
Lithuania	10			3			5		10	12		1		10							5											7	3	1	6	3			1	4			8		90
Austria	2	1	5			10	10	12	12		2	5	8	12	7	7		8	10		8	12	5	12	7	7	12	1	3		10	8	12	10	4	12		4	10	8	10	4	7	12	271
Estonia	3		8	2	3				8		1			7				10	2			3	3		4	8			12	6	4			3	12		5		5	1	2	10	1	6	143
Norway	22					8				5			5	4							2	7			12		7		4	2	7				3		6			2	2			5	60
Portugal	31													3									6				7		2	7		3					3					3			21
United Kingdom	16															3		8												2	2													4	8	23
Serbia	29	3				10				2							8			2										12							3									38
Germany	19	6	5	10	10	2		7	12	7			12	6	1	8	3	7		5		6	8	5	10	3	5		4	12	12	10	12	7	10	4	4	10	10	1	4	7	12	8	204
Albania	11				7	12	7									6	4			10	10	2	8			10	10	8		10			7					1	4					7	126
France	27	7	4				3	5	3	6	3		2		5			4	4			3	4		5	10	10	8				7		5				2	6	5	5	12			114
Czech Republic	36	1	6	1	3		6	7	8	4	5					4	4				3	1						5			6			3				3	4			6			66
Denmark	24						3								3			1	12		12	2	8														6						3		38
Australia	6		2				2						10		2	10					7	7												6				8			8			4	90
Finland	8																		6			6						6								5									23
Bulgaria	35	8		6	5												5	6			10	10	1				2	8															4	8	100
Moldova	32	2	10	2		7			1		8	2	4	1	7	10	2			8					3					8		12	7	5	8	12	7	5	6						94
Sweden	33	4	12	12	8		1	8	2		12	8	4	5	8	5	7	12		8	1	5	10		10	1	8	7	6		8	10	6		10	8		12	12	2		5	6	2	253
Hungary	20					8				4			2					6									2					3													28
Israel	17	5	8	6	12	1		6	4	10		12	3	1	12	12	1	3	1	3	4	6	8		2		6	6	10	5	5	4	8	1		8	12	2	1	10	7	1	10	10	212
Netherlands	39			4	1		10											5	5	4		4	7	6		5	3		3	1			8		8		7		7		8		8		89
Ireland	25		4	4	4								1				4	5	5		3				5		4			5		1	5		8					5	4	6		3	74
Cyprus	14	10	7			4	12	4	3									1	3	12		2	12	3			1	12	6	1	6	5		5	5	7		1	8	12	12	7	3		183
Italy	41	12					8													1								10		4				4		1		8	3						59

2018 Eurovision 63: Lisbon, Portugal

Public Votes — FINAL: 12 May 2018

Country	TOTAL
Ukraine	119
Spain	18
Slovenia	23
Lithuania	91
Austria	71
Estonia	102
Norway	84
Portugal	18
United Kingdom	25
Serbia	75
Germany	136
Albania	58
France	59
Czech Republic	215
Denmark	188
Australia	9
Finland	23
Bulgaria	66
Moldova	115
Sweden	21
Hungary	65
Israel	317
Netherlands	32
Ireland	62
Cyprus	253
Italy	249

Voting countries (columns, left to right): Albania, Armenia, Australia, Austria, Azerbaijan, Belarus, Belgium, Bulgaria, Croatia, Cyprus, Czech Republic, Denmark, Estonia, Finland, France, FYR Macedonia, Georgia, Germany, Greece, Hungary, Iceland, Ireland, Israel, Italy, Latvia, Lithuania, Malta, Moldova, Montenegro, Netherlands, Norway, Poland, Portugal, Romania, Russia, San Marino, Serbia, Slovenia, Spain, Sweden, Switzerland, Ukraine, United Kingdom.

San Marino cannot use televoting as they share Italy's telephone system so, in accordance with the Rules, "a substitute result is calculated by the audience result of a pre-selected group of countries."

(source: eurovision.tv)

2018 Eurovision 63: Lisbon, Portugal
Combined Jury & Public Votes
FINAL: 12 May 2018

	Albania	Armenia	Australia	Austria	Azerbaijan	Belarus	Belgium	Bulgaria	Croatia	Cyprus	Czech Republic	Denmark	Estonia	Finland	France	FYR Macedonia	Georgia	Germany	Greece	Hungary	Iceland	Ireland	Israel	Italy	Latvia	Lithuania	Malta	Moldova	Montenegro	Netherlands	Norway	Poland	Portugal	Romania	Russia	San Marino	Serbia	Slovenia	Spain	Sweden	Switzerland	Ukraine	United Kingdom	TOTAL
Ukraine	4							14	12						4	4	8	6					7	8	3			15	7			12	4		8	5							1	130
Spain		7												5	2							1										2	14	10		7					1		1	61
Slovenia				5	4					7				2	4														6	8			3	1		6	8					5		64
Lithuania		3			5			10	12	6	1											12	4		16		5	1	7	7	15	1	6	6	3					7	8	2	12	181
Austria	2	7	5		10	15	16		2	2	5	18	18	10	7		9	15	8	5	11	17	5	13	7	7	15	1		13	16	12	8	12			4	12	8	12	8	7	12	342
Estonia	4	2	8	2	3			2		5	5	7			7	12	16	2		3	7	7	13	7	18	12	1	3		4			19		9	5	3	5	3		10	4	6	245
Norway	7	1		7	18					5	5	8	6				2	7	3	7	4	7	8	10	2		4	13	4		6	11		3	5		9	5	3	10			5	144
Portugal													3	8								6				7			2							1					13			39
United Kingdom	3		6	8	10							3		3	3			1				10	8	6	2		1	6	2					2										48
Serbia	3			8	10				7	12					1	18			2					1					24				3		3			12			12			113
Germany	14	5	12	16	5	7		7	6	3	3	3	24	1	8	3	7		2	1	14	16	8	13	3	7	4	8		24	18	11	8	8	4	3	4	10	4	13	6	18	3	340
Albania		9	12	7	2	1		8	2		6	6			4		18	4			17	10		12					20			7	10					1	5		7		7	184
France	12	9					11		5	6	4			9			4		5		9	4	6		10	15	8			8		3	5				2	2	10	5		19		173
Czech Republic	1	14	4	15	6	11	8	11	9	13		2	6	5	5	4	9		8	7	8	11	7	12	4	8	8	6		6	4	4		3	2	10	5	11	14	3		14	5	281
Denmark		10	5		10	5			2		7		8	13	2		3	3			24	12	2	6	12	5	10	2	6	8	10	6	2	2	7	6	4	7		12	2	11	2	226
Australia	2		2												10			7	7			2	7		6		9	7			6	4		2	5	2				8		2	1	99
Finland		4														5				3			6																	9			4	46
Bulgaria	14	6	6	1				8	8	5	1	7	1	7	10	7	6		5		10	1		1	2	9	11	4		4		2	7	5		2		5	6	2		14	166
Moldova	2	11	7		11	6		8	8	10	6		6			1	3	11	2		2	1	10	7				11	8				6	19	24	9	6	6		6	4	6	4	209
Sweden	4	12	12	8	2	1	8	2		12	8	11	5	8	5	7	12	8	1	7			10	1	12	12	7	2	8	2	13	6			11	8	12	12	2		5	6	2	274
Hungary		3	8	2			5			4	2		3	8						6			3					2	3	2		10					12	3			1		1	93
Israel	6	18	18	19	13	8	16	14	16	10	22	3	19	24	4		15	11	10		16	13		9	8	7	14	22	1	15	7	10	2	8	18	24	9	1	22	17	6	22	17	529
Netherlands		3	1			22						5	1	2	6		5	5					13		5	3		1	3		9	8		8				7		1		8		121
Ireland	7		12	8		4		4	1	3			2	1		5		15		3	4			5		4				4				1	7		3			6	4	6	13	136
Cyprus	20	19	7	1	14	15	11	15	8		8	6	12	7	3		18	9	24		3	17	2	8	1	7	22	13	6	11	7	8	5	12	11	7	10	14	20	16	10	4	8	436
Italy	24	3		10	5	4	6	6	10	15	2		7	10	10	6	5	12	9	6			5		6	7	22	8	12	7		5	14	6	7	12	14	10	10		8	5		308

2019 Eurovision 64: Tel Aviv, Israel

Semi-final 1: 14 May 2019

Votes are cast by countries participating in each semi-final plus the five automatically qualifying countries decided by draw: France and Spain in semi-final 1, Italy, UK and Germany in semi-final 2. Hosts Israel voted in semi-final 1. Each voting country awards two sets of points, one from their professional jury and one from their public vote. The top 10 countries in each semi-final qualify for the final.

Rank	Start	Country	Artist	Song	Writer	Composer	POINTS
1Q	12	Australia	Kate Miller-Heidke	Zero Gravity	Kate Miller-Heidke, Keir Nuttall	Kate Miller-Heidke, Keir Nuttall, Julian Hamilton	261
2Q	6	Czech Republic	Lake Malawi	Friend of a Friend	Jan Steinsdoerfer, Maciej Mikolaj	Jan Steinsdoerfer, Maciej Mikolaj	242
3Q	13	Iceland	Hatari	Hatrið mun sigra	Hatari	Hatari	221
4Q	14	Estonia	Victor Crone	Storm	Stig Rästa, Victor Crone, Fred Krieger	Stig Rästa, Vallo Kikas, Victor Crone, Sebastian Lestapier	198
5Q	16	Greece	Katerine Duska	Better Love	Katerine Duska, David Sneddon	Katerine Duska, Leon Of Athens, David Sneddon, Phil Cook	185
6Q	5	Slovenia	Zala Kralj & Gašper Šantl	Sebi	Zala Kralj & Gašper Šantl	Zala Kralj & Gašper Šantl	167
7Q	9	Serbia	Nevena Božović	Kruna	Nevena Božović	Nevena Božović, Darko Dimitrov	156
8Q	17	San Marino	Serhat	Say Na Na Na	Serhat, Mary Susan Applegate	Serhat	150
9Q	1	Cyprus	Tamta	Replay	Alex Papaconstantinou, Teddy Sky, Viktor Svensson, Albin Nedler, Kristoffer Fogelmark	Alex Papaconstantinou, Teddy Sky, Viktor Svensson, Albin Nedler, Kristoffer Fogelmark	149
10Q	8	Belarus	ZENA	Like It	Yuliya Kireyeva	Yuliya Kireyeva, Victor Drobysh	122
11	4	Poland	Tulia	Fire of Love (Pali się)	Allan Rich, Jude Friedman, Sonia Krasny	Nadia Dalin	120
12	7	Hungary	Joci Pápai	Az én apám	Ferenc Molnár	Joci Pápai, Ferenc Molnár	97
13	10	Belgium	Eliot	Wake Up	Pierre Dumoulin, Eliot Vassamillet	Pierre Dumoulin, Eliot Vassamillet	70
14	11	Georgia	Oto Nemsadze	Keep on Going	Diana Giorgadze	Roma Giorgadze	62
15	15	Portugal	Conan Osiris	Telemóveis	Conan Osiris	Conan Osiris	51
16	2	Montenegro	D mol	Heaven	Adis Eminić	Dejan Božović	46
17	3	Finland	Darude feat. Sebastian Rejman	Look Away	Sebastian Rejman & Ville Virtanen	Sebastian Rejman & Ville Virtanen	23

2019 Eurovision 64: Tel Aviv, Israel
Jury Votes
Semi-final 1: 14 May 2019

	Australia	Belarus	Belgium	Cyprus	Czech Republic	Estonia	Finland	France	Georgia	Greece	Hungary	Iceland	Israel	Montenegro	Poland	Portugal	San Marino	Serbia	Slovenia	Spain	TOTAL
Cyprus	4	3			10	8		6	5	12		1	4	8	4	1	8	8	7	6	95
Montenegro				4						5							10	12			31
Finland	2									4					1					2	9
Poland	8	6			7	7	10				8					3		3	3		60
Slovenia	4			5	12	5	5	4	7	1	3	5	5	1	8	8	4	7		4	74
Czech Republic	12	7	8	1		12	8	8	12	8	10	10	6	3	7	12	3	10	12	8	157
Hungary	6	2	2			5	1	10	1		12	3	7	6	6	7		6	2		65
Belarus			4		4	10		4	3	7			1			6	1	4	8	7	78
Serbia	3	5	5	6	8	6	3	3	6	6	7	6		7	10	4	5		5	3	91
Belgium				10	3		2		2			4	3	2	3	10	2		6	5	50
Georgia	5	10		7	1			2			2										29
Australia	8	8	12			1	12	7	4	10	5	12	8	5	12	2	6	5		12	121
Iceland	10	1	10	8		2	4	12		2	1	7	10	4	5		7		4		70
Estonia		12	7		2		6	1	8		6					5		1	1	1	65
Portugal			1	3	2										2						8
Greece	7	5	6	12	5	4	7	5	10		4	8	12	12			12	2	10	10	131
San Marino	1	3		2		3						2	2	10		3					26

2019 Eurovision 64: Tel Aviv, Israel

Public Votes — Semi-final 1: 14 May 2019

	Australia	Belarus	Belgium	Cyprus	Czech Republic	Estonia	Finland	France	Georgia	Greece	Hungary	Iceland	Israel	Montenegro	Poland	Portugal	San Marino	Serbia	Slovenia	Spain	TOTAL
Cyprus	3				1				10	12	3		8	4		1	10			1	54
Montenegro																		8	7		15
Finland						12						2									14
Poland	5	5	5		7	2	6	8			6	8	2			5	5		1		60
Slovenia		8	3		5	7	7	2	5	5	7	5		8	8	7	3	10		3	93
Czech Republic	10	3	6	2		8	5		1	1	4	12	6	3	5	4	4	1	5	5	85
Hungary	1				2	3	2					3			3			12	6		32
Belarus	2			6	3	1			7	2		6	4	5	2	3		4	2		44
Serbia		4		5	4		1	6	3	6	2		1	12	4	3	2		12		65
Belgium				3		4		5				1	7		1	2				4	20
Georgia		1		10				4		10				1			1				33
Australia	10	10		4	10	5	8	7	6	8	5	10	12	7	10	10	6	7	4	7	140
Iceland	12	12	7	1	6	6	12	10		7	10		3	6	12	8	7	6	10	10	151
Estonia	7	6	12	7	8		10	1	8	3	8	7	10	2	7	12	8	3	8	6	133
Portugal	4	2	8			3	3	12	2					1						12	43
Greece	8		4	12				3	4		1				1	5	12	2		2	54
San Marino	6	7	2	8	12	10	4		12	4	12	4	5	10	6	6		5	3	8	124

2019 Eurovision 64: Tel Aviv, Israel — Combined Jury & Public Votes — Semi-final 1: 14 May 2019

	Australia	Belarus	Belgium	Cyprus	Czech Republic	Estonia	Finland	France	Georgia	Greece	Hungary	Iceland	Israel	Montenegro	Poland	Portugal	San Marino	Serbia	Slovenia	Spain	TOTAL
Cyprus	3	4	4		11	8		6	15	24	3	1	12	12	4	2	18	8	7	7	149
Montenegro				4						5							10	20	7		46
Finland	2					12				4		2			1					2	23
Poland	13	11	5		14	9	16	8			14	8	7			3	5	3	4		120
Slovenia	4	8	3	5	17	7	12	2	12	6	10	10		9	16	15	7	17		7	167
Czech Republic	22	10	14	3		20	13	8	13	9	14	22	12	6	12	16	7	11	17	13	242
Hungary	7	2	2	6	6	8	3	10	1		self	3	7	6	9	7		18	8		97
Belarus	2		4	11	11	11		4	10	9	12	9	5	5	2	6	1	8	10	7	122
Serbia	3	4	5	13	10	6	4	9	9	12	9	6	1	19	14	7	7		17	3	156
Belgium				17	3	4	2	5	2			5	3			12	2		6	9	70
Georgia	5	11		4	1			6		10	2		7	2	4		1				62
Australia		18	22	9	10	6	20	14	4	18	10	22	20	12	22	12	12	12	4	19	261
Iceland	22	13	17	7	6	8	16	22	6	9	11		3	10	17	8	14	6	14	10	221
Estonia	7	18	19	3	8		16	2	16	3	14	14	20	2	7	17	8	4	9	7	198
Portugal	4	2	9	2	2		3	12	2		5	8	12	13	2		24	4	10	12	51
Greece	15	5	10	24	5	4	7	8	14		5	8		20	6	5					185
San Marino	7	10	2	10	12	13	4		12	4	12	6	7		6	9	5		3	8	150

195

2019 Eurovision 64: Tel Aviv, Israel — Semi-final 2: 16 May 2019

Votes are cast by countries participating in each semi-final plus the five automatically qualifying countries decided by draw: France and Spain in semi-final 1, Italy, UK and Germany in semi-final 2. Hosts Israel voted in semi-final 1. Each voting country awards two sets of points, one from their professional jury and one from their public vote. The top 10 countries in each semi-final qualify for the final.

Rank	Start	Country	Artist	Song	Writer	Composer	POINTS
1Q	16	Netherlands	Duncan Laurence	Arcade	Duncan Laurence, Joel Sjöö, Wouter Hardy	Duncan Laurence, Joel Sjöö, Wouter Hardy	280
2Q	17	North Macedonia	Tamara Todevska	Proud	Kosta Petrov, Sanja Popovska	Robert Bilbilov, Lazar Cvetkoski, Darko Dimitrov	239
3Q	8	Sweden	John Lundvik	Too Late for Love	John Lundvik, Anderz Wrehov, Andreas Stone Johansson	John Lundvik, Anderz Wrehov, Andreas Stone Johansson	238
4Q	4	Switzerland	Luca Hänni	She Got Me	Laurell Barker, Mac Frazer, Luca Hänni, Jon Hällgren, Lukas Hällgren	Laurell Barker, Mac Frazer, Luca Hänni, Jon Hällgren, Lukas Hällgren	232
5Q	18	Azerbaijan	Chingiz	Truth	Borislav Milanov, Trey Campbell, Bo J, Hostess	Borislav Milanov, Trey Campbell, Bo J, Pablo Dinero, Hostess and Chingiz	224
6Q	13	Russia	Sergey Lazarev	Scream	Sharon Vaughn, Dimitris Kontopoulos	Philip Kirkorov, Dimitris Kontopoulos	217
7Q	15	Norway	KEiiNO	Spirit in the Sky	Alexander Olsson, Tom Hugo, Fred Buljo, Alexandra Rotan	Tom Hugo, Henrik Tala, Fred Buljo, Rüdiger Schramm	210
8Q	11	Malta	Michela	Chameleon	Joacim Persson, Paula Winger, Borislav Milanov, Johan Alkenäs	Joacim Persson, Paula Winger, Borislav Milanov, Johan Alkenäs	157
9Q	14	Albania	Jonida Maliqi	Ktheju tokës	Eriona Rushiti	Eriona Rushiti	96
10Q	7	Denmark	Leonora	Love Is Forever	Lise Cabble, Melanie Wehbe, Emil Lei	Lise Cabble, Melanie Wehbe, Emil Lei	94
11	12	Lithuania	Jurij Veklenko	Run with the Lions	Eric Lumiere, Ash Hicklin, Pele Loriano	Eric Lumiere, Ash Hicklin, Pele Loriano	93
12	3	Moldova	Anna Odobescu	Stay	Georgios Kalpakidis, Thomas Reil, Jeppe Reil, Maria Broberg	Georgios Kalpakidis, Thomas Reil, Jeppe Reil, Maria Broberg	85
13	6	Romania	Ester Peony	On a Sunday	Ioana Victoria Badea	Ester Alexandra Crețu, Alexandru Șerbu	71
14	10	Croatia	Roko	The Dream	Jacques Houdek, Charlie Mason, Andrea Čubrić	Jacques Houdek	64
15	5	Latvia	Carousel	That Night	Sabine Žuga	Mārcis Vasiļevskis, Sabine Žuga	50
16	1	Armenia	Srbuk	Walking Out	Garik Papoyan	Lost Capital, tokionine	49
17	9	Austria	PÆNDA	Limits	PÆNDA	PÆNDA	21
18	2	Ireland	Sarah McTernan	22	Janieck van de Polder, Marcia Sondeijker, Roel Rats	Janieck van de Polder, Marcia Sondeijker, Roel Rats	16

2019 Eurovision 64: Tel Aviv, Israel

Jury Votes — Semi-final 2: 16 May 2019

	Albania	Armenia	Austria	Azerbaijan	Croatia	Denmark	Germany	Ireland	Italy	Latvia	Lithuania	Malta	Moldova	Netherlands	North Macedonia	Norway	Romania	Russia	Sweden	Switzerland	United Kingdom	TOTAL
Armenia			1		1			2		2		6	4	2	2			6				26
Ireland									8				5									13
Moldova	3	5	7	3	2							5		6	5	2	12	5	6	5	4	58
Switzerland	5	6		2	10	4	8	10			5			8	3	8	3	2	12			95
Latvia		3		5		6			5		7				3	1				7		37
Romania		2		8			4		2			1	12	1				12			5	47
Denmark		12	4				5	3	12	7				3		5		3	2	2	6	53
Sweden	7		12		4	12	7	12		12	10	10	1	12	4	12	4			10	10	150
Austria	1					2	1		1	1	6						1		8			21
Croatia	2		5			5		1						5							8	26
Malta	6	10	2	6	6		6	4	10	4	3		7	10	7	4	5	8	4	4	1	107
Lithuania			3	1						6		3								3		16
Russia	8	7		12	3	3				3	4	8	8	7	10	3	6		7	1	3	93
Albania				7	5				3				2		12		2	7				38
Norway		1	3			8	2	7				4	3				2		5	6		40
Netherlands	4	4	10	4	8	7	10	8	4	8	12	12		6	6	10	8	1	10	12	2	140
North Macedonia	12	8	8	10	12	10	12	10	7	5	2	2	6	4		7	10	10		8	12	155
Azerbaijan	10		6		7	1	3	5	6	10	8	7	6	1	8	6	7	4	1		7	103

2019 Eurovision 64: Tel Aviv, Israel — Public Votes — Semi-final 2: 16 May 2019

	Albania	Armenia	Austria	Azerbaijan	Croatia	Denmark	Germany	Ireland	Italy	Latvia	Lithuania	Malta	Moldova	Netherlands	North Macedonia	Norway	Romania	Russia	Sweden	Switzerland	United Kingdom	TOTAL
Armenia													2	5	6			10				23
Ireland																					3	3
Moldova		3	12	10		2											12	5		2	6	27
Switzerland	6	8			8	6	12	6	6	3	4	12	6	8	2	7	7	4	4		6	137
Latvia											12		1									13
Romania								1	10				12								1	24
Denmark	1	1	2		1			2		5	3	2		4		8	1	2	10	2		41
Sweden	4	4	1	3	4	10	5	5		4	5	7		10	1	10		2		8	4	88
Austria																						0
Croatia	3	2	8	1			3			1		1			10			3	1	5		38
Malta		7		6	2	5	2	4		2	1	3	3	1	4	3	2				8	50
Lithuania	5		4	2		3	1	12		10			5	2		12		1	7	1	12	77
Russia	2	12		12	3	12	7	7	7	12	10	5	10	3	7	4	8		3	3	2	124
Albania			3	4	6		2		12						12	2	3		2	12		58
Norway	12	5	10	5	10	12	10	10	8	8	8	8	4	12	3		5	8	12	10	10	170
Netherlands	10	10	6	8	7	8	8	8	3	7	6	10	7		8	5	6	7	5	6	5	140
North Macedonia	8	6	5	7	12	1	6		1		2	6		6		1	4	6	6	7		84
Azerbaijan	7		7		5	7	4	3	4	6	7	4	8	7	5	6	10	12	8	4	7	121

198

2019 Eurovision 64: Tel Aviv, Israel — Combined Jury & Public Votes — Semi-final 2: 18 May 2019

	Albania	Armenia	Austria	Azerbaijan	Croatia	Denmark	Germany	Ireland	Italy	Latvia	Lithuania	Malta	Moldova	Netherlands	North Macedonia	Norway	Romania	Russia	Sweden	Switzerland	United Kingdom	TOTAL
Armenia			1		1			2		2		6	6	7	8			16				49
Ireland									8				5								3	16
Moldova	3	8	19	3	2	2	20	16	5	3	9	5	6	6	7	2	24	10	6	5	4	85
Switzerland	11	14		12	18	10			6		19	12	1	16	3	15	10	6	16		6	232
Latvia		3		5		6			5					1		1				7		50
Romania		2		8			4	1	12			1	24	1				12			6	71
Denmark	1	1	6		1		5	5	12	12	3	2	1	7		13		3	12	4	6	94
Sweden	11	16	13	3	8	22	12	17		16	15	17		22	5	22	5	2		18	14	238
Austria	1					2	1	1	1	1	6						1		8			21
Croatia	5	2	13	1		5	3	1		1		1		5	10			3	1	5	8	64
Malta	6	17	2	12	8	5	8	8	10	6	4		10	11	11	7	7	8	4	4	9	157
Lithuania	5		3	3		4	1	12		16		6	5	2		12		1	7	4	12	93
Russia	10	19	4	24	6	6	7	7	7	15	14	13	18	10	17	7	14		10	4	5	217
Albania		3		11	11		2		15				2		24	2	5	7	2	12		96
Norway	12	6	13	5	10	20	12	17	8	8	9	12	7	12	3		5	8	17	16	10	210
Netherlands	14	14	16	12	15	15	18	16	7	15	18	22	7		14	15	14	8	15	18	7	280
North Macedonia	20	14	13	17	24	11	18	10	8	5	4	8	6	10		8	14	16	6	15	12	239
Azerbaijan	17		13		12	8	7	8	10	16	15	11	14	8	13	12	17	16	9	4	14	224

2019 Eurovision 64: Tel Aviv, Israel — FINAL: 18 May 2019

Final qualification rules: Top 10 placed countries from each semi-final. Automatic qualification: United Kingdom, France, Germany, Spain, Italy and hosts Israel. Each of the 43 participating countries awards two sets of points, one from their professional jury and one from their public vote.

Rank	Start	Country	Artist	Song	Writer	Composer	POINTS
1	12	Netherlands	Duncan Laurence	Arcade	Duncan Laurence, Joel Sjöö, Wouter Hardy	Duncan Laurence, Joel Sjöö, Wouter Hardy	498
2	22	Italy	Mahmood	Soldi	Dardust, Mahmood	Dardust, Mahmood, Charlie Charles	472
3	5	Russia	Sergey Lazarev	Scream	Sharon Vaughn, Dimitris Kontopoulos	Philip Kirkorov, Dimitris Kontopoulos	370
4	24	Switzerland	Luca Hänni	She Got Me	Laurell Barker, Mac Frazer, Luca Hänni, Jon Hällgren, Lukas Hällgren	Laurell Barker, Mac Frazer, Luca Hänni, Jon Hällgren, Lukas Hällgren	364
5	9	Sweden	John Lundvik	Too Late for Love	John Lundvik, Anderz Wrehov, Andreas Stone Johansson	John Lundvik, Anderz Wrehov, Andreas Stone Johansson	334
6	15	Norway	KEiiNO	Spirit in the Sky	Alexander Olsson, Tom Hugo, Fred Buljo, Alexandra Rotan	Tom Hugo, Henrik Tala, Fred Buljo, Rüdiger Schramm	331
7	8	North Macedonia	Tamara Todevska	Proud	Kosta Petrov, Sanja Popovska	Robert Bilbilov, Lazar Cvetkoski, Darko Dimitrov	305
8	20	Azerbaijan	Chingiz	Truth	Borislav Milanov, Trey Campbell, Bo J, Hostess	Borislav Milanov, Trey Campbell, Bo J, Pablo Dinero, Hostess and Chingiz	302
9	25	Australia	Kate Miller-Heidke	Zero Gravity	Kate Miller-Heidke, Keir Nuttall	Kate Miller-Heidke, Keir Nuttall, Julian Hamilton	284
10	17	Iceland	Hatari	Hatrið mun sigra	Hatari	Hatari	232
11	3	Czech Republic	Lake Malawi	Friend of a Friend	Jan Steinsdoerfer, Maciej Trybulec, Albert Černý	Jan Steinsdoerfer, Maciej Trybulec, Albert Černý	157
12	6	Denmark	Leonora	Love Is Forever	Lise Cabble, Melanie Wehbe, Emil Lei	Lise Cabble, Melanie Wehbe, Emil Lei	120
13	11	Cyprus	Tamta	Replay	Alex Papaconstantinou, Teddy Sky, Viktor Svensson, Albin Nedler, Kristoffer Fogelmark	Alex Papaconstantinou, Teddy Sky, Viktor Svensson, Albin Nedler, Kristoffer Fogelmark	109
14	1	Malta	Michela	Chameleon	Joacim Perrson, Paula Winger, Borislav Milanov, Johan Alkenäs	Joacim Perrson, Paula Winger, Borislav Milanov, Johan Alkenäs	107
15	10	Slovenia	Zala Kralj & Gašper Šantl	Sebi	Zala Kralj & Gašper Šantl	Zala Kralj & Gašper Šantl	105
16	21	France	Bilal Hassani	Roi	Emilie Satt, Jean-Karl Lucas	Emilie Satt, Jean-Karl Lucas	105
17	2	Albania	Jonida Maliqi	Ktheju tokës	Eriona Rushiti	Eriona Rushiti	90
18	23	Serbia	Nevena Božović	Kruna	Nevena Božović	Nevena Božović, Darko Dimitrov	89
19	7	San Marino	Serhat	Say Na Na Na	Serhat, Mary Susan Applegate	Serhat	77
20	18	Estonia	Victor Crone	Storm	Stig Rästa, Victor Crone, Fred Krieger	Stig Rästa, Vallo Kikas, Victor Crone, Fred Krieger	76
21	13	Greece	Katerine Duska	Better Love	Katerine Duska, David Sneddon	Katerine Duska, Leon of Athens, David Sneddon, Phil Cook	74
22	26	Spain	Miki	La Venda	Adrià Salas	Adrià Salas	54
23	14	Israel	Kobi Marimi	Home	Inbar Wizman, Ohad Shragai	Inbar Wizman, Ohad Shragai	35
24	19	Belarus	ZENA	Like It	Yuliya Kireyeva	Yuliya Kireyeva, Victor Drobysh	31
25	4	Germany	Sisters	Sister	Laurell Barker, Tom Oehler, Marine Kaltenbacher, Thomas Stengaard	Laurell Barker, Tom Oehler, Marine Kaltenbacher, Thomas Stengaard	24
26	16	United Kingdom	Michael Rice	Bigger Than Us	Laurell Barker, Anna-Klara Folin, John Lundvik, Jonas Thander	Laurell Barker, Anna-Klara Folin, John Lundvik, Jonas Thander	11

2019 Eurovision 64: Tel Aviv, Israel — **Jury Votes** — **FINAL: 18 May 2019**

Order votes announced		15	20	23	12	2	19	26	28	22	35	36	8	38	37	32	25	33	16	31	18	41	14	34	29	3	17	7	6	4	10	9	1	21	24	5	30	40	11	27	39	13
	TOTAL	Malta	Albania	Czech Republic	Germany	Russia	Denmark	San Marino	North Macedonia	Sweden	Slovenia	Cyprus	Netherlands	Greece	Israel	Norway	United Kingdom	Iceland	Estonia	Belarus	Azerbaijan	France	Italy	Serbia	Switzerland	Australia	Spain	Montenegro	Netherlands	North Macedonia	Norway	Poland	Portugal	Romania	Russia	San Marino	Serbia	Slovenia	Spain	Sweden	Switzerland	United Kingdom

Receiving country	Order	Total
Malta	15	87
Albania	20	43
Czech Republic	23	150
Germany	12	24
Russia	2	126
Denmark	19	69
San Marino	26	12
North Macedonia	28	247
Sweden	22	241
Slovenia	35	46
Cyprus	36	77
Netherlands	8	237
Greece	38	50
Israel	37	0
Norway	32	40
United Kingdom	25	8
Iceland	33	46
Estonia	16	28
Belarus	31	18
Azerbaijan	18	202
France	41	67
Italy	14	219
Serbia	34	35
Switzerland	29	152
Australia	27	153
Spain	39	1

2019 Eurovision 64: Tel Aviv, Israel — Public Votes — FINAL: 18 May 2019

	Albania	Armenia	Australia	Austria	Azerbaijan	Belarus	Belgium	Croatia	Cyprus	Czech Republic	Denmark	Estonia	Finland	France	Georgia	Germany	Greece	Hungary	Iceland	Ireland	Israel	Italy	Latvia	Lithuania	Malta	Moldova	Montenegro	Netherlands	North Macedonia	Norway	Poland	Portugal	Romania	Russia	San Marino	Serbia	Slovenia	Spain	Sweden	Switzerland	United Kingdom	TOTAL
Malta	6	4																											6													20
Albania								1								5						12					7		12											10		47
Czech Republic		2																								2					1											7
Germany																																										0
Russia	12	12		5	12	12	1		10	12		12	4	3	8	8	8	7		5	12	8	12	12	4	12	10	5	1		1	3	10	7		12	8	2				244
Denmark												6		4		4			4	1	4									5	5		1					3	7	1	6	51
San Marino	10			10	1		2										6	1			1				5	8	8		8													65
North Macedonia	6	3					7								2				8	2					6		6	1								1						58
Sweden	2	8					2				10	3	7		6	1		3		8			3	6			4	8		12						12	12	6		4	5	93
Slovenia				2	5			10			7	1				3		3				2					4		2					6								59
Cyprus																	12																		7	10					1	32
Netherlands	7	10	6	7	7	10	12	4	6	4	7	8	5	5	5	7	6	8	5	8	2	5	5	7	10	6	1		7	8	10	8	12	5	6	3	5	8	6	6	4	261
Greece	2								12				12	4																					10							24
Israel									5	3													7									3		1								35
Norway	5	5	12	8	1	8	7	5	1	10	12	10	10	8		12		10	12	12	10	10	8	8	7	3		12	5		8	6	4	10	3	4	6	7	12	8	12	291
United Kingdom																			3																							3
Iceland	3	10	6		7	3	3			6	4	5	12	1	3	2	2	12		6		7	7	6	1	1	2	7		10	12	3	5	7	2	5	7	3	8	8	8	186
Estonia								8			1		8						3	1			10	4				2			2						1		1	10		48
Belarus			5																								12		10					8		3						13
Azerbaijan	3	1	1		6				7	5					7		2				3	1	4	5	2	10	3	4	1	3	2		6	12	4		1	3		3		100
France	4	3									5					1		1			4	2					5		3			2	1					4		3		38
Italy	8	7	5	10		6	3	8	12		6		3	10	1	6	10	4	6	8	8		3	10	12	5	5	10	3	7	7	7	8	1		8	7	12	4	12		253
Serbia				4		8																					12		10					3			10	7				54
Switzerland	4	8	7	12	8	4	5	6		7	5	6	6	2	10		7	5	7		7		1	2	8	4		6	4		6	5	5		5	6	4	10	2		7	212
Australia	1	1		3			2	4		2		8	2		2	6			10	10	6	6	6	1	3		2		6	4	6	4	2	4	5	6	2	5	5	10		131
Spain			2		6		4		1		7		4								5						3										12		2	5	2	53

San Marino cannot use televoting as they share Italy's telephone system so, in accordance with the Rules, "a substitute result is calculated by the audience result of a pre-selected group of countries."

(source: eurovision.tv)

2019 Eurovision 64: Tel Aviv, Israel

Combined Jury & Public Votes

FINAL: 18 May 2019

Contestant	TOTAL
Malta	107
Albania	90
Czech Republic	157
Germany	24
Russia	370
Denmark	120
San Marino	77
North Macedonia	305
Sweden	334
Slovenia	105
Cyprus	109
Netherlands	498
Greece	74
Israel	35
Norway	331
United Kingdom	11
Iceland	232
Estonia	76
Belarus	31
Azerbaijan	302
France	105
Italy	472
Serbia	89
Switzerland	364
Australia	284
Spain	54

Full voting matrix (41 voting countries × 26 finalists) is presented on the page with points awarded by each of the following voting countries: Albania, Armenia, Australia, Austria, Azerbaijan, Belarus, Belgium, Croatia, Cyprus, Czech Republic, Denmark, Estonia, Finland, France, Georgia, Germany, Greece, Hungary, Iceland, Ireland, Israel, Italy, Latvia, Lithuania, Malta, Moldova, Montenegro, Netherlands, North Macedonia, Norway, Poland, Portugal, Romania, Russia, San Marino, Serbia, Slovenia, Spain, Sweden, Switzerland, United Kingdom.

Eurovision 2019 - Jury Voting Order & National Spokespersons

Order	Country	Spokesperson
15	Albania	Andri Xhahu
20	Armenia	Aram MP3
23	Australia	Electric Fields
12	Austria	Philipp Hansa
2	Azerbaijan	Faig Agayev
19	Belarus	Maria Vasilevich
26	Belgium	David Jeanmotte
28	Croatia	Monika Lelas Halambek
22	Cyprus	Hovig
35	Czech Republic	Radka Rosická
36	Denmark	Rasmussen
8	Estonia	Kelly Sildaru
38	Finland	Christoffer Strandberg
37	France	Julia Molkhou
32	Georgia	Gaga Abashidze
25	Germany	Barbara Schöneberger
33	Greece	Gus G
16	Hungary	Bence Forró
31	Iceland	Jóhannes Haukur Jóhannesson
18	Ireland	Sinéad Kennedy
41	Israel	Izhar Cohen
14	Italy	Ema Stokholma
34	Latvia	Latvia — Laura Rizzotto
29	Lithuania	Andrius Mamontovas
3	Malta	Ben Camille
17	Moldova	Doina Stimpovschi
7	Montenegro	Ajda Šufta
6	Netherlands	Emma Wortelboer
4	North Macedonia	Nikola Trajkovski
10	Norway	Alexander Rybak
9	Poland	Mateusz Szymkowiak
1	Portugal	Inês Lopes Gonçalves
21	Romania	Ilinca
24	Russia	Ivan Bessonov
5	San Marino	Monica Fabbri
30	Serbia	Dragana Kosjerina
40	Slovenia	Lea Sirk
11	Spain	Nieves Álvarez
27	Sweden	Eric Saade
39	Switzerland	Sinplus
13	United Kingdom	Rylan Clark

Eurovision 2019: Final - Round by Round Leaderboard (Jury points)

These tables show the correct jury votes, not the ones broadcast with the incorrect Belarus votes, which leaves North Macedonia rightly top of the leaderboard after the jury voting.

Voting round:

Posn	1 Portugal	Pts	Lead	2 Azerbaijan	Pts	Lead	3 Malta	Pts	Lead	4 North Macedonia	Pts	Lead	5 San Marino	Pts	Lead
1st	Netherlands	12	2	North Macedonia	13	1	Italy	23	1	Italy	35	7	Italy	47	9
2nd	Czech Republic	10	2	Russia	12	0	Russia	22	3	Russia	28	2	Russia	38	9
3rd	Azerbaijan	8	1	Netherlands	12	1	Netherlands	19	3	Netherlands	26	6	Netherlands	29	5
4th	Australia	7	1	Italy	11	1	North Macedonia	16	0	Azerbaijan	20	1	Albania	24	0
5th	Italy	6	1	Czech Republic	10	0	Azerbaijan	16	6	Australia	19	2	Azerbaijan	24	5
6th	North Macedonia	5	1	Malta	10	1	Czech Republic	10	0	Albania	17	1	Australia	19	1
7th	Norway	4	1	Australia	9	1	Malta	10	0	North Macedonia	16	1	Greece	18	1
8th	Slovenia	3	1	Azerbaijan	8	1	Greece	10	1	Malta	15	5	North Macedonia	17	2
9th	Sweden	2	1	Slovenia	7	0	Albania	9	0	Cyprus	10	0	Malta	15	0
10th	Switzerland	1	1	Albania	7	1	Australia	9	0	Greece	10	0	Cyprus	15	5
11th	Malta	0	0	Greece	6	2	Cyprus	9	2	Czech Republic	10	3	Czech Republic	10	2
12th	Albania	0	0	Norway	4	1	Sweden	7	0	Sweden	7	0	Iceland	8	1
13th	Germany	0	0	Cyprus	3	0	Slovenia	7	3	Slovenia	7	3	Sweden	7	0
14th	Russia	0	0	Sweden	2	1	Norway	4	3	Switzerland	4	0	Slovenia	7	1
15th	Denmark	0	0	Belarus	1	0	Belarus	1	0	Norway	4	2	Switzerland	6	2
16th	San Marino	0	0	Switzerland	1	1	San Marino	1	0	Iceland	2	1	Norway	4	3
17th	Cyprus	0	0	Germany	0	0	Switzerland	1	1	Belarus	1	0	Belarus	1	0
18th	Greece	0	0	Denmark	0	0	Germany	0	0	San Marino	1	1	San Marino	1	1
19th	Israel	0	0	San Marino	0	0	Denmark	0	0	Germany	0	0	Germany	0	0
20th	United Kingdom	0	0	Israel	0	0	Israel	0	0	Denmark	0	0	Denmark	0	0
21st	Iceland	0	0	United Kingdom	0	0	United Kingdom	0	0	Israel	0	0	Israel	0	0
22nd	Estonia	0	0	Iceland	0	0	Iceland	0	0	United Kingdom	0	0	United Kingdom	0	0
23rd	Belarus	0	0	Estonia	0	0	Estonia	0	0	Estonia	0	0	Estonia	0	0
24th	France	0	0	France	0	0	France	0	0	France	0	0	France	0	0
25th	Serbia	0	0	Serbia	0	0	Serbia	0	0	Serbia	0	0	Serbia	0	0
26th	Spain	0	0	Spain	0	0	Spain	0	0	Spain	0	0	Spain	0	0

Voting round:

Posn	6 Netherlands	Pts	Lead	7 Montenegro	Pts	Lead	8 Estonia	Pts	Lead	9 Poland	Pts	Lead	10 Norway	Pts	Lead
1st	Italy	53	10	Italy	55	2	Russia	59	4	Russia	59	4	Russia	59	1
2nd	Russia	43	14	Russia	53	21	Italy	55	19	Italy	55	18	Italy	58	13
3rd	Netherlands	29	5	Albania	32	3	Netherlands	36	4	Australia	37	1	North Macedonia	45	2
4th	Albania	24	0	Netherlands	29	0	Albania	32	1	Netherlands	36	1	Netherlands	43	4
5th	Azerbaijan	24	1	Malta	29	2	Sweden	31	2	North Macedonia	35	2	Sweden	39	2
6th	Malta	23	2	North Macedonia	27	2	Azerbaijan	29	0	Malta	33	1	Australia	37	1
7th	Australia	21	1	Australia	25	1	Malta	29	2	Albania	32	1	Azerbaijan	36	1
8th	North Macedonia	20	1	Azerbaijan	24	3	North Macedonia	27	1	Azerbaijan	31	0	Czech Republic	35	2
9th	Sweden	19	1	Cyprus	21	2	Switzerland	26	1	Sweden	31	5	Malta	33	1
10th	Greece	18	2	Sweden	19	1	Australia	25	2	Switzerland	26	3	Switzerland	32	0
11th	Cyprus	16	0	Greece	18	2	Czech Republic	23	2	Czech Republic	23	0	Albania	32	9
12th	Switzerland	16	2	Switzerland	16	1	Cyprus	21	3	Serbia	23	2	Serbia	23	1
13th	Czech Republic	14	6	Czech Republic	15	3	Greece	18	2	Cyprus	21	3	Cyprus	22	1
14th	Iceland	8	1	Serbia	12	2	Serbia	16	4	Greece	18	1	Denmark	21	3
15th	Slovenia	7	0	Denmark	10	2	Denmark	12	4	Denmark	17	0	Greece	18	1
16th	Denmark	7	3	Iceland	8	1	Iceland	8	1	Slovenia	17	6	Slovenia	17	6
17th	Norway	4	0	Slovenia	7	3	Slovenia	7	3	Iceland	11	2	Iceland	11	2
18th	Belarus	1	0	Norway	4	3	Norway	4	1	France	9	4	France	9	4
19th	San Marino	1	1	Belarus	1	0	France	3	1	Norway	5	3	Norway	5	3
20th	Germany	0	0	San Marino	1	0	Belarus	2	1	Belarus	2	1	Belarus	2	0
21st	Israel	0	0	Germany	0	0	San Marino	1	1	San Marino	1	1	United Kingdom	2	1
22nd	United Kingdom	0	0	Israel	0	0	Germany	0	0	Germany	0	0	San Marino	1	1
23rd	Estonia	0	0	United Kingdom	0	0	Israel	0	0	Israel	0	0	Germany	0	0
24th	France	0	0	Estonia	0	0	United Kingdom	0	0	United Kingdom	0	0	Israel	0	0
25th	Serbia	0	0	France	0	0	Estonia	0	0	Estonia	0	0	Estonia	0	0
26th	Spain	0	0	Spain	0	0	Spain	0	0	Spain	0	0	Spain	0	0

Eurovision 2019: Final - Round by Round Leaderboard (Jury points)

Voting round:

	11 Spain			12 Austria			13 United Kingdom			14 Italy			15 Albania		
Posn	Country	Pts	Lead	Country	Pts	Lead	Country	Pts	Lead	Country	Pts	Lead	Country	Pts	Lead
1st	Italy	62	1	Italy	69	8	North Macedonia	69	0	North Macedonia	79	10	North Macedonia	91	16
2nd	Russia	61	10	Russia	61	2	Italy	69	2	Italy	69	0	Sweden	75	1
3rd	Netherlands	51	0	Netherlands	59	2	Sweden	67	2	Sweden	69	4	Italy	74	5
4th	Sweden	51	4	North Macedonia	57	0	Russia	65	0	Russia	65	0	Azerbaijan	69	3
5th	Australia	47	2	Sweden	57	10	Netherlands	65	10	Netherlands	65	4	Russia	66	1
6th	North Macedonia	45	2	Azerbaijan	47	0	Australia	55	1	Azerbaijan	61	0	Netherlands	65	2
7th	Azerbaijan	43	2	Australia	47	2	Azerbaijan	54	4	Australia	61	11	Australia	63	3
8th	Czech Republic	41	6	Switzerland	45	1	Switzerland	50	5	Switzerland	50	1	Switzerland	60	11
9th	Switzerland	35	2	Czech Republic	44	11	Czech Republic	45	12	Czech Republic	49	8	Czech Republic	49	8
10th	Malta	33	1	Malta	33	1	Malta	33	1	Malta	41	5	Malta	41	5
11th	Albania	32	5	Albania	32	5	Albania	32	5	Denmark	36	3	Denmark	36	2
12th	Cyprus	27	4	Cyprus	27	2	Cyprus	27	2	Albania	33	6	Cyprus	34	1
13th	Serbia	23	2	Serbia	25	4	Serbia	25	0	Cyprus	27	2	Albania	33	8
14th	Denmark	21	3	Denmark	21	3	Denmark	24	6	Serbia	25	6	Serbia	25	3
15th	Slovenia	18	0	Slovenia	18	0	Slovenia	18	0	France	19	1	France	22	0
16th	Greece	18	7	Greece	18	4	Greece	18	2	Slovenia	18	0	Greece	22	4
17th	Iceland	11	2	France	14	3	France	16	5	Greece	18	7	Slovenia	18	7
18th	France	9	4	Iceland	11	5	Iceland	11	5	Iceland	11	5	Iceland	11	5
19th	Norway	5	3	Norway	6	4	Norway	6	4	Norway	6	1	Norway	6	1
20th	Belarus	2	0	Belarus	2	0	Belarus	2	0	Estonia	5	3	Estonia	5	3
21st	United Kingdom	2	1	United Kingdom	2	1	United Kingdom	2	1	Belarus	2	0	Belarus	2	0
22nd	San Marino	1	1	San Marino	1	1	San Marino	1	1	United Kingdom	2	1	United Kingdom	2	1
23rd	Germany	0	0	Germany	0	0	Germany	0	0	San Marino	1	1	San Marino	1	1
24th	Israel	0	0	Israel	0	0	Israel	0	0	Germany	0	0	Germany	0	0
25th	Estonia	0	0	Estonia	0	0	Estonia	0	0	Israel	0	0	Israel	0	0
26th	Spain	0	0	Spain	0	0	Spain	0	0	Spain	0	0	Spain	0	0

Voting round:

	16 Hungary			17 Moldova			18 Ireland			19 Belarus			20 Armenia		
Posn	Country	Pts	Lead	Country	Pts	Lead	Country	Pts	Lead	Country	Pts	Lead	Country	Pts	Lead
1st	North Macedonia	101	20	North Macedonia	113	32	North Macedonia	118	25	North Macedonia	128	33	North Macedonia	138	31
2nd	Italy	81	2	Sweden	81	0	Sweden	93	6	Sweden	95	3	Sweden	107	10
3rd	Sweden	79	5	Italy	81	1	Azerbaijan	87	5	Azerbaijan	92	3	Italy	97	5
4th	Azerbaijan	74	8	Azerbaijan	80	7	Italy	82	5	Italy	89	6	Azerbaijan	92	3
5th	Russia	66	0	Australia	73	2	Australia	77	0	Netherlands	83	6	Netherlands	89	5
6th	Netherlands	66	3	Russia	71	2	Netherlands	77	3	Switzerland	77	0	Switzerland	84	4
7th	Switzerland	63	0	Czech Republic	69	0	Russia	74	1	Australia	77	2	Russia	80	3
8th	Australia	63	2	Netherlands	69	6	Switzerland	73	4	Russia	75	6	Australia	77	5
9th	Czech Republic	61	19	Switzerland	63	17	Czech Republic	69	23	Czech Republic	69	15	Czech Republic	72	14
10th	Denmark	42	1	Denmark	46	4	Denmark	46	4	Malta	54	8	Malta	58	12
11th	Malta	41	7	Malta	42	8	Malta	42	8	Denmark	46	4	Denmark	46	4
12th	Cyprus	34	1	Cyprus	34	1	Cyprus	34	1	Cyprus	42	9	Cyprus	42	9
13th	Albania	33	8	Albania	33	8	Albania	33	8	Albania	33	8	Albania	33	8
14th	Serbia	25	3	Serbia	25	3	Serbia	25	3	Greece	25	0	Greece	25	0
15th	France	22	0	France	22	0	France	22	0	Serbia	25	3	Serbia	25	3
16th	Greece	22	4	Greece	22	4	Greece	22	3	France	22	3	France	22	3
17th	Slovenia	18	7	Slovenia	18	5	Norway	19	1	Norway	19	1	Norway	19	1
18th	Iceland	11	1	Norway	13	2	Slovenia	18	7	Slovenia	18	7	Slovenia	18	7
19th	Belarus	10	4	Iceland	11	1	Iceland	11	1	Iceland	11	1	Iceland	11	0
20th	Norway	6	1	Belarus	10	5	Belarus	10	5	Belarus	10	5	Belarus	11	5
21st	Estonia	5	1	Estonia	5	1	Estonia	5	1	Estonia	5	1	United Kingdom	6	1
22nd	United Kingdom	4	3	United Kingdom	4	3	United Kingdom	4	2	United Kingdom	4	2	Estonia	5	3
23rd	San Marino	1	1	San Marino	1	1	Germany	2	1	Germany	2	1	Germany	2	1
24th	Germany	0	0	Germany	0	0	San Marino	1	1	San Marino	1	1	San Marino	1	1
25th	Israel	0	0	Israel	0	0	Israel	0	0	Israel	0	0	Israel	0	0
26th	Spain	0	0	Spain	0	0	Spain	0	0	Spain	0	0	Spain	0	0

Eurovision 2019: Final - Round by Round Leaderboard (Jury points)

Voting round:

21 Romania

Posn	Country	Pts	Lead
1st	North Macedonia	145	37
2nd	Sweden	108	6
3rd	Azerbaijan	102	5
4th	Italy	97	3
5th	Netherlands	94	5
6th	Australia	89	1
7th	Switzerland	88	2
8th	Russia	86	6
9th	Czech Republic	80	22
10th	Malta	58	12
11th	Denmark	46	4
12th	Cyprus	42	7
13th	Albania	35	7
14th	Serbia	28	3
15th	Greece	25	3
16th	France	22	3
17th	Norway	19	1
18th	Slovenia	18	7
19th	Iceland	11	0
20th	Belarus	11	5
21st	United Kingdom	6	1
22nd	Estonia	5	3
23rd	Germany	2	1
24th	San Marino	1	1
25th	Israel	0	0
26th	Spain	0	0

22 Cyprus

Posn	Country	Pts	Lead
1st	North Macedonia	145	30
2nd	Sweden	115	7
3rd	Azerbaijan	108	3
4th	Italy	105	6
5th	Netherlands	99	3
6th	Russia	96	7
7th	Switzerland	89	0
8th	Australia	89	9
9th	Czech Republic	80	19
10th	Malta	61	15
11th	Denmark	46	4
12th	Cyprus	42	5
13th	Albania	37	0
14th	Greece	37	9
15th	Serbia	28	2
16th	France	26	7
17th	Norway	19	1
18th	Slovenia	18	7
19th	Iceland	11	0
20th	Belarus	11	5
21st	United Kingdom	6	1
22nd	Estonia	5	3
23rd	Germany	2	1
24th	San Marino	1	1
25th	Israel	0	0
26th	Spain	0	0

23 Australia

Posn	Country	Pts	Lead
1st	North Macedonia	152	25
2nd	Sweden	127	17
3rd	Azerbaijan	110	5
4th	Netherlands	105	0
5th	Italy	105	5
6th	Russia	100	11
7th	Switzerland	89	0
8th	Australia	89	4
9th	Czech Republic	85	24
10th	Malta	61	15
11th	Denmark	46	4
12th	Cyprus	42	5
13th	Albania	37	0
14th	Greece	37	1
15th	France	36	7
16th	Serbia	29	10
17th	Norway	19	0
18th	Iceland	19	1
19th	Slovenia	18	7
20th	Belarus	11	5
21st	United Kingdom	6	1
22nd	Germany	5	0
23rd	Estonia	5	4
24th	San Marino	1	1
25th	Israel	0	0
26th	Spain	0	0

24 Russia

Posn	Country	Pts	Lead
1st	North Macedonia	156	29
2nd	Sweden	127	5
3rd	Azerbaijan	122	17
4th	Netherlands	105	0
5th	Italy	105	5
6th	Russia	100	11
7th	Switzerland	89	0
8th	Australia	89	4
9th	Czech Republic	85	18
10th	Malta	67	17
11th	Cyprus	50	3
12th	Greece	47	1
13th	Denmark	46	6
14th	Albania	40	4
15th	France	36	7
16th	Serbia	29	8
17th	Iceland	21	2
18th	Norway	19	1
19th	Slovenia	18	0
20th	Belarus	18	12
21st	San Marino	6	0
22nd	United Kingdom	6	1
23rd	Germany	5	0
24th	Estonia	5	4
25th	Spain	1	1
26th	Israel	0	0

25 Germany

Posn	Country	Pts	Lead
1st	North Macedonia	163	34
2nd	Sweden	129	7
3rd	Azerbaijan	122	5
4th	Italy	117	4
5th	Netherlands	113	13
6th	Russia	100	1
7th	Australia	99	4
8th	Switzerland	95	10
9th	Czech Republic	85	15
10th	Malta	70	20
11th	Cyprus	50	3
12th	Denmark	47	0
13th	Greece	47	7
14th	Albania	40	0
15th	France	40	11
16th	Serbia	29	5
17th	Norway	24	3
18th	Iceland	21	3
19th	Slovenia	18	0
20th	Belarus	18	12
21st	San Marino	6	0
22nd	United Kingdom	6	1
23rd	Germany	5	0
24th	Estonia	5	4
25th	Spain	1	1
26th	Israel	0	0

Voting round:

26 Belgium

Posn	Country	Pts	Lead
1st	North Macedonia	163	34
2nd	Sweden	129	0
3rd	Italy	129	7
4th	Azerbaijan	122	3
5th	Netherlands	119	16
6th	Australia	103	1
7th	Switzerland	102	2
8th	Russia	100	10
9th	Czech Republic	90	20
10th	Malta	70	18
11th	Cyprus	52	2
12th	Greece	50	2
13th	Denmark	48	0
14th	France	48	8
15th	Albania	40	9
16th	Iceland	31	2
17th	Serbia	29	5
18th	Norway	24	6
19th	Slovenia	18	0
20th	Belarus	18	12
21st	San Marino	6	0
22nd	United Kingdom	6	1
23rd	Germany	5	0
24th	Estonia	5	4
25th	Spain	1	1
26th	Israel	0	0

27 Sweden

Posn	Country	Pts	Lead
1st	North Macedonia	163	26
2nd	Italy	137	6
3rd	Netherlands	131	2
4th	Sweden	129	2
5th	Azerbaijan	127	15
6th	Switzerland	112	3
7th	Australia	109	6
8th	Russia	103	12
9th	Czech Republic	91	19
10th	Malta	72	13
11th	Cyprus	59	9
12th	Greece	50	2
13th	Denmark	48	0
14th	France	48	8
15th	Albania	40	9
16th	Iceland	31	2
17th	Serbia	29	1
18th	Norway	28	10
19th	Slovenia	18	0
20th	Belarus	18	12
21st	San Marino	6	0
22nd	United Kingdom	6	1
23rd	Germany	5	0
24th	Estonia	5	4
25th	Spain	1	1
26th	Israel	0	0

28 Croatia

Posn	Country	Pts	Lead
1st	Israel	0	-1
2nd	Spain	1	-4
3rd	Germany	5	-1
4th	San Marino	6	0
5th	United Kingdom	6	0
6th	Estonia	6	-12
7th	Slovenia	18	0
8th	Belarus	18	-10
9th	Norway	28	-3
10th	Iceland	31	-2
11th	Serbia	33	-7
12th	Albania	40	-8
13th	Denmark	48	-2
14th	Greece	50	-1
15th	France	51	-8
16th	Cyprus	59	-13
17th	Malta	72	-26
18th	Czech Republic	98	-7
19th	Russia	105	-4
20th	Australia	109	-11
21st	Switzerland	120	-7
22nd	Azerbaijan	127	-7
23rd	Sweden	134	-3
24th	Netherlands	137	-12
25th	Italy	149	-24
26th	North Macedonia	173	173

29 Lithuania

Posn	Country	Pts	Lead
1st	North Macedonia	173	21
2nd	Italy	152	3
3rd	Netherlands	149	7
4th	Sweden	142	5
5th	Azerbaijan	137	17
6th	Switzerland	120	9
7th	Australia	111	5
8th	Russia	106	1
9th	Czech Republic	105	33
10th	Malta	72	13
11th	Cyprus	59	8
12th	France	51	1
13th	Greece	50	2
14th	Denmark	48	8
15th	Albania	40	3
16th	Iceland	37	4
17th	Serbia	33	5
18th	Norway	28	6
19th	Slovenia	22	4
20th	Belarus	18	8
21st	Germany	10	4
22nd	San Marino	6	0
23rd	United Kingdom	6	0
24th	Estonia	6	5
25th	Spain	1	1
26th	Israel	0	0

30 Serbia

Posn	Country	Pts	Lead
1st	North Macedonia	185	23
2nd	Italy	162	12
3rd	Sweden	150	1
4th	Netherlands	149	9
5th	Azerbaijan	140	15
6th	Switzerland	125	7
7th	Australia	118	9
8th	Czech Republic	109	3
9th	Russia	106	34
10th	Malta	72	13
11th	Cyprus	59	7
12th	France	52	2
13th	Denmark	50	0
14th	Greece	50	10
15th	Albania	40	3
16th	Iceland	37	4
17th	Serbia	33	5
18th	Norway	28	6
19th	Slovenia	22	4
20th	Belarus	18	6
21st	Estonia	12	2
22nd	Germany	10	4
23rd	San Marino	6	0
24th	United Kingdom	6	5
25th	Spain	1	1
26th	Israel	0	0

Eurovision 2019: Final - Round by Round Leaderboard (Jury points)

Voting round:

31 Iceland

Posn	Country	Pts	Lead
1st	North Macedonia	193	28
2nd	Italy	165	3
3rd	Sweden	162	6
4th	Netherlands	156	12
5th	Azerbaijan	144	14
6th	Switzerland	130	2
7th	Australia	128	13
8th	Czech Republic	115	9
9th	Russia	106	34
10th	Malta	72	13
11th	Cyprus	59	6
12th	France	53	3
13th	Denmark	50	0
14th	Greece	50	10
15th	Albania	40	3
16th	Iceland	37	2
17th	Serbia	35	7
18th	Norway	28	6
19th	Slovenia	22	4
20th	Belarus	18	6
21st	Estonia	12	2
22nd	Germany	10	4
23rd	San Marino	6	0
24th	United Kingdom	6	5
25th	Spain	1	1
26th	Israel	0	0

32 Georgia

Posn	Country	Pts	Lead
1st	North Macedonia	193	28
2nd	Italy	165	1
3rd	Sweden	164	0
4th	Netherlands	164	10
5th	Azerbaijan	154	21
6th	Switzerland	133	5
7th	Australia	128	1
8th	Czech Republic	127	21
9th	Russia	106	34
10th	Malta	72	7
11th	Cyprus	65	7
12th	France	58	1
13th	Denmark	57	7
14th	Greece	50	10
15th	Albania	40	3
16th	Iceland	37	2
17th	Serbia	35	7
18th	Norway	28	2
19th	Slovenia	26	8
20th	Belarus	18	6
21st	Estonia	12	2
22nd	Germany	10	3
23rd	United Kingdom	7	1
24th	San Marino	6	5
25th	Spain	1	1
26th	Israel	0	0

33 Greece

Posn	Country	Pts	Lead
1st	North Macedonia	194	22
2nd	Italy	172	8
3rd	Sweden	164	0
4th	Netherlands	164	2
5th	Azerbaijan	162	29
6th	Switzerland	133	3
7th	Australia	130	3
8th	Czech Republic	127	11
9th	Russia	116	39
10th	Malta	77	0
11th	Cyprus	77	19
12th	France	58	1
13th	Denmark	57	7
14th	Greece	50	7
15th	Albania	43	6
16th	Iceland	37	2
17th	Serbia	35	5
18th	Slovenia	30	2
19th	Norway	28	10
20th	Belarus	18	6
21st	San Marino	12	0
22nd	Estonia	12	2
23rd	Germany	10	3
24th	United Kingdom	7	6
25th	Spain	1	1
26th	Israel	0	0

34 Latvia

Posn	Country	Pts	Lead
1st	North Macedonia	202	26
2nd	Netherlands	176	2
3rd	Sweden	174	0
4th	Italy	174	6
5th	Azerbaijan	168	35
6th	Switzerland	133	3
7th	Czech Republic	130	0
8th	Australia	130	10
9th	Russia	120	42
10th	Malta	78	1
11th	Cyprus	77	13
12th	Denmark	64	6
13th	France	58	8
14th	Greece	50	7
15th	Albania	43	6
16th	Iceland	37	2
17th	Serbia	35	5
18th	Slovenia	30	2
19th	Norway	28	10
20th	Belarus	18	1
21st	Estonia	17	5
22nd	San Marino	12	2
23rd	Germany	10	3
24th	United Kingdom	7	6
25th	Spain	1	1
26th	Israel	0	0

35 Czech Republic

Posn	Country	Pts	Lead
1st	North Macedonia	209	23
2nd	Sweden	186	4
3rd	Netherlands	182	0
4th	Italy	182	9
5th	Azerbaijan	173	40
6th	Switzerland	133	3
7th	Czech Republic	130	0
8th	Australia	130	10
9th	Russia	120	39
10th	Malta	81	4
11th	Cyprus	77	13
12th	Denmark	64	4
13th	France	60	10
14th	Greece	50	7
15th	Albania	43	2
16th	Iceland	41	1
17th	Slovenia	40	5
18th	Serbia	35	7
19th	Norway	28	10
20th	Estonia	18	0
21st	Belarus	18	6
22nd	San Marino	12	2
23rd	Germany	10	3
24th	United Kingdom	7	6
25th	Spain	1	1
26th	Israel	0	0

Voting round:

36 Denmark

Posn	Country	Pts	Lead
1st	North Macedonia	219	21
2nd	Sweden	198	9
3rd	Netherlands	189	6
4th	Italy	183	6
5th	Azerbaijan	177	38
6th	Switzerland	139	9
7th	Czech Republic	130	0
8th	Australia	130	7
9th	Russia	123	42
10th	Malta	81	4
11th	Cyprus	77	13
12th	Denmark	64	4
13th	France	60	10
14th	Greece	50	7
15th	Albania	43	2
16th	Iceland	41	1
17th	Slovenia	40	5
18th	Serbia	35	2
19th	Norway	33	13
20th	Estonia	20	2
21st	Germany	18	0
22nd	Belarus	18	6
23rd	San Marino	12	5
24th	United Kingdom	7	6
25th	Spain	1	1
26th	Israel	0	0

37 France

Posn	Country	Pts	Lead
1st	North Macedonia	226	18
2nd	Sweden	208	7
3rd	Netherlands	201	10
4th	Italy	191	8
5th	Azerbaijan	183	42
6th	Switzerland	141	7
7th	Australia	134	1
8th	Czech Republic	133	10
9th	Russia	123	42
10th	Malta	81	4
11th	Cyprus	77	12
12th	Denmark	65	5
13th	France	60	10
14th	Greece	50	4
15th	Iceland	46	3
16th	Albania	43	3
17th	Slovenia	40	5
18th	Serbia	35	2
19th	Norway	33	13
20th	Estonia	20	2
21st	Germany	18	0
22nd	Belarus	18	6
23rd	San Marino	12	5
24th	United Kingdom	7	6
25th	Spain	1	1
26th	Israel	0	0

38 Finland

Posn	Country	Pts	Lead
1st	North Macedonia	233	13
2nd	Sweden	220	11
3rd	Netherlands	209	13
4th	Italy	196	11
5th	Azerbaijan	185	41
6th	Switzerland	144	0
7th	Australia	144	7
8th	Czech Republic	137	6
9th	Russia	123	41
10th	Malta	82	5
11th	Cyprus	77	12
12th	Denmark	65	5
13th	France	60	10
14th	Greece	50	4
15th	Slovenia	46	0
16th	Iceland	46	3
17th	Albania	43	8
18th	Serbia	35	2
19th	Norway	33	13
20th	Estonia	20	2
21st	Germany	18	0
22nd	Belarus	18	6
23rd	San Marino	12	5
24th	United Kingdom	7	6
25th	Spain	1	1
26th	Israel	0	0

39 Switzerland

Posn	Country	Pts	Lead
1st	North Macedonia	245	17
2nd	Sweden	228	9
3rd	Netherlands	219	18
4th	Italy	201	16
5th	Azerbaijan	185	37
6th	Australia	148	4
7th	Switzerland	144	7
8th	Czech Republic	137	11
9th	Russia	126	44
10th	Malta	82	5
11th	Cyprus	77	12
12th	Denmark	65	3
13th	France	62	12
14th	Greece	50	7
15th	Slovenia	46	0
16th	Iceland	46	3
17th	Albania	43	3
18th	Norway	40	5
19th	Serbia	35	11
20th	Germany	24	4
21st	Estonia	20	2
22nd	Belarus	18	6
23rd	San Marino	12	4
24th	United Kingdom	8	7
25th	Spain	1	1
26th	Israel	0	0

40 Slovenia

Posn	Country	Pts	Lead
1st	North Macedonia	247	12
2nd	Sweden	235	10
3rd	Netherlands	225	16
4th	Italy	209	14
5th	Azerbaijan	195	46
6th	Czech Republic	149	0
7th	Switzerland	149	1
8th	Australia	148	22
9th	Russia	126	43
10th	Malta	83	6
11th	Cyprus	77	8
12th	Denmark	69	4
13th	France	65	15
14th	Greece	50	4
15th	Slovenia	46	0
16th	Iceland	46	3
17th	Albania	43	3
18th	Norway	40	5
19th	Serbia	35	11
20th	Germany	24	4
21st	Estonia	20	2
22nd	Belarus	18	6
23rd	San Marino	12	4
24th	United Kingdom	8	7
25th	Spain	1	1
26th	Israel	0	0

Eurovision 2019: Final - Round by Round Leaderboard (Jury points)

Voting round: 41 Israel

Posn	Country	Pts	Lead
1st	North Macedonia	247	6
2nd	Sweden	241	4
3rd	Netherlands	237	18
4th	Italy	219	17
5th	Azerbaijan	202	49
6th	Australia	153	1
7th	Switzerland	152	2
8th	Czech Republic	150	24
9th	Russia	126	39
10th	Malta	87	10
11th	Cyprus	77	8
12th	Denmark	69	2
13th	France	67	17
14th	Greece	50	4
15th	Slovenia	46	0
16th	Iceland	46	3
17th	Albania	43	3
18th	Norway	40	5
19th	Serbia	35	7
20th	Estonia	28	4
21st	Germany	24	6
22nd	Belarus	18	6
23rd	San Marino	12	4
24th	United Kingdom	8	7
25th	Spain	1	1
26th	Israel	0	0

Eurovision 2019: Final - Round by Round Leaderboard (Jury points) for top 3 countries overall

Eurovision 2019: Final - Round by Round Leaderboard (Combined Public Voting & Total points)

Public televoting points, announced in ascending order of jury votes as broadcast:

Posn	Spain 53 pts			Israel 35 pts			United Kingdom 3 pts			San Marino 65 pts			Belarus 13 pts		
	Country	Pts	Lead	Country	Pts	Lead	Country	Pts	Lead	Country	Pts	Lead	Country	Pts	Lead
1st	North Macedonia	247	6	North Macedonia	247	6	North Macedonia	247	6	North Macedonia	247	6	North Macedonia	247	6
2nd	Sweden	241	4	Sweden	241	4	Sweden	241	4	Sweden	241	4	Sweden	241	4
3rd	Netherlands	237	18	Netherlands	237	18	Netherlands	237	18	Netherlands	237	18	Netherlands	237	18
4th	Italy	219	17	Italy	219	17	Italy	219	17	Italy	219	17	Italy	219	17
5th	Azerbaijan	202	49	Azerbaijan	202	49	Azerbaijan	202	49	Azerbaijan	202	49	Azerbaijan	202	49
6th	Australia	153	1	Australia	153	1	Australia	153	1	Australia	153	1	Australia	153	1
7th	Switzerland	152	2	Switzerland	152	2	Switzerland	152	2	Switzerland	152	2	Switzerland	152	2
8th	Czech Republic	150	24	Czech Republic	150	24	Czech Republic	150	24	Czech Republic	150	24	Czech Republic	150	24
9th	Russia	126	39	Russia	126	39	Russia	126	39	Russia	126	39	Russia	126	39
10th	Malta	87	10	Malta	87	10	Malta	87	10	Malta	87	10	Malta	87	10
11th	Cyprus	77	8	Cyprus	77	8	Cyprus	77	8	Cyprus	77	8	Cyprus	77	8
12th	Denmark	69	2	Denmark	69	2	Denmark	69	2	San Marino	77	4	San Marino	77	4
13th	France	67	17	France	67	17	France	67	17	Denmark	69	2	Denmark	69	2
14th	Spain	54	1	Spain	54	1	Spain	54	1	France	67	17	France	67	17
15th	Greece	50	4	Greece	50	4	Greece	50	4	Spain	54	1	Spain	54	1
16th	Slovenia	46	0	Slovenia	46	0	Slovenia	46	0	Greece	50	4	Greece	50	4
17th	Iceland	46	3	Iceland	46	3	Iceland	46	3	Slovenia	46	0	Slovenia	46	0
18th	Albania	43	3	Albania	43	3	Albania	43	3	Iceland	46	3	Iceland	46	3
19th	Norway	40	5	Norway	40	5	Norway	40	5	Albania	43	3	Albania	43	3
20th	Serbia	35	7	Serbia	35	7	Serbia	35	7	Norway	40	5	Norway	40	5
21st	Estonia	28	4	Israel	35	0	Israel	35	0	Serbia	35	7	Serbia	35	7
22nd	Germany	24	6	Estonia	28	4	Estonia	28	4	Israel	35	0	Israel	35	0
23rd	Belarus	18	6	Germany	24	6	Germany	24	6	Estonia	28	4	Belarus	31	6
24th	San Marino	12	4	Belarus	18	6	Belarus	18	6	Germany	24	6	Estonia	28	4
25th	United Kingdom	8	7	San Marino	12	4	San Marino	12	4	Belarus	18	6	Germany	24	6
26th	Israel	0	0	United Kingdom	8	7	United Kingdom	11	7	United Kingdom	11	7	United Kingdom	11	7

Public televoting points, announced in ascending order of jury votes as broadcast:

Posn	Germany 0 pts			Estonia 48 pts			Serbia 54 pts			Albania 47pts			Slovenia 59 pts		
	Country	Pts	Lead	Country	Pts	Lead	Country	Pts	Lead	Country	Pts	Lead	Country	Pts	Lead
1st	North Macedonia	247	6	North Macedonia	247	6	North Macedonia	247	6	North Macedonia	247	6	North Macedonia	247	6
2nd	Sweden	241	4	Sweden	241	4	Sweden	241	4	Sweden	241	4	Sweden	241	4
3rd	Netherlands	237	18	Netherlands	237	18	Netherlands	237	18	Netherlands	237	18	Netherlands	237	18
4th	Italy	219	17	Italy	219	17	Italy	219	17	Italy	219	17	Italy	219	17
5th	Azerbaijan	202	49	Azerbaijan	202	49	Azerbaijan	202	49	Azerbaijan	202	49	Azerbaijan	202	49
6th	Australia	153	1	Australia	153	1	Australia	153	1	Australia	153	1	Australia	153	1
7th	Switzerland	152	2	Switzerland	152	2	Switzerland	152	2	Switzerland	152	2	Switzerland	152	2
8th	Czech Republic	150	24	Czech Republic	150	24	Czech Republic	150	24	Czech Republic	150	24	Czech Republic	150	24
9th	Russia	126	39	Russia	126	39	Russia	126	39	Russia	126	39	Russia	126	39
10th	Malta	87	10	Malta	87	10	Serbia	89	7	Albania	90	3	Slovenia	105	0
11th	Cyprus	77	8	Cyprus	77	8	Malta	87	10	Serbia	89	7	Albania	90	3
12th	San Marino	77	4	San Marino	77	4	Cyprus	77	8	Malta	87	10	Serbia	89	7
13th	Denmark	69	2	Estonia	76	4	San Marino	77	4	Cyprus	77	8	Malta	87	10
14th	France	67	17	Denmark	69	2	Estonia	76	4	San Marino	77	4	Cyprus	77	8
15th	Spain	54	1	France	67	17	Denmark	69	2	Estonia	76	4	San Marino	77	4
16th	Greece	50	4	Spain	54	1	France	67	17	Denmark	69	2	Estonia	76	4
17th	Slovenia	46	0	Greece	50	4	Spain	54	1	France	67	17	Denmark	69	2
18th	Iceland	46	3	Slovenia	46	0	Greece	50	4	Spain	54	1	France	67	17
19th	Albania	43	3	Iceland	46	3	Slovenia	46	0	Greece	50	4	Spain	54	1
20th	Norway	40	5	Albania	43	3	Iceland	46	3	Slovenia	46	0	Greece	50	4
21st	Serbia	35	7	Norway	40	5	Albania	43	3	Iceland	46	3	Iceland	46	3
22nd	Israel	35	0	Serbia	35	7	Norway	40	5	Norway	40	5	Norway	40	5
23rd	Belarus	31	6	Israel	35	0	Israel	35	0	Israel	35	0	Israel	35	0
24th	Estonia	28	4	Belarus	31	6	Belarus	31	6	Belarus	31	6	Belarus	31	6
25th	Germany	24	6	Germany	24	6	Germany	24	6	Germany	24	6	Germany	24	6
26th	United Kingdom	11	7	United Kingdom	11	7	United Kingdom	11	7	United Kingdom	11	7	United Kingdom	11	7

Eurovision 2019: Final - Round by Round Leaderboard (Combined Public Voting & Total points)

Public televoting points, announced in ascending order of jury votes as broadcast:

Posn	Greece 24 pts			Norway 291 pts			Iceland 186 pts			France 38 pts			Cyprus 32 pts		
	Country	Pts	Lead	Country	Pts	Lead	Country	Pts	Lead	Country	Pts	Lead	Country	Pts	Lead
1st	North Macedonia	247	6	Norway	331	5	Norway	331	5	Norway	331	5	Norway	331	5
2nd	Sweden	241	4	North Macedonia	247	6	North Macedonia	247	6	North Macedonia	247	6	North Macedonia	247	6
3rd	Netherlands	237	18	Sweden	241	4	Sweden	241	4	Sweden	241	4	Sweden	241	4
4th	Italy	219	17	Netherlands	237	18	Netherlands	237	18	Netherlands	237	18	Netherlands	237	18
5th	Azerbaijan	202	49	Italy	219	17	Iceland	232	3	Iceland	232	3	Iceland	232	3
6th	Australia	153	1	Azerbaijan	202	49	Italy	219	17	Italy	219	17	Italy	219	17
7th	Switzerland	152	2	Australia	153	1	Azerbaijan	202	49	Azerbaijan	202	49	Azerbaijan	202	49
8th	Czech Republic	150	24	Switzerland	152	2	Australia	153	1	Australia	153	1	Australia	153	1
9th	Russia	126	39	Czech Republic	150	24	Switzerland	152	2	Switzerland	152	2	Switzerland	152	2
10th	Slovenia	105	0	Russia	126	39	Czech Republic	150	24	Czech Republic	150	24	Czech Republic	150	24
11th	Albania	90	3	Slovenia	105	0	Russia	126	39	Russia	126	39	Russia	126	39
12th	Serbia	89	7	Albania	90	3	Slovenia	105	0	France	105	17	Cyprus	109	8
13th	Malta	87	10	Serbia	89	7	Albania	90	3	Slovenia	105	0	France	105	17
14th	Cyprus	77	8	Malta	87	10	Serbia	89	7	Albania	90	3	Slovenia	105	0
15th	San Marino	77	4	Cyprus	77	8	Malta	87	10	Serbia	89	7	Albania	90	3
16th	Estonia	76	4	San Marino	77	4	Cyprus	77	8	Malta	87	10	Serbia	89	7
17th	Greece	74	4	Estonia	76	4	San Marino	77	4	Cyprus	77	8	Malta	87	10
18th	Denmark	69	2	Greece	74	4	Estonia	76	4	San Marino	77	4	San Marino	77	4
19th	France	67	17	Denmark	69	2	Greece	74	4	Estonia	76	4	Estonia	76	4
20th	Spain	54	1	France	67	17	Denmark	69	2	Greece	74	4	Greece	74	4
21st	Iceland	46	3	Spain	54	1	France	67	17	Denmark	69	2	Denmark	69	2
22nd	Norway	40	5	Iceland	46	3	Spain	54	1	Spain	54	1	Spain	54	1
23rd	Israel	35	0	Israel	35	0	Israel	35	0	Israel	35	0	Israel	35	0
24th	Belarus	31	6	Belarus	31	6	Belarus	31	6	Belarus	31	6	Belarus	31	6
25th	Germany	24	6	Germany	24	6	Germany	24	6	Germany	24	6	Germany	24	6
26th	United Kingdom	11	7	United Kingdom	11	7	United Kingdom	11	7	United Kingdom	11	7	United Kingdom	11	7

Public televoting points, announced in ascending order of jury votes as broadcast:

Posn	Denmark 51 pts			Malta 20 pts			Russia 244 pts			Switzerland 212 pts			Czech Republic 7 pts		
	Country	Pts	Lead	Country	Pts	Lead	Country	Pts	Lead	Country	Pts	Lead	Country	Pts	Lead
1st	Norway	331	5	Norway	331	5	Russia	370	39	Russia	370	39	Russia	370	39
2nd	North Macedonia	247	6	North Macedonia	247	6	Norway	331	5	Switzerland	364	2	Switzerland	364	2
3rd	Sweden	241	4	Sweden	241	4	North Macedonia	247	6	Norway	331	5	Norway	331	5
4th	Netherlands	237	18	Netherlands	237	18	Sweden	241	4	North Macedonia	247	6	North Macedonia	247	6
5th	Iceland	232	3	Iceland	232	3	Netherlands	237	18	Sweden	241	4	Sweden	241	4
6th	Italy	219	17	Italy	219	17	Iceland	232	3	Netherlands	237	18	Netherlands	237	18
7th	Azerbaijan	202	49	Azerbaijan	202	49	Italy	219	17	Iceland	232	3	Iceland	232	3
8th	Australia	153	1	Australia	153	1	Azerbaijan	202	49	Italy	219	17	Italy	219	17
9th	Switzerland	152	2	Switzerland	152	2	Australia	153	1	Azerbaijan	202	49	Azerbaijan	202	49
10th	Czech Republic	150	24	Czech Republic	150	24	Switzerland	152	2	Australia	153	1	Czech Republic	157	24
11th	Russia	126	39	Russia	126	39	Czech Republic	150	24	Czech Republic	150	24	Australia	153	1
12th	Denmark	120	2	Denmark	120	2	Denmark	120	2	Denmark	120	2	Denmark	120	2
13th	Cyprus	109	8	Cyprus	109	8	Cyprus	109	8	Cyprus	109	8	Cyprus	109	8
14th	France	105	17	Malta	107	10	Malta	107	10	Malta	107	10	Malta	107	10
15th	Slovenia	105	0	France	105	17	France	105	17	France	105	17	France	105	17
16th	Albania	90	3	Slovenia	105	0	Slovenia	105	0	Slovenia	105	0	Slovenia	105	0
17th	Serbia	89	7	Albania	90	3	Albania	90	3	Albania	90	3	Albania	90	3
18th	Malta	87	10	Serbia	89	7	Serbia	89	7	Serbia	89	7	Serbia	89	7
19th	San Marino	77	4	San Marino	77	4	San Marino	77	4	San Marino	77	4	San Marino	77	4
20th	Estonia	76	4	Estonia	76	4	Estonia	76	4	Estonia	76	4	Estonia	76	4
21st	Greece	74	4	Greece	74	4	Greece	74	4	Greece	74	4	Greece	74	4
22nd	Spain	54	1	Spain	54	1	Spain	54	1	Spain	54	1	Spain	54	1
23rd	Israel	35	0	Israel	35	0	Israel	35	0	Israel	35	0	Israel	35	0
24th	Belarus	31	6	Belarus	31	6	Belarus	31	6	Belarus	31	6	Belarus	31	6
25th	Germany	24	6	Germany	24	6	Germany	24	6	Germany	24	6	Germany	24	6
26th	United Kingdom	11	7	United Kingdom	11	7	United Kingdom	11	7	United Kingdom	11	7	United Kingdom	11	7

Eurovision 2019: Final - Round by Round Leaderboard (Combined Public Voting & Total points)

Public televoting points, announced in ascending order of jury votes as broadcast:

	Australia 131 pts			Azerbaijan 100 pts			Italy 253 pts			Netherlands 261 pts			Nth Macedonia 58 pts		
Posn	Country	Pts	Lead	Country	Pts	Lead	Country	Pts	Lead	Country	Pts	Lead	Country	Pts	Lead
1st	Russia	370	39	Russia	370	39	Italy	472	17	Netherlands	498	18	Netherlands	498	18
2nd	Switzerland	364	2	Switzerland	364	2	Russia	370	39	Italy	472	17	Italy	472	17
3rd	Norway	331	5	Norway	331	5	Switzerland	364	2	Russia	370	39	Russia	370	39
4th	Australia	284	1	Azerbaijan	302	49	Norway	331	5	Switzerland	364	2	Switzerland	364	2
5th	North Macedonia	247	6	Australia	284	1	Azerbaijan	302	49	Norway	331	5	Norway	331	5
6th	Sweden	241	4	North Macedonia	247	6	Australia	284	1	Azerbaijan	302	49	North Macedonia	305	6
7th	Netherlands	237	18	Sweden	241	4	North Macedonia	247	6	Australia	284	1	Azerbaijan	302	49
8th	Iceland	232	3	Netherlands	237	18	Sweden	241	4	North Macedonia	247	6	Australia	284	1
9th	Italy	219	17	Iceland	232	3	Netherlands	237	18	Sweden	241	4	Sweden	241	4
10th	Azerbaijan	202	49	Italy	219	17	Iceland	232	3	Iceland	232	3	Iceland	232	3
11th	Czech Republic	157	24	Czech Republic	157	24	Czech Republic	157	24	Czech Republic	157	24	Czech Republic	157	24
12th	Denmark	120	2	Denmark	120	2	Denmark	120	2	Denmark	120	2	Denmark	120	2
13th	Cyprus	109	8	Cyprus	109	8	Cyprus	109	8	Cyprus	109	8	Cyprus	109	8
14th	Malta	107	10	Malta	107	10	Malta	107	10	Malta	107	10	Malta	107	10
15th	France	105	17	France	105	17	France	105	17	France	105	17	France	105	17
16th	Slovenia	105	0	Slovenia	105	0	Slovenia	105	0	Slovenia	105	0	Slovenia	105	0
17th	Albania	90	3	Albania	90	3	Albania	90	3	Albania	90	3	Albania	90	3
18th	Serbia	89	7	Serbia	89	7	Serbia	89	7	Serbia	89	7	Serbia	89	7
19th	San Marino	77	4	San Marino	77	4	San Marino	77	4	San Marino	77	4	San Marino	77	4
20th	Estonia	76	4	Estonia	76	4	Estonia	76	4	Estonia	76	4	Estonia	76	4
21st	Greece	74	4	Greece	74	4	Greece	74	4	Greece	74	4	Greece	74	4
22nd	Spain	54	1	Spain	54	1	Spain	54	1	Spain	54	1	Spain	54	1
23rd	Israel	35	0	Israel	35	0	Israel	35	0	Israel	35	0	Israel	35	0
24th	Belarus	31	6	Belarus	31	6	Belarus	31	6	Belarus	31	6	Belarus	31	6
25th	Germany	24	6	Germany	24	6	Germany	24	6	Germany	24	6	Germany	24	6
26th	United Kingdom	11	7	United Kingdom	11	7	United Kingdom	11	7	United Kingdom	11	7	United Kingdom	11	7

Public televoting points, announced in ascending order of jury votes as broadcast:

Sweden 93 pts

Posn	Country	Pts	Lead
1st	Netherlands	498	18
2nd	Italy	472	17
3rd	Russia	370	39
4th	Switzerland	364	2
5th	Norway	331	5
6th	North Macedonia	305	6
7th	Azerbaijan	302	49
8th	Australia	284	1
9th	Sweden	241	4
10th	Iceland	232	3
11th	Czech Republic	157	24
12th	Denmark	120	2
13th	Cyprus	109	8
14th	Malta	107	10
15th	France	105	17
16th	Slovenia	105	0
17th	Albania	90	3
18th	Serbia	89	7
19th	San Marino	77	4
20th	Estonia	76	4
21st	Greece	74	4
22nd	Spain	54	1
23rd	Israel	35	0
24th	Belarus	31	6
25th	Germany	24	6
26th	United Kingdom	11	7

Eurovision 2019: Final - Round by Round Leaderboard (Positions of overall top 3 during televoting points announcements)

2019 Eurovision 64: Tel Aviv, Israel

Results Table under Previous Scoring System

Semi-final 1: 14 May 2019

	Australia	Belarus	Belgium	Cyprus	Czech Republic	Estonia	Finland	France	Georgia	Greece	Hungary	Iceland	Israel	Montenegro	Poland	Portugal	San Marino	Serbia	Slovenia	Spain	TOTAL
Cyprus			2		6	3		1	10	12			7	6	1		10	4	2	2	66
Montenegro										2							6	12	3		23
Finland						8															8
Poland	7	7	4		10	6	7	5			10	5	3				1				65
Slovenia	1	3		2	12	2	5		5	3	4	7		4	8	8	3	8			75
Czech Republic	10	4	7			12	6	3	7	4	8	12	8	3	6	10	4	6	10	10	130
Hungary	4				1	4		7					2	2	5	2		10	4		41
Belarus			1	3	7	7			4	5	6	6	1	1		1		5	7	1	55
Serbia		1	3	7	4		2	6	3	8	2	2		10	7	3	2		12		72
Belgium				8								1		1	2	6			1	5	23
Georgia	3	6		10				2		7			5								33
Australia	12	12	8	1	5	1	12	10	1	10	3	10	12	7	12	7	7	7		12	141
Iceland	6	8	8	5	2	5	10	12	2	6	5			5	10	4	8	3	8	6	119
Estonia	6	10	10	4	3		8		12		12	8	10		4	12	5	1	5	3	113
Portugal	2		5				1	8												8	24
Greece	8	2	6	12			4	4	8		1	4	6	8			12		6	7	88
San Marino	5	5		6	8	10	3		6	1	7	3	4	12	3	5		2		4	84

There would have been a difference under the old voting system this year. Poland would have qualified for the final ahead of Belarus.

2019 Eurovision 64: Tel Aviv, Israel — Results Table under Previous Scoring System — Semi-final 2: 16 May 2019

	Albania	Armenia	Austria	Azerbaijan	Croatia	Denmark	Germany	Ireland	Italy	Latvia	Lithuania	Malta	Moldova	Netherlands	North Macedonia	Norway	Romania	Russia	Sweden	Switzerland	United Kingdom	TOTAL
Armenia												2	3	3	4			10				22
Ireland									3													3
Moldova		4			1							1		1	3		12	6	1	3		29
Switzerland	6	6	12	8	10	6	12	7		1	4	7	4	10	3	10	5	1	10		2	124
Latvia		2		2		3					12									5		24
Romania				4			1		10				12			7		7			1	35
Denmark			3				2	1	8	5				2		7			7			35
Sweden	5	8	4	1	4	12	6	10		8	7	10		12	2	12	1			12	10	124
Austria											3								4	4		7
Croatia	1	1	7												5						4	22
Malta	3	10		6	3	2	5	4	6	3	1		7	7	6	2	4	3			5	77
Lithuania	2							6		12		3	1			6			3		8	41
Russia	4	12	2		2	4	4	2	2	7	6	8	10	5	10	3	8		6	1		96
Albania			1	5	6				12						12	1	2	2		6		47
Norway	7	3	8	3	5	10	7	12	5	4	5	6	5	8	1		3	5	12	8	6	123
Netherlands	8	7	10	7	8	8	10	8	1	6	10	12	6		8	8	7	4	8	10	3	149
North Macedonia	12	5	5	10	12	7	8	5	4	2	2	4	2	6		4	6	8	2	7	7	118
Azerbaijan	10		6	12	7	5	3	3	7	10	8	5	8	4	7	5	10	12	5	2	12	141

The main difference in the second semi-final is that Lithuania would have qualified for the Final ahead of Denmark.

2019 Eurovision 64: Tel Aviv, Israel

Results Table under Previous Scoring System

FINAL: 18 May 2019

Country	Alb	Arm	Aus	Aut	Aze	Blr	Bel	Cro	Cyp	Cze	Den	Est	Fin	Fra	Geo	Ger	Gre	Hun	Ice	Ire	Isr	Ita	Lat	Lit	Mlt	Mda	Mne	Ned	MKD	Nor	Pol	Por	Rou	Rus	SMR	Srb	Slo	Esp	Swe	Sui	GBR	TOTAL
Malta	4	1																								10	8		4	5	7							3				46
Albania					3																								12						2					5		47
Czech Republic	1	4					2	4																3		6			7			4	4			8	3					71
Germany						2				3														2														3				8
Russia	8	12		2	12	10			10	12					5	5	10	2		5	8	8	10	8	8	8	12	3	2		6	6		12				2			1	202
Denmark												6	5		3	3			2			12	2					6									2		2	3	3	43
San Marino	5			6											6		3									3	6		4					1								34
North Macedonia	12	5	3	7	7	5		10			1	5		2	3	4		6	3	1		6	4		4	8	7	1		4	5	1	3		12	10			7	6		152
Sweden	1	6	12	3				2	4	8	12	8	12	6	4				10	6	1		6	5	7			12		12					5	1	12			6	10	159
Slovenia								6		3	3	3				1											2				8			4	7							37
Cyprus	3			2					12					12	12									2			3							5	7			2	1			49
Netherlands	4	10	6	8	4	12	10	5	7	5	8	10	8	10	8	7	4	5	6	8	10	1	12	12	10	4	3		12	8	10	7	12	2	6			4	10	8	8	305
Greece	2			1			1							8	1										1						7	8		7	8			2	1			32
Israel						2													2																							13
Norway	3	7	6		4	4	3				7	10	6	6	5	10			7	8	12	6	7	5	4	3	7		7		6	5	1	8	1	1		4	10	8	8	190
United Kingdom																																										0
Iceland			10	5		1	7	1		6	2			2		12				3			3	6				4		6	10	2	2	6	4	2	3	4		4	2	111
Estonia											6		5					3			3		8	1											3			5				31
Belarus				2											3													4						10								15
Azerbaijan	6	2		1		7		3	10	4	2			1	10	6	1	1	4	4	4	4	7	10	6	10		4		2		3	10	12	5		5	5	3	4		148
France		8			8		12		5						2	2			1		2	2				1					2				1			1		1		31
Italy	7	8	2	10	8	6	12	12	8		4	1		4	12	12	8	8	5		2	12	10	6	12	1	5	10	10	5	4	10	5		10	10	12	10	8	12		272
Serbia				4				7																		12	6		6		3					3						42
Switzerland	10	7	5	12	5	3	6	8	6	7	7		1		6	2	5	4	7	10	5	2	7	7	5	5	1	8	3	8	1	2	8		3	8	4	6	6		7	185
Australia										2			4						12	7	7							1	2	5	12	7	7		4		7	7	7		12	137
Spain								3	1																			8											2			18

The Netherlands would still have won under the old voting system and only minor changes in positions would have occurred at the top, with Norway finishing 4th instead of Switzerland. At the bottom, the United Kingdom would still have finished last, except with the added embarrassment of 0 points.

Eurovision 2019: Country-by-country history, points scored and final positions for each act.

Albania

			Semi-Final		Final	
Year	Artist	Song	Points	Position	Points	Position
2004	Anjeza Shahini	The Image Of You	167	4	106	7
2005	Ledina Celo	Tomorrow I Go	-	-	53	16
2006	Luiz Ejlli	Zjarr E Ftohtë	58	15	-	-
2007	Aida & Frederik Ndoci	Hear My Plea	49	17	-	-
2008	Olta Boka	Zemrën E Lamë Peng	67	9	55	17
2009	Kejsi Tola	Carry Me In Your Dreams	73	7	48	17
2010	Juliana Pasha	It's All About You	76	6	62	16
2011	Aurela Gaçe	Feel The Passion	47	14	-	-
2012	Rona Nishliu	Suus	146	2	146	5
2013	Adrian Lulgjuraj & Bledar Sejko	Identitet	31	15	-	-
2014	Hersi	One Night's Anger	22	15	-	-
2015	Elhaida Dani	I'm Alive	62	10	34	17
2016	Eneda Tarifa	Fairytale	45	16	-	-
2017	Lindita	World	76	14	-	-
2018	Eugent Bushpepa	Mall	162	8	184	11
2019	Jonida Maliqi	Ktheju tokës	96	9	90	17

Andorra

			Semi-Final		Final	
Year	Artist	Song	Points	Position	Points	Position
2004	Marta Roure	Jugarem A Estimar-nos	12	18	-	-
2005	Marian van de Wal	La Mirada Interior	27	23	-	-
2006	Jennifer	Sense Tu	8	23	-	-
2007	Anonymous	Salvem El Món	80	12	-	-
2008	Gisela	Casanova	22	16	-	-
2009	Susanne Georgi	La Teva Decisió (Get A Life)	8	15	-	-

Armenia

			Semi-Final		Final	
Year	Artist	Song	Points	Position	Points	Position
2006	André	Without Your Love	150	7	129	8
2007	Hayko	Anytime You Need	-	-	138	8
2008	Sirusho	Qele, Qele	139	2	199	4
2009	Inga & Anush	Jan Jan	99	5	92	10
2010	Eva Rivas	Apricot Stone	76	6	141	7
2011	Emmy	Boom Boom	54	12	-	-
2012	-	-	-	-	-	-
2013	Dorians	Lonely Planet	69	7	41	18
2014	Aram MP3	Not Alone	121	4	174	4
2015	Genealogy	Face the Shadow	77	7	34	16
2016	Iveta Mukuchyan	LoveWave	243	2	249	7
2017	Artsvik	Fly With Me	152	7	79	18
2018	Sevak Khanagyan	Qami	79	15	-	-
2019	Srbuk	Walking Out	49	16	-	-

Australia

			Semi-Final		Final	
Year	Artist	Song	Points	Position	Points	Position
2015	Guy Sebastian	Tonight Again	-	-	196	5
2016	Dami Im	Sound of Silence	330	1	511	2
2017	Isaiah	Don't Come Easy	160	6	173	9
2018	Jessica Mauboy	We Got Love	212	4	99	20
2019	Kate Miller-Heidke	Zero Gravity	261	1	284	9

Austria

Year	Artist	Song	Semi-Final Points	Semi-Final Position	Final Points	Final Position
1957	Bob Martin	Wohin, Kleines Pony			3	10
1958	Liane Augustin	Die Ganze Welt Braucht Liebe			8	5
1959	Ferry Graf	Der K. Und K. Kalypso Aus Wien			4	9
1960	Harry Winter	Du Hast Mich So Fasziniert			6	7
1961	Jimmy Makulis	Sehnsucht			1	15
1962	Eleonore Schwarz	Nur In Der Wiener Luft			0	13
1963	Carmela Corren	Vielleicht Geschieht Ein Wunder			16	7
1964	Udo Jürgens	Warum Nur, Warum?			11	6
1965	Udo Jürgens	Sag Ihr, Ich Lass' Sie Grüßen			16	4
1966	Udo Jürgens	Merci Chérie			31	1
1967	Peter Horten	Warum Es Hunderttausend Sterne Gibt			2	14
1968	Karel Gott	Tausend Fenster			2	13
1969	-	-			-	-
1970	-	-			-	-
1971	Marianne Mendt	Musik			66	6
1972	The Milestones	Falter Im Wind			100	5
1973	-	-			-	-
1974	-	-			-	-
1975	-	-			-	-
1976	Waterloo and Robinson	My Little World			80	5
1977	Schmetterlinge	Boom Boom Boomerang			11	17
1978	Springtime	Mrs. Caroline Robinson			14	15
1979	Christina Simon	Heute In Jerusalem			5	18
1980	Blue Danube	Du Bist Musik			64	8
1981	Marty Brem	Wenn Du Da Bist			20	17
1982	Mess	Sonntag			57	9
1983	Westend	Hurricane			53	9
1984	Anita	Einfach Weg			5	19
1985	Gary Lux	Kinder Dieser Welt			60	8
1986	Timna Brauer	Die Zeit Ist Einsam			12	18
1987	Gary Lux	Nur Noch Gefühl			8	20
1988	Wilfried	Lisa Mona Lisa			0	21
1989	Thomas Forstner	Nur Ein Lied			97	5
1990	Simone	Keine Mauern Mehr			58	10
1991	Thomas Forstner	Venedig Im Regen			0	22
1992	Tony Wegas	Zusammen Geh'n			63	9
1993	Tony Wegas	Maria Magdalena			32	14
1994	Petra Frey	Für Den Frieden Der Welt			19	17
1995	Stella Jones	Die Welt Dreht Sich Verkehrt			67	13
1996	George Nußbaumer	Weil's Dr Guat Got			68	10
1997	Bettina Soriat	One Step			12	21
1998	-	-			-	-
1999	Bobbie Singer	Reflection			65	9
2000	The Rounder Girls	All To You			34	14
2001	-	-			-	-
2002	Manuel Ortega	Say A Word			26	18
2003	Alf Poier	Weil Der Mensch Zählt			101	6
2004	Tie Break	Du Bist	-	-	9	21
2005	Global.Kryner	Y Así	30	21	-	-
2006	-	-	-	-	-	-
2007	Eric Papilaya	Get A Life - Get Alive	4	27	-	-
2008	-	-	-	-	-	-
2009	-	-	-	-	-	-
2010	-	-	-	-	-	-
2011	Nadine Beiler	The Secret is Love	69	7	64	18
2012	Trackshittaz	Woki Mit Deim Popo	8	18	-	-
2013	Natália Kelly	Shine	27	14	-	-
2014	Conchita Wurst	Rise Like a Phoenix	169	1	290	1
2015	The Makemakes	I Am Yours	-	-	0	26
2016	ZOË	Loin d'ici	170	7	151	13
2017	Nathan Trent	Running On Air	147	7	93	16
2018	Cesár Sampson	Nobody But You	231	4	342	3
2019	PÆNDA	Limits	21	17	-	-

Azerbaijan

Year	Artist	Song	Semi-Final Points	Semi-Final Position	Final Points	Final Position
2008	Elnur & Samir	Day After Day	96	6	132	8
2009	AySel & Arash	Always	180	2	207	3
2010	Safura	Drip Drop	113	2	145	5
2011	Ell/Nikki	Running Scared	122	2	221	1
2012	Sabina Babayeva	When The Music Dies	-	-	150	4
2013	Farid Mammadov	Hold Me	139	1	234	2
2014	Dilara Kazimova	Start a Fire	57	9	33	22
2015	Elnur Hüseynov	Hour of the Wolf	53	10	49	12
2016	Samra	Miracle	185	6	117	17
2017	Dihaj	Skeletons	150	8	120	14
2018	Aisel	X My Heart	94	11	-	-
2019	Chingiz	Truth	224	5	302	8

Belarus

Year	Artist	Song	Semi-Final Points	Semi-Final Position	Final Points	Final Position
2004	Aleksandra & Konstantin	My Galileo	10	19	-	-
2005	Angelica Agurbash	Love Me Tonight	67	13	-	-
2006	Polina Smolova	Mum	10	22	-	-
2007	Dmitry Koldun	Work Your Magic	176	4	143	6
2008	Ruslan Alenho	Hasta La Vista	27	17	-	-
2009	Petr Elfimov	Eyes That Never Lie	25	13	-	-
2010	3+2	Butterflies	59	9	18	24
2011	Anastasiya Vinnikova	I Love Belarus	45	14	-	-
2012	Litesound	We Are The Heroes	35	16	-	-
2013	Alyona Lanskaya	Solayoh	64	7	48	16
2014	Teo	Cheesecake	87	5	43	16
2015	Uzari & Maimuna	Time	39	12	-	-
2016	IVAN	Help You Fly	84	12	-	-
2017	Naviband	Story Of My Life	110	9	83	17
2018	Alekseev	Forever	65	16	-	-
2019	ZENA	Like It	122	10	31	24

Belgium

Year	Artist	Song	Semi-Final Points	Semi-Final Position	Final Points	Final Position
1956	(1) Mony Marc	Le Plus Beau Jour De Ma Vie			-	2
1956	(2) Fud Leclerc	Messieurs Les Noyés De La Seine			-	2
1957	Bobbejaan Schoepen	Straatdeuntje			5	8
1958	Fud Leclerc	Ma Petite Chatte			8	5
1959	Bob Benny	Hou Toch Van Mij			9	6
1960	Fud Leclerc	Mon Amour Pour Toi			9	6
1961	Bob Benny	September, Gouden Roos			1	15
1962	Fud Leclerc	Ton Nom			0	13
1963	Jacques Raymond	Waarom			4	10
1964	Robert Cogoi	Près De Ma Rivière			2	10
1965	Lize Marke	Als Het Weer Lente Is			0	15
1966	Tonia	Un Peu De Poivre, Un Peu De Sel			14	4
1967	Louis Neefs	Ik Heb Zorgen			8	7
1968	Claude Lombard	Quand Tu Reviendras			8	7
1969	Louis Neefs	Jennifer Jennings			10	7
1970	Jean Vallée	Viens L'oublier			5	8
1971	Lily Castel and Jacques Raymond	Goeie Morgen, Morgen			68	14
1972	Serge and Christine Ghisoland	À La Folie Ou Pas Du Tout			55	17
1973	Nicole and Hugo	Baby, Baby			58	17
1974	Jacques Hustin	Fleur De Liberté			10	9
1975	Ann Christy	Gelukkig Zijn			17	15
1976	Pierre Rapsat	Judy Et Cie.			68	8
1977	Dream Express	A Million In One, Two, Three			69	7
1978	Jean Vallée	L'amour ça Fait Chanter La Vie			125	2
1979	Micha Marah	Hey Nana			5	18
1980	Telex	Euro-vision			14	17

Belgium (continued)

| | | | Semi-Final || Final ||
Year	Artist	Song	Points	Position	Points	Position
1981	Emly Starr	Samson			40	13
1982	Stella	Si Tu Aimes Ma Musique			96	4
1983	Pas de Deux	Rendez-vous			13	18
1984	Jacques Zegers	Avanti La Vie			70	5
1985	Linda Lepomme	Laat Me Nu Gaan			7	19
1986	Sandra Kim	J'aime La Vie			176	1
1987	Liliane Saint-Pierre	Soldiers Of Love			56	11
1988	Reynaert	Laissez Briller Le Soleil			5	18
1989	Ingeborg	Door De Wind			13	19
1990	Philippe Lafontaine	Macédomienne			46	12
1991	Clouseau	Geef Het Op			23	16
1992	Morgane	Nous On Veut Des Violons			11	20
1993	Barbara	Iemand Als Jij			3	25
1994	-	-			-	-
1995	Frédéric Etherlinck	La Voix Est Libre			8	20
1996	Lisa del Bo	Liefde Is Een Kaartspel			22	16
1997	-	-			-	-
1998	Mélanie Cohl	Dis Oui			122	6
1999	Venessa Chinitor	Like The Wind			38	12
2000	Nathalie Sorce	Envie De Vivre			2	24
2001	-	-			-	-
2002	Sergio & the Ladies	Sister			33	13
2003	Urban Trad	Sanomi			165	2
2004	Xandee	1 Life	-	-	7	22
2005	Nuno Resende	Le Grand Soir	29	22	-	-
2006	Kate Ryan	Je T'adore	69	12	-	-
2007	The KMG's	Love Power	14	26	-	-
2008	Ishtar	O Julissi	16	17	-	-
2009	Copycat	Copycat	1	17	-	-
2010	Tom Dice	Me and My Guitar	167	1	143	6
2011	Witloof Bay	With Love Baby	53	11	-	-
2012	Iris	Would You?	16	17	-	-
2013	Roberto Bellarosa	Love Kills	75	5	71	12
2014	Axel Hirsoux	Mother	28	14	-	-
2015	Loïc Nottet	Rhythm Inside	149	2	217	4
2016	Laura Tesoro	What's The Pressure?	274	3	181	10
2017	Blanche	City Lights	165	4	363	4
2018	Sennek	A Matter Of Time	91	12	-	-
2019	Eliot	Wake Up	70	13	-	-

Bosnia & Herzegovina

| | | | Semi-Final || Final ||
Year	Artist	Song	Points	Position	Points	Position
1993	Fazla	Sva Bol Svijeta			27	16
1994	Alma & Dejan	Ostani Kraj Mene			39	15
1995	Davor Popovic	Dvadeset I Prvi Vijek			14	19
1996	Amila Glamocak	Za Našu Ljubav			13	22
1997	Alma Cardzic	Goodbye			22	18
1998	-	-			-	-
1999	Dino & Beatrice	Putnici			86	7
2000	-	-			-	-
2001	Nino	Hano			29	14
2002	Maja	Na Jastuku Za Dvoje			33	13
2003	Mija Martina	Ne Brini			27	16
2004	Deen	In The Disco	133	7	91	9
2005	Feminnem	Call Me	-	-	79	14
2006	Hari Mata Hari	Lejla	267	2	229	3
2007	Marija Sestic	Rijeka Bez Imena	-	-	106	11
2008	Laka	Pokušaj	72	9	110	10
2009	Regina	Bistra Voda	125	3	106	9
2010	Vukašin Brajić	Thunder And Lightning	58	8	51	17
2011	Dino Merlin	Love in Rewind	109	5	125	6
2012	MayaSar	Korake Ti Znam	77	6	55	18

Bosnia & Herzegovina (continued)

Year	Artist	Song	Semi-Final Points	Semi-Final Position	Final Points	Final Position
2013	-	-	-	-	-	-
2014	-	-	-	-	-	-
2015	-	-	-	-	-	-
2016	Dalal & Deen feat. Ana Rucner and Jala	Ljubav Je	104	11	-	-

Bulgaria

Year	Artist	Song	Semi-Final Points	Semi-Final Position	Final Points	Final Position
2005	Kaffe	Lorraine	49	19	-	-
2006	Mariana Popova	Let Me Cry	36	17	-	-
2007	Elitsa Todorova & Stoyan Yankulov	Water	146	6	157	5
2008	Deep Zone & Balthazar	DJ, Take Me Away	56	11	-	-
2009	Krassimir Avramov	Illusion	7	16	-	-
2010	Miro	Angel Si Ti	19	15	-	-
2011	Poli Genova	Na Inat	48	12	-	-
2012	Sofi Marinova	Love Unlimited	45	11	-	-
2013	Elitsa Todorova feat. Stoyan Yankulov	Samo Shampioni (Only Champions)	45	12	-	-
2014	-	-	-	-	-	-
2015	-	-	-	-	-	-
2016	Poli Genova	If Love Was A Crime	220	5	307	4
2017	Kristian Kostov	Beautiful Mess	403	1	615	2
2018	Equinox	Bones	177	7	166	14

Croatia

Year	Artist	Song	Semi-Final Points	Semi-Final Position	Final Points	Final Position
1993	Put	Don't Ever Cry			31	15
1994	Tony Cetinski	Nek'ti Bude Ljubav Sva			27	16
1995	Magazin & Lidija	Nostalgija			91	6
1996	Maja Blagdan	Sveta Ljubav			98	4
1997	ENI	Probudi Me			24	17
1998	Danijela	Neka Mi Ne Svane			131	5
1999	Doris Dragovic	Marija Magdalena			118	4
2000	Goran Karan	Kada Zaspu Andeli			70	9
2001	Vanna	Strings Of My Heart			42	10
2002	Vesna Pisarovic	Everything I Want			44	11
2003	Claudia Beni	Više Nisam Tvoja			29	15
2004	Ivan Mikulic	You Are The Only One	72	9	50	12
2005	Boris Novkovic feat. Lado members	Vukovi Umiru Sami	169	4	115	11
2006	Severina	Moja štikla	-	-	56	12
2007	Dragonfly feat. Dado Topic	Vjerujem U Ljubav	54	16	-	-
2008	Kraljevi Ulice & 75 Cents	Romanca	112	4	44	21
2009	Igor Cukrov featuring Andrea	Lijepa Tena	33	13	45	18
2010	Feminnem	Lako Je Sve	33	13	-	-
2011	Daria	Celebrate	41	15	-	-
2012	Nina Badrić	Nebo	42	12	-	-
2013	Klapa s mora	Mižerja	38	13	-	-
2014	-	-	-	-	-	-
2015	-	-	-	-	-	-
2016	Nina Kraljić	Lighthouse	133	10	73	23
2017	Jacques Houdek	My Friend	141	8	128	13
2018	Franka	Crazy	63	17	-	-
2019	Roko	The Dream	64	17	-	-

Cyprus

			Semi-Final		Final	
Year	Artist	Song	Points	Position	Points	Position
1981	Island	Monika			69	6
1982	Anna Vishy	Mono I Agapi			85	5
1983	Stavros & Constantina	I Agapi Akoma Zi			26	16
1984	Andy Paul	Anna Mari-elena			31	15
1985	Lia Vishy	To Katalava Arga			15	16
1986	Elpida	Tora Zo			4	20
1987	Alexia	Aspro Mavro			80	7
1988	-	-			-	-
1989	Fanny Polymeri & Yiannis Savvidakis	Apopse As Vrethoume			51	11
1990	Haris Anastasiou	Milas Poli			36	14
1991	Elena Patroclou	SOS			60	9
1992	Evridiki	Teriazoume			57	10
1993	Kyriakos Zymboulakis & Demos Van Beke	Mi Stamatas			17	19
1994	Evridiki	Ime Anthropos Ke Ego			51	11
1995	Alexandros Panayi	Sti Fotia			79	9
1996	Constantinos	Mono Gia Mas			72	9
1997	Chara & Andreas Konstantinou	Mana Mou			98	5
1998	Michael Hajiyanni	Genesis			37	11
1999	Marlain Angelidou	Tha'nai Erotas			2	22
2000	Voice	Nomiza			8	21
2001	-	-			-	-
2002	One	Gimme			85	6
2003	Stelios Constantas	Feeling Alive			15	20
2004	Lisa Andreas	Stronger Every Minute	149	5	170	5
2005	Constantinos Christoforou	Ela Ela	-	-	46	18
2006	Annet Artani	Why Angels Cry	57	13	-	-
2007	Evridiki	Comme Ci, Comme ça	65	15	-	-
2008	Evdokia Kadi	Femme Fatale	36	15	-	-
2009	Christina Metaxa	Firefly	32	14	-	-
2010	Jon Lilygreen & The Islanders	Life Looks Better In Spring	67	10	27	21
2011	Christos Mylordos	San Aggelos S'Agapisa	16	18	-	-
2012	Ivi Adamou	La La Love	91	7	65	16
2013	Despina Olympiou	An Me Thimasai	11	15	-	-
2014	-	-	-	-	-	-
2015	John Karayiannis	One Thing I Should Have Done	87	6	11	22
2016	Minus One	Alter Ego	164	8	96	20
2017	Hovig	Gravity	164	5	68	21
2018	Eleni Foureira	Fuego	262	2	436	2
2019	Tamta	Replay	149	9	109	13

Czech Republic

			Semi-Final		Final	
Year	Artist	Song	Points	Position	Points	Position
2007	Kabát	Malá Dáma	1	28	-	-
2008	Tereza Kerndlová	Have Some Fun	9	18	-	-
2009	Gipsy.cz	Aven Romale	0	18	-	-
2010	-	-	-	-	-	-
2011	-	-	-	-	-	-
2012	-	-	-	-	-	-
2013	-	-	-	-	-	-
2014	-	-	-	-	-	-
2015	Marta Jandová & Václav Noid Bárta	Hope Never Dies	33	13	-	-
2016	Gabriela Gunčíková	I Stand	161	9	41	25
2017	Martina Bárta	My Turn	83	13	-	-
2018	Mikolas Josef	Lie To Me	232	3	281	6
2019	Lake Malawi	Friend of a Friend	242	2	157	11

Denmark

Year	Artist	Song	Semi-Final Points	Semi-Final Position	Final Points	Final Position
1957	Birthe Wilke & Gustav Winckler	Skibet Skal Sejle I Nat			10	3
1958	Raquel Rastenni	Jeg Rev Et Blad Ud Af Min Dagbog			3	8
1959	Birthe Wilke	Uh-jeg Ville Ønske Jeg Var Dig			12	5
1960	Katy Bødtger	Det Var En Yndig Tid			4	10
1961	Dario Campeotto	Angelique			12	5
1962	Ellen Winther	Vuggevise			2	10
1963	Grethe & Jørgen Ingmann	Dansevise			42	1
1964	Bjørn Tidmand	Sangen Om Dig			4	9
1965	Birgit Brüel	For Din Skyld			10	7
1966	Ulla Pia	Stop, Ja Stop - Ja Stop, Mens Legen Er Go			4	14
1967	-	-			-	-
1968	-	-			-	-
1969	-	-			-	-
1970	-	-			-	-
1971	-	-			-	-
1972	-	-			-	-
1973	-	-			-	-
1974	-	-			-	-
1975	-	-			-	-
1976	-	-			-	-
1977	-	-			-	-
1978	Mabel	Boom Boom			13	16
1979	Tommy Seebach	Disco Tango			76	6
1980	Bamses Venner	Tænker Altid På Dig			25	14
1981	Debbie Cameron & Tommy Seebach	Krøller Eller Ej			41	11
1982	Brixx	Video-video			5	17
1983	Gry Johansen	Kloden Drejer			16	17
1984	Hot Eyes	Det' Lige Det			101	4
1985	Hot Eyes	Sku' Du Spør Fra No'n			41	11
1986	Lise Haavik & Trax	Du Er Fuld Af Løgn			77	6
1987	Anne-Catherine Herdorf & Bandjo	En Lille Melodi			83	5
1988	Hot Eyes	Ka' Du Se Hva' Jeg Sa'			92	3
1989	Birthe Kjær	Vi Maler Byen Rød			111	3
1990	Lonnie Devantier	Hallo Hallo			64	8
1991	Anders Frandsen	Lige Der Hvor Hjertet Slår			8	19
1992	Lotte Nilsson & Kenny Lübcke	Ålt Det Som Ingen Ser			47	11
1993	Tommy Seebach Band	Under Stjernerne På Himlen			9	22
1994	-	-			-	-
1995	Aud Wilken	Fra Mols Til Skagen			92	5
1996	-	-			-	-
1997	Kølig Kaj	Stemmen I Mit Liv			25	16
1998	-	-			-	-
1999	Trine Jepsen & Michael Teschl	This Time (I Mean It)			71	8
2000	Olsen brothers	Fly On The Wings Of Love			195	1
2001	Rollo & King	Never Ever Let You Go			177	2
2002	Malene	Tell Me Who You Are			7	24
2003	-	-			-	-
2004	Tomas Thordarson	Shame On You	56	13	-	-
2005	Jakob Sveistrup	Talking To You	185	3	125	9
2006	Sidsel Ben Semmane	Twist Of Love	-	-	26	18
2007	DQ	Drama Queen	45	19	-	-
2008	Simon Mathew	All Night Long	112	3	60	15
2009	Brinck	Believe Again	69	8	74	13
2010	Chanée & N'evergreen	In A Moment Like This	101	5	149	4
2011	A Friend in London	New Tomorrow	135	2	134	5
2012	Soluna Samay	Should've Known Better	65	9	21	23
2013	Emmelie de Forest	Only Teardrops	167	1	281	1
2014	Basim	Cliché Love Song	-	-	74	9
2015	Anti Social Media	The Way You Are	33	13	-	-
2016	Lighthouse X	Soldiers Of Love	34	17	-	-
2017	Anja	Where I Am	101	10	77	20

Denmark (continued)

Year	Artist	Song	Semi-Final Points	Semi-Final Position	Final Points	Final Position
2018	Rasmussen	Higher Ground	204	5	226	9
2019	Leonora	Love Is Forever	94	10	120	12

Estonia

Year	Artist	Song	Semi-Final Points	Semi-Final Position	Final Points	Final Position
1994	Silvi Vrait	Nagu Merelaine			2	24
1995	-	-			-	-
1996	Ivo Linna & Maarja-Liis Ilus	Kaelakee Hääl			94	5
1997	Maarja-Liis Ilus	Keelatud Maa			82	8
1998	Koit Toome	Mere Lapsed			36	12
1999	Evelin Samuel & Camille	Diamond Of Night			90	6
2000	Ines	Once In A Lifetime			98	4
2001	Tanel Padar, Dave Benton & 2XL	Everybody			198	1
2002	Sahléne	Runaway			111	3
2003	Ruffus	Eighties Coming Back			14	21
2004	Neiokõsõ	Tii	57	11	-	-
2005	Suntribe	Let's Get Loud	31	20	-	-
2006	Sandra	Through My Window	28	18	-	-
2007	Gerli Padar	Partners In Crime	33	22	-	-
2008	Kreisiraadio	Leto Svet	8	18	-	-
2009	Urban Symphony	Rändajad	115	3	129	6
2010	Malcolm Lincoln	Siren	39	14	-	-
2011	Getter Jaani	Rockefeller Street	60	9	44	24
2012	Ott Lepland	Kuula	100	4	120	6
2013	Birgit Õigemeel	Et Uus Saaks Alguse	52	10	19	20
2014	Tanja	Amazing	36	12	-	-
2015	Elina Born & Stig Rästa	Goodbye to Yesterday	105	3	106	7
2016	Jüri Pootsmann	Play	24	18	-	-
2017	Koit Toome & Laura	Verona	85	14	-	-
2018	Elina Nechayeva	La Forza	201	5	245	8
2019	Victor Crone	Storm	198	4	76	20

Finland

Year	Artist	Song	Semi-Final Points	Semi-Final Position	Final Points	Final Position
1961	Laila Kinnunen	Valoa Ikkunassa			6	10
1962	Marion Rung	Tipi-tii			4	7
1963	Laila Halme	Muistojeni Laulu			0	13
1964	Lasse Mårtenson	Laiskotellen			9	7
1965	Viktor Klimenko	Aurinko Laskee Länteen			0	15
1966	Ann-Christine Nyström	Play-boy			7	10
1967	Fredi	Varjoon-suojaan			3	12
1968	Kristina Hautala	Kun Kello Käy			1	16
1969	Jarkko & Laura	Kuin Silloin Ennen			6	12
1970	-	-			-	-
1971	Markku Aro & Koivisto Sisters	Tie Uuteen Päivään			84	8
1972	Päivi Paunu & Kim Floor	Muistathan			78	12
1973	Marion Rung	Tom Tom Tom			93	6
1974	Carita	Äla Mene Pois (Keep Me Warm)			4	13
1975	Pihasoittajat	Old Man Fiddle			74	7
1976	Fredi & The Friends	Pump-pump			44	11
1977	Monica Aspelund	Lapponia			50	10
1978	Seija Simola	Anna Rakkaudelle Tilaisuus			2	18
1979	Katri-Helena	Katso Sineen Taivaan			38	14
1980	Vesa-Matti Loiri	Huilumies			6	19
1981	Riki Sorsa	Reggae OK			27	16
1982	Kojo	Nuku Pommiin			0	18
1983	Ami Aspelund	Fantasiaa			41	11
1984	Kirka	Hengaillaan			46	9
1985	Sonja Lumme	Eläköön Elämä			58	9
1986	Kari Kuivalainen	Päivä Kahden Ihmisen			22	15

Finland (continued)

Year	Artist	Song	Semi-Final Points	Semi-Final Position	Final Points	Final Position
1987	Vicky Rosti	Sata Salamaa			32	15
1988	Boulevard	Nauravat Silmät Muistetaan			3	20
1989	Anneli Saaristo	La Dolce Vita			76	7
1990	Beat	Fri?			8	21
1991	Kaija	Hullu Yö			6	20
1992	Pave	Yamma Yamma			4	23
1993	Katri-Helena	Tule Luo			20	17
1994	CatCat	Bye Bye Baby			11	22
1995	-	-			-	-
1996	Jasmine	Niin Kaunis On Taivas			9	23
1997	-	-			-	-
1998	Edea	Aava			22	15
1999	-	-			-	-
2000	Nina Åström	A Little Bit			18	18
2001	-	-			-	-
2002	Laura	Addicted To You			24	20
2003	-	-			-	-
2004	Jari Sillanpää	Takes 2 To Tango	51	14	-	-
2005	Geir Rönning	Why?	50	18	-	-
2006	Lordi	Hard Rock Hallelujah	292	1	292	1
2007	Hanna Pakarinen	Leave Me Alone	-	-	53	17
2008	Teräsbetoni	Missä Miehet Ratsastaa	79	8	35	22
2009	Waldo's People	Lose Control	42	12	22	25
2010	Kuunkuiskaajat	Työlki Ellää	49	11	-	-
2011	Paradise Oskar	Da Da Dam	103	3	57	21
2012	Pernilla	När Jag Blundar	41	12	-	-
2013	Krista Siegfrids	Marry Me	64	9	13	24
2014	Softengine	Something Better	97	3	72	11
2015	Pertti Kurikan Nimipäivät	Aina mun pitää	13	16	-	-
2016	Sandhja	Sing It Away	51	15	-	-
2017	Norma John	Blackbird	92	12	-	-
2018	Saara Aalto	Monsters	108	10	46	25
2019	Darude feat. Sebastian Rejman	Look Away	23	17	-	-

France

Year	Artist	Song	Semi-Final Points	Semi-Final Position	Final Points	Final Position
1956	(1) Mathé Altéry	Le Temps Perdu			-	2
1956	(2) Dany Dauberson	Il Est Là			-	2
1957	Paule Desjardins	La Belle Amour			17	2
1958	André Claveau	Dors Mon Amour			27	1
1959	Jean Philippe	Oui, Oui, Oui, Oui			15	3
1960	Jacqueline Boyer	Tom Pillibi			32	1
1961	Jean-Paul Mauric	Printemps (avril Carillonne)			13	4
1962	Isabelle Aubret	Un Premier Amour			26	1
1963	Alain Barrière	Elle était Si Jolie			25	5
1964	Rachel	Le Chant De Mallory			14	4
1965	Guy Mardel	N'avoue Jamais			22	3
1966	Dominique Walter	Chez Nous			1	16
1967	Noëlle Cordier	Il Doit Faire Beau Là-bas			20	3
1968	Isabelle Aubret	La Source			20	3
1969	Frida Boccara	Un Jour, Un Enfant			18	1
1970	Guy Bonnet	Marie Blanche			8	4
1971	Serge Lama	Un Jardin Sur La Terre			83	9
1972	Betty Mars	Comé-comédie			81	11
1973	Martine Clémenceau	Sans Toi			65	15
1974	-				-	-
1975	Nicole Rieu	Et Bonjour à Toi L'artiste			91	4
1976	Catherine Ferry	Un, Deux, Trois			147	2
1977	Marie Myriam	L'oiseau Et L'enfant			136	1
1978	Joël Prévost	Il Y Aura Toujours Des Violons			119	3
1979	Anne-Marie David	Je Suis L'enfant-soleil			106	3
1980	Profil	Hé, Hé M'sieurs Dames			45	11

France (continued)

Year	Artist	Song	Semi-Final Points	Semi-Final Position	Final Points	Final Position
1981	Jean Gabilou	Humanahum			125	3
1982	-	-			-	-
1983	Guy Bonnet	Vivre			56	8
1984	Annick Thoumazeau	Autant D'amoureux Que D'étoiles			61	8
1985	Roger Bens	Femme Dans Ses Rêves Aussi			56	10
1986	Cocktail Chic	Européennes			13	17
1987	Christine Minier	Les Mots D'amour N'ont Pas De Dimanche			44	14
1988	Gérard Lenorman	Chanteur De Charme			64	10
1989	Nathalie Pâque	J'ai Volé La Vie			60	8
1990	Joelle Ursull	White And Black Blues			132	2
1991	Amina	C'est Le Dernier Qui A Parlé Qui A Raison			146	1
1992	Kali	Monté La Riviè			73	8
1993	Patrick Fiori	Mama Corsica			121	5
1994	Nina Morato	Je Suis Un Vrai Garçon			74	7
1995	Nathalie Santamaria	Il Me Donne Rendez-vous			94	4
1996	Dan Ar Braz & l'Héritage des Celtes	Diwanit Bugale			18	19
1997	Fanny	Sentiments Songes			95	7
1998	Marie-Line	Où Aller			3	24
1999	Nayah	Je Veux Donner Ma Voix			14	17
2000	Sofia Mestari	On Aura Le Ciel			5	23
2001	Natasha Saint-Pier	Je N'ai Que Mon âme			142	4
2002	Sandrine François	Il Faut Du Temps			104	5
2003	Louisa Baileche	Monts Et Merveilles			19	18
2004	Jonatan Cerrada	A Chaque Pas	-	-	40	15
2005	Ortal	Chacun Pense à Soi	-	-	11	23
2006	Virginie Pouchin	Il était Temps	-	-	5	22
2007	Les Fatals Picards	L'amour à La Française	-	-	19	22
2008	Sébastien Tellier	Divine	-	-	47	19
2009	Patricia Kaas	Et S'il Fallait Le Faire	-	-	107	8
2010	Jessy Matador	Allez Olla Olé	-	-	82	12
2011	Amaury Vassili	Sognu	-	-	82	15
2012	Anggun	Echo (You And I)	-	-	21	22
2013	Amandine Bourgeois	L'enfer Et Moi	-	-	14	23
2014	Twin Twin	Moustache	-	-	2	26
2015	Lisa Angell	N'oubliez pas	-	-	4	25
2016	Amir	J'ai cherché	-	-	257	6
2017	Alma	Requiem	-	-	135	12
2018	Madame Monsieur	Mercy	-	-	173	13
2019	Bilal Hassani	Roi	-	-	105	16

Georgia

Year	Artist	Song	Semi-Final Points	Semi-Final Position	Final Points	Final Position
2007	Sopho	My Story	123	8	97	12
2008	Diana Gurtskaya	Peace Will Come	107	5	83	11
2009	-	-	-	-	-	-
2010	Sofia Nizharadze	Shine	106	3	136	9
2011	Eldrine	One More Day	74	6	110	9
2012	Anri Jokhadze	I'm A Joker	36	14	-	-
2013	Nodi Tatishvili & Sophie Gelovani	Waterfall	63	10	50	15
2014	The Shin and Mariko	Three Minutes to Earth	15	15	-	-
2015	Nina Sublatti	Warrior	98	4	51	11
2016	Nika Kocharov & Young Georgian Lolitaz	Midnight Gold	123	9	104	20
2017	Tamara Gachechiladze	Keep The Faith	99	11	-	-
2018	Ethno-Jazz Band Iriao	For You	24	18	-	-
2019	Oto Nemsadze	Keep On Going	62	14	-	-

Germany

Year	Artist	Song	Semi-Final Points	Semi-Final Position	Final Points	Final Position
1956	(1) Walter Andreas Schwarz	Im Wartesaal Zum Großen Glück			-	2
1956	(2) Freddy Quinn	So Geht Das Jede Nacht			-	2
1957	Margot Hielscher	Telefon, Telefon			8	4
1958	Margot Hielscher	Für Zwei Groschen Musik			5	7
1959	Alice & Ellen Kessler	Heut' Woll'n Wir Tanzen Geh'n			5	8
1960	Wyn Hoop	Bonne Nuit, Ma Chérie!			11	4
1961	Lale Andersen	Einmal Sehen Wir Uns Wieder			3	13
1962	Conny Froboess	Zwei Kleine Italiener			9	6
1963	Heidi Brühl	Marcel			5	9
1964	Nora Nova	Man Gewöhnt Sich So Schnell An Das Schöne			0	13
1965	Ulla Wiesner	Paradies, Wo Bist Du?			0	15
1966	Margot Eskens	Die Zeiger Der Uhr			7	10
1967	Inge Brück	Anouschka			7	8
1968	Wencke Myhre	Ein Hoch Der Liebe			11	6
1969	Siw Malmkvist	Primaballerina			8	9
1970	Katja Ebstein	Wunder Gibt Es Immer Wieder			12	3
1971	Katja Ebstein	Diese Welt			100	3
1972	Mary Roos	Nur Die Liebe Läßt Uns Leben			107	3
1973	Gitte	Junger Tag			85	8
1974	Cindy & Bert	Die Sommermelodie			3	14
1975	Joy Fleming	Ein Lied Kann Eine Brücke Sein			15	17
1976	Les Humphries Singers	Sing, Sang, Song			12	15
1977	Silver Convention	Telegram			55	8
1978	Ireen Sheer	Feuer			84	6
1979	Dschinghis Khan	Dschinghis Khan			86	4
1980	Katja Ebstein	Theater			128	2
1981	Lena Valaitis	Johnny Blue			132	2
1982	Nicole	Ein Bißchen Frieden			161	1
1983	Hoffmann & Hoffmann	Rücksicht			94	5
1984	Mary Roos	Aufrecht Geh'n			34	13
1985	Wind	Für Alle			105	2
1986	Ingrid Peters	Über Die Brücke Geh'n			62	8
1987	Wind	Laß Die Sonne In Dein Herz			141	2
1988	Maxi & Chris Garden	Lied Für Einen Freund			48	14
1989	Nino de Angelo	Flieger			46	14
1990	Chris Kempers & Daniel Kovac	Frei Zu Leben			60	9
1991	Atlantis 2000	Dieser Traum Darf Niemals Sterben			10	18
1992	Wind	Träume Sind Für Alle Da			27	16
1993	Münchener Freiheit	Viel Zu Weit			18	18
1994	MeKaDo	Wir Geben 'ne Party			128	3
1995	Stone & Stone	Verliebt In Dich			1	23
1996	-	-			-	-
1997	Bianca Shomburg	Zeit			22	18
1998	Guildo Horn	Guildo Hat Euch Lieb			86	7
1999	Sürpriz	Reise Nach Jerusalem - Kudüs'e Seyahat			140	3
2000	Stefan Raab	Wadde Hadde Dudde Da			96	5
2001	Michelle	Wer Liebe Lebt			66	8
2002	Corinna May	I Can't Live Without Music			17	21
2003	Lou	Let's Get Happy			53	11
2004	Max (Maximilian Mutzke)	Can't Wait Until Tonight	-	-	93	8
2005	Gracia	Run & Hide	-	-	4	24
2006	Texas Lightning	No, No, Never	-	-	36	14
2007	Roger Cicero	Frauen Regieren Die Welt	-	-	49	19
2008	No Angels	Disappear	-	-	14	23
2009	Alex Swings Oscar Sings!	Miss Kiss Kiss Bang	-	-	35	20
2010	Lena Meyer-Landrut	Satellite	-	-	246	1
2011	Lena Meyer-Landrut	Taken by a Stranger	-	-	107	10
2012	Roman Lob	Standing Still	-	-	110	8
2013	Cascada	Glorious	-	-	18	21
2014	Elaiza	Is it Right?	-	-	39	18
2015	Ann Sophie	Black Smoke	-	-	0	27
2016	Jamie-Lee	Ghost	-	-	11	26

Germany (continued)

Year	Artist	Song	Semi-Final Points	Semi-Final Position	Final Points	Final Position
2017	Levina	Perfect Life	-	-	6	25
2018	Michael Schulte	You Let Me Walk Alone	-	-	340	4
2019	S!sters	Sister	-	-	24	25

Greece

Year	Artist	Song	Semi-Final Points	Semi-Final Position	Final Points	Final Position
1974	Marinella	Krassi, Thalassa Ke T'agori Mou			7	11
1975	-	-			-	-
1976	Mariza Koch	Panaghia Mou, Panaghia Mou			20	13
1977	Pascalis, Marianna, Robert & Bessy	Mathema Solfege			92	5
1978	Tania Tsanaklidou	Charlie Chaplin			66	8
1979	Elpida	Socrates			69	8
1980	Anna Vishy & the Epikouri	Autostop			30	13
1981	Yiannis Dimitras	Feggari Kalokerino			55	8
1982	-	-			-	-
1983	Christie	Mou Les			32	14
1984	-	-			-	-
1985	Takis Biniaris	Miazoume			15	16
1986	-	-			-	-
1987	Bang	Stop!			64	10
1988	Aphroditi Fryda	Kloun			10	17
1989	Marianna	To Diko Sou Asteri			56	9
1990	Christos Callow & Wave	Horis Skopo			11	9
1991	Sofia Vossou	I Anixi			36	13
1992	Cleopatra	Olou Tou Kosmou I Elpida			94	5
1993	Katerina Garbi	Ellada, Hora Tou Fotos			64	9
1994	Costas Bigalis & the Sea Lovers	To Trehantiri (Diri Diri)			44	14
1995	Elina Constantopoulou	Pia Prossefchi			68	12
1996	Marianna Efstratiou	Emis Forame To Himona Anixiatika			36	14
1997	Marianna Zorba	Horepse			39	12
1998	Dionysia & Thalassa Group	Mia Krifi Evaisthissia			12	20
1999	-	-			-	-
2000	-	-			-	-
2001	Antique	Die For You			147	3
2002	Michalis Rakintzis	SAGAPO			27	17
2003	Mando	Never Let You Go			25	17
2004	Sakis Rouvas	Shake It	238	3	252	3
2005	Helena Paparizou	My Number One	-	-	230	1
2006	Anna Vissi	Everything	-	-	128	9
2007	Sarbel	Yassou Maria	-	-	139	7
2008	Kalomira	Secret Combination	156	1	218	3
2009	Sakis Rouvas	This Is Our Night	110	4	120	7
2010	Giorgos Alkaios & Friends	OPA	133	2	140	8
2011	Loucas Yiorkas feat Stereo Mike	Watch My Dance	133	1	120	7
2012	Eleftheria Eleftheriou	Aphrodisiac	116	4	64	17
2013	Koza Mostra feat. Agathon Iakovidis	Alcohol is Free	121	2	152	6
2014	Freaky Fortune feat. RiskyKidd	Rise Up	74	7	35	20
2015	Maria Elena Kyriakou	One Last Breath	81	6	23	19
2016	Argo	Utopian Land	44	16	-	-
2017	Demy	This Is Love	115	10	77	19
2018	Yianna Terzi	Oniro Mou	81	14	-	-
2019	Katerine Duska	Better Love	185	5	74	21

Hungary

Year	Artist	Song	Semi-Final Points	Semi-Final Position	Final Points	Final Position
1994	Friderika Bayer	Kinek Mondjam El Vétkeimet			122	4
1995	Czaba Szigeti	Új Nèv Egy Règi Hàz Fàlan			3	22
1996	-	-			-	-
1997	VIP	Miert Kell, Hogy Elmenj?			39	12
1998	Charlie	A Holnap Már Ném Lesz Szomorú			4	23
1999	-	-			-	-
2000	-	-			-	-
2001	-	-			-	-
2002	-	-			-	-
2003	-	-			-	-
2004	-	-			-	-
2005	NOX	Forogj Világ			97	12
2006	-	-			-	-
2007	Magdi Rúzsa	Unsubstantial Blues			128	9
2008	Csézy	Candlelight	6	19	-	-
2009	Zoli Ádok	Dance With Me	16	15	-	-
2010	-	-	-	-	-	-
2011	Kati Wolf	What About My Dreams?	72	7	53	22
2012	Compact Disco	Sound of Our Hearts	52	10	19	24
2013	ByeAlex	Kedvesem (Zoohacker Remix)	66	8	84	10
2014	András Kállay-Saunders	Running	127	3	143	5
2015	Boggie	Wars for Nothing	67	8	19	20
2016	Freddie	Pioneer	197	4	108	19
2017	Joci Pápai	Origo	231	2	200	8
2018	AWS	Viszlát Nyár	111	10	93	21
2019	Joci Pápai	Az én apám	97	12	-	-

Iceland

Year	Artist	Song	Semi-Final Points	Semi-Final Position	Final Points	Final Position
1986	Icy	Gleðibankinn			19	16
1987	Halla Margarét	Hægt Og Hljótt			28	16
1988	Beathoven	Sókrates			20	16
1989	Daníel Ágúst Haraldsson	Það Sem Enginn Sér			0	22
1990	Stjórnin	Eitt Lag Enn			124	4
1991	Stefán & Eyfi	Nina			26	15
1992	Heart 2 Heart	Nei Eða Já			80	7
1993	Inga	Þá Veistu Svarið			42	13
1994	Sigga	Nætur			49	12
1995	Bó Halldórsson	Núna			31	15
1996	Anna Mjöll	Sjúbídú			51	13
1997	Paul Oscar	Minn Hinsti Dans			18	20
1998	-	-			-	-
1999	Selma Björnsdóttir	All Out Of Luck			146	2
2000	Einer Ágúst Víðisson & Telma Ágústdóttir	Tell Me!			45	12
2001	TwoTricky	Angel			3	22
2002	-	-			-	-
2003	Birgitta	Open Your Heart			81	8
2004	Jónsi	Heaven	-	-	16	19
2005	Selma	If I Had Your Love	52	16	-	-
2006	Silvia Night	Congratulations	62	13	-	-
2007	Eiríkur Hauksson	Valentine Lost	77	13	-	-
2008	Euroband	This Is My Life	68	8	64	14
2009	Yohanna	Is It True?	174	1	218	2
2010	Hera Björk	Je Ne Sais Quoi	123	3	41	19
2011	Sjonni's Friends	Coming Home	100	4	61	20
2012	Greta Salóme & Jónsi	Never Forget	75	8	46	20
2013	Eythor Ingi	Ég Á Líf	72	6	47	17
2014	Pollapönk	No Prejudice	61	8	58	15
2015	María Ólafs	Unbroken	14	15	-	-
2016	Greta Salóme	Hear Them Calling	51	14	-	-

Iceland (continued)

Year	Artist	Song	Semi-Final Points	Semi-Final Position	Final Points	Final Position
2017	Svala	Paper	60	15	-	-
2018	Ari Ólafsson	Our Choice	15	19	-	-
2019	Hatari	Hatrið mun sigra	221	3	232	10

Ireland

Year	Artist	Song	Semi-Final Points	Semi-Final Position	Final Points	Final Position
1965	Butch Moore	I'm Walking The Streets In The Rain			11	6
1966	Dickie Rock	Come Back To Stay			14	4
1967	Sean Dunphy	If I Could Choose			22	2
1968	Pat McGeegan	Chance Of A Lifetime			18	4
1969	Muriel Day & the Lindsays	The Wages Of Love			10	7
1970	Dana	All Kinds Of Everything			32	1
1971	Angela Farrell	One Day Love			79	11
1972	Sandie Jones	Ceol On Ghrá			72	15
1973	Maxi	Do I Dream?			80	10
1974	Tina	Cross Your Heart			11	7
1975	The Swarbriggs	That's What Friends Are For			68	9
1976	Red Hurley	When			54	10
1977	The Swarbriggs Plus Two	It's Nice To Be In Love Again			119	3
1978	Colm Wilkinson	Born To Sing			86	5
1979	Cathal Dunne	Happy Man			80	5
1980	Johnny Logan	What's Another Year			143	1
1981	Sheeba	Horoscopes			105	5
1982	The Duskeys	Here Today, Gone Tomorrow			49	11
1983	-	-			-	-
1984	Linda Martin	Terminal 3			137	2
1985	Maria Christian	Wait Until The Weekend Comes			91	6
1986	Luv Bug	You Can Count On Me			96	4
1987	Johnny Logan	Hold Me Now			172	1
1988	Jump the Gun	Take Him Home			79	8
1989	Kiev Connolly & the Missing Passengers	The Real Me			21	18
1990	Liam Reilly	Somewhere In Europe			132	2
1991	Kim Jackson	Could It Be That I'm In Love			47	10
1992	Linda Martin	Why Me			155	1
1993	Niamh Kavanagh	In Your Eyes			187	1
1994	Paul Harrington & Charlie McGettigan	Rock 'n' Roll Kids			226	1
1995	Eddie Friel	Dreamin'			44	14
1996	Eimear Quinn	The Voice			162	1
1997	Marc Roberts	Mysterious Woman			157	2
1998	Dawn	Is Always Over Now?			64	9
1999	The Mullans	When You Need Me			18	18
2000	Eamonn Toal	Millennium Of Love			92	6
2001	Gary O'Shaughnessy	Without Your Love			6	21
2002	-	-			-	-
2003	Mickey Harte	We've Got The World			53	11
2004	Chris Doran	If My World Stopped Turning			7	22
2005	Donna & Joseph McCaul	Love?	53	14	-	-
2006	Brian Kennedy	Every Song Is A Cry For Love	79	10	93	10
2007	Dervish	They Can't Stop The Spring	-	-	5	24
2008	Dustin the Turkey	Irelande Douze Pointe	22	15	-	-
2009	Sinéad Mulvey & Black Daisy	Et Cetera	52	11	-	-
2010	Niamh Kavanagh	It's For You	67	9	25	23
2011	Jedward	Lipstick	68	8	119	8
2012	Jedward	Waterline	92	6	46	19
2013	Ryan Dolan	Only Love Survives	54	8	5	26
2014	Can-Linn (feat. Kasey Smith)	Heartbeat	35	12	-	-
2015	Molly Sterling	Playing with Numbers	35	12	-	-
2016	Nicky Byrne	Sunlight	46	15	-	-
2017	Brendan Murray	Dying To Try	86	13	-	-
2018	Ryan O'Shaughnessy	Together	179	6	136	16
2019	Sarah McTernan	22	16	18	-	-

Israel

			Semi-Final		Final	
Year	Artist	Song	Points	Position	Points	Position
1973	Ilanit	Ey-sham			97	4
1974	Poogy	Natati La Khaiai			11	7
1975	Shlomo Artzi	At Ve'ani			40	11
1976	Chocolate, Menta, Mastik	Emor Shalom			77	6
1977	Ilanit	Ah-haa-vah Hee Shir Lish-naa-yim			49	11
1978	Izhar Cohen & the Alphabeta	Abanibi			157	1
1979	Milk & Honey	Hallelujah			125	1
1980	-	-			-	-
1981	Habibi	Halaylah			56	7
1982	Avi Toledano	Hora			100	2
1983	Ofra Haza	Hi			136	2
1984	-	-			-	-
1985	Izhar Cohen	Olé Olé			93	5
1986	Moti Galadi & Sarai Tzuriel	Yavoh Yom			7	19
1987	Datner & Kushnir	Shir Habatlanim			73	8
1988	Yardena Arazi	Ben Adam			85	7
1989	Gili ve Galit	Derech Ha'melech			50	12
1990	Rita	Shara Barechovot			16	18
1991	Duo Datz	Kan			139	3
1992	Dafna	Ze Rak Sport			85	6
1993	Lakahat Shiru	Shiru			4	24
1994	-	-			-	-
1995	Liora	Amen			81	8
1996	-	-			-	-
1997	-	-			-	-
1998	Dana International	Diva			172	1
1999	Eden	Yom Huledeth			93	5
2000	Ping Pong	Sa'me'akh			7	22
2001	Tal Sondak	Ein Davar			25	16
2002	Sarit Hadad	Light A Candle			37	12
2003	Lior Narkis	Words For Love			17	19
2004	David D'or	Le'ha'amin	57	11	-	-
2005	Shiri Maymon	Hasheket Shenish'ar	158	7	154	4
2006	Eddie Butler	Ze Hazman	-	-	4	23
2007	Teapacks	Push The Button	17	24	-	-
2008	Boaz	The Fire In Your Eyes	104	5	124	9
2009	Noa & Mira Awad	There Must Be Another Way	75	7	53	16
2010	Harel Skaat	Milim	71	8	71	14
2011	Dana International	Ding Dong	38	15	-	-
2012	Izabo	Time	33	13	-	-
2013	Moran Mazor	Rak Bishvilo	40	14	-	-
2014	Mei Finegold	Same Heart	19	14	-	-
2015	Nadav Guedj	Golden Boy	151	3	97	9
2016	Hovi Star	Made of Stars	147	7	135	14
2017	IMRI	I Feel Alive	207	3	39	23
2018	Netta	Toy	283	1	529	1
2019	Kobi Marimi	Home	-	-	35	23

Italy

			Semi-Final		Final	
Year	Artist	Song	Points	Position	Points	Position
1956	(1) Tonina Torielli	Amami Se Vuoi			-	2
1956	(2) Franca Raimondi	Aprite Le Finestre			-	2
1957	Nunzio Gallo	Corde Della Mia Chitarra			7	6
1958	Domenico Modugno	Nel Blu Dipinto Di Blu			13	3
1959	Domenico Modugno	Piove			9	6
1960	Renato Rascel	Romantica			5	8
1961	Betty Curtis	Al Di Là			12	5
1962	Claudio Villa	Addio, Addio			3	9
1963	Emilio Pericoli	Uno Per Tutte			37	3
1964	Gigliola Cinquetti	Non Ho L'età			49	1
1965	Bobby Solo	Se Piangi, Se Ridi			15	5
1966	Domenico Modugno	Dio Come Ti Amo			0	17

Italy (continued)

Year	Artist	Song	Semi-Final Points	Semi-Final Position	Final Points	Final Position
1967	Claudio Villa	Non Andare Più Lontano			4	11
1968	Sergio Endrigo	Marianne			7	10
1969	Iva Zanicchi	Due Grosse Lacrime Bianche			5	13
1970	Gianni Morandi	Occhi Di Ragazza			5	8
1971	Massimo Ranieri	L'amore è Un Attimo			91	5
1972	Nicola di Bari	I Giorni Dell' Arcobaleno			92	6
1973	Massimo Ranieri	Chi Sarà Con Te			74	13
1974	Gigliola Cinquetti	Si			18	2
1975	Wess & Dori Ghezzi	Era			115	3
1976	Romina & Al Bano	We'll Live It All Again			69	7
1977	Mia Martini	Liberà			33	13
1978	Ricchi e Poveri	Questo Amore			53	12
1979	Matia Bazar	Raggio Di Luna			27	15
1980	Alan Sorrenti	Non So Che Darei			87	6
1981	-	-			-	-
1982	-	-			-	-
1983	Riccardo Fogli	Per Lucia			41	11
1984	Alice & Battiato	I Treni Di Tozeur			70	5
1985	Al Bano & Romina Power	Magic, Oh Magic			78	7
1986	-	-			-	-
1987	Umberto Tozzi & Raf	Gente Di Mare			103	3
1988	Luca Barbarossa	Ti Scrivo			52	12
1989	Anna Oxa & Fausto Leali	Avrei Voluto			56	9
1990	Toto Cutugno	Insieme: 1992			149	1
1991	Peppino di Capri	Comme E' Ddoce 'o Mare			89	7
1992	Mia Martini	Rapsodia			111	4
1993	Enrico Ruggeri	Sole D'europa			45	12
1994	-	-			-	-
1995	-	-			-	-
1996	-	-			-	-
1997	Jalisse	Fiumi Di Parole			114	4
1998	-	-			-	-
1999	-	-			-	-
2000	-	-			-	-
2001	-	-			-	-
2002	-	-			-	-
2003	-	-			-	-
2004	-	-	-	-	-	-
2005	-	-	-	-	-	-
2006	-	-	-	-	-	-
2007	-	-	-	-	-	-
2008	-	-	-	-	-	-
2009	-	-	-	-	-	-
2010	-	-	-	-	-	-
2011	Raphael Gualazzi	Madness of Love	-	-	189	2
2012	Nina Zilli	L'Amore È Femmina (Out Of Love)	-	-	101	9
2013	Marco Mengoni	L'Essenziale	-	-	126	7
2014	Emma	La Mia Città	-	-	33	21
2015	Il Volo	Grande amore	-	-	292	3
2016	Francesca Michielin	No Degree Of Separation	-	-	124	16
2017	Francesco Gabbani	Occidentali's Karma	-	-	334	6
2018	Ermal Meta e Fabrizio Moro	Non Mi Avete Fatto Niente	-	-	308	5
2019	Mahmood	Soldi	-	-	472	2

Latvia

Year	Artist	Song	Semi-Final Points	Semi-Final Position	Final Points	Final Position
2001	Arnis Mednis	Too Much			16	18
2002	Marie N	I Wanna			176	1
2003	FLY	Hello from Mars			5	24
2004	Fomins & Kleins	Dziesma Par Laimi	23	17	-	-
2005	Walter & Kazha	The War Is Not Over	85	10	153	5
2006	Cosmos	I Hear Your Heart	-	-	30	16
2007	Bonaparti.lv	Questa Notte	168	5	54	16
2008	Pirates Of The Sea	Wolves Of The Sea	86	6	83	12
2009	Intars Busulis	Probka	7	19	-	-
2010	Aisha	What For?	11	17	-	-
2011	Musiqq	Angel in Disguise	25	17	-	-
2012	Anmary	Beautiful Song	17	16	-	-
2013	PeR	Here We Go	13	17	-	-
2014	Aarzemnieki	Cake to Bake	33	13	-	-
2015	Aminata	Love Injected	155	2	186	6
2016	Justs	Heartbeat	132	8	132	15
2017	Triana Park	Line	21	18	-	-
2018	Laura Rizzotto	Funny Girl	106	12	-	-
2019	Carousel	That Night	50	15	-	-

Lithuania

Year	Artist	Song	Semi-Final Points	Semi-Final Position	Final Points	Final Position
1994	Ovidijus Vyšniauskas	Lopšine mylimai			0	25
1995	-	-				
1996	-	-			-	-
1997	-	-			-	-
1998	-	-			-	-
1999	Aiste Smilgeviciute	Strazdas			13	20
2000	-	-			-	-
2001	Skamp	You Got Style			35	13
2002	Aivaras	Happy You			12	23
2003	-	-			-	-
2004	Linas ir Simona	What's Happened To Your Love?	26	16	-	-
2005	Laura & the Lovers	Little By Little	17	25	-	-
2006	LT United	We Are The Winners	163	5	162	6
2007	4Fun	Love Or Leave	-	-	28	21
2008	Jeronimas Milius	Nomads In The Night	30	16	-	-
2009	Sasha Son	Love	66	9	23	23
2010	InCulto	East European Funk	44	12	-	-
2011	Evelina Sašenko	C'est Ma Vie	81	5	63	19
2012	Donny Montell	Love is Blind	107	3	70	14
2013	Andrius Pojavis	Something	53	9	17	22
2014	Vilija Matačiūnaitė	Attention	36	11	-	-
2015	Monika Linkyte & Vaidas Baumila	This Time	67	7	30	18
2016	Donny Montell	I've Been Waiting For This Night	222	4	200	9
2017	Fusedmarc	Rain Of Revolution	42	17	-	-
2018	Ieva Zasimauskaitė	When We're Old	119	9	181	12
2019	Jurij Veklenko	Run With The Lions	93	11	-	-

Luxembourg

Year	Artist	Song	Semi-Final Points	Semi-Final Position	Final Points	Final Position
1956	(1) Michèle Arnaud	Les Amants De Minuit			-	2
1956	(2) Michèle Arnaud	Ne Crois Pas			-	2
1957	Danièle Dupré	Tant De Peine			8	4
1958	Solange Berry	Un Grand Amour			1	9
1959	-	-			-	-
1960	Camillo Felgen	So Laang We's Du Do Bast			1	13
1961	Jean-Claude Pascal	Nous Les Amoureux			31	1
1962	Camillo Felgen	Petit Bonhomme			11	3
1963	Nana Mouskouri	A Force De Prier			13	8

Luxembourg (continued)

Year	Artist	Song	Semi-Final Points	Semi-Final Position	Final Points	Final Position
1964	Hugues Aufray	Dès Que Le Printemps Revient			14	4
1965	France Gall	Poupée De Cire, Poupée De Son			32	1
1966	Michèle Torr	Ce Soir Je T'attendais			7	10
1967	Vicky	L'amour Est Bleu			17	4
1968	Chris Baldo & Sophie Garel	Nous Vivrons D'amour			5	11
1969	Romuald	Cathérine			7	11
1970	David-Alexandre Winter	Je Suis Tombé Du Ciel			0	12
1971	Monique Melsen	Pomme, Pomme, Pomme			70	13
1972	Vicky Leandros	Après Toi			128	1
1973	Anne-Marie David	Tu Te Reconnaîtras			129	1
1974	Ireen Sheer	Bye, Bye, I Love You			14	4
1975	Géraldine	Toi			84	5
1976	Jürgen Marcus	Chansons Pour Ceux Qui S'aiment			17	4
1977	Anne Marie B	Frère Jacques			17	16
1978	Baccara	Parlez-vous Français?			73	7
1979	Jeane Manson	J'ai Déjà Vu ça Dans Tes Yeux			44	13
1980	Sophie & Magaly	Papa Pingouin			56	9
1981	Jean-Claude Pascal	C'est Peut-être Pas L'Amérique			41	11
1982	Svetlana	Cours Après le Temps			78	6
1983	Corinne Hermès	Si La Vie Est Cadeau			142	1
1984	Sophie Carle	100% D'amour			39	10
1985	Margo, Franck Olivier, Diane Solomon, Ireen	Children, Kinder, Enfants			37	13
1986	Sherisse Laurence	L'amour De Ma Vie			117	3
1987	Plastic Bertrand	Amour Amour			4	21
1988	Lara Fabian	Croire			90	4
1989	Park Café	Monsieur			8	20
1990	Céline Carzo	Quand Je Te Rêve			38	13
1991	Sarah Bray	Un Baiser Volé			29	14
1992	Marion Welter & Kontinent	Sou Fräi			10	21
1993	Modern Times	Donne-moi Une Chance			11	20

Malta

Year	Artist	Song	Semi-Final Points	Semi-Final Position	Final Points	Final Position
1971	Joe Grech	Marija L-maltija			52	18
1972	Helen & Joseph	L-imhabba			48	18
1973	-	-			-	-
1974	-	-			-	-
1975	Renato	Singing This Song			32	12
1976	-	-			-	-
1977	-	-			-	-
1978	-	-			-	-
1979	-	-			-	-
1980	-	-			-	-
1981	-	-			-	-
1982	-	-			-	-
1983	-	-			-	-
1984	-	-			-	-
1985	-	-			-	-
1986	-	-			-	-
1987	-	-			-	-
1988	-	-			-	-
1989	-	-			-	-
1990	-	-			-	-
1991	Paul Giordimaina & Georgina	Could It Be			106	6
1992	Mary Spiteri	Little Child			123	3
1993	William Mangion	This Time			69	8
1994	Moira Stafrace & Christopher Scicluna	More Than Love			97	5
1995	Mike Spiteri	Keep Me In Mind			76	10
1996	Miriam Christine	In A Woman's Heart			68	10
1997	Debbie Scerri	Let Me Fly			66	9
1998	Chiara	The One That I Love			165	3
1999	Times 3	Believe 'n Peace			32	15

Malta (continued)

Year	Artist	Song	Semi-Final Points	Semi-Final Position	Final Points	Final Position
2000	Claudette Pace	Desire			73	8
2001	Fabrizio Faniello	Another Summer Night			48	9
2002	Ira Losco	7th Wonder			164	2
2003	Lynn Chircop	To Dream Again			4	25
2004	Julie & Ludwig	On Again... Off Again	74	8	50	12
2005	Chiara	Angel	-	-	192	2
2006	Fabrizio Faniello	I Do	-	-	1	24
2007	Olivia Lewis	Vertigo	15	25	-	-
2008	Morena	Vodka	38	14	-	-
2009	Chiara	What If We	86	6	31	22
2010	Thea Garrett	My Dream	45	12	-	-
2011	Glen Vella	One Life	54	11	-	-
2012	Kurt Calleja	This Is The Night	70	7	41	21
2013	Gianluca	Tomorrow	118	4	120	8
2014	Firelight	Coming Home	63	9	32	23
2015	Amber	Warrior	43	11	-	-
2016	Ira Losco	Walk On Water	209	3	153	12
2017	Claudia Faniello	Breathlessly	55	16	-	-
2018	Christabelle	Taboo	101	13	-	-
2019	Michela	Chameleon	157	8	107	14

Moldova

Year	Artist	Song	Semi-Final Points	Semi-Final Position	Final Points	Final Position
2005	Zdob si Zdub	Boonika Bate Toba	207	2	148	6
2006	Arsenium & Natalia Gordienko	Loca	-	-	22	20
2007	Natalia Barbu	Fight	91	10	109	10
2008	Geta Burlacu	A Century Of Love	36	12	-	-
2009	Nelly Ciobanu	Hora Din Moldova	106	5	69	14
2010	Sunstroke Project & Olia Tira	Run Away	52	10	27	22
2011	Zdob și Zdub	So Lucky	54	10	97	12
2012	Pasha Parfeny	Lăutar	100	5	81	11
2013	Aliona Moon	O Mie	95	4	71	11
2014	Cristina Scarlat	Wild Soul	13	16	-	-
2015	Eduard Romanyuta	I Want Your Love	41	11	-	-
2016	Lidia Isac	Falling Stars	33	17	-	-
2017	Sunstroke Project	Hey Mamma	291	2	374	3
2018	DoReDos	My Lucky Day	235	3	209	10
2019	Anna Odobescu	Stay				

Monaco

Year	Artist	Song	Semi-Final Points	Semi-Final Position	Final Points	Final Position
1959	Jacques Pills	Mon Ami Pierrot			1	11
1960	François Deguelt	Ce Soir-là			15	3
1961	Colette Deréal	Allons, Allons Les Enfants			6	10
1962	François Deguelt	Dis Rien			13	2
1963	Françoise Hardy	L'amour S'en Va			25	5
1964	Romuald	Où Sont-elles Passées?			15	3
1965	Marjorie Noël	Va Dire à L'amour			7	9
1966	Tereza	Bien Plus Fort			0	17
1967	Minouche Barelli	Boum-badaboum			10	5
1968	Line & Willy	A Chacun Sa Chanson			8	7
1969	Jean-Jacques	Maman, Maman			11	6
1970	Dominique Dussault	Marlène			5	8
1971	Séverine	Un Banc, Un Arbre, Une Rue			128	1
1972	Anne-Marie Godart & Peter MacLane	Comme On S'aime			65	16
1973	Marie	Un Train Qui Part			85	8
1974	Romuald	Celui Qui Reste Et Celui Qui S'en Va			14	4
1975	Sophie	Une Chanson C'est Une Lettre			22	13
1976	Mary Christy	Toi, La Musique Et Moi			93	3
1977	Michèle Torr	Une Petite Française			96	4

Monaco (continued)

Year	Artist	Song	Semi-Final Points	Semi-Final Position	Final Points	Final Position
1978	Caline & Olivier Toussaint	Les Jardins De Monaco			107	4
1979	Laurent Vaguener	Notre Vie, C'est La Musique			12	16
1980	-	-			-	-
1981	-	-			-	-
1982	-	-			-	-
1983	-	-			-	-
1984	-	-			-	-
1985	-	-			-	-
1986	-	-			-	-
1987	-	-			-	-
1988	-	-			-	-
1989	-	-			-	-
1990	-	-			-	-
1991	-	-			-	-
1992	-	-			-	-
1993	-	-			-	-
1994	-	-			-	-
1995	-	-			-	-
1996	-	-			-	-
1997	-	-			-	-
1998	-	-			-	-
1999	-	-			-	-
2000	-	-			-	-
2001	-	-			-	-
2002	-	-			-	-
2003	-	-			-	-
2004	Maryon	Notre Planète	10	19	-	-
2005	Lise Darly	Tout De Moi	22	24	-	-
2006	Séverine Ferrer	La Coco-dance	14	21	-	-

Montenegro

Year	Artist	Song	Semi-Final Points	Semi-Final Position	Final Points	Final Position
2007	Stevan Faddy	Ajde Kroci	33	22	-	-
2008	Stefan Filipović	Zauvijek Volim Te	23	14	-	-
2009	Andrea Demirovic	Just Get Out of My Life	44	11	-	-
2010	-	-	-	-	-	-
2011	-	-	-	-	-	-
2012	Rambo Amadeus	Euro Neuro	20	15	-	-
2013	Who See	Igranka	41	12	-	-
2014	Sergej Ćetković	Moj Svijet	63	7	37	19
2015	Knez	Adio	57	9	44	13
2016	Highway	The Real Thing	60	13	-	-
2017	Slavko Kalezić	Space	56	16	-	-
2018	Vanja Radovanović	Inje	40	16	-	-
2019	D mol	Heaven	46	16	-	-

Morocco

Year	Artist	Song	Semi-Final Points	Semi-Final Position	Final Points	Final Position
1980	Samira Bensaïd	Bitakat Hob			7	18

Netherlands

Year	Artist	Song	Semi-Final Points	Semi-Final Position	Final Points	Final Position
1956	(1) Corry Brokken	Voorgoed Voorbij			-	2
1956	(2) Jetty Paerl	De Vogels Van Holland			-	2
1957	Corry Brokken	Net Als Toen			31	1
1958	Corry Brokken	Heel De Wereld			1	9
1959	Teddy Scholten	Een Beetje			21	1
1960	Rudi Carrell	Wat Een Geluk			2	12
1961	Greetje Kauffeld	Wat Een Dag			6	10
1962	De Spelbrekers	Katinka			0	13
1963	Annie Palmen	Een Speeldoos			0	13
1964	Anneke Grönloh	Jij Bent Mijn Leven			2	10
1965	Conny Van den Bos	Het Is Genoeg			5	11
1966	Milly Scott	Fernando En Philippo			2	15
1967	Thérèse Steinmetz	Ring-dinge			2	14
1968	Ronnie Tober	Morgen			1	16
1969	Lenny Kuhr	De Troubadour			18	1
1970	Patricia & Hearts of Soul	Waterman			7	7
1971	Saskia & Serge	De Tijd			85	6
1972	Sandra & Andres	Als Het Om De Liefde Gaat			106	4
1973	Ben Cramer	De Oude Muzikant			69	14
1974	Mouth & MacNeal	I See A Star			15	3
1975	Teach-In	Ding-A-Dong			152	1
1976	Sandra Reemer	The Party's Over Now			56	9
1977	Heddy Lester	De Mallemolen			35	12
1978	Harmony	't Is Ok			37	13
1979	Xandra	Colorado			51	12
1980	Maggie MacNeal	Amsterdam			93	5
1981	Linda Williams	Het Is Een Wonder			51	9
1982	Bill van Dijk	Jij En Ik			8	16
1983	Bernadette	Sing Me A Song			66	7
1984	Maribelle	Ik Hou Van Jou			34	13
1985	-	-			-	-
1986	Frizzle Sizzle	Alles Heeft Ritme			40	13
1987	Marcha	Rechtop In De Wind			83	5
1988	Gerard Joling	Shangri-la			70	9
1989	Justine Pelmelay	Blijf Zoals Je Bent			45	15
1990	Maywood	Ik Wil Alles Met Je Delen			25	15
1991	-	-			-	-
1992	Humphrey Campbell	Wijs Me De Weg			67	13
1993	Ruth Jacott	Vrede			92	6
1994	Willeke Alberti	Waar Is De Zon			4	23
1995	-	-			-	-
1996	Maxine & Franklin Brown	De Eerste Keer			78	7
1997	Mrs Einstein	Niemand Heeft Nog Tijd			5	22
1998	Edsilia Rombley	Hemel En Aarde			150	4
1999	Marlayne	One Good Reason			71	9
2000	Linda Wagenmakers	No Goodbyes			40	13
2001	Michelle	Out On My Own			16	18
2002	-	-			-	-
2003	Esther Hart	One More Night			45	13
2004	Re-union	Without You	146	6	11	20
2005	Glennis Grace	My Impossible Dream	53	14	-	-
2006	Treble	Amambanda	22	19	-	-
2007	Edsilia Rombley	On Top Of The World	38	21	-	-
2008	Hind	Your Heart Belongs To Me	27	13	-	-
2009	The Toppers	Shine	11	17	-	-
2010	Sieneke	Ik Ben Verliefd (Sha-la-lie)	29	14	-	-
2011	3JS	Never Alone	13	19	-	-
2012	Joan Franka	You And Me	35	15	-	-
2013	Anouk	Birds	75	6	114	9
2014	The Common Linnets	Calm After the Storm	150	1	238	2
2015	Trijntje Oosterhuis	Walk Along	33	14	-	-

Netherlands (continued)

Year	Artist	Song	Semi-Final Points	Semi-Final Position	Final Points	Final Position
2016	Douwe Bob	Slow Down	197	5	153	11
2017	OG3NE	Lights And Shadows	200	4	150	11
2018	Waylon	Outlaw In 'Em	174	7	121	18
2019	Duncan Laurence	Arcade	280	1	498	1

North Macedonia

Year	Artist	Song	Semi-Final Points	Semi-Final Position	Final Points	Final Position
1998	Vlado Janevski	Ne Zori, Zoro			16	19
1999	-				-	-
2000	XXL	100% Te Ljubam			29	15
2001	-				-	-
2002	Karolina	Od Nas Zavisi			25	19
2003	-				-	-
2004	Tose Proeski	Life	71	10	47	14
2005	Martin Vucic	Make My Day	97	9	52	17
2006	Elena Risteska	Ninanajna	76	8	56	12
2007	Karolina	Mojot Svet	97	9	73	14
2008	Tamara, Vrčak & Adrijan	Let Me Love You	64	10	-	-
2009	Next Time	Neshto Shto Ke Ostane	45	10	-	-
2010	Gjoko Taneski	Jas Ja Imam Silata	37	15	-	-
2011	Vlatko Ilievski	Rusinka	36	16	-	-
2012	Kaliopi	Crno I Belo	53	9	71	13
2013	Esma & Lozano	Pred Da Se Razdeni	28	16	-	-
2014	Tijana	To The Sky	33	13	-	-
2015	Daniel Kajmakoski	Autumn Leaves	28	15	-	-
2016	Kaliopi	Dona	88	11	-	-
2017	Jana Burčeska	Dance Alone	69	15	-	-
2018	Eye Cue	Lost And Found	24	18	-	-
2019	Tamara Todevska	Proud	239	2	305	7

Norway

Year	Artist	Song	Semi-Final Points	Semi-Final Position	Final Points	Final Position
1960	Nora Brockstedt	Voi-voi			11	4
1961	Nora Brockstedt	Sommer I Palma			10	7
1962	Inger Jacobsen	Kom Sol, Kom Regn			2	10
1963	Anita Thallaug	Solhverv			0	13
1964	Arne Bendiksen	Spiral			6	8
1965	Kirsti Sparboe	Karusell			1	13
1966	Åse Kleveland	Intet Er Nytt Under Solen			15	3
1967	Kirsti Sparboe	Dukkemann			2	14
1968	Odd Børre	Stress			2	13
1969	Kirsti Sparboe	Oj, Oj, Oj, Så Glad, Jeg Skal Bli			1	16
1970	-	-			-	-
1971	Hanne Krogh	Lykken Er...			65	17
1972	Grethe Kausland & Benny Borg	Småting			73	14
1973	Bendik Singers	It's Just A Game			89	7
1974	Anne-Karine Ström & the Bendik Singers	The First Day Of Love			3	14
1975	Ellen Nikolaysen	You Touched My Life With Summer			11	18
1976	Anne-Karine Ström	Mata Hari			7	17
1977	Anita Skorgan	Casanova			18	14
1978	Jahn Teigen	Mil Etter Mil			0	20
1979	Anita Skorgan	Oliver			57	11
1980	Sverre Kjellsberg & Mattis Hætta	Sámiid Ædnan			15	16
1981	Finn Kalvik	Aldri I Livet			0	20
1982	Jahn Teigen & Anita Skorgan	Adieu			40	12
1983	Jahn Teigen	Do Re Mi			53	9
1984	Dollie de Luxe	Lenge Leve Livet			29	17
1985	Bobbysocks	La Det Swinge			123	1
1986	Ketil Stokkan	Romeo			44	12
1987	Kate Gulbrandsen	Mitt Liv			65	9

Norway (continued)

Year	Artist	Song	Semi-Final Points	Semi-Final Position	Final Points	Final Position
1988	Karoline Krüger	For Vår Jord			88	5
1989	Britt Synnøve Johansen	Venners Nærhet			30	17
1990	Ketil Stokkan	Brandenburger Tor			8	21
1991	Just 4 Fun	Mrs Thompson			14	17
1992	Merethe Trøan	Visjoner			23	18
1993	Silje Vige	Alle Mine Tankar			120	4
1994	Elisabeth Andreasson & Jan Werner Danielsen	Duett			76	6
1995	Secret Garden	Nocturne			148	1
1996	Elisabeth Andreasson	I Evighet			114	2
1997	Tor Endresen	San Francisco			0	24
1998	Lars Fredriksen	Alltid Sommer			79	8
1999	Stig André Van Eijk	Living My Life Without You			35	13
2000	Charmed	My Heart Goes Boom			57	11
2001	Haldor Lægreid	On My Own			3	22
2002	-	-			-	-
2003	Jostein Hasselgård	I'm Not Afraid To Move On			123	4
2004	Knut Anders Sørum	High	-	-	3	24
2005	Wig Wam	In My Dreams	164	6	125	9
2006	Christine Guldbrandsen	Alvedansen	-	-	36	14
2007	Guri Schanke	Ven A Bailar Conmigo	48	18	-	-
2008	Maria	Hold On Be Strong	106	4	182	5
2009	Alexander Rybak	Fairytale	201	1	387	1
2010	Didrik Solli-Tangen	My Heart Is Yours	-	-	35	20
2011	Stella Mwangi	Haba Haba	30	17	-	-
2012	Tooji	Stay	45	10	7	26
2013	Margaret Berger	I Feed You My Love	120	3	191	4
2014	Carl Espen	Silent Storm	77	6	88	8
2015	Mørland & Debrah Scarlett	A Monster Like Me	123	4	102	8
2016	Agnete	Icebreaker	63	13	-	-
2017	JOWST	Grab The Moment	189	5	158	10
2018	Alexander Rybak	That's How You Write A Song	266	1	144	15
2019	KEiiNO	Spirit In The Sky	210	7	331	6

Poland

Year	Artist	Song	Semi-Final Points	Semi-Final Position	Final Points	Final Position
1994	Edyta Górniak	To Nie Ja!			166	2
1995	Justyna	Sama			15	18
1996	Kasia Kowalska	Chce Znac Swój Grzech			31	15
1997	Anna Maria Jopek	Ale Jestem			54	11
1998	Sixteen	To Takie Proste			19	17
1999	Mietek (Mieczyslaw) Szczesniak	Przytul Mnie Mocno			17	19
2000	-	-			-	-
2001	Piasek	2 Long			11	20
2002	-	-			-	-
2003	Ich Troje	Keine Grenzen - Zadnych Granic			90	7
2004	Blue Cafe	Love Song	-	-	27	17
2005	Ivan & Delfin	Czarna Dziewczyna	81	11	-	-
2006	Ich Troje	Follow My Heart	70	11	-	-
2007	The Jet Set	Time To Party	75	14	-	-
2008	Isis Gee	For Life	42	10	14	24
2009	Lidia Kopania	I Don't Wanna Leave	43	12	-	-
2010	Marcin Mroziński	Legenda	44	13	-	-
2011	Magdalena Tul	Jestem	18	19	-	-
2012	-	-	-	-	-	-
2013	-	-	-	-	-	-
2014	Donatan & Cleo	My Słowianie - We Are Slavic	70	8	62	14
2015	Monika Kuszynska	In the Name of Love	57	8	10	23
2016	Michał Szpak	Color Of Your Life	151	6	229	8
2017	Kasia Moś	Flashlight	119	9	64	22
2018	Gromee feat. Lukas Meijer	Light Me Up	81	14	-	-
2019	Tulia	Fire of Love (Pali się)	120	11	-	-

Portugal

Year	Artist	Song	Semi-Final Points	Semi-Final Position	Final Points	Final Position
1964	António Calvário	Oração			0	13
1965	Simone de Oliviera	Sol De Inverno			1	13
1966	Madalena Iglesias	Ele E Ela			6	13
1967	Eduardo Nascimento	O Vento Mudou			3	12
1968	Carlos Mendes	Verão			5	11
1969	Simone de Oliveira	Desfolhada Portuguesa			4	15
1970	-	-			-	-
1971	Tonicha	Menina Do Alto Da Serra			83	9
1972	Carlos Mendes	A Festa Da Vida			90	7
1973	Fernando Tordo	Tourada			80	10
1974	Paulo de Carvalho	E Depois Do Adeus			3	14
1975	Duarte Mendes	Madrugada			16	16
1976	Carlos do Carmo	Uma Flor De Verde Pinho			24	12
1977	Os Amigos	Portugal No Coração			18	14
1978	Gemini	Dai-li-dou			5	17
1979	Manuela Bravo	Sobe, Sobe, Balão Sobe			64	9
1980	José Cid	Um Grande, Grande Amor			71	7
1981	Carlos Paião	Play-back			9	18
1982	Doce	Bem-bom			32	13
1983	Armando Gama	Esta Balada Que Te Dou			33	13
1984	Maria Guinot	Silêncio E Tanta Gente			38	11
1985	Adelaïde	Penso Em Ti, Eu Sei			9	18
1986	Dora	Não Sejas Mau Para Mim			28	14
1987	Nevada	Neste Barco à Vela			15	18
1988	Dora	Voltarei			5	18
1989	Da Vinci	Conquistador			39	16
1990	Nucha	Há Sempre Alguém			9	20
1991	Dulce	Lusitana Paixão			62	8
1992	Diná	Amor D'água Fresca			26	17
1993	Anabela	A Cidade Até Ser Dia			60	10
1994	Sara Tavares	Chamar A Música			73	8
1995	Tó Cruz	Baunilha E Chocolate			5	21
1996	Lúcia Moniz	O Meu Coração Não Tem Cor			92	6
1997	Célia Lawson	Antes Do Adeus			0	24
1998	Alma Lusa	Se Eu Te Pudesse Abraçar			36	12
1999	Rui Bandeira	Como Tudo Começou			12	21
2000	-	-			-	-
2001	MTM	Só Sei Ser Feliz Assim			18	17
2002	-	-			-	-
2003	Rita Guerra	Deixa-me Sonhar			13	22
2004	Sofia	Foi Magia	38	15	-	-
2005	2B	Amar	51	17	-	-
2006	Nonstop	Coisas De Nada	26	19	-	-
2007	Sabrina	Dança Comigo (vem Ser Feliz)	88	11	-	-
2008	Vânia Fernandes	Senhora Do Mar (Negras Águas)	120	2	69	13
2009	Flor-de-lis	Todas As Ruas Do Amor	70	8	57	15
2010	Filipa Azevedo	Há Dias Assim	89	4	43	18
2011	Homens Da Luta	Luta É Alegria	22	18	-	-
2012	Filipa Sousa	Vida Minha	39	13	-	-
2013	-	-	-	-	-	-
2014	Suzy	Quero Ser Tua	39	11	-	-
2015	Leonor Andrade	Há um mar que nos separa	19	14	-	-
2016	-	-	-	-	-	-
2017	Salvador Sobral	Amar Pelos Dois	370	1	758	1
2018	Cláudia Pascoal	O Jardim	-	-	39	26
2019	Conan Osiris	Telemóveis	51	15	-	-

Romania

Year	Artist	Song	Semi-Final Points	Semi-Final Position	Final Points	Final Position
1994	Dan Bittman	Dincolo De Nori			14	21
1995	-	-			-	-
1996	-	-			-	-
1997	-	-			-	-
1998	Malina Olinescu	Eu Cred			6	22
1999	-	-			-	-
2000	Taxi	The Moon			25	17
2001	-	-			-	-
2002	Monica Anghel & Marcel Pavel	Tell Me Why			72	8
2003	Nicola	Don't Break My Heart			73	10
2004	Sanda Ladosi	I Admit			18	18
2005	Luminita Anghel & Sistem	Let Me Try	235	1	158	3
2006	Mihai Traistariu	Tornero	-	-	172	4
2007	Todomondo	Liubi, Liubi, I Love You	-	-	84	13
2008	Nico & Vlad	Pe-o Margine De Lume	94	7	45	20
2009	Elena	The Balkan Girls	67	9	40	19
2010	Paula Seling & Ovi	Playing With Fire	104	4	162	3
2011	Hotel FM	Change	111	4	77	17
2012	Mandinga	Zaleilah	120	3	71	12
2013	Cezar	It's My Life	83	5	65	13
2014	Paul Seling & Ovi	Miracle	125	2	72	12
2015	Voltaj	De la capat (All over Again)	89	5	35	15
2016	-	-	-	-	-	-
2017	Ilinca ft. Alex Florea	Yodel It!	174	6	282	7
2018	The Humans	Goodbye	107	11	-	-
2019	Ester Peony	On A Sunday	71	13	-	-

Russia

Year	Artist	Song	Semi-Final Points	Semi-Final Position	Final Points	Final Position
1994	Youddiph	Vechni Stranik			70	9
1995	Philipp Kirkorov	Kolybelnaya Dlya Vulkana			18	17
1996	-	-			-	-
1997	Alla Pugachova	Primadonna			33	15
1998	-	-			-	-
1999	-	-			-	-
2000	Alsou	Solo			155	2
2001	Mumiy Troll	Lady Alpine Blue			37	12
2002	Prime Minister	Northern Girl			55	10
2003	t.A.T.u.	Ne Ver', Ne Boisia			164	3
2004	Julia Savicheva	Believe Me	-	-	67	11
2005	Natalia Podolskaya	Nobody Hurt No One	-	-	57	15
2006	Dima Bilan	Never Let You Go	217	3	248	2
2007	Serebro	Song # 1	-	-	207	3
2008	Dima Bilan	Believe	135	3	272	1
2009	Anastasia Prikhodko	Mamo	-	-	91	11
2010	Peter Nalitch & Friends	Lost And Forgotten	74	7	90	11
2011	Alexej Vorobjov	Get You	64	9	77	16
2012	Buranovskiye Babushki	Party for Everybody	152	1	259	2
2013	Dina Garipova	What If	156	2	174	5
2014	Tolmachevy Sisters	Shine	63	6	89	7
2015	Polina Gagarina	A Million Voices	182	1	303	2
2016	Sergey Lazarev	You Are The Only One	342	1	491	3
2017	-	-	-	-	-	-
2018	Julia Samoylova	I Won't Break	65	15	-	-
2019	Sergey Lazarev	Scream	217	6	370	3

San Marino

Year	Artist	Song	Semi-Final Points	Semi-Final Position	Final Points	Final Position
2008	Miodio	Complice	5	19	-	-
2009	-	-	-	-	-	-
2010	-	-	-	-	-	-
2011	Senit	Stand By	34	16	-	-
2012	Valentina Monetta	The Social Network Song (Oh Oh - Uh - Oh Oh)	31	14	-	-
2013	Valentina Monetta	Crisalide (Vola)	47	11	-	-
2014	Valentina Monetta	Maybe (Forse)	40	10	14	24
2015	Michele Perniola & Anita Simoncini	Chain of Lights	11	16	-	-
2016	Serhat	I Didn't Know	68	12	-	-
2017	Valentina Monetta & Jimmie Wilson	Spirit Of The Night	1	18	-	-
2018	Jessika feat. Jenifer Brening	Who We Are	28	17	-	-
2019	Serhat	Say Na Na Na	150	8	77	19

Serbia

Year	Artist	Song	Semi-Final Points	Semi-Final Position	Final Points	Final Position
2007	Marija Šerifović	Molitva	298	1	268	1
2008	Jelena Tomašević feat Bora Dugic	Oro	-	-	160	6
2009	Marko Kon & Milaan	Cipela	60	10	-	-
2010	Milan Stanković	Ovo Je Balkan	79	5	72	13
2011	Nina	Čaroban	67	8	85	14
2012	Željko Joksimović	Nije Ljubav Stvar	159	2	214	3
2013	Moje 3	Ljubav Je Svuda	46	11	-	-
2014	-	-	-	-	-	-
2015	Bojana Stamenov	Beauty Never Lies	63	9	53	10
2016	Sanja Vučić ZAA	Goodbye (Shelter)	105	10	115	18
2017	Tijana Bogićević	In Too Deep	98	11	-	-
2018	Sanja Ilić & Balkanika	Nova Deca	117	9	113	19
2019	Nevena Božović	Kruna	156	7	89	18

Serbia & Montenegro

Year	Artist	Song	Semi-Final Points	Semi-Final Position	Final Points	Final Position
2004	Željko Joksimović	Lane Moje	263	1	263	2
2005	No Name	Zauvijek Moja	-	-	137	7
2006	-	-	-	-	-	-

Slovakia

Year	Artist	Song	Semi-Final Points	Semi-Final Position	Final Points	Final Position
1994	Martin Durinda & Tublatanka	Nekovecná Piesen			15	19
1995	-	-			-	-
1996	Marcel Palonder	Kým Nás Máš			19	18
1997	-	-			-	-
1998	Katarína Hasprová	Modlitba			8	21
1999	-	-			-	-
2000	-	-			-	-
2001	-	-			-	-
2002	-	-			-	-
2003	-	-			-	-
2004	-	-	-	-	-	-
2005	-	-	-	-	-	-
2006	-	-	-	-	-	-
2007	-	-	-	-	-	-
2008	-	-	-	-	-	-
2009	Kamil Mikulčík & Nela Pocisková	Leť Tmou	8	18	-	-
2010	Kristina Pelakova	Horehronie	24	16	-	-
2011	TWiiNS	I'm Still Alive	48	13	-	-
2012	Max Jason Mai	Don't Close Your Eyes	22	18	-	-

Slovenia

Year	Artist	Song	Semi-Final Points	Semi-Final Position	Final Points	Final Position
1993	1X Band	Tih Dezeven Dan			9	22
1994	-	-			-	-
1995	Darja Svajger	Prisluhni Mi			83	7
1996	Regina	Dan Najlepših Sanj			16	21
1997	Tanja Ribic	Zbudi Se			60	10
1998	Vili Resnik	Naj Bogovi Slišijo			17	18
1999	Darja Svajger	For A Thousand Years			50	11
2000	-	-			-	-
2001	Nuša Derenda	Energy			70	7
2002	Sestre	Samo Ljubezen			32	15
2003	Karmen	Nanana			7	23
2004	Platin	Stay Forever	5	21	-	-
2005	Omar Naber	Stop	69	12	-	-
2006	Anžej Dežan	Mr Nobody	49	16	-	-
2007	Alenka Gotar	Cvet Z Juga	140	7	66	15
2008	Rebeka Dremelj	Vrag Naj Vzame	36	11	-	-
2009	Quartissimo featuring Martina	Love Symphony	14	16	-	-
2010	Ansambel Žlindra & Kalamari	Narodnozabavni Rock	6	16	-	-
2011	Maja Keuc	No One	112	3	96	13
2012	Eva Boto	Verjamem	31	17	-	-
2013	Hannah	Straight Into Love	8	16	-	-
2014	Tinkara Kovač	Round and Round	52	10	9	17
2015	Maraaya	Here for You	92	5	39	14
2016	ManuElla	Blue And Red	57	14	-	-
2017	Omar Naber	On My Way	36	17	-	-
2018	Lea Sirk	Hvala, ne!	132	8	64	22
2019	Zala Kralj & Gašper Šantl	Sebi	167	6	105	15

Spain

Year	Artist	Song	Semi-Final Points	Semi-Final Position	Final Points	Final Position
1961	Conchita Bautista	Estando Contigo			8	9
1962	Victor Balaguer	Llámame			0	13
1963	José Guardiola	Algo Prodigioso			2	12
1964	Tim, Nelly & Tony	Caracola			1	12
1965	Conchita Bautista	Qué Bueno, Qué Bueno			0	15
1966	Raphael	Yo Soy Aquél			9	7
1967	Raphael	Hablemos Del Amor			9	6
1968	Massiel	La, La, La...			29	1
1969	Salomé	Vivo Cantando			18	1
1970	Julio Iglesias	Gwendolyne			8	4
1971	Karina	En Un Mundo Nuevo			115	2
1972	Jaime Morey	Amanece			83	10
1973	Mocedades	Eres Tú			125	2
1974	Peret	Canta Y Se Feliz			10	9
1975	Sergio & Estíbaliz	Tú Volverás			53	10
1976	Braulio	Sobran Las Palabras			11	16
1977	Micky	Enséñame A Cantar			52	9
1978	José Vélez	Bailemos Un Vals			65	9
1979	Betty Missiego	Su Canción			116	2
1980	Trigo Limpio	Qué Date Esta Noche			38	12
1981	Bacchelli	Y Solo Tú			38	14
1982	Lucía	Él			52	10
1983	Remedios Amaya	¿Quién Maneja Mi Barca?			0	9
1984	Bravo	Lady, Lady			106	3
1985	Paloma San Basilio	La Fiesta Terminó			36	14
1986	Cadillac	Valentino			51	10
1987	Patricia Kraus	No Estás Solo			10	19
1988	La Década	La Chica Que Yo Quiero (Made In Spain)			58	11
1989	Nina	Nacida Para Amar			88	6
1990	Azúcar Moreno	Bandido			96	5
1991	Sergio Dalma	Bailar Pegados			119	4
1992	Serafin	Todo Esto Es La Música			37	14

Spain (continued)

Year	Artist	Song	Semi-Final Points	Semi-Final Position	Final Points	Final Position
1993	Eva Santamaria	Hombres			58	11
1994	Alejandro Abad	Ella No Es Ella			17	18
1995	Anabel Conde	Vuelve Conmigo			119	2
1996	Antonio Carbonell	¡Ay, Qué Deseo!			17	20
1997	Marcos Llunas	Sin Rencor			96	6
1998	Mikel Herzog	¿Qué Voy A Hacer Sin Ti?			21	16
1999	Lydia	No Quiero Escuchar			1	23
2000	Serafín Zubiri	Colgado De Un Sueño			18	18
2001	David Civera	Dile Que La Quiero			76	6
2002	Rosa	Europe's Living A Celebration			81	7
2003	Beth	Dime			81	8
2004	Ramón	Para Llenarme De Ti	-	-	87	10
2005	Son de sol	Brujería	-	-	28	21
2006	Las Ketchup	Bloody Mary	-	-	18	21
2007	NASH	I Love You Mi Vida	-	-	43	20
2008	Rodolfo Chikilicuatre	Baila El Chiki Chiki	-	-	55	16
2009	Soraya	La Noche Es Para Mí	-	-	23	24
2010	Daniel Diges	Algo Pequeñito (Something Tiny)	-	-	68	15
2011	Lucía Pérez	Que Me Quiten Lo Bailao	-	-	50	23
2012	Pastora Soler	Quédate Conmigo (Stay With Me)	-	-	97	10
2013	ESDM	Contigo Hasta El Final (With You Until The End)	-	-	8	25
2014	Ruth Lorenzo	Dancing in the Rain	-	-	74	10
2015	Edurne	Amanecer	-	-	15	21
2016	Barei	Say Yay!	-	-	77	22
2017	Manel Navarro	Do It For Your Lover	-	-	5	26
2018	Amaia y Alfred	Tu Canción	-	-	61	23
2019	Miki	La Venda	-	-	54	22

Sweden

Year	Artist	Song	Semi-Final Points	Semi-Final Position	Final Points	Final Position
1958	Alice Babs	Lilla Stjärna			10	4
1959	Brita Borg	Augustin			4	9
1960	Siw Malmkvist	Alla Andra Får Varann			4	10
1961	Lill-Babs	April, April			2	14
1962	Inger Berggren	Sol Och Vår			4	7
1963	Monica Zetterlund	En Gång I Stockholm			0	13
1964	-				-	-
1965	Ingvar Wixell	Absent Friend			6	10
1966	Lill Lindfors & Svante Thuresson	Nygammal Vals Eller Hip Man Svinaherde			16	2
1967	Östen Warnebring	Som En Dröm			7	8
1968	Claes-Göran Hederström	Det Börjar Verka Kärlek, Banne Mej			15	5
1969	Tommy Körberg	Judy, Min Vän			8	9
1970	-				-	-
1971	Family Four	Vita Vidder			85	6
1972	Family Four	Härliga Sommardag			75	13
1973	The Nova & The Dolls	You're Summer			94	5
1974	ABBA	Waterloo			24	1
1975	Lars Berghagen & The Dolls	Jennie, Jennie			72	8
1976	-				-	-
1977	Forbes	Beatles			2	18
1978	Björn Skifs	Det Blir Alltid Värre Framåt Natter			26	14
1979	Ted Gärdestad	Satellit			8	17
1980	Tomas Ledin	Just Nu!			47	10
1981	Björn Skifs	Fångad I En Dröm			50	10
1982	Chips	Dag Efter Dag			67	8
1983	Carola Häggkvist	Främling			126	3
1984	Herrey's	Diggi-loo Diggy-ley			145	1
1985	Kikki Danielsson	Bra Vibrationer			103	3
1986	Lasse Holm and Monica Törnell	E' De' Det Här Du Kallar Kärlek			78	5
1987	Lotta Engberg	Boogaloo			50	12
1988	Tommy Körberg	Stad I Ljus			52	12
1989	Tommy Nilsson	En Dag			110	4

Sweden (continued)

Year	Artist	Song	Semi-Final Points	Semi-Final Position	Final Points	Final Position
1990	Edin-Ådahl	Som En Vind			24	16
1991	Carola	Fångad Av En Stormvind			146	1
1992	Christer Björkmann	I Morgon är En Annan Dag			9	22
1993	Arvingarna	Eloïse			89	7
1994	Marie Bergman & Roger Pontare	Stjärnorna			48	13
1995	Jan Johansen	Se På Mej			100	3
1996	One More Time	Den Vilda			100	3
1997	Blond	Bara Hon älskar Mig			36	14
1998	Jill Johnson	Kärleken är			53	10
1999	Charlotte Nilsson	Take Me To Your Heaven			163	1
2000	Roger Pontare	When Spirits Are Calling My Name			88	7
2001	Friends	Listen To Your Heartbeat			100	5
2002	Afro-dite	Never Let It Go			72	8
2003	Fame	Give Me Your Love			107	5
2004	Lena Philipsson	It Hurts	-	-	170	5
2005	Martin Stenmarck	Las Vegas	-	-	30	19
2006	Carola	Invincible	214	4	170	5
2007	The Ark	The Worrying Kind	-	-	51	18
2008	Charlotte Perrelli	Hero	54	12	47	18
2009	Malena Ernman	La Voix	105	4	33	21
2010	Anna Bergendahl	This Is My Life	62	11	-	-
2011	Eric Saade	Popular	155	1	185	3
2012	Loreen	Euphoria	181	1	372	1
2013	Robin Stjernberg	You	-	-	62	14
2014	Sanna Nielsen	Undo	131	2	218	3
2015	Måns Zelmerlöw	Heroes	217	1	365	1
2016	Frans	If I Were Sorry	-	-	261	5
2017	Robin Bengtsson	I Can't Go On	227	3	344	5
2018	Benjamin Ingrosso	Dance You Off	254	2	274	7
2019	John Lundvik	Too Late For Love	238	3	334	5

Switzerland

Year	Artist	Song	Semi-Final Points	Semi-Final Position	Final Points	Final Position
1956	(1) Lys Assia	Refrain			-	1
1956	(2) Lys Assia	Das Alte Karussell			-	2
1957	Lys Assia	L'enfant Que J'étais			5	8
1958	Lys Assia	Giorgio			24	2
1959	Christa Williams	Irgendwoher			14	4
1960	Anita Traversi	Cielo E Terra			5	8
1961	Franca di Rienzo	Nous Aurons Demain			16	13
1962	Jean Philippe	Le Retour			2	10
1963	Esther Ofarim	T'en Va Pas			40	2
1964	Anita Traversi	I Miei Pensieri			0	13
1965	Yovanna	Non à Jamais Sans Toi			8	8
1966	Madeleine Pascal	Ne Vois-tu Pas?			12	6
1967	Géraldine	Quel Coeur Vas-tu Briser?			0	17
1968	Gianni Mascolo	Guardando Il Sole			2	13
1969	Paola del Medico	Bonjour, Bonjour			13	5
1970	Henri Dès	Retour			8	4
1971	Peter, Sue & Marc	Les Illusions De Nos Vingt Ans			78	12
1972	Véronique Müller	C'est La Chanson De Mon Amour			88	8
1973	Patrick Juvet	Je Me Vais Marier, Marie			79	12
1974	Piera Martell	Mein Ruf Nach Dir			3	14
1975	Simone Drexel	Mikado			77	6
1976	Peter, Sue & Marc	Djambo, Djambo			91	4
1977	Pepe Lienhard Band	Swiss Lady			71	6
1978	Carole Vinci	Vivre			65	9
1979	Peter, Sue & Marc & Pfuri, Gorps & Kniri	Trödler Und Co			60	10
1980	Paola	Cinéma			104	4
1981	Peter, Sue & Marc	Io Senza Tei			121	4
1982	Arlette Zola	Amour On T'aime			97	3
1983	Mariella Farré	Io Così Non Ci Sto			28	15

Switzerland (continued)

Year	Artist	Song	Semi-Final Points	Semi-Final Position	Final Points	Final Position
1984	Rainy Day	Welche Farbe Hat Der Sonnenschein			30	16
1985	Mariella Farré & Pino Gasparini	Piano Piano			39	12
1986	Daniela Simons	Pas Pour Moi			140	2
1987	Carole Rich	Moitié Moitié			26	17
1988	Céline Dion	Ne Partez Pas Sans Moi			137	1
1989	Furbaz	Viver Senza Tei			47	13
1990	Egon Egemann	Musik Klingt In Die Welt Hinaus			51	11
1991	Sandra Simò	Canzone Per Te			118	5
1992	Daisy Auvray	Mister Music Man			32	15
1993	Annie Cotton	Moi, Tout Simplement			148	3
1994	Duilio	Sto Pregando			15	19
1995	-				-	-
1996	Cathy Leander	Mon Coeur L'aime			22	16
1997	Barbara Berta	Dentro Di Me			5	22
1998	Gunvor	Lass Ihn			0	25
1999	-				-	-
2000	Jane Bogaert	La Vita Cos'è?			14	20
2001	-				-	-
2002	Francine Jordi	Dans Le Jardin De Mon Âme			15	22
2003	-	-			-	-
2004	Piero Esteriore & the MusicStars	Celebrate	0	22	-	-
2005	Vanilla Ninja	Cool Vibes	114	8	128	8
2006	Six4One	If We All Give A Little	-	-	30	16
2007	DJ BoBo	Vampires Are Alive	40	20	-	-
2008	Paolo Meneguzzi	Era Stupendo	47	13	-	-
2009	Lovebugs	The Highest Heights	15	14	-	-
2010	Michael von der Heide	Il Pleut de L'Or	2	17	-	-
2011	Anna Rossinelli	In Love For A While	55	10	19	25
2012	Sinplus	Unbreakable	45	11	-	-
2013	Takasa	You And Me	41	13	-	-
2014	Sebalter	Hunter of Stars	92	4	64	13
2015	Mélanie René	Time to Shine	4	17	-	-
2016	Rykka	The Last Of Our Kind	28	18	-	-
2017	Timebelle	Apollo	97	12	-	-
2018	ZiBBZ	Stones	86	13	-	-
2019	Luca Hänni	She Got Me	232	4	364	4

Turkey

Year	Artist	Song	Semi-Final Points	Semi-Final Position	Final Points	Final Position
1975	Semiha Yanki	Seninle Bir Dakika			3	19
1976	-	-			-	-
1977	-				-	-
1978	Nazar	Sevinçe			2	18
1979	-				-	-
1980	Ajda Pekkan	Petr'oil			23	15
1981	Modern Folk Trio & Aysegül	Dönme Dolap			9	18
1982	Neço	Hani			20	15
1983	Çetin Alp & the Short Wave	Opera			0	19
1984	Bes Yil Önce, On Yil Sonra	Halay			37	12
1985	MFÖ	Di Dai Di Dai Dai (A'sik Oldum			36	14
1986	Klips ve Onlar	Halley			53	9
1987	Seyyal Tanner & Lokomotif	Sarkim Sevgi üstüne			0	22
1988	MFÖ	Sufi (Hey Ya Hey)			37	15
1989	Pan	Bana Bana			5	21
1990	Kayahan	Gözlerinin Hapsindeyim			21	17
1991	Izel Çeliköz, Rayhan Soykarçi & Can Ugurluér	Iki Dakika			44	12
1992	Aylin Vatankos	Yaz Bitti			17	19
1993	Burak Aydos, Öztürk Baybora & Serter	Esmer Yarim			10	21
1994	-	-			-	-
1995	Arzu Ece	Sev!			21	16
1996	Sebnem Paker	Besinçi Mevsim			57	12
1997	Sebnem Paker & Group Etnic	Dinle			121	3

Turkey (continued)

Year	Artist	Song	Semi-Final Points	Semi-Final Position	Final Points	Final Position
1998	Tüzmen	Unutamazsin			25	14
1999	Tuba Önal & Grup Mystik	Dön Artik			21	16
2000	Pinar Ayhan & SOS Band	Yorgunum Anla			59	10
2001	Sedat Yüce	Sevgiliye Son			41	11
2002	Buket Bengisu & Saphire	Leylaklar Soldu Kalbinde			29	16
2003	Sertab Erener	Everyway That I Can			167	1
2004	Athena	For Real	-	-	195	4
2005	Gülseren	Rimi Rimi Ley	-	-	92	13
2006	Sibel Tüzün	Superstar	91	9	91	11
2007	Kenan Dogulu	Shake It Up Shekerim	197	3	163	4
2008	Mor ve Ötesi	Deli	85	7	138	7
2009	Hadise	Düm Tek Tek	172	2	177	4
2010	maNga	We Could Be The Same	118	1	170	2
2011	Yüksek Sadakat	Live It Up	47	13	-	-
2012	Can Bonomo	Love Me Back	80	5	112	7

Ukraine

Year	Artist	Song	Semi-Final Points	Semi-Final Position	Final Points	Final Position
2003	Olexandr	Hasta La Vista			30	14
2004	Ruslana	Wild Dances	256	2	280	1
2005	Greenjolly	Razom Nas Bahato	-	-	30	19
2006	Tina Karol	Show Me Your Love	146	6	145	7
2007	Verka Serduchka	Dancing Lasha Tumbai	-	-	235	2
2008	Ani Lorak	Shady Lady	152	1	230	2
2009	Svetlana Loboda	Be my Valentine! (Anti-crisis Girl)	80	6	76	12
2010	Alyosha	Sweet People	77	7	108	10
2011	Mika Newton	Angel	81	6	159	4
2012	Gaitana	Be My Guest	64	8	65	15
2013	Zlata Ognevich	Gravity	140	3	214	3
2014	Mariya Yaremchuk	Tick-Tock	118	5	113	6
2015	-	-	-	-	-	-
2016	Jamala	1944	287	2	534	1
2017	O Torvald	Time	-	-	36	24
2018	Melovin	Under The Ladder	179	6	130	17

United Kingdom

Year	Artist	Song	Semi-Final Points	Semi-Final Position	Final Points	Final Position
1957	Patricia Bredin	All			6	7
1958	-	-			-	-
1959	Pearl Carr & Teddy Johnson	Sing Little Birdie			16	2
1960	Bryan Johnson	Looking High, High, High			25	2
1961	The Allisons	Are You Sure?			24	2
1962	Ronnie Carroll	Ring-a-ding Girl			10	4
1963	Ronnie Carroll	Say Wonderful Things			28	4
1964	Matt Monro	I Love The Little Things			17	2
1965	Kathy Kirby	I Belong			26	2
1966	Kenneth McKellar	A Man Without Love			8	9
1967	Sandie Shaw	Puppet On A String			47	1
1968	Cliff Richard	Congratulations			28	2
1969	Lulu	Boom Bang-a-bang			18	1
1970	Mary Hopkin	Knock, Knock (Who's There?)			26	2
1971	Clodagh Rodgers	Jack In The Box			98	4
1972	The New Seekers	Beg, Steal Or Borrow			114	2
1973	Cliff Richard	Power To All Our Friends			123	3
1974	Olivia Newton-John	Long Live Love			14	4
1975	The Shadows	Let Me Be The One			138	2
1976	Brotherhood of Man	Save Your Kisses For Me			164	1
1977	Lynsey de Paul & Mike Moran	Rock Bottom			121	2
1978	Co-Co	The Bad Old Days			61	11
1979	Black Lace	Mary Ann			73	7

United Kingdom (continued)

			Semi-Final		Final	
Year	Artist	Song	Points	Position	Points	Position
1980	Prima Donna	Love Enough For Two			106	3
1981	Bucks Fizz	Making Your Mind Up			136	1
1982	Bardo	One Step Further			76	7
1983	Sweet Dreams	I'm Never Giving Up			79	6
1984	Belle & The Devotions	Love Games			63	7
1985	Vikki	Love Is...			100	4
1986	Ryder	Runner In The Night			72	7
1987	Rikki	Only The Light			47	13
1988	Scott Fitzgerald	Go			136	2
1989	Live Report	Why Do I Always Get It Wrong			130	2
1990	Emma	Give A Little Love Back To The World			87	6
1991	Samantha Janus	A Message To Your Heart			47	10
1992	Michael Ball	One Step Out Of Time			139	2
1993	Sonia	Better The Devil You Know			164	2
1994	Frances Ruffelle	We Will Be Free (Lonely Symphony)			63	10
1995	Love City Groove	Love City Groove			76	10
1996	Gina G	Just A Little Bit			77	8
1997	Katrina & The Waves	Love Shine A Light			227	1
1998	Imaani	Where Are You?			166	2
1999	Precious	Say It Again			38	14
2000	Nicki French	Don't Play That Song Again			28	16
2001	Lindsay D	No Dream Impossible			28	15
2002	Jessica Garlick	Come Back			111	3
2003	Jemini	Cry Baby			0	26
2004	James Fox	Hold On To Our Love	-	-	29	16
2005	Javine	Touch My Fire	-	-	18	22
2006	Daz Sampson	Teenage Life	-	-	25	19
2007	Scooch	Flying The Flag (For You)	-	-	19	22
2008	Andy Abraham	Even If	-	-	14	25
2009	Jade Ewen	It's My Time	-	-	173	5
2010	Josh Dubovie	That Sounds Good To Me	-	-	10	25
2011	Blue	I Can	-	-	100	11
2012	Engelbert Humperdinck	Love Will Set You Free	-	-	12	25
2013	Bonnie Tyler	Believe in Me	-	-	23	19
2014	Molly	Children of the Universe	-	-	40	17
2015	Electro Velvet	Still in Love with You	-	-	5	24
2016	Joe And Jake	You're Not Alone	-	-	62	24
2017	Lucie Jones	Never Give Up On You	-	-	111	15
2018	SuRie	Storm	-	-	48	24
2019	Michael Rice	Bigger Than Us	-	-	11	26

Yugoslavia

			Semi-Final		Final	
Year	Artist	Song	Points	Position	Points	Position
1961	Ljiljana Petrovic	Neke Davne Zvezde			9	8
1962	Lola Novakovic	Ne Pali Svetlo U Sumrak			10	4
1963	Vice Vukov	Brodovi			3	11
1964	Sabahudin Kurt	Zivot Je Sklopio Krug			0	13
1965	Vice Vukov	Ceznja			2	12
1966	Berta Ambroz	Brez Besed			9	7
1967	Lado Leskovar	Vse Roze Sveta			7	8
1968	Luci Kapurso & Hamo Hajdarhodzic	Jedan Dan			8	7
1969	Ivan	Pozdrav Svijetu			5	13
1970	Eva Sršen	Pridi, Dala Ti Bom Cvet			4	11
1971	Krunoslav Slabinac	Tvoj Djecak Je Tuzan			68	14
1972	Tereza	Muzika I Ti			87	9
1973	Zdravko Colic	Gori Vatra			65	15
1974	Korni	Generacija 42			6	12
1975	Pepel In Kri	Dan Ljubezni			22	13
1976	Ambasadori	Ne Mogu Skriti Svoju Bol			10	18
1977	-	-			-	-
1978	-	-			-	-
1979	-	-			-	-

Yugoslavia (continued)

Year	Artist	Song	Semi-Final Points	Semi-Final Position	Final Points	Final Position
1980	-	-			-	-
1981	Seid-Memic Vajta	Leila			35	15
1982	Aska	Halo Halo			21	14
1983	Danijel	Dzuli			125	4
1984	Vlado & Isolda	Ciao Amore			26	18
1985	-	-			-	-
1986	Doris Dragovic	Zeljo Moja			49	11
1987	Novi Fosili	Ja Sam Za Ples			92	4
1988	Srebrna Krila	Mangup			87	6
1989	Riva	Rock Me			137	1
1990	Tajci	Hajde Da Ludujemo			81	7
1991	Baby Doll	Brazil			1	21
1992	Extra Nena	Ljubim Te Pesmama			44	12

SECTION 3

Statistics and Records

Facts & Figures and Full Analysis of the Results

Eurovision Winners - Who is the best and worst at predicting the winner?

1. Under the 1975-2015 scoring system

	Netherlands 1975	United Kingdom 1976	France 1977	Israel 1978	Israel 1979	Ireland 1980	United Kingdom 1981	Germany 1982	Luxembourg 1983	Sweden 1984	Norway 1985	Belgium 1986	Ireland 1987	Switzerland 1988	Yugoslavia 1989	Italy 1990	Sweden 1991	Ireland 1992	Ireland 1993	Ireland 1994	Norway 1995	Ireland 1996	United Kingdom 1997
Albania	-	-	-	-	-	-	-	-	-	-	-	-	-	-	-	-	-	-	-	-	-	-	-
Andorra	-	-	-	-	-	-	-	-	-	-	-	-	-	-	-	-	-	-	-	-	-	-	-
Armenia	-	-	-	-	-	-	-	-	-	-	-	-	-	-	-	-	-	-	-	-	-	-	-
Australia	-	-	-	-	-	-	-	-	-	-	-	-	-	-	-	-	-	-	-	-	-	-	-
Austria	-	10	7	8	8	10	4	1	5	12	12	6	12	0	10	7	10	10	8	10	0	7	12
Azerbaijan	-	-	-	-	-	-	-	-	-	-	-	-	-	-	-	-	-	-	-	-	-	-	-
Belarus	-	-	-	-	-	-	-	-	-	-	-	-	-	-	-	-	-	-	-	-	-	-	-
Belgium	3	12	4	12	2	12	8	10	8	7	12	W	12	4	10	8	10	7	2	-	5	3	-
Bosnia-H	-	-	-	-	-	-	-	-	-	-	-	-	-	-	-	-	-	-	8	10	1	12	10
Bulgaria	-	-	-	-	-	-	-	-	-	-	-	-	-	-	-	-	-	-	-	-	-	-	-
Croatia	-	-	-	-	-	-	-	-	-	-	-	-	-	-	-	-	-	-	6	12	0	0	12
Cyprus	-	-	-	-	-	-	4	12	10	12	0	10	8	-	5	12	6	5	7	8	7	6	7
Czech Republic	-	-	-	-	-	-	-	-	-	-	-	-	-	-	-	-	-	-	-	-	-	-	-
Denmark	-	-	-	6	6	12	10	12	2	12	12	10	5	0	10	6	12	10	6	-	2	-	12
Estonia	-	-	-	-	-	-	-	-	-	-	-	-	-	-	-	-	-	-	-	10	-	12	10
Finland	10	10	12	10	12	8	3	10	8	8	4	12	12	5	7	8	8	10	3	7	-	10	-
France	5	7	W	8	1	8	7	-	12	6	2	12	1	1	3	4	0	0	10	8	10	6	12
Georgia	-	-	-	-	-	-	-	-	-	-	-	-	-	-	-	-	-	-	-	-	-	-	-
Germany	8	8	12	12	0	12	4	W	8	12	12	1	6	12	1	6	12	10	5	12	4	-	10
Greece	-	12	7	5	4	12	6	-	12	-	1	-	0	10	0	10	0	12	6	0	12	10	10
Hungary	-	-	-	-	-	-	-	-	-	-	-	-	-	-	-	-	-	-	-	10	6	-	12
Iceland	-	-	-	-	-	-	-	-	-	-	10	0	7	6	3	12	7	3	12	12	0	8
Ireland	8	3	10	8	12	W	10	12	-	12	12	12	W	10	12	12	3	W	W	W	10	W	12
Israel	12	12	10	W	W	-	12	12	12	-	12	5	4	4	12	1	10	0	5	-	10	-	-
Italy	1	4	10	8	0	1	-	-	12	6	6	-	12	7	0	W	0	2	12	-	-	-	8
Latvia	-	-	-	-	-	-	-	-	-	-	-	-	-	-	-	-	-	-	-	-	-	-	-
Lithuania	-	-	-	-	-	-	-	-	-	-	-	-	-	-	-	-	-	-	-	-	10	-	-
Luxembourg	10	8	10	12	8	7	5	0	W	6	7	10	10	1	5	10	7	10	7	-	-	-	-
Malta	12	-	-	-	-	-	-	-	-	-	-	-	-	-	-	-	0	12	12	5	6	4	1
Moldova	-	-	-	-	-	-	-	-	-	-	-	-	-	-	-	-	-	-	-	-	-	-	-
Monaco	10	10	4	3	8	-	-	-	-	-	-	-	-	-	-	-	-	-	-	-	-	-	-
Montenegro	-	-	-	-	-	-	-	-	-	-	-	-	-	-	-	-	-	-	-	-	-	-	-
Morocco	-	-	-	-	0	-	-	-	-	-	-	-	-	-	-	-	-	-	-	-	-	-	-
Netherlands	W	10	8	12	1	6	12	6	1	10	-	10	12	10	8	8	-	10	10	12	-	12	12
Nth Macedonia	-	-	-	-	-	-	-	-	-	-	-	-	-	-	-	-	-	-	-	-	-	-	-
Norway	12	12	3	8	12	12	3	10	0	10	0	8	8	8	7	0	8	7	12	12	W	10	6
Poland	-	-	-	-	-	-	-	-	-	-	-	-	-	-	-	-	-	-	-	8	12	12	10
Portugal	7	12	5	10	12	5	6	12	12	4	0	12	8	12	4	10	10	4	6	12	12	8	7
Romania	-	-	-	-	-	-	-	-	-	-	-	-	-	-	-	-	-	-	-	8	-	-	-
Russia	-	-	-	-	-	-	-	-	-	-	-	-	-	-	-	-	-	-	-	12	12	-	12
San Marino	-	-	-	-	-	-	-	-	-	-	-	-	-	-	-	-	-	-	-	-	-	-	-
Serbia**	8	10	-	-	-	-	10	12	12	4	-	10	6	6	W	6	6	2	-	-	-	-	-
Slovakia	-	-	-	-	-	-	-	-	-	-	-	-	-	-	-	-	-	-	-	6	-	7	-
Slovenia	-	-	-	-	-	-	-	-	-	-	-	-	-	-	-	-	-	-	12	-	7	12	8
Spain	12	12	10	6	12	7	8	12	7	4	1	10	10	8	0	12	4	1	10	10	4	0	5
Sweden	12	-	6	0	10	7	8	8	10	W	12	6	12	12	8	10	W	10	12	10	0	7	12
Switzerland	6	12	12	12	5	12	8	12	3	10	6	10	12	W	5	8	10	6	12	12	-	12	12
Turkey	4	-	-	12	-	0	8	12	8	3	0	12	10	10	12	8	6	12	1	-	12	12	7
Ukraine	-	-	-	-	-	-	-	-	-	-	-	-	-	-	-	-	-	-	-	-	-	-	-
United Kingdom	12	W	6	5	12	12	W	8	0	7	12	10	12	10	12	0	12	8	12	10	4	0	W

*W denotes the winner, which is excluded from the average calcuations. **Serbia includes Serbia-Montenegro & Yugoslavia

Contest & Winner

Israel 1998	Sweden 1999	Denmark 2000	Estonia 2001	Latvia 2002	Turkey 2003	Ukraine 2004	Greece 2005	Finland 2006	Serbia 2007	Russia 2008	Norway 2009	Germany 2010	Azerbaijan 2011	Sweden 2012	Denmark 2013	Austria 2014	Sweden 2015	Average points given to winner*	% of times 12 points given to winner	% of times 0 points given to winner	Country
-	-	-	-	-	-	5	12	0	1	6	7	10	8	5	1	5	7	5.6	8%	8%	Albania
-	-	-	-	-	-	10	4	10	0	5	10	-	-	-	-	-	-	6.5	0%	17%	Andorra
-	-	-	-	-	-	-	-	0	7	12	8	0	0	-	4	0	7	4.2	11%	44%	Armenia
-	-	-	-	-	-	-	-	-	-	-	-	-	-	-	-	-	12	12.0	100%	0%	Australia
-	6	10	-	10	12	4	4	-	12	-	-	-	8	12	5	W	7	7.8	21%	6%	Austria
-	-	-	-	-	-	-	-	-	-	8	8	1	W	7	5	1	6	5.1	0%	0%	Azerbaijan
-	-	-	-	-	-	10	0	7	7	12	12	0	6	6	1	0	10	5.9	17%	25%	Belarus
10	7	10	-	8	12	5	12	8	7	3	10	10	3	12	10	12	12	8.2	27%	0%	Belgium
-	12	-	4	5	12	6	6	7	12	4	10	8	8	8	-	-	-	7.9	22%	0%	Bosnia-H
-	-	-	-	-	-	-	12	5	6	6	2	3	0	8	2	-	-	4.9	11%	11%	Bulgaria
0	0	0	2	2	10	8	5	10	12	6	8	6	10	7	10	-	-	6.0	14%	24%	Croatia
10	6	4	-	4	8	8	12	5	3	8	10	4	8	10	7	-	10	7.2	12%	3%	Cyprus
-	-	-	-	-	-	-	-	8	7	3	-	-	-	-	-	-	10	7.0	0%	0%	Czech Republic
-	10	W	8	7	-	5	2	12	6	0	12	12	0	12	W	8	12	7.8	34%	9%	Denmark
7	12	8	W	12	0	12	0	12	0	12	12	8	12	12	8	4	10	8.7	45%	15%	Estonia
10	-	10	-	6	-	8	3	W	12	10	8	12	5	12	7	12	12	8.7	26%	0%	Finland
12	3	7	8	8	10	2	8	8	8	1	8	3	6	12	12	10	8	6.6	15%	5%	France
-	-	-	-	-	-	-	-	6	8	-	0	8	8	7	10	7	7	6.8	0%	13%	Georgia
7	2	12	10	12	10	6	12	10	8	7	12	W	0	12	10	7	10	8.3	34%	5%	Germany
10	-	-	12	10	7	7	W	12	4	7	10	2	5	6	7	12	4	7.2	24%	12%	Greece
0	-	-	-	-	-	-	12	-	12	10	12	-	7	12	10	10	10	9.5	38%	8%	Hungary
-	10	12	10	-	3	12	2	12	7	0	12	3	8	12	10	10	12	7.8	36%	11%	Iceland
6	5	12	10	-	0	7	2	10	4	5	8	8	0	12	12	12	10	8.5	36%	6%	Ireland
W	8	12	6	12	7	12	7	7	3	12	12	0	4	12	8	12	10	8.4	42%	6%	Israel
-	-	-	-	-	-	-	-	-	-	-	-	0	0	12	12	12	12	6.0	29%	24%	Italy
-	12	12	W	0	12	0	8	3	12	12	12	2	12	6	6	-	12	8.6	57%	14%	Latvia
-	3	-	12	12	-	12	1	10	0	12	12	10	8	10	2	10	10	8.4	31%	6%	Lithuania
-	-	-	-	-	-	-	-	-	-	-	-	-	-	-	-	-	-	7.4	6%	6%	Luxembourg
12	12	8	12	7	4	8	6	7	8	8	8	4	12	6	6	10	10	7.7	27%	4%	Malta
-	-	-	-	-	-	-	4	6	5	10	8	0	10	7	6	7	8	6.5	0%	9%	Moldova
-	-	-	-	-	-	6	0	0	-	-	-	-	-	-	-	-	-	5.1	0%	25%	Monaco
-	-	-	-	-	-	-	-	-	12	8	10	-	-	7	10	2	5	7.7	14%	0%	Montenegro
-	-	-	-	-	-	-	-	-	-	-	-	-	-	-	-	-	-	0.0	0%	100%	Morocco
6	8	10	12	-	12	7	10	7	8	1	12	4	6	12	10	12	10	8.8	31%	0%	Netherlands
8	-	0	-	7	-	8	7	6	12	6	8	0	6	12	3	3	5	6.4	13%	13%	Nth Macedonia
3	12	10	10	-	10	7	4	12	10	5	W	12	0	12	7	10	12	8.0	29%	11%	Norway
10	6	-	12	-	2	12	1	12	8	6	12	7	8	-	-	0	12	8.3	39%	6%	Poland
12	10	-	0	-	8	10	3	6	5	5	1	8	3	-	12	8	8	9.3	32%	6%	Portugal
7	-	1	-	0	10	6	10	4	6	10	5	3	10	10	6	8	8	6.6	0%	6%	Romania
-	-	12	6	10	0	12	4	8	5	W	12	6	12	12	4	5	8	8.4	44%	6%	Russia
-	-	-	-	-	-	-	-	-	0	-	-	10	3	0	0	-	7	3.3	0%	50%	San Marino
-	-	-	-	-	-	-	-	W	10	10	8	0	10	12	-	-	8	7.9	16%	5%	Serbia**
0	-	-	-	-	-	-	-	-	-	10	12	7	12	-	-	-	-	7.7	29%	14%	Slovakia
7	7	-	12	5	10	8	2	8	12	7	12	10	0	10	12	12	12	8.8	38%	5%	Slovenia
12	6	10	8	12	3	8	8	10	1	5	12	12	0	12	8	12	8	7.6	27%	7%	Spain
5	0	12	8	5	8	10	12	12	10	0	12	12	3	W	10	12	W	8.4	33%	11%	Sweden
10	-	10	-	8	-	0	7	8	12	0	8	12	1	7	3	12	12	8.5	39%	6%	Switzerland
5	6	1	12	6	W	12	12	7	0	5	3	10	12	6	-	-	-	7.5	33%	9%	Turkey
-	-	-	-	2	W	0	7	6	12	5	10	6	5	8	-	-	-	7.3	20%	10%	Ukraine
5	12	12	12	8	7	5	12	12	0	0	10	4	0	12	12	12	12	8.2	45%	16%	United Kingdom

Eurovision Winners - Who is the best and worst at predicting the winner?

2. Under the current scoring system, showing separate jury and public voting for each year's winner

	Jury voting							Public voting						
	Ukraine 2016	Portugal 2017	Israel 2018	Netherlands 2019	Average points given to winner*	% of times 12 points given to winner	% of times 0 points given to winner	Ukraine 2016	Portugal 2017	Israel 2018	Netherlands 2019	Average points given to winner*	% of times 12 points given to winner	% of times 0 points given to winner
Albania	0	6	5	0	2.8	0%	50%	6	8	1	7	5.5	0%	0%
Andorra	-	-	-	-	-	-	-	-	-	-	-	-	-	-
Armenia	0	12	8	6	6.5	25%	25%	10	10	10	10	10.0	0%	0%
Australia	2	7	6	6	5.3	0%	0%	8	7	12	6	8.3	25%	0%
Austria	0	8	12	8	7.0	25%	25%	10	12	7	7	9.0	25%	0%
Azerbaijan	10	8	1	0	4.8	0%	25%	10	8	12	7	9.3	25%	0%
Belarus	7	10	0	6	5.8	0%	25%	10	7	8	10	8.8	0%	0%
Belgium	3	8	6	6	5.8	0%	0%	2	12	10	12	9.0	50%	0%
Bosnia-H	12	-	-	-	12.0	100%	0%	7	-	-	-	7.0	0%	0%
Bulgaria	0	0	4	-	1.3	0%	67%	10	7	10	-	9.0	0%	0%
Croatia	0	7	10	6	5.8	0%	25%	10	10	6	4	7.5	0%	0%
Cyprus	0	8	0	5	3.3	0%	50%	7	7	10	6	7.5	0%	0%
Czech Republic	0	12	12	6	7.5	50%	25%	12	8	10	4	8.5	25%	0%
Denmark	12	10	3	7	8.0	25%	0%	3	5	0	7	3.8	0%	25%
Estonia	7	8	0	7	5.5	0%	25%	8	10	0	8	6.5	0%	25%
Finland	0	8	12	8	7.0	25%	25%	12	12	7	5	9.0	50%	0%
France	0	12	12	12	9.0	75%	25%	10	12	12	5	9.8	50%	0%
Georgia	12	12	3	8	8.8	50%	0%	10	8	12	5	8.8	25%	0%
Germany	7	10	1	8	6.5	0%	0%	6	12	10	7	8.8	25%	0%
Greece	2	5	4	0	2.8	0%	25%	6	8	6	6	6.5	0%	0%
Hungary	0	12	6	1	4.8	25%	25%	12	7	10	8	9.3	25%	0%
Iceland	0	12	8	7	6.8	25%	25%	0	12	7	5	6.0	25%	25%
Ireland	0	5	7	8	5.0	0%	25%	4	10	6	8	7.0	0%	0%
Israel	12	12	W	12	12.0	100%	0%	8	12	W	2	7.3	33%	0%
Italy	10	5	2	0	4.3	0%	25%	12	5	7	5	7.3	25%	0%
Latvia	12	12	0	12	9.0	75%	25%	10	10	8	5	8.3	0%	0%
Lithuania	8	12	6	12	9.5	50%	0%	10	12	1	7	7.5	25%	0%
Luxembourg	-	-	-	-	-	-	-	-	-	-	-	-	-	-
Malta	0	10	6	7	5.8	0%	25%	4	8	8	10	7.5	0%	0%
Moldova	12	7	10	3	8.0	25%	0%	10	6	12	6	8.5	25%	0%
Monaco	-	-	-	-	-	-	-	-	-	-	-	-	-	-
Montenegro	0	0	0	0	0.0	0%	100%	8	8	1	1	4.5	0%	0%
Morocco	-	-	-	-	-	-	-	-	-	-	-	-	-	-
Netherlands	3	12	5	W	6.7	33%	0%	7	12	10	W	9.7	33%	0%
Nth Macedonia	12	10	1	7	7.5	25%	0%	6	7	3	7	5.8	0%	0%
Norway	4	10	0	7	5.3	0%	25%	4	12	7	8	7.8	25%	0%
Poland	12	12	0	0	6.0	50%	50%	12	10	10	10	10.5	25%	0%
Portugal	-	W	1	12	6.5	50%	0%	-	W	1	8	4.5	0%	0%
Romania	-	6	0	5	3.7	0%	33%	-	7	8	12	9.0	33%	0%
Russia	0	-	8	0	2.7	0%	67%	10	-	10	5	8.3	0%	0%
San Marino	12	12	12	3	9.8	75%	0%	12	7	12	6	9.3	50%	0%
Serbia	12	12	2	0	6.5	50%	25%	7	8	7	3	6.3	0%	0%
Slovakia	-	-	-	-	-	-	-	-	-	-	-	-	-	-
Slovenia	12	12	1	6	7.8	50%	0%	7	8	0	5	5.0	0%	25%
Spain	0	12	10	8	7.5	25%	25%	7	12	12	8	9.8	50%	0%
Sweden	0	12	7	12	7.8	50%	25%	7	10	10	6	8.3	0%	0%
Switzerland	6	12	1	10	7.3	25%	0%	4	12	5	6	6.8	25%	0%
Turkey	-	-	-	-	-	-	-	-	-	-	-	-	-	-
Ukraine	W	10	10	-	10.0	0%	0%	W	10	12	-	11.0	50%	0%
United Kingdom	10	12	10	6	9.5	25%	0%	5	8	7	4	6.0	0%	0%

*W denotes the winner, which is excluded from the average calcuations.

Eurovision 2019: Marcel Bezençon Awards

Press Award (given to the best act as judged by the accredited press and media)

Year	Country	Song	Artist	Position
2002	France	Il faut du temps	Sandrine François	5th
2003	Turkey	Everyway That I Can	Sertab Erener	1st
2004	Serbia & Montenegro	Lane moje	Željko Joksimović	2nd
2005	Malta	Angel	Chiara	2nd
2006	Finland	Hard Rock Hallelujah	Lordi	1st
2007	Ukraine	Dancing Lasha Tumbai	Verka Serduchka	2nd
2008	Portugal	Senhora do mar (Negras águas)	Vânia Fernandes	13th
2009	Norway	Fairytale	Alexander Rybak	1st
2010	Israel	Milim	Harel Skaat	14th
2011	Finland	Da Da Dam	Paradise Oskar	21st
2012	Azerbaijan	When the Music Dies	Sabina Babayeva	4th
2013	Georgia	Waterfall	Nodi and Sophie	15th
2014	Austria	Rise Like a Phoenix	Conchita Wurst	1st
2015	Italy	Grande amore	Il Volo	3rd
2016	Russia	You Are the Only One	Sergey Lazarev	3rd
2017	Italy	Occidentali's Karma	Francesco Gabbani	6th
2018	France	Mercy	Madame Monsieur	13th
2019	Netherlands	Arcade	Duncan Laurence	1st

Artistic Award (given to the best artist as judged by the commentators)

Year	Country	Song	Artist	Position
2002*	Sweden	Never Let It Go	Afro-dite	8th
2003*	Netherlands	One More Night	Esther Hart	13th
2004*	Ukraine	Wild Dances	Ruslana	1st
2005*	Greece	My Number One	Helena Paparizou	1st
2006*	Sweden	Invincible	Carola	5th
2007*	Serbia	Molitva	Marija Šerifović	1st
2008*	Ukraine	Shady Lady	Ani Lorak	2nd
2009*	France	Et s'il fallait le faire	Patricia Kaas	8th
2010	Israel	Milim	Harel Skaat	14th
2011	Ireland	Lipstick	Jedward	8th
2012	Sweden	Euphoria	Loreen	1st
2013	Azerbaijan	Hold Me	Farid Mammadov	2nd
2014	Netherlands	Calm After the Storm	The Common Linnets	2nd
2015	Sweden	Heroes	Måns Zelmerlöw	1st
2016	Ukraine	1944	Jamala	1st
2017	Portugal	Amar pelos dois	Salvador Sobral	1st
2018	Cyprus	Fuego	Eleni Foureira	2nd
2019	Australia	Zero Gravity	Kate Miller-Heidke	9th

* Awarded by previous winners until 2010

Composer Award (given to the best song as judged by a jury of participating composers)

Year	Country	Song	Artist	Position
2004	Cyprus	Lisa Andreas	Stronger Every Minute	5th
2005	Serbia & Montenegro	No Name	Zauvijek moja	7th
2006	Bosnia & Herzegovina	Hari Mata Hari	Lejla	3rd
2007	Hungary	Magdi Rúzsa	Unsubstantial Blues	9th
2008	Romania	Nico & Vlad	Pe-o margine de lume	20th
2009	Bosnia & Herzegovina	Regina	Bistra voda	9th
2010	Israel	Harel Skaat	Milim	14th
2011	France	Amaury Vassili	Sognu	15th
2012	Sweden	Loreen	Euphoria	1st
2013	Sweden	Robin Stjernberg	You	14th
2014	Netherlands	The Common Linnets	Calm After the Storm	2nd
2015	Norway	Mørland & Debrah Scarlett	A Monster Like Me	8th
2016	Australia	Dami Im	Sound of Silence	2nd
2017	Portugal	Amar pelos dois	Salvador Sobral	1st
2018	Bulgaria	Equinox	Bones	14th
2019	Italy	Soldi	Mahmood	2nd

Eurovision 2019: OGAE Poll Results

How do the votes by members of OGAE compare to the final result? (Top ten countries shown)

	2013	
Position	OGAE Poll	Contest Position
1	Denmark	1
2	San Marino	SF
3	Norway	4
4	Germany	21
5	Italy	7
6	Netherlands	9
7	Ukraine	3
8	United Kingdom	19
9	Sweden	14
10	Russia	5

	2014	
Position	OGAE Poll	Contest Position
1	Sweden	3
2	Hungary	5
3	Israel	SF
4	Austria	1
5	United Kingdom	17
6	Armenia	4
7	Norway	8
8	Spain	10
9	Greece	20
10	Montenegro	19

	2015	
Position	OGAE Poll	Contest Position
1	Italy	3
2	Sweden	1
3	Estonia	7
4	Norway	8
5	Slovenia	14
6	Australia	5
7	Israel	9
8	Spain	21
9	Azerbaijan	12
10	Belgium	4

	2016	
Position	OGAE Poll	Contest Position
1	France	6
2	Russia	3
3	Australia	2
4	Bulgaria	4
5	Italy	16
6	Spain	22
7	Austria	13
8	Latvia	15
9	Ukraine	1
10	Hungary	19

	2017	
Position	OGAE Poll	Contest Position
1	Italy	6
2	Belgium	4
3	Sweden	5
4	France	12
5	Estonia	SF
6	Portugal	1
7	Bulgaria	2
8	FYR Macedonia	SF
9	Israel	23
10	Finland	SF

	2018	
Position	OGAE Poll	Contest Position
1	Israel	1
2	France	13
3	Finland	25
4	Australia	20
5	Czech Republic	6
6	Bulgaria	14
7	Belgium	SF
8	Greece	SF
9	Cyprus	2
10	Denmark	9

	2019	
Position	OGAE Poll	Contest Position
1	Italy	2
2	Switzerland	4
3	Netherlands	1
4	Norway	6
5	Cyprus	13
6	Sweden	5
7	Azerbaijan	8
8	Iceland	10
9	Russia	3
10	Greece	21

Source: OGAEinternational.com. OGAE is an international Eurovision fan organisation.

Eurovision 2019: Internal Selection or National Competition?

Which method of choosing a representative is most popular? And which is most successful? (Artists only)

Country	2019	Position
Albania	Competition	17
Armenia	Internal	SF
Australia	Competition	9
Austria	Internal	SF
Azerbaijan	Internal	8
Belarus	Competition	24
Belgium	Internal	SF
Croatia	Competition	SF
Cyprus	Internal	13
Czech Republic	Competition	11
Denmark	Competition	12
Estonia	Competition	20
Finland	Internal	SF
France	Competition	16
Georgia	Competition	SF
Germany	Competition	25
Greece	Internal	21
Hungary	Competition	SF
Iceland	Competition	10
Ireland	Internal	SF
Israel	Competition	23
Italy	Competition	2
Latvia	Competition	SF
Lithuania	Competition	SF
Malta	Competition	14
Moldova	Competition	SF
Montenegro	Competition	SF
Netherlands	Internal	1
North Macedonia	Internal	7
Norway	Competition	6
Poland	Internal	SF
Portugal	Competition	SF
Romania	Competition	SF
Russia	Internal	3
San Marino	Internal	19
Serbia	Competition	18
Slovenia	Competition	15
Spain	Competition	22
Sweden	Competition	5
Switzerland	Internal	4
United Kingdom	Competition	26

% Internal Selection	34%	(2018: 33%)
% National Competition	66%	(2018: 67%)

Previous Years' Top 3 (in final)

Year	Winner	2nd	3rd
2018	competition	internal	internal
2017	competition	internal	competition
2016	competition	internal	internal
2015	competition	internal	competition
2014	internal	internal	competition
2013	competition	competition	competition
2012	competition	competition	internal
2011	competition	competition	competition
2010	competition	internal	competition
2009	competition	competition	internal
2008	competition	internal	competition
2007	competition	competition	internal
2006	competition	internal	internal

Previous Years' Bottom 3 (in final)

Year	Last	2nd Last	3rd Last
2018	competition	internal	competition
2017	competition	competition	competition
2016	competition	internal	competition
2015	competition	competition	internal
2014	competition	competition	internal
2013	competition	internal	competition
2012	competition	internal	competition
2011	competition	competition	competition
2010	competition	internal	competition
2009	competition	competition	competition
2008	competition	competition	competition
2007	internal	competition	competition
2006	competition	competition	competition

Eurovision Winners - Average age and gender (solo performers & duos only)

Year	Winner	Performer	Date of Contest	Date of Birth	Age
1956	Switzerland	Lys Assia	24 May 1956	03 March 1924	32
1957	Netherlands	Corry Brokken	03 March 1957	03 December 1932	24
1958	France	André Claveau	12 March 1958	17 December 1911	46
1959	Netherlands	Teddy Scholten	11 March 1959	11 May 1926	32
1960	France	Jacqueline Boyer	29 March 1960	23 April 1941	18
1961	Luxembourg	Jean-Claude Pascal	18 March 1961	24 October 1927	33
1962	France	Isabelle Aubret	18 March 1962	28 July 1938	23
1963	Denmark	Grethe and Jørgen Ingmann - Grethe	23 March 1963	17 June 1938	24
		Grethe and Jørgen Ingmann - Jørgen	23 March 1963	26 April 1925	37
1964	Italy	Gigliola Cinquetti	21 March 1964	20 December 1947	16
1965	Luxembourg	France Gall	20 March 1965	09 October 1947	17
1966	Austria	Udo Jürgens	05 March 1966	30 September 1934	31
1967	United Kingdom	Sandie Shaw	08 April 1967	26 February 1947	20
1968	Spain	Massiel	06 April 1968	02 August 1947	20
1969	Spain	Salomé	29 March 1969	21 June 1943	25
	United Kingdom	Lulu	29 March 1969	03 November 1948	20
	Netherlands	Lenny Kuhr	29 March 1969	22 February 1950	19
	France	Frida Boccara	29 March 1969	29 October 1940	28
1970	Ireland	Dana	21 March 1970	30 August 1951	18
1971	Monaco	Séverine	03 April 1971	10 October 1948	22
1972	Luxembourg	Vicky Leandros	25 March 1972	23 August 1949	22
1973	Luxembourg	Anne-Marie David	07 April 1973	23 May 1952	20
1974	Sweden	ABBA	06 April 1974	-	-
1975	Netherlands	Teach-In	22 March 1975	-	-
1976	United Kingdom	Brotherhood of Man	03 April 1976	-	-
1977	France	Marie Myriam	07 May 1977	08 May 1957	19
1978	Israel	Izhar Cohen and the Alphabeta	22 April 1978	13 May 1951	26
1979	Israel	Gali Atari and Milk and Honey	31 March 1979	29 December 1953	25
1980	Ireland	Johnny Logan	19 April 1980	13 May 1954	25
1981	United Kingdom	Bucks Fizz	04 April 1981	-	-
1982	Germany	Nicole	24 April 1982	25 October 1964	17
1983	Luxembourg	Corinne Hermès	23 April 1983	16 November 1961	21
1984	Sweden	Herreys	05 May 1984	-	-
1985	Norway	Bobbysocks! - Hanne Krogh	04 May 1985	24 January 1956	29
		Bobbysocks! - Elisabeth Andreassen	04 May 1985	28 March 1958	27
1986	Belgium	Sandra Kim	03 May 1986	15 October 1972	13
1987	Ireland	Johnny Logan	09 May 1987	13 May 1954	32
1988	Switzerland	Celine Dion	30 April 1988	30 March 1968	20
1989	Yugoslavia	Riva	06 May 1989	-	-
1990	Italy	Toto Cutugno	05 May 1990	07 July 1943	46
1991	Sweden	Carola	04 May 1991	08 September 1966	24
1992	Ireland	Linda Martin	09 May 1992	17 April 1947	45
1993	Ireland	Niamh Kavanagh	15 May 1993	13 February 1968	25
1994	Ireland	Paul Harrington & Charlie McGettigan - Paul	30 April 1994	08 May 1960	33
		Paul Harrington & Charlie McGettigan - Charlie	30 April 1994	07 December 1950	43
1995	Norway	Secret Garden - Fionnuala Sherry	13 May 1995	20 September 1962	32
		Secret Garden - Rolf Løvland	13 May 1995	19 April 1955	40

Eurovision Winners - Average age and gender (solo performers & duos only)

Year	Winner	Performer	Date of Contest	Date of Birth	Age
1996	Ireland	Eimear Quinn	18 May 1996	01 January 1973	23
1997	United Kingdom	Katrina and the Waves	03 May 1997	-	-
1998	Israel	Dana International	09 May 1998	02 February 1969	29
1999	Sweden	Charlotte Nilsson	29 May 1999	07 October 1974	24
2000	Denmark	Olsen Brothers - Jørgen	13 May 2000	15 March 1950	50
		Olsen Brothers - Niels	13 May 2000	13 April 1954	46
2001	Estonia	Tanel Padar, Dave Benton and 2XL - Tanel	12 May 2001	27 October 1980	20
		Tanel Padar, Dave Benton and 2XL - Dave	12 May 2001	31 January 1951	50
2002	Latvia	Marie N	25 May 2002	23 June 1973	28
2003	Turkey	Sertab Erener	24 May 2003	04 December 1964	38
2004	Ukraine	Ruslana	15 May 2004	24 May 1973	30
2005	Greece	Helena Paparizou	21 May 2005	31 January 1982	23
2006	Finland	Lordi	20 May 2006	-	-
2007	Serbia	Marija Šerifović	12 May 2007	14 November 1984	22
2008	Russia	Dima Bilan	24 May 2008	24 December 1981	26
2009	Norway	Alexander Rybak	16 May 2009	13 May 1986	23
2010	Germany	Lena Meyer-Landrut	29 May 2010	23 May 1991	19
2011	Azerbaijan	Ell/Nikki - Eldar Gasimov	14 May 2011	04 June 1989	21
		Ell/Nikki - Nigar Jamal	14 May 2011	07 September 1980	30
2012	Sweden	Loreen	26 May 2012	16 October 1983	28
2013	Denmark	Emmelie de Forest	18 May 2013	28 February 1993	20
2014	Austria	Conchita Wurst (performs as female)	10 May 2014	06 November 1988	25
2015	Sweden	Måns Zelmerlöw	23 May 2015	13 June 1986	28
2016	Ukraine	Jamala	14 May 2016	27 August 1983	32
2017	Portugal	Salvador Sobral	13 May 2017	28 December 1989	27
2018	Israel	Netta	12 May 2018	22 January 1993	25
2019	Netherlands	Duncan Laurence	18 May 2019	11 April 1994	25
			66 performers	Average:	27
			50 solo acts	Average (solo acts):	25
			21 male performers	Average (men):	33
			45 female performers	Average (women):	24

Eurovision 2019: What type of act?

Following last year's winning solo male artist, what did each country choose to send to this year's Contest?

Country	Represented by	Accompanied by*
Albania	solo female	mixed backing singers
Armenia	solo female	none
Australia	solo female	female performers
Austria	solo female	none
Azerbaijan	solo male	none
Belarus	solo female	male dancers
Belgium	solo male	mixed musicians
Croatia	solo male	male dancers
Cyprus	solo female	male dancers
Czech Republic	mixed group	none
Denmark	solo female	male dancers & female singers
Estonia	solo male	none
Finland	mixed duo	female dancer
France	solo male	female dancers
Georgia	solo male	male singers
Germany	female duo	none
Greece	solo female	female singers & female dancers
Hungary	solo male	none
Iceland	mixed group	mixed dancers
Ireland	solo female	female dancers
Israel	solo male	mixed singers
Italy	solo male	male dancers
Latvia	mixed group	none
Lithuania	solo male	none
Malta	solo female	mixed dancers
Moldova	solo female	female performers
Montenegro	mixed group	none
Netherlands	solo male	none
North Macedonia	solo female	none
Norway	mixed group	none
Poland	female group	none
Portugal	solo male	male dancer
Romania	solo female	male musician
Russia	solo male	female singers & male dancers
San Marino	solo male	female singers & male dancers
Serbia	solo female	none
Slovenia	mixed duo	none
Spain	solo male	mixed singers
Sweden	solo male	female singers
Switzerland	solo male	mixed dancers
United Kingdom	solo male	mixed singers
	solo female	14 (34%)
	solo male	18 (44%)
	others	9

* only includes clearly visible backing singers

Eurovision 2019: Language selection over 9 year period (predominant language only)

Country	2011	2012	2013	2014	2015	2016	2017	2018	2019
Albania	English	Albanian	Albanian	English	English	English	English	Albanian	Albanian
Armenia	English		English	English	English	English	English	Armenian	English
Australia				English	English	English	English	English	English
Austria	English	German	English	English	English	French	English	English	English
Azerbaijan	English	English	English	English	English	English	English	English	English
Belarus	English	English	English	English	English	English	Belarusian	English	English
Belgium	English	English	English	English	English	English	English	English	English
Bosnia & H	English	Bosnian				Bosnian			
Bulgaria	Bulgarian	Bulgarian	Bulgarian			English	English	English	
Croatia	English	Croatian	Croatian			English	English	English	English
Cyprus	Greek	English	Greek		English	English	English	English	English
Czech Republic					English	English	English	English	English
Denmark	English	English	English	English	English	English	English	English	English
Estonia	English	Estonian	Estonian	English	English	English	English	Italian	English
Finland	English	Swedish	English	English	Finnish	English	English	English	English
France	Corsican	French	French	French	French	French	French	French	French
Georgia	English	English	English	English	English	English	English	Georgian	Georgian
Germany	English	English	English	English	English	English	English	English	English
Greece	English	English	Greek	English	English	English	English	Greek	English
Hungary	English	English	Hungarian	English	English	English	Hungarian	Hungarian	Hungarian
Iceland	English	English	Icelandic	English	English	English	English	English	Icelandic
Ireland	English	English	English	English	English	English	English	English	English
Israel	Hebrew	English	Hebrew	English	English	English	English	English	English
Italy	Italian	English	Italian	Italian	Italian	Italian	Italian	Italian	Italian
Latvia	English	English	English	English	English	English	English	English	English
Lithuania	English	English	English	English	English	English	English	English	English
Malta	English	English	English	English	English	English	English	English	English
Moldova	English	English	Romanian	English	English	English	English	English	English
Montenegro		English	Montenegrin	Montenegrin	Montenegrin	English	English	Montenegrin	English
Netherlands	English	English	English	English	English	English	English	English	English
Nth Macedonia	Macedonian	Macedonian	Macedonian	English	English	Macedonian	English	English	English
Norway	English	English	English	English	English	English	English	English	English
Poland	Polish			Polish	English	English	English	English	Polish
Portugal	Portuguese	Portuguese		Portuguese	Portuguese		Portuguese	Portuguese	Portuguese
Romania	English	Spanish	English	English	Romanian		English	English	English
Russia	English	Udmurt	English	English	English	English		English	English
San Marino	English	English	Italian	English	English	English	English	English	English
Serbia	Serbian	Serbian	Serbian			English	English	Serbian	Serbian
Slovakia	English	English							
Slovenia	English	Slovene	English	English	English	English	English	Slovene	Slovene
Spain	Spanish	Spanish	Spanish	English	Spanish	English	Spanish	Spanish	Spanish
Sweden	English	English	English	English	English	English	English	English	English
Switzerland	English	English	English	English	English	English	English		English
Turkey	English	English							
Ukraine	English	English	English	English		English	English	English	
United Kingdom	English	English	English	English	English	English	English	English	English
Number of songs:	43	42	39	37	40	42	42	43	41
Sung in English:	33	27	22	32	33	37	36	29	30
Percentage:	77%	64%	56%	86%	83%	88%	86%	67%	73%

denotes winner

The Most Successful Countries in Eurovision history....

Rank 2019	Rank 2018	Change	Country	Winners	2nd	3rd	4th	5th
1	1	0	Ireland	7	3	2	3	3
2	2	0	Sweden	6	1	6	2	9
3	3	0	United Kingdom	5	15	3	4	1
4	4	0	France	5	4	7	6	3
5	7	+2	Netherlands	5	1	1	2	2
6	5	-1	Luxembourg	5	0	2	2	4
7	6	-1	**Israel**	4	2	1	2	2
8	8	0	Denmark	3	1	3	2	3
9	9	0	Norway	3	1	1	4	3
10	10	0	**Germany**	2	4	5	3	3
11	11	0	Spain	2	4	1	2	1
12	13	+1	**Italy**	2	3	5	2	4
13	12	-1	Switzerland	2	3	3	5	2
14	14	0	Ukraine	2	2	1	1	0
15	15	0	**Austria**	2	0	1	1	4
16	16	0	Russia	1	4	4	0	1
17	17	0	Belgium	1	2	0	3	2
18	18	0	Monaco	1	1	3	3	1
19	19	0	Turkey	1	1	1	3	0
20	20	0	Azerbaijan	1	1	1	1	1
21	21	0	Greece	1	0	3	0	2
22	22	0	Latvia	1	0	1	0	1
23	23	0	Serbia	1	0	1	0	0
24	24	0	Estonia	1	0	0	2	1
24	24	0	Yugoslavia	1	0	0	2	1
26	26	0	Finland	1	0	0	0	0
26	26	0	Portugal	1	0	0	0	0
28	28	0	Malta	0	2	2	0	1
29	29	0	Iceland	0	2	0	1	0
30	30	0	Bulgaria	0	1	0	1	1
31	31	0	**Cyprus**	0	1	0	0	3
32	32	0	Australia	0	1	0	0	1
33	33	0	Poland	0	1	0	0	0
33	33	0	Serbia & Montenegro	0	1	0	0	0
35	35	0	Romania	0	0	2	1	0
36	36	0	Bosnia & Herzegovina	0	0	1	0	0
36	36	0	Moldova	0	0	1	0	0
38	38	0	Croatia	0	0	0	2	1
39	39	0	Armenia	0	0	0	2	0
40	40	0	Hungary	0	0	0	1	1
41	41	0	Albania	0	0	0	0	1
42	42	0	Andorra	0	0	0	0	0
42	42	0	Belarus	0	0	0	0	0
42	42	0	Czech Republic	0	0	0	0	0
42	42	0	North Macedonia	0	0	0	0	0
42	42	0	Georgia	0	0	0	0	0
42	42	0	Lithuania	0	0	0	0	0
42	42	0	Montenegro	0	0	0	0	0
42	42	0	Morocco	0	0	0	0	0
42	42	0	San Marino	0	0	0	0	0
42	42	0	Slovakia	0	0	0	0	0
42	42	0	Slovenia	0	0	0	0	0

...And The Least Successful Countries in Eurovision history

(although, they at least made it to the Final...)

Rank 2019	Rank 2018	Change	Country	Last	2nd last	3rd Last	4th Last	5th Last
1	1	0	Norway	9	3	2	4	1
2	2	0	Austria	6	3	5	3	1
3	3	0	Belgium	6	2	7	4	2
4	4	0	**Finland**	5	4	5	2	7
5	5	0	Germany	4	2	4	4	1
6	9	3	**United Kingdom**	4	2	3	2	0
7	6	-1	Switzerland	4	1	1	3	3
8	7	-1	**Spain**	3	3	2	6	5
9	8	-1	Turkey	3	3	0	1	4
10	10	0	Luxembourg	3	1	3	0	1
11	11	0	Malta	3	1	0	2	0
12	12	0	Sweden	2	2	2	1	2
13	13	0	Ireland	2	1	2	1	1
14	14	0	Yugoslavia	1	5	0	1	2
15	15	0	**Portugal**	1	4	4	4	4
16	16	0	Netherlands	1	4	3	3	2
17	17	0	France	1	3	5	2	3
18	18	0	Denmark	1	1	3	3	3
19	19	0	Cyprus	1	1	1	2	2
20	20	0	Lithuania	1	1	1	2	1
21	21	0	Monaco	1	1	1	1	1
22	22	0	Iceland	1	1	0	0	1
23	23	0	Italy	1	0	1	1	4
24	24	0	Israel	0	3	1	2	1
25	25	0	Estonia	0	2	0	0	0
26	26	0	Hungary	0	1	2	1	0
27	27	0	**Slovenia**	0	1	1	2	1
28	30	2	Belarus	0	1	1	0	0
29	28	-1	Poland	0	1	0	1	2
30	29	-1	Bosnia & Herzegovina	0	1	0	0	1
31	30	-1	Morocco	0	1	0	0	0
31	30	-1	Czech Republic	0	1	0	0	0
33	33	0	Latvia	0	0	1	0	0
33	33	0	San Marino	0	0	1	0	0
33	33	0	Ukraine	0	0	1	0	0
36	36	0	Greece	0	0	0	2	1
37	37	0	Moldova	0	0	0	1	2
38	38	0	Romania	0	0	0	1	1
38	38	0	Croatia	0	0	0	1	1
40	40	0	Slovakia	0	0	0	0	1
40	40	0	Azerbaijan	0	0	0	0	1
42	42	0	Albania	0	0	0	0	0
42	42	0	Andorra	0	0	0	0	0
42	42	0	Armenia	0	0	0	0	0
42	42	0	Bulgaria	0	0	0	0	0
42	42	0	North Macedonia	0	0	0	0	0
42	42	0	Georgia	0	0	0	0	0
42	42	0	Montenegro	0	0	0	0	0
42	42	0	Russia	0	0	0	0	0
42	42	0	Serbia	0	0	0	0	0
42	42	0	Serbia & Montenegro	0	0	0	0	0

The Most Finishes in the Top 3...

Country	Top 3	Winners	2nd	3rd
United Kingdom	23	5	15	3
France	16	5	4	7
Sweden	13	6	1	6
Ireland	12	7	3	2
Germany	11	2	4	5
Italy	10	2	3	5
Switzerland	8	2	3	3
Russia	9	1	4	4
Netherlands	7	5	1	1
Luxembourg	7	5	0	2
Israel	7	4	2	1
Denmark	7	3	1	3
Spain	7	2	4	1

... And the Most Finishes in the Bottom 3

Country	Bottom 3	Last	2nd last	3rd Last
Belgium	15	6	2	7
Norway	14	9	3	2
Austria	14	6	3	5
Finland	14	5	4	5
Germany	11	4	3	4
United Kingdom	9	4	2	3
Portugal	9	1	4	4
France	9	1	3	5
Spain	8	3	3	2
Netherlands	8	1	4	3
Luxembourg	7	3	1	3
Switzerland	6	4	1	1
Turkey	6	3	3	0
Sweden	6	2	2	2

Failing to Qualify for the Final
Who has been eliminated at the semi-final stage the most times?

Country	Failures	Appearances	Failure rate
Andorra	6	6	100%
Slovakia	4	4	100%
Monaco	3	3	100%
San Marino	8	9	89%
Montenegro	9	11	82%
Switzerland	11	14	79%
Bulgaria	8	11	73%
Portugal	9	12	75%
Czech Republic	5	7	71%
Belarus	10	14	71%
Belgium	10	14	71%
Slovenia	10	15	67%
North Macedonia	10	15	67%
Netherlands	9	14	64%
Latvia	10	15	67%
Poland	8	12	67%
Estonia	9	15	60%
Croatia	7	12	58%
Ireland	8	14	57%
Malta	7	13	54%
Cyprus	6	12	50%
Albania	7	14	50%
Finland	8	15	53%
Iceland	7	14	50%
Israel	6	13	46%
Lithuania	7	15	47%
Moldova	5	13	38%
Austria	5	14	36%
Denmark	4	13	31%
Serbia	3	10	30%
Norway	3	11	27%
Georgia	4	12	33%
Hungary	3	10	30%
Armenia	3	11	27%
Greece	2	11	18%
Turkey	1	7	14%
Bosnia & H	1	8	13%
Russia	1	10	10%
Sweden	1	11	9%
Romania	2	12	17%
Azerbaijan	1	11	9%

..And the Most Successful Semi-Finalists

Country	Failures	Appearances	Success Rate
Ukraine	0	11	100%
Australia	0	4	100%

The Best Semi-Final to Compete In
(Analysis of Semi-Finalists since the introduction of the two Semi-Finals in 2008)

Year	Winner	Second	Third	Last place
2008	Semi-final 1	Semi-final 2	Semi-final 1	n/a (United Kingdom)
2009	Semi-final 2	Semi-final 1	Semi-final 2	Semi-final 1
2010	n/a (Germany)	Semi-final 2	Semi-final 2	n/a (United Kingdom)
2011	Semi-final 1	n/a (Italy)	Semi-final 2	Semi-final 1
2012	Semi-final 2	Semi-final 1	Semi-final 2	Semi-final 2
2013	Semi-final 1	Semi-final 2	Semi-final 1	Semi-final 1
2014	Semi-final 2	Semi-final 1	Semi-final 1	n/a (France)
2015	Semi-final 2	Semi-final 1	n/a (Italy)	n/a (Germany)
2016	Semi-final 2	Semi-final 2	Semi-final 1	n/a (Germany)
2017	Semi-final 1	Semi-final 2	Semi-final 1	n/a (Spain)
2018	Semi-final 1	Semi-final 1	Semi-final 1	n/a (Portugal)
2019	Semi-final 2	n/a (Italy)	Semi-final 2	n/a (United Kingdom)

Year	Average points received in the Final by SF Qualifiers		Average position in Final by SF Qualifiers	
	Semi-final 1	Semi-final 2	Semi-final 1	Semi-final 2
2008	133	87	10	13
2009	83	118	14	11
2010	69	113	15	10
2011	87	110	15	11
2012	82	113	15	12
2013	101	100	13	12
2014	111	76	10	14
2015	87	93	12	12
2016	163	245	15	10
2017	242	183	12	13
2018	254	134	10	14
2019	279	124	14	8

The Best Semi-Final to Compete In
(Analysis of Semi-Finalists since the introduction of the two Semi-Finals in 2008)

Winner's position in the Semi-finals

Year	Winner	Position in SF
2008	Russia	3rd
2009	Norway	1st
2010	Germany	n/a
2011	Azerbaijan	2nd
2012	Sweden	1st
2013	Denmark	1st
2014	Austria	1st
2015	Sweden	1st
2016	Ukraine	2nd
2017	Portugal	1st
2018	Israel	1st
2019	Netherlands	1st

Performance by SF Winners in Final

Semi-final winners	Finished in Final
Greece & Ukraine	3rd & 2nd
Iceland & Norway	2nd & 1st
Belgium & Turkey	6th & 2nd
Greece & Sweden	7th & 3rd
Russia & Sweden	2nd & 1st
Denmark & Azerbaijan	1st & 2nd
Netherlands & Austria	2nd & 1st
Russia & Sweden	2nd & 1st
Russia & Australia	3rd & 2nd
Portugal & Bulgaria	1st & 2nd
Israel & Norway	1st & 15th
Australia & Netherlands	9th & 1st

Most semi-final consecutive failures

Country	Number of Years	Last Final appearance*
Andorra	6	Never qualified
Slovakia	4	Never qualified
Montenegro	4	2015
Monaco	3	Never qualified
Georgia	3	2016
Latvia	3	2016
Romania	2	2017
Bosnia & H	1	2012
Poland	2	2017
Armenia	2	2017
Belgium	2	2017
Croatia	2	2017
Hungary	1	2018
Portugal	1	2018
Finland	1	2018
Lithuania	1	2018
Moldova	1	2018
Austria	1	2018
Ireland	1	2018

This year saw the qualification for the Final by these countries for the first time for at least 3 years:

Country	Last Final appearance*
Nth Macedonia	2012
San Marino	2014
Switzerland	2014
Iceland	2014
Malta	2016

* Includes only the years when semi-finals were held.

Eurovision 2019: Jinxed Semi-finalists

Do countries despair when they've been drawn in their 'unlucky' semi-final?

Country	2008	2009	2010	2011	2012	2013	2014	2015	2016	2017	2018	2019	Appearances in: SF1	SF2	Qualification %: SF1	SF2	Difference
Finland	1	1	1	1	1	2	2	1	1	1	1	1	10	2	40%	100%	60%
Czech Republic	2	1	-	-	-	-	-	2	1	1	1	1	5	2	60%	0%	60%
Lithuania	2	2	2	1	2	1	2	2	2	2	1	2	3	9	100%	44%	56%
Turkey	2	1	2	1	2	-	-	-	-	-	-	-	2	3	50%	100%	50%
Ireland	1	2	2	2	1	1	2	2	2	2	1	2	4	8	75%	25%	50%
Russia	1	AQ	1	1	1	1	1	1	1	-	2	2	8	2	100%	50%	50%
Cyprus	2	2	2	2	1	1	-	2	1	1	1	1	6	5	83%	40%	43%
Norway	1	2	AQ	1	2	2	2	2	2	2	2	2	2	9	50%	89%	39%
Latvia	2	2	1	2	1	2	1	2	2	1	2	2	4	8	0%	38%	38%
Montenegro	1	1	-	-	1	1	1	2	1	1	2	1	8	2	13%	50%	38%
San Marino	1	-	-	1	1	2	1	2	1	2	2	1	6	4	33%	0%	33%
Romania	1	1	2	2	1	2	2	1	-	2	2	2	4	7	100%	71%	29%
Austria	-	-	-	2	1	1	2	AQ	1	2	1	2	4	4	50%	75%	25%
Moldova	1	2	1	2	1	1	1	1	1	1	2	2	8	4	50%	75%	25%
Slovenia	1	2	2	2	2	1	2	2	2	1	2	1	4	8	25%	50%	25%
Croatia	2	2	2	1	2	1	-	-	1	2	1	2	4	6	25%	50%	25%
Estonia	1	2	2	2	1	2	1	1	1	2	1	1	8	4	50%	75%	25%
Bosnia-H	1	1	1	2	2	-	-	-	1	-	-	-	4	2	75%	100%	25%
Nth Macedonia	2	1	1	2	2	2	2	1	2	2	1	2	4	8	0%	25%	25%
Hungary	2	2	-	1	1	2	1	1	1	2	2	1	6	5	83%	60%	23%
Greece	1	2	1	1	1	2	2	1	1	1	1	1	9	3	78%	100%	22%
Bulgaria	2	1	2	2	2	2	-	-	2	2	1	-	2	7	50%	29%	21%
Denmark	2	2	2	2	1	1	AQ	1	2	2	2	2	3	8	67%	88%	21%
Serbia	AQ	2	1	1	2	1	-	1	2	2	2	1	5	5	80%	60%	20%
Poland	1	2	1	1	-	-	2	2	2	1	2	1	5	5	40%	60%	20%
Israel	1	1	2	2	1	2	2	2	2	2	1	AQ	4	7	75%	57%	18%
Netherlands	1	2	2	2	2	1	1	1	1	2	2	2	5	7	60%	43%	17%
Portugal	2	1	1	1	2	-	1	2	-	1	AQ	1	6	3	50%	33%	17%
Belarus	2	1	1	2	2	1	2	1	2	2	1	1	6	6	50%	33%	17%
Azerbaijan	1	2	2	1	AQ	2	1	2	1	1	1	2	6	5	83%	100%	17%
Sweden	2	1	2	2	2	AQ	1	2	AQ	1	2	2	3	7	100%	86%	14%
Belgium	1	1	1	2	1	1	1	1	2	1	1	1	10	2	40%	50%	10%
Armenia	1	1	2	1	-	2	1	1	1	1	1	2	8	3	75%	67%	8%
Georgia	2	-	2	1	2	2	2	1	2	1	2	1	4	7	50%	57%	7%
Albania	2	2	1	1	1	2	1	1	2	1	1	2	7	5	57%	60%	3%
Switzerland	2	1	2	1	1	2	2	2	2	2	1	2	4	8	25%	25%	0%
Malta	2	1	1	1	2	2	2	2	1	2	2	2	4	8	50%	50%	0%
Iceland	2	1	1	1	1	2	1	2	1	1	1	1	9	3	67%	67%	0%
Slovakia	-	2	1	2	2	-	-	-	-	-	-	-	1	3	0%	0%	0%
Ukraine	2	2	2	2	2	1	1	-	2	AQ	2	-	2	7	100%	100%	0%
Australia	-	-	-	-	-	-	-	-	2	1	2	1	2	2	100%	100%	0%
Andorra	1	1	-	-	-	-	-	-	-	-	-	-	2	0	0%	-	-

Qualification shown in **bold**.

Performance of the "Big 5"

Since automatic qualification to the final was introduced in 2004.

Contest	Countries in Final		France		Germany		Spain		United Kingdom		Italy	
Final	Voting	Max pts	Points	% of max	Points	% of max	Points	% of max	Points	% of max	Points	% of max
2004	36	420	40	10%	93	22%	87	21%	29	7%	-	0%
2005	39	456	11	2%	4	1%	28	6%	18	4%	-	0%
2006	38	444	5	1%	36	8%	18	4%	25	6%	-	0%
2007	42	492	19	4%	49	10%	43	9%	19	4%	-	0%
2008	43	504	47	9%	14	3%	55	11%	14	3%	-	0%
2009	42	492	107	22%	35	7%	23	5%	173	35%	-	0%
2010	38	444	82	18%	246	55%	68	15%	10	2%	-	0%
2011	43	504	82	16%	107	21%	50	10%	100	20%	189	38%
2012	42	492	21	4%	110	22%	97	20%	12	2%	101	21%
2013	39	456	14	3%	18	4%	8	2%	23	5%	126	28%
2014	37	432	2	0%	39	9%	74	17%	40	9%	33	8%
2015	40	468	4	1%	0	0%	15	3%	5	1%	292	62%
2016	42	984	257	26%	11	1%	77	8%	62	6%	124	13%
2017	42	984	135	14%	6	1%	5	1%	111	11%	334	34%
2018	42	984	173	18%	340	35%	61	6%	48	5%	308	31%
2019	41	960	105	11%	24	3%	54	6%	11	1%	472	49%

The Best & Worst Positions in the Order of Performance: 1975-2015

(Finals only. From the introduction of the modern points system in 1975 until the change to two sets of votes in 2016.)

Running Order	Points received and frequency awarded (Finals only)												Total Points		Average Points	
	0 pts	1 pt	2 pts	3 pts	4 pts	5 pts	6 pts	7 pts	8 pts	10 pts	12 pts	Any	Points	Rank	Av Pts	Rank
1	617	60	42	54	58	48	45	43	46	48	46	490	2749	10	2.483	16
2	765	45	32	32	36	43	37	37	37	20	23	342	1817	24	1.641	26
3	680	55	46	49	44	36	38	44	40	38	37	427	2330	15	2.105	20
4	681	41	44	51	51	43	51	41	34	40	30	426	2326	16	2.101	21
5	689	48	48	41	44	44	43	40	40	29	41	418	2303	19	2.080	24
6	699	39	50	51	36	41	47	32	47	35	30	408	2233	21	2.017	25
7	635	46	61	51	50	45	51	48	35	52	33	472	2584	13	2.334	18
8	656	41	59	46	47	58	38	48	40	41	33	451	2465	14	2.227	19
9	622	48	57	53	44	44	35	48	56	49	51	485	2813	8	2.541	14
10	581	35	49	35	57	63	45	55	61	57	69	526	3322	3	3.001	6
11	613	50	48	50	48	65	53	53	43	39	45	494	2776	9	2.508	15
12	606	53	51	47	48	39	55	46	51	65	46	501	2945	4	2.660	11
13	641	46	39	36	54	43	39	50	47	59	53	466	2849	6	2.574	13
14	626	53	42	50	58	42	52	47	39	58	40	481	2742	11	2.477	17
15	693	52	39	46	31	51	37	44	39	35	40	414	2319	17	2.095	22
16	691	45	44	41	40	47	46	47	41	32	34	417	2312	18	2.087	23
17	571	44	44	38	46	50	63	63	54	55	79	536	3429	1	3.098	3
18	537	46	53	71	51	53	68	61	59	51	57	570	3335	2	3.013	5
19	559	50	49	45	53	41	55	42	61	48	50	494	2892	5	2.746	9
20	516	34	48	43	38	34	29	47	41	60	68	442	2828	7	2.952	7
21	466	49	37	40	46	42	51	43	38	30	36	412	2280	20	2.597	12
22	428	42	39	48	37	46	30	34	46	52	55	429	2608	12	3.043	4
23	400	39	28	32	47	34	41	34	36	44	33	368	2157	22	2.809	8
24	292	25	29	30	27	30	27	27	42	42	47	326	2102	23	3.401	2
25	250	14	22	21	12	19	22	23	23	25	20	201	1231	25	2.729	10
26	149	5	5	4	4	4	3	4	3	1	2	35	167	27	0.908	27
27	1	2	2	2	0	2	6	6	8	2	9	39	292	26	7.300	1
First 3	2062	160	120	135	138	127	120	124	123	106	106	1259	6896		2.076	
Top Half	311	528	562	537	544	539	513	522	516	489	465	5213	29457		5.333	
Bottom Half	369	579	546	571	564	569	594	585	591	618	642	5857	34749		5.581	
Last 3	1651	142	140	156	144	167	160	166	184	190	211	1660	10327		3.119	
Last	565	40	51	43	49	47	44	56	60	58	72	520	3282		3.025	

Notes:

The change to the way points were awarded in the 2016 Contest, meaning that the number of points was effectively been doubled, made comparisons with previous years almost meaningless. A simple inclusion of the total points awarded from 2016 onwards would distort the statistics calculated under the old system. We have therefore presented two sets of figures, one for the "old" scoring system from 1975 to 2015 and one for 2016 onwards under the new scoring system.

The average points awarded figure has been recalculated to take account of the times no votes were given.

Countries performing second in the running order have received no votes from individual countries 765 times, making it by far the worst place to perform. In fact, performing in the first 3 is pretty much fatal for your chances, compared to performing in the last 3.

On average the act performing first has received the 16th highest average votes and the act performing last has received the 5th highest average votes.

Performing in the second half of the contest remains a big advantage, with three of the top five acts this year performing in the last five places in the running order.

Best & Worst Positions in the Order of Performance: 2016 onwards

(Finals only. Since the change to the points system in 2016.)

Running Order	Frequency each points score was awarded																
	0 pts	1 pt	2 pts	3 pts	4 pts	5 pts	6 pts	7 pts	8 pts	9 pts	10 pts	11 pts	12 pts	13 pts	14 pts	15 pts	16 pts
1	99	8	4	5	10	8	3	5	8	1	5	1	5	0	2	1	2
2	115	11	10	6	4	3	4	6	1	0	4	0	0	1	1	1	0
3	86	11	6	12	11	6	7	10	7	0	3	0	5	0	2	0	0
4	96	13	7	9	4	6	7	7	4	2	4	0	4	0	0	1	2
5	56	9	10	12	9	8	4	7	10	1	7	2	7	8	1	3	3
6	70	8	7	11	13	9	5	11	8	5	6	0	8	1	0	1	2
7	66	8	7	10	6	9	8	13	14	3	8	1	3	2	2	0	2
8	56	9	11	6	12	9	7	13	7	1	8	2	9	4	3	2	1
9	54	11	14	7	6	5	10	10	4	1	6	4	7	2	4	6	1
10	118	4	6	8	6	5	2	4	4	0	4	0	3	1	1	0	0
11	40	9	3	10	7	5	7	7	10	1	6	3	3	7	5	3	4
12	53	8	5	2	8	14	7	10	2	5	16	3	8	2	3	5	5
13	72	6	4	6	6	9	10	3	3	8	4	5	5	3	2	8	1
14	80	6	4	7	12	11	6	11	7	3	7	5	3	1	3	1	0
15	79	3	10	3	6	9	5	7	6	2	13	3	9	1	1	1	1
16	114	7	11	4	3	3	3	6	5	1	4	1	2	0	1	1	1
17	85	7	10	12	4	7	8	10	6	2	4	2	5	2	1	1	1
18	63	10	7	5	7	10	11	6	11	1	9	3	5	1	7	3	0
19	108	9	7	3	5	4	10	4	5	1	3	3	1	0	0	1	0
20	36	5	11	10	11	9	13	13	18	1	12	7	10	3	0	2	2
21	81	6	10	11	6	6	4	4	5	0	11	0	4	2	0	3	0
22	56	6	4	4	8	7	6	9	6	3	9	4	2	6	2	5	7
23	80	6	4	8	6	13	6	6	11	3	6	1	4	3	4	0	0
24	35	10	7	11	18	7	11	13	10	5	5	7	8	3	8	2	4
25	39	3	9	8	7	3	4	8	11	2	9	6	4	6	12	6	5
26	64	7	11	6	12	12	9	10	4	1	11	3	7	0	3	1	1
First 3	300	30	20	23	25	17	14	21	16	1	12	1	10	1	5	2	2
Top Half	981	115	94	104	102	96	81	106	82	28	81	21	67	31	26	31	23
Bottom Half	920	85	105	92	105	101	96	107	105	25	103	45	64	28	42	18	22
Last 3	138	20	27	25	37	22	24	33	34	8	25	16	19	0	0	0	0
Last	64	7	11	6	12	12	9	10	10	1	11	3	7	0	0	0	0

Notes:

Now that we've had 4 contests using the new scoring system, it is easier to see trends emerging. Perhaps not surprisingly, the best and worst places in the running order are already similar to those under the previous system. Performing 2nd is still the worst, although it does not hold the award for receiving votes the least number of times - that belongs to 10th place.

Perform 24th and you can expect to receive some votes more times than any other place in the line-up.

If you perform in the bottom half, you are likely to score 6% more points than in the top half, and performing last so far has scored 21% more than being the first to perform.

The Best & Worst Positions in the Order of Performance: 2016 onwards

(Finals only. Since the change to the points system in 2016.)

Running Order	Frequency each points score was awarded							Total Points		Average Points	
	17 pts	18 pts	19 pts	20 pts	22 pts	24 pts	Any	Points	Rank	Av Pts	Rank
1	0	0	0	0	0	1	70	457	20	2.70	20
2	0	0	0	1	0	0	55	256	26	1.51	26
3	0	1	0	1	0	0	85	457	20	2.67	21
4	1	0	0	0	1	0	76	415	22	2.41	22
5	3	4	0	2	1	1	117	899	8	5.20	7
6	0	2	1	0	0	0	104	639	17	3.67	16
7	0	2	0	3	1	0	109	730	15	4.17	12
8	1	3	0	1	1	2	120	851	10	4.84	10
9	0	6	1	4	3	2	123	977	7	5.52	5
10	0	1	0	0	0	1	60	306	25	1.72	24
11	4	5	3	10	6	10	139	1464	1	8.18	1
12	5	3	1	2	1	0	127	1031	4	5.73	4
13	5	3	1	1	0	3	109	886	9	4.90	9
14	0	0	0	1	0	0	102	585	18	3.21	18
15	3	2	1	1	0	2	104	749	12	4.09	13
16	0	1	0	0	0	0	70	315	24	1.71	25
17	0	1	0	0	0	0	100	509	19	2.75	19
18	1	2	2	0	2	2	123	844	11	4.54	11
19	0	0	2	0	0	2	79	385	23	2.06	23
20	1	0	1	1	0	2	152	990	6	5.27	6
21	1	3	3	2	4	2	108	738	14	3.90	14
22	6	6	2	2	4	4	134	1190	3	6.26	3
23	1	2	0	0	3	1	111	677	16	3.54	17
24	1	1	0	0	1	1	157	995	5	5.18	8
25	4	9	3	5	2	3	154	1397	2	7.24	2
26	0	2	0	1	1	2	130	746	13	3.85	15
First 3	0	1	0	2	0	1	210	1170		2.294	
Top Half	19	30	7	25	14	20	1203	9368		4.289	
Bottom Half	18	29	14	13	17	21	1255	9985		4.591	
Last 3	0	0	0	0	0	0	290	1532		3.579	
Last	0	0	0	0	0	0	99	553		3.393	

vision Winners & Losers by Order of Performance

By Contest Year

Contest	Finalists	Position in Running Order			
		Winner	Second	Third	Last
1975	19	1	9	19	13
1976	18	1	17	16	18
1977	18	18	9	1	13
1978	20	18	10	6	2
1979	19	10	19	11	18
1980	19	17	12	13	10
1981	20	14	3	9	13
1982	18	18	15	7	6
1983	20	20	16	4	6 & 7
1984	19	1	9	4	13
1985	19	13	10	16	8
1986	20	13	10	1	5
1987	22	20	16	7	10
1988	21	9	4	13	12
1989	22	22	7	12	20
1990	22	19	14	17	9
1991	22	8	9	15	6
1992	23	17	16	10	12
1993	25	14	19	4	7
1994	25	3	24	14	16
1995	23	5	9	18	3
1996	23	17	12	23	18
1997	25	24	5	2	3
1998	25	8	16	10	5
1999	23	15	13	21	3
2000	24	14	9	21	10
2001	23	20	23	22	4
2002	24	23	20	2	14
2003	26	4	22	11	15
2004	24	10	5	16	3
2005	24	19	3	4	17
2006	24	17	10	13	7
2007	24	17	18	15	4
2008	25	24	18	21	2
2009	25	20	7	11	24
2010	25	22	14	19	12
2011	25	19	12	7	13
2012	26	17	6	24	12
2013	26	18	20	22	26
2014	26	11	24	13	14
2015	27	10	25	27	17
2016	26	21	13	18	10
2017	26	11	25	7	16
2018	26	22	25	5	8
2019	26	12	22	5	16

(Since the introduction of the modern points scoring system in 1975)

By Position in Running Order

Running Order	Number of times:	
	Winner	Last
1	3	0
2	0	2
3	1	4
4	1	2
5	1	2
6	0	3
7	0	3
8	2	2
9	1	1
10	3	4
11	2	0
12	1	4
13	2	5
14	3	2
15	1	1
16	0	3
17	6	2
18	4	3
19	3	0
20	4	1
21	1	0
22	3	0
23	1	0
24	2	1
25	0	0
26	0	1
27	0	0

This was the first time a country performing 12th has won the contest.

Double Douze! Countries receiving the maximum 24 points in a Final since 2016

Country	Contest	Performer	24 points	Out of	%	Position
Portugal	2017	Salvador Sobral	7	41	17%	1
Ukraine	2016	Jamala	2	41	5%	1
Australia	2016	Dami Im	2	41	5%	2
Bulgaria	2017	Kristian Kostov	2	41	5%	2
Russia	2016	Sergey Lazarev	2	41	5%	3
Italy	2017	Francesco Gabbani	2	41	5%	6
Israel	2018	Netta	2	42	5%	1
Germany	2018	Michael Schulte	2	42	5%	4
Italy	2019	Mahmood	2	42	5%	2
Sweden	2017	Robin Bengtsson	1	41	2%	5
Armenia	2016	Iveta Mukuchyan	1	41	2%	7
Romania	2017	Ilinca ft. Alex Florea	1	41	2%	7
Hungary	2017	Joci Pápai	1	41	2%	8
Belgium	2016	Laura Tesoro	1	41	2%	10
Greece	2017	Demy	1	41	2%	19
Cyprus	2017	Hovig	1	41	2%	21
Cyprus	2018	Eleni Foureira	1	42	2%	2
Denmark	2018	Rasmussen	1	42	2%	9
Italy	2018	Ermal Meta & Fabrizio Moro	1	42	2%	5
Moldova	2018	DoReDoS	1	42	2%	10
Serbia	2018	Sanja Ilić & Balkanika	1	42	2%	19
Russia	2019	Sergey Lazarev	1	42	2%	3
North Macedonia	2019	Tamara Todevska	1	42	2%	7
Cyprus	2019	Tamta	1	42	2%	13
Greece	2019	Katerine Duska	1	42	2%	21
Azerbaijan	2019	Chingiz	1	42	2%	8
Serbia	2019	Nevena Božović	1	42	2%	18

Quadruple Douze! When juries & public both gave maximum points in semi-finals & finals in 2019

Voting country	Points given to	Jury (SF)	Public (SF)	Jury (F)	Public (F)
Greece	Cyprus	12	12	12	12

Are You Sure? Countries whose juries gave the complete opposite to their voting public in 2019

Voting country	Points given to	By jury	By public	SF/Final
Hungary	Belarus	12	0	Semi-final 1
Israel	Greece	12	0	Semi-final 1
Russia	Romania	12	0	Semi-final 2
Italy	Denmark	12	0	Semi-final 2
United Kingdom	North Macedonia	12	0	Semi-final 2
Belarus	Malta	12	0	Final
Georgia	Czech Republic	12	0	Final
Hungary	Czech Republic	12	0	Final
Norway	Czech Republic	12	0	Final
Slovenia	Czech Republic	12	0	Final
Austria	North Macedonia	12	0	Final
Moldova	North Macedonia	12	0	Final
United Kingdom	North Macedonia	12	0	Final
Czech Republic	Sweden	12	0	Final
Estonia	Finland	0	12	Semi-final 1
France	Portugal	0	12	Semi-final 1
Spain	Portugal	0	12	Semi-final 1
Czech Republic	San Marino	0	12	Semi-final 1
Georgia	San Marino	0	12	Semi-final 1
Hungary	San Marino	0	12	Semi-final 1
Malta	Switzerland	0	12	Semi-final 2
Ireland	Lithuania	0	12	Semi-final 2
Norway	Lithuania	0	12	Semi-final 2
United Kingdom	Lithuania	0	12	Semi-final 2
Switzerland	Albania	0	12	Semi-final 2
Albania	Norway	0	12	Semi-final 2
Netherlands	Norway	0	12	Semi-final 2
Czech Republic	Russia	0	12	Final
Israel	Russia	0	12	Final
France	Israel	0	12	Final
Australia	Norway	0	12	Final
Iceland	Norway	0	12	Final
Netherlands	Norway	0	12	Final
United Kingdom	Norway	0	12	Final
Finland	Iceland	0	12	Final
Hungary	Iceland	0	12	Final

Highest number of 12 points scored by one entry

1. Under the old scoring system from 1975 to 2015, including semi-finals.

Country	Contest	Performer	12 points	Out of	%	Position
Portugal	2017 Final (Jury)	Salvadore Sobral	18	41	44%	1
Sweden	2012 Final	Loreen	18	41	44%	1
Norway	2009 Final	Alexander Rybak	16	41	39%	1
Sweden	2015 Semi	Måns Zelmerlöw	14	20	70%	1
Austria	2014 Final	Conchita Wurst	13	36	36%	1
Sweden	2015 Final	Måns Zelmerlöw	12	39	31%	1
United Kingdom	1997	Katrina and The Waves	10	24	42%	1
Azerbaijan	2013 Final	Farid Mammadov	10	38	26%	2
Greece	2005 Final	Helena Paparizou	10	38	26%	1
Germany	1982	Nicole	9	17	53%	1
Estonia	2001	Tanel Padar, Dave Benton & 2XL	9	22	41%	1
Serbia & Montenegro	2004 Semi	Željko Joksimović	9	35	26%	1
Bosnia & Herzegovina	2006 Semi	Hari Mata Hari	9	37	24%	2
Germany	2010 Final	Lena Meyer-Landrut	9	38	24%	1
Italy	2015 Final	Il Volo	9	39	23%	3
Serbia	2007 Semi	Marija Šerifović	9	41	22%	1
Serbia	2007 Final	Marija Šerifović	9	41	22%	1

2. Under the current scoring system from 2016 onwards, including semi-finals, with separate jury and public scores.

Country	Contest	Performer	12 points	Out of	%	Position
Portugal	2017 Final (Jury)	Salvadore Sobral	18	41	44%	1
Portugal	2017 Final (Public)	Salvadore Sobral	12	41	29%	1
Russia	2019 Final (Public)	Sergey Lazarev	11	40	28%	3
Ukraine	2016 Final (Jury)	Jamala	11	41	27%	2
Sweden	2019 Final (Public)	John Lundvik	10	40	25%	5
Russia	2016 Final (Public)	Sergey Lazarev	10	41	24%	1
Portugal	2017 Semi (Public)	Salvadore Sobral	9	20	45%	1
Australia	2016 Semi (Jury)	Dami Im	9	20	45%	1
Sweden	2018 Semi (Jury)	Benjamin Ingrosso	9	20	45%	1
Australia	2016 Final (Jury)	Dami Im	9	41	22%	1
Austria	2018 Final (Jury)	Cesár Sampson	9	42	21%	3
Norway	2019 Final (Public)	KEiiNO	8	40	20%	6
Israel	2018 Final (Public)	Netta	8	42	19%	1
Sweden	2018 Final (Jury)	Benjamin Ingrosso	8	42	19%	7

Final winners with the lowest number of 12 points

Country	Contest	Performer	12 points	Out of	%
Netherlands	2019 (Public)	Duncan Laurence	2	40	5%
United Kingdom	1981	Bucks Fizz	2	19	11%
Azerbaijan	2011	Ell/Nikki	3	42	7%
Israel	1998	Dana International	3	24	13%
Ireland	1992	Linda Martin	3	22	14%
Italy	1990	Toto Cutugno	3	21	14%
Switzerland	1988	Céline Dion	3	20	15%
France	1977	Marie Myriam	3	17	18%
Turkey	2003	Sertab Erener	4	25	16%
Yugoslavia	1989	Riva	4	21	19%
Sweden	1991	Carola	4	21	19%
Latvia	2002	Marie N	5	23	22%
Sweden	1999	Charlotte Nilsson	5	22	23%
Belgium	1986	Sandra Kim	5	19	26%
Sweden	1984	Herrey's	5	18	28%

Maximum/Most Points: Recent Final History

Who has received the maximum/most points from each country in Finals in the last 10 years? As the 12 point maximum no longer applies from 2016, the recipient of the most points is shown. Double 12 recipients are highlighted in **bold**, those countries who received the maximum 12 points from the jury and public televoting of the same country.

Voting country	Oslo 2010	Düsseldorf 2011	Baku 2012	Malmö 2013	Copenhagen 2014	Vienna 2015	Stockholm 2016	Kiev 2017	Lisbon 2018	Tel Aviv 2019
Albania	Greece	Italy	Greece	Italy	Spain	Italy	**Australia**	**Italy**	**Italy**	North Macedonia
Andorra	-	-	-	-	-	-	-	-	-	-
Armenia	Georgia	Ukraine	-	Ukraine	Montenegro	Russia	France	Portugal	Cyprus	Russia
Australia	-	-	-	-	-	Sweden	**Belgium**	Moldova	Israel	Sweden
Austria	-	Bosnia & H	Sweden	Azerbaijan	Armenia	Australia	Sweden & Aus	Portugal	Israel	Switzerland
Azerbaijan	Turkey	Ukraine	Turkey	Ukraine	Russia	Russia	**Russia**	Moldova	Ukraine & Cyprus	**Russia**
Belarus	Russia	Georgia	Russia	Ukraine	Russia	Russia	**Russia**	**Bulgaria**	Cyprus	Netherlands
Belgium	Greece	France	Sweden	Netherlands	Austria	Sweden	France & Aus	Portugal	Netherlands	Italy
Bosnia & H	Serbia	Slovenia	FYR Macedonia	-	-	-	Serbia	-	-	-
Bulgaria	Azerbaijan	United Kingdom	Serbia	Azerbaijan	-	-	Armenia	Austria & France	Austria	-
Croatia	Turkey	Slovenia	Serbia	Ukraine	-	-	Australia	**Hungary**	Israel	**Italy**
Cyprus	Greece	Greece	Greece	Greece	-	Italy	Russia	**Greece**	Italy	**Greece**
Czech Rep	-	-	-	-	-	Azerbaijan	Sweden	Portugal	Israel	Russ, Swe & Aze
Denmark	Germany	Ireland	Sweden	Norway	Sweden	Sweden	Australia	**Sweden**	**Germany**	Sweden
Estonia	Germany	Sweden	Sweden	Russia	Netherlands	Russia	Sweden	Bulgaria	Lithuania	Russia
Finland	Germany	Hungary	Sweden	Norway	Austria	Sweden	Sweden	Portugal	Israel	Sweden
France	Turkey	Spain	Sweden	Denmark	Armenia	Belgium	Austria	Portugal	**Israel**	Italy
Georgia	Belarus	Lithuania	Lithuania	Azerbaijan	Armenia	Armenia	Ukraine	Azerbaijan	Estonia	Cyprus
Germany	Belgium	Austria	Sweden	Hungary	Netherlands	Russia	Sweden	Portugal	Austria & Ireland	Italy
Greece	Cyprus	France	Cyprus	Azerbaijan	Austria	Italy	Russia	**Cyprus**	**Cyprus**	**Cyprus**
Hungary	-	Iceland	Sweden	Azerbaijan	Netherlands	Belgium	Australia	Bulgaria	**Denmark**	Czech & Iceland
Iceland	Denmark	Denmark	Sweden	Denmark	Netherlands	Sweden	Swe, Neth & Aus	**Portugal**	Austria	Swe & Australia
Ireland	Denmark	Denmark	Sweden	Denmark	Austria	Latvia	Bulgaria	Romania	Cyprus	Norway
Israel	Armenia	Sweden	Sweden	Azerbaijan	Austria	Italy	France & Ukraine	**Portugal**	Austria	Italy
Italy	-	Romania	Albania	Denmark	Austria	Sweden	Ukraine	Moldova	Germany	Albania
Latvia	Germany	Italy	Sweden	Russia	Netherlands	Sweden	Ukraine	Port & Belgium	Estonia	Netherlands
Lithuania	Georgia	Georgia	Azerbaijan	Azerbaijan	Netherlands	Latvia	Latvia	**Portugal**	Austria & France	Netherlands
Malta	Azerbaijan	Azerbaijan	Azerbaijan	Azerbaijan	Italy	Italy	Bulgaria	**Italy**	Cyprus & Italy	**Italy**
Moldova	Romania	Romania	Romania	Ukraine	Romania	Romania	Ukraine	Romania	Israel	Russia

Maximum/Most Points: Recent Final History

Who has received the maximum/most points from each country in Finals in the last 10 years? As the 12 point maximum no longer applies from 2016, the recipients of the most points is shown. Double 12 recipients are highlighted in bold, those countries who received the maximum 12 points from the jury and public televoting of the same country.

Voting country	Oslo 2010	Düsseldorf 2011	Baku 2012	Malmö 2013	Copenhagen 2014	Vienna 2015	Stockholm 2016	Kiev 2017	Lisbon 2018	Tel Aviv 2019
Montenegro	-	-	Serbia	Azerbaijan	Hungary	Serbia	Serbia & Russia	Italy	**Serbia**	**Serbia**
Netherlands	Armenia	Denmark	Sweden	Belgium	Austria	Belgium	Australia	**Portugal**	**Germany**	Sweden
North Macedonia	Albania	Bosnia & H	Albania	Denmark	Montenegro	Albania	Bulgaria	**Bulgaria**	Serb, Alb & Cyp	Albania
Norway	Finland	Denmark	Sweden	Sweden	Netherlands	Sweden	Australia	Portugal	Germany	Sweden
Poland	Denmark	Lithuania	-	-	Netherlands	Sweden	**Ukraine**	Port & Belgium	Ukraine & Austria	Australia
Portugal	Spain	Spain	Spain	-	Austria	Italy	-	Mold & Belgium	Estonia	Netherlands
Romania	Denmark	Moldova	Moldova	Moldova	Sweden	Italy	-	Moldova	**Moldova**	Netherlands
Russia	Armenia	Azerbaijan	Sweden	Azerbaijan	Belarus	Italy	**Armenia**	-	**Israel**	**Azerbaijan**
San Marino	-	Italy	Albania	Greece	Azerbaijan	Latvia	**Ukraine**	Portugal	Italy	Russia
Serbia	Bosnia & H	Bosnia & H	FYR Macedonia	Denmark	-	Montenegro	Ukraine	Hungary	-	**North Macedonia**
Slovakia	Germany	Ukraine	Sweden	-	-	-	-	-	-	-
Slovenia	Denmark	Bosnia & H	Serbia	Denmark	Austria	Sweden	Ukraine	Portugal	Cyprus	Italy
Spain	Germany	Italy	Sweden	Italy	Austria	Italy	Armenia	**Portugal**	Israel	Sweden
Sweden	Germany	Ireland	Cyprus	Norway	Austria	Australia	**Australia**	Portugal	Israel	Netherlands
Switzerland	Germany	Bosnia & H	Albania	Italy	Austria	Sweden	Austria	**Portugal**	Germany	Italy
Turkey	Azerbaijan	Azerbaijan	Azerbaijan	-	-	-	-	-	-	-
Ukraine	Azerbaijan	Georgia	Azerbaijan	Belarus	Sweden	-	Azerbaijan	Port & Belarus	Israel	-
United Kingdom	Greece	Ireland	Sweden	Denmark	Austria	Sweden	Lithuania	Portugal	Israel	Australia

Number of times the winner received the most votes from each country:

| 8 | 3 | 18 | 8 | 13 | 12 | 9 | 20 | 12 | 6 |

Maximum Points: Public & Jury Voting in Finals since 2016

Who has received the maximum 12 points from countries' public and juries each year since the change to the voting system in 2016? Countries whose jury and public awarded 12 points to the same act are highlighted in bold.

Public voting

Voting country	2016	2017	2018	2019
Albania	Australia	Italy	Italy	Russia
Armenia	Russia	Cyprus	Cyprus	Russia
Australia	**Belgium**	Moldova	Israel	Norway
Austria	Poland	Portugal	Czech Rep	Switzerland
Azerbaijan	**Russia**	Bulgaria	Israel	**Russia**
Belarus	**Russia**	**Bulgaria**	Ukraine	Russia
Belgium	Poland	Portugal	Netherlands	Netherlands
Bosnia & H	Serbia	-	-	-
Bulgaria	Russia	France	Cyprus	-
Croatia	Serbia	**Hungary**	Serbia	**Italy**
Cyprus	Bulgaria	Greece	Bulgaria	**Greece**
Czech Rep	Ukraine	Bulgaria	Ukraine	Russia
Denmark	Sweden	**Sweden**	Germany	Norway
Estonia	Russia	Belgium	Lithuania	Russia
Finland	Ukraine	Portugal	Estonia	Iceland
France	Armenia	**Portugal**	**Israel**	Israel
Georgia	Armenia	Azerbaijan	Israel	Cyprus
Germany	Russia	Portugal	Italy	Norway
Greece	Cyprus	**Cyprus**	**Cyprus**	**Cyprus**
Hungary	Ukraine	Bulgaria	**Denmark**	Iceland
Iceland	Sweden	**Portugal**	Denmark	Norway
Ireland	Lithuania	Romania	Lithuania	Norway
Israel	France	**Portugal**	Czech Rep	Russia
Italy	Ukraine	Moldova	Albania	Albania
Latvia	Russia	Belgium	Lithuania	Russia
Lithuania	Latvia	**Portugal**	Estonia	Russia
Malta	Australia	**Italy**	Italy	**Italy**
Moldova	Russia	**Romania**	Israel	Russia
Montenegro	Serbia	Croatia	**Serbia**	Serbia
Netherlands	Belgium	**Portugal**	Germany	Norway
Nth Macedonia	Serbia	**Bulgaria**	Albania	Albania
Norway	Lithuania	Portugal	Lithuania	Sweden
Poland	**Ukraine**	Belgium	Ukraine	Iceland
Portugal	-	Moldova	Spain	Spain
Romania	-	Moldova	Moldova	Netherlands
Russia	Armenia	-	Moldova	Azerbaijan
San Marino	Ukraine	Bulgaria	Israel	Russia
Serbia	Russia	Hungary	Hungary	**N Macedonia**
Slovenia	Serbia	Croatia	Serbia	N Macedonia
Spain	Bulgaria	**Portugal**	Israel	Italy
Sweden	**Australia**	Belgium	Denmark	Norway
Switzerland	Serbia	**Portugal**	Serbia	Italy
Ukraine	Russia	Moldova	Israel	-
United Kingdom	Lithuania	Bulgaria	Lithuania	Norway

Jury voting

Voting country	2016	2017	2018	2019
Albania	Australia	Italy	Italy	N Macedonia
Armenia	France	Portugal	Sweden	Sweden
Australia	**Belgium**	UK	Sweden	Sweden
Austria	Australia	Netherlands	Israel	N Macedonia
Azerbaijan	**Russia**	Belarus	Albania	**Russia**
Belarus	**Russia**	**Bulgaria**	Cyprus	Malta
Belgium	Australia	Sweden	Austria	Italy
Bosnia & H	Ukraine	-	-	-
Bulgaria	Armenia	Austria	Austria	-
Croatia	Australia	**Hungary**	Lithuania	**Italy**
Cyprus	Russia	Greece	Sweden	**Greece**
Czech Rep	Sweden	Portugal	Israel	Sweden
Denmark	Ukraine	**Sweden**	Germany	Sweden
Estonia	Sweden	Bulgaria	Austria	Sweden
Finland	Sweden	Sweden	Israel	Sweden
France	Italy	**Portugal**	**Israel**	Netherlands
Georgia	Ukraine	Portugal	Sweden	Czech Rep
Germany	Israel	Norway	Sweden	Italy
Greece	Russia	**Cyprus**	**Cyprus**	**Cyprus**
Hungary	Australia	Portugal	**Denmark**	Czech Rep
Iceland	Netherlands	**Portugal**	Austria	Sweden
Ireland	Belgium	Belgium	Cyprus	Sweden
Israel	Ukraine	**Portugal**	Austria	Netherlands
Italy	Spain	Azerbaijan	Norway	Denmark
Latvia	Ukraine	Portugal	Sweden	Netherlands
Lithuania	Australia	**Portugal**	Austria	Netherlands
Malta	UK	**Italy**	Cyprus	**Italy**
Moldova	Ukraine	**Romania**	Estonia	N Macedonia
Montenegro	Malta	Greece	**Serbia**	Serbia
Netherlands	Australia	**Portugal**	Germany	Sweden
Nth Macedonia	Ukraine	**Bulgaria**	Estonia	Italy
Norway	Italy	Bulgaria	Germany	Czech Rep
Poland	**Ukraine**	Portugal	Austria	Australia
Portugal	-	Azerbaijan	Estonia	Netherlands
Romania	-	Netherlands	Austria	Australia
Russia	Armenia	-	Moldova	Azerbaijan
San Marino	Ukraine	Portugal	Israel	Italy
Serbia	Ukraine	Portugal	Sweden	**N Macedonia**
Slovenia	Ukraine	Portugal	Sweden	Czech Rep
Spain	Armenia	**Portugal**	Cyprus	Sweden
Sweden	**Australia**	Portugal	Cyprus	Netherlands
Switzerland	Australia	**Portugal**	Germany	N Macedonia
Ukraine	Lithuania	Belarus	France	-
United Kingdom	Georgia	Portugal	Austria	N Macedonia

Eurovision 2019 - Sharing the Love

Which countries spread their votes in the Final around the most?

Voting country	Countries receiving votes	Average points to top 3			Average points to rest		
		Jury	Public	Combined	Jury	Public	Combined
Albania	12	2.00	9.00	11.00	2.26	1.3	3.61
Armenia	13	6.33	9.67	16.00	1.70	1.3	2.96
Australia	13	3.33	3.67	7.00	2.09	2.0	4.13
Austria	13	5.00	7.33	12.33	1.87	1.6	3.43
Azerbaijan	14	5.67	8.33	14.00	1.78	1.4	3.22
Belarus	14	4.67	8.33	13.00	1.91	1.4	3.35
Belgium	13	6.00	7.00	13.00	1.74	1.6	3.35
Croatia	14	6.67	5.33	12.00	1.65	1.8	3.48
Cyprus	13	7.67	8.00	15.67	1.52	1.5	3.00
Czech Republic	14	4.67	6.00	10.67	1.91	1.7	3.65
Denmark	12	3.67	3.33	7.00	2.04	2.1	4.13
Estonia	13	4.33	6.67	11.00	1.96	1.7	3.61
Finland	13	4.33	4.00	8.33	1.96	2.0	3.96
France	13	6.67	6.00	12.67	1.65	1.7	3.39
Georgia	15	2.67	4.67	7.33	2.17	1.9	4.09
Germany	12	6.67	7.00	13.67	1.65	1.6	3.26
Greece	14	5.67	8.00	13.67	1.78	1.5	3.26
Hungary	15	2.67	6.33	9.00	2.17	1.7	3.87
Iceland	13	3.33	3.67	7.00	2.09	2.0	4.13
Ireland	12	4.00	5.67	9.67	2.00	1.8	3.78
Israel	13	7.33	7.33	14.67	1.57	1.6	3.13
Italy	14	0.00	4.33	4.33	2.52	2.0	4.48
Latvia	14	6.00	6.67	12.67	1.74	1.7	3.39
Lithuania	12	5.33	9.67	15.00	1.83	1.3	3.09
Malta	13	9.67	8.67	18.33	1.26	1.4	2.65
Moldova	14	2.67	7.67	10.33	2.17	1.5	3.70
Montenegro	14	4.00	5.33	9.33	2.00	1.8	3.83
Netherlands	13	3.67	3.33	7.00	2.04	2.1	4.13
North Macedonia	13	8.33	3.33	11.67	1.43	2.1	3.52
Norway	13	3.33	5.33	8.67	2.09	1.8	3.91
Poland	14	0.00	6.67	6.67	2.52	1.7	4.17
Portugal	14	6.00	8.33	14.33	1.74	1.4	3.17
Romania	14	3.67	9.00	12.67	2.04	1.3	3.39
Russia	16	0.00	2.00	2.00	2.52	2.3	4.78
San Marino	11	8.33	8.67	17.00	1.43	1.4	2.83
Serbia	16	3.33	6.00	9.33	2.09	1.7	3.83
Slovenia	14	4.67	4.33	9.00	1.91	2.0	3.87
Spain	12	4.67	7.33	12.00	1.91	1.6	3.48
Sweden	13	7.67	3.33	11.00	1.52	2.1	3.61
Switzerland	13	6.00	6.00	12.00	1.74	1.7	3.48
United Kingdom	13	3.33	1.33	4.67	2.09	2.3	4.43

Notes:

We've simplified the table this year, concentrating now on the average points awarded by each country.

So, the combined public and juries of Russia and Serbia this year gave some points to 16 different countries, whereas San Marino focussed their points on just 11 countries.

Poland's jury gave no points to any of the top 3. Neither did Italy and Russa but they were themselves in the top 3.

The UK's public gave an average of 1.33 points to the top 3 but Armenia and Lithuania gave them an average of 9.67 points each.

In this table, "top 3" refers to the final overall standings, so Netherlands, Italy and Russia in 2019.

Eurovision Hosts Performance

Since the introduction of the modern points system in 1975. Two sets of points were awarded from 2016 onwards.

Year	Host Country	Points	% of max	Finished	Out of	Countries voting
1975	Sweden	72	33%	8	19	19
1976	Netherlands	56	27%	9	18	18
1977	United Kingdom	121	59%	2	18	18
1978	France	119	52%	3	20	20
1979	Israel	125	58%	1	19	19
1980	Netherlands	93	43%	5	19	19
1981	Ireland	105	46%	5	20	20
1982	United Kingdom	76	37%	7	18	18
1983	Germany	94	41%	5	20	20
1984	Luxembourg	39	18%	10	19	19
1985	Sweden	103	48%	3	19	19
1986	Norway	44	19%	12	20	20
1987	Belgium	56	22%	11	22	22
1988	Ireland	79	33%	8	21	21
1989	Switzerland	47	19%	13	22	22
1990	Yugoslavia	81	32%	7	22	22
1991	Italy	89	35%	7	22	22
1992	Sweden	9	3%	22	23	23
1993	Ireland	187	65%	1	25	25
1994	Ireland	226	78%	1	25	25
1995	Ireland	44	17%	14	23	23
1996	Norway	114	43%	2	23	23
1997	Ireland	157	55%	2	25	25
1998	United Kingdom	166	58%	2	25	25
1999	Israel	93	35%	5	23	23
2000	Sweden	88	32%	7	24	24
2001	Denmark	177	67%	2	23	23
2002	Estonia	111	40%	4	24	24
2003	Latvia	5	2%	24	26	26
2004	Turkey	195	46%	4	24	36
2005	Ukraine	30	7%	19	24	39
2006	Greece	128	29%	9	24	38
2007	Finland	53	11%	17	24	42
2008	Serbia	160	32%	6	25	43
2009	Russia	91	18%	11	25	42
2010	Norway	35	8%	20	25	39
2011	Germany	107	21%	10	25	43
2012	Azerbaijan	150	30%	4	26	42
2013	Sweden	62	14%	14	26	39
2014	Denmark	74	17%	9	26	37
2015	Austria	0	0%	26	27	40
2016	Sweden	261	27%	5	26	42
2017	Ukraine	36	4%	24	26	42
2018	Portugal	39	4%	26	26	43
2019	Israel	35	4%	23	26	41

(% of max is based on the number of countries voting, less one. It also reflects the maximum possible points that each country can award, 12 from 1975 to 2015 and 24 from 2016 onwards.)

Nul Points! Countries finishing with No Points

1. Under the old scoring system from 1975 to 2015

Year	Country	Performer	Song
1962	Belgium	Fud Leclerc	Ton nom
1962	Spain	Victor Balaguer	Llámame
1962	Austria	Eleonore Schwarz	Nur in der Wiener Luft
1962	Netherlands	De Spelbrekers	Katinka
1963	Netherlands	Annie Palmen	Een speeldoos
1963	Norway	Anita Thallaug	Solhverv
1963	Finland	Laila Halme	Muistojeni laulu
1963	Sweden	Monica Zetterlund	En gång i Stockholm
1964	Germany	Nora Nova	Man gewöhnt sich so schnell an das Schöne
1964	Portugal	António Calvário	Oração
1964	Yugoslavia	Sabahudin Kurt	Život je sklopio krug
1964	Switzerland	Anita Traversi	I miei pensieri
1965	Spain	Conchita Bautista	¡Qué bueno, qué bueno!
1965	Germany	Ulla Wiesner	Paradies, wo bist du?
1965	Belgium	Lize Marke	Als het weer lente is
1965	Finland	Viktor Klimenko	Aurinko laskee länteen
1966	Monaco	Tereza Kesovija	Bien plus fort
1966	Italy	Domenico Modugno	Dio, come ti amo
1967	Switzerland	Géraldine	Quel cœur vas-tu briser?
1970	Luxembourg	David Alexandre Winter	Je suis tombé du ciel
1978	Norway	Jahn Teigen	Mil etter mil
1981	Norway	Finn Kalvik	Aldri i livet
1982	Finland	Kojo	Nuku pommiin
1983	Turkey	Çetin Alp and The Short Waves	Opera
1983	Spain	Remedios Amaya	Quién maneja mi barca?
1987	Turkey	Seyyal Taner and Grup Locomotif	Şarkım Sevgi Üstüne
1988	Austria	Wilfried	Lisa Mona Lisa
1989	Iceland	Daníel Ágúst	Það sem enginn sér
1991	Austria	Thomas Forstner	Venedig im Regen
1994	Lithuania	Ovidijus Vyšniauskas	Lopšinė mylimai
1997	Norway	Tor Endresen	San Francisco
1997	Portugal	Célia Lawson	Antes do adeus
1998	Switzerland	Gunvor	Lass' ihn
2003	United Kingdom	Jemini	Cry Baby
2004 Semi	Switzerland	Piero & The MusicStars	Celebrate
2009 Semi	Czech Republic	Gypsy.cz	Aven Romale
2015	Germany	Ann Sophie	Black Smoke
2015	Austria	The Makemakes	I Am Yours

2. Under the current scoring system from 2016 onwards

Year	Country	Performer	Song
2016 Final (Public)	Czech Republic	Gabriela Gunčíková	I Stand
2017 Final (Jury)	Spain	Manel Navarro	Do It For Your Lover
2017 Final (Public)	Austria	Nathan Trent	Running On Air
2018 Semi (Public)	Iceland	Ari Ólafsson	Our Choice
2019 Semi (Public)	Austria	PÆNDA	Limits
2019 Final (Jury)	Israel	Kobi Marimi	Home
2019 Final (Public)	Germany	S!sters	Sister

Highest Scores in Finals

Including the points awarded by juries and public televoting from 2016 onwards as separate totals:

Year	Country	Performer	Song	Points	Position
2009	Norway	Alexander Rybak	Fairytale	387	1
2017 Juries	Portugal	Salvador Sobral	Amar Pelos Dois	382	1
2017 Public	Portugal	Salvador Sobral	Amar Pelos Dois	376	1
2012	Sweden	Loreen	Euphoria	372	1
2015	Sweden	Måns Zelmerlöw	Heroes	365	1
2016 Public	Russia	Sergey Lazarev	You Are The Only One	361	1
2017 Public	Bulgaria	Kristian Kostov	Beautiful Mess	337	2
2016 Public	Ukraine	Jamala	1944	323	2
2016 Juries	Australia	Dami Im	Sound of Silence	320	1
2018 Public	Israel	Netta	Toy	317	1
2015	Russia	Polina Gagarina	A Million Voices	303	2
2006	Finland	Lordi	Hard Rock Hallelujah	292	1
2015	Italy	Il Volo	Grande Amore	292	3
2014	Austria	Conchita Wurst	Rise Like a Phoenix	290	1
2013	Denmark	Emmelie de Forest	Only Teardrops	281	1
2004	Ukraine	Ruslana	Wild Dances	280	1
2017 Juries	Bulgaria	Kristian Kostov	Beautiful Mess	278	2
2008	Russia	Dima Bilan	Believe	272	1
2018 Juries	Austria	Cesár Sampson	Nobody But You	271	3
2007	Serbia	Marija Šerifovic	Molitva	268	1
2017 Public	Moldova	Sunstroke Project	Hey, Mamma!	264	3
2019 Public	Netherlands	Duncan Laurence	Arcade	261	1

With combined final points totals from 2016 onwards:

Year	Country	Performer	Song	Points	Position
2017	Portugal	Salvador Sobral	Amar Pelos Dois	758	1
2017	Bulgaria	Kristian Kostov	Beautiful Mess	615	2
2016	Ukraine	Jamala	1944	534	1
2018	Israel	Netta	Toy	529	1
2019	Netherlands	Duncan Laurence	Arcade	498	1

Eurovision Winners - Winning Margins

(since the introduction of the modern points system in 1975)

Year	Winner	Points	Runner-up	Points	Winning Margin	Margin as Percentage
2009	Norway	387	Iceland	218	169	78%
1982	Germany	161	Israel	100	61	61%
2010	Germany	246	Turkey	170	76	45%
1997	United Kingdom	227	Ireland	157	70	45%
2012	Sweden	372	Russia	259	113	44%
1996	Ireland	162	Norway	114	48	42%
1994	Ireland	226	Poland	166	60	36%
2000	Denmark	195	Russia	155	40	26%
1986	Belgium	176	Switzerland	140	36	26%
1978	Israel	157	Belgium	125	32	26%
1995	Norway	148	Spain	119	29	24%
2017	Portugal	758	Bulgaria	615	143	23%
1987	Ireland	172	Germany	141	31	22%
2014	Austria	290	Netherlands	238	52	22%
2018	Israel	529	Cyprus	436	93	21%
2015	Sweden	365	Russia	303	62	20%
2013	Denmark	281	Azerbaijan	234	47	20%
2005	Greece	230	Malta	192	38	20%
2008	Russia	272	Ukraine	230	42	18%
2006	Finland	292	Russia	248	44	18%
1985	Norway	123	Germany	105	18	17%
2011	Azerbaijan	221	Italy	189	32	17%
2007	Serbia	268	Ukraine	235	33	14%
1993	Ireland	187	United Kingdom	164	23	14%
1990	Italy	149	France	132	17	13%
1977	France	136	United Kingdom	121	15	12%
2001	Estonia	198	Denmark	177	21	12%
1980	Ireland	143	Germany	128	15	12%
1999	Sweden	163	Iceland	146	17	12%
1976	United Kingdom	164	France	147	17	12%
1992	Ireland	155	United Kingdom	139	16	12%
1975	Netherlands	152	United Kingdom	138	14	10%
1979	Israel	125	Spain	116	9	8%
2002	Latvia	176	Malta	164	12	7%
2019	Netherlands	498	Italy	472	26	6%
2004	Ukraine	280	Serbia & Mont	263	17	6%
1998	Israel	176	United Kingdom	166	10	6%
1984	Sweden	145	Ireland	137	8	6%
1989	Yugoslavia	137	United Kingdom	130	7	5%
2016	Ukraine	534	Australia	511	23	5%
1983	Luxembourg	142	Israel	136	6	4%
1981	United Kingdom	136	Germany	132	4	3%
2003	Turkey	167	Belgium	165	2	1%
1988	Switzerland	137	United Kingdom	136	1	1%
1991	Sweden	146	France	146	0	0%

Performance on Debut

Country	Debut Year	First Artist	Finish
Serbia	2007	Marija Šerifović	Winner
Serbia & Montenegro	2004	Željko Joksimović & Ad-Hoc Orchestra	2nd in final
Belgium	1956	Fud Leclerc	2nd
France	1956	Mathé Altéry	2nd
Germany	1956	Walter Andreas Schwarz	2nd
Italy	1956	Franca Raimondi	2nd
Luxembourg	1956	Michèle Arnaud	2nd
Netherlands	1956	Corry Brokken	2nd
Poland	1994	Edyta Górniak	2nd
Switzerland	1956	Lys Assia	2nd (with first song)
Denmark	1957	Birthe Wilke & Gustav Winckler	3rd
Latvia	2000	Brainstorm	3rd
Hungary	1994	Friderika Bayer	4th
Israel	1973	Ilanit	4th
Norway	1960	Nora Brockstedt	4th
Sweden	1958	Alice Babs	4th
San Marino	2008	Sirusho	4th in final
Australia	2015	Guy Sebastian	5th in final
Cyprus	1981	Island	6th
Ireland	1965	Butch Moore	6th
Moldova	2005	Zdob și Zdub	6th in final
United Kingdom	1957	Patricia Bredin	7th
Albania	2004	Anjeza Shahini	7th in final
Yugoslavia	1961	Ljiljana Petrović	8th
Armenia	2006	André	8th in final
Azerbaijan	2008	Elnur & Samir	8th in final
Russia	1994	Youddiph	9th
Spain	1961	Conchita Bautista	9th
Finland	1961	Laila Kinnunen	10th
Austria	1957	Bob Martin	10th (last)
Greece	1974	Marinella	11th
Monaco	1959	Jacques Pills	11th (last)
Georgia	2007	Sopho	12th in final
Portugal	1964	António Calvário	13th
Ukraine	2003	Olexandr	14th
Croatia	1993	Put	15th
Bosnia & Herzegovina	1993	Fazla	16th
Iceland	1986	ICY	16th
Morocco	1980	Samira Bensaïd	18th
Malta	1971	Joe Grech	18th (last)
Andorra	2004	Marta Roure	18th in semi-final
North Macedonia	1998	Vlado Janevski	19th
Slovakia	1994	Tublatanka	19th
Turkey	1975	Semiha Yankı	19th (last)
Belarus	2004	Aleksandra and Konstantin	19th in semi-final
Bulgaria	2005	Kaffe	19th in semi-final
Romania	1994	Dan Bittman	21st
Slovenia	1993	1X Band	22nd
Montenegro	2007	Stevan Faddy	22nd in semi-final
Estonia	1994	Silvi Vrait	24th
Lithuania	1994	Ovidijus Vyšniauskas	25th (last)
Czech Republic	2007	Kabát	28th in semi-final (last)

League Table of Appearances

Country	Years entered
Germany	63
France	62
United Kingdom	62
Belgium	61
Netherlands	60
Switzerland	60
Sweden	59
Spain	59
Norway	58
Ireland	53
Finland	53
Austria	52
Portugal	51
Denmark	48
Italy	45
Israel	42
Greece	40
Luxembourg	37
Cyprus	36
Turkey	34
Iceland	32
Malta	32
Yugoslavia	27
Croatia	25
Slovenia	25
Estonia	25
Monaco	24
Poland	22
Russia	22
Romania	20
Lithuania	20
Latvia	19
Bosnia & Herzegovina	19
North Macedonia	19
Hungary	17
Albania	16
Belarus	16
Moldova	15
Ukraine	15
Armenia	13
Serbia	12
Azerbaijan	12
Georgia	12
Bulgaria	12
Montenegro	11
San Marino	10
Czech Republic	8
Slovakia	7
Andorra	6
Australia	5
Serbia & Montenegro	2
Morocco	1

Top 5 closest voting relationships

Since the introduction of the modern points scoring system in 1975, including semi-finals.
"% of max" is the percentage of the maximum one country could give to the other in all contests.

1) Most Points Awarded Between Two Countries

Pos	Country	Gave to	Total	% of max	Country	Gave to	Total	% of max	Average Total	Average % of max
1	Cyprus	Greece	467	93%	Greece	Cyprus	458	89%	463	91%
2	Denmark	Sweden	437	73%	Sweden	Denmark	289	50%	363	62%
3	Norway	Sweden	416	64%	Sweden	Norway	286	47%	351	56%
4	Denmark	Norway	269	47%	Norway	Denmark	291	49%	280	48%
5	United Kingdom	Ireland	302	52%	Ireland	United Kingdom	219	38%	261	45%

2) Highest Percentage of Possible Points Awarded Between Two Countries

Pos	Country	Gave to	Total	% of max	Country	Gave to	Total	% of max	Average Total	Average % of max
1	Turkey	Azerbaijan	72	100%	Azerbaijan	Turkey	84	100%	78	100%
2	Romania	Moldova	245	93%	Moldova	Romania	257	97%	251	95%
3	Cyprus	Greece	467	93%	Greece	Cyprus	458	89%	463	91%
4	Montenegro	Serbia	179	93%	Serbia	Montenegro	69	82%	124	88%
5	Andorra	Spain	60	83%	Spain	Andorra	54	90%	57	87%

3) Most Number of Times Any Points Awarded Between Two Countries

Pos	Country	Voted for	Times	% of max	Country	Voted for	Times	% of max	Average Times	Average % of max
1	Sweden	Denmark	38	88%	Denmark	Sweden	40	91%	39	90%
2	Norway	Sweden	42	88%	Sweden	Norway	35	76%	39	82%
3	Ireland	United Kingdom	37	84%	United Kingdom	Ireland	37	84%	37	84%
4	Greece	Cyprus	34	97%	Cyprus	Greece	36	100%	35	99%
5	Denmark	Norway	30	73%	Norway	Denmark	35	83%	33	78%

4) Highest Percentage of Possible Times Two Countries Have Awarded Points to each Other

Pos	Country	Voted for	Times	% of max	Country	Voted for	Times	% of max	Average Times	Average % of max
1	Albania	Greece	23	100%	Greece	Albania	20	100%	22	100%
2	Russia	Ukraine	19	100%	Ukraine	Russia	17	100%	18	100%
3	Moldova	Romania	18	100%	Romania	Moldova	17	100%	18	100%
4	Croatia	FYR Macedonia	18	100%	FYR Macedonia	Croatia	16	100%	17	100%
5	Albania	FYR Macedonia	15	100%	FYR Macedonia	Albania	17	100%	16	100%
6	Armenia	Russia	17	100%	Russia	Armenia	15	100%	16	100%

.. And the Bottom 5 (or the Countries who receive points but don't reciprocate)

Since the introduction of the modern points scoring system in 1975, including semi-finals.
"% of max" is the percentage of the maximum one country could give to the other in all contests.

1) The Most One-Sided Points Totals

Pos	Gave to		Total	% of max	Gave to		Total	% of max	Difference Total	% of max
1	Russia	Latvia	30	12%	Latvia	Russia	229	68%	-199	-56%
2	Russia	Estonia	64	21%	Estonia	Russia	245	68%	-181	-47%
3	Turkey	France	38	10%	France	Turkey	190	44%	-152	-34%
4	Lithuania	United Kingdom	22	8%	United Kingdom	Lithuania	181	49%	-159	-41%
5	Sweden	Denmark	289	50%	Denmark	Sweden	437	73%	-148	-23%

2) The Most One-Sided Points as a percentage of the total points possible

Pos	Gave to		Total	% of max	Gave to		Total	% of max	Difference Total	% of max
1	Andorra	Portugal	10	17%	Portugal	Andorra	64	76%	-54	-59%
2	Armenia	Turkey	16	13%	Turkey	Switzerland	75	69%	-59	-56%
3	Russia	Latvia	30	12%	Latvia	Russia	229	68%	-199	-56%
4	Ukraine	Andorra	0	0%	Andorra	Ukraine	49	51%	-49	-51%
5	Ukraine	Italy	9	8%	Italy	Ukraine	110	57%	-101	-49%

3) The biggest difference between the number of times countries vote for each other

Pos	Voted for		Times	% of max	Voted for		Times	% of max	Difference Times	% of max
1	Sweden	Spain	8	18%	Spain	Sweden	30	65%	-22	-47%
2	Sweden	United Kingdom	21	48%	United Kingdom	Sweden	40	78%	-19	-30%
3	Sweden	Slovenia	6	23%	Slovenia	Sweden	24	77%	-18	-54%
4	Ireland	Portugal	6	17%	Portugal	Ireland	24	65%	-18	-48%
5	Israel	Germany	11	28%	Germany	Israel	29	64%	-18	-36%

4) Countries who keep voting for others but get nothing in return - based on percentage of maximum possible

The change to the voting system in 2016 and the inclusion of jury and public sets of points separately in the voting stats has meant that there are no instances remaining where a currently participating country has always voted for another but received nothing from either the jury or public from that country at every opportunity.

5) Countries who keep voting for others but are never voted for in return

Pos	Voted for		Times	% of max	Voted for		Times	% of max	Difference Times	% of max
1	Sweden	San Marino	0	0%	San Marino	Sweden	10	77%	-10	-77%
2	Norway	San Marino	0	0%	San Marino	Norway	10	71%	-10	-71%
3	Belgium	North Macedonia	0	0%	North Macedonia	Belgium	8	44%	-8	-44%
4	United Kingdom	San Marino	0	0%	San Marino	United Kingdom	7	70%	-7	-70%
5	Denmark	San Marino	0	0%	San Marino	Denmark	7	64%	-7	-64%

(Excludes statistics for Yugoslavia and Serbia & Montenegro - as those entities no longer exist, their figures will be permanent, and also excludes those for Morocco whose appearance in 1980 looks to be one-off.)

Each Country's Closest Voting Partners

The highest total points received from the same country since the start of the 1975 voting system, including semi-finals, and how many points those countries awarded in Finals over the last ten years. "% of max" is the percentage of the total points it has been possible for the awarding country to give.

Based on total points received

Country	Received most points from:	Total Points	% of max
Albania	North Macedonia	253	88%
Andorra	Spain	54	90%
Armenia	Russia	187	82%
Australia	Poland	115	56%
Austria	Belgium	131	26%
Azerbaijan	Russia	187	78%
Belarus	Ukraine	155	72%
Belgium	Netherlands	210	45%
Bosnia & H	Croatia	194	70%
Bulgaria	North Macedonia	160	63%
Croatia	Slovenia	184	61%
Cyprus	Greece	458	89%
Czech Republic	Iceland	76	35%
Denmark	Norway	291	49%
Estonia	Finland	204	63%
Finland	Sweden	179	37%
France	Israel	157	30%
Georgia	Lithuania	147	77%
Germany	Spain	203	35%
Greece	Cyprus	467	93%
Hungary	Serbia	156	59%
Iceland	Sweden	190	43%
Ireland	United Kingdom	302	52%
Israel	France	247	48%
Italy	Spain	211	59%
Latvia	Lithuania	189	83%
Lithuania	Ireland	194	52%
Luxembourg	Portugal	76	33%
Malta	United Kingdom	146	35%
Moldova	Romania	245	93%
Monaco	Italy	33	55%
Montenegro	Serbia	69	82%
Netherlands	Belgium	249	48%
North Macedonia	Albania	183	73%
Norway	Sweden	286	47%
Poland	Germany	140	45%
Portugal	France	242	48%
Romania	Moldova	257	97%
Russia	Estonia	245	68%
San Marino	Azerbaijan	41	31%
Serbia	Slovenia	185	70%
Slovakia	Malta	27	45%
Slovenia	Croatia	135	49%
Spain	Portugal	184	35%
Sweden	Denmark	437	73%
Switzerland	Austria	159	34%
Turkey	Germany	208	48%
Ukraine	Belarus	215	72%
United Kingdom	Ireland	219	38%

Based on % of maximum possible points

Country	Received most points from:	Total Points	% of max
Albania	North Macedonia	253	88%
Andorra	Spain	54	90%
Armenia	Russia	187	82%
Australia	Sweden	96	62%
Austria	Bulgaria	75	45%
Azerbaijan	Turkey	84	100%
Belarus	Ukraine	155	72%
Belgium	Australia	70	49%
Bosnia & H	Serbia	78	81%
Bulgaria	Cyprus	120	67%
Croatia	Bosnia & H	176	67%
Cyprus	Greece	458	89%
Czech Republic	Croatia	64	44%
Denmark	Sweden	289	50%
Estonia	Latvia	190	75%
Finland	Estonia	168	54%
France	Monaco	53	55%
Georgia	Armenia	141	78%
Germany	Denmark	191	38%
Greece	Cyprus	467	93%
Hungary	Serbia	156	59%
Iceland	Australia	42	50%
Ireland	United Kingdom	302	52%
Israel	France	247	48%
Italy	Albania	132	85%
Latvia	Lithuania	189	83%
Lithuania	Latvia	183	66%
Luxembourg	Malta	25	52%
Malta	Luxembourg	27	56%
Moldova	Romania	245	93%
Monaco	Italy	33	55%
Montenegro	Serbia	69	82%
Netherlands	Belgium	249	48%
North Macedonia	Serbia	135	87%
Norway	Slovakia	47	49%
Poland	Germany	140	45%
Portugal	Andorra	64	76%
Romania	Moldova	257	97%
Russia	Belarus	212	88%
San Marino	Albania	39	46%
Serbia	Montenegro	179	93%
Slovakia	Malta	27	45%
Slovenia	Bosnia & H	110	54%
Spain	Andorra	60	83%
Sweden	Denmark	437	73%
Switzerland	Luxembourg	80	35%
Turkey	Azerbaijan	72	100%
Ukraine	Belarus	215	72%
United Kingdom	Luxembourg	123	54%

Which Countries Have Never Awarded Points To Another?

(In semi-finals and finals, where voting for the recipient would have been possible, due to being drawn in the same semi-final). Includes either Jury or Public votes since 2016.)

	Countries never voted for:	Change on 2018	The Unfortunates:	First time awarded points in 2019
Albania	0	0	none	
Andorra	8	0	Belarus, Bulgaria, Croatia, Czech Republic, Estonia, FYR Macedonia, Georgia, Serbia	
Armenia	2	0	Andorra, Monaco	
Australia	1	0	Albania	
Austria	3	0	Andorra, Montenegro, Morocco	
Azerbaijan	3	0	Andorra, Armenia, Slovakia	
Belarus	1	-1	Monaco	San Marino
Belgium	4	-2	Andorra, North Macedonia, Montenegro, Morocco	Belarus, San Marino
Bosnia-H	3	0	Andorra, Luxembourg, San Marino	
Bulgaria	5	0	Andorra, Monaco, Montenegro, San Marino, Slovakia	
Croatia	2	0	Luxembourg, Monaco	
Cyprus	2	-1	Andorra, Slovakia	San Marino
Czech Republic	1	-1	Spain	San Marino
Denmark	4	0	Andorra, Morocco, San Marino, Slovakia	
Estonia	1	0	Montenegro	
Finland	1	0	Morocco	
France	2	0	Andorra, Morocco	
Georgia	4	0	Andorra, Ireland, Montenegro, Slovakia	
Germany	3	0	Andorra, Morocco, Slovakia	
Greece	1	0	Morocco	
Hungary	3	0	Andorra, Monaco, Slovakia	
Iceland	2	0	Monaco, Morocco	
Ireland	3	-1	Montenegro, Morocco, San Marino	North Macedonia
Israel	1	0	Slovakia	
Italy	1	-1	Slovakia	Czech Republic
Latvia	3	-1	Andorra, Monaco, Slovakia	North Macedonia
Lithuania	4	-1	Monaco, Montenegro, San Marino, Slovakia	North Macedonia
Luxembourg	4	0	Bosnia, Croatia, Morocco, Slovenia	
Malta	0	0	none	
Moldova	0	0	none	
Monaco	8	0	Andorra, Armenia, Bulgaria, Hungary, Moldova, Poland, Russia, Yugoslavia	
Montenegro	2	0	Andorra, Germany	
Morocco	8	0	Belgium, Finland, Greece, Ireland, Italy, Luxembourg, Netherlands, Portugal	
Netherlands	2	0	Morocco, Slovakia	
North Macedonia	1	0	Monaco	
Norway	3	0	Morocco, San Marino, Slovakia	
Poland	1	-2	San Marino	North Macedonia, San Marino
Portugal	1	-2	Morocco	North Macedonia, San Marino
Romania	2	0	Andorra, Monaco	
Russia	1	0	Monaco	
San Marino	2	0	Andorra, Bosnia & H	
Serbia	1	-2	Andorra	San Marino, Spain
Serbia & Mont	15	0	Andorra, Armenia, Austria, Belarus, Belgium, Denmark, France, Germany, Latvia, Malta, Monaco, Poland, Portugal, Spain, United Kingdom	

Which Countries Have Never Awarded Points To Another?

(In semi-finals and finals, where voting for the recipient would have been possible, due to being drawn in the same semi-final). Includes either Jury or Public votes since 2016.)

	Countries never voted for:	Change on 2018	The Unfortunates:	First time awarded points in 2019
Slovakia	4	0	Bulgaria, France, Georgia, Latvia	
Slovenia	1	-1	Monaco	San Marino
Spain	2	-1	North Macedonia, Morocco	Belarus
Sweden	2	0	Morocco, San Marino	
Switzerland	4	0	Andorra, Morocco, San Marino, Slovakia	
Turkey	3	0	Morocco, Serbia, Slovakia	
Ukraine	2	0	Andorra, Monaco	
United Kingdom	5	-1	Andorra, Montenegro, Morocco, San Marino, Slovakia	North Macedonia
Yugoslavia	0	0	-	

(Net change takes into account the first time one country could vote for another, so the number of countries never voted for can increase depending on the semi-final draw).

The Least Friendly Pairs - Public Voting (2016 onwards)

Using the new points allocation system from 2016, which countries' voting public have shunned each other? (Includes semi-finals)

Country	Voting public have never awarded points to or received points from:	Total
Albania	Serbia, Latvia, Malta, Georgia, Belarus	5
Armenia	Azerbaijan, Lithuania, United Kingdom, Ireland, Slovenia	5
Australia	-	0
Austria	United Kingdom, Montenegro	2
Azerbaijan	Serbia, Armenia, Finland	3
Belarus	Germany, Spain, Malta, United Kingdom, North Macedonia, Albania	6
Belgium	Bosnia & H	1
Bosnia & H	Belgium, Italy, Israel, Germany, Poland, Lithuania, Spain, Latvia, Georgia, United Kingdom, Finland, Greece, Moldova, Estonia, Iceland	15
Bulgaria	-	0
Croatia	Georgia	1
Cyprus	-	0
Czech Republic	-	0
Denmark	Serbia, Spain	2
Estonia	Bosnia & H	1
Finland	Azerbaijan, Germany, Malta, Georgia, Greece, Bosnia & H	6
France	Germany, Latvia, United Kingdom, San Marino	4
Georgia	Croatia, Spain, Malta, Switzerland, Ireland, Albania, Bosnia & H, Montenegro	8
Germany	France, Belarus, Bosnia & H, Finland, Montenegro	5
Greece	Lithuania, Latvia, Bosnia & H	3
Hungary	-	0
Iceland	Ukraine, Bosnia & H	2
Ireland	Serbia, Georgia, Armenia, Slovenia	4
Israel	Bosnia & H	1
Italy	Bosnia & H	1
Latvia	Serbia, Albania, Bosnia & H, France, Greece, Montenegro	6
Lithuania	Serbia, Armenia, Slovenia, Bosnia & H, Greece	5
Malta	Serbia, Georgia, Albania, Belarus, Finland, Slovenia	6
Moldova	United Kingdom, Bosnia & H	2
Montenegro	Germany, Poland, Latvia, Georgia, Austria, United Kingdom	7
Netherlands	-	0
North Macedonia	Spain, United Kingdom, Belarus	3
Norway	Spain, Armenia	2
Poland	Bosnia & H, Montenegro	2
Portugal	United Kingdom, Albania	2
Romania	Spain, Lithuania, United Kingdom, Albania, Finland, Slovenia	6
Russia	-	0
San Marino	France	1
Serbia	Azerbaijan, Lithuania, Latvia, Malta, United Kingdom, Albania, Ireland	7
Slovenia	Lithuania, Malta, United Kingdom, Armenia, Ireland	5
Spain	Georgia, Bosnia & H, Belarus, Denmark, North Macedonia	5
Sweden	Georgia	1
Switzerland	Georgia	1
Ukraine	-	0
United Kingdom	France, Serbia, Austria, Armenia, Belarus, North Macedonia, Slovenia, Bosnia & H, Montenegro	9

(As 2016 was the first year the public vote was treated separately from the jury vote, this list will include losing semi-finalists to whom some of the finalists will not yet have had an opportunity to award points.)

Jury/Public Vote Points Split in Finals since 2016

Country	Public	Jury
Albania	38%	62%
Armenia	47%	53%
Australia	31%	69%
Austria	33%	67%
Azerbaijan	40%	60%
Belarus	40%	60%
Belgium	56%	44%
Bosnia & Herzegovina		
Bulgaria	54%	46%
Croatia	68%	32%
Cyprus	52%	48%
Czech Republic	46%	54%
Denmark	58%	42%
Estonia	47%	53%
Finland	50%	50%
France	44%	56%
Georgia	23%	77%
Germany	39%	61%
Greece	35%	65%
Hungary	68%	32%
Iceland	80%	20%

Jury/Public Vote Points Split in Finals since 2016

Ireland — Jury 54%, Public 46%
Israel — Jury 50%, Public 50%
Italy — Jury 40%, Public 60%
Latvia — Jury 52%, Public 48%
Lithuania — Jury 51%, Public 49%
Malta — Jury 86%, Public 14%
Moldova — Jury 35%, Public 65%
Montenegro —
Netherlands — Jury 62%, Public 38%
North Macedonia — Jury 81%, Public 19%
Norway — Jury 36%, Public 64%
Poland — Jury 10%, Public 90%
Portugal — Jury 51%, Public 49%
Romania — Jury 21%, Public 79%
Russia — Jury 30%, Public 70%
San Marino — Jury 16%, Public 84%
Serbia — Jury 34%, Public 66%
Slovenia — Jury 51%, Public 49%
Spain — Jury 56%, Public 44%
Sweden — Jury 69%, Public 31%
Switzerland — Jury 42%, Public 58%
Ukraine — Jury 33%, Public 67%
United Kingdom — Jury 79%, Public 21%

Most Points Received Since 1975

Despite most of Eastern Europe only joining in the 1990's, the results are not quite what you'd think....
(includes combined jury/public voting points since 2016)

Semi-finals

Country	Total Points Received	Contests	Average Points
Albania	1177	9	131
Andorra	157	6	26
Armenia	1308	12	109
Australia	963	4	241
Austria	876	10	88
Azerbaijan	1413	11	128
Belarus	1025	16	64
Belgium	1217	15	81
Bosnia & H	945	8	118
Bulgaria	1251	12	104
Croatia	995	13	77
Cyprus	1350	14	96
Czech Republic	761	8	95
Denmark	1401	14	100
Estonia	1172	16	73
Finland	1155	15	77
France	-	-	-
Georgia	930	12	78
Germany	-	-	-
Greece	1587	13	122
Hungary	1042	11	95
Iceland	1225	15	82
Ireland	884	14	63
Israel	1400	14	100
Italy	-	-	-
Latvia	932	11	85
Lithuania	1166	12	97
Luxembourg	-	-	-
Malta	1128	14	81
Moldova	1439	14	103
Monaco	46	3	15
Montenegro	483	11	44
Morocco	-	-	-
Netherlands	1483	16	93
North Macedonia	1085	16	68
Norway	1642	13	126
Poland	971	13	75
Portugal	1022	13	79
Romania	1380	12	115
Russia	1667	11	152
San Marino	415	10	42
Serbia	1248	11	113
Serbia & Mont	263	1	263
Slovakia	102	4	26
Slovenia	1006	16	63
Spain	-	-	-
Sweden	1838	11	167
Switzerland	898	15	60
Turkey	790	7	113
Ukraine	1580	11	144
United Kingdom	-	-	-
Yugoslavia	-	-	-

Finals

Country	Total Points Received	Contests	Average Points
Albania	778	15	52
Andorra	-	-	-
Armenia	1276	10	128
Australia	1821	5	364
Austria	1980	33	60
Azerbaijan	1710	11	155
Belarus	366	6	61
Belgium	2229	32	70
Bosnia & H	1242	18	69
Bulgaria	1245	4	311
Croatia	1216	18	68
Cyprus	2006	30	67
Czech Republic	479	3	160
Denmark	2743	34	81
Estonia	1464	16	92
Finland	1231	32	38
France	3267	44	74
Georgia	631	7	90
Germany	3059	44	70
Greece	2884	37	78
Hungary	1112	14	79
Iceland	1546	25	62
Ireland	3079	35	88
Israel	2965	34	87
Italy	3271	26	126
Latvia	835	13	64
Lithuania	834	11	76
Luxembourg	935	19	49
Malta	1850	23	80
Moldova	1207	10	121
Monaco	330	5	66
Montenegro	81	2	41
Morocco	7	1	7
Netherlands	2699	32	84
North Macedonia	674	9	75
Norway	3169	41	77
Poland	809	14	58
Portugal	1778	32	56
Romania	1471	18	82
Russia	3327	21	158
San Marino	91	2	46
Serbia	1169	9	130
Serbia & Mont	400	2	200
Slovakia	42	3	14
Slovenia	723	15	48
Spain	2374	45	53
Sweden	4987	44	113
Switzerland	2158	30	72
Turkey	1996	33	60
Ukraine	2385	15	159
United Kingdom	3453	45	77
Yugoslavia	730	13	56

Eurovision 2019 East v West

(With 22 countries from the "west" and 19 from the "east" taking part this year, how strong was geographical voting?)

Semi-Final 1 (9 "eastern" voting countries, 11 "western" voting countries)

East		Points received from Juries				Points received from Public				
	Total	East	% of max	West	% of max	Total	East	% of max	West	% of max
Montenegro	31	12	13%	19	14%	15	15	16%	0	0%
Poland	60	34	35%	26	20%	60	21	22%	39	30%
Slovenia	74	38	40%	36	27%	93	58	60%	35	27%
Czech Republic	157	73	76%	84	64%	85	30	31%	55	42%
Hungary	65	32	33%	33	25%	32	26	27%	6	5%
Belarus	78	45	47%	33	25%	44	24	25%	20	15%
Serbia	91	47	49%	44	33%	65	41	43%	24	18%
Georgia	29	15	16%	14	11%	33	1	1%	32	24%
Estonia	65	28	29%	37	28%	133	50	52%	83	63%
Average		**36**	**33%**	**36.2**	**25%**		**29.6**	**27%**	**32.7**	**23%**

West	Total	East	% of max	West	% of max	Total	East	% of max	West	% of max
Finland	9	1	1%	8	7%	14	12	9%	2	2%
Belgium	50	14	11%	36	33%	20	5	4%	15	14%
Cyprus	95	54	41%	41	38%	54	18	14%	36	33%
Australia	121	40	30%	81	75%	140	58	44%	82	76%
Iceland	70	17	13%	53	49%	151	74	56%	77	71%
Portugal	8	4	3%	4	4%	43	4	3%	39	36%
Greece	131	52	39%	79	73%	54	8	6%	46	43%
San Marino	26	16	12%	10	9%	124	77	58%	47	44%
Average		**24.8**	**19%**	**39.0**	**33%**		**32.0**	**30%**	**43.0**	**30%**

Semi-Final 2 (10 "eastern" voting countries, 11 "western" voting countries)

East		Points received from Juries				Points received from Public				
	Total	East	% of max	West	% of max	Total	East	% of max	West	% of max
Lithuania	16	7	6%	9	7%	77	23	21%	54	41%
Russia	93	61	56%	32	24%	124	76	70%	48	36%
Armenia	26	15	14%	11	8%	23	18	17%	5	4%
Latvia	37	18	17%	19	14%	13	13	12%	0	0%
Romania	47	34	31%	13	10%	24	12	11%	12	9%
Croatia	26	2	2%	24	18%	38	20	19%	18	14%
Moldova	58	30	28%	28	21%	27	20	19%	7	5%
Albania	38	35	32%	3	2%	58	25	23%	33	25%
North Macedonia	155	75	69%	80	61%	84	45	42%	39	30%
Azerbaijan	103	60	56%	43	33%	121	60	56%	61	46%
Average		**33.7**	**28%**	**26.2**	**22%**		**31.2**	**26%**	**27.7**	**23%**

West	Total	East	% of max	West	% of max	Total	East	% of max	West	% of max
Ireland	13	5	4%	8	7%	3	0	0%	3	3%
Switzerland	95	38	32%	57	48%	137	58	48%	79	66%
Norway	40	5	4%	35	29%	170	68	57%	102	85%
Netherlands	140	55	46%	85	71%	140	76	63%	64	53%
Denmark	53	11	9%	42	35%	41	11	9%	30	25%
Sweden	150	53	44%	97	81%	88	28	23%	60	50%
Austria	21	9	8%	12	10%	0	0	0%	0	0%
Malta	107	62	52%	45	38%	50	27	23%	23	19%
Average		**29.8**	**23%**	**47.6**	**44%**		**33.5**	**25%**	**45.1**	**42%**

Eurovision 2019 - East v West

(With 22 countries from the "west" and 19 from the "east" taking part this year, how strong was geographical voting?)

FINAL (19 "eastern" voting countries, 22 "western" voting countries)

Finalists

East		Points received from Juries				Points received from Public			
	Total	East	% of max	West	% of max	Total	East	% of max	West	% of max
Albania	43	28	12%	15	6%	47	20	8%	27	10%
Czech Republic	150	85	35%	65	25%	7	3	1%	4	2%
Russia	126	59	25%	67	25%	244	151	63%	93	35%
North Macedonia	247	127	53%	120	45%	58	48	20%	10	4%
Slovenia	46	32	13%	14	5%	59	53	22%	6	2%
Estonia	28	13	5%	15	6%	48	16	7%	32	12%
Belarus	18	18	8%	0	0%	13	13	5%	0	0%
Azerbaijan	202	101	42%	101	38%	100	69	29%	31	12%
Serbia	35	30	13%	5	2%	54	43	18%	11	4%
Average		54.8	23%	44.7	17%		46.2	19%	23.8	9%

West	Total	East	% of max	West	% of max	Total	East	% of max	West	% of max
Germany	24	5	2%	19	8%	0	0	0%	0	0%
France	67	26	10%	41	16%	38	6	2%	32	13%
Denmark	69	40	16%	29	12%	51	9	4%	42	17%
San Marino	12	5	2%	7	3%	65	64	25%	1	0%
Sweden	241	91	36%	150	60%	93	14	6%	79	31%
Malta	87	53	21%	34	13%	20	16	6%	4	2%
Cyprus	77	38	15%	39	15%	32	12	5%	20	8%
Netherlands	237	85	34%	152	60%	261	124	49%	137	54%
Greece	50	23	9%	27	11%	24	2	1%	22	9%
Israel	0	0	0%	0	0%	35	17	7%	18	7%
Norway	40	8	3%	32	13%	291	110	44%	181	72%
United Kingdom	8	5	2%	3	1%	3	0	0%	3	1%
Iceland	46	17	7%	29	12%	186	91	36%	95	38%
Italy	219	89	35%	130	52%	253	100	40%	153	61%
Switzerland	152	62	25%	90	36%	212	82	33%	130	52%
Australia	153	61	24%	92	37%	131	35	14%	96	38%
Spain	1	1	0%	0	0%	53	4	2%	49	19%
Average		35.8	14%	51.4	20%		40.4	16%	62.5	25%

Notes:
"% of max" is the most points a country could have received, so for example there were 22 "western" countries voting in the final, so the most points a "western" country could have received from other "western" countries was 21 x 12 points, but "eastern" countries could have received 22 x 12 points.

The stats show that "eastern" and "western" countries continued to vote for their own blocs and that applied to both the juries and the public.
This year though, the public of the western countries gave much fewer points to eastern countries than they did to western ones, the largest difference since we started compiling these statistics.

Whether a country falls into the category of "western" or "eastern" is of course, fairly arbitrary. The above statistics allocate countries along what is normally considered traditional east and west groupings, with Australia, Israel, Greece and Cyprus being included in the "western" category.

Eurovision 2019 Bloc Voting in Final

Jury voting

Balkan bloc

Country	Average points received from	
	Balkan bloc	Other countries
Albania	3.20	0.77
North Macedonia	8.60	5.83
Serbia	3.20	0.54
Slovenia	0.00	1.31
Total	**15.00**	**8.46**

Public voting

Balkan bloc

Country	Average points received from	
	Balkan bloc	Other countries
Albania	4.00	0.77
North Macedonia	8.60	0.43
Serbia	8.00	0.40
Slovenia	5.20	0.94
Total	**25.80**	**2.54**

Scandinavian bloc (Jury voting)

Country	Average points received from	
	Scandinavian bloc	Other countries
Denmark	1.33	1.76
Norway	3.00	0.84
Sweden	10.67	5.65
Iceland	0.00	1.24
Total	**15.00**	**9.49**

Scandinavian bloc (Public voting)

Country	Average points received from	
	Scandinavian bloc	Other countries
Denmark	5.33	0.95
Norway	12.00	6.89
Sweden	10.00	1.70
Iceland	7.33	4.43
Total	**34.67**	**13.97**

Former Soviet Union bloc (Jury voting)

Country	Average points received from	
	Former Soviet bloc	Other countries
Russia	1.25	2.88
Estonia	6.50	0.72
Belarus	0.50	0.25
Azerbaijan	1.50	4.63
Total	**9.75**	**8.47**

Former Soviet Union bloc (Public voting)

Country	Average points received from	
	Former Soviet bloc	Other countries
Russia	11.50	4.75
Estonia	1.75	1.06
Belarus	1.63	0.00
Azerbaijan	5.63	1.72
Total	**20.50**	**7.53**

Notes on voting countries in each bloc:

Balkan bloc:

Albania, Croatia, North Macedonia, Montenegro, Serbia, Slovenia

Scandinavian bloc:

Denmark, Iceland, Norway, Sweden

Former Soviet Union bloc:

Armenia, Azerbaijan, Belarus, Estonia, Georgia, Latvia, Lithuania, Moldova, Russia

Eurovision 2019: Who Votes for Who? (And Who Doesn't)

Since the introduction of the modern points scoring system in 1975, including semi-finals. Since 2008, this figure is based on which semi-final each country was drawn to vote/perform in and which countries then made the final. Previous voting arrangements are also taken into account, including the 2004 voting boycott by France, Poland & Russia. "% of max" is the percentage of the maximum one country could have given to the other in the semi-finals and final. From 2016 the analysis of the awarding of 12 points includes the jury and public televoting points separately but the total points and the frequency that any points have been awarded are based on the final combined score.

Albania

	Albania awarded points to:				Frequency		Albania received points from:				Frequency	
	Total	% of max	12's	% of max	Times	% of max	Total	% of max	12's	% of max	Times	% of max
Albania	-	-	-	-	-	-	-	-	-	-	-	-
Andorra	6	13%	0	0%	1	25%	6	7%	0	0%	1	14%
Armenia	42	15%	0	0%	8	44%	6	3%	0	0%	2	13%
Australia	56	36%	2	15%	6	86%	0	0%	0	0%	0	0%
Austria	16	8%	0	0%	5	42%	60	31%	1	6%	10	83%
Azerbaijan	102	35%	0	0%	13	72%	72	30%	2	10%	10	67%
Belarus	13	6%	0	0%	3	20%	24	10%	1	5%	3	18%
Belgium	42	17%	0	0%	9	56%	63	22%	0	0%	12	63%
Bosnia & Herzegovina	70	49%	1	8%	8	67%	43	36%	0	0%	9	90%
Bulgaria	88	46%	0	0%	9	82%	21	12%	0	0%	5	42%
Croatia	38	17%	0	0%	8	53%	100	42%	0	0%	16	100%
Cyprus	87	32%	2	9%	10	59%	30	12%	0	0%	6	35%
Czech Republic	3	2%	0	0%	2	29%	15	10%	0	0%	3	33%
Denmark	18	6%	0	0%	6	29%	31	11%	0	0%	6	32%
Estonia	16	7%	0	0%	5	31%	3	1%	0	0%	3	18%
Finland	22	9%	0	0%	5	28%	31	11%	0	0%	6	32%
France	41	17%	0	0%	9	56%	21	9%	0	0%	6	35%
Georgia	5	2%	0	0%	2	14%	13	6%	0	0%	3	23%
Germany	49	20%	0	0%	9	56%	31	13%	0	0%	8	50%
Greece	230	71%	9	33%	23	100%	206	72%	2	8%	20	100%
Hungary	59	22%	0	0%	10	53%	35	17%	0	0%	6	40%
Iceland	23	8%	0	0%	4	20%	51	18%	1	4%	8	40%
Ireland	20	9%	0	0%	4	27%	11	4%	0	0%	5	29%
Israel	58	21%	0	0%	11	65%	13	5%	0	0%	3	19%
Italy	132	85%	7	54%	9	100%	87	56%	5	38%	7	88%
Latvia	1	0%	0	0%	1	6%	11	4%	0	0%	4	19%
Lithuania	14	5%	0	0%	4	22%	1	0%	0	0%	1	6%
Luxembourg	0	-	0	-	0	-	0	-	0	-	0	-
Malta	51	22%	0	0%	12	75%	27	11%	0	0%	5	29%
Moldova	37	13%	1	4%	7	37%	24	10%	0	0%	5	29%
Monaco	2	6%	0	0%	1	33%	3	6%	0	0%	1	25%
Montenegro	43	51%	2	29%	5	83%	121	78%	3	23%	10	100%
Morocco	0	-	0	-	0	-	0	-	0	-	0	-
Netherlands	40	17%	0	0%	7	47%	8	4%	0	0%	4	25%
North Macedonia	183	73%	8	38%	17	100%	253	88%	16	67%	19	100%
Norway	54	18%	1	4%	9	45%	21	8%	0	0%	5	29%
Poland	23	10%	0	0%	5	33%	19	8%	0	0%	4	27%
Portugal	48	27%	1	7%	6	46%	23	9%	0	0%	5	29%
Romania	42	18%	0	0%	8	44%	20	9%	0	0%	7	44%
Russia	72	25%	1	4%	10	48%	19	8%	0	0%	6	33%
San Marino	39	46%	0	0%	5	83%	51	39%	1	9%	7	78%
Serbia	31	14%	0	0%	11	73%	12	6%	0	0%	4	29%
Serbia & Montenegro	17	47%	0	0%	3	100%	22	46%	0	0%	3	75%
Slovakia	4	17%	0	0%	1	50%	4	7%	0	0%	1	20%
Slovenia	24	12%	0	0%	4	31%	35	15%	0	0%	10	67%
Spain	55	23%	2	10%	8	50%	25	8%	0	0%	5	24%
Sweden	89	29%	0	0%	16	80%	27	11%	0	0%	7	44%
Switzerland	46	20%	0	0%	7	47%	160	56%	3	13%	18	95%
Turkey	113	78%	3	25%	12	100%	60	45%	0	0%	11	100%
Ukraine	38	13%	0	0%	7	35%	7	4%	0	0%	3	21%
United Kingdom	31	13%	0	0%	6	38%	29	10%	0	0%	8	44%
Yugoslavia	0	-	0	-	0	-	0	-	0	-	0	-

Eurovision 2019: Who Votes for Who? (And Who Doesn't)

Andorra

	Andorra awarded points to:				Frequency		Andorra received points from:				Frequency	
	Total	% of max	12's	% of max	Times	% of max	Total	% of max	12's	% of max	Times	% of max
Albania	6	7%	0	0%	1	14%	6	13%	0	0%	1	25%
Andorra	-	-	-	-	-	-	-	-	-	-	-	-
Armenia	3	4%	0	0%	1	14%	0	0%	0	0%	0	0%
Australia	0	-	0	-	0	-	0	-	0	-	0	-
Austria	8	22%	0	0%	2	67%	0	0%	0	0%	0	0%
Azerbaijan	15	42%	0	0%	2	67%	0	0%	0	0%	0	0%
Belarus	0	0%	0	0%	0	0%	4	7%	0	0%	1	20%
Belgium	8	11%	0	0%	2	33%	0	0%	0	0%	0	0%
Bosnia & Herzegovina	6	5%	0	0%	2	20%	0	0%	0	0%	0	0%
Bulgaria	0	0%	0	0%	0	0%	0	0%	0	0%	0	0%
Croatia	0	0%	0	0%	0	0%	2	4%	0	0%	1	25%
Cyprus	6	10%	0	0%	2	40%	0	0%	0	0%	0	0%
Czech Republic	0	0%	0	0%	0	0%	7	29%	0	0%	1	50%
Denmark	18	21%	0	0%	4	57%	0	0%	0	0%	0	0%
Estonia	0	0%	0	0%	0	0%	8	13%	0	0%	2	40%
Finland	49	45%	1	11%	7	78%	5	7%	0	0%	1	17%
France	26	36%	0	0%	5	83%	0	0%	0	0%	0	0%
Georgia	0	0%	0	0%	0	0%	0	0%	0	0%	0	0%
Germany	5	7%	0	0%	1	17%	0	0%	0	0%	0	0%
Greece	34	35%	0	0%	6	75%	4	7%	0	0%	1	20%
Hungary	17	35%	0	0%	4	100%	0	0%	0	0%	0	0%
Iceland	24	29%	0	0%	3	43%	6	10%	0	0%	1	20%
Ireland	6	8%	0	0%	2	33%	5	8%	0	0%	2	40%
Israel	45	42%	1	11%	6	67%	6	8%	0	0%	2	33%
Italy	0	-	0	-	0	-	0	-	0	-	0	-
Latvia	12	14%	0	0%	2	29%	0	0%	0	0%	0	0%
Lithuania	13	18%	0	0%	3	50%	2	4%	0	0%	1	25%
Luxembourg	0	-	0	-	0	-	0	-	0	-	0	-
Malta	18	21%	0	0%	4	57%	3	5%	0	0%	1	20%
Moldova	5	6%	0	0%	2	29%	4	8%	0	0%	1	25%
Monaco	17	47%	0	0%	3	100%	0	0%	0	0%	0	0%
Montenegro	1	3%	0	0%	1	33%	0	0%	0	0%	0	0%
Morocco	0	-	0	-	0	-	0	-	0	-	0	-
Netherlands	19	26%	0	0%	4	67%	7	12%	0	0%	1	20%
North Macedonia	0	0%	0	0%	0	0%	1	2%	0	0%	1	20%
Norway	26	27%	0	0%	5	63%	2	3%	0	0%	1	20%
Poland	10	14%	0	0%	1	17%	7	15%	0	0%	2	50%
Portugal	64	76%	4	57%	6	86%	10	17%	0	0%	2	40%
Romania	34	31%	0	0%	6	67%	0	0%	0	0%	0	0%
Russia	22	23%	0	0%	5	63%	4	8%	0	0%	1	25%
San Marino	2	17%	0	0%	1	100%	0	0%	0	0%	0	0%
Serbia	0	0%	0	0%	0	0%	0	0%	0	0%	0	0%
Serbia & Montenegro	3	8%	0	0%	2	67%	0	0%	0	0%	0	0%
Slovakia	0	-	0	-	0	-	0	-	0	-	0	-
Slovenia	8	11%	0	0%	1	17%	5	8%	0	0%	2	40%
Spain	60	83%	5	83%	5	83%	54	90%	3	60%	5	100%
Sweden	32	33%	0	0%	6	75%	2	3%	0	0%	1	20%
Switzerland	9	13%	0	0%	3	50%	0	0%	0	0%	0	0%
Turkey	15	14%	0	0%	3	33%	3	5%	0	0%	2	40%
Ukraine	49	51%	1	13%	6	75%	0	0%	0	0%	0	0%
United Kingdom	6	8%	0	0%	2	33%	0	0%	0	0%	0	0%
Yugoslavia	0	-	0	-	0	-	0	-	0	-	0	-

Eurovision 2019: Who Votes for Who? (And Who Doesn't)

Armenia

	Armenia awarded points to:				Frequency		Armenia received points from:				Frequency	
	Total	% of max	12's	% of max	Times	% of max	Total	% of max	12's	% of max	Times	% of max
Albania	6	3%	0	0%	2	13%	42	15%	0	0%	8	44%
Andorra	0	0%	0	0%	0	0%	3	4%	0	0%	1	14%
Armenia	-	-	-	-	-	-	-	-	-	-	-	-
Australia	13	10%	0	0%	5	83%	11	11%	0	0%	2	40%
Austria	30	16%	0	0%	6	60%	39	22%	1	7%	6	60%
Azerbaijan	3	1%	0	0%	2	11%	0	0%	0	0%	0	0%
Belarus	58	35%	1	7%	8	73%	92	45%	1	6%	13	93%
Belgium	36	18%	0	0%	8	62%	126	50%	5	24%	14	82%
Bosnia & Herzegovina	19	14%	0	0%	5	50%	25	17%	0	0%	5	50%
Bulgaria	31	18%	0	0%	6	60%	102	53%	1	6%	12	92%
Croatia	17	9%	0	0%	5	45%	13	6%	0	0%	3	21%
Cyprus	121	53%	5	26%	9	75%	111	49%	2	11%	12	86%
Czech Republic	43	26%	0	0%	6	75%	85	47%	4	27%	10	100%
Denmark	18	8%	0	0%	6	43%	8	4%	0	0%	3	20%
Estonia	24	12%	0	0%	4	31%	15	6%	0	0%	4	25%
Finland	14	6%	0	0%	2	12%	29	10%	0	0%	7	37%
France	73	36%	1	6%	12	92%	142	66%	7	39%	15	100%
Georgia	141	78%	4	27%	13	100%	146	76%	5	31%	13	100%
Germany	11	5%	0	0%	2	15%	59	27%	0	0%	10	67%
Greece	146	53%	0	0%	17	94%	158	57%	3	13%	16	89%
Hungary	10	5%	0	0%	3	21%	28	15%	0	0%	6	46%
Iceland	26	11%	1	5%	6	38%	25	9%	0	0%	7	39%
Ireland	4	2%	0	0%	2	18%	4	2%	0	0%	2	13%
Israel	68	28%	1	5%	7	47%	110	48%	2	11%	13	81%
Italy	37	26%	0	0%	6	75%	11	8%	0	0%	3	43%
Latvia	5	3%	0	0%	2	20%	31	14%	0	0%	7	47%
Lithuania	6	3%	0	0%	2	15%	10	4%	0	0%	4	27%
Luxembourg	0	-	0	-	0	-	0	-	0	-	0	-
Malta	85	44%	1	6%	8	67%	52	22%	1	5%	8	50%
Moldova	81	34%	0	0%	10	67%	88	33%	0	0%	14	82%
Monaco	0	0%	0	0%	0	0%	0	0%	0	0%	0	0%
Montenegro	44	37%	1	10%	6	75%	68	33%	1	6%	9	69%
Morocco	0	-	0	-	0	-	0	-	0	-	0	-
Netherlands	62	26%	0	0%	8	57%	141	56%	7	33%	14	82%
North Macedonia	39	25%	0	0%	4	40%	41	17%	0	0%	9	56%
Norway	61	27%	0	0%	13	87%	7	3%	0	0%	2	13%
Poland	14	8%	0	0%	5	45%	68	35%	2	13%	12	92%
Portugal	49	34%	1	8%	5	50%	20	10%	0	0%	5	38%
Romania	26	12%	0	0%	9	56%	56	26%	0	0%	11	69%
Russia	217	82%	12	55%	18	100%	187	82%	10	53%	16	100%
San Marino	14	13%	0	0%	4	57%	54	32%	1	7%	9	82%
Serbia	26	15%	0	0%	5	45%	16	11%	0	0%	4	40%
Serbia & Montenegro	0	-	0	-	0	-	0	0%	0	0%	0	0%
Slovakia	0	-	0	-	0	-	7	29%	0	0%	2	100%
Slovenia	6	4%	0	0%	2	18%	18	9%	0	0%	5	36%
Spain	13	6%	0	0%	4	31%	121	42%	2	8%	14	74%
Sweden	100	35%	3	13%	13	72%	47	18%	0	0%	11	65%
Switzerland	42	25%	0	0%	6	55%	7	3%	0	0%	3	18%
Turkey	16	13%	0	0%	3	30%	75	69%	1	11%	9	100%
Ukraine	102	50%	3	18%	12	86%	78	46%	1	7%	11	92%
United Kingdom	15	7%	0	0%	4	31%	15	6%	0	0%	4	24%
Yugoslavia	0	-	0	-	0	-	0	-	0	-	0	-

Eurovision 2019: Who Votes for Who? (And Who Doesn't)

Australia

	Australia awarded points to:				Frequency		Australia received points from:				Frequency	
	Total	% of max	12's	% of max	Times	% of max	Total	% of max	12's	% of max	Times	% of max
Albania	0	0%	0	0%	0	0%	56	36%	2	15%	6	86%
Andorra	0	-	0	-	0	-	0	-	0	-	0	-
Armenia	11	11%	0	0%	2	40%	13	10%	0	0%	5	83%
Australia	-	-	-	-	-	-	-	-	-	-	-	-
Austria	11	13%	0	0%	3	75%	30	28%	2	22%	3	60%
Azerbaijan	9	8%	0	0%	3	50%	20	15%	0	0%	3	50%
Belarus	8	7%	0	0%	2	40%	57	37%	0	0%	7	100%
Belgium	70	49%	4	33%	6	86%	89	49%	3	20%	7	88%
Bosnia & Herzegovina	0	-	0	-	0	-	13	54%	0	0%	1	100%
Bulgaria	49	51%	0	0%	3	75%	32	33%	1	13%	2	50%
Croatia	2	4%	0	0%	2	100%	23	24%	1	13%	2	50%
Cyprus	22	13%	0	0%	4	50%	38	24%	0	0%	6	86%
Czech Republic	37	28%	1	9%	4	67%	41	26%	1	8%	5	71%
Denmark	46	35%	1	9%	5	83%	92	59%	2	15%	7	100%
Estonia	23	24%	0	0%	4	80%	34	26%	0	0%	5	83%
Finland	15	18%	0	0%	3	75%	74	47%	1	8%	6	86%
France	26	24%	0	0%	2	40%	62	40%	1	8%	7	100%
Georgia	13	9%	0	0%	3	43%	31	15%	0	0%	4	44%
Germany	15	14%	0	0%	2	40%	77	49%	0	0%	7	100%
Greece	25	21%	0	0%	3	50%	40	26%	0	0%	4	57%
Hungary	16	11%	0	0%	3	43%	60	38%	1	8%	6	86%
Iceland	42	50%	1	14%	3	75%	94	60%	1	8%	6	86%
Ireland	19	32%	0	0%	2	67%	39	30%	0	0%	4	67%
Israel	53	37%	1	8%	5	71%	84	54%	3	23%	6	86%
Italy	15	14%	0	0%	3	60%	47	26%	1	7%	6	75%
Latvia	27	23%	0	0%	4	67%	73	41%	1	7%	8	100%
Lithuania	30	31%	0	0%	4	80%	41	31%	2	18%	5	83%
Luxembourg	0	-	0	-	0	-	0	-	0	-	0	-
Malta	23	27%	0	0%	4	100%	50	38%	1	9%	5	83%
Moldova	71	66%	2	22%	4	80%	61	39%	0	0%	7	100%
Monaco	0	-	0	-	0	-	0	-	0	-	0	-
Montenegro	7	7%	0	0%	1	20%	27	15%	0	0%	5	63%
Morocco	0	-	0	-	0	-	0	-	0	-	0	-
Netherlands	21	16%	0	0%	4	67%	41	31%	1	9%	5	83%
North Macedonia	16	27%	0	0%	3	100%	37	28%	0	0%	4	67%
Norway	44	31%	1	8%	6	86%	79	51%	1	8%	7	100%
Poland	28	17%	1	7%	4	50%	115	56%	2	12%	9	100%
Portugal	34	35%	0	0%	3	60%	34	26%	0	0%	4	67%
Romania	11	15%	0	0%	2	50%	29	27%	1	11%	5	100%
Russia	29	30%	0	0%	4	80%	23	21%	0	0%	5	100%
San Marino	9	11%	0	0%	2	50%	31	20%	0	0%	5	71%
Serbia	26	15%	0	0%	5	63%	57	32%	0	0%	7	88%
Serbia & Montenegro	0	-	0	-	0	-	0	-	0	-	0	-
Slovakia	0	-	0	-	0	-	0	-	0	-	0	-
Slovenia	19	11%	0	0%	4	50%	56	27%	1	6%	8	89%
Spain	14	13%	0	0%	2	40%	69	44%	1	8%	6	86%
Sweden	104	62%	5	36%	7	88%	96	62%	4	31%	7	100%
Switzerland	8	13%	0	0%	2	67%	47	36%	2	18%	5	83%
Turkey	0	-	0	-	0	-	0	-	0	-	0	-
Ukraine	25	21%	0	0%	3	60%	38	32%	1	10%	5	100%
United Kingdom	29	27%	1	11%	3	60%	76	49%	0	0%	7	100%
Yugoslavia	0	-	0	-	0	-	0	-	0	-	0	-

Eurovision 2019: Who Votes for Who? (And Who Doesn't)

Austria

	Austria awarded points to:				Frequency		Austria received points from:				Frequency	
	Total	% of max	12's	% of max	Times	% of max	Total	% of max	12's	% of max	Times	% of max
Albania	60	31%	1	6%	10	83%	16	8%	0	0%	5	42%
Andorra	0	0%	0	0%	0	0%	8	22%	0	0%	2	67%
Armenia	39	22%	1	7%	6	60%	30	16%	0	0%	6	60%
Australia	30	28%	2	22%	3	60%	11	13%	0	0%	3	75%
Austria	-	-	-	-	-	-	-	-	-	-	-	-
Azerbaijan	46	23%	1	6%	6	55%	12	6%	0	0%	3	30%
Belarus	25	12%	0	0%	3	21%	32	14%	0	0%	5	36%
Belgium	77	16%	0	0%	19	51%	131	26%	4	10%	21	55%
Bosnia & Herzegovina	108	50%	4	22%	12	71%	53	26%	1	6%	8	53%
Bulgaria	71	42%	1	7%	8	89%	75	45%	3	21%	7	78%
Croatia	117	35%	1	4%	16	73%	44	13%	0	0%	9	43%
Cyprus	32	7%	0	0%	9	26%	58	13%	0	0%	13	39%
Czech Republic	51	39%	1	9%	5	83%	30	21%	0	0%	5	71%
Denmark	113	21%	2	5%	19	49%	111	23%	0	0%	20	57%
Estonia	55	16%	0	0%	13	57%	87	27%	2	7%	11	52%
Finland	37	8%	0	0%	8	24%	97	20%	2	5%	14	39%
France	124	25%	4	10%	17	45%	101	20%	2	5%	15	41%
Georgia	2	2%	0	0%	1	13%	37	28%	0	0%	5	63%
Germany	129	26%	1	2%	22	58%	112	22%	2	5%	19	50%
Greece	57	12%	0	0%	15	41%	96	20%	3	8%	18	51%
Hungary	79	27%	1	4%	12	63%	57	25%	0	0%	8	57%
Iceland	51	15%	0	0%	12	46%	92	18%	1	2%	11	30%
Ireland	196	39%	4	10%	24	63%	129	23%	3	6%	20	49%
Israel	123	24%	3	7%	20	56%	106	22%	3	8%	13	37%
Italy	106	30%	0	0%	15	60%	78	21%	4	13%	13	48%
Latvia	24	13%	0	0%	5	36%	33	14%	0	0%	7	47%
Lithuania	6	2%	0	0%	3	17%	71	26%	1	4%	8	47%
Luxembourg	47	22%	0	0%	9	50%	14	6%	0	0%	3	17%
Malta	71	20%	1	3%	13	52%	44	12%	1	3%	9	38%
Moldova	34	15%	0	0%	8	53%	26	12%	0	0%	6	46%
Monaco	14	19%	0	0%	3	50%	10	14%	0	0%	2	33%
Montenegro	0	0%	0	0%	0	0%	3	2%	0	0%	2	22%
Morocco	0	0%	0	0%	0	0%	3	25%	0	0%	1	100%
Netherlands	168	30%	3	7%	23	59%	104	21%	1	2%	15	42%
North Macedonia	37	15%	1	5%	6	38%	14	5%	0	0%	4	25%
Norway	81	15%	1	2%	16	40%	67	13%	0	0%	11	30%
Poland	59	29%	2	12%	9	60%	40	18%	1	5%	7	44%
Portugal	39	10%	1	3%	5	16%	78	18%	1	3%	13	39%
Romania	86	31%	1	4%	13	65%	44	17%	2	10%	7	41%
Russia	106	34%	1	4%	13	59%	27	10%	0	0%	5	28%
San Marino	8	8%	0	0%	2	40%	12	7%	0	0%	3	33%
Serbia	81	45%	2	13%	11	100%	17	12%	0	0%	4	50%
Serbia & Montenegro	36	100%	3	100%	3	100%	0	0%	0	0%	0	0%
Slovakia	3	8%	0	0%	1	33%	9	19%	0	0%	3	75%
Slovenia	35	13%	0	0%	9	45%	77	29%	1	5%	11	58%
Spain	68	13%	0	0%	12	31%	97	19%	2	5%	15	39%
Sweden	188	35%	4	9%	24	60%	101	20%	1	2%	20	53%
Switzerland	159	34%	3	8%	23	66%	121	23%	3	7%	16	43%
Turkey	70	21%	1	4%	11	39%	71	23%	1	4%	13	50%
Ukraine	30	15%	0	0%	7	50%	16	8%	0	0%	3	25%
United Kingdom	168	33%	7	16%	24	62%	131	25%	3	7%	21	54%
Yugoslavia	24	17%	0	0%	5	42%	23	16%	0	0%	5	42%

Eurovision 2019: Who Votes for Who? (And Who Doesn't)

Azerbaijan

	Azerbaijan awarded points to:				Frequency		Azerbaijan received points from:				Frequency	
	Total	% of max	12's	% of max	Times	% of max	Total	% of max	12's	% of max	Times	% of max
Albania	72	30%	2	10%	10	67%	102	35%	0	0%	13	72%
Andorra	0	0%	0	0%	0	0%	15	42%	0	0%	2	67%
Armenia	0	0%	0	0%	0	0%	3	1%	0	0%	2	11%
Australia	20	15%	0	0%	3	50%	9	8%	0	0%	3	50%
Austria	12	6%	0	0%	3	30%	46	23%	1	6%	6	55%
Azerbaijan	-	-	-	-	-	-	-	-	-	-	-	-
Belarus	56	52%	3	33%	5	83%	71	37%	0	0%	9	75%
Belgium	17	10%	0	0%	4	40%	37	15%	0	0%	8	53%
Bosnia & Herzegovina	24	25%	0	0%	4	57%	53	44%	0	0%	7	88%
Bulgaria	46	38%	1	10%	5	83%	70	42%	3	21%	9	82%
Croatia	12	7%	0	0%	5	50%	73	29%	0	0%	9	60%
Cyprus	39	15%	0	0%	7	50%	112	42%	0	0%	14	88%
Czech Republic	23	15%	0	0%	4	57%	109	57%	2	13%	10	100%
Denmark	17	8%	0	0%	4	29%	40	18%	0	0%	6	40%
Estonia	26	14%	0	0%	7	58%	49	19%	0	0%	8	50%
Finland	6	3%	0	0%	2	15%	24	9%	0	0%	7	41%
France	9	5%	0	0%	2	17%	38	17%	0	0%	7	47%
Georgia	89	62%	1	8%	10	100%	166	77%	6	33%	14	100%
Germany	6	3%	0	0%	2	17%	20	9%	0	0%	4	27%
Greece	97	35%	1	4%	14	78%	114	40%	3	13%	16	89%
Hungary	69	32%	0	0%	9	64%	110	48%	5	26%	12	80%
Iceland	7	3%	0	0%	2	13%	60	21%	0	0%	12	67%
Ireland	17	9%	0	0%	5	42%	43	16%	0	0%	9	53%
Israel	91	40%	1	5%	11	79%	92	38%	2	10%	13	81%
Italy	31	20%	0	0%	5	56%	42	22%	2	13%	4	36%
Latvia	31	20%	0	0%	6	60%	64	24%	0	0%	12	71%
Lithuania	30	15%	0	0%	8	62%	104	39%	2	9%	12	71%
Luxembourg	0	-	0	-	0	-	0	-	0	-	0	-
Malta	89	49%	1	7%	9	82%	124	49%	5	24%	13	81%
Moldova	93	41%	0	0%	12	86%	172	62%	3	13%	17	100%
Monaco	0	-	0	-	0	-	0	-	0	-	0	-
Montenegro	34	28%	0	0%	5	63%	81	36%	1	5%	11	79%
Morocco	0	-	0	-	0	-	0	-	0	-	0	-
Netherlands	28	13%	0	0%	5	42%	57	22%	0	0%	12	71%
North Macedonia	34	35%	0	0%	3	60%	55	24%	0	0%	9	64%
Norway	53	22%	1	5%	10	63%	50	19%	0	0%	7	39%
Poland	21	13%	0	0%	6	55%	67	31%	1	6%	10	71%
Portugal	40	37%	1	11%	4	57%	56	27%	1	6%	8	62%
Romania	73	38%	0	0%	12	86%	89	44%	1	6%	10	71%
Russia	182	76%	10	50%	15	94%	187	78%	6	30%	16	100%
San Marino	41	31%	0	0%	6	67%	72	32%	1	5%	10	67%
Serbia	12	8%	0	0%	2	20%	21	12%	0	0%	5	42%
Serbia & Montenegro	0	-	0	-	0	-	0	-	0	-	0	-
Slovakia	0	0%	0	0%	0	0%	29	48%	1	20%	4	80%
Slovenia	20	13%	1	8%	4	40%	43	18%	0	0%	8	50%
Spain	4	2%	0	0%	3	25%	44	15%	0	0%	9	47%
Sweden	36	14%	0	0%	9	56%	53	19%	0	0%	8	47%
Switzerland	24	15%	0	0%	4	40%	23	9%	0	0%	7	41%
Turkey	72	100%	6	100%	6	100%	84	100%	7	100%	7	100%
Ukraine	138	72%	3	19%	13	100%	117	70%	4	29%	12	100%
United Kingdom	7	4%	0	0%	2	17%	33	12%	0	0%	5	29%
Yugoslavia	0	-	0	-	0	-	0	-	0	-	0	-

Eurovision 2019: Who Votes for Who? (And Who Doesn't)

Belarus

	Belarus awarded points to:				Frequency		Belarus received points from:				Frequency	
	Total	% of max	12's	% of max	Times	% of max	Total	% of max	12's	% of max	Times	% of max
Albania	24	10%	1	5%	3	18%	13	6%	0	0%	3	20%
Andorra	4	7%	0	0%	1	20%	0	0%	0	0%	0	0%
Armenia	92	45%	1	6%	13	93%	58	35%	1	7%	8	73%
Australia	57	37%	0	0%	7	100%	8	7%	0	0%	2	40%
Austria	32	14%	0	0%	5	36%	25	12%	0	0%	3	21%
Azerbaijan	71	37%	0	0%	9	75%	56	52%	3	33%	5	83%
Belarus	-	-	-	-	-	-	-	-	-	-	-	-
Belgium	53	20%	1	5%	8	47%	4	1%	0	0%	1	6%
Bosnia & Herzegovina	21	12%	0	0%	5	33%	8	7%	0	0%	3	30%
Bulgaria	78	33%	4	20%	7	50%	40	19%	1	6%	9	64%
Croatia	36	16%	0	0%	7	47%	17	8%	0	0%	3	21%
Cyprus	49	18%	1	4%	7	41%	45	21%	0	0%	8	57%
Czech Republic	39	25%	0	0%	3	38%	22	15%	0	0%	5	63%
Denmark	36	12%	0	0%	9	43%	5	2%	0	0%	3	19%
Estonia	64	22%	1	4%	11	58%	50	18%	0	0%	10	56%
Finland	27	11%	0	0%	6	35%	14	6%	0	0%	3	19%
France	11	5%	0	0%	2	13%	18	8%	0	0%	3	19%
Georgia	88	43%	1	6%	12	86%	87	43%	3	18%	11	85%
Germany	8	3%	0	0%	1	6%	2	1%	0	0%	1	6%
Greece	66	23%	1	4%	13	65%	51	22%	0	0%	10	67%
Hungary	37	15%	0	0%	9	56%	31	17%	1	7%	5	45%
Iceland	53	22%	2	10%	9	53%	19	8%	0	0%	5	33%
Ireland	11	5%	0	0%	4	25%	14	6%	0	0%	5	31%
Israel	83	27%	1	4%	14	74%	63	23%	2	9%	11	65%
Italy	18	12%	0	0%	4	44%	8	6%	0	0%	2	25%
Latvia	47	26%	0	0%	10	77%	53	26%	0	0%	8	57%
Lithuania	101	35%	0	0%	14	74%	83	31%	1	5%	14	82%
Luxembourg	0	-	0	-	0	-	0	-	0	-	0	-
Malta	57	24%	1	5%	11	65%	51	22%	0	0%	10	63%
Moldova	104	48%	1	6%	14	88%	77	43%	1	7%	11	85%
Monaco	0	0%	0	0%	0	0%	1	3%	0	0%	1	33%
Montenegro	5	6%	0	0%	2	33%	24	17%	0	0%	7	78%
Morocco	0	-	0	-	0	-	0	-	0	-	0	-
Netherlands	36	14%	0	0%	5	31%	6	3%	0	0%	3	20%
North Macedonia	22	8%	0	0%	5	25%	44	15%	0	0%	9	45%
Norway	99	34%	1	4%	13	68%	4	2%	0	0%	2	14%
Poland	60	29%	0	0%	10	77%	40	21%	0	0%	8	67%
Portugal	34	16%	0	0%	4	27%	15	7%	0	0%	4	27%
Romania	27	11%	0	0%	10	53%	14	6%	0	0%	5	33%
Russia	212	88%	15	75%	18	100%	89	62%	4	33%	10	91%
San Marino	11	13%	0	0%	2	50%	1	1%	0	0%	1	17%
Serbia	44	16%	0	0%	9	53%	25	11%	0	0%	6	43%
Serbia & Montenegro	20	56%	0	0%	3	100%	0	0%	0	0%	0	0%
Slovakia	3	8%	0	0%	1	33%	4	8%	0	0%	2	50%
Slovenia	31	13%	0	0%	7	44%	22	9%	0	0%	4	25%
Spain	2	1%	0	0%	1	6%	7	3%	0	0%	1	7%
Sweden	80	28%	0	0%	13	65%	4	2%	0	0%	2	13%
Switzerland	33	15%	0	0%	6	43%	2	1%	0	0%	2	13%
Turkey	18	12%	0	0%	5	38%	8	7%	0	0%	2	22%
Ukraine	215	72%	8	32%	20	95%	155	72%	8	44%	14	93%
United Kingdom	6	3%	0	0%	3	19%	4	2%	0	0%	2	12%
Yugoslavia	0	-	0	-	0	-	0	-	0	-	0	-

Eurovision 2019: Who Votes for Who? (And Who Doesn't)

Belgium

	Belgium awarded points to:				Frequency		Belgium received points from:				Frequency	
	Total	% of max	12's	% of max	Times	% of max	Total	% of max	12's	% of max	Times	% of max
Albania	63	22%	0	0%	12	63%	42	17%	0	0%	9	56%
Andorra	0	0%	0	0%	0	0%	8	11%	0	0%	2	33%
Armenia	126	50%	5	24%	14	82%	36	18%	0	0%	8	62%
Australia	89	49%	3	20%	7	88%	70	49%	4	33%	6	86%
Austria	131	26%	4	10%	21	55%	77	16%	0	0%	19	51%
Azerbaijan	37	15%	0	0%	8	53%	17	10%	0	0%	4	40%
Belarus	4	1%	0	0%	1	6%	53	20%	1	5%	8	47%
Belgium	-	-	-	-	-	-	-	-	-	-	-	-
Bosnia & Herzegovina	26	10%	0	0%	7	32%	22	10%	0	0%	3	18%
Bulgaria	51	27%	0	0%	7	64%	52	29%	1	7%	5	45%
Croatia	19	7%	0	0%	8	38%	15	6%	0	0%	5	26%
Cyprus	96	18%	0	0%	18	47%	73	15%	0	0%	13	37%
Czech Republic	52	31%	0	0%	6	75%	34	22%	0	0%	6	75%
Denmark	115	22%	1	2%	20	50%	120	26%	2	5%	14	40%
Estonia	50	14%	1	3%	10	38%	93	28%	1	4%	16	67%
Finland	46	8%	0	0%	11	26%	126	22%	3	6%	20	48%
France	156	28%	1	2%	21	50%	165	32%	6	14%	24	60%
Georgia	32	17%	0	0%	8	67%	53	29%	1	7%	7	70%
Germany	141	26%	0	0%	22	52%	114	22%	2	5%	18	45%
Greece	157	27%	2	4%	27	63%	82	16%	1	2%	13	34%
Hungary	52	19%	1	4%	10	53%	37	19%	1	6%	5	38%
Iceland	98	22%	1	3%	14	42%	82	15%	1	2%	12	29%
Ireland	178	34%	5	11%	29	71%	148	27%	5	11%	19	46%
Israel	156	27%	1	2%	26	62%	92	17%	0	0%	17	44%
Italy	93	27%	1	3%	13	52%	64	18%	0	0%	10	40%
Latvia	43	17%	1	5%	6	33%	78	30%	1	5%	9	50%
Lithuania	32	12%	0	0%	5	28%	64	28%	0	0%	9	60%
Luxembourg	53	23%	0	0%	8	42%	48	21%	1	5%	8	42%
Malta	53	16%	0	0%	8	32%	37	12%	1	4%	5	22%
Moldova	38	14%	0	0%	9	45%	39	17%	0	0%	8	50%
Monaco	16	17%	0	0%	3	38%	26	27%	1	13%	3	38%
Montenegro	0	0%	0	0%	0	0%	18	9%	0	0%	5	42%
Morocco	0	0%	0	0%	0	0%	0	0%	0	0%	0	0%
Netherlands	249	48%	8	19%	30	77%	210	45%	5	13%	27	73%
North Macedonia	0	0%	0	0%	0	0%	39	15%	0	0%	8	44%
Norway	133	24%	1	2%	25	58%	94	20%	0	0%	17	46%
Poland	62	20%	2	8%	9	43%	106	37%	4	17%	11	58%
Portugal	111	23%	2	5%	16	42%	160	32%	3	7%	20	53%
Romania	75	25%	0	0%	13	54%	40	18%	0	0%	7	39%
Russia	87	26%	1	4%	16	62%	63	26%	0	0%	9	47%
San Marino	2	2%	0	0%	1	17%	26	20%	0	0%	5	63%
Serbia	26	11%	0	0%	6	40%	44	24%	0	0%	8	73%
Serbia & Montenegro	10	28%	0	0%	2	67%	0	0%	0	0%	0	0%
Slovakia	4	7%	0	0%	2	40%	26	36%	0	0%	3	50%
Slovenia	22	7%	0	0%	6	26%	82	25%	1	4%	12	55%
Spain	128	23%	3	6%	25	58%	138	23%	2	4%	21	48%
Sweden	200	33%	5	10%	31	67%	94	18%	1	2%	16	40%
Switzerland	119	25%	3	8%	18	50%	83	17%	0	0%	11	30%
Turkey	140	34%	6	18%	18	53%	63	18%	1	3%	10	34%
Ukraine	58	19%	0	0%	10	48%	41	21%	0	0%	5	38%
United Kingdom	149	26%	7	15%	21	49%	120	22%	1	2%	21	51%
Yugoslavia	45	29%	1	8%	7	54%	32	21%	0	0%	5	38%

Eurovision 2019: Who Votes for Who? (And Who Doesn't)

Bosnia & Herzegovina

	Bosnia awarded points to:				Frequency		Bosnia received points from:				Frequency	
	Total	% of max	12's	% of max	Times	% of max	Total	% of max	12's	% of max	Times	% of max
Albania	43	36%	0	0%	9	90%	70	49%	1	8%	8	67%
Andorra	0	0%	0	0%	0	0%	6	5%	0	0%	2	20%
Armenia	25	17%	0	0%	5	50%	19	14%	0	0%	5	50%
Australia	13	54%	0	0%	1	100%	0	-	0	-	0	-
Austria	53	26%	1	6%	8	53%	108	50%	4	22%	12	71%
Azerbaijan	53	44%	0	0%	7	88%	24	25%	0	0%	4	57%
Belarus	8	7%	0	0%	3	30%	21	12%	0	0%	5	33%
Belgium	22	10%	0	0%	3	18%	26	10%	0	0%	7	32%
Bosnia & Herzegovina	-	-	-	-	-	-	-	-	-	-	-	-
Bulgaria	18	17%	0	0%	5	63%	31	22%	0	0%	6	50%
Croatia	176	67%	6	27%	18	90%	194	70%	6	26%	21	95%
Cyprus	2	1%	0	0%	1	6%	7	3%	0	0%	2	10%
Czech Republic	22	31%	1	17%	2	50%	22	31%	0	0%	4	80%
Denmark	12	6%	0	0%	4	24%	76	35%	1	6%	12	67%
Estonia	19	8%	0	0%	5	26%	2	1%	0	0%	2	9%
Finland	20	10%	0	0%	5	31%	53	21%	1	5%	8	40%
France	59	25%	1	5%	10	53%	71	25%	0	0%	13	57%
Georgia	5	5%	0	0%	2	29%	2	3%	0	0%	1	17%
Germany	33	14%	0	0%	6	33%	79	27%	0	0%	13	54%
Greece	63	24%	0	0%	12	57%	20	7%	0	0%	4	18%
Hungary	14	9%	0	0%	6	55%	1	1%	0	0%	1	10%
Iceland	9	4%	0	0%	3	15%	18	7%	0	0%	5	23%
Ireland	54	25%	1	6%	9	50%	24	9%	0	0%	7	32%
Israel	34	15%	0	0%	7	39%	6	3%	0	0%	3	15%
Italy	12	17%	0	0%	2	40%	11	18%	0	0%	3	60%
Latvia	5	3%	0	0%	1	8%	4	2%	0	0%	2	13%
Lithuania	4	2%	0	0%	2	14%	7	4%	0	0%	2	13%
Luxembourg	0	0%	0	0%	0	0%	0	0%	0	0%	0	0%
Malta	68	25%	2	9%	12	57%	30	10%	0	0%	8	33%
Moldova	10	6%	0	0%	2	15%	21	13%	0	0%	5	38%
Monaco	0	0%	0	0%	0	0%	28	47%	2	40%	3	60%
Montenegro	38	63%	1	20%	4	100%	77	80%	4	50%	7	100%
Morocco	0	-	0	-	0	-	0	-	0	-	0	-
Netherlands	21	9%	0	0%	6	35%	90	33%	0	0%	14	64%
North Macedonia	114	68%	1	8%	13	93%	116	60%	3	19%	16	100%
Norway	44	19%	0	0%	10	53%	92	37%	3	14%	11	52%
Poland	25	13%	0	0%	4	27%	20	9%	0	0%	4	22%
Portugal	12	6%	0	0%	5	28%	20	8%	0	0%	4	18%
Romania	24	13%	0	0%	6	38%	24	12%	1	6%	3	18%
Russia	57	22%	0	0%	10	50%	15	6%	0	0%	3	16%
San Marino	10	28%	0	0%	1	50%	6	8%	0	0%	1	20%
Serbia	110	92%	6	60%	9	100%	78	81%	5	63%	8	100%
Serbia & Montenegro	34	94%	2	67%	3	100%	41	68%	2	40%	5	100%
Slovakia	11	18%	0	0%	2	40%	41	38%	1	11%	6	67%
Slovenia	110	54%	2	12%	17	100%	151	57%	5	23%	17	77%
Spain	30	13%	0	0%	5	26%	12	4%	0	0%	4	17%
Sweden	74	27%	2	9%	14	64%	127	42%	1	4%	17	71%
Switzerland	8	6%	0	0%	3	25%	84	41%	3	18%	12	71%
Turkey	133	55%	4	20%	16	80%	175	69%	6	29%	19	90%
Ukraine	54	28%	1	6%	9	60%	22	13%	0	0%	3	21%
United Kingdom	33	14%	0	0%	7	37%	16	6%	0	0%	5	23%
Yugoslavia	0	-	0	-	0	-	0	-	0	-	0	-

Eurovision 2019: Who Votes for Who? (And Who Doesn't)

Bulgaria

	Bulgaria awarded points to:				Frequency		Bulgaria received points from:				Frequency	
	Total	% of max	12's	% of max	Times	% of max	Total	% of max	12's	% of max	Times	% of max
Albania	21	12%	0	0%	5	42%	88	46%	0	0%	9	82%
Andorra	0	0%	0	0%	0	0%	0	0%	0	0%	0	0%
Armenia	102	53%	1	6%	12	92%	31	18%	0	0%	6	60%
Australia	32	33%	1	13%	2	50%	49	51%	0	0%	3	75%
Austria	75	45%	3	21%	7	78%	71	42%	1	7%	8	89%
Azerbaijan	70	42%	3	21%	9	82%	46	38%	1	10%	5	83%
Belarus	40	19%	1	6%	9	64%	78	33%	4	20%	7	50%
Belgium	52	29%	1	7%	5	45%	51	27%	0	0%	7	64%
Bosnia & Herzegovina	31	22%	0	0%	6	50%	18	17%	0	0%	5	63%
Bulgaria	-	-	-	-	-	-	-	-	-	-	-	-
Croatia	36	18%	0	0%	7	54%	60	29%	0	0%	8	67%
Cyprus	76	40%	2	13%	10	83%	120	67%	3	20%	11	100%
Czech Republic	21	19%	0	0%	2	33%	52	36%	1	8%	7	88%
Denmark	29	12%	1	5%	6	35%	53	26%	1	6%	6	50%
Estonia	15	8%	0	0%	5	42%	56	29%	2	13%	5	45%
Finland	17	10%	0	0%	4	33%	44	26%	0	0%	6	60%
France	17	9%	1	7%	2	17%	69	36%	0	0%	10	83%
Georgia	37	22%	0	0%	8	67%	34	20%	0	0%	6	60%
Germany	21	12%	1	7%	3	25%	64	30%	1	6%	8	62%
Greece	112	67%	4	29%	12	100%	71	46%	1	8%	9	100%
Hungary	47	23%	0	0%	8	62%	72	46%	3	23%	7	78%
Iceland	11	7%	0	0%	2	15%	15	8%	0	0%	2	18%
Ireland	13	6%	0	0%	5	36%	88	41%	1	6%	7	58%
Israel	78	28%	0	0%	11	65%	72	30%	1	5%	7	50%
Italy	6	6%	0	0%	1	17%	34	31%	0	0%	4	80%
Latvia	1	1%	0	0%	1	9%	30	17%	0	0%	5	45%
Lithuania	44	17%	0	0%	9	56%	47	21%	0	0%	6	46%
Luxembourg	0	-	0	-	0	-	0	-	0	-	0	-
Malta	26	15%	0	0%	5	42%	83	43%	2	13%	8	67%
Moldova	40	22%	0	0%	8	62%	51	39%	0	0%	7	88%
Monaco	0	0%	0	0%	0	0%	0	0%	0	0%	0	0%
Montenegro	0	0%	0	0%	0	0%	29	27%	0	0%	5	83%
Morocco	0	-	0	-	0	-	0	-	0	-	0	-
Netherlands	26	14%	0	0%	4	36%	45	25%	2	13%	4	36%
North Macedonia	109	50%	2	11%	14	93%	160	63%	4	19%	15	100%
Norway	25	11%	0	0%	9	60%	80	39%	3	18%	6	50%
Poland	19	16%	0	0%	3	43%	31	22%	0	0%	4	50%
Portugal	14	9%	0	0%	3	27%	41	26%	0	0%	8	80%
Romania	53	25%	0	0%	11	69%	46	27%	0	0%	6	55%
Russia	66	46%	2	17%	8	73%	4	4%	0	0%	1	17%
San Marino	0	0%	0	0%	0	0%	45	42%	2	22%	4	80%
Serbia	69	38%	2	13%	9	82%	76	45%	0	0%	9	100%
Serbia & Montenegro	4	33%	0	0%	1	100%	1	4%	0	0%	1	50%
Slovakia	0	0%	0	0%	0	0%	0	0%	0	0%	0	0%
Slovenia	14	10%	0	0%	3	30%	52	29%	0	0%	6	55%
Spain	9	5%	0	0%	3	25%	81	52%	1	8%	9	100%
Sweden	33	14%	0	0%	7	41%	25	14%	0	0%	4	33%
Switzerland	11	6%	0	0%	3	25%	45	19%	1	5%	6	43%
Turkey	96	62%	2	15%	13	100%	49	51%	1	13%	8	100%
Ukraine	95	36%	2	9%	15	83%	40	19%	0	0%	8	62%
United Kingdom	19	11%	1	7%	2	17%	99	46%	2	11%	9	69%
Yugoslavia	0	-	0	-	0	-	0	-	0	-	0	-

Eurovision 2019: Who Votes for Who? (And Who Doesn't)

Croatia

	Croatia awarded points to:				Frequency		Croatia received points from:				Frequency	
	Total	% of max	12's	% of max	Times	% of max	Total	% of max	12's	% of max	Times	% of max
Albania	100	42%	0	0%	16	100%	38	17%	0	0%	8	53%
Andorra	2	4%	0	0%	1	25%	0	0%	0	0%	0	0%
Armenia	13	6%	0	0%	3	21%	17	9%	0	0%	5	45%
Australia	23	24%	1	13%	2	50%	2	4%	0	0%	2	100%
Austria	44	13%	0	0%	9	43%	117	35%	1	4%	16	73%
Azerbaijan	73	29%	0	0%	9	60%	12	7%	0	0%	5	50%
Belarus	17	8%	0	0%	3	21%	36	16%	0	0%	7	47%
Belgium	15	6%	0	0%	5	26%	19	7%	0	0%	8	38%
Bosnia & Herzegovina	194	70%	6	26%	21	95%	176	67%	6	27%	18	90%
Bulgaria	60	29%	0	0%	8	67%	36	18%	0	0%	7	54%
Croatia	-	-	-	-	-	-	-	-	-	-	-	-
Cyprus	87	22%	2	6%	14	52%	54	15%	0	0%	12	46%
Czech Republic	64	44%	1	8%	6	86%	19	13%	0	0%	3	38%
Denmark	65	17%	2	6%	12	44%	10	3%	0	0%	3	13%
Estonia	30	8%	0	0%	7	28%	27	8%	0	0%	8	32%
Finland	23	9%	0	0%	3	16%	21	7%	0	0%	7	35%
France	48	14%	0	0%	9	36%	34	10%	0	0%	6	24%
Georgia	16	11%	0	0%	3	27%	11	9%	0	0%	3	38%
Germany	35	10%	0	0%	10	42%	83	26%	0	0%	17	74%
Greece	72	20%	0	0%	13	50%	40	12%	0	0%	10	43%
Hungary	112	39%	3	13%	12	63%	44	18%	0	0%	7	44%
Iceland	18	6%	0	0%	6	25%	44	14%	0	0%	10	43%
Ireland	70	19%	1	3%	15	58%	37	10%	0	0%	10	37%
Israel	57	16%	1	3%	7	30%	36	12%	0	0%	11	52%
Italy	64	41%	2	15%	7	78%	6	6%	0	0%	1	17%
Latvia	31	15%	0	0%	7	47%	25	10%	0	0%	6	35%
Lithuania	40	11%	1	3%	8	33%	27	8%	0	0%	7	30%
Luxembourg	0	0%	0	0%	0	0%	0	0%	0	0%	0	0%
Malta	113	29%	3	9%	18	67%	92	24%	2	6%	11	41%
Moldova	29	12%	0	0%	9	56%	19	10%	0	0%	5	42%
Monaco	0	0%	0	0%	0	0%	16	27%	0	0%	3	60%
Montenegro	17	35%	0	0%	3	100%	60	50%	1	10%	7	100%
Morocco	0	-	0	-	0	-	0	-	0	-	0	-
Netherlands	76	19%	1	3%	10	38%	54	15%	0	0%	11	42%
North Macedonia	157	59%	4	17%	18	100%	152	55%	2	9%	18	100%
Norway	73	18%	1	3%	13	46%	33	9%	0	0%	11	42%
Poland	14	6%	0	0%	3	18%	24	10%	0	0%	7	37%
Portugal	41	15%	0	0%	5	24%	41	15%	0	0%	14	67%
Romania	27	10%	0	0%	6	30%	38	16%	0	0%	6	35%
Russia	113	34%	2	7%	16	67%	33	12%	0	0%	9	45%
San Marino	3	4%	0	0%	2	50%	18	15%	0	0%	4	67%
Serbia	156	72%	7	39%	14	100%	89	53%	3	21%	11	100%
Serbia & Montenegro	36	100%	3	100%	3	100%	42	70%	1	20%	5	100%
Slovakia	8	13%	0	0%	1	20%	32	44%	2	33%	4	67%
Slovenia	135	49%	2	9%	20	95%	184	61%	7	28%	21	91%
Spain	36	10%	0	0%	7	28%	35	10%	2	7%	7	28%
Sweden	59	14%	0	0%	13	45%	27	7%	1	3%	9	33%
Switzerland	56	19%	0	0%	10	50%	101	30%	0	0%	20	87%
Turkey	56	19%	1	4%	11	46%	55	21%	0	0%	9	41%
Ukraine	82	28%	1	4%	13	62%	61	25%	0	0%	11	65%
United Kingdom	71	20%	2	7%	12	48%	34	9%	0	0%	15	54%
Yugoslavia	0	-	0	-	0	-	0	-	0	-	0	-

Eurovision 2019: Who Votes for Who? (And Who Doesn't)

Cyprus

	Cyprus awarded points to:				Frequency		Cyprus received points from:				Frequency	
	Total	% of max	12's	% of max	Times	% of max	Total	% of max	12's	% of max	Times	% of max
Albania	30	12%	0	0%	6	35%	87	32%	2	9%	10	59%
Andorra	0	0%	0	0%	0	0%	6	10%	0	0%	2	40%
Armenia	111	49%	2	11%	12	86%	121	53%	5	26%	9	75%
Australia	38	24%	0	0%	6	86%	22	13%	0	0%	4	50%
Austria	58	13%	0	0%	13	39%	32	7%	0	0%	9	26%
Azerbaijan	112	42%	0	0%	14	88%	39	15%	0	0%	7	50%
Belarus	45	21%	0	0%	8	57%	49	18%	1	4%	7	41%
Belgium	73	15%	0	0%	13	37%	96	18%	0	0%	18	47%
Bosnia & Herzegovina	7	3%	0	0%	2	10%	2	1%	0	0%	1	6%
Bulgaria	120	67%	3	20%	11	100%	76	40%	2	13%	10	83%
Croatia	54	15%	0	0%	12	46%	87	22%	2	6%	14	52%
Cyprus	0	-	0	-	-	-	-	-	-	-	-	-
Czech Republic	30	15%	0	0%	5	50%	40	17%	0	0%	5	42%
Denmark	81	17%	0	0%	17	46%	80	17%	0	0%	15	43%
Estonia	47	13%	0	0%	9	36%	81	20%	0	0%	11	42%
Finland	44	10%	0	0%	10	31%	108	21%	0	0%	16	46%
France	102	22%	0	0%	20	57%	57	11%	1	2%	12	33%
Georgia	57	32%	1	7%	8	67%	63	29%	1	6%	6	50%
Germany	55	12%	2	5%	9	26%	56	12%	0	0%	13	38%
Greece	467	93%	34	81%	36	100%	458	89%	30	70%	34	97%
Hungary	46	15%	0	0%	7	35%	44	16%	1	4%	8	47%
Iceland	48	11%	1	3%	10	31%	104	19%	3	7%	16	42%
Ireland	103	23%	1	3%	17	47%	105	20%	2	5%	17	44%
Israel	115	24%	1	3%	20	57%	94	19%	0	0%	19	54%
Italy	119	45%	2	9%	15	83%	65	21%	0	0%	12	57%
Latvia	24	10%	0	0%	7	39%	32	10%	0	0%	8	38%
Lithuania	45	16%	0	0%	11	52%	34	11%	0	0%	9	43%
Luxembourg	32	22%	0	0%	5	42%	8	6%	0	0%	2	17%
Malta	72	21%	0	0%	14	56%	119	31%	4	13%	18	67%
Moldova	58	22%	0	0%	11	61%	38	14%	0	0%	6	38%
Monaco	4	11%	0	0%	1	33%	24	50%	1	25%	3	75%
Montenegro	6	5%	0	0%	2	25%	40	17%	0	0%	7	54%
Morocco	0	-	0	-	0	-	0	-	0	-	0	-
Netherlands	50	11%	0	0%	11	34%	83	18%	1	3%	10	29%
North Macedonia	5	2%	0	0%	2	13%	33	12%	0	0%	4	22%
Norway	92	20%	0	0%	17	47%	68	15%	1	3%	14	40%
Poland	21	8%	0	0%	7	37%	34	10%	0	0%	8	38%
Portugal	59	14%	1	3%	9	29%	64	13%	0	0%	16	46%
Romania	91	34%	1	5%	16	76%	49	19%	0	0%	10	53%
Russia	169	54%	3	12%	20	87%	66	23%	0	0%	11	55%
San Marino	10	10%	0	0%	1	20%	57	30%	0	0%	6	60%
Serbia	43	21%	0	0%	8	62%	35	17%	0	0%	7	58%
Serbia & Montenegro	30	83%	0	0%	3	100%	6	13%	0	0%	3	75%
Slovakia	0	0%	0	0%	0	0%	3	4%	0	0%	3	43%
Slovenia	26	8%	0	0%	6	25%	64	16%	0	0%	12	44%
Spain	123	26%	1	3%	19	53%	112	20%	1	2%	15	38%
Sweden	163	30%	4	9%	24	59%	99	18%	2	4%	17	43%
Switzerland	74	19%	0	0%	16	53%	68	14%	0	0%	17	49%
Turkey	12	3%	0	0%	2	6%	10	3%	0	0%	3	10%
Ukraine	107	37%	1	4%	16	76%	28	12%	0	0%	6	38%
United Kingdom	80	17%	0	0%	21	58%	158	29%	2	4%	25	64%
Yugoslavia	59	49%	1	10%	9	90%	52	43%	1	10%	8	80%

Eurovision 2019: Who Votes for Who? (And Who Doesn't)
Czech Republic

	Czech Rep awarded points to:				Frequency		Czech Rep received points from:				Frequency	
	Total	% of max	12's	% of max	Times	% of max	Total	% of max	12's	% of max	Times	% of max
Albania	15	10%	0	0%	3	33%	3	2%	0	0%	2	29%
Andorra	7	29%	0	0%	1	50%	0	0%	0	0%	0	0%
Armenia	85	47%	4	27%	10	100%	43	26%	0	0%	6	75%
Australia	41	26%	1	8%	5	71%	37	28%	1	9%	4	67%
Austria	30	21%	0	0%	5	71%	51	39%	1	9%	5	83%
Azerbaijan	109	57%	2	13%	10	100%	23	15%	0	0%	4	57%
Belarus	22	15%	0	0%	5	63%	39	25%	0	0%	3	38%
Belgium	34	22%	0	0%	6	75%	52	31%	0	0%	6	75%
Bosnia & Herzegovina	22	31%	0	0%	4	80%	22	31%	1	17%	2	50%
Bulgaria	52	36%	1	8%	7	88%	21	19%	0	0%	2	33%
Croatia	19	13%	0	0%	3	38%	64	44%	1	8%	6	86%
Cyprus	40	17%	0	0%	5	42%	30	15%	0	0%	5	50%
Czech Republic	-	-	-	-	-	-	-	-	-	-	-	-
Denmark	25	21%	0	0%	4	57%	6	6%	0	0%	1	20%
Estonia	20	13%	0	0%	4	50%	47	30%	1	8%	6	86%
Finland	15	9%	0	0%	4	44%	42	22%	0	0%	6	67%
France	7	5%	0	0%	2	25%	19	13%	0	0%	4	57%
Georgia	18	14%	0	0%	5	63%	26	18%	2	17%	3	43%
Germany	3	2%	0	0%	1	13%	12	11%	0	0%	2	33%
Greece	13	7%	0	0%	3	30%	27	15%	0	0%	4	50%
Hungary	48	29%	1	7%	6	67%	47	33%	1	8%	5	71%
Iceland	36	19%	0	0%	6	55%	76	35%	2	11%	7	64%
Ireland	31	43%	0	0%	3	75%	18	15%	0	0%	4	67%
Israel	61	32%	3	19%	7	64%	48	31%	2	15%	5	63%
Italy	20	19%	0	0%	4	80%	4	4%	0	0%	1	20%
Latvia	25	21%	0	0%	6	75%	15	11%	0	0%	4	57%
Lithuania	8	6%	0	0%	4	50%	27	20%	0	0%	3	43%
Luxembourg	0	-	0	-	0	-	0	-	0	-	0	-
Malta	35	27%	0	0%	6	75%	15	10%	0	0%	4	50%
Moldova	30	23%	0	0%	3	43%	27	20%	0	0%	3	50%
Monaco	0	-	0	-	0	-	0	-	0	-	0	-
Montenegro	8	7%	0	0%	2	29%	15	8%	0	0%	5	56%
Morocco	0	-	0	-	0	-	0	-	0	-	0	-
Netherlands	38	29%	0	0%	4	67%	16	15%	0	0%	3	60%
North Macedonia	25	26%	0	0%	5	83%	28	21%	0	0%	3	43%
Norway	20	15%	0	0%	3	38%	16	17%	1	13%	2	40%
Poland	38	26%	0	0%	4	50%	32	22%	0	0%	6	86%
Portugal	52	36%	1	8%	6	67%	45	27%	2	14%	5	56%
Romania	6	7%	0	0%	1	17%	11	15%	0	0%	2	50%
Russia	59	49%	1	10%	7	100%	8	7%	0	0%	2	40%
San Marino	12	14%	1	14%	1	25%	27	20%	0	0%	4	67%
Serbia	39	27%	1	8%	5	63%	20	17%	0	0%	3	50%
Serbia & Montenegro	0	-	0	-	0	-	0	-	0	-	0	-
Slovakia	0	-	0	-	0	-	0	-	0	-	0	-
Slovenia	42	29%	1	8%	6	75%	53	37%	2	17%	5	71%
Spain	0	0%	0	0%	0	0%	67	37%	0	0%	6	75%
Sweden	81	40%	3	18%	8	67%	19	11%	0	0%	5	67%
Switzerland	11	11%	0	0%	2	33%	11	8%	0	0%	1	13%
Turkey	7	10%	0	0%	3	50%	1	3%	0	0%	1	33%
Ukraine	68	57%	4	40%	7	100%	14	19%	0	0%	1	25%
United Kingdom	15	10%	0	0%	3	38%	16	10%	0	0%	4	44%
Yugoslavia	0	-	0	-	0	-	0	-	0	-	0	-

Eurovision 2019: Who Votes for Who? (And Who Doesn't)
Denmark

	Denmark awarded points to:				Frequency		Denmark received points from:				Frequency	
	Total	% of max	12's	% of max	Times	% of max	Total	% of max	12's	% of max	Times	% of max
Albania	31	11%	0	0%	6	32%	18	6%	0	0%	6	29%
Andorra	0	0%	0	0%	0	0%	18	21%	0	0%	4	57%
Armenia	8	4%	0	0%	3	20%	18	8%	0	0%	6	43%
Australia	92	59%	2	15%	7	100%	46	35%	1	9%	5	83%
Austria	111	23%	0	0%	20	57%	113	21%	2	5%	19	49%
Azerbaijan	40	18%	0	0%	6	40%	17	8%	0	0%	4	29%
Belarus	5	2%	0	0%	3	19%	36	12%	0	0%	9	43%
Belgium	120	26%	2	5%	14	40%	115	22%	1	2%	20	50%
Bosnia & Herzegovina	76	35%	1	6%	12	67%	12	6%	0	0%	4	24%
Bulgaria	53	26%	1	6%	6	50%	29	12%	1	5%	6	35%
Croatia	10	3%	0	0%	3	13%	65	17%	2	6%	12	44%
Cyprus	80	17%	0	0%	15	43%	81	17%	0	0%	17	46%
Czech Republic	6	6%	0	0%	1	20%	25	21%	0	0%	4	57%
Denmark	-	-	-	-	-	-	-	-	-	-	-	-
Estonia	86	29%	0	0%	17	77%	136	39%	2	7%	20	80%
Finland	64	17%	1	3%	11	35%	109	23%	1	3%	18	50%
France	70	14%	1	2%	16	43%	124	22%	2	4%	22	54%
Georgia	5	3%	0	0%	1	8%	30	13%	0	0%	7	47%
Germany	191	38%	6	14%	27	71%	148	25%	2	4%	23	55%
Greece	42	9%	0	0%	13	37%	45	10%	1	3%	10	28%
Hungary	50	16%	1	4%	10	48%	112	37%	4	16%	15	75%
Iceland	161	46%	3	10%	23	82%	248	50%	10	24%	28	74%
Ireland	187	37%	4	10%	28	74%	195	33%	8	16%	29	66%
Israel	79	15%	0	0%	18	49%	144	27%	2	5%	24	62%
Italy	26	8%	0	0%	7	30%	104	26%	3	9%	13	48%
Latvia	70	24%	0	0%	13	65%	124	33%	2	6%	18	72%
Lithuania	53	16%	0	0%	10	45%	71	19%	0	0%	16	64%
Luxembourg	32	17%	0	0%	9	56%	26	14%	0	0%	6	38%
Malta	84	24%	1	3%	14	58%	93	23%	0	0%	19	68%
Moldova	40	14%	0	0%	6	30%	30	10%	1	4%	7	33%
Monaco	14	23%	0	0%	2	40%	33	46%	0	0%	4	67%
Montenegro	5	5%	0	0%	1	14%	31	16%	0	0%	5	42%
Morocco	0	0%	0	0%	0	0%	2	17%	0	0%	1	100%
Netherlands	188	35%	1	2%	23	61%	205	36%	6	13%	28	68%
North Macedonia	24	9%	0	0%	4	22%	31	9%	1	3%	5	22%
Norway	269	47%	10	21%	30	73%	291	49%	8	16%	35	83%
Poland	26	10%	0	0%	7	41%	74	26%	1	4%	13	68%
Portugal	31	8%	0	0%	7	23%	77	17%	0	0%	21	60%
Romania	64	20%	0	0%	13	57%	84	23%	1	3%	16	67%
Russia	87	24%	2	7%	14	54%	61	18%	1	4%	10	42%
San Marino	0	0%	0	0%	0	0%	34	18%	1	6%	7	64%
Serbia	22	8%	0	0%	5	31%	43	16%	1	4%	8	47%
Serbia & Montenegro	17	47%	0	0%	2	67%	0	0%	0	0%	0	0%
Slovakia	0	0%	0	0%	0	0%	16	22%	0	0%	3	50%
Slovenia	22	7%	0	0%	3	14%	122	32%	2	6%	15	56%
Spain	38	8%	1	2%	11	29%	93	18%	0	0%	18	45%
Sweden	437	73%	18	36%	40	91%	289	50%	10	21%	38	88%
Switzerland	117	26%	1	3%	21	64%	71	13%	0	0%	20	50%
Turkey	90	23%	0	0%	14	42%	32	8%	0	0%	12	36%
Ukraine	80	23%	1	3%	14	58%	51	16%	0	0%	8	36%
United Kingdom	141	28%	2	5%	25	66%	163	29%	4	9%	26	62%
Yugoslavia	52	39%	2	18%	6	55%	7	5%	0	0%	2	18%

Eurovision 2019: Who Votes for Who? (And Who Doesn't)

Estonia

	Estonia awarded points to:				Frequency		Estonia received points from:				Frequency	
	Total	% of max	12's	% of max	Times	% of max	Total	% of max	12's	% of max	Times	% of max
Albania	3	1%	0	0%	3	18%	16	7%	0	0%	5	31%
Andorra	8	13%	0	0%	2	40%	0	0%	0	0%	0	0%
Armenia	15	6%	0	0%	4	25%	24	12%	0	0%	4	31%
Australia	34	26%	0	0%	5	83%	23	24%	0	0%	4	80%
Austria	87	27%	2	7%	11	52%	55	16%	0	0%	13	57%
Azerbaijan	49	19%	0	0%	8	50%	26	14%	0	0%	7	58%
Belarus	50	18%	0	0%	10	56%	64	22%	1	4%	11	58%
Belgium	93	28%	1	4%	16	67%	50	14%	1	3%	10	38%
Bosnia & Herzegovina	2	1%	0	0%	2	9%	19	8%	0	0%	5	26%
Bulgaria	56	29%	2	13%	5	45%	15	8%	0	0%	5	42%
Croatia	27	8%	0	0%	8	32%	30	8%	0	0%	7	28%
Cyprus	81	20%	0	0%	11	42%	47	13%	0	0%	9	36%
Czech Republic	47	30%	1	8%	6	86%	20	13%	0	0%	4	50%
Denmark	136	39%	2	7%	20	80%	86	29%	0	0%	17	77%
Estonia	-	-	-	-	-	-	-	-	-	-	-	-
Finland	168	54%	5	19%	19	86%	204	63%	8	30%	21	95%
France	50	14%	1	3%	11	44%	76	19%	0	0%	13	46%
Georgia	42	27%	0	0%	8	73%	46	29%	0	0%	6	60%
Germany	48	14%	1	4%	11	46%	51	16%	0	0%	11	46%
Greece	33	8%	0	0%	9	31%	56	16%	1	3%	9	36%
Hungary	107	33%	1	4%	16	76%	55	20%	0	0%	9	50%
Iceland	91	27%	1	4%	16	67%	103	31%	1	4%	16	70%
Ireland	96	30%	1	4%	15	63%	121	34%	0	0%	20	77%
Israel	25	7%	0	0%	7	30%	84	26%	0	0%	12	55%
Italy	28	17%	0	0%	5	50%	34	26%	1	9%	5	56%
Latvia	136	63%	2	11%	17	100%	190	75%	7	33%	18	95%
Lithuania	101	34%	1	4%	14	67%	141	49%	4	17%	18	90%
Luxembourg	0	-	0	-	0	-	0	-	0	-	0	-
Malta	70	21%	0	0%	15	63%	46	14%	1	4%	8	33%
Moldova	21	8%	0	0%	6	30%	51	20%	1	5%	11	61%
Monaco	2	6%	0	0%	1	33%	5	14%	0	0%	1	33%
Montenegro	0	0%	0	0%	0	0%	8	4%	0	0%	3	25%
Morocco	0	-	0	-	0	-	0	-	0	-	0	-
Netherlands	119	29%	3	9%	15	54%	69	18%	1	3%	12	43%
North Macedonia	2	1%	0	0%	1	5%	32	11%	1	4%	6	30%
Norway	152	41%	2	6%	21	78%	63	20%	0	0%	12	52%
Poland	29	10%	1	4%	5	24%	59	22%	1	5%	9	47%
Portugal	29	11%	0	0%	5	25%	93	30%	4	15%	10	45%
Romania	33	11%	1	4%	7	30%	17	6%	0	0%	6	30%
Russia	245	68%	8	27%	27	100%	64	21%	0	0%	11	48%
San Marino	20	15%	0	0%	3	43%	13	7%	0	0%	2	18%
Serbia	13	5%	0	0%	5	29%	21	9%	0	0%	6	40%
Serbia & Montenegro	1	3%	0	0%	1	33%	4	11%	0	0%	1	33%
Slovakia	6	7%	0	0%	1	14%	50	42%	1	10%	6	60%
Slovenia	30	10%	0	0%	6	26%	56	17%	1	4%	11	46%
Spain	13	4%	0	0%	4	16%	62	16%	1	3%	13	46%
Sweden	219	57%	8	25%	25	89%	119	35%	3	11%	17	68%
Switzerland	45	20%	2	11%	6	38%	24	9%	1	4%	3	16%
Turkey	14	6%	0	0%	3	16%	22	11%	1	6%	3	19%
Ukraine	113	38%	2	8%	16	73%	41	19%	0	0%	10	63%
United Kingdom	53	15%	0	0%	11	44%	81	26%	1	4%	13	57%
Yugoslavia	0	-	0	-	0	-	0	-	0	-	0	-

Eurovision 2019: Who Votes for Who? (And Who Doesn't)
Finland

	Finland awarded points to:				Frequency		Finland received points from:				Frequency	
	Total	% of max	12's	% of max	Times	% of max	Total	% of max	12's	% of max	Times	% of max
Albania	31	11%	0	0%	6	32%	22	9%	0	0%	5	28%
Andorra	5	7%	0	0%	1	17%	49	45%	1	11%	7	78%
Armenia	29	10%	0	0%	7	37%	14	6%	0	0%	2	12%
Australia	74	47%	1	8%	6	86%	15	18%	0	0%	3	75%
Austria	97	20%	2	5%	14	39%	37	8%	0	0%	8	24%
Azerbaijan	24	9%	0	0%	7	41%	6	3%	0	0%	2	15%
Belarus	14	6%	0	0%	3	19%	27	11%	0	0%	6	35%
Belgium	126	22%	3	6%	20	48%	46	8%	0	0%	11	26%
Bosnia & Herzegovina	53	21%	1	5%	8	40%	20	10%	0	0%	5	31%
Bulgaria	44	26%	0	0%	6	60%	17	10%	0	0%	4	33%
Croatia	21	7%	0	0%	7	35%	23	9%	0	0%	3	16%
Cyprus	108	21%	0	0%	16	46%	44	10%	0	0%	10	31%
Czech Republic	42	22%	0	0%	6	67%	15	9%	0	0%	4	44%
Denmark	109	23%	1	3%	18	50%	64	17%	1	3%	11	35%
Estonia	204	63%	8	30%	21	95%	168	54%	5	19%	19	86%
Finland	-	-	-	-	-	-	-	-	-	-	-	-
France	122	23%	3	7%	23	58%	50	10%	0	0%	11	29%
Georgia	20	10%	0	0%	5	36%	1	1%	0	0%	1	8%
Germany	81	15%	2	5%	16	40%	82	17%	2	5%	18	46%
Greece	94	15%	0	0%	21	47%	87	15%	1	2%	15	36%
Hungary	114	37%	3	12%	15	71%	36	16%	1	5%	6	38%
Iceland	169	38%	5	14%	20	63%	164	29%	5	11%	23	55%
Ireland	129	28%	1	3%	25	69%	98	20%	1	3%	14	37%
Israel	203	38%	4	9%	28	70%	91	18%	1	2%	18	47%
Italy	155	45%	4	14%	21	84%	28	9%	0	0%	4	17%
Latvia	39	19%	1	6%	8	53%	45	20%	0	0%	8	47%
Lithuania	28	12%	0	0%	5	29%	43	20%	0	0%	7	44%
Luxembourg	55	24%	1	5%	9	47%	21	9%	0	0%	6	32%
Malta	55	15%	0	0%	13	48%	35	10%	0	0%	8	31%
Moldova	33	13%	0	0%	5	28%	22	10%	0	0%	4	25%
Monaco	17	18%	0	0%	4	50%	27	25%	0	0%	4	44%
Montenegro	3	2%	0	0%	1	11%	5	3%	0	0%	2	17%
Morocco	0	0%	0	0%	0	0%	0	0%	0	0%	0	0%
Netherlands	109	23%	1	3%	16	46%	48	11%	0	0%	12	34%
North Macedonia	9	4%	0	0%	3	16%	34	13%	0	0%	8	40%
Norway	170	31%	6	13%	23	53%	147	31%	4	10%	22	58%
Poland	31	11%	0	0%	4	21%	64	25%	2	10%	11	61%
Portugal	82	17%	2	5%	16	43%	52	11%	0	0%	10	27%
Romania	30	10%	0	0%	7	29%	22	8%	0	0%	6	29%
Russia	128	38%	2	7%	19	76%	35	14%	1	5%	5	26%
San Marino	8	6%	0	0%	3	38%	17	10%	0	0%	4	36%
Serbia	39	18%	1	6%	7	50%	7	5%	0	0%	2	20%
Serbia & Montenegro	20	56%	0	0%	2	67%	15	31%	0	0%	2	50%
Slovakia	2	4%	0	0%	1	25%	2	3%	0	0%	1	17%
Slovenia	39	14%	0	0%	9	47%	31	12%	0	0%	5	26%
Spain	80	15%	0	0%	14	34%	85	14%	0	0%	18	40%
Sweden	287	51%	8	17%	32	76%	179	37%	3	8%	23	62%
Switzerland	148	31%	2	5%	24	63%	87	17%	1	2%	16	39%
Turkey	55	14%	0	0%	13	39%	40	11%	0	0%	9	30%
Ukraine	43	19%	1	5%	8	50%	13	9%	0	0%	2	18%
United Kingdom	106	20%	0	0%	18	44%	84	16%	2	5%	13	33%
Yugoslavia	35	22%	1	8%	7	54%	22	14%	0	0%	5	38%

Eurovision 2019: Who Votes for Who? (And Who Doesn't)

France

	France awarded points to:				Frequency		France received points from:				Frequency	
	Total	% of max	12's	% of max	Times	% of max	Total	% of max	12's	% of max	Times	% of max
Albania	21	9%	0	0%	6	35%	41	17%	0	0%	9	56%
Andorra	0	0%	0	0%	0	0%	26	36%	0	0%	5	83%
Armenia	142	66%	7	39%	15	100%	73	36%	1	6%	12	92%
Australia	62	40%	1	8%	7	100%	26	24%	0	0%	2	40%
Austria	101	20%	2	5%	15	41%	124	25%	4	10%	17	45%
Azerbaijan	38	17%	0	0%	7	47%	9	5%	0	0%	2	17%
Belarus	18	8%	0	0%	3	19%	11	5%	0	0%	2	13%
Belgium	165	32%	6	14%	24	60%	156	28%	1	2%	21	50%
Bosnia & Herzegovina	71	25%	0	0%	13	57%	59	25%	1	5%	10	53%
Bulgaria	69	36%	0	0%	10	83%	17	9%	1	7%	2	17%
Croatia	34	10%	0	0%	6	24%	48	14%	0	0%	9	36%
Cyprus	57	11%	1	2%	12	33%	102	22%	0	0%	20	57%
Czech Republic	19	13%	0	0%	4	57%	7	5%	0	0%	2	25%
Denmark	124	22%	2	4%	22	54%	70	14%	1	2%	16	43%
Estonia	76	19%	0	0%	13	46%	50	14%	1	3%	11	44%
Finland	50	10%	0	0%	11	29%	122	23%	3	7%	23	58%
France	-	-	-	-	-	-	-	-	-	-	-	-
Georgia	10	5%	0	0%	2	14%	18	9%	0	0%	5	42%
Germany	116	21%	1	2%	18	42%	119	21%	3	6%	18	42%
Greece	115	20%	0	0%	22	51%	146	28%	2	5%	24	62%
Hungary	68	18%	0	0%	15	60%	15	6%	0	0%	5	29%
Iceland	68	15%	1	3%	12	35%	103	19%	1	2%	16	38%
Ireland	102	21%	0	0%	22	56%	130	23%	1	2%	21	49%
Israel	247	48%	6	14%	32	84%	157	30%	2	5%	23	59%
Italy	157	44%	2	7%	21	81%	122	34%	1	3%	16	62%
Latvia	28	11%	0	0%	4	21%	31	11%	0	0%	7	35%
Lithuania	10	4%	0	0%	3	16%	58	20%	0	0%	9	45%
Luxembourg	56	26%	2	11%	9	50%	89	41%	3	17%	12	67%
Malta	68	16%	0	0%	14	45%	33	8%	0	0%	7	23%
Moldova	52	19%	1	4%	10	53%	13	6%	0	0%	3	20%
Monaco	27	32%	0	0%	5	71%	53	55%	2	25%	7	88%
Montenegro	7	6%	0	0%	1	14%	12	7%	0	0%	3	27%
Morocco	0	0%	0	0%	0	0%	1	8%	0	0%	1	100%
Netherlands	161	27%	3	6%	23	55%	128	24%	4	9%	20	50%
North Macedonia	15	6%	0	0%	2	11%	15	5%	0	0%	4	21%
Norway	74	12%	0	0%	15	32%	143	25%	3	6%	27	63%
Poland	77	25%	1	4%	15	68%	49	16%	1	4%	9	41%
Portugal	242	48%	8	19%	28	72%	130	25%	3	7%	24	60%
Romania	94	29%	1	4%	15	63%	15	5%	0	0%	4	20%
Russia	71	19%	0	0%	14	52%	60	20%	1	4%	9	41%
San Marino	5	3%	0	0%	1	13%	12	7%	0	0%	3	30%
Serbia	103	37%	3	13%	13	76%	10	5%	0	0%	4	33%
Serbia & Montenegro	16	67%	0	0%	2	100%	0	0%	0	0%	0	0%
Slovakia	1	1%	0	0%	1	14%	0	0%	0	0%	0	0%
Slovenia	32	10%	0	0%	9	39%	38	11%	0	0%	9	36%
Spain	150	26%	2	4%	25	57%	127	22%	0	0%	20	45%
Sweden	168	26%	3	6%	32	67%	120	21%	0	0%	24	56%
Switzerland	93	22%	1	3%	15	44%	156	30%	4	9%	24	60%
Turkey	190	44%	8	22%	21	58%	38	10%	0	0%	12	36%
Ukraine	30	10%	0	0%	8	36%	38	18%	1	6%	4	27%
United Kingdom	152	26%	5	10%	23	52%	91	16%	0	0%	20	45%
Yugoslavia	21	15%	0	0%	7	58%	56	39%	3	25%	7	58%

Eurovision 2019: Who Votes for Who? (And Who Doesn't)

Georgia

	Georgia awarded points to:				Frequency		Georgia received points from:				Frequency	
	Total	% of max	12's	% of max	Times	% of max	Total	% of max	12's	% of max	Times	% of max
Albania	13	6%	0	0%	3	23%	5	2%	0	0%	2	14%
Andorra	0	0%	0	0%	0	0%	0	0%	0	0%	0	0%
Armenia	146	76%	5	31%	13	100%	141	78%	4	27%	13	100%
Australia	31	15%	0	0%	4	44%	13	9%	0	0%	3	43%
Austria	37	28%	0	0%	5	63%	2	2%	0	0%	1	13%
Azerbaijan	166	77%	6	33%	14	100%	89	62%	1	8%	10	100%
Belarus	87	43%	3	18%	11	85%	88	43%	1	6%	12	86%
Belgium	53	29%	1	7%	7	70%	32	17%	0	0%	8	67%
Bosnia & Herzegovina	2	3%	0	0%	1	17%	5	5%	0	0%	2	29%
Bulgaria	34	20%	0	0%	6	60%	37	22%	0	0%	8	67%
Croatia	11	9%	0	0%	3	38%	16	11%	0	0%	3	27%
Cyprus	63	29%	1	6%	6	50%	57	32%	1	7%	8	67%
Czech Republic	26	18%	2	17%	3	43%	18	14%	0	0%	5	63%
Denmark	30	13%	0	0%	7	47%	5	3%	0	0%	1	8%
Estonia	46	29%	0	0%	6	60%	42	27%	0	0%	8	73%
Finland	1	1%	0	0%	1	8%	20	10%	0	0%	5	36%
France	18	9%	0	0%	5	42%	10	5%	0	0%	2	14%
Georgia	-	-	-	-	-	-	-	-	-	-	-	-
Germany	15	8%	0	0%	4	36%	24	13%	0	0%	3	25%
Greece	51	21%	0	0%	11	69%	83	41%	0	0%	14	100%
Hungary	28	11%	0	0%	7	44%	26	14%	0	0%	9	69%
Iceland	13	7%	0	0%	4	31%	15	8%	0	0%	4	31%
Ireland	0	0%	0	0%	0	0%	14	9%	0	0%	4	36%
Israel	47	23%	1	6%	9	75%	48	25%	0	0%	9	69%
Italy	34	22%	0	0%	7	78%	17	12%	0	0%	3	38%
Latvia	65	39%	0	0%	8	80%	55	27%	0	0%	8	62%
Lithuania	99	52%	2	13%	12	92%	147	77%	6	38%	14	100%
Luxembourg	0	-	0	-	0	-	0	-	0	-	0	-
Malta	31	17%	0	0%	6	50%	29	15%	0	0%	5	36%
Moldova	53	29%	1	7%	8	73%	52	31%	0	0%	9	82%
Monaco	0	-	0	-	0	-	0	-	0	-	0	-
Montenegro	0	0%	0	0%	0	0%	4	3%	0	0%	2	22%
Morocco	0	-	0	-	0	-	0	-	0	-	0	-
Netherlands	33	17%	0	0%	6	55%	13	8%	0	0%	4	33%
North Macedonia	6	4%	0	0%	4	40%	15	8%	0	0%	5	36%
Norway	46	18%	0	0%	8	50%	2	1%	0	0%	2	13%
Poland	27	13%	0	0%	5	42%	56	26%	0	0%	8	62%
Portugal	51	33%	2	15%	5	50%	18	13%	0	0%	4	40%
Romania	25	13%	0	0%	4	29%	6	4%	0	0%	2	17%
Russia	77	40%	0	0%	12	92%	70	45%	0	0%	11	100%
San Marino	24	22%	1	11%	4	67%	17	12%	0	0%	5	56%
Serbia	35	13%	0	0%	5	31%	17	7%	0	0%	4	27%
Serbia & Montenegro	0	-	0	-	0	-	0	-	0	-	0	-
Slovakia	0	0%	0	0%	0	0%	0	0%	0	0%	0	0%
Slovenia	25	10%	0	0%	5	36%	16	7%	0	0%	5	33%
Spain	2	1%	0	0%	1	8%	13	7%	0	0%	4	31%
Sweden	91	34%	3	14%	11	69%	15	8%	0	0%	4	31%
Switzerland	13	9%	0	0%	4	40%	2	1%	0	0%	2	14%
Turkey	37	34%	0	0%	8	89%	65	60%	0	0%	9	100%
Ukraine	157	65%	4	20%	15	100%	115	64%	2	13%	12	100%
United Kingdom	7	4%	0	0%	3	25%	27	13%	2	11%	4	27%
Yugoslavia	0	-	0	-	0	-	0	-	0	-	0	-

Eurovision 2019: Who Votes for Who? (And Who Doesn't)

Germany

	Germany awarded points to:				Frequency		Germany received points from:				Frequency	
	Total	% of max	12's	% of max	Times	% of max	Total	% of max	12's	% of max	Times	% of max
Albania	31	13%	0	0%	8	50%	49	20%	0	0%	9	56%
Andorra	0	0%	0	0%	0	0%	5	7%	0	0%	1	17%
Armenia	59	27%	0	0%	10	67%	11	5%	0	0%	2	15%
Australia	77	49%	0	0%	7	100%	15	14%	0	0%	2	40%
Austria	112	22%	2	5%	19	50%	129	26%	1	2%	22	58%
Azerbaijan	20	9%	0	0%	4	27%	6	3%	0	0%	2	17%
Belarus	2	1%	0	0%	1	6%	8	3%	0	0%	1	6%
Belgium	114	22%	2	5%	18	45%	141	26%	0	0%	22	52%
Bosnia & Herzegovina	79	27%	0	0%	13	54%	33	14%	0	0%	6	33%
Bulgaria	64	30%	1	6%	8	62%	21	12%	1	7%	3	25%
Croatia	83	26%	0	0%	17	74%	35	10%	0	0%	10	42%
Cyprus	56	12%	0	0%	13	38%	55	12%	2	5%	9	26%
Czech Republic	12	11%	0	0%	2	33%	3	2%	0	0%	1	13%
Denmark	148	25%	2	4%	23	55%	191	38%	6	14%	27	71%
Estonia	51	16%	0	0%	11	46%	48	14%	1	4%	11	46%
Finland	82	17%	2	5%	18	46%	81	15%	2	5%	16	40%
France	119	21%	3	6%	18	42%	116	21%	1	2%	18	42%
Georgia	24	13%	0	0%	3	25%	15	8%	0	0%	4	36%
Germany	-	-	-	-	-	-	-	-	-	-	-	-
Greece	148	29%	3	7%	22	54%	36	7%	0	0%	10	26%
Hungary	67	23%	1	4%	10	53%	24	10%	1	5%	4	24%
Iceland	75	20%	1	3%	14	45%	75	14%	1	2%	12	29%
Ireland	159	28%	2	4%	27	63%	148	26%	1	2%	27	63%
Israel	183	30%	4	8%	29	64%	79	15%	2	5%	11	28%
Italy	100	28%	3	10%	18	69%	86	24%	1	3%	14	54%
Latvia	62	22%	1	4%	8	40%	44	15%	1	4%	8	40%
Lithuania	19	6%	0	0%	6	27%	32	11%	0	0%	7	35%
Luxembourg	42	18%	1	5%	7	37%	67	29%	2	11%	11	58%
Malta	92	20%	0	0%	20	61%	32	8%	0	0%	10	34%
Moldova	26	10%	0	0%	5	29%	10	4%	0	0%	2	13%
Monaco	23	21%	0	0%	4	44%	32	33%	1	13%	5	63%
Montenegro	2	2%	0	0%	1	14%	0	0%	0	0%	0	0%
Morocco	0	0%	0	0%	0	0%	10	83%	0	0%	1	100%
Netherlands	178	31%	1	2%	25	61%	149	28%	5	11%	24	60%
North Macedonia	30	10%	1	4%	4	18%	11	4%	0	0%	2	11%
Norway	184	26%	5	9%	27	53%	102	18%	2	4%	18	42%
Poland	140	45%	4	15%	19	86%	64	21%	1	4%	9	43%
Portugal	105	21%	2	5%	17	44%	165	32%	4	9%	23	58%
Romania	59	16%	0	0%	12	44%	37	13%	1	4%	8	40%
Russia	107	30%	2	7%	17	65%	38	13%	0	0%	7	32%
San Marino	1	1%	0	0%	1	14%	14	8%	0	0%	1	10%
Serbia	70	28%	0	0%	10	67%	18	9%	0	0%	2	17%
Serbia & Montenegro	25	69%	1	33%	3	100%	0	0%	0	0%	0	0%
Slovakia	0	0%	0	0%	0	0%	27	38%	1	17%	3	50%
Slovenia	31	9%	0	0%	8	32%	34	10%	0	0%	7	29%
Spain	84	15%	2	4%	13	30%	203	35%	8	17%	28	64%
Sweden	234	35%	9	16%	32	65%	124	22%	2	4%	19	44%
Switzerland	145	28%	3	7%	21	54%	160	30%	5	11%	25	63%
Turkey	208	48%	8	22%	22	61%	86	22%	3	9%	13	39%
Ukraine	45	14%	0	0%	6	29%	10	5%	0	0%	2	13%
United Kingdom	153	27%	2	4%	25	57%	147	26%	1	2%	27	61%
Yugoslavia	16	10%	0	0%	6	46%	33	21%	1	8%	6	46%

Eurovision 2019: Who Votes for Who? (And Who Doesn't)

Greece

	Greece awarded points to:				Frequency		Greece received points from:				Frequency	
	Total	% of max	12's	% of max	Times	% of max	Total	% of max	12's	% of max	Times	% of max
Albania	206	72%	2	8%	20	100%	230	71%	9	33%	23	100%
Andorra	4	7%	0	0%	1	20%	34	35%	0	0%	6	75%
Armenia	158	57%	3	13%	16	89%	146	53%	0	0%	17	94%
Australia	40	26%	0	0%	4	57%	25	21%	0	0%	3	50%
Austria	96	20%	3	8%	18	51%	57	12%	0	0%	15	41%
Azerbaijan	114	40%	3	13%	16	89%	97	35%	1	4%	14	78%
Belarus	51	22%	0	0%	10	67%	66	23%	1	4%	13	65%
Belgium	82	16%	1	2%	13	34%	157	27%	2	4%	27	63%
Bosnia & Herzegovina	20	7%	0	0%	4	18%	63	24%	0	0%	12	57%
Bulgaria	71	46%	1	8%	9	100%	112	67%	4	29%	12	100%
Croatia	40	12%	0	0%	10	43%	72	20%	0	0%	13	50%
Cyprus	458	89%	30	70%	34	97%	467	93%	34	81%	36	100%
Czech Republic	27	15%	0	0%	4	50%	13	7%	0	0%	3	30%
Denmark	45	10%	1	3%	10	28%	42	9%	0	0%	13	37%
Estonia	56	16%	1	3%	9	36%	33	8%	0	0%	9	31%
Finland	87	15%	1	2%	15	36%	94	15%	0	0%	21	47%
France	146	28%	2	5%	24	62%	115	20%	0	0%	22	51%
Georgia	83	41%	0	0%	14	100%	51	21%	0	0%	11	69%
Germany	36	7%	0	0%	10	26%	148	29%	3	7%	22	54%
Greece	-	-	-	-	-	-	-	-	-	-	-	-
Hungary	45	13%	0	0%	8	35%	71	23%	1	4%	12	55%
Iceland	59	13%	0	0%	12	36%	67	13%	0	0%	15	42%
Ireland	108	23%	2	5%	14	38%	61	12%	0	0%	15	37%
Israel	68	13%	0	0%	15	39%	134	25%	2	5%	21	53%
Italy	112	33%	1	4%	16	67%	61	18%	1	4%	14	56%
Latvia	15	7%	0	0%	4	24%	25	8%	0	0%	6	26%
Lithuania	11	4%	0	0%	4	21%	35	12%	0	0%	7	32%
Luxembourg	24	13%	1	6%	5	31%	29	16%	0	0%	6	40%
Malta	86	24%	0	0%	18	67%	130	32%	2	6%	21	68%
Moldova	86	31%	0	0%	14	74%	66	23%	0	0%	14	70%
Monaco	16	19%	1	14%	2	29%	31	32%	0	0%	4	50%
Montenegro	18	14%	0	0%	3	38%	77	34%	3	16%	9	64%
Morocco	0	0%	0	0%	0	0%	0	0%	0	0%	0	0%
Netherlands	73	15%	1	3%	15	43%	119	24%	0	0%	22	58%
North Macedonia	8	4%	0	0%	3	18%	58	19%	0	0%	12	55%
Norway	84	15%	2	4%	16	37%	87	16%	0	0%	20	48%
Poland	44	14%	0	0%	13	57%	56	16%	0	0%	14	54%
Portugal	73	16%	0	0%	16	44%	111	21%	1	2%	17	43%
Romania	113	39%	1	4%	16	70%	166	53%	5	19%	20	83%
Russia	171	48%	3	10%	21	78%	112	33%	0	0%	20	77%
San Marino	24	18%	0	0%	7	88%	111	51%	6	33%	9	64%
Serbia	50	22%	0	0%	9	60%	72	33%	0	0%	11	73%
Serbia & Montenegro	24	67%	0	0%	3	100%	35	73%	1	25%	4	100%
Slovakia	7	12%	0	0%	2	40%	23	21%	0	0%	4	44%
Slovenia	27	8%	0	0%	6	26%	65	17%	0	0%	12	43%
Spain	140	27%	0	0%	23	58%	192	29%	3	5%	29	59%
Sweden	66	12%	0	0%	13	33%	68	13%	2	5%	15	38%
Switzerland	81	19%	1	3%	17	50%	105	20%	1	2%	21	53%
Turkey	36	10%	0	0%	6	19%	81	23%	2	7%	14	47%
Ukraine	68	27%	0	0%	12	67%	35	18%	0	0%	6	40%
United Kingdom	85	16%	2	5%	15	38%	149	27%	5	11%	21	50%
Yugoslavia	30	25%	0	0%	7	70%	17	16%	0	0%	4	44%

Eurovision 2019: Who Votes for Who? (And Who Doesn't)

Hungary

	Hungary awarded points to:				Frequency		Hungary received points from:				Frequency	
	Total	% of max	12's	% of max	Times	% of max	Total	% of max	12's	% of max	Times	% of max
Albania	35	17%	0	0%	6	40%	59	22%	0	0%	10	53%
Andorra	0	0%	0	0%	0	0%	17	35%	0	0%	4	100%
Armenia	28	15%	0	0%	6	46%	10	5%	0	0%	3	21%
Australia	60	38%	1	8%	6	86%	16	11%	0	0%	3	43%
Austria	57	25%	0	0%	8	57%	79	27%	1	4%	12	63%
Azerbaijan	110	48%	5	26%	12	80%	69	32%	0	0%	9	64%
Belarus	31	17%	1	7%	5	45%	37	15%	0	0%	9	56%
Belgium	37	19%	1	6%	5	38%	52	19%	1	4%	10	53%
Bosnia & Herzegovina	1	1%	0	0%	1	10%	14	9%	0	0%	6	55%
Bulgaria	72	46%	3	23%	7	78%	47	23%	0	0%	8	62%
Croatia	44	18%	0	0%	7	44%	112	39%	3	13%	12	63%
Cyprus	44	16%	1	4%	8	47%	46	15%	0	0%	7	35%
Czech Republic	47	33%	1	8%	5	71%	48	29%	1	7%	6	67%
Denmark	112	37%	4	16%	15	75%	50	16%	1	4%	10	48%
Estonia	55	20%	0	0%	9	50%	107	33%	1	4%	16	76%
Finland	36	16%	1	5%	6	38%	114	37%	3	12%	15	71%
France	15	6%	0	0%	5	29%	68	18%	0	0%	15	60%
Georgia	26	14%	0	0%	9	69%	28	11%	0	0%	7	44%
Germany	24	10%	1	5%	4	24%	67	23%	1	4%	10	53%
Greece	71	23%	1	4%	12	55%	45	13%	0	0%	8	35%
Hungary	-		-		-		-		-		-	
Iceland	109	41%	3	14%	14	74%	91	28%	1	4%	13	59%
Ireland	48	27%	0	0%	7	54%	37	13%	1	4%	7	37%
Israel	51	21%	0	0%	7	47%	56	20%	1	4%	8	44%
Italy	35	21%	0	0%	7	70%	15	8%	0	0%	4	36%
Latvia	22	12%	0	0%	6	46%	32	12%	0	0%	9	50%
Lithuania	13	6%	0	0%	3	21%	29	12%	0	0%	7	41%
Luxembourg	0	-	0	-	0	-	0	-	0	-	0	-
Malta	56	20%	1	4%	7	39%	34	10%	0	0%	9	41%
Moldova	46	19%	0	0%	9	56%	27	10%	0	0%	8	44%
Monaco	0	0%	0	0%	0	0%	0	0%	0	0%	0	0%
Montenegro	4	3%	0	0%	1	13%	46	19%	1	5%	7	50%
Morocco	0	-	0	-	0	-	0	-	0	-	0	-
Netherlands	119	41%	3	13%	12	71%	82	25%	0	0%	12	57%
North Macedonia	12	8%	0	0%	2	18%	29	12%	0	0%	5	29%
Norway	106	34%	1	4%	15	71%	57	18%	0	0%	11	52%
Poland	65	27%	0	0%	11	69%	95	34%	2	9%	11	61%
Portugal	32	16%	1	6%	3	21%	47	20%	0	0%	9	53%
Romania	65	26%	2	10%	10	56%	136	52%	1	5%	17	94%
Russia	102	35%	1	4%	13	65%	54	18%	0	0%	11	52%
San Marino	36	20%	1	7%	6	60%	64	23%	0	0%	10	63%
Serbia	62	25%	2	10%	9	60%	156	59%	8	36%	14	88%
Serbia & Montenegro	2	17%	0	0%	1	100%	14	58%	0	0%	2	100%
Slovakia	0	0%	0	0%	0	0%	10	17%	0	0%	2	40%
Slovenia	41	19%	0	0%	7	50%	42	15%	0	0%	8	44%
Spain	18	7%	0	0%	4	24%	66	19%	0	0%	11	46%
Sweden	86	29%	1	4%	14	70%	65	22%	1	4%	11	55%
Switzerland	38	20%	0	0%	8	57%	62	22%	1	4%	10	50%
Turkey	30	23%	0	0%	7	64%	25	19%	0	0%	6	55%
Ukraine	63	28%	1	5%	10	67%	61	24%	0	0%	11	69%
United Kingdom	38	15%	1	5%	7	41%	28	11%	0	0%	7	39%
Yugoslavia	0	-	0	-	0	-	0	-	0	-	0	-

Eurovision 2019: Who Votes for Who? (And Who Doesn't)

Iceland

	Iceland awarded points to:				Frequency		Iceland received points from:				Frequency	
	Total	% of max	12's	% of max	Times	% of max	Total	% of max	12's	% of max	Times	% of max
Albania	51	18%	1	4%	8	40%	23	8%	0	0%	4	20%
Andorra	6	10%	0	0%	1	20%	24	29%	0	0%	3	43%
Armenia	25	9%	0	0%	7	39%	26	11%	1	5%	6	38%
Australia	94	60%	1	8%	6	86%	42	50%	1	14%	3	75%
Austria	92	18%	1	2%	11	30%	51	15%	0	0%	12	46%
Azerbaijan	60	21%	0	0%	12	67%	7	3%	0	0%	2	13%
Belarus	19	8%	0	0%	5	33%	53	22%	2	10%	9	53%
Belgium	82	15%	1	2%	12	29%	98	22%	1	3%	14	42%
Bosnia & Herzegovina	18	7%	0	0%	5	23%	9	4%	0	0%	3	15%
Bulgaria	15	8%	0	0%	2	18%	11	7%	0	0%	2	15%
Croatia	44	14%	0	0%	10	43%	18	6%	0	0%	6	25%
Cyprus	104	19%	3	7%	16	42%	48	11%	1	3%	10	31%
Czech Republic	76	35%	2	11%	7	64%	36	19%	0	0%	6	55%
Denmark	248	50%	10	24%	28	74%	161	46%	3	10%	23	82%
Estonia	103	31%	1	4%	16	70%	91	27%	1	4%	16	67%
Finland	164	29%	5	11%	23	55%	169	38%	5	14%	20	63%
France	103	19%	1	2%	16	38%	68	15%	1	3%	12	35%
Georgia	15	8%	0	0%	4	31%	13	7%	0	0%	4	31%
Germany	75	14%	1	2%	12	29%	75	20%	1	3%	14	45%
Greece	67	13%	0	0%	15	42%	59	13%	0	0%	12	36%
Hungary	91	28%	1	4%	13	59%	109	41%	3	14%	14	74%
Iceland	-	-	-	-	-	-	-	-	-	-	-	-
Ireland	82	22%	1	3%	15	52%	63	16%	1	3%	11	35%
Israel	81	15%	0	0%	12	30%	66	16%	1	3%	11	35%
Italy	47	13%	0	0%	8	31%	36	17%	0	0%	8	50%
Latvia	55	22%	0	0%	11	58%	70	24%	0	0%	13	59%
Lithuania	32	12%	0	0%	7	37%	54	21%	0	0%	9	47%
Luxembourg	9	4%	0	0%	3	16%	13	14%	0	0%	2	25%
Malta	54	14%	0	0%	11	37%	77	20%	3	9%	10	33%
Moldova	30	12%	0	0%	4	24%	28	12%	0	0%	6	38%
Monaco	0	0%	0	0%	0	0%	6	17%	0	0%	2	67%
Montenegro	2	1%	0	0%	1	10%	29	13%	0	0%	5	36%
Morocco	0	0%	0	0%	0	0%	0	-	0	-	0	-
Netherlands	108	21%	4	10%	13	35%	58	16%	0	0%	10	36%
North Macedonia	9	4%	0	0%	2	13%	11	5%	0	0%	5	28%
Norway	202	35%	7	15%	27	60%	167	43%	3	9%	25	81%
Poland	55	18%	0	0%	12	55%	62	21%	2	8%	11	50%
Portugal	115	22%	4	9%	12	29%	106	23%	2	5%	17	50%
Romania	46	18%	0	0%	9	45%	25	11%	0	0%	3	17%
Russia	94	27%	1	3%	17	65%	31	10%	0	0%	9	39%
San Marino	12	8%	0	0%	4	44%	48	25%	0	0%	6	46%
Serbia	38	19%	0	0%	8	62%	22	13%	0	0%	4	33%
Serbia & Montenegro	7	19%	0	0%	1	33%	2	6%	0	0%	1	33%
Slovakia	5	14%	0	0%	1	33%	24	29%	0	0%	5	71%
Slovenia	29	10%	0	0%	7	35%	46	15%	0	0%	9	41%
Spain	26	5%	0	0%	9	21%	120	24%	1	2%	21	57%
Sweden	288	46%	7	13%	34	72%	190	43%	3	8%	27	79%
Switzerland	87	18%	1	3%	16	42%	71	18%	0	0%	13	42%
Turkey	31	7%	0	0%	8	22%	34	10%	0	0%	7	26%
Ukraine	60	23%	1	5%	9	47%	8	5%	0	0%	3	21%
United Kingdom	44	8%	1	2%	9	21%	109	25%	2	5%	18	53%
Yugoslavia	48	31%	1	8%	6	46%	4	5%	0	0%	1	14%

Eurovision 2019: Who Votes for Who? (And Who Doesn't)
Ireland

	Ireland awarded points to:				Frequency		Ireland received points from:				Frequency	
	Total	% of max	12's	% of max	Times	% of max	Total	% of max	12's	% of max	Times	% of max
Albania	11	4%	0	0%	5	29%	20	9%	0	0%	4	27%
Andorra	5	8%	0	0%	2	40%	6	8%	0	0%	2	33%
Armenia	4	2%	0	0%	2	13%	4	2%	0	0%	2	18%
Australia	39	30%	0	0%	4	67%	19	32%	0	0%	2	67%
Austria	129	23%	3	6%	20	49%	196	39%	4	10%	24	63%
Azerbaijan	43	16%	0	0%	9	53%	17	9%	0	0%	5	42%
Belarus	14	6%	0	0%	5	31%	11	5%	0	0%	4	25%
Belgium	148	27%	5	11%	19	46%	178	34%	5	11%	29	71%
Bosnia & Herzegovina	24	9%	0	0%	7	32%	54	25%	1	6%	9	50%
Bulgaria	88	41%	1	6%	7	58%	13	6%	0	0%	5	36%
Croatia	37	10%	0	0%	10	37%	70	19%	1	3%	15	58%
Cyprus	105	20%	2	5%	17	44%	103	23%	1	3%	17	47%
Czech Republic	18	15%	0	0%	4	67%	31	43%	0	0%	3	75%
Denmark	195	33%	8	16%	29	66%	187	37%	4	10%	28	74%
Estonia	121	34%	0	0%	20	77%	96	30%	1	4%	15	63%
Finland	98	20%	1	3%	14	37%	129	28%	1	3%	25	69%
France	130	23%	1	2%	21	49%	102	21%	0	0%	22	56%
Georgia	14	9%	0	0%	4	36%	0	0%	0	0%	0	0%
Germany	148	26%	1	2%	27	63%	159	28%	2	4%	27	63%
Greece	61	12%	0	0%	15	37%	108	23%	2	5%	14	38%
Hungary	37	13%	1	4%	7	37%	48	27%	0	0%	7	54%
Iceland	63	16%	1	3%	11	35%	82	22%	1	3%	15	52%
Ireland	-	-	-	-	-	-	-	-	-	-	-	-
Israel	146	23%	1	2%	20	44%	90	17%	1	2%	20	49%
Italy	98	28%	3	10%	15	60%	108	30%	5	17%	15	56%
Latvia	122	46%	5	23%	14	74%	55	21%	0	0%	11	58%
Lithuania	194	52%	11	35%	22	88%	86	27%	2	7%	12	55%
Luxembourg	65	30%	1	6%	10	56%	96	44%	0	0%	14	78%
Malta	107	27%	2	6%	18	62%	94	26%	2	7%	15	56%
Moldova	38	15%	0	0%	10	56%	9	4%	0	0%	4	27%
Monaco	17	18%	0	0%	3	38%	31	29%	0	0%	4	44%
Montenegro	0	0%	0	0%	0	0%	4	4%	0	0%	3	38%
Morocco	0	0%	0	0%	0	0%	0	0%	0	0%	0	0%
Netherlands	178	31%	2	4%	28	67%	150	28%	3	7%	25	61%
North Macedonia	15	5%	0	0%	2	11%	16	6%	0	0%	4	22%
Norway	212	32%	3	5%	31	63%	179	30%	5	10%	32	71%
Poland	93	31%	1	4%	12	55%	53	19%	1	4%	12	57%
Portugal	40	9%	0	0%	6	17%	128	27%	0	0%	24	65%
Romania	110	32%	2	7%	18	69%	47	16%	0	0%	10	48%
Russia	125	36%	0	0%	16	62%	39	14%	1	4%	6	29%
San Marino	0	0%	0	0%	0	0%	23	19%	1	10%	4	50%
Serbia	14	6%	0	0%	3	21%	3	2%	0	0%	1	10%
Serbia & Montenegro	9	25%	0	0%	2	67%	1	2%	0	0%	1	25%
Slovakia	6	10%	0	0%	2	40%	29	30%	1	13%	5	63%
Slovenia	39	11%	1	3%	7	26%	42	13%	1	4%	13	50%
Spain	48	8%	0	0%	11	25%	151	29%	3	7%	23	56%
Sweden	223	36%	7	13%	29	62%	223	43%	6	14%	30	73%
Switzerland	143	26%	2	4%	22	55%	197	36%	7	15%	29	71%
Turkey	24	6%	0	0%	7	20%	124	32%	2	6%	22	69%
Ukraine	61	20%	0	0%	13	59%	12	5%	0	0%	6	35%
United Kingdom	219	38%	1	2%	37	84%	302	52%	8	17%	37	84%
Yugoslavia	34	24%	1	8%	8	67%	38	26%	0	0%	10	83%

Eurovision 2019: Who Votes for Who? (And Who Doesn't)

Israel

	Israel awarded points to:				Frequency		Israel received points from:				Frequency	
	Total	% of max	12's	% of max	Times	% of max	Total	% of max	12's	% of max	Times	% of max
Albania	13	5%	0	0%	3	19%	58	21%	0	0%	11	65%
Andorra	6	8%	0	0%	2	33%	45	42%	1	11%	6	67%
Armenia	110	48%	2	11%	13	81%	68	28%	1	5%	7	47%
Australia	84	54%	3	23%	6	86%	53	37%	1	8%	5	71%
Austria	106	22%	3	8%	13	37%	123	24%	3	7%	20	56%
Azerbaijan	92	38%	2	10%	13	81%	91	40%	1	5%	11	79%
Belarus	63	23%	2	9%	11	65%	83	27%	1	4%	14	74%
Belgium	92	17%	0	0%	17	44%	156	27%	1	2%	26	62%
Bosnia & Herzegovina	6	3%	0	0%	3	15%	34	15%	0	0%	7	39%
Bulgaria	72	30%	1	5%	7	50%	78	28%	0	0%	11	65%
Croatia	36	12%	0	0%	11	52%	57	16%	1	3%	7	30%
Cyprus	94	19%	0	0%	19	54%	115	24%	1	3%	20	57%
Czech Republic	48	31%	2	15%	5	63%	61	32%	3	19%	7	64%
Denmark	144	27%	2	5%	24	62%	79	15%	0	0%	18	49%
Estonia	84	26%	0	0%	12	55%	25	7%	0	0%	7	30%
Finland	91	18%	1	2%	18	47%	203	38%	4	9%	28	70%
France	157	30%	2	5%	23	59%	247	48%	6	14%	32	84%
Georgia	48	25%	0	0%	9	69%	47	23%	1	6%	9	75%
Germany	79	15%	2	5%	11	28%	183	30%	4	8%	29	64%
Greece	134	25%	2	5%	21	53%	68	13%	0	0%	15	39%
Hungary	56	20%	1	4%	8	44%	51	21%	0	0%	7	47%
Iceland	66	16%	1	3%	11	35%	81	15%	0	0%	12	30%
Ireland	90	17%	1	2%	20	49%	146	23%	1	2%	20	44%
Israel	-	-	-	-	-	-	-	-	-	-	-	-
Italy	73	23%	1	4%	12	52%	78	22%	1	3%	13	54%
Latvia	54	23%	1	5%	9	50%	22	7%	0	0%	8	36%
Lithuania	27	9%	0	0%	8	38%	46	13%	0	0%	10	45%
Luxembourg	35	17%	1	6%	6	35%	76	37%	1	6%	11	65%
Malta	67	19%	0	0%	13	48%	119	29%	1	3%	15	52%
Moldova	56	27%	0	0%	11	73%	47	21%	1	5%	6	40%
Monaco	19	20%	0	0%	4	50%	43	40%	2	22%	6	67%
Montenegro	8	7%	0	0%	2	25%	26	14%	0	0%	7	58%
Morocco	0	-	0	-	0	-	0	-	0	-	0	-
Netherlands	139	29%	3	8%	24	69%	177	35%	3	7%	27	73%
North Macedonia	21	7%	0	0%	5	25%	54	15%	0	0%	12	52%
Norway	119	20%	2	4%	21	48%	156	27%	1	2%	27	63%
Poland	23	8%	0	0%	5	26%	72	23%	0	0%	10	48%
Portugal	44	10%	2	5%	6	18%	149	30%	2	5%	21	57%
Romania	182	54%	3	11%	23	88%	87	26%	0	0%	18	75%
Russia	170	59%	6	25%	20	91%	68	27%	0	0%	9	50%
San Marino	11	8%	0	0%	2	25%	52	27%	2	13%	7	64%
Serbia	13	6%	0	0%	4	31%	49	24%	0	0%	7	64%
Serbia & Montenegro	15	42%	0	0%	2	67%	6	13%	0	0%	2	50%
Slovakia	0	0%	0	0%	0	0%	20	42%	0	0%	3	75%
Slovenia	45	13%	0	0%	12	50%	41	11%	0	0%	10	38%
Spain	118	22%	3	7%	22	55%	156	28%	3	7%	23	56%
Sweden	201	36%	5	11%	26	60%	121	23%	1	2%	21	53%
Switzerland	94	19%	1	2%	20	54%	186	32%	1	2%	30	71%
Turkey	42	11%	0	0%	11	33%	63	17%	2	6%	11	35%
Ukraine	144	50%	2	8%	18	90%	72	29%	1	5%	10	63%
United Kingdom	146	28%	4	9%	23	58%	173	29%	3	6%	28	65%
Yugoslavia	52	36%	3	25%	6	50%	54	38%	2	17%	8	67%

Eurovision 2019: Who Votes for Who? (And Who Doesn't)

Italy

	Italy awarded points to:				Frequency		Italy received points from:				Frequency	
	Total	% of max	12's	% of max	Times	% of max	Total	% of max	12's	% of max	Times	% of max
Albania	87	56%	5	38%	7	88%	132	85%	7	54%	9	100%
Andorra	0	-	0	-	0	-	0	-	0	-	0	-
Armenia	11	8%	0	0%	3	43%	37	26%	0	0%	6	75%
Australia	47	26%	1	7%	6	75%	15	14%	0	0%	3	60%
Austria	78	21%	4	13%	13	48%	106	30%	0	0%	15	60%
Azerbaijan	42	22%	2	13%	4	36%	31	20%	0	0%	5	56%
Belarus	8	6%	0	0%	2	25%	18	12%	0	0%	4	44%
Belgium	64	18%	0	0%	10	40%	93	27%	1	3%	13	52%
Bosnia & Herzegovina	11	18%	0	0%	3	60%	12	17%	0	0%	2	40%
Bulgaria	34	31%	0	0%	4	80%	6	6%	0	0%	1	17%
Croatia	6	6%	0	0%	1	17%	64	41%	2	15%	7	78%
Cyprus	65	21%	0	0%	12	57%	119	45%	2	9%	15	83%
Czech Republic	4	4%	0	0%	1	20%	20	19%	0	0%	4	80%
Denmark	104	26%	3	9%	13	48%	26	8%	0	0%	7	30%
Estonia	34	26%	1	9%	5	56%	28	17%	0	0%	5	50%
Finland	28	9%	0	0%	4	17%	155	45%	4	14%	21	84%
France	122	34%	1	3%	16	62%	157	44%	2	7%	21	81%
Georgia	17	12%	0	0%	3	38%	34	22%	0	0%	7	78%
Germany	86	24%	1	3%	14	54%	100	28%	3	10%	18	69%
Greece	61	18%	1	4%	14	56%	112	33%	1	4%	16	67%
Hungary	15	8%	0	0%	4	36%	35	21%	0	0%	7	70%
Iceland	36	17%	0	0%	8	50%	47	13%	0	0%	8	31%
Ireland	108	30%	5	17%	15	56%	98	28%	3	10%	15	60%
Israel	78	22%	1	3%	13	54%	73	23%	1	4%	12	52%
Italy	-	-	-	-	-	-	-	-	-	-	-	-
Latvia	17	10%	0	0%	3	33%	34	22%	1	8%	5	56%
Lithuania	24	13%	0	0%	5	45%	48	31%	0	0%	6	67%
Luxembourg	41	21%	2	13%	7	44%	64	33%	1	6%	9	56%
Malta	74	34%	0	0%	12	86%	151	70%	7	39%	12	86%
Moldova	103	54%	2	13%	11	100%	29	19%	0	0%	5	56%
Monaco	33	55%	1	20%	5	100%	15	25%	0	0%	3	60%
Montenegro	9	8%	0	0%	2	29%	61	42%	0	0%	8	100%
Morocco	7	58%	0	0%	1	100%	0	0%	0	0%	0	0%
Netherlands	69	19%	0	0%	15	60%	68	20%	1	4%	10	42%
North Macedonia	23	21%	0	0%	5	83%	55	35%	1	8%	9	100%
Norway	93	22%	2	6%	14	48%	86	24%	2	7%	14	54%
Poland	62	34%	0	0%	10	100%	37	26%	0	0%	5	63%
Portugal	50	19%	0	0%	9	45%	197	61%	6	22%	22	92%
Romania	85	51%	3	21%	10	91%	39	30%	1	9%	6	75%
Russia	51	27%	0	0%	8	67%	27	19%	1	8%	4	44%
San Marino	14	17%	0	0%	3	60%	88	56%	2	15%	8	89%
Serbia	36	21%	0	0%	8	89%	58	40%	0	0%	6	75%
Serbia & Montenegro	0	-	0	-	0	-	0	-	0	-	0	-
Slovakia	0	0%	0	0%	0	0%	5	21%	0	0%	1	50%
Slovenia	27	12%	0	0%	5	36%	73	41%	0	0%	9	82%
Spain	95	26%	2	7%	14	54%	211	59%	9	30%	23	88%
Sweden	93	21%	1	3%	15	50%	62	18%	0	0%	10	40%
Switzerland	90	27%	1	4%	17	68%	156	43%	2	7%	23	88%
Turkey	23	13%	0	0%	3	20%	76	40%	0	0%	12	75%
Ukraine	110	57%	3	19%	11	100%	9	8%	0	0%	2	29%
United Kingdom	100	28%	1	3%	16	62%	35	10%	0	0%	8	31%
Yugoslavia	17	14%	0	0%	3	30%	62	52%	1	10%	8	80%

Eurovision 2019: Who Votes for Who? (And Who Doesn't)

Latvia

	Latvia awarded points to:				Frequency		Latvia received points from:				Frequency	
	Total	% of max	12's	% of max	Times	% of max	Total	% of max	12's	% of max	Times	% of max
Albania	11	4%	0	0%	4	19%	1	0%	0	0%	1	6%
Andorra	0	0%	0	0%	0	0%	12	14%	0	0%	2	29%
Armenia	31	14%	0	0%	7	47%	5	3%	0	0%	2	20%
Australia	73	41%	1	7%	8	100%	27	23%	0	0%	4	67%
Austria	33	14%	0	0%	7	47%	24	13%	0	0%	5	36%
Azerbaijan	64	24%	0	0%	12	71%	31	20%	0	0%	6	60%
Belarus	53	26%	0	0%	8	57%	47	26%	0	0%	10	77%
Belgium	78	30%	1	5%	9	50%	43	17%	1	5%	6	33%
Bosnia & Herzegovina	4	2%	0	0%	2	13%	5	3%	0	0%	1	8%
Bulgaria	30	17%	0	0%	5	45%	1	1%	0	0%	1	9%
Croatia	25	10%	0	0%	6	35%	31	15%	0	0%	7	47%
Cyprus	32	10%	0	0%	8	38%	24	10%	0	0%	7	39%
Czech Republic	15	11%	0	0%	4	57%	25	21%	0	0%	6	75%
Denmark	124	33%	2	6%	18	72%	70	24%	0	0%	13	65%
Estonia	190	75%	7	33%	18	95%	136	63%	2	11%	17	100%
Finland	45	20%	0	0%	8	47%	39	19%	1	6%	8	53%
France	31	11%	0	0%	7	35%	28	11%	0	0%	4	21%
Georgia	55	27%	0	0%	8	62%	65	39%	0	0%	8	80%
Germany	44	15%	1	4%	8	40%	62	22%	1	4%	8	40%
Greece	25	8%	0	0%	6	26%	15	7%	0	0%	4	24%
Hungary	32	12%	0	0%	9	50%	22	12%	0	0%	6	46%
Iceland	70	24%	0	0%	13	59%	55	22%	0	0%	11	58%
Ireland	55	21%	0	0%	11	58%	122	46%	5	23%	14	74%
Israel	22	7%	0	0%	8	36%	54	23%	1	5%	9	50%
Italy	34	22%	1	8%	5	56%	17	10%	0	0%	3	33%
Latvia	-	-	-	-	-	-	-	-	-	-	-	-
Lithuania	183	66%	3	13%	18	95%	189	83%	10	53%	16	100%
Luxembourg	0	-	0	-	0	-	0	-	0	-	0	-
Malta	64	21%	0	0%	14	67%	69	26%	2	9%	9	47%
Moldova	67	22%	0	0%	9	45%	30	13%	1	5%	8	50%
Monaco	0	0%	0	0%	0	0%	10	21%	0	0%	2	50%
Montenegro	2	2%	0	0%	1	13%	5	3%	0	0%	2	20%
Morocco	0	-	0	-	0	-	0	-	0	-	0	-
Netherlands	75	25%	3	12%	8	42%	23	10%	0	0%	5	29%
North Macedonia	13	5%	0	0%	2	11%	31	13%	0	0%	7	41%
Norway	128	36%	2	7%	18	75%	64	24%	1	5%	11	61%
Poland	37	13%	0	0%	9	50%	67	28%	1	5%	8	50%
Portugal	65	34%	3	19%	6	43%	48	25%	0	0%	8	53%
Romania	22	7%	0	0%	6	27%	13	6%	0	0%	4	25%
Russia	229	68%	10	36%	22	92%	30	12%	0	0%	9	50%
San Marino	4	4%	0	0%	2	29%	35	29%	1	10%	5	63%
Serbia	13	6%	0	0%	4	29%	6	4%	0	0%	3	30%
Serbia & Montenegro	10	28%	0	0%	3	100%	0	0%	0	0%	0	0%
Slovakia	0	0%	0	0%	0	0%	0	0%	0	0%	0	0%
Slovenia	37	13%	0	0%	10	53%	63	24%	0	0%	9	50%
Spain	13	5%	0	0%	3	15%	27	11%	1	5%	5	26%
Sweden	181	44%	5	15%	20	74%	53	18%	0	0%	11	55%
Switzerland	37	16%	1	5%	8	50%	46	19%	0	0%	9	53%
Turkey	2	1%	0	0%	1	7%	6	4%	0	0%	1	8%
Ukraine	164	49%	4	14%	18	78%	45	21%	0	0%	8	53%
United Kingdom	30	10%	0	0%	10	50%	82	31%	0	0%	13	72%
Yugoslavia	0	-	0	-	0	-	0	-	0	-	0	-

Eurovision 2019: Who Votes for Who? (And Who Doesn't)

Lithuania

	Lithuania awarded points to:				Frequency		Lithuania received points from:				Frequency	
	Total	% of max	12's	% of max	Times	% of max	Total	% of max	12's	% of max	Times	% of max
Albania	1	0%	0	0%	1	6%	14	5%	0	0%	4	22%
Andorra	2	4%	0	0%	1	25%	13	18%	0	0%	3	50%
Armenia	10	4%	0	0%	4	27%	6	3%	0	0%	2	15%
Australia	41	31%	2	18%	5	83%	30	31%	0	0%	4	80%
Austria	71	26%	1	4%	8	47%	6	2%	0	0%	3	17%
Azerbaijan	104	39%	2	9%	12	71%	30	15%	0	0%	8	62%
Belarus	83	31%	1	5%	14	82%	101	35%	0	0%	14	74%
Belgium	64	28%	0	0%	9	60%	32	12%	0	0%	5	28%
Bosnia & Herzegovina	7	4%	0	0%	2	13%	4	2%	0	0%	2	14%
Bulgaria	47	21%	0	0%	6	46%	44	17%	0	0%	9	56%
Croatia	27	8%	0	0%	7	30%	40	11%	1	3%	8	33%
Cyprus	34	11%	0	0%	9	43%	45	16%	0	0%	11	52%
Czech Republic	27	20%	0	0%	3	43%	8	6%	0	0%	4	50%
Denmark	71	19%	0	0%	16	64%	53	16%	0	0%	10	45%
Estonia	141	49%	4	17%	18	90%	101	34%	1	4%	14	67%
Finland	43	20%	0	0%	7	44%	28	12%	0	0%	5	29%
France	58	20%	0	0%	9	45%	10	4%	0	0%	3	16%
Georgia	147	77%	6	38%	14	100%	99	52%	2	13%	12	92%
Germany	32	11%	0	0%	7	35%	19	6%	0	0%	6	27%
Greece	35	12%	0	0%	7	32%	11	4%	0	0%	4	21%
Hungary	29	12%	0	0%	7	41%	13	6%	0	0%	3	21%
Iceland	54	21%	0	0%	9	47%	32	12%	0	0%	7	37%
Ireland	86	27%	2	7%	12	55%	194	52%	11	35%	22	88%
Israel	46	13%	0	0%	10	45%	27	9%	0	0%	8	38%
Italy	48	31%	0	0%	6	67%	24	13%	0	0%	5	45%
Latvia	189	83%	10	53%	16	100%	183	66%	3	13%	18	95%
Lithuania	-	-	-	-	-	-	-	-	-	-	-	-
Luxembourg	0	-	0	-	0	-	0	-	0	-	0	-
Malta	45	14%	0	0%	13	59%	34	10%	0	0%	8	35%
Moldova	37	17%	0	0%	6	40%	28	14%	0	0%	6	43%
Monaco	0	0%	0	0%	0	0%	11	23%	0	0%	2	50%
Montenegro	0	0%	0	0%	0	0%	3	2%	0	0%	2	22%
Morocco	0	-	0	-	0	-	0	-	0	-	0	-
Netherlands	83	27%	3	12%	12	60%	30	10%	0	0%	7	33%
North Macedonia	4	1%	0	0%	1	6%	16	5%	0	0%	4	20%
Norway	137	36%	3	9%	17	65%	138	40%	4	14%	16	67%
Poland	71	30%	1	5%	12	71%	57	24%	2	10%	9	53%
Portugal	36	17%	2	11%	4	25%	46	20%	1	5%	6	35%
Romania	23	8%	0	0%	7	35%	10	4%	0	0%	3	18%
Russia	166	58%	4	17%	20	95%	47	19%	0	0%	11	61%
San Marino	0	0%	0	0%	0	0%	17	12%	0	0%	3	33%
Serbia	16	6%	0	0%	5	31%	27	12%	0	0%	5	33%
Serbia & Montenegro	3	8%	0	0%	2	67%	6	13%	0	0%	2	50%
Slovakia	0	0%	0	0%	0	0%	7	10%	0	0%	1	17%
Slovenia	34	12%	0	0%	8	40%	19	6%	0	0%	5	23%
Spain	12	4%	0	0%	2	10%	14	5%	0	0%	5	26%
Sweden	144	40%	0	0%	20	80%	36	12%	0	0%	8	36%
Switzerland	56	19%	0	0%	9	47%	40	11%	0	0%	7	30%
Turkey	16	8%	0	0%	4	24%	4	2%	0	0%	2	13%
Ukraine	150	48%	3	12%	18	82%	59	22%	1	5%	11	61%
United Kingdom	22	8%	0	0%	5	25%	181	49%	6	19%	21	81%
Yugoslavia	0	-	0	-	0	-	0	-	0	-	0	-

Eurovision 2019: Who Votes for Who? (And Who Doesn't)

Luxembourg

	Luxembourg awarded points to				Frequency		Luxembourg received points from:				Frequency	
	Total	% of max	12's	% of max	Times	% of max	Total	% of max	12's	% of max	Times	% of max
Albania	0	-	0	-	0	-	0	-	0	-	0	-
Andorra	0	-	0	-	0	-	0	-	0	-	0	-
Armenia	0	-	0	-	0	-	0	-	0	-	0	-
Australia	0	-	0	-	0	-	0	-	0	-	0	-
Austria	14	6%	0	0%	3	17%	47	22%	0	0%	9	50%
Azerbaijan	0	-	0	-	0	-	0	-	0	-	0	-
Belarus	0	-	0	-	0	-	0	-	0	-	0	-
Belgium	48	21%	1	5%	8	42%	53	23%	0	0%	8	42%
Bosnia & Herzegovina	0	0%	0	0%	0	0%	0	0%	0	0%	0	0%
Bulgaria	0	-	0	-	0	-	0	-	0	-	0	-
Croatia	0	0%	0	0%	0	0%	0	0%	0	0%	0	0%
Cyprus	8	6%	0	0%	2	17%	32	22%	0	0%	5	42%
Czech Republic	0	-	0	-	0	-	0	-	0	-	0	-
Denmark	26	14%	0	0%	6	38%	32	17%	0	0%	9	56%
Estonia	0	-	0	-	0	-	0	-	0	-	0	-
Finland	21	9%	0	0%	6	32%	55	24%	1	5%	9	47%
France	89	41%	3	17%	12	67%	56	26%	2	11%	9	50%
Georgia	0	-	0	-	0	-	0	-	0	-	0	-
Germany	67	29%	2	11%	11	58%	42	18%	1	5%	7	37%
Greece	29	16%	0	0%	6	40%	24	13%	1	6%	5	31%
Hungary	0	-	0	-	0	-	0	-	0	-	0	-
Iceland	13	14%	0	0%	2	25%	9	4%	0	0%	3	16%
Ireland	96	44%	0	0%	14	78%	65	30%	1	6%	10	56%
Israel	76	37%	1	6%	11	65%	35	17%	1	6%	6	35%
Italy	64	33%	1	6%	9	56%	41	21%	2	13%	7	44%
Latvia	0	-	0	-	0	-	0	-	0	-	0	-
Lithuania	0	-	0	-	0	-	0	-	0	-	0	-
Luxembourg	-	-	-	-	-	-	-	-	-	-	-	-
Malta	27	56%	1	25%	3	75%	25	52%	0	0%	3	75%
Moldova	0	-	0	-	0	-	0	-	0	-	0	-
Monaco	17	28%	1	20%	3	60%	10	17%	0	0%	2	40%
Montenegro	0	-	0	-	0	-	0	-	0	-	0	-
Morocco	0	0%	0	0%	0	0%	0	0%	0	0%	0	0%
Netherlands	61	30%	2	12%	11	65%	45	22%	1	6%	8	47%
North Macedonia	0	-	0	-	0	-	0	-	0	-	0	-
Norway	33	14%	0	0%	9	47%	38	17%	1	5%	6	32%
Poland	0	-	0	-	0	-	0	-	0	-	0	-
Portugal	51	22%	0	0%	10	53%	76	33%	2	11%	12	63%
Romania	0	-	0	-	0	-	0	-	0	-	0	-
Russia	0	-	0	-	0	-	0	-	0	-	0	-
San Marino	0	-	0	-	0	-	0	-	0	-	0	-
Serbia	0	-	0	-	0	-	0	-	0	-	0	-
Serbia & Montenegro	0	-	0	-	0	-	0	-	0	-	0	-
Slovakia	0	-	0	-	0	-	0	-	0	-	0	-
Slovenia	0	0%	0	0%	0	0%	1	8%	0	0%	1	100%
Spain	67	29%	0	0%	12	63%	51	22%	1	5%	9	47%
Sweden	59	27%	0	0%	11	61%	52	24%	0	0%	8	44%
Switzerland	80	35%	3	16%	15	79%	26	11%	1	5%	5	26%
Turkey	19	10%	0	0%	4	25%	26	14%	0	0%	7	44%
Ukraine	0	-	0	-	0	-	0	-	0	-	0	-
United Kingdom	123	54%	4	21%	18	95%	57	25%	0	0%	10	53%
Yugoslavia	24	15%	0	0%	5	38%	37	24%	1	8%	6	46%

Eurovision 2019: Who Votes for Who? (And Who Doesn't)

Malta

	Malta awarded points to:				Frequency		Malta received points from:				Frequency	
	Total	% of max	12's	% of max	Times	% of max	Total	% of max	12's	% of max	Times	% of max
Albania	27	11%	0	0%	5	29%	51	22%	0	0%	12	75%
Andorra	3	5%	0	0%	1	20%	18	21%	0	0%	4	57%
Armenia	52	22%	1	5%	8	50%	85	44%	1	6%	8	67%
Australia	50	38%	1	9%	5	83%	23	27%	0	0%	4	100%
Austria	44	12%	1	3%	9	38%	71	20%	1	3%	13	52%
Azerbaijan	124	49%	5	24%	13	81%	89	49%	1	7%	9	82%
Belarus	51	22%	0	0%	10	63%	57	24%	1	5%	11	65%
Belgium	37	12%	1	4%	5	22%	53	16%	0	0%	8	32%
Bosnia & Herzegovina	30	10%	0	0%	8	33%	68	25%	2	9%	12	57%
Bulgaria	83	43%	2	13%	8	67%	26	15%	0	0%	5	42%
Croatia	92	24%	2	6%	11	41%	113	29%	3	9%	18	67%
Cyprus	119	31%	4	13%	18	67%	72	21%	0	0%	14	56%
Czech Republic	15	10%	0	0%	4	50%	35	27%	0	0%	6	75%
Denmark	93	23%	0	0%	19	68%	84	24%	1	3%	14	58%
Estonia	46	14%	1	4%	8	33%	70	21%	0	0%	15	63%
Finland	35	10%	0	0%	8	31%	55	15%	0	0%	13	48%
France	33	8%	0	0%	7	23%	68	16%	0	0%	14	45%
Georgia	29	15%	0	0%	5	36%	31	17%	0	0%	6	50%
Germany	32	8%	0	0%	10	34%	92	20%	0	0%	20	61%
Greece	130	32%	2	6%	21	68%	86	24%	0	0%	18	67%
Hungary	34	10%	0	0%	9	41%	56	20%	1	4%	7	39%
Iceland	77	20%	3	9%	10	33%	54	14%	0	0%	11	37%
Ireland	94	26%	2	7%	15	56%	107	27%	2	6%	18	62%
Israel	119	29%	1	3%	15	52%	67	19%	0	0%	13	48%
Italy	151	70%	7	39%	12	86%	74	34%	0	0%	12	86%
Latvia	69	26%	2	9%	9	47%	64	21%	0	0%	14	67%
Lithuania	34	10%	0	0%	8	35%	45	14%	0	0%	13	59%
Luxembourg	25	52%	0	0%	3	75%	27	56%	1	25%	3	75%
Malta	-	-	-	-	-	-	-	-	-	-	-	-
Moldova	27	11%	0	0%	6	38%	27	13%	0	0%	5	38%
Monaco	1	2%	0	0%	1	25%	5	8%	0	0%	1	20%
Montenegro	18	17%	0	0%	3	43%	50	28%	1	7%	6	55%
Morocco	0	-	0	-	0	-	0	-	0	-	0	-
Netherlands	128	30%	2	6%	17	63%	71	18%	0	0%	15	56%
North Macedonia	40	14%	0	0%	9	43%	91	29%	2	8%	13	59%
Norway	114	23%	1	2%	22	61%	87	20%	2	5%	14	44%
Poland	21	7%	0	0%	6	27%	29	10%	0	0%	7	33%
Portugal	29	8%	0	0%	6	22%	50	15%	1	4%	12	46%
Romania	108	31%	1	3%	15	60%	61	20%	0	0%	11	52%
Russia	110	29%	2	6%	16	59%	64	20%	1	4%	8	36%
San Marino	39	27%	1	8%	5	63%	62	32%	1	6%	10	91%
Serbia	26	11%	0	0%	8	53%	37	19%	0	0%	7	58%
Serbia & Montenegro	10	28%	0	0%	2	67%	0	0%	0	0%	0	0%
Slovakia	27	45%	1	20%	3	60%	31	37%	1	14%	5	71%
Slovenia	29	9%	0	0%	8	35%	49	15%	2	7%	8	33%
Spain	48	12%	1	3%	9	30%	86	22%	1	3%	15	52%
Sweden	206	41%	4	10%	26	72%	95	21%	2	5%	18	56%
Switzerland	90	26%	3	10%	14	54%	62	16%	0	0%	12	41%
Turkey	87	27%	1	4%	12	44%	93	32%	1	4%	15	63%
Ukraine	85	30%	0	0%	14	70%	28	13%	0	0%	6	40%
United Kingdom	128	31%	2	6%	21	70%	146	35%	3	9%	23	72%
Yugoslavia	4	11%	0	0%	2	67%	13	36%	0	0%	3	100%

Eurovision 2019: Who Votes for Who? (And Who Doesn't)

Moldova

	Moldova awarded points to:				Frequency		Moldova received points from:				Frequency	
	Total	% of max	12's	% of max	Times	% of max	Total	% of max	12's	% of max	Times	% of max
Albania	24	10%	0	0%	5	29%	37	13%	1	4%	7	37%
Andorra	4	8%	0	0%	1	25%	5	6%	0	0%	2	29%
Armenia	88	33%	0	0%	14	82%	81	34%	0	0%	10	67%
Australia	61	39%	0	0%	7	100%	71	66%	2	22%	4	80%
Austria	26	12%	0	0%	6	46%	34	15%	0	0%	8	53%
Azerbaijan	172	62%	3	13%	17	100%	93	41%	0	0%	12	86%
Belarus	77	43%	1	7%	11	85%	104	48%	1	6%	14	88%
Belgium	39	17%	0	0%	8	50%	38	14%	0	0%	9	45%
Bosnia & Herzegovina	21	13%	0	0%	5	38%	10	6%	0	0%	2	15%
Bulgaria	51	39%	0	0%	7	88%	40	22%	0	0%	8	62%
Croatia	19	10%	0	0%	5	42%	29	12%	0	0%	9	56%
Cyprus	38	14%	0	0%	6	38%	58	22%	0	0%	11	61%
Czech Republic	27	20%	0	0%	3	50%	30	23%	0	0%	3	43%
Denmark	30	10%	1	4%	7	33%	40	14%	0	0%	6	30%
Estonia	51	20%	1	5%	11	61%	21	8%	0	0%	6	30%
Finland	22	10%	0	0%	4	25%	33	13%	0	0%	5	28%
France	13	6%	0	0%	3	20%	52	19%	1	4%	10	53%
Georgia	52	31%	0	0%	9	82%	53	29%	1	7%	8	73%
Germany	10	4%	0	0%	2	13%	26	10%	0	0%	5	29%
Greece	66	23%	0	0%	14	70%	86	31%	0	0%	14	74%
Hungary	27	10%	0	0%	8	44%	46	19%	0	0%	9	56%
Iceland	28	12%	0	0%	6	38%	30	12%	0	0%	4	24%
Ireland	9	4%	0	0%	4	27%	38	15%	0	0%	10	56%
Israel	47	21%	1	5%	6	40%	56	27%	0	0%	11	73%
Italy	29	19%	0	0%	5	56%	103	54%	2	13%	11	100%
Latvia	30	13%	1	5%	8	50%	67	22%	0	0%	9	45%
Lithuania	28	14%	0	0%	6	43%	37	17%	0	0%	6	40%
Luxembourg	0	-	0	-	0	-	0	-	0	-	0	-
Malta	27	13%	0	0%	5	38%	27	11%	0	0%	6	38%
Moldova	-	-	-	-	-	-	-	-	-	-	-	-
Monaco	2	8%	0	0%	1	50%	0	0%	0	0%	0	0%
Montenegro	19	12%	0	0%	3	30%	56	25%	0	0%	9	64%
Morocco	0	-	0	-	0	-	0	-	0	-	0	-
Netherlands	31	10%	0	0%	6	33%	31	10%	0	0%	5	24%
North Macedonia	24	14%	1	7%	5	42%	49	21%	0	0%	9	56%
Norway	77	28%	0	0%	13	72%	30	13%	0	0%	7	44%
Poland	13	6%	0	0%	5	36%	43	19%	0	0%	8	53%
Portugal	46	32%	1	8%	5	50%	126	62%	4	24%	13	93%
Romania	257	97%	20	91%	19	100%	245	93%	16	73%	18	100%
Russia	223	66%	6	21%	22	96%	170	57%	7	28%	19	90%
San Marino	21	18%	0	0%	5	71%	51	30%	0	0%	6	60%
Serbia	28	12%	0	0%	6	40%	52	25%	0	0%	9	64%
Serbia & Montenegro	1	8%	0	0%	1	100%	11	31%	0	0%	2	67%
Slovakia	7	19%	0	0%	1	33%	16	19%	0	0%	3	43%
Slovenia	15	7%	0	0%	4	27%	52	20%	0	0%	10	56%
Spain	13	6%	0	0%	3	20%	86	30%	0	0%	13	65%
Sweden	86	27%	0	0%	15	75%	51	17%	0	0%	6	32%
Switzerland	18	14%	0	0%	3	33%	14	7%	0	0%	3	21%
Turkey	11	10%	0	0%	2	22%	42	39%	1	11%	6	67%
Ukraine	178	64%	3	13%	18	95%	121	50%	4	20%	14	82%
United Kingdom	5	2%	0	0%	2	13%	55	24%	1	5%	7	47%
Yugoslavia	0	-	0	-	0	-	0	-	0	-	0	-

Eurovision 2019: Who Votes for Who? (And Who Doesn't)

Monaco

	Monaco awarded points to:				Frequency		Monaco received points from:				Frequency	
	Total	% of max	12's	% of max	Times	% of max	Total	% of max	12's	% of max	Times	% of max
Albania	3	6%	0	0%	1	25%	2	6%	0	0%	1	33%
Andorra	0	0%	0	0%	0	0%	17	47%	0	0%	3	100%
Armenia	0	0%	0	0%	0	0%	0	0%	0	0%	0	0%
Australia	0	-	0	-	0	-	0	-	0	-	0	-
Austria	10	14%	0	0%	2	33%	14	19%	0	0%	3	50%
Azerbaijan	0	-	0	-	0	-	0	-	0	-	0	-
Belarus	1	3%	0	0%	1	33%	0	0%	0	0%	0	0%
Belgium	26	27%	1	13%	3	38%	16	17%	0	0%	3	38%
Bosnia & Herzegovina	28	47%	2	40%	3	60%	0	0%	0	0%	0	0%
Bulgaria	0	0%	0	0%	0	0%	0	0%	0	0%	0	0%
Croatia	16	27%	0	0%	3	60%	0	0%	0	0%	0	0%
Cyprus	24	50%	1	25%	3	75%	4	11%	0	0%	1	33%
Czech Republic	0	0%	0	-	0	-	0	0%	0	-	0	-
Denmark	33	46%	0	0%	4	67%	14	23%	0	0%	2	40%
Estonia	5	14%	0	0%	1	33%	2	6%	0	0%	1	33%
Finland	27	25%	0	0%	4	44%	17	18%	0	0%	4	50%
France	53	55%	2	25%	7	88%	27	32%	0	0%	5	71%
Georgia	0	-	0	-	0	-	0	-	0	-	0	-
Germany	32	33%	1	13%	5	63%	23	21%	0	0%	4	44%
Greece	31	32%	0	0%	4	50%	16	19%	1	14%	2	29%
Hungary	0	0%	0	0%	0	0%	0	0%	0	0%	0	0%
Iceland	6	17%	0	0%	2	67%	0	0%	0	0%	0	0%
Ireland	31	29%	0	0%	4	44%	17	18%	0	0%	3	38%
Israel	43	40%	2	22%	6	67%	19	20%	0	0%	4	50%
Italy	15	25%	0	0%	3	60%	33	55%	1	20%	5	100%
Latvia	10	21%	0	0%	2	50%	0	0%	0	0%	0	0%
Lithuania	11	23%	0	0%	2	50%	0	0%	0	0%	0	0%
Luxembourg	10	17%	0	0%	2	40%	17	28%	1	20%	3	60%
Malta	5	8%	0	0%	1	20%	1	2%	0	0%	1	25%
Moldova	0	0%	0	0%	0	0%	2	8%	0	0%	1	50%
Monaco	-	-	-	-	-	-	-	-	-	-	-	-
Montenegro	0	-	0	-	0	-	0	-	0	-	0	-
Morocco	0	-	0	-	0	-	0	-	0	-	0	-
Netherlands	32	30%	0	0%	6	67%	18	19%	0	0%	2	25%
North Macedonia	4	6%	0	0%	2	33%	0	0%	0	0%	0	0%
Norway	9	8%	0	0%	3	33%	10	10%	0	0%	3	38%
Poland	0	0%	0	0%	0	0%	1	4%	0	0%	1	50%
Portugal	8	8%	0	0%	3	38%	18	19%	0	0%	5	63%
Romania	11	23%	0	0%	2	50%	0	0%	0	0%	0	0%
Russia	0	0%	0	0%	0	0%	0	0%	0	0%	0	0%
San Marino	0	-	0	-	0	-	0	-	0	-	0	-
Serbia	0	-	0	-	0	-	0	-	0	-	0	-
Serbia & Montenegro	14	39%	0	0%	3	100%	0	0%	0	0%	0	0%
Slovakia	0	-	0	-	0	-	0	-	0	-	0	-
Slovenia	7	19%	0	0%	2	67%	0	0%	0	0%	0	0%
Spain	14	15%	0	0%	4	50%	17	18%	0	0%	3	38%
Sweden	22	23%	0	0%	4	50%	22	26%	1	14%	2	29%
Switzerland	29	27%	0	0%	7	78%	16	17%	0	0%	3	38%
Turkey	11	15%	0	0%	2	33%	5	8%	0	0%	1	20%
Ukraine	15	25%	0	0%	4	80%	0	0%	0	0%	0	0%
United Kingdom	42	44%	2	25%	5	63%	24	25%	0	0%	4	50%
Yugoslavia	0	0%	0	0%	0	0%	4	17%	0	0%	1	50%

Eurovision 2019: Who Votes for Who? (And Who Doesn't)

Montenegro

	Montenegro awarded points to:				Frequency		Montenegro received points from:				Frequency	
	Total	% of max	12's	% of max	Times	% of max	Total	% of max	12's	% of max	Times	% of max
Albania	121	78%	3	23%	10	100%	43	51%	2	29%	5	83%
Andorra	0	0%	0	0%	0	0%	1	3%	0	0%	1	33%
Armenia	68	33%	1	6%	9	69%	44	37%	1	10%	6	75%
Australia	27	15%	0	0%	5	63%	7	7%	0	0%	1	20%
Austria	3	2%	0	0%	2	22%	0	0%	0	0%	0	0%
Azerbaijan	81	36%	1	5%	11	79%	34	28%	0	0%	5	63%
Belarus	24	17%	0	0%	7	78%	5	6%	0	0%	2	33%
Belgium	18	9%	0	0%	5	42%	0	0%	0	0%	0	0%
Bosnia & Herzegovina	77	80%	4	50%	7	100%	38	63%	1	20%	4	100%
Bulgaria	29	27%	0	0%	5	83%	0	0%	0	0%	0	0%
Croatia	60	50%	1	10%	7	100%	17	35%	0	0%	3	100%
Cyprus	40	17%	0	0%	7	54%	6	5%	0	0%	2	25%
Czech Republic	15	8%	0	0%	5	56%	8	7%	0	0%	2	29%
Denmark	31	16%	0	0%	5	42%	5	5%	0	0%	1	14%
Estonia	8	4%	0	0%	3	25%	0	0%	0	0%	0	0%
Finland	5	3%	0	0%	2	17%	3	2%	0	0%	1	11%
France	12	7%	0	0%	3	27%	7	6%	0	0%	1	14%
Georgia	4	3%	0	0%	2	22%	0	0%	0	0%	0	0%
Germany	0	0%	0	0%	0	0%	2	2%	0	0%	1	14%
Greece	77	34%	3	16%	9	64%	18	14%	0	0%	3	38%
Hungary	46	19%	1	5%	7	50%	4	3%	0	0%	1	13%
Iceland	29	13%	0	0%	5	36%	2	1%	0	0%	1	10%
Ireland	4	4%	0	0%	3	38%	0	0%	0	0%	0	0%
Israel	26	14%	0	0%	7	58%	8	7%	0	0%	2	25%
Italy	61	42%	0	0%	8	100%	9	8%	0	0%	2	29%
Latvia	5	3%	0	0%	2	20%	2	2%	0	0%	1	13%
Lithuania	3	2%	0	0%	2	22%	0	0%	0	0%	0	0%
Luxembourg	0	-	0	-	0	-	0	-	0	-	0	-
Malta	50	28%	1	7%	6	55%	18	17%	0	0%	3	43%
Moldova	56	25%	0	0%	9	64%	19	12%	0	0%	3	30%
Monaco	0	-	0	-	0	-	0	-	0	-	0	-
Montenegro	-	-	-	-	-	-	-	-	-	-	-	-
Morocco	0	-	0	-	0	-	0	-	0	-	0	-
Netherlands	15	7%	0	0%	6	50%	6	5%	0	0%	1	13%
North Macedonia	51	71%	0	0%	5	100%	27	56%	1	25%	4	100%
Norway	44	22%	0	0%	7	54%	3	4%	0	0%	1	17%
Poland	6	3%	0	0%	3	25%	0	0%	0	0%	0	0%
Portugal	26	20%	0	0%	4	50%	12	10%	0	0%	3	38%
Romania	32	19%	0	0%	5	42%	7	7%	0	0%	1	14%
Russia	123	54%	0	0%	13	87%	8	6%	0	0%	2	22%
San Marino	39	25%	0	0%	5	56%	29	20%	0	0%	4	44%
Serbia	179	93%	13	81%	11	100%	69	82%	3	43%	5	100%
Serbia & Montenegro	0	-	0	-	0	-	0	-	0	-	0	-
Slovakia	0	-	0	-	0	-	0	-	0	-	0	-
Slovenia	91	45%	1	6%	12	100%	63	44%	0	0%	8	89%
Spain	6	3%	0	0%	2	18%	5	3%	0	0%	2	22%
Sweden	54	20%	0	0%	9	56%	15	10%	0	0%	5	50%
Switzerland	5	6%	0	0%	1	17%	3	4%	0	0%	2	33%
Turkey	15	21%	0	0%	4	67%	5	21%	0	0%	1	50%
Ukraine	65	34%	1	6%	8	67%	12	17%	0	0%	3	60%
United Kingdom	2	1%	0	0%	1	9%	0	0%	0	0%	0	0%
Yugoslavia	0	-	0	-	0	-	0	-	0	-	0	-

Eurovision 2019: Who Votes for Who? (And Who Doesn't)
Morocco

	Morocco awarded points to:				Frequency		Morocco received points from :				Frequency	
	Total	% of max	12's	% of max	Times	% of max	Total	% of max	12's	% of max	Times	% of max
Albania	0	-	0	-	0	-	0	-	0	-	0	-
Andorra	0	-	0	-	0	-	0	-	0	-	0	-
Armenia	0	-	0	-	0	-	0	-	0	-	0	-
Australia	0	-	0	-	0	-	0	-	0	-	0	-
Austria	3	25%	0	0%	1	100%	0	0%	0	0%	0	0%
Azerbaijan	0	-	0	-	0	-	0	-	0	-	0	-
Belarus	0	-	0	-	0	-	0	-	0	-	0	-
Belgium	0	0%	0	0%	0	0%	0	0%	0	0%	0	0%
Bosnia & Herzegovina	0	-	0	-	0	-	0	-	0	-	0	-
Bulgaria	0	-	0	-	0	-	0	-	0	-	0	-
Croatia	0	-	0	-	0	-	0	-	0	-	0	-
Cyprus	0	-	0	-	0	-	0	-	0	-	0	-
Czech Republic	0	-	0	-	0	-	0	-	0	-	0	-
Denmark	2	17%	0	0%	1	100%	0	0%	0	0%	0	0%
Estonia	0	-	0	-	0	-	0	-	0	-	0	-
Finland	0	0%	0	0%	0	0%	0	0%	0	0%	0	0%
France	1	8%	0	0%	1	100%	0	0%	0	0%	0	0%
Georgia	0	-	0	-	0	-	0	-	0	-	0	-
Germany	10	83%	0	0%	1	100%	0	0%	0	0%	0	0%
Greece	0	0%	0	0%	0	0%	0	0%	0	0%	0	0%
Hungary	0	-	0	-	0	-	0	-	0	-	0	-
Iceland	0	-	0	-	0	-	0	0%	0	0%	0	0%
Ireland	0	0%	0	0%	0	0%	0	0%	0	0%	0	0%
Israel	0	-	0	-	0	-	0	-	0	-	0	-
Italy	0	0%	0	0%	0	0%	7	58%	0	0%	1	100%
Latvia	0	-	0	-	0	-	0	-	0	-	0	-
Lithuania	0	-	0	-	0	-	0	-	0	-	0	-
Luxembourg	0	0%	0	0%	0	0%	0	0%	0	0%	0	0%
Malta	0	-	0	-	0	-	0	-	0	-	0	-
Moldova	0	-	0	-	0	-	0	-	0	-	0	-
Monaco	0	-	0	-	0	-	0	-	0	-	0	-
Montenegro	0	-	0	-	0	-	0	-	0	-	0	-
Morocco	-	-	-	-	-	-	--	-	-	-	-	-
Netherlands	0	0%	0	0%	0	0%	0	0%	0	0%	0	0%
North Macedonia	0	-	0	-	0	-	0	-	0	-	0	-
Norway	4	33%	0	0%	1	100%	0	0%	0	0%	0	0%
Poland	0	-	0	-	0	-	0	-	0	-	0	-
Portugal	0	0%	0	0%	0	0%	0	0%	0	0%	0	0%
Romania	0	-	0	-	0	-	0	-	0	-	0	-
Russia	0	-	0	-	0	-	0	-	0	-	0	-
San Marino	0	-	0	-	0	-	0	-	0	-	0	-
Serbia	0	-	0	-	0	-	0	-	0	-	0	-
Serbia & Montenegro	0	-	0	-	0	-	0	-	0	-	0	-
Slovakia	0	-	0	-	0	-	0	-	0	-	0	-
Slovenia	0	-	0	-	0	-	0	-	0	-	0	-
Spain	5	42%	0	0%	1	100%	0	0%	0	0%	0	0%
Sweden	6	50%	0	0%	1	100%	0	0%	0	0%	0	0%
Switzerland	7	58%	0	0%	1	100%	0	0%	0	0%	0	0%
Turkey	12	100%	1	100%	1	100%	0	0%	0	0%	0	0%
Ukraine	0	-	0	-	0	-	0	-	0	-	0	-
United Kingdom	8	67%	0	0%	1	100%	0	0%	0	0%	0	0%
Yugoslavia	0	-	0	-	0	-	0	-	0	-	0	-

Eurovision 2019: Who Votes for Who? (And Who Doesn't)

Netherlands

	Netherlands awarded points to:				Frequency		Netherlands received points from:				Frequency	
	Total	% of max	12's	% of max	Times	% of max	Total	% of max	12's	% of max	Times	% of max
Albania	8	4%	0	0%	4	25%	40	17%	0	0%	7	47%
Andorra	7	12%	0	0%	1	20%	19	26%	0	0%	4	67%
Armenia	141	56%	7	33%	14	82%	62	26%	0	0%	8	57%
Australia	41	31%	1	9%	5	83%	21	16%	0	0%	4	67%
Austria	104	21%	1	2%	15	42%	168	30%	3	7%	23	59%
Azerbaijan	57	22%	0	0%	12	71%	28	13%	0	0%	5	42%
Belarus	6	3%	0	0%	3	20%	36	14%	0	0%	5	31%
Belgium	210	45%	5	13%	27	73%	249	48%	8	19%	30	77%
Bosnia & Herzegovina	90	33%	0	0%	14	64%	21	9%	0	0%	6	35%
Bulgaria	45	25%	2	13%	4	36%	26	14%	0	0%	4	36%
Croatia	54	15%	0	0%	11	42%	76	19%	1	3%	10	38%
Cyprus	83	18%	1	3%	10	29%	50	11%	0	0%	11	34%
Czech Republic	16	15%	0	0%	3	60%	38	29%	0	0%	4	67%
Denmark	205	36%	6	13%	28	68%	188	35%	1	2%	23	61%
Estonia	69	18%	1	3%	12	43%	119	29%	3	9%	15	54%
Finland	48	11%	0	0%	12	34%	109	23%	1	3%	16	46%
France	128	24%	4	9%	20	50%	161	27%	3	6%	23	55%
Georgia	13	8%	0	0%	4	33%	33	17%	0	0%	6	55%
Germany	149	28%	5	11%	24	60%	178	31%	1	2%	25	61%
Greece	119	24%	0	0%	22	58%	73	15%	1	3%	15	43%
Hungary	82	25%	0	0%	12	57%	119	41%	3	13%	12	71%
Iceland	58	16%	0	0%	10	36%	108	21%	4	10%	13	35%
Ireland	150	28%	3	7%	25	61%	178	31%	2	4%	28	67%
Israel	177	35%	3	7%	27	73%	139	29%	3	8%	24	69%
Italy	68	20%	1	4%	10	42%	69	19%	0	0%	15	60%
Latvia	23	10%	0	0%	5	29%	75	25%	3	12%	8	42%
Lithuania	30	10%	0	0%	7	33%	83	27%	3	12%	12	60%
Luxembourg	45	22%	1	6%	8	47%	61	30%	2	12%	11	65%
Malta	71	18%	0	0%	15	56%	128	30%	2	6%	17	63%
Moldova	31	10%	0	0%	5	24%	31	10%	0	0%	6	33%
Monaco	18	19%	0	0%	2	25%	32	30%	0	0%	6	67%
Montenegro	6	5%	0	0%	1	13%	15	7%	0	0%	6	50%
Morocco	0	0%	0	0%	0	0%	0	0%	0	0%	0	0%
Netherlands	-	-	-	-	-	-	-	-	-	-	-	-
North Macedonia	18	8%	0	0%	4	24%	54	19%	0	0%	9	50%
Norway	200	32%	4	8%	32	70%	162	27%	2	4%	22	51%
Poland	43	16%	0	0%	9	45%	61	21%	1	4%	7	37%
Portugal	90	20%	3	8%	15	43%	108	24%	2	5%	16	46%
Romania	52	15%	0	0%	12	48%	89	27%	3	11%	12	57%
Russia	78	20%	0	0%	16	59%	32	10%	1	4%	7	32%
San Marino	4	3%	0	0%	1	14%	79	37%	2	11%	10	91%
Serbia	72	29%	0	0%	13	81%	34	16%	0	0%	6	50%
Serbia & Montenegro	26	72%	1	33%	3	100%	1	2%	0	0%	1	25%
Slovakia	0	0%	0	0%	0	0%	5	7%	0	0%	1	17%
Slovenia	38	12%	0	0%	7	29%	81	23%	0	0%	15	60%
Spain	60	11%	0	0%	13	32%	133	24%	1	2%	23	56%
Sweden	240	38%	6	12%	27	59%	171	29%	3	6%	24	56%
Switzerland	138	32%	1	3%	17	52%	149	30%	2	5%	23	64%
Turkey	168	42%	7	21%	23	70%	95	28%	1	4%	19	68%
Ukraine	61	18%	0	0%	11	46%	40	14%	1	4%	6	32%
United Kingdom	112	21%	2	4%	20	49%	115	21%	1	2%	24	60%
Yugoslavia	25	17%	0	0%	4	33%	40	28%	0	0%	7	58%

Eurovision 2019: Who Votes for Who? (And Who Doesn't)

North Macedonia

	Nth Macedonia awarded points to:				Frequency		Nth Macedonia received points from:				Frequency	
	Total	% of max	12's	% of max	Times	% of max	Total	% of max	12's	% of max	Times	% of max
Albania	253	88%	16	67%	19	100%	183	73%	8	38%	17	100%
Andorra	1	2%	0	0%	1	20%	0	0%	0	0%	0	0%
Armenia	41	17%	0	0%	9	56%	39	25%	0	0%	4	40%
Australia	37	28%	0	0%	4	67%	16	27%	0	0%	3	100%
Austria	14	5%	0	0%	4	25%	37	15%	1	5%	6	38%
Azerbaijan	55	24%	0	0%	9	64%	34	28%	0	0%	3	60%
Belarus	44	15%	0	0%	9	45%	22	8%	0	0%	5	25%
Belgium	39	15%	0	0%	8	44%	0	0%	0	0%	0	0%
Bosnia & Herzegovina	116	60%	3	19%	16	100%	114	79%	1	8%	13	93%
Bulgaria	160	63%	4	19%	15	100%	109	50%	2	11%	14	93%
Croatia	152	55%	2	9%	18	100%	157	55%	4	17%	18	100%
Cyprus	33	12%	0	0%	4	22%	5	2%	0	0%	2	13%
Czech Republic	28	21%	0	0%	3	43%	25	30%	0	0%	5	83%
Denmark	31	9%	1	3%	5	22%	24	8%	0	0%	4	22%
Estonia	32	11%	1	4%	6	30%	2	1%	0	0%	1	5%
Finland	34	13%	0	0%	8	40%	9	4%	0	0%	3	16%
France	15	5%	0	0%	4	21%	15	6%	0	0%	2	11%
Georgia	15	8%	0	0%	5	36%	6	4%	0	0%	4	40%
Germany	11	4%	0	0%	2	11%	30	10%	1	4%	4	18%
Greece	58	19%	0	0%	12	55%	8	4%	0	0%	3	18%
Hungary	29	12%	0	0%	5	29%	12	7%	0	0%	2	18%
Iceland	11	5%	0	0%	5	28%	9	5%	0	0%	2	13%
Ireland	16	6%	0	0%	4	22%	15	5%	0	0%	2	11%
Israel	54	15%	0	0%	12	52%	21	7%	0	0%	5	25%
Italy	55	35%	1	8%	9	100%	23	21%	0	0%	5	83%
Latvia	31	13%	0	0%	7	41%	13	5%	0	0%	2	11%
Lithuania	16	5%	0	0%	4	20%	4	1%	0	0%	1	6%
Luxembourg	0	-	0	-	0	-	0	-	0	-	0	-
Malta	91	29%	2	8%	13	59%	40	15%	0	0%	9	43%
Moldova	49	21%	0	0%	9	56%	24	14%	1	7%	5	42%
Monaco	0	0%	0	0%	0	0%	4	6%	0	0%	2	33%
Montenegro	27	56%	1	25%	4	100%	51	85%	0	0%	5	100%
Morocco	0	-	0	-	0	-	0	-	0	-	0	-
Netherlands	54	19%	0	0%	9	50%	18	8%	0	0%	4	24%
North Macedonia	-	-	-	-	-	-	-	-	-	-	-	-
Norway	41	12%	0	0%	9	39%	21	7%	0	0%	3	17%
Poland	13	7%	0	0%	5	38%	8	5%	0	0%	1	8%
Portugal	23	11%	0	0%	3	20%	5	3%	0	0%	1	6%
Romania	79	24%	2	7%	13	54%	59	21%	1	4%	10	50%
Russia	92	33%	0	0%	13	65%	28	15%	0	0%	4	29%
San Marino	13	18%	0	0%	2	50%	7	10%	0	0%	3	75%
Serbia	184	77%	7	35%	15	100%	135	87%	7	54%	10	100%
Serbia & Montenegro	30	83%	0	0%	3	100%	59	82%	2	33%	6	100%
Slovakia	3	6%	0	0%	1	25%	6	10%	0	0%	3	60%
Slovenia	69	30%	0	0%	13	81%	119	50%	2	10%	15	94%
Spain	5	2%	0	0%	2	11%	0	0%	0	0%	0	0%
Sweden	64	18%	0	0%	14	58%	18	8%	0	0%	6	33%
Switzerland	26	9%	0	0%	7	37%	102	33%	1	4%	16	76%
Turkey	125	65%	2	13%	16	100%	72	40%	0	0%	12	80%
Ukraine	92	32%	1	4%	14	70%	27	13%	0	0%	6	43%
United Kingdom	28	10%	0	0%	5	26%	24	8%	2	8%	2	10%
Yugoslavia	0	-	0	-	0	-	0	-	0	-	0	-

Eurovision 2019: Who Votes for Who? (And Who Doesn't)

Norway

	Norway awarded points to:				Frequency		Norway received points from:				Frequency	
	Total	% of max	12's	% of max	Times	% of max	Total	% of max	12's	% of max	Times	% of max
Albania	21	8%	0	0%	5	29%	54	18%	1	4%	9	45%
Andorra	2	3%	0	0%	1	20%	26	27%	0	0%	5	63%
Armenia	7	3%	0	0%	2	13%	61	27%	0	0%	13	87%
Australia	79	51%	1	8%	7	100%	44	31%	1	8%	6	86%
Austria	67	13%	0	0%	11	30%	81	15%	1	2%	16	40%
Azerbaijan	50	19%	0	0%	7	39%	53	22%	1	5%	10	63%
Belarus	4	2%	0	0%	2	14%	99	34%	1	4%	13	68%
Belgium	94	20%	0	0%	17	46%	133	24%	1	2%	25	58%
Bosnia & Herzegovina	92	37%	3	14%	11	52%	44	19%	0	0%	10	53%
Bulgaria	80	39%	3	18%	6	50%	25	11%	0	0%	9	60%
Croatia	33	9%	0	0%	11	42%	73	18%	1	3%	13	46%
Cyprus	68	15%	1	3%	14	40%	92	20%	0	0%	17	47%
Czech Republic	16	17%	1	13%	2	40%	20	15%	0	0%	3	38%
Denmark	291	49%	8	16%	35	83%	269	47%	10	21%	30	73%
Estonia	63	20%	0	0%	12	52%	152	41%	2	6%	21	78%
Finland	147	31%	4	10%	22	58%	170	31%	6	13%	23	53%
France	143	25%	3	6%	27	63%	74	12%	0	0%	15	32%
Georgia	2	1%	0	0%	2	13%	46	18%	0	0%	8	50%
Germany	102	18%	2	4%	18	42%	184	26%	5	9%	27	53%
Greece	87	16%	0	0%	20	48%	84	15%	2	4%	16	37%
Hungary	57	18%	0	0%	11	52%	106	34%	1	4%	15	71%
Iceland	167	43%	3	9%	25	81%	202	35%	7	15%	27	60%
Ireland	179	30%	5	10%	32	71%	212	32%	3	5%	31	63%
Israel	156	27%	1	2%	27	63%	119	20%	2	4%	21	48%
Italy	86	24%	2	7%	14	54%	93	22%	2	6%	14	48%
Latvia	64	24%	1	5%	11	61%	128	36%	2	7%	18	75%
Lithuania	138	40%	4	14%	16	67%	137	36%	3	9%	17	65%
Luxembourg	38	17%	1	5%	6	32%	33	14%	0	0%	9	47%
Malta	87	20%	2	5%	14	44%	114	23%	1	2%	22	61%
Moldova	30	13%	0	0%	7	44%	77	28%	0	0%	13	72%
Monaco	10	10%	0	0%	3	38%	9	8%	0	0%	3	33%
Montenegro	3	4%	0	0%	1	17%	44	22%	0	0%	7	54%
Morocco	0	0%	0	0%	0	0%	4	33%	0	0%	1	100%
Netherlands	162	27%	2	4%	22	51%	200	32%	4	8%	32	70%
North Macedonia	21	8%	0	0%	3	17%	41	12%	0	0%	9	39%
Norway	-	-	-	-	-	-	-	-	-	-	-	-
Poland	82	24%	0	0%	16	67%	126	32%	2	6%	19	68%
Portugal	65	13%	2	5%	9	23%	102	18%	1	2%	23	53%
Romania	89	26%	0	0%	14	56%	76	20%	0	0%	15	60%
Russia	81	23%	0	0%	17	68%	113	32%	2	7%	13	52%
San Marino	0	0%	0	0%	0	0%	77	34%	0	0%	10	71%
Serbia	66	25%	0	0%	10	63%	63	24%	0	0%	9	56%
Serbia & Montenegro	16	44%	0	0%	2	67%	6	13%	0	0%	2	50%
Slovakia	0	0%	0	0%	0	0%	47	49%	0	0%	6	75%
Slovenia	28	8%	0	0%	6	23%	98	23%	1	3%	17	57%
Spain	59	10%	0	0%	14	32%	92	15%	3	6%	18	38%
Sweden	416	64%	15	28%	42	88%	286	47%	10	20%	35	76%
Switzerland	132	25%	1	2%	22	55%	145	23%	0	0%	23	50%
Turkey	59	13%	0	0%	16	43%	57	14%	1	3%	11	31%
Ukraine	54	17%	0	0%	11	50%	78	27%	1	4%	12	63%
United Kingdom	122	21%	2	4%	23	52%	131	20%	3	6%	21	43%
Yugoslavia	31	20%	1	8%	5	38%	11	7%	0	0%	2	15%

Eurovision 2019: Who Votes for Who? (And Who Doesn't)

Poland

	Poland awarded points to:				Frequency		Poland received points from:				Frequency	
	Total	% of max	12's	% of max	Times	% of max	Total	% of max	12's	% of max	Times	% of max
Albania	19	8%	0	0%	4	27%	23	10%	0	0%	5	33%
Andorra	7	15%	0	0%	2	50%	10	14%	0	0%	1	17%
Armenia	68	35%	2	13%	12	92%	14	8%	0	0%	5	45%
Australia	115	56%	2	12%	9	100%	28	17%	1	7%	4	50%
Austria	40	18%	1	5%	7	44%	59	29%	2	12%	9	60%
Azerbaijan	67	31%	1	6%	10	71%	21	13%	0	0%	6	55%
Belarus	40	21%	0	0%	8	67%	60	29%	0	0%	10	77%
Belgium	106	37%	4	17%	11	58%	62	20%	2	8%	9	43%
Bosnia & Herzegovina	20	9%	0	0%	4	22%	25	13%	0	0%	4	27%
Bulgaria	31	22%	0	0%	4	50%	19	16%	0	0%	3	43%
Croatia	24	10%	0	0%	7	37%	14	6%	0	0%	3	18%
Cyprus	34	10%	0	0%	8	38%	21	8%	0	0%	7	37%
Czech Republic	32	22%	0	0%	6	86%	38	26%	0	0%	4	50%
Denmark	74	26%	1	4%	13	68%	26	10%	0	0%	7	41%
Estonia	59	22%	1	5%	9	47%	29	10%	1	4%	5	24%
Finland	64	25%	2	10%	11	61%	31	11%	0	0%	4	21%
France	49	16%	1	4%	9	41%	77	25%	1	4%	15	68%
Georgia	56	26%	0	0%	8	62%	27	13%	0	0%	5	42%
Germany	64	21%	1	4%	9	43%	140	45%	4	15%	19	86%
Greece	56	16%	0	0%	14	54%	44	14%	0	0%	13	57%
Hungary	95	34%	2	9%	11	61%	65	27%	0	0%	11	69%
Iceland	62	21%	2	8%	11	50%	55	18%	0	0%	12	55%
Ireland	53	19%	1	4%	12	57%	93	31%	1	4%	12	55%
Israel	72	23%	0	0%	10	48%	23	8%	0	0%	5	26%
Italy	37	26%	0	0%	5	63%	62	34%	0	0%	10	100%
Latvia	67	28%	1	5%	8	50%	37	13%	0	0%	9	50%
Lithuania	57	24%	2	10%	9	53%	71	30%	1	5%	12	71%
Luxembourg	0	-	0	-	0	-	0	-	0	-	0	-
Malta	29	10%	0	0%	7	33%	21	7%	0	0%	6	27%
Moldova	43	19%	0	0%	8	53%	13	6%	0	0%	5	36%
Monaco	1	4%	0	0%	1	50%	0	0%	0	0%	0	0%
Montenegro	0	0%	0	0%	0	0%	6	3%	0	0%	3	25%
Morocco	0	-	0	-	0	-	0	-	0	-	0	-
Netherlands	61	21%	1	4%	7	37%	43	16%	0	0%	9	45%
North Macedonia	8	5%	0	0%	1	8%	13	7%	0	0%	5	38%
Norway	126	32%	2	6%	19	68%	82	24%	0	0%	16	67%
Poland	-	-	-	-	-	-	-	-	-	-	-	-
Portugal	61	22%	3	13%	6	30%	16	7%	0	0%	6	33%
Romania	45	19%	0	0%	8	44%	23	14%	0	0%	4	31%
Russia	77	26%	0	0%	12	55%	32	13%	0	0%	7	37%
San Marino	6	5%	0	0%	1	14%	25	14%	0	0%	5	45%
Serbia	51	20%	0	0%	8	53%	7	4%	0	0%	3	27%
Serbia & Montenegro	5	21%	0	0%	1	50%	0	0%	0	0%	0	0%
Slovakia	5	8%	0	0%	1	20%	7	12%	0	0%	2	40%
Slovenia	83	23%	0	0%	13	54%	43	12%	0	0%	11	46%
Spain	21	7%	0	0%	6	27%	33	10%	0	0%	9	38%
Sweden	132	35%	3	10%	16	64%	45	15%	0	0%	10	48%
Switzerland	42	21%	1	6%	7	47%	27	11%	0	0%	5	29%
Turkey	11	5%	0	0%	3	18%	8	5%	0	0%	2	15%
Ukraine	171	65%	9	41%	17	100%	77	38%	1	6%	10	77%
United Kingdom	37	12%	0	0%	8	36%	85	27%	2	8%	13	59%
Yugoslavia	0	-	0	-	0	-	0	-	0	-	0	-

Eurovision 2019: Who Votes for Who? (And Who Doesn't)

Portugal

	Portugal awarded points to:				Frequency		Portugal received points from:				Frequency	
	Total	% of max	12's	% of max	Times	% of max	Total	% of max	12's	% of max	Times	% of max
Albania	23	9%	0	0%	5	29%	48	27%	1	7%	6	46%
Andorra	10	17%	0	0%	2	40%	64	76%	4	57%	6	86%
Armenia	20	10%	0	0%	5	38%	49	34%	1	8%	5	50%
Australia	34	26%	0	0%	4	67%	34	35%	0	0%	3	60%
Austria	78	18%	1	3%	13	39%	39	10%	1	3%	5	16%
Azerbaijan	56	27%	1	6%	8	62%	40	37%	1	11%	4	57%
Belarus	15	7%	0	0%	4	27%	34	16%	0	0%	4	27%
Belgium	160	32%	3	7%	20	53%	111	23%	2	5%	16	42%
Bosnia & Herzegovina	20	8%	0	0%	4	18%	12	6%	0	0%	5	28%
Bulgaria	41	26%	0	0%	8	80%	14	9%	0	0%	3	27%
Croatia	41	15%	0	0%	14	67%	41	15%	0	0%	5	24%
Cyprus	64	13%	0	0%	16	46%	59	14%	1	3%	9	29%
Czech Republic	45	27%	2	14%	5	56%	52	36%	1	8%	6	67%
Denmark	77	17%	0	0%	21	60%	31	8%	0	0%	7	23%
Estonia	93	30%	4	15%	10	45%	29	11%	0	0%	5	25%
Finland	52	11%	0	0%	10	27%	82	17%	2	5%	16	43%
France	130	25%	3	7%	24	60%	242	48%	8	19%	28	72%
Georgia	18	13%	0	0%	4	40%	51	33%	2	15%	5	50%
Germany	165	32%	4	9%	23	58%	105	21%	2	5%	17	44%
Greece	111	21%	1	2%	17	43%	73	16%	0	0%	16	44%
Hungary	47	20%	0	0%	9	53%	32	16%	1	6%	3	21%
Iceland	106	23%	2	5%	17	50%	115	22%	4	9%	12	29%
Ireland	128	27%	0	0%	24	65%	40	9%	0	0%	6	17%
Israel	149	30%	2	5%	21	57%	44	10%	2	5%	6	18%
Italy	197	61%	6	22%	22	92%	50	19%	0	0%	9	45%
Latvia	48	25%	0	0%	8	53%	65	34%	3	19%	6	43%
Lithuania	46	20%	1	5%	6	35%	36	17%	2	11%	4	25%
Luxembourg	76	33%	2	11%	12	63%	51	22%	0	0%	10	53%
Malta	50	15%	1	4%	12	46%	29	8%	0	0%	6	22%
Moldova	126	62%	4	24%	13	93%	46	32%	1	8%	5	50%
Monaco	18	19%	0	0%	5	63%	8	8%	0	0%	3	38%
Montenegro	12	10%	0	0%	3	38%	26	20%	0	0%	4	50%
Morocco	0	0%	0	0%	0	0%	0	0%	0	0%	0	0%
Netherlands	108	24%	2	5%	16	46%	90	20%	3	8%	15	43%
North Macedonia	5	2%	0	0%	1	6%	23	11%	0	0%	3	20%
Norway	102	18%	1	2%	23	53%	65	13%	2	5%	9	23%
Poland	16	7%	0	0%	6	33%	61	22%	3	13%	6	30%
Portugal	-	-	-	-	-	-	-	-	-	-	-	-
Romania	85	39%	1	6%	13	76%	28	16%	0	0%	3	23%
Russia	71	28%	0	0%	14	70%	4	2%	0	0%	1	7%
San Marino	9	11%	0	0%	1	20%	24	22%	1	11%	2	33%
Serbia	32	18%	0	0%	7	58%	35	19%	1	7%	6	50%
Serbia & Montenegro	17	47%	0	0%	2	67%	0	0%	0	0%	0	0%
Slovakia	9	15%	0	0%	2	40%	11	13%	0	0%	3	43%
Slovenia	49	16%	0	0%	10	45%	50	18%	2	9%	6	30%
Spain	184	35%	8	18%	23	56%	224	43%	8	19%	27	68%
Sweden	190	32%	2	4%	27	59%	90	18%	2	5%	14	36%
Switzerland	103	23%	1	3%	21	60%	169	37%	4	11%	22	61%
Turkey	21	5%	0	0%	4	11%	48	12%	1	3%	10	29%
Ukraine	117	49%	5	25%	15	83%	34	20%	0	0%	4	33%
United Kingdom	156	30%	4	9%	25	61%	78	15%	1	2%	12	29%
Yugoslavia	11	7%	0	0%	3	23%	14	9%	0	0%	3	23%

Eurovision 2019: Who Votes for Who? (And Who Doesn't)

Romania

	Romania awarded points to:				Frequency		Romania received points from:				Frequency	
	Total	% of max	12's	% of max	Times	% of max	Total	% of max	12's	% of max	Times	% of max
Albania	20	9%	0	0%	7	44%	42	18%	0	0%	8	44%
Andorra	0	0%	0	0%	0	0%	34	31%	0	0%	6	67%
Armenia	56	26%	0	0%	11	69%	26	12%	0	0%	9	56%
Australia	29	27%	1	11%	5	100%	11	15%	0	0%	2	50%
Austria	44	17%	2	10%	7	41%	86	31%	1	4%	13	65%
Azerbaijan	89	44%	1	6%	10	71%	73	38%	0	0%	12	86%
Belarus	14	6%	0	0%	5	33%	27	11%	0	0%	10	53%
Belgium	40	18%	0	0%	7	39%	75	25%	0	0%	13	54%
Bosnia & Herzegovina	24	12%	1	6%	3	18%	24	13%	0	0%	6	38%
Bulgaria	46	27%	0	0%	6	55%	53	25%	0	0%	11	69%
Croatia	38	16%	0	0%	6	35%	27	10%	0	0%	6	30%
Cyprus	49	19%	0	0%	10	53%	91	34%	1	5%	16	76%
Czech Republic	11	15%	0	0%	2	50%	6	7%	0	0%	1	17%
Denmark	84	23%	1	3%	16	67%	64	20%	0	0%	13	57%
Estonia	17	6%	0	0%	6	30%	33	11%	1	4%	7	30%
Finland	22	8%	0	0%	6	29%	30	10%	0	0%	7	29%
France	15	5%	0	0%	4	20%	94	29%	1	4%	15	63%
Georgia	6	4%	0	0%	2	17%	25	13%	0	0%	4	29%
Germany	37	13%	1	4%	8	40%	59	16%	0	0%	12	44%
Greece	166	53%	5	19%	20	83%	113	39%	1	4%	16	70%
Hungary	136	52%	1	5%	17	94%	65	26%	2	10%	10	56%
Iceland	25	11%	0	0%	3	17%	46	18%	0	0%	9	45%
Ireland	47	16%	0	0%	10	48%	110	32%	2	7%	18	69%
Israel	87	26%	0	0%	18	75%	182	54%	3	11%	23	88%
Italy	39	30%	1	9%	6	75%	85	51%	3	21%	10	91%
Latvia	13	6%	0	0%	4	25%	22	7%	0	0%	6	27%
Lithuania	10	4%	0	0%	3	18%	23	8%	0	0%	7	35%
Luxembourg	0	-	0	-	0	-	0	-	0	-	0	-
Malta	61	20%	0	0%	11	52%	108	31%	1	3%	15	60%
Moldova	245	93%	16	73%	18	100%	257	97%	20	91%	19	100%
Monaco	0	0%	0	0%	0	0%	11	23%	0	0%	2	50%
Montenegro	7	7%	0	0%	1	14%	32	19%	0	0%	5	42%
Morocco	0	-	0	-	0	-	0	-	0	-	0	-
Netherlands	89	27%	3	11%	12	57%	52	15%	0	0%	12	48%
North Macedonia	59	21%	1	4%	10	50%	79	24%	2	7%	13	54%
Norway	76	20%	0	0%	15	60%	89	26%	0	0%	14	56%
Poland	23	14%	0	0%	4	31%	45	19%	0	0%	8	44%
Portugal	28	16%	0	0%	3	23%	85	39%	1	6%	13	76%
Romania	-	-	-	-	-	-	-	-	-	-	-	-
Russia	128	41%	2	8%	16	70%	68	24%	3	13%	13	59%
San Marino	9	8%	0	0%	2	29%	27	15%	0	0%	5	42%
Serbia	37	19%	0	0%	6	50%	22	12%	0	0%	6	50%
Serbia & Montenegro	24	67%	0	0%	3	100%	12	25%	0	0%	3	75%
Slovakia	3	8%	0	0%	1	33%	7	8%	0	0%	2	29%
Slovenia	35	14%	0	0%	8	44%	38	13%	0	0%	8	36%
Spain	48	17%	0	0%	9	45%	169	59%	6	25%	19	83%
Sweden	92	26%	2	7%	15	60%	48	15%	0	0%	10	42%
Switzerland	63	24%	0	0%	8	42%	33	10%	0	0%	8	32%
Turkey	107	56%	1	6%	15	94%	55	29%	0	0%	12	75%
Ukraine	54	20%	0	0%	12	63%	29	12%	0	0%	9	50%
United Kingdom	20	7%	1	4%	4	20%	59	20%	1	4%	9	39%
Yugoslavia	0	-	0	-	0	-	0	-	0	-	0	-

Eurovision 2019: Who Votes for Who? (And Who Doesn't)

Russia

	Russia awarded points to:				Frequency		Russia received points from:				Frequency	
	Total	% of max	12's	% of max	Times	% of max	Total	% of max	12's	% of max	Times	% of max
Albania	19	8%	0	0%	6	33%	72	25%	1	4%	10	48%
Andorra	4	8%	0	0%	1	25%	22	23%	0	0%	5	63%
Armenia	187	82%	10	53%	16	100%	217	82%	12	55%	18	100%
Australia	23	21%	0	0%	5	100%	29	30%	0	0%	4	80%
Austria	27	10%	0	0%	5	28%	106	34%	1	4%	13	59%
Azerbaijan	187	78%	6	30%	16	100%	182	76%	10	50%	15	94%
Belarus	89	62%	4	33%	10	91%	212	88%	15	75%	18	100%
Belgium	63	26%	0	0%	9	47%	87	26%	1	4%	16	62%
Bosnia & Herzegovina	15	6%	0	0%	3	16%	57	22%	0	0%	10	50%
Bulgaria	4	4%	0	0%	1	17%	66	46%	2	17%	8	73%
Croatia	33	12%	0	0%	9	45%	113	34%	2	7%	16	67%
Cyprus	66	23%	0	0%	11	55%	169	54%	3	12%	20	87%
Czech Republic	8	7%	0	0%	2	40%	59	49%	1	10%	7	100%
Denmark	61	18%	1	4%	10	42%	87	24%	2	7%	14	54%
Estonia	64	21%	0	0%	11	48%	245	68%	8	27%	27	100%
Finland	35	14%	1	5%	5	26%	128	38%	2	7%	19	76%
France	60	20%	1	4%	9	41%	71	19%	0	0%	14	52%
Georgia	70	45%	0	0%	11	100%	77	40%	0	0%	12	92%
Germany	38	13%	0	0%	7	32%	107	30%	2	7%	17	65%
Greece	112	33%	0	0%	20	77%	171	48%	3	10%	21	78%
Hungary	54	18%	0	0%	11	52%	102	35%	1	4%	13	65%
Iceland	31	10%	0	0%	9	39%	94	27%	1	3%	17	65%
Ireland	39	14%	1	4%	6	29%	125	36%	0	0%	16	62%
Israel	68	27%	0	0%	9	50%	170	59%	6	25%	20	91%
Italy	27	19%	1	8%	4	44%	51	27%	0	0%	8	67%
Latvia	30	12%	0	0%	9	50%	229	68%	10	36%	22	92%
Lithuania	47	19%	0	0%	11	61%	166	58%	4	17%	20	95%
Luxembourg	0	-	0	-	0	-	0	-	0	-	0	-
Malta	64	20%	1	4%	8	36%	110	29%	2	6%	16	59%
Moldova	170	57%	7	28%	19	90%	223	66%	6	21%	22	96%
Monaco	0	0%	0	0%	0	0%	0	0%	0	0%	0	0%
Montenegro	8	6%	0	0%	2	22%	123	54%	0	0%	13	87%
Morocco	0	-	0	-	0	-	0	-	0	-	0	-
Netherlands	32	10%	1	4%	7	32%	78	20%	0	0%	16	59%
North Macedonia	28	15%	0	0%	4	29%	92	33%	0	0%	13	65%
Norway	113	32%	2	7%	13	52%	81	23%	0	0%	17	68%
Poland	32	13%	0	0%	7	37%	77	26%	0	0%	12	55%
Portugal	4	2%	0	0%	1	7%	71	28%	0	0%	14	70%
Romania	68	24%	3	13%	13	59%	128	41%	2	8%	16	70%
Russia	-	-	-	-	-	-	-	-	-	-	-	-
San Marino	9	7%	0	0%	3	38%	68	31%	2	11%	7	50%
Serbia	49	20%	0	0%	9	56%	100	46%	1	6%	13	87%
Serbia & Montenegro	16	67%	0	0%	2	100%	12	25%	0	0%	3	75%
Slovakia	1	3%	0	0%	1	33%	9	13%	0	0%	2	33%
Slovenia	50	20%	0	0%	10	56%	92	29%	2	8%	12	52%
Spain	22	7%	0	0%	6	27%	102	27%	1	3%	14	48%
Sweden	73	20%	1	3%	14	56%	103	27%	0	0%	14	52%
Switzerland	22	11%	0	0%	5	36%	30	10%	0	0%	6	27%
Turkey	25	12%	0	0%	6	35%	50	25%	0	0%	9	53%
Ukraine	148	56%	1	5%	19	100%	144	63%	5	26%	17	100%
United Kingdom	38	13%	1	4%	8	36%	65	19%	0	0%	11	44%
Yugoslavia	0	-	0	-	0	-	0	-	0	-	0	-

Eurovision 2019: Who Votes for Who? (And Who Doesn't)

San Marino

	San Marino awarded points to:				Frequency		San Marino received points from:				Frequency	
	Total	% of max	12's	% of max	Times	% of max	Total	% of max	12's	% of max	Times	% of max
Albania	51	39%	1	9%	7	78%	39	46%	0	0%	5	83%
Andorra	0	0%	0	0%	0	0%	2	17%	0	0%	1	100%
Armenia	54	32%	1	7%	9	82%	14	13%	0	0%	4	57%
Australia	31	20%	0	0%	5	71%	9	11%	0	0%	2	50%
Austria	12	7%	0	0%	3	33%	8	8%	0	0%	2	40%
Azerbaijan	72	32%	1	5%	10	67%	41	31%	0	0%	6	67%
Belarus	1	1%	0	0%	1	17%	11	13%	0	0%	2	50%
Belgium	26	20%	0	0%	5	63%	2	2%	0	0%	1	17%
Bosnia & Herzegovina	6	8%	0	0%	1	20%	10	28%	0	0%	1	50%
Bulgaria	45	42%	2	22%	4	80%	0	0%	0	0%	0	0%
Croatia	18	15%	0	0%	4	67%	3	4%	0	0%	2	50%
Cyprus	57	30%	0	0%	6	60%	10	10%	0	0%	1	20%
Czech Republic	27	20%	0	0%	4	67%	12	14%	1	14%	1	25%
Denmark	34	18%	1	6%	7	64%	0	0%	0	0%	0	0%
Estonia	13	7%	0	0%	2	18%	20	15%	0	0%	3	43%
Finland	17	10%	0	0%	4	36%	8	6%	0	0%	3	38%
France	12	7%	0	0%	3	30%	5	3%	0	0%	1	13%
Georgia	17	12%	0	0%	5	56%	24	22%	1	11%	4	67%
Germany	14	8%	0	0%	1	10%	1	1%	0	0%	1	14%
Greece	111	51%	6	33%	9	64%	24	18%	0	0%	7	88%
Hungary	64	23%	0	0%	10	63%	36	20%	1	7%	6	60%
Iceland	48	25%	0	0%	6	46%	12	8%	0	0%	4	44%
Ireland	23	19%	1	10%	4	50%	0	0%	0	0%	0	0%
Israel	52	27%	2	13%	7	64%	11	8%	0	0%	2	25%
Italy	88	56%	2	15%	8	89%	14	17%	0	0%	3	60%
Latvia	35	29%	1	10%	5	63%	4	4%	0	0%	2	29%
Lithuania	17	12%	0	0%	3	33%	0	0%	0	0%	0	0%
Luxembourg	0	-	0	-	0	-	0	-	0	-	0	-
Malta	62	32%	1	6%	10	91%	39	27%	1	8%	5	63%
Moldova	51	30%	0	0%	6	60%	21	18%	0	0%	5	71%
Monaco	0	-	0	-	0	-	0	-	0	-	0	-
Montenegro	29	20%	0	0%	4	44%	39	25%	0	0%	5	56%
Morocco	0	-	0	-	0	-	0	-	0	-	0	-
Netherlands	79	37%	2	11%	10	91%	4	3%	0	0%	1	14%
North Macedonia	7	10%	0	0%	3	75%	13	18%	0	0%	2	50%
Norway	77	34%	0	0%	10	71%	0	0%	0	0%	0	0%
Poland	25	14%	0	0%	5	45%	6	5%	0	0%	1	14%
Portugal	24	22%	1	11%	2	33%	9	11%	0	0%	1	20%
Romania	27	15%	0	0%	5	42%	9	8%	0	0%	2	29%
Russia	68	31%	2	11%	7	50%	9	7%	0	0%	3	38%
San Marino	-	-	-	-	-	-	-	-	-	-	-	-
Serbia	32	16%	0	0%	7	64%	6	6%	0	0%	2	40%
Serbia & Montenegro	0	-	0	-	0	-	0	-	0	-	0	-
Slovakia	0	-	0	-	0	-	0	-	0	-	0	-
Slovenia	21	13%	0	0%	5	56%	3	3%	0	0%	1	17%
Spain	1	1%	0	0%	1	10%	19	13%	0	0%	3	33%
Sweden	72	33%	2	11%	10	77%	0	0%	0	0%	0	0%
Switzerland	13	11%	0	0%	3	38%	0	0%	0	0%	0	0%
Turkey	19	53%	0	0%	3	100%	5	42%	0	0%	1	100%
Ukraine	44	26%	2	14%	4	40%	4	6%	0	0%	1	25%
United Kingdom	31	18%	0	0%	7	70%	0	0%	0	0%	0	0%
Yugoslavia	0	-	0	-	0	-	0	-	0	-	0	-

Eurovision 2019: Who Votes for Who? (And Who Doesn't)

Serbia

	Serbia awarded points to:				Frequency		Serbia received points from:				Frequency	
	Total	% of max	12's	% of max	Times	% of max	Total	% of max	12's	% of max	Times	% of max
Albania	12	6%	0	0%	4	29%	31	14%	0	0%	11	73%
Andorra	0	0%	0	0%	0	0%	0	0%	0	0%	0	0%
Armenia	16	11%	0	0%	4	40%	26	15%	0	0%	5	45%
Australia	57	32%	0	0%	7	88%	26	15%	0	0%	5	63%
Austria	17	12%	0	0%	4	50%	81	45%	2	13%	11	100%
Azerbaijan	21	12%	0	0%	5	42%	12	8%	0	0%	2	20%
Belarus	25	11%	0	0%	6	43%	44	16%	0	0%	9	53%
Belgium	44	24%	0	0%	8	73%	26	11%	0	0%	6	40%
Bosnia & Herzegovina	78	81%	5	63%	8	100%	110	92%	6	60%	9	100%
Bulgaria	76	45%	0	0%	9	100%	69	38%	2	13%	9	82%
Croatia	89	53%	3	21%	11	100%	156	72%	7	39%	14	100%
Cyprus	35	17%	0	0%	7	58%	43	21%	0	0%	8	62%
Czech Republic	20	17%	0	0%	3	50%	39	27%	1	8%	5	63%
Denmark	43	16%	1	4%	8	47%	22	8%	0	0%	5	31%
Estonia	21	9%	0	0%	6	40%	13	5%	0	0%	5	29%
Finland	7	5%	0	0%	2	20%	39	18%	1	6%	7	50%
France	10	5%	0	0%	4	33%	103	37%	3	13%	13	76%
Georgia	17	7%	0	0%	4	27%	35	13%	0	0%	5	31%
Germany	18	9%	0	0%	2	17%	70	28%	0	0%	10	67%
Greece	72	33%	0	0%	11	73%	50	22%	0	0%	9	60%
Hungary	156	59%	8	36%	14	88%	62	25%	2	10%	9	60%
Iceland	22	13%	0	0%	4	33%	38	19%	0	0%	8	62%
Ireland	3	2%	0	0%	1	10%	14	6%	0	0%	3	21%
Israel	49	24%	0	0%	7	64%	13	6%	0	0%	4	31%
Italy	58	40%	0	0%	6	75%	36	21%	0	0%	8	89%
Latvia	6	4%	0	0%	3	30%	13	6%	0	0%	4	29%
Lithuania	27	12%	0	0%	5	33%	16	6%	0	0%	5	31%
Luxembourg	0	-	0	-	0	-	0	-	0	-	0	-
Malta	37	19%	0	0%	7	58%	26	11%	0	0%	8	53%
Moldova	52	25%	0	0%	9	64%	28	12%	0	0%	6	40%
Monaco	0	-	0	-	0	-	0	-	0	-	0	-
Montenegro	69	82%	3	43%	5	100%	179	93%	13	81%	11	100%
Morocco	0	-	0	-	0	-	0	-	0	-	0	-
Netherlands	34	16%	0	0%	6	50%	72	29%	0	0%	13	81%
North Macedonia	135	87%	7	54%	10	100%	184	77%	7	35%	15	100%
Norway	63	24%	0	0%	9	56%	66	25%	0	0%	10	63%
Poland	7	4%	0	0%	3	27%	51	20%	0	0%	8	53%
Portugal	35	19%	1	7%	6	50%	32	18%	0	0%	7	58%
Romania	22	12%	0	0%	6	50%	37	19%	0	0%	6	50%
Russia	100	46%	1	6%	13	87%	49	20%	0	0%	9	56%
San Marino	6	6%	0	0%	2	40%	32	16%	0	0%	7	64%
Serbia	-	-	-	-	-	-	-	-	-	-	-	-
Serbia & Montenegro	0	-	0	-	0	-	0	-	0	-	0	-
Slovakia	7	19%	0	0%	2	67%	21	29%	0	0%	3	50%
Slovenia	97	48%	0	0%	11	92%	185	70%	11	50%	16	100%
Spain	2	1%	0	0%	1	8%	26	11%	0	0%	7	47%
Sweden	69	30%	2	11%	12	86%	59	29%	0	0%	8	62%
Switzerland	22	18%	0	0%	4	57%	143	66%	8	44%	13	100%
Turkey	3	3%	0	0%	1	11%	0	0%	0	0%	0	0%
Ukraine	87	35%	1	5%	12	75%	29	13%	0	0%	6	43%
United Kingdom	10	5%	0	0%	2	17%	11	5%	0	0%	4	29%
Yugoslavia	0	-	0	-	0	-	0	-	0	-	0	-

Eurovision 2019: Who Votes for Who? (And Who Doesn't)

Serbia & Montenegro

	Serbia & Mont awarded points to:				Frequency		Serbia & Mont received points from:				Frequency	
	Total	% of max	12's	% of max	Times	% of max	Total	% of max	12's	% of max	Times	% of max
Albania	22	46%	0	0%	3	75%	17	47%	0	0%	3	100%
Andorra	0	0%	0	0%	0	0%	3	8%	0	0%	2	67%
Armenia	0	0%	0	0%	0	0%	0	-	0	-	0	-
Australia	0	-	0	-	0	-	0	-	0	-	0	-
Austria	0	0%	0	0%	0	0%	36	100%	3	100%	3	100%
Azerbaijan	0	-	0	-	0	-	0	-	0	-	0	-
Belarus	0	0%	0	0%	0	0%	20	56%	0	0%	3	100%
Belgium	0	0%	0	0%	0	0%	10	28%	0	0%	2	67%
Bosnia & Herzegovina	41	68%	2	40%	5	100%	34	94%	2	67%	3	100%
Bulgaria	1	4%	0	0%	1	50%	4	33%	0	0%	1	100%
Croatia	42	70%	1	20%	5	100%	36	100%	3	100%	3	100%
Cyprus	6	13%	0	0%	3	75%	30	83%	0	0%	3	100%
Czech Republic	0	-	0	-	0	-	0	-	0	-	0	-
Denmark	0	0%	0	0%	0	0%	17	47%	0	0%	2	67%
Estonia	4	11%	0	0%	1	33%	1	3%	0	0%	1	33%
Finland	15	31%	0	0%	2	50%	20	56%	0	0%	2	67%
France	0	0%	0	0%	0	0%	16	67%	0	0%	2	100%
Georgia	0	-	0	-	0	-	0	-	0	-	0	-
Germany	0	0%	0	0%	0	0%	25	69%	1	33%	3	100%
Greece	35	73%	1	25%	4	100%	24	67%	0	0%	3	100%
Hungary	14	58%	0	0%	2	100%	2	17%	0	0%	1	100%
Iceland	2	6%	0	0%	1	33%	7	19%	0	0%	1	33%
Ireland	1	2%	0	0%	1	25%	9	25%	0	0%	2	67%
Israel	6	13%	0	0%	2	50%	15	42%	0	0%	2	67%
Italy	0	-	0	-	0	-	0	-	0	-	0	-
Latvia	0	0%	0	0%	0	0%	10	28%	0	0%	3	100%
Lithuania	6	13%	0	0%	2	50%	3	8%	0	0%	2	67%
Luxembourg	0	-	0	-	0	-	0	-	0	-	0	-
Malta	0	0%	0	0%	0	0%	10	28%	0	0%	2	67%
Moldova	11	31%	0	0%	2	67%	1	8%	0	0%	1	100%
Monaco	0	0%	0	0%	0	0%	14	39%	0	0%	3	100%
Montenegro	0	-	0	-	0	-	0	-	0	-	0	-
Morocco	0	-	0	-	0	-	0	-	0	-	0	-
Netherlands	1	2%	0	0%	1	25%	26	72%	1	33%	3	100%
North Macedonia	59	82%	2	33%	6	100%	30	83%	0	0%	3	100%
Norway	6	13%	0	0%	2	50%	16	44%	0	0%	2	67%
Poland	0	0%	0	0%	0	0%	5	21%	0	0%	1	50%
Portugal	0	0%	0	0%	0	0%	17	47%	0	0%	2	67%
Romania	12	25%	0	0%	3	75%	24	67%	0	0%	3	100%
Russia	12	25%	0	0%	3	75%	16	67%	0	0%	2	100%
San Marino	0	-	0	-	0	-	0	-	0	-	0	-
Serbia	0	-	0	-	0	-	0	-	0	-	0	-
Serbia & Montenegro	-	-	-	-	-	-	-	-	-	-	-	-
Slovakia	0	-	0	-	0	-	0	-	0	-	0	-
Slovenia	14	39%	0	0%	2	67%	34	94%	2	67%	3	100%
Spain	0	0%	0	0%	0	0%	14	39%	0	0%	2	67%
Sweden	9	19%	0	0%	3	75%	28	78%	2	67%	3	100%
Switzerland	2	4%	0	0%	1	25%	36	100%	3	100%	3	100%
Turkey	2	4%	0	0%	1	25%	15	42%	0	0%	2	67%
Ukraine	25	42%	0	0%	4	80%	27	75%	2	67%	3	100%
United Kingdom	0	0%	0	0%	0	0%	11	31%	0	0%	2	67%
Yugoslavia	0	-	0	-	0	-	0	-	0	-	0	-

Eurovision 2019: Who Votes for Who? (And Who Doesn't)

Slovakia

	Slovakia awarded points to:				Frequency		Slovakia received points from:				Frequency	
	Total	% of max	12's	% of max	Times	% of max	Total	% of max	12's	% of max	Times	% of max
Albania	4	7%	0	0%	1	20%	4	17%	0	0%	1	50%
Andorra	0	-	0	-	0	-	0	-	0	-	0	-
Armenia	7	29%	0	0%	2	100%	0	-	0	-	0	-
Australia	0	-	0	-	0	-	0	-	0	-	0	-
Austria	9	19%	0	0%	3	75%	3	8%	0	0%	1	33%
Azerbaijan	29	48%	1	20%	4	80%	0	0%	0	0%	0	0%
Belarus	4	8%	0	0%	2	50%	3	8%	0	0%	1	33%
Belgium	26	36%	0	0%	3	50%	4	7%	0	0%	2	40%
Bosnia & Herzegovina	41	38%	1	11%	6	67%	11	18%	0	0%	2	40%
Bulgaria	0	0%	0	0%	0	0%	0	0%	0	0%	0	0%
Croatia	32	44%	2	33%	4	67%	8	13%	0	0%	1	20%
Cyprus	3	4%	0	0%	3	43%	0	0%	0	0%	0	0%
Czech Republic	0	-	0	-	0	-	0	-	0	-	0	-
Denmark	16	22%	0	0%	3	50%	0	0%	0	0%	0	0%
Estonia	50	42%	1	10%	6	60%	6	7%	0	0%	1	14%
Finland	2	3%	0	0%	1	17%	2	4%	0	0%	1	25%
France	0	0%	0	0%	0	0%	1	1%	0	0%	1	14%
Georgia	0	0%	0	0%	0	0%	0	0%	0	0%	0	0%
Germany	27	38%	1	17%	3	50%	0	0%	0	0%	0	0%
Greece	23	21%	0	0%	4	44%	7	12%	0	0%	2	40%
Hungary	10	17%	0	0%	2	40%	0	0%	0	0%	0	0%
Iceland	24	29%	0	0%	5	71%	5	14%	0	0%	1	33%
Ireland	29	30%	1	13%	5	63%	6	10%	0	0%	2	40%
Israel	20	42%	0	0%	3	75%	0	0%	0	0%	0	0%
Italy	5	21%	0	0%	1	50%	0	0%	0	0%	0	0%
Latvia	0	0%	0	0%	0	0%	0	0%	0	0%	0	0%
Lithuania	7	10%	0	0%	1	17%	0	0%	0	0%	0	0%
Luxembourg	0	-	0	-	0	-	0	-	0	-	0	-
Malta	31	37%	1	14%	5	71%	27	45%	1	20%	3	60%
Moldova	16	19%	0	0%	3	43%	7	19%	0	0%	1	33%
Monaco	0	-	0	-	0	-	0	-	0	-	0	-
Montenegro	0	-	0	-	0	-	0	-	0	-	0	-
Morocco	0	-	0	-	0	-	0	-	0	-	0	-
Netherlands	5	7%	0	0%	1	17%	0	0%	0	0%	0	0%
North Macedonia	6	10%	0	0%	3	60%	3	6%	0	0%	1	25%
Norway	47	49%	0	0%	6	75%	0	0%	0	0%	0	0%
Poland	7	12%	0	0%	2	40%	5	8%	0	0%	1	20%
Portugal	11	13%	0	0%	3	43%	9	15%	0	0%	2	40%
Romania	7	8%	0	0%	2	29%	3	8%	0	0%	1	33%
Russia	9	13%	0	0%	2	33%	1	3%	0	0%	1	33%
San Marino	0	-	0	-	0	-	0	-	0	-	0	-
Serbia	21	29%	0	0%	3	50%	7	19%	0	0%	2	67%
Serbia & Montenegro	0	-	0	-	0	-	0	-	0	-	0	-
Slovakia	-	-	-	-	-	-	-	-	-	-	-	-
Slovenia	9	13%	0	0%	2	33%	3	5%	0	0%	1	20%
Spain	4	5%	0	0%	2	29%	2	3%	0	0%	1	20%
Sweden	48	50%	2	25%	5	63%	3	5%	0	0%	1	20%
Switzerland	6	13%	0	0%	2	50%	0	0%	0	0%	0	0%
Turkey	3	4%	0	0%	1	17%	0	0%	0	0%	0	0%
Ukraine	30	36%	1	14%	5	71%	14	39%	1	33%	2	67%
United Kingdom	15	18%	0	0%	3	43%	0	0%	0	0%	0	0%
Yugoslavia	0	-	0	-	0	-	0	-	0	-	0	-

Eurovision 2019: Who Votes for Who? (And Who Doesn't)

Slovenia

	Slovenia awarded points to:				Frequency		Slovenia received points from:				Frequency	
	Total	% of max	12's	% of max	Times	% of max	Total	% of max	12's	% of max	Times	% of max
Albania	35	15%	0	0%	10	67%	24	12%	0	0%	4	31%
Andorra	5	8%	0	0%	2	40%	8	11%	0	0%	1	17%
Armenia	18	9%	0	0%	5	36%	6	4%	0	0%	2	18%
Australia	56	27%	1	6%	8	89%	19	11%	0	0%	4	50%
Austria	77	29%	1	5%	11	58%	35	13%	0	0%	9	45%
Azerbaijan	43	18%	0	0%	8	50%	20	13%	1	8%	4	40%
Belarus	22	9%	0	0%	4	25%	31	13%	0	0%	7	44%
Belgium	82	25%	1	4%	12	55%	22	7%	0	0%	6	26%
Bosnia & Herzegovina	151	57%	5	23%	17	77%	110	54%	2	12%	17	100%
Bulgaria	52	29%	0	0%	6	55%	14	10%	0	0%	3	30%
Croatia	184	61%	7	28%	21	91%	135	49%	2	9%	20	95%
Cyprus	64	16%	0	0%	12	44%	26	8%	0	0%	6	25%
Czech Republic	53	37%	2	17%	5	71%	42	29%	1	8%	6	75%
Denmark	122	32%	2	6%	15	56%	22	7%	0	0%	3	14%
Estonia	56	17%	1	4%	11	46%	30	10%	0	0%	6	26%
Finland	31	12%	0	0%	5	26%	39	14%	0	0%	9	47%
France	38	11%	0	0%	9	36%	32	10%	0	0%	9	39%
Georgia	16	7%	0	0%	5	33%	25	10%	0	0%	5	36%
Germany	34	10%	0	0%	7	29%	31	9%	0	0%	8	32%
Greece	65	17%	0	0%	12	43%	27	8%	0	0%	6	26%
Hungary	42	15%	0	0%	8	44%	41	19%	0	0%	7	50%
Iceland	46	15%	0	0%	9	41%	29	10%	0	0%	7	35%
Ireland	42	13%	1	4%	13	50%	39	11%	1	3%	7	26%
Israel	41	11%	0	0%	10	38%	45	13%	0	0%	12	50%
Italy	73	41%	0	0%	9	82%	27	12%	0	0%	5	36%
Latvia	63	24%	0	0%	9	50%	37	13%	0	0%	10	53%
Lithuania	19	6%	0	0%	5	23%	34	12%	0	0%	8	40%
Luxembourg	1	8%	0	0%	1	100%	0	0%	0	0%	0	0%
Malta	49	15%	2	7%	8	33%	29	9%	0	0%	8	35%
Moldova	52	20%	0	0%	10	56%	15	7%	0	0%	4	27%
Monaco	0	0%	0	0%	0	0%	7	19%	0	0%	2	67%
Montenegro	63	44%	0	0%	8	89%	91	45%	1	6%	12	100%
Morocco	0	-	0	-	0	-	0	-	0	-	0	-
Netherlands	81	23%	0	0%	15	60%	38	12%	0	0%	7	29%
North Macedonia	119	55%	2	10%	15	94%	69	30%	0	0%	13	81%
Norway	98	23%	1	3%	17	57%	28	8%	0	0%	6	23%
Poland	43	12%	0	0%	11	46%	83	23%	0	0%	13	54%
Portugal	50	18%	2	9%	6	30%	49	16%	0	0%	10	45%
Romania	38	13%	0	0%	8	36%	35	14%	0	0%	8	44%
Russia	92	29%	2	8%	12	52%	50	20%	0	0%	10	56%
San Marino	3	3%	0	0%	1	17%	21	13%	0	0%	5	56%
Serbia	185	70%	11	50%	16	100%	97	48%	0	0%	11	92%
Serbia & Montenegro	34	94%	2	67%	3	100%	14	39%	0	0%	2	67%
Slovakia	3	5%	0	0%	1	20%	9	13%	0	0%	2	33%
Slovenia	-	-	-	-	-	-	-	-	-	-	-	-
Spain	20	6%	0	0%	7	28%	34	10%	0	0%	9	39%
Sweden	177	40%	4	11%	24	77%	30	8%	0	0%	6	23%
Switzerland	49	21%	0	0%	9	53%	12	5%	0	0%	3	16%
Turkey	18	7%	0	0%	4	19%	18	9%	0	0%	4	24%
Ukraine	89	26%	2	7%	13	54%	32	14%	0	0%	6	38%
United Kingdom	50	14%	0	0%	10	40%	18	5%	0	0%	3	12%
Yugoslavia	0	-	0	-	0	-	0	-	0	-	0	-

Eurovision 2019: Who Votes for Who? (And Who Doesn't)

Spain

	Spain awarded points to:				Frequency		Spain received points from:				Frequency	
	Total	% of max	12's	% of max	Times	% of max	Total	% of max	12's	% of max	Times	% of max
Albania	25	8%	0	0%	5	24%	55	23%	2	10%	8	50%
Andorra	54	90%	3	60%	5	100%	60	83%	5	83%	5	83%
Armenia	121	42%	2	8%	14	74%	13	6%	0	0%	4	31%
Australia	69	44%	1	8%	6	86%	14	13%	0	0%	2	40%
Austria	97	19%	2	5%	15	39%	68	13%	0	0%	12	31%
Azerbaijan	44	15%	0	0%	9	47%	4	2%	0	0%	3	25%
Belarus	7	3%	0	0%	1	7%	2	1%	0	0%	1	6%
Belgium	138	23%	2	4%	21	48%	128	23%	3	6%	25	58%
Bosnia & Herzegovina	12	4%	0	0%	4	17%	30	13%	0	0%	5	26%
Bulgaria	81	52%	1	8%	9	100%	9	5%	0	0%	3	25%
Croatia	35	10%	2	7%	7	28%	36	10%	0	0%	7	28%
Cyprus	112	20%	1	2%	15	38%	123	26%	1	3%	19	53%
Czech Republic	67	37%	0	0%	6	75%	0	0%	0	0%	0	0%
Denmark	93	18%	0	0%	18	45%	38	8%	1	2%	11	29%
Estonia	62	16%	1	3%	13	46%	13	4%	0	0%	4	16%
Finland	85	14%	0	0%	18	40%	80	15%	0	0%	14	34%
France	127	22%	0	0%	20	45%	150	26%	2	4%	25	57%
Georgia	13	7%	0	0%	4	31%	2	1%	0	0%	1	8%
Germany	203	35%	8	17%	28	64%	84	15%	2	4%	13	30%
Greece	192	29%	3	5%	29	59%	140	27%	0	0%	23	58%
Hungary	66	19%	0	0%	11	46%	18	7%	0	0%	4	24%
Iceland	120	24%	1	2%	21	57%	26	5%	0	0%	9	21%
Ireland	151	29%	3	7%	23	56%	48	8%	0	0%	11	25%
Israel	156	28%	3	7%	23	56%	118	22%	3	7%	22	55%
Italy	211	59%	9	30%	23	88%	95	26%	2	7%	14	54%
Latvia	27	11%	1	5%	5	26%	13	5%	0	0%	3	15%
Lithuania	14	5%	0	0%	5	26%	12	4%	0	0%	2	10%
Luxembourg	51	22%	1	5%	9	47%	67	29%	0	0%	12	63%
Malta	86	22%	1	3%	15	52%	48	12%	1	3%	9	30%
Moldova	86	30%	0	0%	13	65%	13	6%	0	0%	3	20%
Monaco	17	18%	0	0%	3	38%	14	15%	0	0%	4	50%
Montenegro	5	3%	0	0%	2	22%	6	3%	0	0%	2	18%
Morocco	0	0%	0	0%	0	0%	5	42%	0	0%	1	100%
Netherlands	133	24%	1	2%	23	56%	60	11%	0	0%	13	32%
North Macedonia	0	0%	0	0%	0	0%	5	2%	0	0%	2	11%
Norway	92	15%	3	6%	18	38%	59	10%	0	0%	14	32%
Poland	33	10%	0	0%	9	38%	21	7%	0	0%	6	27%
Portugal	224	43%	8	19%	27	68%	184	35%	8	18%	23	56%
Romania	169	59%	6	25%	19	83%	48	17%	0	0%	9	45%
Russia	102	27%	1	3%	14	48%	22	7%	0	0%	6	27%
San Marino	19	13%	0	0%	3	33%	1	1%	0	0%	1	10%
Serbia	26	11%	0	0%	7	47%	2	1%	0	0%	1	8%
Serbia & Montenegro	14	39%	0	0%	2	67%	0	0%	0	0%	0	0%
Slovakia	2	3%	0	0%	1	20%	4	5%	0	0%	2	29%
Slovenia	34	10%	0	0%	9	39%	20	6%	0	0%	7	28%
Spain	-	-	-	-	-	-	-	-	-	-	-	-
Sweden	169	28%	3	6%	30	65%	43	7%	0	0%	8	18%
Switzerland	61	13%	0	0%	14	38%	158	29%	3	7%	29	71%
Turkey	55	13%	1	3%	14	39%	118	29%	2	6%	19	56%
Ukraine	85	32%	0	0%	14	74%	6	3%	0	0%	2	13%
United Kingdom	133	23%	1	2%	25	56%	65	11%	0	0%	20	44%
Yugoslavia	22	14%	0	0%	4	31%	26	17%	0	0%	7	54%

Eurovision 2019: Who Votes for Who? (And Who Doesn't)

Sweden

	Sweden awarded points to:				Frequency		Sweden received points from:				Frequency	
	Total	% of max	12's	% of max	Times	% of max	Total	% of max	12's	% of max	Times	% of max
Albania	27	11%	0	0%	7	44%	89	29%	0	0%	16	80%
Andorra	2	3%	0	0%	1	20%	32	33%	0	0%	6	75%
Armenia	47	18%	0	0%	11	65%	100	35%	3	13%	13	72%
Australia	96	62%	4	31%	7	100%	104	62%	5	36%	7	88%
Austria	101	20%	1	2%	20	53%	188	35%	4	9%	24	60%
Azerbaijan	53	19%	0	0%	8	47%	36	14%	0	0%	9	56%
Belarus	4	2%	0	0%	2	13%	80	28%	0	0%	13	65%
Belgium	94	18%	1	2%	16	40%	200	33%	5	10%	31	67%
Bosnia & Herzegovina	127	42%	1	4%	17	71%	74	27%	2	9%	14	64%
Bulgaria	25	14%	0	0%	4	33%	33	14%	0	0%	7	41%
Croatia	27	7%	1	3%	9	33%	59	14%	0	0%	13	45%
Cyprus	99	18%	2	4%	17	43%	163	30%	4	9%	24	59%
Czech Republic	19	11%	0	0%	6	67%	81	40%	3	18%	8	67%
Denmark	289	50%	10	21%	38	88%	437	73%	18	36%	40	91%
Estonia	119	35%	3	11%	17	68%	219	57%	8	25%	25	89%
Finland	179	37%	3	8%	23	62%	287	51%	8	17%	32	76%
France	120	21%	0	0%	24	56%	168	26%	3	6%	32	67%
Georgia	15	8%	0	0%	4	31%	91	34%	3	14%	11	69%
Germany	124	22%	2	4%	19	44%	234	35%	9	16%	32	65%
Greece	68	13%	2	5%	15	38%	66	12%	0	0%	13	33%
Hungary	65	22%	1	4%	11	55%	86	29%	1	4%	14	70%
Iceland	190	43%	3	8%	27	79%	288	46%	7	13%	34	72%
Ireland	223	43%	6	14%	30	73%	223	36%	7	13%	29	62%
Israel	121	23%	1	2%	21	53%	201	36%	5	11%	26	60%
Italy	62	18%	0	0%	10	40%	93	21%	1	3%	15	50%
Latvia	53	18%	0	0%	11	55%	181	44%	5	15%	20	74%
Lithuania	36	12%	0	0%	8	36%	144	40%	0	0%	20	80%
Luxembourg	52	24%	0	0%	8	44%	59	27%	0	0%	11	61%
Malta	95	21%	2	5%	18	56%	206	41%	4	10%	26	72%
Moldova	51	17%	0	0%	6	32%	86	27%	0	0%	15	75%
Monaco	22	26%	1	14%	2	29%	22	23%	0	0%	4	50%
Montenegro	15	10%	0	0%	5	50%	54	20%	0	0%	9	56%
Morocco	0	0%	0	0%	0	0%	6	50%	0	0%	1	100%
Netherlands	171	29%	3	6%	24	56%	240	38%	6	12%	27	59%
North Macedonia	18	8%	0	0%	6	33%	64	18%	0	0%	14	58%
Norway	286	47%	10	20%	35	76%	416	64%	15	28%	42	88%
Poland	45	15%	0	0%	10	48%	132	35%	3	10%	16	64%
Portugal	90	18%	2	5%	14	36%	190	32%	2	4%	27	59%
Romania	48	15%	0	0%	10	42%	92	26%	2	7%	15	60%
Russia	103	27%	0	0%	14	52%	73	20%	1	3%	14	56%
San Marino	0	0%	0	0%	0	0%	72	33%	2	11%	10	77%
Serbia	59	29%	0	0%	8	62%	69	30%	2	11%	12	86%
Serbia & Montenegro	28	78%	2	67%	3	100%	9	19%	0	0%	3	75%
Slovakia	3	5%	0	0%	1	20%	48	50%	2	25%	5	63%
Slovenia	30	8%	0	0%	6	23%	177	40%	4	11%	24	77%
Spain	43	7%	0	0%	8	18%	169	28%	3	6%	30	65%
Sweden	-	-	-	-	-	-	-	-	-	-	-	-
Switzerland	83	18%	3	8%	14	38%	190	32%	3	6%	26	58%
Turkey	91	19%	0	0%	15	38%	97	21%	1	3%	20	53%
Ukraine	55	16%	0	0%	12	50%	87	29%	1	4%	14	67%
United Kingdom	133	23%	3	6%	21	48%	261	38%	4	7%	40	78%
Yugoslavia	35	24%	1	8%	6	50%	49	34%	1	8%	9	75%

Eurovision 2019: Who Votes for Who? (And Who Doesn't)

Switzerland

	Switzerland awarded points to:				Frequency		Switzerland received points from:				Frequency	
	Total	% of max	12's	% of max	Times	% of max	Total	% of max	12's	% of max	Times	% of max
Albania	160	56%	3	13%	18	95%	46	20%	0	0%	7	47%
Andorra	0	0%	0	0%	0	0%	9	13%	0	0%	3	50%
Armenia	7	3%	0	0%	3	18%	42	25%	0	0%	6	55%
Australia	47	36%	2	18%	5	83%	8	13%	0	0%	2	67%
Austria	121	23%	3	7%	16	43%	159	34%	3	8%	23	66%
Azerbaijan	23	9%	0	0%	7	41%	24	15%	0	0%	4	40%
Belarus	2	1%	0	0%	2	13%	33	15%	0	0%	6	43%
Belgium	83	17%	0	0%	11	30%	119	25%	3	8%	18	50%
Bosnia & Herzegovina	84	41%	3	18%	12	71%	8	6%	0	0%	3	25%
Bulgaria	45	19%	1	5%	6	43%	11	6%	0	0%	3	25%
Croatia	101	30%	0	0%	20	87%	56	19%	0	0%	10	50%
Cyprus	68	14%	0	0%	17	49%	74	19%	0	0%	16	53%
Czech Republic	11	8%	0	0%	1	13%	11	11%	0	0%	2	33%
Denmark	71	13%	0	0%	20	50%	117	26%	1	3%	21	64%
Estonia	24	9%	1	4%	3	16%	45	20%	2	11%	6	38%
Finland	87	17%	1	2%	16	39%	148	31%	2	5%	24	63%
France	156	30%	4	9%	24	60%	93	22%	1	3%	15	44%
Georgia	2	1%	0	0%	2	14%	13	9%	0	0%	4	40%
Germany	160	30%	5	11%	25	63%	145	28%	3	7%	21	54%
Greece	105	20%	1	2%	21	53%	81	19%	1	3%	17	50%
Hungary	62	22%	1	4%	10	50%	38	20%	0	0%	8	57%
Iceland	71	18%	0	0%	13	42%	87	18%	1	3%	16	42%
Ireland	197	36%	7	15%	29	71%	143	26%	2	4%	22	55%
Israel	186	32%	1	2%	30	71%	94	19%	1	2%	20	54%
Italy	156	43%	2	7%	23	88%	90	27%	1	4%	17	68%
Latvia	46	19%	0	0%	9	53%	37	16%	1	5%	8	50%
Lithuania	40	11%	0	0%	7	30%	56	19%	0	0%	9	47%
Luxembourg	26	11%	1	5%	5	26%	80	35%	3	16%	15	79%
Malta	62	16%	0	0%	12	41%	90	26%	3	10%	14	54%
Moldova	14	7%	0	0%	3	21%	18	14%	0	0%	3	33%
Monaco	16	17%	0	0%	3	38%	29	27%	0	0%	7	78%
Montenegro	3	4%	0	0%	2	33%	5	6%	0	0%	1	17%
Morocco	0	0%	0	0%	0	0%	7	58%	0	0%	1	100%
Netherlands	149	30%	2	5%	23	64%	138	32%	1	3%	17	52%
North Macedonia	102	33%	1	4%	16	76%	26	9%	0	0%	7	37%
Norway	145	23%	0	0%	23	50%	132	25%	1	2%	22	55%
Poland	27	11%	0	0%	5	29%	42	21%	1	6%	7	47%
Portugal	169	37%	4	11%	22	61%	103	23%	1	3%	21	60%
Romania	33	10%	0	0%	8	32%	63	24%	0	0%	8	42%
Russia	30	10%	0	0%	6	27%	22	11%	0	0%	5	36%
San Marino	0	0%	0	0%	0	0%	13	11%	0	0%	3	38%
Serbia	143	66%	8	44%	13	100%	22	18%	0	0%	4	57%
Serbia & Montenegro	36	100%	3	100%	3	100%	2	4%	0	0%	1	25%
Slovakia	0	0%	0	0%	0	0%	6	13%	0	0%	2	50%
Slovenia	12	5%	0	0%	3	16%	49	21%	0	0%	9	53%
Spain	158	29%	3	7%	29	71%	61	13%	0	0%	14	38%
Sweden	190	32%	3	6%	26	58%	83	18%	3	8%	14	38%
Switzerland	-	-	-	-	-	-	-	-	-	-	-	-
Turkey	154	37%	3	9%	21	60%	60	16%	0	0%	11	35%
Ukraine	25	9%	0	0%	5	26%	7	4%	0	0%	2	18%
United Kingdom	143	26%	2	4%	23	56%	150	27%	3	7%	22	52%
Yugoslavia	18	12%	0	0%	4	31%	61	39%	1	8%	9	69%

Eurovision 2019: Who Votes for Who? (And Who Doesn't)

Turkey

	Turkey awarded points to:				Frequency		Turkey received points from:				Frequency	
	Total	% of max	12's	% of max	Times	% of max	Total	% of max	12's	% of max	Times	% of max
Albania	60	45%	0	0%	11	100%	113	78%	3	25%	12	100%
Andorra	3	5%	0	0%	2	40%	15	14%	0	0%	3	33%
Armenia	75	69%	1	11%	9	100%	16	13%	0	0%	3	30%
Australia	0	-	0	-	0	-	0	-	0	-	0	-
Austria	71	23%	1	4%	13	50%	70	21%	1	4%	11	39%
Azerbaijan	84	100%	7	100%	7	100%	72	100%	6	100%	6	100%
Belarus	8	7%	0	0%	2	22%	18	12%	0	0%	5	38%
Belgium	63	18%	1	3%	10	34%	140	34%	6	18%	18	53%
Bosnia & Herzegovina	175	69%	6	29%	19	90%	133	55%	4	20%	16	80%
Bulgaria	49	51%	1	13%	8	100%	96	62%	2	15%	13	100%
Croatia	55	21%	0	0%	9	41%	56	19%	1	4%	11	46%
Cyprus	10	3%	0	0%	3	10%	12	3%	0	0%	2	6%
Czech Republic	1	3%	0	0%	1	33%	7	10%	0	0%	3	50%
Denmark	32	8%	0	0%	12	36%	90	23%	0	0%	14	42%
Estonia	22	11%	1	6%	3	19%	14	6%	0	0%	3	16%
Finland	40	11%	0	0%	9	30%	55	14%	0	0%	13	39%
France	38	10%	0	0%	12	36%	190	44%	8	22%	21	58%
Georgia	65	60%	0	0%	9	100%	37	34%	0	0%	8	89%
Germany	86	22%	3	9%	13	39%	208	48%	8	22%	22	61%
Greece	81	23%	2	7%	14	47%	36	10%	0	0%	6	19%
Hungary	25	19%	0	0%	6	55%	30	23%	0	0%	7	64%
Iceland	34	10%	0	0%	7	26%	31	7%	0	0%	8	22%
Ireland	124	32%	2	6%	22	69%	24	6%	0	0%	7	20%
Israel	63	17%	2	6%	11	35%	42	11%	0	0%	11	33%
Italy	76	40%	0	0%	12	75%	23	13%	0	0%	3	20%
Latvia	6	4%	0	0%	1	8%	2	1%	0	0%	1	7%
Lithuania	4	2%	0	0%	2	13%	16	8%	0	0%	4	24%
Luxembourg	26	14%	0	0%	7	44%	19	10%	0	0%	4	25%
Malta	93	32%	1	4%	15	63%	87	27%	1	4%	12	44%
Moldova	42	39%	1	11%	6	67%	11	10%	0	0%	2	22%
Monaco	5	8%	0	0%	1	20%	11	15%	0	0%	2	33%
Montenegro	5	21%	0	0%	1	50%	15	21%	0	0%	4	67%
Morocco	0	0%	0	0%	0	0%	12	100%	1	100%	1	100%
Netherlands	95	28%	1	4%	19	68%	168	42%	7	21%	23	70%
North Macedonia	72	40%	0	0%	12	80%	125	65%	2	13%	16	100%
Norway	57	14%	1	3%	11	31%	59	13%	0	0%	16	43%
Poland	8	5%	0	0%	2	15%	11	5%	0	0%	3	18%
Portugal	48	12%	1	3%	10	29%	21	5%	0	0%	4	11%
Romania	55	29%	0	0%	12	75%	107	56%	1	6%	15	94%
Russia	50	25%	0	0%	9	53%	25	12%	0	0%	6	35%
San Marino	5	42%	0	0%	1	100%	19	53%	0	0%	3	100%
Serbia	0	0%	0	0%	0	0%	3	3%	0	0%	1	11%
Serbia & Montenegro	15	42%	0	0%	2	67%	2	4%	0	0%	1	25%
Slovakia	0	0%	0	0%	0	0%	3	4%	0	0%	1	17%
Slovenia	18	9%	0	0%	4	24%	18	7%	0	0%	4	19%
Spain	118	29%	2	6%	19	56%	55	13%	1	3%	14	39%
Sweden	97	21%	1	3%	20	53%	91	19%	0	0%	15	38%
Switzerland	60	16%	0	0%	11	35%	154	37%	3	9%	21	60%
Turkey	-	-	-	-	-	-	-	-	-	-	-	-
Ukraine	69	38%	2	13%	10	67%	39	23%	0	0%	9	64%
United Kingdom	126	31%	2	6%	21	62%	143	30%	4	10%	24	60%
Yugoslavia	80	56%	4	33%	10	83%	42	29%	1	8%	6	50%

Eurovision 2019: Who Votes for Who? (And Who Doesn't)

Ukraine

	Ukraine awarded points to:				Frequency		Ukraine received points from:				Frequency	
	Total	% of max	12's	% of max	Times	% of max	Total	% of max	12's	% of max	Times	% of max
Albania	7	4%	0	0%	3	21%	38	13%	0	0%	7	35%
Andorra	0	0%	0	0%	0	0%	49	51%	1	13%	6	75%
Armenia	78	46%	1	7%	11	92%	102	50%	3	18%	12	86%
Australia	38	32%	1	10%	5	100%	25	21%	0	0%	3	60%
Austria	16	8%	0	0%	3	25%	30	15%	0	0%	7	50%
Azerbaijan	117	70%	4	29%	12	100%	138	72%	3	19%	13	100%
Belarus	155	72%	8	44%	14	93%	215	72%	8	32%	20	95%
Belgium	41	21%	0	0%	5	38%	58	19%	0	0%	10	48%
Bosnia & Herzegovina	22	13%	0	0%	3	21%	54	28%	1	6%	9	60%
Bulgaria	40	19%	0	0%	8	62%	95	36%	2	9%	15	83%
Croatia	61	25%	0	0%	11	65%	82	28%	1	4%	13	62%
Cyprus	28	12%	0	0%	6	38%	107	37%	1	4%	16	76%
Czech Republic	14	19%	0	0%	1	25%	68	57%	4	40%	7	100%
Denmark	51	16%	0	0%	8	36%	80	23%	1	3%	14	58%
Estonia	41	19%	0	0%	10	63%	113	38%	2	8%	16	73%
Finland	13	9%	0	0%	2	18%	43	19%	1	5%	8	50%
France	38	18%	1	6%	4	27%	30	10%	0	0%	8	36%
Georgia	115	64%	2	13%	12	100%	157	65%	4	20%	15	100%
Germany	10	5%	0	0%	2	13%	45	14%	0	0%	6	29%
Greece	35	18%	0	0%	6	40%	68	27%	0	0%	12	67%
Hungary	61	24%	0	0%	11	69%	63	28%	1	5%	10	67%
Iceland	8	5%	0	0%	3	21%	60	23%	1	5%	9	47%
Ireland	12	5%	0	0%	6	35%	61	20%	0	0%	13	59%
Israel	72	29%	1	5%	10	63%	144	50%	2	8%	18	90%
Italy	9	8%	0	0%	2	29%	110	57%	3	19%	11	100%
Latvia	45	21%	0	0%	8	53%	164	49%	4	14%	18	78%
Lithuania	59	22%	1	5%	11	61%	150	48%	3	12%	18	82%
Luxembourg	0	-	0	-	0	-	0	-	0	-	0	-
Malta	28	13%	0	0%	6	40%	85	30%	0	0%	14	70%
Moldova	121	50%	4	20%	14	82%	178	64%	3	13%	18	95%
Monaco	0	0%	0	0%	0	0%	15	25%	0	0%	4	80%
Montenegro	12	17%	0	0%	3	60%	65	34%	1	6%	8	67%
Morocco	0	-	0	-	0	-	0	-	0	-	0	-
Netherlands	40	14%	1	4%	6	32%	61	18%	0	0%	11	46%
North Macedonia	27	14%	0	0%	6	43%	92	32%	1	4%	14	70%
Norway	78	27%	1	4%	12	63%	54	17%	0	0%	11	50%
Poland	77	38%	1	6%	10	77%	171	65%	9	41%	17	100%
Portugal	34	20%	0	0%	4	33%	117	49%	5	25%	15	83%
Romania	29	12%	0	0%	9	50%	54	20%	0	0%	12	63%
Russia	144	63%	5	26%	17	100%	148	56%	1	5%	19	100%
San Marino	4	6%	0	0%	1	25%	44	26%	2	14%	4	40%
Serbia	29	13%	0	0%	6	43%	87	35%	1	5%	12	75%
Serbia & Montenegro	27	75%	2	67%	3	100%	25	42%	0	0%	4	80%
Slovakia	14	39%	1	33%	2	67%	30	36%	1	14%	5	71%
Slovenia	32	14%	0	0%	6	38%	89	26%	2	7%	13	54%
Spain	6	3%	0	0%	2	13%	85	32%	0	0%	14	74%
Sweden	87	29%	1	4%	14	67%	55	16%	0	0%	12	50%
Switzerland	7	4%	0	0%	2	18%	25	9%	0	0%	5	26%
Turkey	39	23%	0	0%	9	64%	69	38%	2	13%	10	67%
Ukraine	-	-	-	-	-	-	-	-	-	-	-	-
United Kingdom	9	4%	0	0%	2	13%	67	21%	0	0%	12	55%
Yugoslavia	0	-	0	-	0	-	0	-	0	-	0	-

Eurovision 2019: Who Votes for Who? (And Who Doesn't)

United Kingdom

	UK awarded points to:				Frequency		UK received points from:				Frequency	
	Total	% of max	12's	% of max	Times	% of max	Total	% of max	12's	% of max	Times	% of max
Albania	29	10%	0	0%	8	44%	31	13%	0	0%	6	38%
Andorra	0	0%	0	0%	0	0%	6	8%	0	0%	2	33%
Armenia	15	6%	0	0%	4	24%	15	7%	0	0%	4	31%
Australia	76	49%	0	0%	7	100%	29	27%	1	11%	3	60%
Austria	131	25%	3	7%	21	54%	168	33%	7	16%	24	62%
Azerbaijan	33	12%	0	0%	5	29%	7	4%	0	0%	2	17%
Belarus	4	2%	0	0%	2	12%	6	3%	0	0%	3	19%
Belgium	120	22%	1	2%	21	51%	149	26%	7	15%	21	49%
Bosnia & Herzegovina	16	6%	0	0%	5	23%	33	14%	0	0%	7	37%
Bulgaria	99	46%	2	11%	9	69%	19	11%	1	7%	2	17%
Croatia	34	9%	0	0%	15	54%	71	20%	2	7%	12	48%
Cyprus	158	29%	2	4%	25	64%	80	17%	0	0%	21	58%
Czech Republic	16	10%	0	0%	4	44%	15	10%	0	0%	3	38%
Denmark	163	29%	4	9%	26	62%	141	28%	2	5%	25	66%
Estonia	81	26%	1	4%	13	57%	53	15%	0	0%	11	44%
Finland	84	16%	2	5%	13	33%	106	20%	0	0%	18	44%
France	91	16%	0	0%	20	45%	152	26%	5	10%	23	52%
Georgia	27	13%	2	11%	4	27%	7	4%	0	0%	3	25%
Germany	147	26%	1	2%	27	61%	153	27%	2	4%	25	57%
Greece	149	27%	5	11%	21	50%	85	16%	2	5%	15	38%
Hungary	28	11%	0	0%	7	39%	38	15%	1	5%	7	41%
Iceland	109	25%	2	5%	18	53%	44	8%	1	2%	9	21%
Ireland	302	52%	8	17%	37	84%	219	38%	1	2%	37	84%
Israel	173	29%	3	6%	28	65%	146	28%	4	9%	23	58%
Italy	35	10%	0	0%	8	31%	100	28%	1	3%	16	62%
Latvia	82	31%	0	0%	13	72%	30	10%	0	0%	10	50%
Lithuania	181	49%	6	19%	21	81%	22	8%	0	0%	5	25%
Luxembourg	57	25%	0	0%	10	53%	123	54%	4	21%	18	95%
Malta	146	35%	3	9%	23	72%	128	31%	2	6%	21	70%
Moldova	55	24%	1	5%	7	47%	5	2%	0	0%	2	13%
Monaco	24	25%	0	0%	4	50%	42	44%	2	25%	5	63%
Montenegro	0	0%	0	0%	0	0%	2	1%	0	0%	1	9%
Morocco	0	0%	0	0%	0	0%	8	67%	0	0%	1	100%
Netherlands	115	21%	1	2%	24	60%	112	21%	2	4%	20	49%
North Macedonia	24	8%	2	8%	2	10%	28	10%	0	0%	5	26%
Norway	131	20%	3	6%	21	43%	122	21%	2	4%	23	52%
Poland	85	27%	2	8%	13	59%	37	12%	0	0%	8	36%
Portugal	78	15%	1	2%	12	29%	156	30%	4	9%	25	61%
Romania	59	20%	1	4%	9	39%	20	7%	1	4%	4	20%
Russia	65	19%	0	0%	11	44%	38	13%	1	4%	8	36%
San Marino	0	0%	0	0%	0	0%	31	18%	0	0%	7	70%
Serbia	11	5%	0	0%	4	29%	10	5%	0	0%	2	17%
Serbia & Montenegro	11	31%	0	0%	2	67%	0	0%	0	0%	0	0%
Slovakia	0	0%	0	0%	0	0%	15	18%	0	0%	3	43%
Slovenia	18	5%	0	0%	3	12%	50	14%	0	0%	10	40%
Spain	65	11%	0	0%	20	44%	133	23%	1	2%	25	56%
Sweden	261	38%	4	7%	40	78%	133	23%	3	6%	21	48%
Switzerland	150	27%	3	7%	22	52%	143	26%	2	4%	23	56%
Turkey	143	30%	4	10%	24	60%	126	31%	2	6%	21	62%
Ukraine	67	21%	0	0%	12	55%	9	4%	0	0%	2	13%
United Kingdom	-	-	-	-	-	-	-	-	-	-	-	-
Yugoslavia	47	30%	2	15%	6	46%	57	37%	1	8%	8	62%

Eurovision 2019: Who Votes for Who? (And Who Doesn't)

Yugoslavia

	Yugoslavia awarded points to:				Frequency		Yugoslavia received points from:				Frequency	
	Total	% of max	12's	% of max	Times	% of max	Total	% of max	12's	% of max	Times	% of max
Albania	0	-	0	-	0	-	0	-	0	-	0	-
Andorra	0	-	0	-	0	-	0	-	0	-	0	-
Armenia	0	-	0	-	0	-	0	-	0	-	0	-
Australia	0	-	0	-	0	-	0	-	0	-	0	-
Austria	23	16%	0	0%	5	42%	24	17%	0	0%	5	42%
Azerbaijan	0	-	0	-	0	-	0	-	0	-	0	-
Belarus	0	-	0	-	0	-	0	-	0	-	0	-
Belgium	32	21%	0	0%	5	38%	45	29%	1	8%	7	54%
Bosnia & Herzegovina	0	-	0	-	0	-	0	-	0	-	0	-
Bulgaria	0	-	0	-	0	-	0	-	0	-	0	-
Croatia	0	-	0	-	0	-	0	-	0	-	0	-
Cyprus	52	43%	1	10%	8	80%	59	49%	1	10%	9	90%
Czech Republic	0	-	0	-	0	-	0	-	0	-	0	-
Denmark	7	5%	0	0%	2	18%	52	39%	2	18%	6	55%
Estonia	0	-	0	-	0	-	0	-	0	-	0	-
Finland	22	14%	0	0%	5	38%	35	22%	1	8%	7	54%
France	56	39%	3	25%	7	58%	21	15%	0	0%	7	58%
Georgia	0	-	0	-	0	-	0	-	0	-	0	-
Germany	33	21%	1	8%	6	46%	16	10%	0	0%	6	46%
Greece	17	16%	0	0%	4	44%	30	25%	0	0%	7	70%
Hungary	0	-	0	-	0	-	0	-	0	-	0	-
Iceland	4	5%	0	0%	1	14%	48	31%	1	8%	6	46%
Ireland	38	26%	0	0%	10	83%	34	24%	1	8%	8	67%
Israel	54	38%	2	17%	8	67%	52	36%	3	25%	6	50%
Italy	62	52%	1	10%	8	80%	17	14%	0	0%	3	30%
Latvia	0	-	0	-	0	-	0	-	0	-	0	-
Lithuania	0	-	0	-	0	-	0	-	0	-	0	-
Luxembourg	37	24%	1	8%	6	46%	24	15%	0	0%	5	38%
Malta	13	36%	0	0%	3	100%	4	11%	0	0%	2	67%
Moldova	0	-	0	-	0	-	0	-	0	-	0	-
Monaco	4	17%	0	0%	1	50%	0	0%	0	0%	0	0%
Montenegro	0	-	0	-	0	-	0	-	0	-	0	-
Morocco	0	-	0	-	0	-	0	-	0	-	0	-
Netherlands	40	28%	0	0%	7	58%	25	17%	0	0%	4	33%
North Macedonia	0	-	0	-	0	-	0	-	0	-	0	-
Norway	11	7%	0	0%	2	15%	31	20%	1	8%	5	38%
Poland	0	-	0	-	0	-	0	-	0	-	0	-
Portugal	14	9%	0	0%	3	23%	11	7%	0	0%	3	23%
Romania	0	-	0	-	0	-	0	-	0	-	0	-
Russia	0	-	0	-	0	-	0	-	0	-	0	-
San Marino	0	-	0	-	0	-	0	-	0	-	0	-
Serbia	0	-	0	-	0	-	0	-	0	-	0	-
Serbia & Montenegro	0	-	0	-	0	-	0	-	0	-	0	-
Slovakia	0	-	0	-	0	-	0	-	0	-	0	-
Slovenia	0	-	0	-	0	-	0	-	0	-	0	-
Spain	26	17%	0	0%	7	54%	22	14%	0	0%	4	31%
Sweden	49	34%	1	8%	9	75%	35	24%	1	8%	6	50%
Switzerland	61	39%	1	8%	9	69%	18	12%	0	0%	4	31%
Turkey	42	29%	1	8%	6	50%	80	56%	4	33%	10	83%
Ukraine	0	-	0	-	0	-	0	-	0	-	0	-
United Kingdom	57	37%	1	8%	8	62%	47	30%	2	15%	6	46%
Yugoslavia	-	-	-	-	-	-	-	-	-	-	-	-